CONTENTS

PART 2

Creating a Research Design 67

Marketing

Research

Essentials

Carl McDaniel, Jr.
UNIVERSITY OF TEXAS AT ARLINGTON

Roger Gates
UNIVERSITY OF TEXAS AT ARLINGTON

Marketing Research Essentials

WEST PUBLISHING COMPANY
MINNEAPOLIS/ST. PAUL   NEW YORK   LOS ANGELES   SAN FRANCISCO

PRODUCTION CREDITS

Copyediting: Bonnie Gruen

Composition: Graphic World, Inc.

Text design: Roslyn Stendahl

Cover art: David Bishop

Cover design: Gary Hespenheide

Index: Terry Casey

Production, prepress, printing, and binding by West Publishing Company

WEST'S COMMITMENT TO THE ENVIRONMENT

In 1906, West Publishing Company began recycling materials left over from the production of books. This began a tradition of efficient and responsible use of resources. Today, up to 95 percent of our legal books and 70 percent of our college and school texts are printed on recycled, acid-free stock. West also recycles nearly 22 million pounds of scrap paper annually—the equivalent of 181,717 trees. Since the 1960s, West has devised ways to capture and recycle waste inks, solvents, oils, and vapors created in the printing process. We also recycle plastics of all kinds, wood, glass, corrugated cardboard, and batteries, and have eliminated the use of Styrofoam book packaging. We at West are proud of the longevity and the scope of our commitment to the environment.

British Library Cataloguing-in-Publication Data. A catalogue record for this book is available from the British Library.

COPYRIGHT ©1995   By WEST PUBLISHING COMPANY
610 Opperman Drive
P.O. Box 64526
St. Paul, MN 55164-0526

Library of Congress Cataloging-in-Publication Data

McDaniel, Carl D.
    Marketing research essentials/Carl McDaniel, Jr., Roger Gates.
        p. cm.
    Includes bibliographical references and index.
    ISBN 0-314-04283-0 (pbk.)
    1. Marketing research.   I. Gates, Roger H., 1942-   . II. Title.
HF5415.2.M3825 1995
658.8'3--dc20   94-20227
                                                                          CIP

CONTENTS IN BRIEF

v

PART 3

Data Acquisition 237

PART 4

Data Analysis 361

PREFACE

This text was written in response to requests from a number of users of our highly successful *Contemporary Marketing Research*. Professors teaching on the quarter system found that there was simply not enough time to cover all twenty chapters in the book. Some instructors like to place most of the emphasis on a class marketing research project. In this case, the text becomes a reference tool. Other professors, including the authors, are concerned about the increased price of textbooks. *Marketing Research Essentials* has been created to address the needs and concerns of our new market. It is concise and value priced.

Our objective in each edition of *Contemporary Marketing Research* has been to create a lively, stimulating, real-world perspective based upon our 30-plus years of experience in the industry. You will find that we have maintained this standard in *Marketing Research Essentials*.

We, the authors, are active in the marketing research industry, which enables us to offer students unique, practical insights into trends, technology, and methodology found in contemporary marketing research practice. Yet, as academicians, we demand that a research textbook be rigorous, demanding, and challenging to the student. Because of our dual backgrounds in marketing research and in academics, we offer a truly unique perspective not found elsewhere. We recognize that most readers of this text will be users of marketing research information rather than professional researchers. Accordingly, our goal is to help the reader become a more effective decision maker through the use of marketing research information and a more sophisticated buyer of marketing research. This demands a thorough knowledge of the research process and of proper statistical applications to research data.

Marketing Research Essentials covers the essence of what every student should learn in the first marketing research class. In Part One we detail the role of marketing research in management decision making, the research process, ethics in marketing research, and information on how the industry is structured. In Part Two we cover data sources. We begin with secondary data and decision support systems, then follow with chapters on qualitative, observation, and survey research. Part Two concludes with a discussion of experimentation.

In Part Three we outline the data acquisition process. We begin by explaining the concept of measurement and describe various attitude scales and how to use them. We then move to sampling issues such as developing a sampling plan and a description of probability and nonprobability sampling methods. The final chapter in Part Three explains sample size determination.

In Part Four we focus on data analysis. Data processing activities introduce the subject. We then explain descriptive statistics and statistical testing of differences. Part Four concludes with a chapter on correlation and regression. Part Five discusses the importance of effectively communicating the research results to decision makers. We explain how to organize and present the report. Most importantly, we offer tips on getting managers to use the research information.

A RELEVANT AND ENJOYABLE BOOK TO READ

As we noted in *Contemporary Marketing Research,* there is probably no greater hindrance to learning than a dull textbook. With this in mind, we've strived to make *Marketing Research Essentials* a truly pleasurable reading experience. This has been accomplished by:

- *Opening each chapter with a real-world marketing research example.* At the conclusion of each opening vignette we pose a few teaser questions designed to pique the students' interest in the material about to be covered.
- *Writing in a lively, informal style developed over the years by two highly experienced and successful authors.* Careful attention to language, sentence structure, and the use of hundreds of real-world examples make *Marketing Research Essentials* engrossing while at the same time rigorous.
- *Implementing a research user's orientation.* A number of features have been incorporated into the text to aid future managers in effectively utilizing marketing research. In Chapter 1 we offer an extensive discussion on when to conduct marketing research and when not to. Chapter 2 discusses not only the research process but also where and how managers get involved, that is, the research request. Chapter 3 will help future managers understand "the players" in the research industry. Chapter 15 tells the reader what to look for in a marketing research report and how to help managers use marketing research data.

A PROFESSIONAL LEARNING TOOL

Creating a book that's a pleasure to read is an important step in developing an effective learning tool. Still, pedagogical devices are necessary to complete the task. *Marketing Research Essentials* offers:

- Chapter learning objectives that challenge the student to explain, discuss, understand, and clarify the concepts to be presented
- An opening vignette, photos and illustrations, and special in-text sections to amplify and clarify text material
- A comprehensive chapter summary
- Key terms—bold-faced in the text and listed at the end of the chapter, as well as defined in the margins
- Review questions, recalling key points in the chapter
- Discussion questions—probing, thought-provoking questions designed to stimulate class discussion
- A case study in each chapter—short, real-world, written in a lively style to enhance student learning and enjoyment
- Ethics cases at the end of each part that pose real-world ethical dilemmas faced by marketing researchers and managers

AN EXTENSIVE AND USEFUL SET OF SUPPLEMENTS

The key variables in creating a motivational and enthusiastic learning environment are the textbook, the instructor's lectures, and supplemental material used to augment and reinforce the textbook material. Because *Marketing Research Essentials* is being used in the only marketing research course most students will ever take, we want to maximize the students' understanding and appreciation of marketing research. At the same time, we hope to minimize unnecessary classroom and project preparation time for the instructor. We want to thank Shiva Nandan of Missouri Western State College for his contribution in the development of the Instructor's Manual, and Dave Andrus of Kansas State University for preparing the Test Bank. Also, we would like to thank Glen Jarboe for creating the second edition of *The Marketing Research Project Manual* and Chip Miller of Pacific Lutheran University, for his preparation of a marketing workbook. Supplements for *Marketing Research Essentials* are:

- *Marketing Research Workbook*. This student workbook includes hands-on activities for appropriate chapters of the book to help students improve their research skills and managerial decision making, such as which market to target, when to make decisions, and what type of research to use.
- *The Marketing Research Project Manual*, second edition. This highly popular manual offers a detailed, step-by-step procedure for students to follow in the conducting of a market research project. The second edition contains more vignettes about alternative projects and a complete data set keyed to the results reported in the manual. Instructors who require a real-world marketing research project have found that the manual saves valuable class time and provides lucid explanations of the research process.
- *Instructor's Manual with Video Guide*. Insightful comments from users have enabled us to create the most comprehensive instructor's manual available for the marketing research course. The complete lecture outline for each chapter with supplemental notes is designed so that instructors can use the material during class lectures and discussions. The manual also includes video summaries for the video library which includes a description, running times, key points, and discussion questions.
- *Test Bank*. The new classroom-tested and validated test bank contains over 1500 multiple choice, true/false, and case questions. The questions are designed to test the student's knowledge of the most salient points of each chapter. A computerized version, WESTEST, is also available.
- Marketing research computer programs. Several excellent practitioner-oriented software packages are available to adopters of the text:
  1. Sawtooth Ci2 Lab System software for the IBM PC and compatibles allows instructors and students to construct and administer questionnaires for market research. It is designed for academic use, but contains all of the features used in the Ci2 system for the commercial market research industry. It also includes an introduction that prepares students for designing their own questionnaires. Questionnaires may be used for personal interviewing where the respondent sits at the computer or for telephone interviewing where the interviewer is at the computer. This software is the most widely used interviewing software in the marketing research industry.
  2. MYSTAT is a student version of the popular SYSTAT package. It runs on the IBM PC and compatibles or the Macintosh and is consistently rated in the top tier of statistical packages in reviews conducted by personal computer periodicals. It has a full screen data editor, algebraic variable transformations, sorting, ranking, multi-way tabulations, and more.

3. Microtab is a crosstabulation software available for IBM PCs and compatibles that comes with a comprehensive users' manual. It is fully menu-driven and user-friendly.
4. UNCLE was developed by World Research Systems, Inc. It is, in our opinion, the most powerful and flexible tabulation package available today. It has a large number of devotees in the research industry.

■ Videos. We offer an excellent and expanded video package.
1. *One on One: Getting It Right* covers interviewing techniques used by marketing researchers. Questions for discussion follow the discussion and illustration of each interviewing topic.
2. *Focus Group on Women's Shoes* shows the conduction of a focus group by a professional moderator trainer for Riva Marketing Research, Chicago.
3. *Focus Group on a New Deodorant* shows the conduction of a focus group by a professional moderator trainer for Riva Marketing Research, Chicago.
4. *Marketing Research and the Interview* contains discussion and demonstration of proper marketing research interviewing techniques.
5. *Developing Crystal Pepsi* illustrates the research that went into the development of Crystal Pepsi.
6. *A. C. Nielsen Grocery Category Management* covers grocery audits and information outputs from A. C. Nielsen in 1991.
7. *Chilton Research Services* illustrates the capabilities and resources of one of the largest full service marketing research firms in the United States.
8. *Behind the Scenes (Advertising Education Foundation)* shows the role of marketing research in the campaign development process. It includes strategy/concept discussions and focus group shots.
9. *Depth Interview with a Homemaker on Nutritious Snacks (DDB Needham)* shows a middle-class homemaker discussing products for her family as part of a lifestyle study.
10. In *How to Conduct a Focus Group* a professional moderator trainer explains how to conduct a focus group.

■ Transparencies to enhance classroom presentations. Approximately one hundred transparencies accompany the book. These include key figures from the text as well as alternate transparencies of new material.

ACKNOWLEDGMENTS

Every textbook owes its knowledge, personality, and features not just to the authors but a team of hardworking individuals behind the scenes. A special thanks goes to RoseAnn Reddick for typing the manuscript and the revisions. We are especially indebted to our editor, Rick Leyh, who brought focus to the project and offered many creative suggestions and ideas. It is always a pleasure to work with someone who will only settle for the best. We also could not have done without the advice and help of Jessica Evans at West Publishing. We want to give a special thanks to Laura Evans for helping the production process move smoothly. We are also indebted to the following colleagues who acted as reviewers and whose advice and counsel was deeply appreciated.

Joseph Cangelosi
University of Central Arkansas

Gilberto De Los Santos
University of Texas, Pan American

Raj Javalgi
Cleveland State University

Thomas Kotka
Central Washington University

Chip E. Miller
Pacific Lutheran University

Rick Netemeyer
Louisiana State University

Wes Roehl
University of Nevada, Las Vegas

Dan Toy
California State University, Chico

Raja Velu
University of Wisconsin, Whitewater

Clyde Vollmers
Morehead State University

Richard Yalch
University of Washington

PART 1

An Introduction to Marketing Research

CHAPTER 1

The Role of Marketing Research in Management Decision Making

LEARNING OBJECTIVES

1. To review the marketing concept and the marketing mix.

2. To comprehend the marketing environment within which managers must make decisions.

3. To define marketing research.

4. To understand the importance of marketing research in shaping marketing decisions.

5. To learn when marketing research should and should not be conducted.

6. To understand the history of marketing research.

It was a bold concept—a sleek airplane made not from metal but carbon-plastic, with startling L-shaped wings and twin turboprop engines mounted aft to push rather than pull. Raytheon Company's Beech unit invested a decade and a small fortune on it, called it Starship, and marketed it as a flashy but fuel-efficient alternative to the corporate jet.

But Starship has made a hard landing in the marketplace. In one of the most expensive flops in commercial aviation, Raytheon officials now concede they have quietly written off much of the development cost of the plane, estimated by some analysts to approach $500 million. Only twenty-three Starships have been sold—fewer than half of the fifty orders claimed by Raytheon before the first sale in 1990. Not one Starship was sold in 1993.

"For the pilot and the passenger, it has really got everything," says Dennis Murphy, sales manager at Elliott Flying Services, in Des Moines, Iowa. But "for the money, the performance isn't there," Mr. Murphy adds. "For $5 million, you can buy a jet. Starship just doesn't fit in today's market."

Starship's space-age design was also thought of as an attraction for corporate chiefs. But it "turns out the older-generation CEO-level manager is very conservative—he doesn't want people pointing at him when he lands," a Raytheon executive says. Burt Rutan, who designed the first Starship models and helped flight-test the plane, says manufacturing costs were so high "they'll never recover their investment....They expected break-even at about 500 units."[1]

The Starship story makes several important points about marketing research. First, engineering and design can be excellent, but if the resulting product doesn't meet the needs of the marketplace, the product will fail. Second, marketing research could have alerted management to a "lack of fit" between product and market needs early in the design process. Third, spending a little on marketing research (probably less than $100,000) could have saved Raytheon about a half-billion dollars.

In this chapter we begin by reviewing how and where marketing research fits into the overall marketing process. Next, the role of marketing research in management decision making is discussed. We then describe the various opportunities available in the research industry.

THE NATURE OF MARKETING

Marketing is the process of planning and executing the conception, pricing, promotion, and distribution of ideas, goods, and services to create exchanges that satisfy individual and organizational objectives.[2] The potential for exchange exists when there are at least two parties and each has something of potential value to the other. When the two parties can communicate and deliver the desired goods or services, exchange can take place. How do marketing managers attempt to stimulate exchange? They follow the "right" principle. They attempt to get the right goods or services to the right people at the right place at the right time at the right price using the right promotion techniques. This principle tells you that marketing managers control many factors that ultimately determine marketing success. In order to make the "right" decisions, management must have timely decision-making information. Marketing research is a primary channel for providing that information.

Marketing
The process of planning and executing the conception, pricing, promotion, and distribution of ideas, goods, and services that satisfy individual and organizational objectives.

The Marketing Concept

To efficiently accomplish their goals, firms today have adopted the **marketing concept**, which requires (1) a consumer orientation, (2) a goal orientation, and (3) a systems orientation. **Consumer orientation** means that firms strive to identify the group of people (or firms) most likely to buy their product (the target market) and to produce a good or offer a service that will meet the needs of the target customers most effectively. The second tenet of the marketing concept is **goal orientation**; that is, a firm must be consumer oriented only to the extent that it also accomplishes corporate goals. These goals in profit-making firms usually center on financial criteria, such as a 15 percent return on investment.

The third component of the marketing concept is a **systems orientation**. A system is an organized whole—or a group of diverse units that form an integrated whole—functioning or operating in unison. It is one thing for a firm to say it is consumer oriented and another actually to be consumer oriented. Systems must be established first to find out what consumers want and to identify market opportunities. As you will see later, identifying target market needs and market opportunities are the tasks of marketing research. Next, this information must be fed back to the firm. Without feedback from the marketplace, a firm is not truly consumer oriented.

Marketing concept
A business philosophy based on consumer orientation, goal orientation, and systems orientation.

Consumer orientation
Identification of and focus on the group of people or firms most likely to buy a product and production of a good or service that will meet their needs most effectively.

Goal orientation
A focus on the accomplishment of corporate goals; a limit set on consumer orientation.

Systems orientation
Creation of systems to monitor the external environment and deliver the marketing mix to the target market.

Researching the Marketing Mix

Establishing the marketing concept is the first step in developing a marketing-oriented organization. Within the marketing department, a **marketing mix**, based upon the marketing concept, must be created. This mix is the unique blend of product pricing, promotion, offerings, and distribution designed to reach a specific group of consumers.

Each element within the marketing mix can be controlled by the marketing manager. A strategy for each element must be uniquely constructed and blended with other elements by the marketing manager to achieve an optimum mix. Any mix is only as good as its weakest component. For example, a weak product with

Marketing mix
The unique blend of product pricing, promotion, offerings, and distribution designed to meet the needs of a specific group of consumers.

an excellent distribution system is often doomed to failure. Campbell, for example, has an excellent distribution system that reaches over 95 percent of all retail grocers. Yet, its Red Kettle soups were an ill-conceived product that failed in the marketplace because of poor positioning.

Marketing research can help find and eliminate "weak links" in the marketing mix. New product research, for example, could have evaluated the general concept of Red Kettle soups. Also, taste tests and packaging tests to evaluate the design, size, and color of the can should have been conducted.

The External Marketing Environment

Over time, the marketing mix must be altered because of changes in the environment in which consumers live, work, and make purchasing decisions. This means that some new consumers will become part of the target market, others will drop out of the market, and those who remain may have different tastes, needs, incomes, lifestyles, and purchase habits than the original target consumers.

Although managers can control the marketing mix, they cannot control elements in the external environment that continually mold and reshape the target market. Unless management understands the external environment, the firm cannot intelligently plan its future. An organization is often unaware of the forces that influence its future. Marketing research is a key means for understanding the environment. Knowledge of the environment helps a firm to not only alter its present marketing mix, but also to identify new opportunities. For example, America's growing interest in personal health led Con Agra to develop Healthy Choice frozen dinners. Unlike most low calorie frozen dinners, Healthy Choice products are low in sodium and cholesterol.

THE ROLE OF MARKETING RESEARCH IN DECISION MAKING

Marketing research plays two key roles in the marketing system. First, it is part of the marketing intelligence feedback process. It provides decision makers with data on the effectiveness of the current marketing mix and provides insights for necessary changes. Market research also is the primary tool for exploring new opportunities in the marketplace. Segmentation research and new product research help identify the most lucrative opportunities for marketing managers.

Marketing Research Defined

Marketing research
The planning, collection, and analysis of data relevant to marketing decision making and the communication of the results of this analysis to management.

Now that you have an understanding of how **marketing research** fits into the overall marketing system, we can proceed with a formal definition of the term as specified by the American Marketing Association:

Marketing research is the function which links the consumer, customer, and public to the marketer through information—information used to identify and define marketing opportunities and problems; generate, refine, and evaluate marketing actions; monitor marketing performance; and improve understanding of marketing as a process. Marketing research specifies the information required to address these issues; designs the method for collecting information; manages and implements the data collection process; analyzes the results; and communicates the findings and their implications.[3]

We like a shorter definition: marketing research is the planning for, collection, and analysis of data relevant to marketing decision making and the communication of the results of this analysis to management.

The Importance of Marketing Research to Management

Marketing research can be viewed as playing three functional roles: descriptive, diagnostic, and predictive. Its **descriptive function** includes gathering and presenting statements of fact. For example, what is the historic sales trend in the industry? What are consumers' attitudes toward a product and its advertising? The second role of research is the **diagnostic function**, wherein data or actions are explained. What was the impact on sales when we changed the design on the package? The final role of research is the **predictive function**. How can the researcher use the descriptive and diagnostic research to predict the results of a planned marketing decision?

Descriptive function
The gathering and presentation of statements of fact.

Diagnostic function
The explanation of data or actions.

Predictive function
Specification of how to use the descriptive and diagnostic research to predict the results of a planned marketing decision.

Improving the Quality of Decision Making.   Marketing research is an invaluable tool to the marketing manager. Most important, it improves the quality of marketing decision making by shedding light on the desirability of various marketing alternatives. Consider the case of Dad's Root Beer, which faced several packaging and taste alternatives for the product:

> A market research study noted that respondents tended to describe their favorite root beer brand as possessing attributes such as "great tasting," "refreshing," and "flavorful." Dad's graphics tended to reinforce attributes like "attractive package," "looks good," "distinctive," "clear," and "fresh" but detracted from the image of "foamy."
>
> The study determined that earth tones, not white, connoted root beer, so the package graphics were redesigned and tested in Rockford, Illinois, and Oshkosh, Wisconsin. In Oshkosh, sales increased more than 10 percent with the new graphics. In Rockford, sales increased 14 percent. Additionally, the light blue color of Dad's sugar-free root beer package no longer appealed to the "upscale, young, mostly female" audience for diet drinks, so that packaging was changed to silver.
>
> Taste testing showed that while Dad's was perceived as having "real root beer" taste, the contemporary youth market wanted a "more mellow" or "smoother" taste. The goal in reformulating Dad's, therefore, was to retain its distinctive taste, but make it lighter. This was done primarily by making it sweeter and adding more vanilla flavoring. The new taste scored considerably higher than all competitors.[4]

Finding Out What Went Wrong.   A second way in which managers use research is to find out why something did not work out as planned. Was this decision incorrect to begin with? Did an unforeseen change in the external environment cause it to fail? How can we avoid making the same mistake again? Alcon Laboratories, a major manufacturer of ophthalmic products, introduced an eye drop for the over-the-counter market called Happy Eyes. In blind package tests (showing no brand names), consumers preferred Happy Eyes over both Murine and Visine. Subsequent introduction of the product nationally proved to be a total disaster. Follow-up market research found that consumers were uncomfortable with the product's name. "Happy Eyes" sounded too frivolous and flippant. One interviewee said that "it sounded like something a guy concocted in his garage in an old wash tub." Consumers wanted to make sure that anything they put into their eyes was only of the highest quality. The name Happy Eyes did not project a high-quality image.

Understanding the Marketplace.   The third basic use of marketing research by managers is to understand what is going on in the marketplace. Historically, marketing research has been practiced for as long as marketing has existed. The early Phoenicians carried out market demand studies as they traded in the various ports of the Mediterranean Sea. Marco Polo's diary indicates he was performing a marketing research function as he traveled to China. There is even evidence that the Spanish systematically conducted "market surveys" as they explored the New World, and there was reported one example of marketing research conducted during the Renaissance. Today, a marketing manager might, for example, consider offering coupons with the introduction of a new frozen pastry. The coupon will be used along with network television advertising to induce trial of the new pastry. The question arises as to who should receive the coupons. The sales promotion expenditure will be more effective if coupons are mailed to those households most likely to redeem them. Previous experience with frozen pastry coupon redemptions suggests that heavy coupon users in general are most likely to redeem the new pastry coupons. The next logical question for the marketing manager to ask would be, "Are there any identifiable demographic characteristics of

Marketing research helps determine the packaging colors and graphics that will reinforce the attributes of a product. Sales of Dad's Root Beer increased after a redesign of its packaging. (Courtesy of The Monarch Company, Inc.)

TABLE 1.1   *Demographics of Heavy Coupon Users*

	HEAVY (TOP 20%)	MEDIUM–LIGHT	NONUSER
Average Household Size	3.6	3.2	3.4
Average Age Female Head	43.1	45.2	41.9
Household Income ($000)	$30.9	$29.1	$28.7
Female Head Attended College	51%	50%	52%
Average Monthly Grocery Bill	$334	$292	$303
Female Head Does Not Work Outside or Works Part Time	65%	61%	55%

heavy coupon users versus light users?" Market research revealed that the only statistically significant difference is that the female head of household is not employed full time (see Table 1.1). The marketing manager would then specify this characteristic when purchasing the mailing list for the new frozen pastry coupons.

The Proactive Role of Marketing Research

Understanding the nature of the marketing system is a necessity for a successful marketing orientation. By having a thorough knowledge of factors that have an impact on the target market and the marketing mix, management can be proactive rather than reactive. A proactive management alters the marketing mix to fit newly emerging patterns in economic, social, and competitive environments whereas a reactive management waits for change to have a major impact on the firm before deciding to take action. It is the difference between viewing the turbulent marketing environment as a threat (a reactive stance) or an opportunity (a proactive stance). Procter & Gamble, for example, was reactive in the 1980s in the disposable diaper market, when it attempted to defend itself against environmentalist claims of nonbiodegradability. A proactive stance would have been to create a biodegradable diaper. Marketing research plays a key role in proactive management by anticipating changes in the market and consumer desires and then designing goods and services to meet those needs.

In the early 1980s, attempts to diversify Pitney Bowes into computer applications such as word processing failed. The chairman decided to focus the company's efforts on its mainstay, the mailroom, where it faced less competition. He tripled the market research budget to find a way to push past the basic postage machine and return to double-digit profit growth. The market research yielded a clear conclusion: the paperless society is a pipe dream; paper will continue to clog desks and mailboxes. So Pitney's chairman decided to find ways to automate the paper handling. Pitney Bowes has doubled its software and electronic engineering staff since 1985. R&D spending shot from $48 million in 1985 to over $100 million in 1993. Out came a string of new products to change the way companies mail and ship products.

A proactive manager not only makes short-term adjustments (tactics) in the marketing mix to meet market changes but also seeks, through strategic planning, to develop a long-run **marketing strategy** for the firm. A strategic plan guides the

Marketing strategy
Guiding the long-run use of the firm's resources based on its existing and projected capabilities and on projected changes in the external environment.

long-run use of the firm's resources based on the firm's existing and projected internal capabilities and on projected changes in the external environment. A good strategic plan, like that of Pitney Bowes, is based upon good marketing research. It helps the firm meet long-run profit and market share goals. Poor strategic planning can threaten survival of the firm. Montgomery Ward, floundering for almost a decade due to inadequate planning and lack of understanding of the marketplace, had to give up its once-dominant catalog sales division.

Applied Research versus Basic Research

Applied research
Research aimed at solving a specific, pragmatic problem—better understanding of the marketplace, determination of why a strategy or tactic failed, reduction of uncertainty in management decision making.

Basic research
Research aimed at expanding the frontiers of knowledge rather than solving a specific, pragmatic problem.

Virtually all marketing research is conducted to better understand the marketplace, to find out why a strategy failed, or to reduce uncertainty in management decision making. All research conducted for these purposes is called **applied research**. For example, should the price of frozen dinners be raised 40 cents? What name should Ford select for the new sedan? Which commercial has the highest level of recall: A or B? On the other hand, **basic** or pure **research** attempts to expand the frontiers of knowledge; it is research not aimed at a specific pragmatic problem. Basic research hopes to provide further confirmation to an existing theory or to learn more about a concept or phenomenon. For example, basic research might test a hypothesis on high-involvement decision making or consumer information processing. In the long run, basic research helps us understand more about the world in which we live. The findings of basic research usually cannot be implemented by managers in the short run. Most basic research is now conducted in universities. In contrast, most research undertaken by businesses is applied research because it must be cost effective and of demonstrable value to the decision maker.

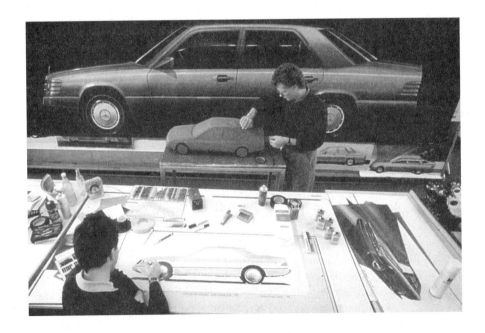

Applied research is conducted by automobile manufacturers to determine names for their new vehicles. (R. Bossu/Sygma)

DECIDING WHETHER TO CONDUCT MARKET RESEARCH

A manager who is faced with several alternative solutions to a particular problem should not instinctively call for applied marketing research. In fact, the first decision to be made is whether to conduct marketing research at all. In a number of situations it is best not to conduct marketing research.

A Lack of Resources.   There are two situations when a lack of resources should preclude marketing research from being undertaken. First, an organization may lack the funds to do the research properly. If a project calls for a sample of 800 respondents but the budget allows for only 50 interviews, the quality of the information would be highly suspect. Second, funds may be available to do the research properly but insufficient to implement any decisions resulting from the research. Sometimes small organizations in particular lack the necessary resources to create an effective marketing mix. We once conducted a project for a performing arts guild. The director was in complete agreement with our recommendations, but two years later nothing had been done because the money was not available.

Research Results Would Not Be Useful.   Some types of marketing research studies measure lifestyle and personality factors of customers and potential customers. Assume that a study finds introverted people with a poor self-concept yet a high need for achievement are most likely to patronize a discount brokerage service. Management of Charles Schwab discount brokerage might be hardpressed to use this information.

Poor Timing in the Marketplace.   Marketing research should not be undertaken if the opportunity for successful entry into a market has already passed. If a product is in the late maturity or decline stage of the product life cycle, such as record turntables or console black and white television, it would be foolish to do research for new product entry. The same is true for markets rapidly approaching saturation, such as super premium ice cream; that is, Häagen-Dazs, Ben and Jerry's, Schraffts, and Blue Bell. For products already in the market, however, research is needed to modify the products as tastes, competition, and other factors change.

The Decision Already Has Been Made.   In the real world of management decision making and company politics, marketing research has sometimes been used improperly. Several years ago we conducted a large marketing research study for a bank with over $300 million in deposits. The purpose of the research project was to guide top management in mapping a strategic direction for the bank during the next five years. After presenting the report to the president he said, "I fully agree with your recommendations because that was what I was going to do anyway! I'm going to use your study tomorrow when I present my strategic plan to the board of directors." The question was then asked by the researcher, "What if my recommendations had been counter to your decision?" The bank president laughed and said, "They would have never known that I had conducted a marketing research study!" Not only was the project a waste of money, but it certainly raised a number of ethical questions in the researcher's mind.

When Managers Cannot Agree On What They Need to Know to Make a Decision. Although it may seem obvious that research should not be undertaken until objectives are specified, it sometimes happens. Although preliminary or exploratory studies are commonly done to better understand the nature of the problem, a large, major research project should not be. It is faulty logic to say, "Well, let's just go ahead and do the study and then we will better understand the problem and know what steps to take." The wrong phenomena might be studied or key elements needed for management decision making may not be included.

When Decision-Making Information Already Exists. Some companies have been conducting research in certain markets for many years. They understand the characteristics of the target customers and what they like and dislike about existing products. Under these circumstances, further research would be redundant and a waste of money. Procter & Gamble, for example, has extensive knowledge of the coffee market. After it conducted initial taste tests, P&G went into national distribution with Folger's Instant Coffee without further research. The Sara Lee Corporation did the same thing with its frozen croissants, as did Quaker Oats with Chewy Granola Bars. This tactic, however, does not always work. P&G thought they understood the pain reliever market thoroughly, so they bypassed market research for Encaprin encapsulated aspirin. The product failed because it lacked a distinct competitive advantage over existing products and was withdrawn from the market.

When the Costs of Conducting Research Outweigh the Benefits. There are rarely situations where a manager has such tremendous confidence in his or her judgment that additional information relative to a pending decision would not be accepted if it were available and free. The manager might have sufficient confidence to be unwilling to pay very much for it or wait long to receive it. Willingness to acquire additional decision-making information depends upon a manager's perception of its quality, price, and timing. The manager would be willing to pay more for perfect information, that is, data that left no doubt on which alternative to follow, than information that still left uncertainty as to what to do. In summary, research should be undertaken only when the expected value of the information is greater than the cost of obtaining the data.[5]

TABLE 1.2 *The Decision Whether to Conduct Market Research*

MARKET SIZE	SMALL PROFIT MARGIN	LARGE PROFIT MARGIN
Small	Cost likely to be greater than benefit, e.g., eyeglasses replacement screw, tire valve extension	Possible benefits greater than cost, e.g., ultraexpensive Lambeggehni-type sportswear; larger specialized industrial equipment, e.g., Joy Manufacturing, computer-aided metal stamping machines
Large	Benefits likely to be greater than costs, e.g., Stouffers frozen entrees, Crest's tartar control toothpastes	Benefits most likely to be greater than costs, e.g., medical equipment like C.A.T. scanners, Toshiba's high-definition television

Note: The decision on whether to conduct marketing research depends on whether the perceived cost is greater than the benefit. Two important determinants of potential benefit are profit margins and market size.

Generally speaking, potential new products with large profit margins are going to have greater potential benefit than products with smaller profit margins, assuming that both items have the same sales potential. Also, new product opportunities in large markets are going to offer greater potential benefits than those in smaller markets if competitive intensity is the same in both markets (see Table 1.2).

SUMMARY

Marketing is a process of planning and executing the conception, pricing, promotion, and distribution of ideas, goods, and services to create exchanges that satisfy individual and organizational objectives. Marketing managers attempt to get the right goods or services to the right people at the right place at the right time at the right price, using the right promotion technique. This may be accomplished by following the marketing concept. The marketing concept is based on consumer orientation, goal orientation, and systems orientation.

The marketing manager must work within an internal environment of the organization and understand the external environment over which he or she has little, if any, control. The primary variables over which the marketing manager has control are place, price, promotion, and product decisions. The unique combination of these four variables is called the *marketing mix*.

Marketing research plays a key part in providing the information for managers to shape the marketing mix. Marketing research plays several important roles for the marketing manager: it helps reduce uncertainty, it aids managers in determining what went wrong, and it helps managers understand the marketplace. Marketing research should be undertaken only when the perceived benefits are greater than the costs.

KEY TERMS

Marketing
Marketing concept
Consumer orientation
Goal orientation
Systems orientation
Marketing mix
Marketing research

Descriptive function
Diagnostic function
Predictive function
Marketing strategy
Applied research
Basic research

REVIEW AND DISCUSSION QUESTIONS

1. The role of marketing is to create exchanges. What role might marketing research play in the facilitation of the exchange process?
2. Marketing research has traditionally been associated with manufacturers of consumer goods. Today, we are experiencing an increasing number of organizations, both profit making and nonprofit, using marketing research. Why do you think this trend exists? Give some examples.

3. Explain the relationship between marketing research and the marketing concept.
4. Name two consumer goods, two services, and two nonprofit concepts that might have logically been developed with marketing research.
5. Comment on the following statement: "I own a restaurant in the downtown area. I see customers everyday whom I know on a first name basis. I understand their likes and dislikes. If I put something on the menu and it doesn't sell, I know that they didn't like it. I also read the magazine *Modern Restaurants,* so I know what the trends are in the industry. This is all of the marketing research I need to do."
6. Why is marketing research important to marketing executives? Give several reasons.
7. How do you think marketing research might differ between (a) a retailer, (b) a consumer goods manufacturer, (c) an industrial goods manufacturer, and (d) a charitable organization?
8. Ralph Moran is planning to invest $1.5 million in a new restaurant in St. Louis. When Ralph applied for a construction financing loan, the bank officer asked if he had conducted any research. Ralph replied, "I checked on research and a marketing research company wanted $20,000 to do the work. I decided that with all the other expenses of opening a new business, research was a luxury that I could do without." Comment.
9. Describe three situations in which marketing research should not be undertaken. Explain why this is true.
10. Give an example of (a) the descriptive role of marketing research, (b) the diagnostic role, and (c) the predictive function of marketing research.

CASE

Fairfield Inns

The hotel glut has produced a tremendous windfall for business travelers. Service is up but prices are not. Because of overbuilding, hotel chains are engaging in an all-out service war to pamper the business traveler. Business persons spend about $34 billion a year at hotels and motels and account for nearly all the occupancy except at resorts.

The number of available rooms increased 40 percent during the 1980s, resulting in an average occupancy rate of 63.8 percent by the end of the decade. The breakeven point for the industry is 65 percent, thus about 60 percent of America's hotels lost money in the early 1990s. To make matters worse for the profit margin, corporate discounts have become increasingly popular and the size of the discount is going up. In the past five years the average corporate discount rose from 18 percent off regular rates to 25 percent.

Yet despite this difficult environment, economy hotels are thriving. When corporations began tightening expense accounts for lower-level employees, demand surged for rooms priced at $40 per night and under. The low-end segment of the market was once characterized by seedy independents offering run-down facilities on roads long bypassed by interstate highways. The big chains like Marriott, stymied by lower growth in their traditional markets, moved into the economy market segment and began upgrading its image.

Marriott's entry into the economy market is Fairfield Inns. For a price lower than most hotels, the business traveler receives a king-size or two double-size beds, a large work area, free cable TV, and a bathroom with a separate vanity area so the traveler will not fog up the mirror with steam from a shower. When guests check out of a Fairfield

Inn, they can rate their stay on two computers at either end of the reception desk. Four questions pop up on the screen dealing with cleanliness, service, value for the price, and overall rating; the guest punches a key to indicate excellent, average, or poor. Employee bonuses are pegged to the ratings.[6]

1. Would you say that the data gathered at the two computers at the reception desk was marketing research? Why?
2. What kind of market research information do you think Marriott gathered before it developed the Fairfield Inn concept? Would it be applied or basic research? Why?
3. Now that Fairfield Inns are a viable, ongoing operation, do you see the need for other marketing research information? If yes, give some examples.

APPENDIX A

A Career in Marketing Research

Marketing research offers a variety of career paths depending upon one's education level, interests, and personality. Most jobs are to be found with either research suppliers (firms that conduct research for clients) or research users (corporations that depend on market research for decision-making guidance). A limited number of market research positions are also available with advertising agencies and various branches of government.

Positions with research suppliers tend to be concentrated in a few large cities, for example, New York, Chicago, Los Angeles, San Francisco, and Dallas. Although research suppliers are found throughout the country, a majority of the larger firms (and entry-level jobs) are found in these cities. Research users, on the other hand, tend to be more widely scattered and found in communities of various size, for example, General Mills in Minneapolis, Tyson Foods in Springdale, Arkansas.

Women have long been accepted as equals in the marketing research industry. Senior-level positions are increasingly filled by women executives. At the college entry-level position of junior analyst, women are twice as prevalent as men! Obviously, young women increasingly are recognizing the opportunities that await them in the exciting field of marketing research.

There was a time when a decision to go into marketing research represented a lifetime career commitment. Once you were a marketing researcher, there was a good chance you would always be a marketing researcher. Today this inflexibility is not so prevalent. Now it is more common to see people transfer into and out of the marketing research department as part of a career in marketing.

Table A.1 presents a comparative summary of career positions within the research industry. Not all companies have all positions, but you will find people with these titles across the industry. The table also lists the minimum experience and education typical for each position.

Positions within Supplier Organizations

Research suppliers offer a majority of the entry-level career positions in the market research field. Many of the newer firms are entrepreneurial in nature and headed by a founder or partners. In smaller companies the founder-owner not only manages the company but typically is involved in selling and conducting research projects.

TABLE A.1   *Career Opportunities in Marketing Research: General Duties and Qualifications*

POSITION	LEVEL OF RESPONSIBILITY	MINIMUM EXPERIENCE	MINIMUM EDUCATION
Director	Department Administration	10+ years	Graduate Degree
Assistant Director	Projects Administration	5+ years	Graduate Degree
Senior Analyst	Project Supervision	3–5 years	College Degree (may require graduate degree)
Analyst	Project Analysis and Expediting	2–4 years	College Degree (may require graduate degree)
Statistician	Statistical Analysis	0 years	College Degree (may require graduate degree)
Clerical Supervisor	Office Management	3–5 years	Vocational Degree
Junior Analyst	Project Assistance	0 years	College Degree
Field Director	Data Collection Supervisor	3–5+ years	High School
Librarian	Library Management	0 years	College Degree
Interviewer	Questionnaire Administration	0 years	Some High School
Tabulator and Clerk	Simple Tabulation, Filing, and Organizing	0 years	Some High School

Owners of larger supplier organizations perform basically the same functions as top managers in other large corporations, such as creating strategic plans and developing broad corporate policies. It is also common in large supplier organizations to have managers that specialize in either a specific industry or type of research, for example, manager of health care research, manager of financial research, or political polling. Firms also may have a director of qualitative research or a director of multivariate studies. Nonmanagerial jobs found in supplier firms follow.

Statistician—Data Processing Specialist.   A person holding this position is viewed as internal expert on statistical techniques, sampling methods, and market research software programs such as SPSS, SAS, or UNCLE. Normally, a masters degree or even a Ph.D. is required.

Senior Analyst.   A senior analyst is usually found in larger firms. The individual typically works with an account executive to plan a research project and then supervises several analysts who execute the projects. Senior analysts work with a minimal level of supervision themselves. They often work with analysts in developing questionnaires and may help in analyzing difficult data sets. The final report is usually written by an analyst but reviewed, with comments, by the senior analyst. People in this position are usually given budgetary control over projects and responsibility for meeting time schedules.

Analyst.   The analyst usually handles the bulk of the work required for executing research projects. An analyst normally reports to a senior analyst. He or she assists in questionnaire preparation, pretests, then does data analysis, and writes the preliminary report. Much of the secondary data work is performed by the analyst.

Junior Analyst.   This job is typically at the entry level for a degreed person. A junior analyst works under close supervision on rather mundane tasks, for example, editing and coding questionnaires, performing basic statistical analysis, conducting secondary data searches, and writing rough draft reports on simple projects.

Account Executive.   An account executive is responsible for making sales to client firms and keeping client organizations satisfied enough to continue funneling work to the research supplier. An account executive works on a day-to-day basis with clients and serves as liaison between the client and the research organization. Account managers must understand each client's problems and know what research techniques should be employed to provide the right data. He or she must be able to explain to the client what research techniques are needed in a nontechnical manner. Moreover, the account executive must be able to sell the firm's services and abilities over competing suppliers. Account executives work hand in hand with the research analysts to develop the research methodology to solve the client's problems. This position often requires an MBA degree.

Field Work Director.   Most market research firms do not have their own interviewers. Instead, they rely on market research field services throughout the United States to conduct the actual interviews. Field services are the production line of the market research industry. They hire, train, and supervise interviewers within a specific geographic area. A field work director is responsible for obtaining completed interviews in the proper geographic area, using the specified sampling instructions, within a specified budget and on time. Field work directors keep in close touch with field services throughout the United States. They know which field services have the best interviewers and can maintain time schedules. After a study has been fielded, the field service director obtains daily reports from the field service. Typical data reported includes the number of completed interviews; the number of refusals; interviewing hours, travel time, and mileage; and problems, if any.

Clerical Supervisor.   Large research suppliers usually have a clerical supervisor. This person is in charge of the centralized handling and processing of statistical data. Duties include scheduling work, maintaining accuracy, and supervising data entry clerks and other clerical help.

Positions within Research Departments and Advertising Agencies

Only a handful of manufacturers and retailers have full-blown research departments. These companies, like Kraft General Foods, Sears, and Procter & Gamble, have organization structures similar to research suppliers. Often these departments compete against outside suppliers for the company's research work. A new product manager at General Mills, who finds that an outside supplier is cheaper or offers a superior methodology is usually free to award the contract to the supplier. In addition to the positions just listed, a full-service research department will have a research director and an assistant director.

Research Director.   The research director (sometimes vice-president of research) is responsible for the entire research program of the company. The director may conduct strategic research for top management or accept work from new product managers, brand managers, or other internal clients. In some cases, the director may initiate proposals for studies but typically responds to requests. He or she has full responsibility for the market research budget and, where resources are limited, may have to set priorities regarding projects undertaken. The director hires the professional staff and exercises general supervision of the research department. He or she normally presents the findings of strategic research projects to top management. This position often requires a masters degree and, in some companies, a Ph.D. The director often is viewed as the top technical expert in the department as well.

Theodore Dunn, research director of Benton & Bowles Advertising, one of the world's largest agencies, provides a glimpse of the job of ad agency researchers:

> Their job is to understand current and potential customer needs and to help translate it into advertising strategy. Then, through research, they provide creative information that helps in the creation of selling advertising. The effort is directed more against the development of the agency's product and less against the development of the client's product. In so doing, agency research departments are now better able to concentrate their efforts and then do it with fewer people.
>
> The staffs of agency research departments today are better trained in the social sciences. Their training better enables them to measure and understand consumer needs and reactions. But more important than their training, they are better integrated into the process of developing advertising than was true just five years ago. It's this integration of research into the agency process of developing advertising that makes for greater utility.
>
> At Benton & Bowles, we have a formal system for coordinating the various services in the agency. There are five associate research directors, each of whom is responsible for research on specific brands and assigned to a core group, for each of his or her accounts. The core group is made up of account management and an associate research director. The group is charged by our management with developing agency advertising and marketing strategies for its brand. Its purpose is not only to take advantage of the individual services input but also to profit by the interaction of all people involved.
>
> Because we have this system at B&B, the specific research tools we use are geared to the right problems. In fact, the creative person in the core group very often requests certain kinds of information from research which is needed to develop advertising. When he asks for a study, he is looking for information, and you can bet he'll use it and use it better than when someone just drops a research report on his desk, and that is the first he has ever heard of the project.
>
> What kinds of research does the core group want? They want to know all they can about their consumers. Who are their best customers? How do consumers feel about existing products and brands? What are they like demographically? What are they like psychographically? Socially? Does their product cater better to one demographic or psychographic subgroup? How do consumers use the product? With what frequency do they use it? Who accounts for what volume? What's the best position/promise for the brand?
>
> From this they develop an advertising strategy. Creative people then use research to help guide them in making judgments about the best executions for the strategy. They want to know, for example, which of several initial executions on which they are working has the best chance of breaking through the mass of communications impinging on the consumer and being remembered. They want to know which best communicates what they want to say. Which does it most convincingly? Which best predisposes the consumer to buy? Sometimes they decide to combine elements of several commercials to develop a better one than any of their

original alternatives. Sometimes they decide not to pursue another execution direction in favor of their original.[7]

Assistant Research Director.   This position is normally found only in large full-scale research departments. This person is second in command and reports to the research director. Senior analysts, statisticians, and data processing specialists usually report to the assistant director, who performs many of the same functions as the director.

Research Directors and Others in Limited Function Research Departments

Most research departments in corporations or advertising agencies are limited in their functions. Therefore, they do not conduct the research or analyze the data. Instead, they formulate requests for research proposals, analyze the proposals, award contracts to research suppliers, and evaluate the supplier's work. Internally, they work with brand managers and new product specialists in formulating research problems and interpreting and implementing the recommendations of the research reports provided by the suppliers.

The research director and assistant director (if any) function in a manner similar to their positions described earlier. Analysts formulate and evaluate proposals and the work of research suppliers. They also help implement the recommendations. With the exception of a secretary, there is usually no other personnel in a limited function research department.

A Career in Marketing Research at 3M

In order to gain an appreciation for a career in marketing research, we'll examine the career path in one company.

The challenges are tough and the opportunities available to marketing researchers at 3M are almost limitless. The biggest challenge is that each researcher has an annual goal of a set percentage of time that must be sold on approved projects. The opportunities presented by a large number of businesses, with thousands of products that need research information, are obvious.

The Corporate Marketing Research Department consists of about twenty-nine people, organized as in Figure A.1. The marketing research project work is carried out by the analysts, senior analysts, supervisors, and the two research managers. (The research manager for Corporate Planning Services works solely for the Corporate Planning and Strategy Committee.) Projects are obtained through requests from marketing personnel in the operating units or from sales calls made by analysts and senior analysts. A sales call may be the result of follow-up from a previous project, introduction of a new research service, information on new or expanded activity in the operating unit, or the introduction of a new analyst. All project requests take the form of a proposal that outlines the marketing situation, the information needed, how the information will be obtained, timing, and costs. The signed proposal, with an operating unit designated to be charged for the costs, is the authorization to proceed with the project.

The analysts are recruited from university MBA programs and from among 3M employees in other disciplines (i.e., engineering, laboratory, etc.) who have

FIGURE A.1   *Organization of Corporate Marketing Research Department at 3M*

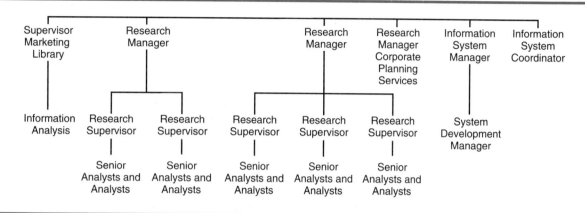

obtained an MBA while working at 3M and want to make a career change. The analysts' career goals are in marketing management but they are interested in, and have an aptitude for, spending three years in marketing research. Just about all of the analysts have postbaccalaureate business experience with 3M or other companies.

In the first year about 60 percent of an analyst's time is spent on research projects for operating units. The remainder of the time is spent in development seminars and classes covering sampling, study design, questionnaire design, focus groups, and other relevant subjects. The classes taken depend on prior experience and aptitude. All analysts take sales training from one of 3M's divisional sales trainers. (They are expected to sell their time to cover their costs, so they are given sales training. Also, managers believe that sales training is very beneficial in developing the personal interviewing techniques required in many projects.)

One year as an analyst, with good performance, qualifies a person for a position as a senior analyst. This is a promotion and the senior positions require selling close to 100 percent of one's time. The senior analyst is the workhorse of the project system, devoting time entirely to getting projects sold, completed, and reported.

The researchers' projects, for the most part, are divided along sector and group lines. Therefore, an individual's work will have an emphasis in a particular area such as industrial, health care, or imaging. However, if a project in one sector calls for an area of expertise that resides with someone assigned to another sector, that person can cross over for the project. Flexibility is an important element in the personal development of the analysts.

The senior analyst becomes a supervisor in about one year and is given one or two of the beginning analysts to develop into a competent researcher and future 3M marketer. The supervisor still does operating unit work, handling some of the more complex projects, selling time in the 60–80 percent range.

Supervisors will have developed a special rapport with several operating units over the years and will invariably be offered a marketing position in one of the line units at about the time three years have been completed. Alternatively, the managers of Corporate Marketing Research will be asked for a recommendation to fill an operating unit marketing position and the available supervisors will be recommended for interviews.[8]

CHAPTER 2

The Marketing Research Process

LEARNING OBJECTIVES

1. To learn the steps involved in the marketing research process.

2. To understand the components of the research request.

3. To become familiar with the nature of management within a research department.

4. To learn the advantages and disadvantages of survey, observation, and experimental research techniques.

Honda uses all the standard marketing research tools. The company even videotapes drivers as they test new cars. In response to all this customer input, Honda has made thousands of changes in the Accord since introducing it in 1976. The new wrinkles range from installing a suspension system used on racing cars for improved handling to changing the shape of the rear window so that a large soft drink can be passed into the car without spilling. In the process Honda just happened to produce the best-selling car in America from 1989 until 1992, when the Ford Taurus edged it out. Says Ben Knight, vice president for R&D of Honda North America, "We believe that the market and the customer will always find the truth."

Honda's manufacturing unit recently kicked off its most extensive customer research effort yet—the E. T. Phone Home Project (the name and the notion were lifted from the film *E.T.*). Over a three month period, factory workers who actually bolt and bang the Accord together called over 47,000 recent Accord buyers, or about half the owners who registered their cars with the company the previous spring. Honda's goal: to find out if customers were happy with their autos and to get ideas from improvements. The impact was seen in the 1994 Accords.[1]

Understanding customer's desires is a function of marketing research. In a small company, the procedure and tools for conducting the research can be pretty simple. Yet, several logical steps in the research process have to be taken before reliable decision-making information can be obtained. What are the basic steps in the market research process? How is marketing research managed in a company like Honda? These are the issues we will address in Chapter 2.

THE RESEARCH PROCESS

The research process builds a foundation for the remainder of the text. Every subsequent chapter will examine some specific aspect of this procedure. The marketing research process is shown in Figure 2.1.

Problem/Opportunity Identification and Formulation

The research process begins with the recognition of a marketing problem or opportunity. As changes occur in the firm's external environment, marketing managers are faced with the questions, "Should we change the existing marketing

FIGURE 2.1   *The Marketing Research Process*

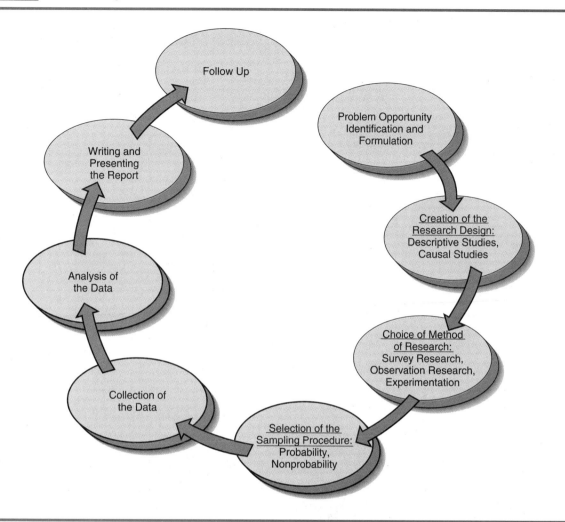

mix?" and, if so, "How?" Marketing research may be used to evaluate product, promotion, distribution, or pricing alternatives. In addition, it is used to find and evaluate new market opportunities.

For example, Taco Bell, a Mexican fast-food chain, serves typical Americanized Mexican food. Executives of the firm have noted from trade publications that American diets are changing to healthier, lighter fare. This trend could represent a problem or opportunity for Taco Bell.

Once a problem has been sensed, the marketing researcher comes into the picture. The first responsibility of the researcher, whether from an internal staff or outside consulting firm, is to work with the marketing manager to precisely define or uncover the problem whose symptoms have been observed. Certainly, no area of marketing research requires more insight and creativity than the process of problem definition. It is the first step in arriving at a solution. It is also the most critical part of the marketing research process. Proper definition of a problem also provides guidance and direction for the entire research process. Truly, a well-defined problem is "half the battle" of conducting research.

Anthony Miles, vice-president of the Boston Consulting Group, discusses three key questions he always seeks to answer at the problem definition stage:

1. Why is the information being sought?
2. Does this information already exist?
3. Can the question really be answered?

Find Out Why the Information Is Being Sought.   Large amounts of money, effort, and time are wasted because requests for marketing information are poorly formulated or misunderstood. For example, managers may not have a clear idea of what they want or may not phrase the question properly. Therefore, the following activities may answer the first question:

- Discuss what the information is to be used for and what decisions might be made as a result. Go through examples in detail.
- Try to get the client or manager to set priorities among the questions. This helps sort out the central questions from those of incidental interest.
- Rephrase the questions in several slightly different forms and discuss the differences.
- Create sample data and ask if they would help answer the questions. Simulate the decision process.
- Remember that the more clear-cut you think the questions are and the more quickly you come to feel that the question is straightforward, the more you should doubt that you have understood the real need.

As changes occur in a firm's external environment, marketing managers are faced with the questions: Should we change the existing marketing mix? If so, how? Executives of Taco Bell had to decide how to respond to the trend toward lighter, healthier diets. (Photo copyright Taco Bell Corp.)

Determine if the Information Already Exists. It often seems easier and more interesting to develop new information than to delve through old reports and data files to see if it already exists. There is a tendency to assume that current data are superior to data collected in the past.

Current data appear to be a "fix on today's situation." One has more control over the format and comprehensiveness of fresh data—they promise to be easier to work with.

Determine if the Question Really Can Be Answered. In companies where research is in discredit, a frequent reason is that too much was promised from prior pieces of work. It is extremely important to avoid being impelled by overeagerness to please or managerial macho into an effort that one knows has a limited probability of success. In most cases, it is possible to discern in advance the likelihood of success by identifying the following:

- Instances where you know for certain that information of the type required exists or can be readily obtained.
- Situations where you are fairly sure, but not fully certain, that the information can be gathered, based on similar prior experiences.
- Cases where you know you are trying something quite new and where there is a real risk of drawing a complete blank.

Use Exploratory Research to Define the Problem. Once a problem is recognized, it is extremely important for the researcher to understand exactly what needs to be examined. Obviously, the Taco Bell management cannot change America's eating habits. So, the firm is going to use marketing research to help guide its decision making. At this early stage of the research process, it is often necessary to conduct exploratory research. **Exploratory research** is usually small-scale research undertaken to define the exact nature of the problem and to gain a better understanding of the environment within which the problem has occurred. The Taco Bell researcher, for example, might review several existing studies and articles on trends in American eating habits. Competing chains could be visited to see how they are coping with the problem. A small-scale survey of consumers might be developed along with interviews of company executives. In addition, small groups of consumers may be brought together to discuss eating habits. This type of qualitative research is the subject of Chapter 5.

Exploratory research tends to be highly flexible with researchers following ideas, clues, and hunches as long as time and money constraints permit. Often ideas and clues can be obtained from so-called experts in the field. According to one industrial marketing research expert, "It is not uncommon to find that less than 1 percent of the 'knowledgeable' persons associated with an industrial market possess virtually all of the relevant information about the market . . .[therefore] careful attention should be given to the selection of knowledgeable persons." The researcher for Taco Bell could seek out nutritional experts at the Federal Department of Human Resources and at major research universities. He or she should also seek information from persons within the firm who might have insight into nutritional trends.

As the researcher moves through the exploratory research process, a list of problems and subproblems should be developed. The investigator should discern what all the probable factors are that seem to be somehow related to the problem

Exploratory research
Preliminary research to clarify the exact nature of the problem to be solved.

area. These are probable research topics. This stage of problem definition requires a brainstorming-type approach, but one guided by the previous stage's findings. All possibilities should be listed without regard to the feasibility of addressing them via research.

Unfortunately, given the natural desire of managers to get something going and the short time frame available for marketing research projects, the problem definition phase of the project is often not given proper attention. In many instances, this phase can be time consuming and seem to be heading nowhere. The tendency to short-circuit problem definition is unfortunate, for it can be very costly. The value of this phase of the research process lies in getting efforts off on the right track. A considerable amount of time and effort can be wasted in pursuit of the wrong problem.

Define Research Objectives.   The culmination of the problem/opportunity formulation process is a statement of the research objectives. These objectives are stated in terms of the precise information necessary and desired to solve the marketing management problem.

Diane Schmalensee, director of research operations, Marketing Science Institute, offers the following insights on research objectives.

> Objectives guide the researcher in developing good research, and they help the client evaluate the final product. So the client should be convinced of the importance of objectives.
>
> Even when clients seem to know the objectives, keep digging until the true purpose of the project has been uncovered. Otherwise, the research method may be at odds with the research objective, resulting in off-target findings.
>
> Objectives must be specific. Clients frequently state objectives in vague, general terms, and they must be prodded into providing details. For example, a client may want to determine if its advertising has been effective. The researcher must learn what the client means by "effective" and the purpose of the advertising. Research mechanics will differ considerably between measuring brand awareness for a new line of cosmetics among women age 15–25 and convincing men age 18–40 that one's light beer has lusty flavor.
>
> Limit the number of objectives. The fewer the study objectives, the easier it is to keep track of them, make sure each is addressed fully, and determine the most appropriate methodology.
>
> Once the research objectives have been established, research design and analysis are fairly straightforward.[2]

Research Objectives Must Avoid the "Nice to Know" Syndrome.   Even after conducting exploratory research, managers often tend to discuss research objectives in terms of broad areas of ignorance. They say, in effect, "Here are some things I don't know." Taco Bell management might say, "Who is eating this lighter, healthier food?" Managers are implicitly thinking, "When the research results come in, it will be nice to know more about this new eating trend. Once I have more knowledge, then I can make some decisions." Unfortunately, this scenario will usually lead to disappointment. There is nothing wrong with interesting findings, but they must also be "actionable." That is, the findings must provide decision-making information.

Accomplishment of a research objective must do more than reduce management's level of ignorance. Unless all the research is exploratory, it should lead to a decision. Perhaps the best way to assure actionable research is to determine how the research results will be implemented. In the case of Taco Bell, exploratory research uncovered a number of reports and news articles that confirmed the notion that Americans are eating lighter foods. Brainstorming among company executives led to a number of ideas including developing "lite lunches" and a number of specialty items, for example, chicken fajitas, that would offer an alternative to the standard menu items. Creation of new food items, however, is a lengthy process whereby new ideas are converted to recipes, recipes are then tried in the company's test kitchens, variations are developed, and finally those judged to be best are tested in company-owned stores. Management felt that Taco Bell needed a rapid response to changing eating habits. The easiest and quickest partial solution to the problem would be to add salad bars to Taco Bell restaurants. Thus, assume that the management decisions were (1) to determine if salad bars should be added to Taco Bell stores, and (2) if so, what items should be featured in the salad bar.

Determine Management Decisions and Formulate Research Objectives. Research objectives are basically a restatement of what management needs to know to make a decision in research terms. In the Taco Bell case, the research objectives are

1. To determine the portion of Taco Bell customers that eat at salad bars.
2. To determine how often Taco Bell customers and noncustomers eat at salad bars.
3. To examine what Taco Bell customers and noncustomers eat at salad bars and the items they like most and least.
4. To evaluate the desirability of specific Mexican-oriented food items on a Taco Bell salad bar.
5. To assess the stated desirability of a salad bar by Taco Bell customers and noncustomers.

State Research Objectives as Hypotheses. Often researchers state research objectives in the form of a hypothesis. A hypothesis is a conjectural statement about a relationship between two or more variables that can be tested with empirical data. Hypotheses are tentative statements that are considered to be plausible given the available information. A good hypothesis will contain clear implications for testing stated relationships. For example, based on exploratory research, a researcher might hypothesize that the addition of salad bars will result in current customers patronizing Taco Bell two additional times per month and increase each store's customer base (new customers) by 12 percent. A second hypothesis might be that new customers will be predominantly adults between 21 and 35 years of age with average household incomes of $25,000–40,000. The development of research hypotheses sets the stage for creating the research design.

Creating the Research Design

The **research design** is the plan to be followed to answer the research objectives or hypotheses. In essence, the researcher develops a structure or framework to solve a specific problem. There is no single, best research design. Instead, the investigator faces an array of choices, each with certain advantages and disadvantages. Ultimately, trade-offs are typically involved. A common trade-off is between research costs and the quality of decision-making information provided. Generally

Research design
The plan to be followed to answer the research objectives; the structure or framework to solve a specific problem.

speaking, the more precise and error free the information obtained, the higher the cost. Another common trade-off is between time constraints and the type of research design selected. In summary, the researcher must attempt to provide management with the best information possible subject to the various constraints under which he or she must operate.

Descriptive studies
These studies answer the questions who, what, where, when, and how.

Descriptive Studies.   The researcher's first task is to decide whether the research will be descriptive or causal. **Descriptive studies** are conducted to answer who, what, when, where, and how questions. Implicit in descriptive research is that management already knows or understands the underlying relationships of the problem area. Returning to our Taco Bell example, it is assumed, based on the exploratory research, that salads are perceived by consumers as lighter, healthier foods and that those consumers who seek a healthier diet sometimes choose a salad for a meal. Without knowledge of relationships, descriptive research would have little value for decision makers. For example, it would be of little value to Taco Bell to conduct a descriptive study of a new market area, for example, St. Louis, that provided age, income, ethnic, and educational levels of various segments of the city

Taco Bell management can use marketing research to determine if salad bars should be added to their stores. (Harriet Newman-Brown/Monkmeyer Press)

if Taco Bell had no idea what relationship, if any, these variables had to the success of a Taco Bell store.

Causal Studies.   In **causal studies** the researcher investigates whether one variable causes or determines the value of another variable. A variable is simply a symbol or concept that can assume any one of a set of values. An independent variable in a research project is a presumed cause of the dependent variable, the presumed effect. For example, does the level of advertising (independent variable) determine the level of sales (dependent variable) at a Taco Bell store? A **dependent variable** is a variable expected to be predicted or explained. An **independent variable** is a variable in an experiment that the market researcher can, to some extent, manipulate, change, or alter. An independent variable is expected to influence the dependent variable. Descriptive research can tell us that two variables seem to be somehow associated, such as advertising and sales, but cannot provide reasonable proof that the high levels of advertising cause high sales. Because descriptive research can shed light on associations or relationships, it helps the researcher in selecting variables for a causal study. For example, without the descriptive data, the Taco Bell researcher wouldn't know whether to examine age, occupation, income, or a host of other variables.

A causal study for Taco Bell might involve changing one independent variable (for example, in-store display for chips and cheese dip) and then observing the effect on the dependent variable (sales of chips and dip). Given that chips and dip sales go up when the displays are placed in the stores, there is an appropriate causal order of events called **temporal sequence**. The concept of temporal sequence is one criterion for causality that must be met.

A second criterion for causality is the necessity of concomitant variation. The degree to which a cause (in-store display) and effect (chips and dip sales) occur together or vary together is called **concomitant variation**. If in-store displays are considered a cause of increased sales of chips and dip, then when the displays go up sales should increase, and when the displays are removed chips and dip sales should fall to around the predisplay level or a little higher (new triers induced by the display may now become loyal consumers of chips and dip, thus creating a permanent increase in sales). If, however, erection of the in-store displays does not result in an increase in chips and dip sales, the researcher must conclude that the hypothesis about the relationship between in-store displays and sales of chips and dip is not correct.

An ideal situation would be one where sales increased markedly in every Taco Bell store when the in-store displays were put in place. But, alas, we live in a world where perfection is rarely achieved. There would probably be a few stores where little, if any, sales increases occurred with the erection of displays. In fact, sales might even drop in one or two stores! Yet out of hundreds of stores, this would be inconsequential. Perhaps the sales of chips and dip dropped in a small town where there had been a recent outbreak of food poisoning attributed to cheese products.

Remember, even perfect concomitant variation would not prove that A causes B. All that the researcher could say is that the association makes the hypothesis more likely but does not prove it.

The third issue of causality is to recognize the possibility of **spurious association**. This means that another variable or other variables might possibly cause changes in the dependent variable. The ideal situation would be one in which the researcher demonstrates that there is a total absence of other causal factors. In the

Causal studies
These studies examine whether one variable causes or determines the value of another variable.

Dependent variable
A symbol or concept expected to be explained or caused by the independent variable.

Independent variable
The symbol or concept over which the researcher has some control or can manipulate to some extent and that is hypothesized to cause or influence the dependent variable.

Temporal sequence
Appropriate causal order of events.

Concomitant variation
The degree to which a cause and effect occur or vary together.

Spurious association
Another variable or variables may cause changes in the dependent variable.

real world of marketing research, it is very difficult to identify and control all other potential causal factors. Think for a moment of all of the variables that could cause the sales of chips and cheese dip at Taco Bell to increase or decrease.

The researcher may lower spurious associations by holding constant other factors that could influence sales of chips and dip: for example, prices, newspaper and television advertising, coupons, discounts, size of the containers, and the receipts for cheese dip and the chips. Alternatively, the researcher may look at changes in sales by stores of approximately equal sales volume or by stores located in similar socioeconomic areas.

Choosing a Basic Method of Research

A research design, either descriptive or causal, is chosen according to a project's objectives. The next step is to select a means of gathering data. There are three basic research methods: survey, observation, and experiment. Survey research is often descriptive in nature, but can be causal. Experiments are almost always causal, whereas observation research is typically descriptive.

Survey research
Research where an interviewer interacts with respondents to obtain facts, opinions, and attitudes.

Survey.   **Survey research** involves an interviewer (except in mail surveys) interacting with respondents to obtain facts, opinions, and attitudes. A questionnaire is used to provide an orderly and structured approach to data gathering. Face-to-face interviews may take place within the respondent's home, in a shopping mall, or in a place of business.

Observation research
Descriptive research that monitors respondents' actions without direct interaction.

Observation.   The fastest growing form of **observation research** involves the use of cash registers with scanners, which read tags with bar codes to identify the item being purchased. The future of observation research is somewhat mind boggling. For example, A. C. Nielsen has been using black boxes for years on television sets to silently siphon off information on a family's viewing habits. But what if the set is on and no one is in the room? To overcome that problem, researchers say TVs might be equipped with heat sensors that will feel when the viewer is watching. Or participants might wear rings or watches with a transmitter that would signal the presence of "person A in the room while the television is on." Some have even talked of surgically implanting a transmitter into the body of a test subject. Far-fetched? The technology is already available.[3]

Experiments
Research to measure causality in which one or more variables are changed while observing the effect of the change on another variable.

Experiments.   **Experiments** are the third method researchers use to gather data. An experiment is distinguished by the researcher's changing one or more variables—price, package, design, shelf space, advertising theme, or advertising expenditures—while observing the effects of those changes on another variable (usually sales). The objective of experiments is to measure causality. The best experiments are those in which all factors are held constant except the ones being manipulated. This enables the researcher to observe that changes in sales, for example, can be caused by changes in the amount of money spent on advertising. Holding all other factors constant in the external environment is a monumental and costly, if not impossible, task. Factors such as competitors' actions in various markets, weather, and economic conditions are beyond the control of the researcher.

One way researchers attempt to control factors that might influence the dependent variable is to use a laboratory experiment; that is, an experiment conducted in a test facility rather than the natural environment. Researchers sometimes create simulated supermarket environments, give consumers script (play money), and then ask them to shop as they normally would for groceries. By varying package design or color over several time periods, for example, the researcher can determine which package is most likely to stimulate sales. Although laboratory techniques can provide valuable information, one must realize that the consumer is not in a natural environment. How a person acts in a laboratory may be different from an actual shopping situation. We will discuss experiments in detail in Chapter 8.

Selecting the Sampling Procedure

The sample is actually part of the research design but is a separate step in the research process. A sample is a subset from a larger population. Several questions must be answered before a sampling plan is selected. First, the population or universe of interest must be defined. This is the group from which the sample will be drawn. It should include all the people whose opinions, behavior, preferences, attitudes, and so on will aid the marketer's decision making. An example would be all persons who eat Mexican food at least once every sixty days. After the population has been defined, the next question is whether to use a probability sample or a nonprobability sample.

A **probability sample** is characterized by every element in the population having a known nonzero probability of being selected. Such samples allow the researcher to estimate how much sampling error is present in a given study. **Nonprobability samples** include all samples that cannot be considered probability samples. Specifically, any sample in which little or no attempt is made to ensure that a representative cross section of the population is obtained can be considered a nonprobability sample. The researchers cannot statistically calculate the reliability of the sample; that is, they cannot determine the degree of sampling error that can be expected. Sampling is the topic of Chapters 11 and 12.

Probability samples
Subsets of a population that ensure a representative cross section by giving every element in the population a known nonzero chance of being selected.

Nonprobability samples
Subsets of a population in which little or no attempt is made to ensure a representative cross section.

Collecting the Data

Most data collection is done by marketing research field services. Field service firms, found throughout the country, specialize in providing interviewing for data collection on a subcontract basis. A typical research study involves data collection in several cities and requires working with a comparable number of field service firms. To ensure that all subcontractors do everything exactly the same way, detailed field instructions should be developed for every job. Nothing should be left to chance; no interpretations of procedures should be left to the subcontractors.

Besides interviewing, field service firms provide group research facilities, mall intercept locations, test product storage, and kitchen facilities to prepare test food products. They also conduct retail audits (counting the amount of product sold from retail shelves). After an in-home interview has been completed, field service supervisors validate the survey by recontacting about 15 percent of the respondents to make sure certain responses were recorded properly and the person was actually interviewed.

Analyzing the Data

After the data have been collected, the next step in the research process is data analysis. The purpose of this analysis is to interpret and draw conclusions from the mass of collected data. The marketing researcher may use techniques beginning with simple frequency analysis and ultimately culminating in complex multivariate techniques. Data analysis will be discussed in Chapters 13 and 14.

Preparing and Writing the Report

After data analysis is completed, the researcher must prepare the report and communicate the conclusions and recommendations to management. This is a key step in the process because a marketing researcher who wants conclusions acted upon must convince the manager that the results are credible and justified by the data collected.

The researcher will ordinarily be required to present both written and oral reports on the project. When preparing and presenting these reports, the research- ers should keep in mind the nature of the audience. The reports should begin with a clear, concise statement of the research objectives, followed by a complete, but brief and simple, explanation of the research design or methodology employed. A summary of major findings should come next. The report should end with a presentation of conclusions and recommendations for management.

Because most people who enter marketing become research users rather than research suppliers, it is important to know what to look for in a report. Evaluating research will be a much greater portion of one's job than other aspects of marketing research. Like many other items we purchase, quality is not always readily apparent. Nor does a high price for the project necessarily guarantee superior quality. The basis for measuring quality is to return to the research proposal. Did the report meet the objectives established in the proposal? Was the methodology outlined in the proposal followed? Are the conclusions based on logical deductions from the data analysis? Do the recommendations seem prudent, given the conclusions?

Is the writing style crisp and lucid? It has been said that a reader who is offered the slightest opportunity to misunderstand probably will. The report should also be as concise as possible. It should follow the format outlined earlier so that important findings and recommendations can be found quickly and determined easily.

Follow-Up

After a company has spent a considerable amount of effort and money conducting marketing research and preparing a report, it is important for the findings to be utilized. Management should determine whether the recommendations were followed and why or why not. One way to help ensure that the research will be used is to minimize conflict between the marketing research department and other departments.

MANAGEMENT OF MARKETING RESEARCH

The Research Request

Prior to conducting the research project, Taco Bell requires approval of a formal **research request**. Moderate and large-size retailers, manufacturers, and nonprofit organizations often utilize the research request as a basis for determining which projects will be funded. Typically, in larger organizations there are far more requests by managers for marketing research information than monies available to conduct such research. The research request step is a formalized approach to allocating scarce research dollars.

It is very important for the brand manager, new product specialist, or whoever is in need of research information to clearly state in the formal research request why the desired information is critical to the organization. Otherwise, the person with approval authority may fail to see why the research expenditure is necessary.

In smaller organizations, the communication link between the brand managers and the market researchers is much closer. The day-to-day contact often removes the need for a formal research request. Instead, decisions to fund research are made on an ad hoc basis by the marketing manager or the director of marketing research.

Completion and approval of the request represents a disciplined approach to identifying research problems and obtaining funding to solve them. The degree of effort expended at this step in the research process will be reflected in the quality of information provided the decision maker because it will guide the design, data gathering, analysis, and reporting of the research toward a highly focused objective. The components of a formal research request are as follows:

Research request
Document used in large organizations that describes a potential research project, its benefits to the organization, and estimated costs. A project cannot begin until the research request has been formally approved.

1. *Action.* The decision maker must describe the action to be taken on the basis of the research. This will help the decision maker focus on what information makes sense and guide the researcher in creating the research design and in analyzing the results.
2. *Origin.* This is a statement of the events that led to a need for a decision to act. It helps the researcher understand more deeply the nature of the research problem.
3. *Information.* The decision maker must list the questions that he or she needs to have answered to take the action. Carefully considering this area improves the efficiency of the research and ensures that the questions make sense in light of the action to be taken.
4. *Use.* This section explains how each piece of information will be used to help make the actual decision. It gives logical reasons for each piece of the research and ensures that the questions make sense in light of the action to be taken.
5. *Targets and subgroups.* This section describes from whom the information must be gathered for the action to be taken. This helps the researcher design the sample for the research project.
6. *Logistics.* Time and budget constraints always affect the research technique that is chosen for a project. For this reason, approximations of the amount of money required and the amount of time that exists before results are needed must be stated as a part of the research request.
7. *Comments.* Any other comments relevant to the research project must be stated so that, once again, the researcher can fully understand the nature of the problem.[4]

GLOBAL MARKETING RESEARCH

In contrast to Western practice, Japanese executives don't give managers sole responsibility for a research area. They conduct research and make decisions by consensus, and they lean toward their intuitive judgment. Rarely do Japanese executives call in an outside professional, and when they do, they often disregard the consultant's report if it goes against their instincts about the best course of action. When Kozo Ohsone, the executive in charge of developing Sony's portable, compact Discman, heard that the company's marketing people were thinking about commissioning a research study, he told them not to waste their money.[5]

Manager-Researcher Conflict

Complaints about ineffectiveness, uselessness, and even interference in the decision process are all too common by product managers and corporate executives.[6] On the other hand, many researchers do not respect product managers because they do not act on the researcher's recommendations. Some managers have research studies conducted because it is expected of them. Other managers are unsure of what to do so they request research to avoid or postpone a decision. New product managers will sometimes request a study and then publicize the results only if it confirms their preconceived notions about the product concept.

Resolution of these problems is not a simple task. The first step is a clear delineation of authority and responsibility. A researcher's job is to conduct research and provide information; a manager's job is to make decisions. Thus, researchers must recognize that their job is to provide actionable information to decision makers. In turn, the managers must clearly define what information is needed for strategy and tactics and what format will be most useful for decision making.[7]

Factors Influencing a Manager's Decision to Use Research Information.   It is important for a researcher to have knowledge of what factors influence a manager to use research data. These factors are (1) conformity to prior expectations; (2) clarity of presentation; (3) research quality; (4) political acceptability within the firm; and (5) challenge to the status quo.[8] Managers and researchers both agree that technical quality is the most important determinant of research use. However, managers are less likely to utilize research that does not conform to preconceived notions or is not politically acceptable.[9] This does not mean, of course, that researchers should alter their findings to meet management's preconceived notions. Also, marketing managers in industrial firms tend to use research findings more than their counterparts in consumer goods organizations.[10] This is attributed to a greater exploratory objective in information collection, a greater degree of formalization of organizational structure, and a lesser degree of surprise in the information collection.

SUMMARY

The steps in the market research process are

1. Problem/opportunity identification and formulation
2. Creation of the research design
3. Choice of the method of research
4. Selection of the sampling procedure
5. Collection of data
6. Analysis of data
7. Preparation of the research report
8. Follow-up

In larger organizations, it is often common to have a research request prepared after the definition of research objectives. The research request generally describes the action to be taken on the basis of the research, the reason for the need for the information, how the information will be used, the target groups from whom the information should be gathered, the amount of time and money needed to complete the research project, and any other information pertinent to the request.

In specifying a research design, the researcher must determine whether the research will be descriptive or causal. Descriptive studies are conducted to answer who, what, when, and how questions. Causal studies are those in which the researcher investigates whether one variable (independent) causes or determines the value of another variable (dependent). The next step in creating a research design is to select a research method: survey, observation, or experiment. Survey research involves an interviewer interacting with a respondent to obtain facts, opinions, and attitudes. Observation research, in contrast, does not rely on direct interaction with people. An experiment is distinguished by the researcher changing one or more variables while observing the effects of those changes on another variable (usually sales). The objective of most experiments is to measure causality.

A sample is a subset from a larger population. A probability sample is characterized by every element in the population having a known nonzero probability of being selected. Nonprobability samples include all samples that cannot be considered probability samples. Any sample in which little or no attempt is made to ensure that a representative cross section of the population is obtained can be considered a nonprobability sample.

KEY TERMS

Exploratory research
Research design
Descriptive studies
Causal studies
Dependent variable
Independent variable
Temporal sequence
Concomitant variation

Spurious association
Survey research
Observation research
Experiments
Probability samples
Nonprobability samples
Research request

REVIEW AND DISCUSSION QUESTIONS

1. The definition of the research problem is one of the most critical steps in the research process. Why? Who should be involved in this process?
2. What role does exploratory research play in the market research process? How does exploratory research differ from other forms of market research?
3. In the absence of company problems, is there any need to conduct marketing research?
4. Are there any situations in which it would be better to take a census of the population rather than a sample? Give several examples.
5. Critique the following methodologies and suggest more appropriate alternatives:
   (a) A supermarket was interested in determining its image. It dropped a short questionnaire in the grocery bag of each customer prior to sacking the groceries.
   (b) To assess the extent of its trade area, a shopping mall stationed interviewers in the parking lot every Monday and Friday evening. Interviewers walked up to persons after they had parked their car and asked them for their zip codes.
   (c) To assess the popularity of a new movie, a major studio invited people to call a 900 number and vote yes, they would see it again or no, they would not. Each caller was billed a $2 charge.
6. You have been charged with determining how to attract more business majors to your school. Outline the steps you would take, including the sampling procedures, to accomplish this task.
7. What are the conditions for causality? Discuss the criteria.
8. Do you think market researchers should always use probability samples? Why or why not?

CASE

Pizza Heaven

Pizza Heaven is a small West Coast independent chain of pizza restaurants that caters primarily to college students. Accordingly, the restaurants are usually located near a campus and promote their offerings extensively in college newspapers. In the last year, Pizza Heaven sales have slipped, and management feels that the national chains such as Pizza Hut, Pizza Inn, and Domino's are making inroads into its market, along with single-store, independent pizza restaurants.

Pizza Heaven decided to conduct marketing research to determine its image among its customers and to see if the company needed to reposition itself. The first step was to do exploratory research. The exploratory research consisted of a pilot study with forty students. According to the pilot study, the college students expected to find a dark, informal, fun atmosphere in a pizza restaurant. They did not want noisy games or movies at the restaurant. College students claimed they used coupons extensively. The respondents particularly liked the two-for-one coupons offered by Pizza Inn and Domino's. Pizza was considered an intermediate food—something between a fast hamburger and a formal restaurant. Study participants thought of pizza primarily as a group activity rather than a dating situation. They noted that pizza was also a mood or an impulse food because of its distinct taste. They enjoyed eating other foods at pizza restaurants. College students usually ate pizza with more than one person, and not everyone wanted pizza. Submarine sandwiches came up quite frequently as food that many ordered as an alternate. Convenience played a big part in where the students chose to eat pizza.

Naturally, the most important feature in a pizza restaurant was the quality of the pizza. A good pizza was defined as hot, with a lot of fresh ingredients. It should have a large quantity of cheese, sauce, and meat. Some students claimed they would drive farther to get a favorite pizza (which was usually produced by an independent pizza restaurant). They said the independent's pizza was typically thicker and had more ingredients for the same amount of money than the average chain pizza.

The college students were generally negative toward luncheon specials. They said the pizzas were usually cold and dry. Also, they noted that the selection was often poor. Many of them did not think of pizza for lunch.

1. Now that Pizza Heaven is armed with the information from the exploratory research, should it begin implementing the findings? Why or why not?
2. If additional research should be undertaken, what topics should be covered? Why?
3. Outline the procedure for implementing additional market research.

CHAPTER 3

The Marketing Research Industry and Research Ethics

LEARNING OBJECTIVES

1. To appreciate the structure of the marketing research industry.

2. To comprehend the nature of corporate marketing research departments.

3. To learn about the various types of firms and their functions in the market research industry.

4. To understand the functions of the advertising agency research department.

5. To review contemporary ethics in the marketing research industry.

6. To discover methods by which the level of professionalism in marketing research can be raised.

P rincess Cruises' famous fleet of Love Boats sails to destinations around the world. The company is the third largest in the industry based on market share and carries approximately 450,000 passengers annually.

The company's marketing research department analyzes over 185,000 customer satisfaction questionnaires each year. The on-board survey is distributed one per cabin prior to the last day of the cruise, and passengers are asked to place the completed surveys in a locked box. The very detailed, forty-five-question survey solicits opinions about precruise documents and about logistics such as airport transfers to the ships, airline flights, and shore excursions. It also contains questions about presentation of food, quality of ingredients, variety of menu items, and issues such as stateroom service, housekeeping, and front desk performance. The surveys are distributed on every voyage of each of the nine ships in the Princess fleet.

The marketing research department produces a monthly summary report that examines on-board performance by cruise destination and vessel and identifies any specific problem areas that need to be addressed. For example, the ongoing survey has led to changes in the menu items and the on-board buffets.

Princess Cruises often turns to Pine Company, a Santa Monica, California, marketing research company, to conduct customized research studies. One recent study examined customers' satisfaction with two ways of booking shore excursions: either prior to the cruise through a travel agent or Princess or through the shore excursion office on each Princess vessel. "From our standard on-board surveys we've gotten some feedback that (the booking process) is one of our weaker areas. In response we designed a survey that looked in detail at the various attributes affecting shore excursions to try to remedy any problems we might be having," notes Jaime Goldfarb, Ph.D., a senior market researcher for Princess Cruises.[1]

P rincess Cruises' marketing research department is just one type of marketing research organization in the industry. What types of companies conduct marketing research? What types of specialized services and support firms exist in the research industry? What are the basic characteristics of the industry today? What are the ethical standards that have developed in the marketing research industry? We will examine these questions in this chapter.

THE EVOLVING STRUCTURE OF THE MARKETING RESEARCH INDUSTRY

Today, about $8.1 billion a year is spent on marketing/advertising/public opinion research services around the world, according to estimates developed by the European Society for Opinion and Marketing Research. That estimate puts U.S. spending at $2.9 billion.[2]

Over the past two decades, the marketing research industry has become highly concentrated. About 39 percent of the world's spending for research services goes to the ten largest marketing research organizations. About 51 percent is held by the twenty-five largest worldwide organizations.[3] The other half is shared by a thousand or more small research firms.

This concentration is even more pronounced in the United States, where the ten largest firms account for 59 percent of the total U.S. spending for marketing/advertising/public opinion research. The twenty largest firms account for 72 percent, and the top thirty account for 79 percent. If anything, this trend toward concentration continues, largely due to mergers. The wave of mergers in the late 1980s that resulted in the consolidation of marketing departments at top package-goods companies has had an immediate impact on the competitive environment. "When a Philip Morris absorbs a General Foods and then a Kraft, or when an R. J. Reynolds acquires a Nabisco, there's only a certain number of service companies and a certain amount of service those [conglomerates] are going to use," says David Learner, president of MRCA Information Services.[4] "One of the efficiencies of combining companies is the elimination of duplicate services, and the most damage that has been done to marketing research has been done [from mergers]," he says.

Corporate mergers, more than the economy, have spurred consolidations and alliances among research companies as they battle for business among a smaller client universe. This also intensified price competition among researchers, with earnings for some top companies sliding even as revenues grew. "Research has been moving into a third phase that will be challenging, certainly, but also provide opportunities," says John Costello, president of Nielsen Marketing Research USA.[5] "The first phase was collecting information. The second was turning that information into insights. This third phase will be converting those insights into results."

Because of the recession of the early 1990s, that third phase was hastened along, Mr. Costello says. It focused research user attention on productivity and cost of sales more than pure growth.

The various types of organizations encountered in the research industry are summarized in Table 3.1. The structure of the marketing research industry is summarized in Figure 3.1. This diagram shows the process for survey-based research operating at five levels. It depicts companies at Levels 1 and 2 as the ultimate consumers of marketing research data, the information users. The information they need rests with individual consumers and those who make business purchase decisions at Level 5, the respondents. Companies at Level 3 are the research designers and providers, and companies at Level 4 are the data collectors.

TABLE 3.1 *General Categories of Institutions Involved in Marketing Research*

INSTITUTION	ACTIVITIES, FUNCTIONS, AND SERVICES
Level 1. Corporate Marketing Research Departments	Marketing research departments in firms such as Kraft General Foods or Procter & Gamble
Level 2. Ad Agency Research Departments	Marketing research departments in advertising agencies such as J. Walter Thompson, Young and Rubicam, or Foote, Cone and Belding
Level 3. Custom or Ad Hoc Research Firms	Marketing research consulting firms such as Market Facts, Data Development, or MARC, which do customized marketing research projects addressing specific problems for individual clients
Level 3. Syndicated Service Firms	Marketing research data gathering and reporting firms like A. C. Nielsen, Arbitron, or Information Resources Incorporated, which collect data of general interest to many firms but for no one firm in particular; anyone can buy the data they collect; prominent in the media audience field and scanner-based research
Level 4. Field Service Firms	Collect data only, on a subcontract basis for corporate marketing research departments, ad agency research departments, custom research firms, or syndicated research firms
Specialized Service Firms*	Provide specialized support service to the marketing research industry, such as Survey Sampling, Inc.
Others*	Governmental agencies, university research bureaus, individual university professors, and others

* These organizations typically operate at levels 1, 2, or 3.

Level 1. Primary Information Providers (Corporate Marketing Research Departments)

Level 1 organizations are the ultimate users of marketing research data provided by their marketing research departments. Their primary business is the sale of products and services. They use marketing research data to support the marketing decision-making process. They need marketing research data on an ongoing basis to

1. Determine how various target groups will react to alternative marketing mixes.
2. Evaluate the ongoing success of operational marketing strategies.
3. Assess changes in the external or uncontrollable environment and their implications for their product or service strategy.

Figure 3.1 shows that these companies, and their marketing research departments, may work with a combination of custom and syndicated research firms, go directly to ad agencies, or use all or some combination of these alternatives to satisfy their many marketing research needs.

Level 2. Information Users (Ad Agencies)

Ad agencies (Level 2) are also in the position of serving corporate clients, but they may also be ultimate consumers of marketing research data. Their main business is the development and execution of ad campaigns. To properly fulfill this role, they often need marketing research data. They may obtain data from custom and syndicated research firms, field service firms, or they may use some combination of these alternatives.

Level 3. Research Designers and Suppliers

Custom and syndicated marketing research firms (Level 3) represent the front line
of the research industry. They sell research services, design research studies, analyze
the results, and make recommendations to their clients. They design research,
manage its execution, and buy data collection and other services from firms down
the line (see Figure 3.1).

FIGURE 3.1   *The Marketing Research Industry*

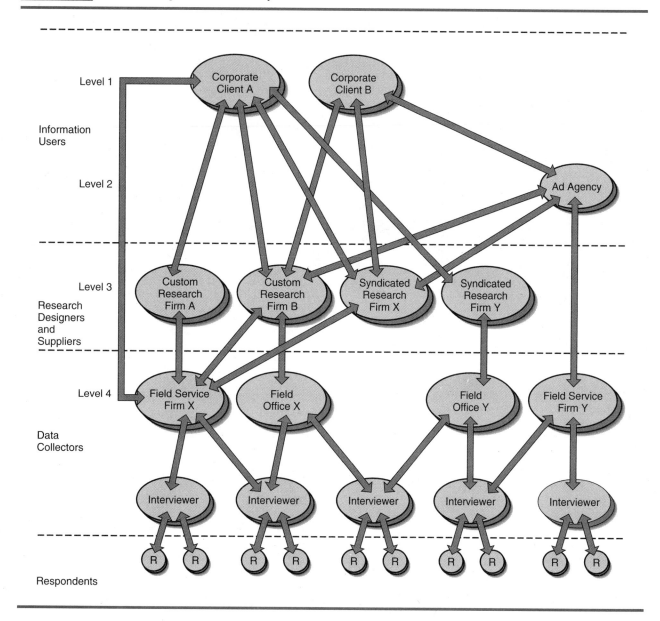

GLOBAL MARKETING RESEARCH

The passage of the North American Free Trade Agreement (NAFTA) in 1993 has focused increased attention on conducting marketing research in Mexico. About $5.5 million a year is spent on marketing research in Mexico. The Mexican subsidiary of Nielsen Marketing Research is, by far, the largest marketing research firm operating in Mexico, controlling about one-half of total research expenditures. Founded in 1967, Nielsen Mexico is a conglomerate with about 386 employees, plus interviewing staff.

In addition to continuous audits of product movement through panels of retail stores (food, drug, liquor, etc.), Nielsen does surveys and operates a diary-type purchase panel. Like all other Mexican research firms, it is headquartered in Mexico City.

After Nielsen, there is a sharp drop-off. The two largest survey research firms—Asesoria e Investigaciones Gamma and IMOP (Gallup Mexico)—have annual revenues in the $4 million to $5 million range, and after that a firm doing $1.5 million to $2 million a year is considered big in Mexico.

One of the first things U.S. researchers operating in Mexico have to face up to is that they cannot rely on telephone and mail service for data collection. Most data collection is door-to-door and is concentrated in three or four of the largest cities (markets), namely Matamoros, Monterrey, Guadalajara, and Mexico City, which—with a metropolitan population of 17 million—is the world's second largest city (after Tokyo) and home to one out of every five Mexicans.

Mexican research firms either have their own interviewers in the major markets or make use of local field services there. Even with diary panels, most interviewers work door-to-door with respondent households, dropping off and picking up the diaries to ensure compliance with data collection requests.[6]

Level 4. Data Collectors

Field service firms (Level 4) collect data for syndicated research firms, custom research firms, ad agencies, and corporations. Field offices are data collection operations run by custom or syndicated research firms; however, these are rare today. Most custom and many syndicated research firms depend on field services for their survey data collection needs.

At Level 4 are the interviewers who actually collect the data. They typically work on a part-time, as-needed basis and may work for several different field service firms, depending on the amount of business the various field services have at any given time.

Measurement of the opinions, preferences, intentions, behavior, and so on of respondents, or potential buyers is the goal of the research process. What potential buyers feel, think, do, and intend to do are the focus of the entire marketing research industry.

Callers at central telephone interviewing facilities collect data through phone surveys. (© 1990, Comstock)

CORPORATE MARKETING RESEARCH DEPARTMENTS

Because corporations are the final consumers and the initiators of most marketing research, they are the logical starting point in developing an understanding of how the research industry operates.

Because different corporations have different information needs, marketing research departments are often quite different from company to company. Some departments, like the one at Delta Airlines, concern themselves almost exclusively with the analysis of internal operating data. Other departments, such as the one at American Airlines, are more concerned with collecting and analyzing customer and noncustomer data. Still other research departments, like the ones at Frito-Lay or Radio Shack, buy virtually all their survey and analysis work from outside suppliers. At the other end of the spectrum, companies such as Kraft General Foods, Procter & Gamble, Pillsbury, General Mills, and others, though purchasing many research services externally, have the capability to design and execute all phases of a marketing research project.

Because we cannot deal with all types of marketing research departments, attention will be devoted to those found in the more sophisticated, larger companies. In these companies, research is a staff department and the director of the department will likely report to the top marketing executive. Although the research manager reports to a high-level marketing executive, most of the work of the department will be with product or brand managers, new product development managers, and other front-line managers. With the possible exception of various recurring studies that may be programmed into the firm's marketing information

Corporate marketing research departments Departments of major firms that produce or oversee collection and analysis of information relevant to marketing the firm's present or future products or services.

system, the marketing research department typically does not initiate studies. In fact, the research director may control little or no actual budget. Instead, line managers have funds in their budgets earmarked for research.

When brand managers perceive that they have a problem requiring research, they go to the marketing research department for help. Working with the marketing research manager or a senior analyst, they go through a series of steps that may lead to the design and execution of a marketing research project (see Chapter 2).

Jack Honomichl, a prolific writer about the marketing research industry and president of Marketing Aid Center, talks about the marketing research department of the future in the feature on page 49.

THE MARKETING RESEARCH INDUSTRY

Level 3. The Big Marketing Research Companies

Although the marketing research industry is characterized by hundreds of small firms, there are some giants in the industry. Table 3.2 shows 1992 sales for the thirty largest marketing research firms. It should be noted that the four largest firms in the industry—namely, Nielsen, IMS, Arbitron, and Information Resources—are all syndicated service firms or largely syndicated service firms. Most of the remaining firms are either primarily custom research firms or combination firms offering some syndicated services along with their custom research services.

Level 3. Custom Research Firms

Custom, or ad hoc, marketing research firms
Research companies that carry out customized marketing research to address specific projects for corporate clients.

Custom, or ad hoc, marketing research firms, as noted earlier, are primarily in the business of executing custom, one-of-a-kind marketing research projects for corporate clients. If the corporation has a new product or service idea, packaging idea, ad concept, new pricing strategy, product reformulation, or other related marketing problems or opportunities that need to be dealt with, the custom research firm is the place to go for research help.

There are thousands of custom marketing research firms in this country. However, the overwhelming majority of these firms are small with billings of less than $1 million and less than ten employees. They may serve clients only in their local areas. They may or may not specialize by type of industry or type of research.

Level 3. Syndicated Service Firms

Syndicated service research firms
Companies that collect, package, and sell the same general market research data to many firms.

Audience data syndicated services
Companies that collect, package, and sell general data on media audiences to many firms.

In sharp contrast to the custom research company example, **syndicated service research firms** collect and sell the same marketing research data to many firms. Anyone willing to pay the price can buy the data these firms collect, package, and sell. Syndicated service firms are relatively few in number and, in comparison to custom research firms, relatively large. They deal primarily with media audience and product movement data and are based on serving information needs that many companies have in common. For example, many companies advertise on

MARKETING RESEARCH IN PRACTICE

In enlightened companies, there will come to be a new corporate unit headed by a chief information officer. This CIO will rank right up there in the corporate hierarchy with the CFO and report to the CEO. This new corporate information unit will formalize top management's realization that timely, accurate information from the marketplace is a make-or-break proposition; what you don't know can kill you.

As differences between competing products narrow, profitable differentiation comes from an intimate (hopefully, real time) understanding of what's going on in the marketplace, and the ability to capitalize on windows of opportunity. The CIO would coordinate all the corporation's information sources, distill and analyze the "findings," and continually brief the corporate CEO. The CIO's unit would have several deputy directors, depending on the corporation's main business activity. These could include the following:

■ *Business intelligence officer:* Many corporations have one now. Their main function is to monitor closely anything a competitor does: personnel changes, new construction, financials, acquisitions, etc. Input comes mostly from public domain sources, and the concept is to know, and to try to understand, every move a competitor makes. A plant expansion, for example, might reveal plans a competitor has for a product.

■ *Syndicated data source officer:* As appropriate for the corporation's industry, this unit would constantly monitor the syndicated marketing services available and make buy recommendations. Also, this unit would tap into corporate data sources (for example, factory shipments) and tailor them to meld with external data sources.

■ *Management information systems officer:* This position would be the same as what now exists in many corporations. Main function: establishing systems and software that expedite the timely processing and distillation of data—from internal and external sources—and making it easily accessible to top operating management; making relevant make or buy decisions regarding required software.

■ *Customer satisfaction measurement officer:* Depending on the nature of the corporation's product or service, this person would be a key member of the team. As top management realizes that the cost of obtaining new customers is very high, it is critical to prevent the loss of existing customers as much as possible.

■ *Custom research officer:* This is a unit to design and conduct ad hoc research as required to obtain data unavailable from sources mentioned above. Test marketing would be the responsibility of this unit.[7]

network television. Their problem is to select shows that reach their target customers most efficiently. They need information on the size and demographic composition of the audiences for different television programs. It would be extremely inefficient for each firm to collect these data individually.

Product movement data syndicated services Companies that collect, package, and sell retail sales data to many firms.

TABLE 3.2   *Top Thirty U.S. Research Organizations in 1993*

1993 RANK	ORGANIZATION	HEADQUARTERS	TOTAL RESEARCH REVENUES (MILLIONS)	PERCENT REVENUES FROM OUTSIDE U.S.
1	D&B Marketing Information Systems	Cham, Switzerland	$1,868.3	61.0%
2	Information Resources Inc.	Chicago, IL	334.5	15.0
3	The Arbitron Co.	New York, NY	172.0	
4	Walsh International/PMSI	Phoenix, AZ	115.4	34.4
5	Westat, Inc.	Rockville, MD	113.1	
6	Maritz Marketing Research Inc.	St. Louis, MO	74.4	
7	The NPD Group	Port Washington, NY	66.0	23.8
8	NFO Research Inc.	Greenwich, CT	51.9	
9	Elrick & Lavidge Inc.	Atlanta, GA	47.1	
10	Market Facts Inc.	Arlington Heights, IL	45.6	
11	The M/A/R/C Group	Las Colinas, TX	44.7	
12	Walker Group	Indianapolis, IN	38.1	1.9
13	Abt Associates Inc.	Cambridge, MA	36.4	
14	MRB Group	London, England	35.0	
15	The National Research Group Inc.	Los Angeles, CA	34.5	15.0
16	NOP Information Group	Livingston, NJ	33.0	
17	Intersearch Corp.	Horsham, PA	32.2	
18	The BASES Group	Covington, KY	31.0	5.0
19	Millward Brown Inc.	Naperville, IL	29.0	
20	Opinion Research Corp.	Princeton, NJ	26.6	27.9
21	Burke Marketing Research	Cincinnati, OH	26.1	2.9
22	Roper Starch Worldwide Inc.	Mamaroneck, NY	24.9	4.0
23	J.D. Powers & Associates	Agoura Hills, CA	24.5	
24	Creative & Response Research Svcs.	Chicago, IL	23.8	
25	Research International USA	New York, NY	22.7	30.4
26	Louis Harris and Associates Inc.	New York, NY	22.0	68.2
27	Chilton Research Services	Radnor, PA	22.0	
28	Mercer Mgt. Consulting/Decision Research	Lexington, MA	20.7	
29	Yankelovich Partners	Westport, CT	20.1	8.0
30	ASI Market Research	Stamford, CT	17.5	

Source: "The Honomichl 50," *Marketing News* (June 6, 1994), p. H4.

Level 4. Field Service Firms

Field service firms
Companies that only collect survey data for corporate clients or research firms.

A true **field service firm** does nothing but collect survey data—no research design, no analysis. Field service firms are data collection specialists who collect data on a subcontract basis for corporate marketing research departments, custom research firms, syndicated service research firms, and ad agency research departments.

The following description of the sequence of activities undertaken by a typical field service company provides a good idea of how they operate:

Client contact

Client (custom research firm, syndicated research firm, corporate or ad agency research department) alerts field service firm that it has a particular type of study (telephone interview, mail interview, etc.), seeking a particular type of respondent (e.g., women with children between ages 3 and 8 who have served a canned spaghetti product to their children in the last thirty days), for a particular date, requiring a certain number of interviewers for a certain number of days

GLOBAL MARKETING RESEARCH

A.C. Nielsen Company has picked up its first pan-European TV contract, increasing its profile in a region where commercial TV growth is increasing the demand for TV audience measurement research. In 1990 Nielsen began conducting Pan-European Television Audience Research (PETAR) in eleven European countries. The company collects data through diaries from 3,500 households representing Europe's cable audience of 15–20 million households.

PETAR is sponsored by an industry group including McDonald's Corp., the British Broadcasting Corp., Cable News Network, MTV: Music Television, Italian state broadcaster RAI, and the two German-language satellite channels, RTL Plus and Sat 1. It covers about 100 channels delivered via satellite.

Nielsen selects communities receiving a selection of channels representative of the national viewing choice in each country. Households are selected randomly and family members four and older asked to keep diaries recording programs watched every fifteen minutes. The results show viewership on a country-by-country basis of channels including Rupert Murdoch's Sky Television and MTV Europe. The findings help advertisers decide whether to buy time on cable and satellite channels. The contract previously was held by Research Services, Ltd.

Nielsen's main business in Europe still will be retail panels. One U.K. service, HomeScan, may be extended to other European markets. HomeScan is a national purchasing panel started in 1989 using 7,000 homes equipped with portable scanners. Consumers scan the Universal Product Codes of grocery and other household purchases, recording the product, price, purchase point, quantity, and any promotions used. Nielsen retrieves the information via telephone modem.

HomeScan measures consumer purchasing trends such as brand switching, brand loyalty, and "household repertoire—like if you buy Kellogg's corn flakes, what other breakfast cereals do you have?" said Colin Buckingham, Nielsen's U.K. marketing director.[8]

Estimate cost bid	The field service indicates that it can or cannot handle the job; it may be asked to provide a bid or cost estimate at this point
Interviewer recruiting	The field service lines up interviewers from their pool to work on the particular job
Interviewer training	The day the job is to begin, a briefing or training session is held to acquaint interviewers with the requirements of the particular job or questionnnaire
Interviewing status reports	Daily reports are made to the client regarding progress, number of interviews completed, and costs, which permit the client to determine whether the job is on schedule and within budget; the field service can advise their client of any problem in either area
Quality control	Interviewers bring in their completed assignments and the interviews are edited and validated (editing refers to checking interviews to see that they were completed

correctly; validation entails calling a certain percentage of each interviewer's respondents to determine whether the interview took place and if it was done in the prescribed manner)

Ship to client Finally, the completed, edited, and validated interviews are shipped to the client

The field service provides interviewing and supervisory service. Most custom research firms rely on field services because it is uneconomical for them to handle the work themselves. There are too many cities to cover, and it is always uncertain as to which cities will be needed over time. On the other hand, field service firms located in particular cities maintain a steady work flow by having many research firms, corporate, and ad agency research departments as their clients.

Until about twenty years ago, most field service firms were operated by women out of their homes. Their major asset was typically a pool of a dozen or so interviewers available for assignment. Though field service firms of this type still exist, the trend is toward larger, more professional, and better equipped organizations.

The major field service firm of today has a permanent office. It probably has one or more permanent mall test centers, focus group facilities, a central location telephone interviewing facility, other specialized facilities and equipment, and possibly even WATS (wide area telephone service) lines for interviewing thoughout the country from a single location. Another recent trend in the field service business is the emergence of multicity operations.

Specialized Service and Support Firms

Specialized service or support firms
Companies that handle a specific facet of research, such as data processing or statistical analysis, for many corporate clients.

Finally, in the marketing research industry there are a number of very **specialized service or support firms**. These firms provide various types of support services to marketing research and other firms.

Data Processing. First are those firms that offer various computer and data processing services. They take completed questionnaires and handle all editing, coding, and computer data entry and run all tabulations and other analysis required by their clients. These companies are often called "tab houses" in the industry.

Sample Generation. A second realm where specialized service firms are found is in the sample generation area. Firms such as Survey Sampling, Inc., of Westport, Connecticut, provide samples of households and businesses to their clients. They maintain massive databases with information on millions of households and businesses from which they generate samples to their clients' specifications.

Secondary Data. A third area of specialized service to the research industry is provided by firms providing access to specialized databases via computer. For example, no company needs to purchase all U.S. census tapes when it needs a demographic profile of a single metro area. The secondary data firms provide access to the data via on-line computer networks or provide the desired data on floppy diskettes so their clients can process it on their own PCs.

Statistical Analysis. With the growing use of sophisticated statistical techniques, a new type of marketing research support firm, the data analysis specialist, has emerged. Firms such as Sophisticated Data Research in Atlanta provide sophisticated consulting services to marketing research firms and corporate marketing research departments regarding the selection and use of various statistical techniques for the analysis of marketing research data.

Other. A number of other assorted and miscellaneous types of specialized service or support firms are found in the marketing research industry. Each has found its niche through the cultivation of expertise in a very specific facet of the marketing research process where researchers are likely to seek outside assistance. An example of a specialized firm is Survey Sampling, Incorporated. This organization is used to draw sophisticated and complex samples or hard to find respondents.

AD AGENCY RESEARCH DEPARTMENTS

Ad agency marketing research departments are a cross between the corporate marketing research department and the custom marketing research firm. They are similar to corporate marketing research departments in that they are parts of organizations (ad agencies) whose major business is something other than the sale of marketing research services. They are similar to custom research firms in the sense that they also do research for external clients.

> Ad agency marketing research departments Departments of advertising agencies that produce or oversee research to support the development and evaluation of advertising for the agency's clients.

A check of the *Standard Directory of Advertising Agencies*[9] shows that over 90 percent of all agencies with billings of more than $10 million have a marketing research department. The major use of research by ad agencies is to support the development and evaluation of advertising for their clients. Different ideas or approaches to ad campaigns and rough, simulated commercials are tested. Various cuts of finished commercials are frequently evaluated and ongoing campaigns are monitored via research. Though much ad agency research is oriented toward testing ads at various stages, agency research departments may initiate more fundamental types of research. For example, the agency may recommend that the client do market segmentation research through the agency to better identify advertising audiences so as to assist the agency in selecting media and message.

An example of an ambitious form of basic research undertaken by an advertising agency is the annual lifestyle survey conducted by the DDB Needham Worldwide agency. In this survey, a representative national sample of several thousand consumers is interviewed. Each is administered a very lengthy questionnaire with detailed questions regarding their activities, interests, opinions, buying habits, and demographics. The results are compiled and translated into profiles of several lifestyle market segments. The agency has even gone so far as to hire actors to portray the "typical" person from each lifestyle segment. These video tapes are reviewed by the agency's copywriters and other creative personnel to help them gain a mental picture of the consumers they are communicating to for clients such as McDonald's and Budweiser.

The scope of marketing research at some of the largest advertising agencies is changing. Traditionally, advertising agencies conducted "endless copy tests and endless group discussions." Today the focus is switching from evaluating output (finished advertisements) to guiding input (overall strategy development).

Most ad agencies (and their research departments) are relatively small. They, therefore, lean heavily on outside contractors to execute all or major parts of studies. The agency research people often work with their corporate clients to design the study and then contract out the interviewing to field service firms and data processing and tabulation to a tab house.[10] The agency research people complete the process by preparing a report. Another approach might involve farming out the entire study, once research objectives have been agreed upon, to a custom research firm, depending on the scope, complexity, and specialized nature of the project.

OTHER ORGANIZATIONS AND INDIVIDUALS

Finally, we must mention various other organizations and individuals, although they are not truly part of the marketing research industry, because of their special contribution to it. Included here are various government agencies at the federal, state, and local levels; university bureaus of business and economic research; individual university professors that serve as marketing research consultants; and research units associated with various industry groups and others. In the case of all but the university professors, these institutions serve primarily as sources of extremely valuable and useful data for the marketing research industry. University professors, primarily those in marketing departments, who also are marketing research consultants, provide a pool of sophisticated talent that is tapped on an as-needed basis by corporate marketing research departments, companies with no internal marketing research capabilities, custom research firms, and others.

The role of various government agencies is important, though they serve primarily as providers of secondary data. Specific examples of agencies and the types of data they provided are presented and discussed in Chapter 4.

THE GROWING ROLE OF STRATEGIC PARTNERING

Marketing research is becoming a team effort. Under pressure from clients and the cost of increasingly sophisticated technology, research companies are forming strategic alliances, sharing data or capabilities as a cost-effective way to grow. The trend toward **strategic partnering**—even with competitors—will continue, industry executives say.

Strategic partnering
Two or more marketing research firms with unique skills and resources form an alliance to offer a new service for clients, provide strategic support for each firm, or in some other manner create mutual benefits.

"The '90s are the decade of the strategic alliance agreement," said Tom Daley, president of Spectra Marketing, Chicago. "The technology is so expensive and leadership positions so vulnerable that it's the way business has to go. It used to be that when you introduced a new [research] product or service, it was two or three years before everyone matched it. Now Nielsen can have it in the marketplace next week. So everyone's asking, 'How can I get smarter, faster?' And strategic alliances are the answer."[11]

Spectra, a geodemographic research company founded in 1988, has been built through a series of strategic alliances. It has deals with several major companies, including Information Resources Incorporated (IRI), Claritas Corporation, Market

Facts, and Donnelly Marketing's Carol Wright unit. IRI has been one of the most active in forming alliances, having set deals with Arbitron Company, BASES Burke Institute, Citicorp, VideOCart, and others. "In 1979 we introduced BehaviorScan on an investment of a few million dollars. You couldn't even begin to think of duplicating that system for anywhere near that cost," said IRI Chairman-CEO Gian Fulgoni. "The cost of doing business and the complexity of the business are driving the trend to strategic alliances."[12] Other recent examples of strategic partnering include

- Nielsen Marketing Research USA bought an interest in Market Simulations and then joined GTE Interactive Services to create and test Retail Alliance, an integrated service for retailers and manufacturers.
- Acxiom Corporation, Conway, Arizona, formed a research and development alliance with Young & Rubicam, New York, providing the agency with database management services and direct marketing software.
- Market Facts, Chicago, and M/A/R/C Group, Las Colinas, Texas, formed a strategic alliance covering consumer mail surveys. Market Facts will buy the mail panel operation of a M/A/R/C subsidiary, merging it with its larger, 360,000-household panel. M/A/R/C can use the combined panel for ten years, but the two companies will design studies and analyze panel data independently.

There is no doubt that strategic partnering will continue to be an important trend in the marketing research industry throughout the remainder of the 1990s.

MAKING ETHICAL DECISIONS IN MARKETING RESEARCH

The foundation of strategic partnering is mutual trust. Trust exists when an organization develops and practices high ethical standards. Today's business ethics are actually a subset of the values held by society as a whole. The values used by marketing people to make decisions have been acquired through family, educational, and religious institutions, as well as social movements (e.g., antinuclear, women's rights). A market researcher with a mature set of ethical values accepts personal responsibility for decisions that affect the full community, including responsibility for

1. Employees' needs and desires and the long-range best interests of the organization.
2. Persons directly affected by company activities and their long-range goodwill and best interests (this creates good publicity for the firm).
3. Social values and conditions for society at large that provide values, sanctions, and a social structure that enables the company to exist.

Ethics and Professionalism

A high standard of ethics and professionalism go hand in hand. Good ethics provide a solid foundation for professionalism and striving for a lofty level of professionalism necessitates proper ethics on the part of researchers.

Indications of a Lack of Professionalism

Phone-In Polls. There are numerous signs that professionalism has not reached a desired level in the marketing research industry. One example is the phone-in poll in which viewers or listeners are encouraged to volunteer their opinions by calling a toll-free (or nominal charge) number. In such surveys, sample selection based upon probability theory is nonexistent. One poll, for example, conducted by *USA Today* showed that Americans loved Donald Trump. A month later, *USA Today* reported that 5,640 of the 7,800 calls came from offices owned by one man, Cincinnati financier Carl Lindner. Lindner would not comment, but a spokesperson told *USA Today* that Lindner's employees admire Trump. *USA Today* says its call-in polls are not meant to be scientific and are "strictly for fun." Yet, the information derived is widely reported by the media and is often assumed by the public to be representative.[13]

Council for Marketing and Opinion Research (CMOR) An umbrella organization for survey research companies designed to protect the research industry against unnecessarily restrictive legislation, deal with reduced respondent cooperation, and fight selling disguised as research.

Sales Pitches Disguised as Research. Another serious problem is the use of sales pitches disguised as marketing research. Although the latter problem is caused by persons outside the research industry, it still casts a negative light on legitimate researchers.

The Council of American Survey Research Organizations (CASRO) has been fighting firms who use sales pitches disguised as marketing research. CASRO is a trade association representing approximately 130 full-service marketing research firms. Yet firms who conduct marketing research and other organizations that conduct survey research realized that more needed to be done. In 1992, the Council for Marketing and Opinion Research (CMOR) was created. It is sponsored by the American Marketing Association, CASRO, the Marketing Research Association, and the Advertising Research Foundation. CMOR is an umbrella organization for survey research companies designed to speak as a unified voice to respondents, legislators, and regulators. CMOR's objectives are to protect the research industry against unnecessarily restrictive legislation, deal with waning respondent cooperation, and fight selling disguised as research. CMOR, for example, has asked "sugging marketers" (firms selling under the guise of research) to use more forthright and honest marketing techniques (see the Marketing Research in Practice box on page 58). It has succeeded with some groups, such as the Sierra Club, which agreed not to use the survey technique again, even though it was a successful fund-raising tool for the organization.

The Better Business Bureau has issued a memorandum describing legitimate marketing research, stating that "real" marketing research does not sell. The U.S. Postal Service has issued cease and desist orders to two companies that conducted fraudulent operations under the guise of research.[14]

A marketing malpractice suit in 1987 concerned a major marketing research firm's report on potential market share for Delicare Cold Water Wash, marketed by Beecham, Inc. (Courtesy Benckieser Consumer Products)

Lawsuits Involving Researchers. A third indication of a lack of professionalism is the growing number of lawsuits in the marketing research industry. In the late 1980s Yankelovich, Skelly and White/Clancy Shulman, one of America's premier research organizations, was sued by Beecham, Inc., for negligence, negligent misrepresentation, professional malpractice, and breech of contract in its handling of Delicare Cold Water Wash. Yankelovich had conducted a simulated test market and then claimed that Delicare could achieve a 45 to 52 percent market share if Beecham spent $18 million to advertise the brand. Beecham followed the researcher's recommendations, but never achieved over 20 percent market share. It seems that the researcher used a figure of 75 percent of all U.S. homes used a fine-fabric detergent such as Woolite. The correct figure, provided initially by Beecham, was 30 percent. Beecham sought $24 million in damages.[15] The suit was settled out of court, and no facts of the settlement were made public.

In the wake of the Beecham-Yankelovich malpractice case, the American Marketing Association has drafted the following sample arbitration provision that marketing research firms may add to their contracts:

"Disputes or controversies arising with respect to the interpretation of this agreement or any transaction or action undertaken or contemplated pursuant to this agreement shall be resolved through arbitration conducted at [a blank is left for insertion of the location, such as the firm's headquarters city or a neutral location], in accordance with the Commercial Arbitration Rules of the American Arbitration Association then in effect. The decision of the arbitrator shall be final and binding on each of the parties and may not be appealed. Costs and charges assessed by the American Arbitration Association pursuant to such arbitration shall be borne by the party assessed such costs by the arbitrator; and in the absence of such assessment, such charges shall be borne equally by the parties. Each party shall bear its own costs for counsel, witnesses and experts with respect to the arbitration proceedings."[16]

Another recent lawsuit was based more on unethical behavior than research malpractice. Minneapolis television station WCCO sued station KARE and Atkinson Research charging that the two organizations conspired to manipulate the May A.C. Nielsen ratings period.

PROACTIVE EFFORTS TO ENHANCE THE LEVEL OF PROFESSIONALISM IN THE MARKET RESEARCH INDUSTRY

Several positive steps have been taken recently to improve the level of professionalism in the marketing research industry. For example, the Council of American Survey Research Organizations (CASRO) has sponsored several symposiums that deal with ethical issues in survey research. CASRO has also created a code of ethics that has been widely disseminated to research professionals. The CASRO board has worked with other groups such as the Marketing Research Association to provide input to legislatures considering antimarketing research legislation. According to John Rupp, general council to CASRO, "Our effort, ultimately, must be to preserve survey research for research professionals."[17]

The Creation of CMOR

In January 1992, research industry leaders decided to band together to address the critical issues of government affairs and respondent cooperation, because no existing association could adequately move forward alone on either of these two initiatives. Further, it was clear that these issues required broad industry support, involvement, and substantial funding. Separate fund-raising efforts for each initiative would seriously compromise the viability of both initiatives.

MARKETING RESEARCH IN PRACTICE

You've got something that's worth $1,500 to me. . . . Your opinion is valuable. You've always given it away freely. But I'll reward you for it. I'll give you up to $1,500 worth of FREE Gifts in exchange for your opinion of the TV programs that you watch." This is an excerpt from a direct mail letter soliciting "TV Raters" sent by John Westcott, vice president of American Media Research Corporation (AMRC). It sounds wonderful, doesn't it?

And the more you read Westcott's letter, the more wonderful it sounds. All you have to do to receive up to $1,500 worth of FREE gifts is to fill out a "TV Survey" form every month for thirty-six months. Then, John Westcott writes, "We'll take your survey answers and match them up with similar responses from all over the country. This report, profiling the viewing habits and consumer preferences of our TV Raters, will be delivered to top executives in the Television, Entertainment and Consumer Goods industries. This important data will be marketed to some of America's largest and most powerful media, mailing list and consumer product companies."

Yes, this sounds great! Even the "small enrollment fee" of up to $20 and "a modest shipping and processing charge of about $2.00 or so, each month" for the FREE gift you get when you send in the monthly TV survey doesn't dampen your enthusiasm. *And* if you enroll within the next eleven days, you'll get a "Promptness Gift worth not $25, not $50, not $75, but $95!" If you're a bargain hunter and a public-spirited citizen, interested both in FREE gifts and in having your opinions count ("Your Answers May Affect Millions"), why not join up?

The scheme worked. People enrolled as "TV Raters" by the thousands. After all, to the inexperienced, unknowing eye, there doesn't seem to be anything wrong with this program—not really.

But there is a lot wrong with this scheme. And soon after this letter hit people's mailboxes, many questions and complaints were brought up by consumer and industry watchdogs, including the survey research industry, by the knowing public, *and* even by disillusioned "TV Raters" themselves.

Several times CASRO sent letters to AMRC, asking about the TV Rater survey, explaining survey research industry standards on respondent confidentiality and protection from harassment and misrepresentation, and questioning the validity of the data being collected. Finally, CASRO received a response from Donald Pickman, president and CEO of American Media Research Corporation. Mr. Pickman wrote, "We at American Media are definitely interested in structuring our business to maximize its potential to output the information contained in the database. It is my intention to further review with you any input you and your organization can provide that will help achieve our goals and not offend your standards of practice." I never did figure out what Mr. Pickman meant, though I suspect his intentions were as questionable as his sentence structure.

Within a week of receiving the letter from Mr. Pickman, I got a call from Stacy Ludwig, an attorney with the United States Postal Service. It seemed

—Continued

—Continued

that the USPS had received a number of complaints from individuals and from organizations, including CASRO, questioning the legitimacy of the AMRC operation, both as a seller of "free" products and as a survey research company. CASRO was asked to participate in the USPS investigation of AMRC. Ms. Ludwig wanted to learn all about the research industry and how surveys are conducted.

Harry W. O'Neill, vice chairman of The Roper Organization; David Lapovsky, vice president of Arbitron Ratings Company; and Diane Bowers provided written affidavits on legitimate survey research and industry standards, and they were prepared to testify against AMRC before an Administrative Law Judge in Washington, D.C. In his affidavit to the USPS, Harry O'Neill described different types of survey research, sampling and statistical measures, and reporting arrangements. He also wrote:

The conduct of survey research has become more difficult in recent years because of such factors as (1) the increase of working women and families with both heads in the workforce, thereby making it harder to reach a respondent at a convenient time, (2) the increase in crime and dangerous neighborhoods, making door-to-door interviewing less desirable for the interviewer and a cause for suspicion on the part of potential respondents, (3) the increase of telemarketing, which often is conducted by using research as a guise and, even when legitimate, competes for the time of potential survey respondents, (4) the increase of mail solicitations for contributions using research as a guise. Given [these] problems, coupled with the increase in legitimate survey research, we are very sensitive to any activity that can cast a bad light on our industry. AMRC is such an activity, for the following reasons:

1. It charges respondents for participation—a practice no legitimate survey company engages in.
2. It leads respondents to believe their opinions are being sought by top executives in the entertainment and consumer products industries when the service has no clients.
3. It not only promises gifts for participation whose value falls short of that which is promised, but charges shipping and handling for the gifts. If a legitimate survey firm rewards a respondent with a gift, there is never a charge.
4. Most seriously, while claiming to be a survey research company, AMRC violates respondent anonymity. Respondent names are put into a direct marketing file and respondents obviously will be solicited at some future date. Legitimate research firms, on the contrary, assure respondents that survey participation never will result in a future sales contact. To the extent respondents are not treated well by AMRC, are told untruths, find their names on mailing lists—and all of this is associated with a company claiming to be a research company— the credibility of our industry will suffer.

On January 22, 1990, a Cease and Desist Order was signed by the USPS Judicial Officer. The Cease and Desist Order covered AMRC, its officers, directors, owners, and employees and extended to AMRC's promotional materials and "to any promotion that seeks to obtain remittances of money or property through the mail in connection with a survey." Furthermore, the order directed that "If any purpose of [the AMRC] program is to solicit money, to compile mailing lists or to sell products, [AMRC] is hereby further ordered not to represent, identify or describe their promotion as a survey."[18]

GLOBAL MARKETING RESEARCH

Concerns about restrictive government policies and regulations for the marketing research industry extend beyond U.S. borders. For example, the European Commission, a pan-European governing body based in Brussels, issues what it terms "directives" that could come to prevail throughout the twelve EC member countries. One such directive, aimed at data privacy, decrees that respondents cannot be asked questions about "sensitive subjects" without the respondent's writen permission.

In Ireland, the marketing research community is banding together to try to thwart a government ruling that political poll results could not be published during a specified time period (say, two weeks) immediately before an election. The polls can be conducted, but the findings can't be made known to the general public. Some other governments have toyed with the same restriction.

The United Kingdom has the Data Protection Act, which is designed primarily to prevent abuse of household financial records and information stored by database marketers. But it also covers marketing research databases and records of all individual survey respondents. It says a firm cannot gather data on individuals, coupled with their address, without written consent, and individuals have the right to see data on themselves in a database.

British research firms must be licensed (that is, registered) to collect data but can request an exemption to the written consent provision which is what large British research firms do. Of course, there is always the possibility that a change of government might deny exemptions.

It became evident that the marketing and opinion research industry needed to take action to protect itself from unreasonable government prohibitions, to bolster its image among the public and legislators, to promote self-regulation, and to develop a means to differentiate the research industry from other industries that appear to be similar.

The January 1992 meeting of research professionals led to the creation of the Council for Marketing and Opinion Research (CMOR). The organization initially raised $500,000 to help meet the following objectives:

1. Establish a single, unified voice for the research industry to speak to respondents, legislators, and regulators. This unified voice would have three major characteristics: (1) broad enough to be all-encompassing in terms of who it represents; (2) focused in its objectives to remain solely dedicated to this mission; (3) nonpartisan to make it possible to speak for every facet of the industry.
2. Monitor state and federal legislation and lobby on behalf ofthe interests of the research industry to prevent passage of unnecessarily restrictive legislation.
3. Work proactively with government leaders to protect the industry from abuses of the research process.
4. Develop a means for the public to determine the legitimacy of a research interaction.
5. Differentiate the research industry from other kinds of unsolicited contacts with the public.

6. Create an educational platform that will strengthen and expand research industry alliances to increase and mobilize the support for CMOR.
7. Provide support to and complement the efforts of other industry associations.[19]

SUMMARY

The research industry may be categorized as follows:

1. Corporate marketing research departments—marketing research departments in major firms such as Kraft General Foods and Ralston Purina.
2. Ad agency research departments—marketing research departments in advertising agencies such as J. Walter Thompson and Grey Advertising.
3a. Custom or ad hoc research firms—firms that handle customized marketing research projects addressing specific problems for individual clients.
3b. Syndicated service firms—firms that collect data of general interest. Anyone can purchase the information. These firms are prominent in the media audience field and scanner data research.
4. Field service firms—data collection firms.

Today's business ethics are a subset of the values held by society as a whole. A marketing researcher with mature ethical values assumes responsibility for employees' needs and desires, persons directly affected by company activities, and social values and conditions for society at large.

The level of professionalism in the marketing research industry has been raised by the efforts of CASRO and CMOR. CMOR is primarily concerned with respondent cooperation and legislation that curtails or prohibits various forms of survey research.

KEY TERMS

Corporate marketing research
departments
Custom, or ad hoc, marketing research
firms
Syndicated service research firms
Audience data syndicated services
Product movement data syndicated
services

Field service firms
Specialized service or support firms
Ad agency marketing research
departments
Strategic partnering
Council for Marketing and Opinion
Research (CMOR)

REVIEW AND DISCUSSION QUESTIONS

1. Compare and contrast custom and syndicated marketing research firms.
2. What is the role of field services in marketing research?
3. Discuss several types of support service firms in the research industry.
4. Describe the levels of the marketing research industry.
5. List several key characteristics of corporate marketing research departments.
6. Discuss the different "product offerings" of syndicated service firms.
7. Explain the role of ad agency research departments.

8. Define strategic partnering. Why has it become so prominent in the marketing research industry?
9. What role should the federal government play in establishing ethical standards for the marketing research industry? How would this be enforced?
10. What is the relationship between ethics and professionalism? What do you think can be done to raise the level of professionalism within the marketing research industry?

CASE

Anchor Marketing Research

Anchor Marketing Research is a custom marketing research firm located in Detroit. Allen Mayberry, president, is concerned about a new type of strategic partnering that is occurring within the marketing research industry. Traditional strategic partnering occurs when two marketing research firms with unique skills and resources form an alliance to offer a new service for clients, provide strategic support for each, or in some other manner create mutual benefits. In the new form of strategic partnering, a large research user, such as Kraft General Foods, decides to work closely with a very limited number of custom and syndicated research firms rather than getting competitive bids from a large number of firms. Once a partnership is established it is quite difficult for a new firm to break the bond between research supplier and user.

Anchor was founded in 1990 and has quickly grown to a $12 million-a-year firm. The firm's primary competitive advantage is its expertise in multivariate statistical techniques and mathematical modeling for new products. Allen Mayberry is concerned that despite Anchor's talents it may have limited opportunity to showcase them because of the new type of strategic partnering. Presently the firm is not engaged in strategic partnering. Allen decided that the best way to assess the situation is to do marketing research. Anchor interviewed 100 marketing research directors from large research user organizations. The sample consisted of consumer products companies, 54 percent; service organizations, 36 percent; and business-to-business firms, 10 percent. The findings were as follows:

Partnering trends (base = 100)	%
Partnering more now	59
Will partner more in future	38
Other companies will partner more	73

Three-fourths of all firms claim to be doing some kind of partnering. It is widespread among all types and sizes of companies, though particularly strong among the larger organizations. For those that are not partnering with their research firms, respondents say they don't need to or mention cost considerations.

Reasons not to partner (base = 25)	%
No need	60
Bid out projects	28
Depends on cost	20

The twenty-five firms not partnering are more sensitive to cost considerations, and they worry slightly more about giving the research firm too much power. The same does not seem to be true among the ones that are partnering, however.

Advantages of partnering (base = 75)	%
Know our needs	51
Replicate studies	45
Consistency/ongoing relationships	43
Saves money/more value	33
Faster turnaround	32
Provide expertise	21

Ratings of partnering benefits (5 = agree strongly)

Benefit	"Now partnering" mean (base = 75)	"Not partnering" mean (base = 25)
Helps a research firm learn about the client's business	4.6	4.4
Makes it more efficient and simple to work with a research firm	4.7	3.8
Helps a research firm provide better design and analysis	4.3	3.8
Helps develop standard procedures and norms	4.3	3.7

Reasons to partner center around making client researchers more efficient and effective—research firms know their needs and can replicate studies, be more consistent, give faster turnaround, and provide expertise. Also, one-third of respondents believe they are getting a better value so partnering works during budget crunches.

Ratings of partnering drawbacks (5 = agree strongly)

Drawback	"Now partnering" mean (base = 75)	"Not partnering" mean (base = 25)
Risks having the research firm overcharge the client	2.8	3.9
Risks making the research firm too powerful at the client company	2.8	3.4
Cannot work because the client and research firm have different goals	1.8	1.6

How partnering works (base = 75)	%
Informal agreement	71
Limited number of suppliers	37
Don't bid out	9
Contract	7

Very few clients and research firms have formal contracts—only 7 percent of those partnering. Most have an informal agreement or have decided on their own to limit the number of research firms with which they work.[20]

1. You are Allen Mayberry. Would you enter into strategic partnering?
2. If so, how would you go about it?

Ethical Dilemma——PART ONE

J. D. Power's Syndicated Research

In 1971, J. D. Power decided to create small-scale mail surveys that would focus on automobiles. The first consisted of the initial 1,000 buyers of the new Mazda rotary-engine vehicle. The second was a survey of the buyers of front-wheel drive passenger cars such as the Honda 600 and other entries from Saab, Renault, Peugeot, and Subaru. The studies were low cost, low priced, and an immediate success.

Mazda Motors of America did not subscribe to the first survey, but Mazda Japan did as well as GM, Ford, Chrysler, VW, and a host of other Japanese car manufacturers. At $1,800 per subscribing company, J. D. Power felt that he had the key to success, and he sent out the first press release with topline results. Mazda Motors America used the headline from the press release without attribution for a television commercial: "Nine out of ten owners of Mazda rotary engine cars would recommend them to their friends." This was J. D. Power's first indication that he was creating advertisable research. A year later, at the request of several subscribers to the first Mazda Rotary Engine Owner Survey, the company conducted another to gauge the acceptance of the product after a year of ownership. He also raised the price to $2,500.

The results of the follow-up survey revealed that one out of five owners experienced an "O" ring failure that resulted in the need for an engine overhaul. One of the Detroit-based subscribers leaked the findings to the *Wall Street Journal*, which confronted Mazda Motors America. Mazda subscribed to the study and challenged J. D. Power's findings, methodology, and general capabilities to project from a sample of 500 returns. Within twenty-four hours the story was in every newspaper throughout the world. The rest is history—all the other automobile manufacturers, including GM and Ford, scuttled their development work on rotary engines and Mazda went to work on correcting the deficiencies.

By 1991, J. D. Power and Associates was grossing over $18 million per year. Now Power, who was 60 years old in 1991, wants to become the quality judge for everything from computers to airlines to phone companies. But his capricious management style has prompted several key employees to leave recently. And Power plays conflicting roles—providing advice to consumers while selling research and advertising claims to manufacturers—that could undermine the company's credibility.

Both problems were evident in the resignation of Christopher Cedergren, J. D. Power's chief market-competition analyst. Power told Cedergren, who is often quoted by auto writers, to stop publicly criticizing car makers because he was upsetting clients. "We muzzled him," says Power bluntly. Because of that and other differences, Cedergren quit.

Power's methods were evident in his company's first survey of satisfaction among personal computer users. Power officials phoned Dell Computer Corporation in Austin, Texas, with the good news that Dell had topped the Power computer survey. Then the Power people told Dell it would cost them $72,000 to buy the syndicated survey and another $40,000 to advertise its results. Dell paid up. "One has to understand that a survey of this nature will pay for itself in a fairly short order of time," explains Barry Rumac, Dell's director of advertising. Indeed, Dell's computer sales quickly jumped an additional 10 percent.

Power perfected this formula in the auto industry. He charges auto makers up to $130,000 for a major survey—notably the Customer Satisfaction Index, which tracks the experiences of car buyers during the year after their purchase, and the Initial Quality Survey, which measures defects in the first ninety days of a car's life. Then Power announces the top finishers—and charges them thousands of dollars more to advertise how well they did. The companies who do not do well can rest assured that Power will not publicly disclose their names. Instead, the company offers to sell them consulting advice—to help them do better on the next J. D. Power survey, of course. "We'll coach every company that wants us to coach them," Power declares.

Nobody questions the basic validity of J. D. Power's research. For the two major surveys, J. D. Power mails out about 80,000 questionnaires and gets back close to 30,000 responses. Mr. Power dismisses the notion that his methods lead to conflicts of interest. He views his surveys as "the voice of the consumer." Being a cheerleader instead of a critic allows him to be effective, he says. "Maybe it would be ideal to [release] the ratings on everybody," Power acknowledges. But that would require selling the surveys directly to consumers instead of to car makers, he says. He adds, "We've done more for market research in the auto industry than anyone else—I, personally, and we, the company—by getting top management to focus on the consumer."

Auto makers pay because the surveys can sound impressive—at times maybe too much so. In 1989, Power's quality survey named the Buick LeSabre the most trouble-free domestic model, with only 89 defects per 100 cars. Never mind that Ford's Crown Victoria had just 91 defects per 100 cars, a difference Power says was within the margin of error and statistically meaningless. Buick heavily advertised its victory, and LeSabre sales surged more than 40 percent.

In 1990, GM's Chevrolet division used the Power survey to tout its Lumina coupe as "the most trouble-free car in its class." But the class—midsize specialty cars—included only seven vehicles, all domestic. The Lumina coupe beat the other six but had more defects than the average for all cars. Criticism of the Chevy ad prompted Power to ban such "best of class" advertising this year.

1. Is it ethical for J. D. Power to provide information to consumers about product quality while charging manufacturers to advertise J. D. Power survey results?
2. Discuss the ethical issues involved in J. D. Power's handling of Christopher Cedergren.
3. Are the actions that J. D. Power took when Dell Computer finished at the top of the satisfaction survey ethical? Why or why not?
4. Should complete survey results be made public? Is it unethical to withhold such information?
5. Does the banning of "best of class" advertising by J. D. Power provide evidence that the company is one of high ethical standards?

This case was developed from Neal Templin, "Expanding Beyond Automobile Surveys, J. D. Power Defends Its Business Methods," *The Wall Street Journal* (September 5, 1991), pp. B1, B4; and J. D. Power, "A Different Kind of Marketing Research Firm," *CASRO Journal 1991*, pp. 75–78.

PART 2

Creating a Research Design

CHAPTER 4

Published Secondary Data, Computerized Databases, and Decision Support Systems

LEARNING OBJECTIVES

1. To understand how to create an internal database.
2. To distinguish between primary and secondary data and understand the advantages and disadvantages of each.
3. To understand the growth and types of on-line databases.
4. To learn the nature of decision support systems.

T he marketing research function at Samsonite Corporation combines traditional research methods with newer database-oriented approaches, all within a "customer-oriented" environment. Databases provide a unique marketing research tool to aid in decision making and help position Samsonite to cope with the challenges of retail consolidation, blurring of traditional channels, development of new distribution channels, and better informed, proactive consumers.

Robert Bengen, director of direct marketing and research at Samsonite, describes the role of Samsonite's database in its marketing research.

The consumer database is the main source of information about our consumers. It is "driven" by the consumer response card—asking for demographic, lifestyle, and purchase information—inserted into all Samsonite luggage and business cases. After about two years of operation [late 1993], we had nearly a half-million records, and the monthly numbers are increasing steadily.

The consumer database has provided a wealth of information for marketing planning. By analyzing the characteristics of purchasers of our different products, say, Silhouette 4 products vs. Ultralite products, we have been able to target our products and our planning more exactly. Also, by examining our consumers against the population as a whole, we have been able to understand where we are *underrepresented* and have produced products for these targets. One good example of this is our Esteem luggage, which is targeted toward professional women.

Second, our consumer and prospect databases have also aided our sales department in increasing sales to our retail accounts. For example, the Samsonite purchasers' profile shows that our consumers are nicely *overrepresented* in the key twenty-five- to fifty-four-year-old age group, are upscale, educated, active, and do lots of traveling, especially air travel and foreign travel. This profile is a very powerful one and has been used successfully by our salespeople to drive home the point to retailers that "Samsonite's the type of business you want."

In addition, analyses of Samsonite purchasers in different retail accounts (account profiles) have enabled our salespeople to (1) understand our accounts better and work with them more effectively, and (2) show accounts how taking on additional Samsonite luggage lines will target different shoppers. As one salesperson said, "If we show that we know as much or more about the account than does the account itself, then we are in a great position to make additional sales."

One other thing we have done—and will do more of in the future—is retail trading area analyses. Using Workbench, we have been able to profile both the census population and the Samsonite purchaser population around a store or group of stores so we can work cooperatively with accounts to develop highly targeted direct marketing programs to key target groups.[1]

The use of databases in marketing research has mushroomed in the past decade. Will massive databases eliminate the need for primary research? What are the advantages and pitfalls of secondary data? These are some of the questions we will answer in Chapter 4.

THE NATURE OF SECONDARY DATA

Secondary data is information that has been gathered and only *might* be relevant to the problem at hand. **Primary data**, in contrast, is survey, observation, or experiment data collected to solve the particular problem under investigation. In other words, it is highly unlikely that any marketing research problem is entirely unique or has never occurred before. It also is probable that someone else has investigated this problem or one similar to it in the past. There are two basic sources of secondary data: the company itself (**internal databases**) and other organizations or persons (external databases).

Secondary data
Data that has been previously gathered.

Primary data
New data gathered to help solve the problem at hand.

Internal database
Database developed from data within the organization.

Creating an Internal Database

For many companies like Samsonite, a computerized database containing information about customers and prospects has become an essential marketing tool. A database is simply a collection of related information. A good starting point for creating an internal secondary database is to pull information from the firm's sales or inquiry processing and tracking system. Typically, such a system is built upon a salesperson's "call report." Call reports provide a blueprint of a salesperson's daily activities. A report details the number of calls made, characteristics of each firm visited, sales activity resulting from the call, and information picked up regarding competitors such as price changes, new products, credit term modifications, and new features stressed by competitors.

Creating an internal marketing secondary database built upon sales results and customer preferences can be a powerful marketing tool. Catalog companies such as Speigel's and L. L. Bean have become masters at building and utilizing internal databases. The story of how Cabela's, a major fishing tackle and outdoors products company, uses its database follows on page 72.

Keys to a Successful Internal Database

To achieve the levels of success that Cabela's and other organizations have with their internal databases, several steps must be taken. First, you must create a **database management system**. This involves capturing data on the computer, organizing it for effective use, updating and maintaining it, and being able to readily retrieve information from it for marketing decision making. This is no simple task. With today's technology, storing data on a computer is trivial. Creating an internal secondary database system with the proper blend of experienced people, hardware, and software to make it usable is a complex task.

Database management system
The system in which data are captured on the computer, organized for effective use, updated, and maintained to provide information for decision making.

Second, database users must be trained on how to retrieve needed information and how to manipulate the data using **database management software**. Some of the basic abilities a manager will acquire by using such software include

Database management software
Computer programs for the retrieval and manipulation of data.

- Inputing: Adding new data to the database.
- Querying: Looking for specific pieces of information, such as sales prospects not called on in two years.
- Sorting: Taking an alphabetical list of sales prospects and sorting them by zip code, for distribution to sales representatives in those regions for follow-up.
- Extracting: A researcher might want to evaluate the rough potential for a new product with the firm's current base of customers.

A researcher who believed that each employee in an office or plant would create a market for seven units of the new product per year could quickly determine the product's potential, by location, by extracting the key fields from the database—company name, location, number of employees—and inserting a column that multiplies each employee by a factor of seven.

A manager would also typically learn spreadsheet applications for the database. Spreadsheet software is designed to reflect the format of a standard business spreadsheet. Rows and columns of data, each with their applicable labels, can be added, subtracted, divided, multiplied, and formulated in as many ways as the user likes. The final tabulated results can be printed as a finished report. The software's obvious advantage is the incredible speed at which these calculations can be accomplished. Thus, a number of different scenarios can be postulated and their

MARKETING RESEARCH IN PRACTICE

Cabela's depends on its database to control the distribution costs of its four-color catalogs. In a typical year, Cabela's sends out at least nine mailings of between 300,000 and 3 million catalogs each.

Cabela's constantly winnows out the people who do not respond. It also sends specific kinds of catalogs to buyers based on their purchasing patterns, says marketing director Sharon Robison. The company divides customers into ten major categories, from the buyers of footwear to buyers of gifts and fishing and bow-hunting equipment. Cabela's gathers new names by sharing its mailing list with similar catalog companies such as Gander Mountain, by renting address lists from magazines, by advertising in hunting and fishing publications, and by soliciting new names from current catalog recipients.[2]

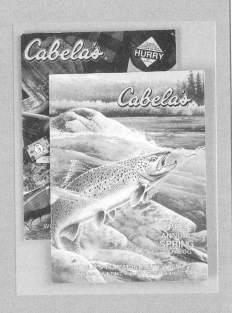

TABLE 4.1   *How Electronic Spreadsheets Answer "What If" Questions*

	BASE		8% SALES INCREASE/15% GM		11% SALES INCREASE/12% GM	
Sales	12,000	100%	12,960	100%	13,320	100%
Cost of Sales	10,200	85%	11,016	85%	11,722	88%
Gross Profit	1,800	15%	1,944	15%	1,598	12%
Sales Expenses	600	5%	648	5%	666	5%
Administration	480	4%	518	4%	533	4%
Profit	720	6%	778	6%	400	3%

impacts examined. For example, Jim Clancy opened a small deli across the street from the college he is attending (see Table 4.1). Last quarter Jim had sales of $12,000, a gross profit margin of 15 percent, and a net profit of $720. Using an electronic spreadsheet, Jim can determine what will happen next quarter if sales increase 8 percent and his gross margin remains the same. Jim may be faced with an increase in meat costs that will cut his gross margin to 12 percent. However, he feels that advertising in the college newspaper may begin paying off so that sales could rise 11 percent over the previous quarter. Under this scenario, net profit will fall to $400.

The Growing Importance of Internal Database Marketing

Perhaps the fastest-growing use of an internal database is database marketing. *Database marketing* is the creation of a large computerized file of customers' and potential customers' profiles and purchase patterns. Specifically, database marketing can

- Evaluate sales territories.
- Identify most profitable and least profitable customers.
- Identify most profitable market segments and target efforts with greater efficiency and effectiveness.
- Aim marketing efforts to those products, services, and segments that require the most support.
- Increase revenue through repackaging and repricing products for various market segments.
- Evaluate opportunities for offering new products or services.
- Identify products or services that are best sellers or most profitable.
- Evaluate existing marketing programs.

In the 1950s, network television enabled advertisers to "get the same message to everyone simultaneously." Database marketing can get a customized, individual message to everyone simultaneously through direct mail. This is why database marketing is sometimes called "micro marketing."

The size of many databases is somewhat mind boggling: Ford Motor Company's is about 50 million names; Kraft/General Foods, 25 million; Citicorp, 30 million; and Kimberly Clark, maker of Huggies diapers, 10 million new mothers. American Express, for example, can pull from its database all card holders who made purchases at golf pro-shops in the past six months, or who attended symphony concerts, or who traveled to Europe more than once in the last year, or the very few people who did all three activities.

MARKETING RESEARCH IN PRACTICE

A utility company recently added Equifax Marketing Decision Systems' VISION codes to its customer database. VISION is a geodemographic segmentation system that assigns each census block group to one of forty-eight categories based on its demographic characteristics. It describes these segments with unique nicknames, giving the company a vivid picture of its 1.2 million customers.

After the initial coding project was complete, the research department used the information to target a campaign aimed at persuading current oil-burner owners to evaluate electric heat pumps for their homes. VISION segments were selected that matched the demographics of its customers who already owned electric heat pumps. This approach saved the company thousands of dollars in mailing costs.

Next, the utility's communications department and advertising agency looked at the customer profiles. The data called for a basic change in the company's advertising. Their television spots had been very upscale and "homey." But the profiles indicated that a different approach might work better. Based on the strong presence of mid- to down-scale town and rural segments such as "Tom Sawyerville" and "Appalachian Trail," the new campaign portrayed heat-pump installers who shared the target audience's working-class demeanor. The result was a significant increase in awareness of the product.

The company has decided to expand its research program. It may add individual demographic characteristics to its customer lists to make even smaller levels of segmentation possible. It may also switch to a PC-based system that will allow it greater analytical flexibility.

Electric utilities must manage the demand for power. Power plants are expensive to build. Reducing the demand for electricity during the peak periods of the day can postpone the need to build new plants. With the help of lifestyle information, they have put together conservation programs aimed at lowering demand during peak periods. Homeowners volunteer, and are compensated, to let the utility company shut off their air conditioning and hot water when the system is operating at full capacity—usually during the day. "You wouldn't want to target people who are gone all day," says the utility company's manager of consumer research, "because they aren't using electricity during those times anyway."

Two primary groups should be interested in this kind of program: the ecology minded and the cost conscious. "Some people really care about the environment," explains the manager. "They are societally conscious and don't care about the money. Other people would be just delighted to get $5 every time we shut off their air conditioning."[3]

A technique of growing popularity for building a database is the creation of "customer clubs." Kraft, for example, has been inviting kids to join the Cheese & Macaroni Club. For three proofs-of-purchase, $2.95, and a completed membership form with the child's (and, of course, Mom's) address, Kraft will send a painter's cap, bracelet, shoelaces, a book of stickers, and other goodies.[4] Burger King Corporation is signing up 50,000 kids a day for its Kids Club, and Coors Brewing Co. has begun locating its loyal buyers through a Club Coors program.[5]

Quaker, in late 1990, mailed over 18 million packages containing sixteen pages of coupons and promotional offers. Each coupon was coded with an individual household identification number. When consumers redeemed the coupons, the grocery stores' electronic scanners automatically sent detailed information about the purchase back to Quaker. With that data, Quaker then determined who has a dog, say, or a child, and can then specifically target the next round of coupons it mails to that particular household. A Quaker marketing manager noted, "Every time a coupon is redeemed, customers participate in a two-way communication."[6] Quaker planned not only to target future mailings based upon demographics, but also to offer higher incentives to resistent shoppers. After two mailings, however, the program was put on hold due to high cost.[7]

Some experts feel that personalized database marketing will not really take off until marketers can electronically deliver their promotions to individual households—a method that is much less expensive than direct mail. Others, however, disagree. George Mrkonic is president of K-Mart's $7 billion specialty stores division, which includes Waldenbooks, Pace Membership Warehouses, Sports Authority, Builders Square, and Pay Less Drug Stores. He plans to increase the division's sales from 22 percent to 30 percent of company sales by 1996. The key to the success of his plan, according to Mrkonic, is database marketing.[8]

Through its Club Coors program, the Coors Brewing Company pulls together a database of buyers while offering consumers coupons, special offers, feature stories, and opportunities for involvement in conservation efforts. Courtesy of the Coors Brewing Company.

PUBLISHED SECONDARY DATA

Internal

Published secondary information originating within the company includes documents such as annual reports, reports to stockholders, product testing results perhaps made available to the news media, and house periodicals composed by the company's personnel for communication to employees, customers, or others. Often this information is incorporated into a company's internal database.

External

Innumerable outside sources of secondary information also exist, principally in the forms of government (federal, state, and local) departments and agencies who compile and publish summaries of business data. Trade and industry associations also provide published secondary data. Still another set is composed of all business periodicals and other news media that regularly publish studies and articles on the economy, specific industries, and even individual companies. The unpublished summarized secondary information from these sources corresponds to internal reports, memos, or special-purpose analyses with limited circulation. Economic considerations or priorities in the organization may preclude publication of these summaries. Finally, it is conceivable that pockets of raw data may reside in these organizations just as they occur in the marketing researcher's own (client) firm. It should be evident that each type of secondary information requires that unique tasks be performed to render it useful to the researcher.

ADVANTAGES OF SECONDARY DATA

Marketing researchers use secondary information because it can be obtained at a fraction of the cost, time, and inconvenience of primary data collection. Additional advantages for using secondary information include the following.

1. *Secondary information may help to clarify or redefine the definition of the problem as part of the exploratory research process.* As you learned in Chapter 2, secondary data plays a key role in exploratory research. A local YMCA was concerned about its stagnant level of membership and a lack of participation in many traditional YMCA programs. It decided to survey members and nonmembers. Secondary data revealed a tremendous influx of young, single persons into the target market whereas the number of "traditional families" remained constant. The problem was redefined to examine how the YMCA could attract a significant share of the young single adult market while maintaining its traditional family base.

2. *Secondary information may actually provide a solution to the problem.* It is highly unlikely that a problem faced by a manager and communicated to the marketing researcher will never before have been encountered; there is always a possibility that someone else has addressed the identical problem or a very similar one. Someone may have collected the precise information desired, but not for the same purpose as the problem faced by the manager.

   Many states publish a directory of manufacturers that contains information on the location, markets, product lines, number of plants, names of key personnel, number of employees, and sales levels of companies. For example, a consulting company specializing in long-range strategic planning for members of the semiconductor industry desired a regional profile of its potential clients. Individual state directories were used to compile the profile. No primary data collection was necessary.

3. *Secondary information may provide primary data research method alternatives.* Each primary research endeavor is custom designed for the situation at hand; consequently, the marketing researcher should always be open to information that offers research alternatives. For example, we conducted a research project for a large southwestern city's convention and visitor's bureau. A research report prepared by *Meeting and Convention Planners* magazine was obtained prior to designing the questionnaire. The secondary report published by the magazine contained the original questionnaire. A series of scaling questions were used in our questionnaire. Not only were the scales well-designed, but results from our study could be compared with the magazine's data.

4. *Secondary information may alert the marketing researcher to potential problems or difficulties.* Apart from alternatives, secondary information may divulge potential dangers. Unpopular collection methods, sample selection difficulties, or respondent hostility may be uncovered. For example, examination of a study of anesthesiologists by a researcher planning to conduct a study to measure the level of satisfaction with certain existing drugs used in the profession uncovered a high refusal rate in a telephone survey. The researcher had also planned a telephone study, but switched to a mail questionnaire with a response incentive.

5. *Secondary information may provide necessary background information and build creativity for the research report.* Secondary information can often provide a wealth of background data for planning a research project. It may offer a profile of potential buyers versus nonbuyers, industry data, new product features desired, language used by purchasers to describe the industry, existing products and their advantages and disadvantages. Language used by target consumers can aid in phrasing questions that will be understood correctly and be meaningful to respondents. Background data also can often meet some research objectives, eliminating the need to ask the questions in a present study. Shorter questionnaires typically have higher completion rates. Secondary data can sometimes enrich research findings by providing additional insights into what the data mean or by corroborating current findings. Finally, secondary data can serve as a reference base for subsequent research projects.

LIMITATIONS OF SECONDARY DATA

Despite the many advantages of secondary data, it also poses some dangers and pitfalls. The disadvantages are lack of availability, lack of relevance, inaccuracy, and insufficiency.[9]

Lack of Availability

For some research questions there is simply no available data. If Kraft General Foods wants to evaluate the taste, texture, and color of three new gourmet brownie mixes, there is no secondary data that would answer these questions. Consumers must try each mix and then evaluate it. If McDonald's wants to evaluate its image in Phoenix, Arizona, it must gather primary data. If Ford wants to know the reaction of college students to a new two-seater sports car design, it must show prototypes to the students and evaluate their opinions. Of course, secondary data may have played a major role in the engineer's design plan for the car.

Lack of Relevance

It is not uncommon for secondary data to be expressed in units or measures that cannot be used by the researcher. For example, Joan Dermott is a retailer of oriental rugs, who determined that the primary customers for her wares are families with total household incomes of $40,000–80,000. Higher-income consumers tend to purchase rugs beyond the price range carried by the dealer. In attempting to decide whether to open a store in another Florida city, she cannot find useful income data. One source offered class breakdowns from $30,000–50,000, $50,000–70,000, $70,000–90,000, and so forth. A second secondary source breaks down incomes as under $15,000, $15,000–30,000, and over $30,000. Even if the income brackets had met Joan's needs, she encountered another problem: lack of publication currency. One study was conducted in 1980 and the other in 1982. In Florida's dynamic markets, the percentages probably were no longer relevant. This is often the case with U.S. census data, which is historically nearly two years old before it is available in publications. However, computer disks for the 1990 census were available much sooner.

Inaccurate Data

Users of secondary data should always be suspicious of the accuracy of the data. There are a number of potential sources of error when a researcher gathers, codes, analyzes, and presents data. Any report that does not mention possible sources of error and ranges of error should be suspect.

Using secondary data does not relieve the researcher from attempting to assess its accuracy.[10] A few guidelines for determining secondary data accuracy are as follows.

1. *Who gathered the data?* The source of the secondary data is a key to its accuracy. Federal agencies, most state agencies, and large commercial market research firms can generally be counted on to have conducted their research as professionally as possible. One should always be on guard when examining data where a hidden agenda might be present. A Chamber of Commerce, for instance, is always going to put its best foot forward. Similarly, trade associations often advocate one position or another.
2. *What was the purpose of the study?* Data are always collected for some reason. Understanding the motivation for the research can provide clues in assessing the quality of the data. A Chamber of Commerce study conducted to provide data that can be used to attract new industry to the area should be viewed with a great deal of scrutiny and caution. We know of situations where advertising agencies were hired by their clients to assess the impact of its advertising program. In other words, the advertising agency was asked to evaluate the quality of the job it was doing for the client!

3. *What information was collected?* A researcher should always identify exactly what information was gathered. For example, in a dog food study, were purchasers of canned, dry, and semimoist food interviewed or just one or two types of dog food purchasers surveyed? In a voters' survey were only Democrats or Republicans interviewed? Were the respondents evaluated to make certain they are registered voters? Was any attempt made to ascertain the respondent's likelihood of voting in the next election? Was self-reported data used to infer actual behavior?

4. *When was the information collected?* A shopping mall study that surveyed shoppers only on weekends would not reflect the "typical" mall patrons. A telephone survey conducted from 9:00 A.M. to 5:00 P.M. would vastly underrepresent working persons. A survey of Florida visitors conducted during the summer would probably reveal different motivations and interests from winter visitors.

5. *How was the information obtained?* Was the data collected by mail, telephone, or personal interview? Each of these techniques offers advantages and disadvantages. What was the refusal rate? Were decision makers interviewed or a representative of the decision maker? In short, the researcher must attempt to discern the amount of bias injected into the data by the information-gathering process. A mail survey with a 1 percent response rate (where only 1 percent of those who received the survey mailed it back) probably contains a lot of self-selection bias.

6. *Is the information consistent with other information?* A lack of consistency between secondary data sets should serve as a caution sign. The researcher should delve into possible causes of the discrepancy. A different sample frame, time factors, sampling methodology, questionnaire structure, and other factors can lead to variations in studies. If possible, the researcher should assess the reliability of the studies as a basis of determining which, if any, study should be used for decision making.

Insufficient Data

A researcher may determine that data is available, relevant, and accurate but still is not sufficient to make a decision or bring complete closure to a problem. A manager for WalMart discount stores may have sufficient secondary data on incomes, family sizes, number of competitors, and growth potential to determine, among five Iowa towns with a population of under 20,000, in which one it wishes to locate its next store. However, as no traffic counts exist for the selected town, primary data will have to be gathered to select a specific site for the store.

THE NEW AGE OF SECONDARY INFORMATION—ON-LINE DATABASES

Gathering traditional secondary data was often an arduous task. It meant writing for government, trade association, or other reports—then waiting several weeks for a reply. Many times one or more trips to the library were required, and then needed reports may have been checked out or missing. Today, the rapid development of **on-line** computerized **databases** have alleviated much of the drudgery associated with gathering secondary data. An on-line database is a public information database accessible to anyone with proper communication facilities. With over 10,000

On-line database
A public information database accessible to anyone with proper communication facilities.

databases available in 1994 virtually every topic of interest to a marketing researcher can be found in some database.

Data communication requires a computer system on one end as the sender or receiver and either another computer system or terminal on the other. A **modem** is used to convert digital to analog data so that the data can be transferred over a telephone system. At the receiving end another modem converts the sounds back into electrical impulses. Some day, a fiber optic telephone cable will be able to transmit 100 trillion bits per second!

An example of how an on-line database can affect decision making is shown in the true, but disguised, scenario on page 83.

Modem
A modulator-demodulator used to convert digital to analog data so that the data can be transmitted over a telephone system.

Types of Databases

Databases cover a variety of different subjects, geographic areas, and frequency of database update. Databases can be divided into four major categories: numeric, bibliographic, directory, and full text.[11]

Numeric databases contain original survey data such as the VALS2 database. Over 12,000 respondents are reported with data describing their attitudes, wants, beliefs in the eight VALS (values and lifestyles) categories developed by the Stanford Research Institute. This data is melded with Medimark Research Incorporated's study of 20,000 adults regarding magazines they read, the radio programs they listen to, and the television they watch. In addition, purchase habits on 5,700 individual brands are available.

Numeric database
Database containing original survey data on a wide variety of general topics.

One of the most valuable **bibliographic databases** for marketing is FIND/SVP. Over 11,000 studies done by more than 500 research firms are indexed. The database offers instant access to citations of market research reports, consumer and product studies, store audit reports, subscription research services, and surveys of fifty-five industries worldwide. A sample report is shown in Figure 4.1. FIND/SVP is composed of two divisions: quick information service and the strategic research division. The latter handles assignments that require more in-depth explanation and analysis. A summary of the offerings of the two divisions are shown in Table 4.2 on page 82.

Bibliographic database
An index of published studies and reports, may include explanation and analysis.

A popular **directory database** used to get a "quick picture" of a company is Standard and Poor's Corporate Descriptions. It contains information on 8,000 publicly held U.S. corporations. Some of the information provided includes capital expenditures; number of employees, officers, and directors; names of principal stockholders; and two years of balance sheet data.

Directory database
Data available through directories or indexes of directory-type data.

As the name implies, **full text databases** contain the complete text of the source documents making up the database. For example, the *Harvard Business Review* database contains the full text of articles from 1976 to the present. Searches can be conducted in a number of ways: by subject, title, company, industry, product, service, and others.

Full text database
Index containing the full text of source documents, such as articles.

On-Line Vendors

An **on-line** database **vendor** is an intermediary that acquires databases from a variety of database creators. Such databases offer electronic mail, news, finance, sports, weather, airline schedules, software, encyclopedias, bibliographies, directories, full

On-line vendor
An intermediary that acquires databases from a variety of database creators.

text information, and numeric databases. Thus, a user can go to a single on-line vendor and gain access to a variety of databases. Billing is simplified because a single invoice covers the use of a variety of databases on the vendor's system. Also, searching is simplified because it is standardized for all databases offered by the

FIGURE 4.1   *A Sample On-Line Citation from FIND/SVP*

236757 ON-LINE DATABASES IN EUROPE
361 P. $1495   ONE-TIME
Publ: Market Intelligence Research Corp, Mountain View, CA 415-961-9000
Availability: Publisher
Report No.: 490B-60
   Deregulation, coupled with heavy merger and acquisition activity among vendors, is prompting tremendous growth in the European online database market. This report focuses on two general categories of databases: referral and source. Referral databases point users to other sources for complete information. Source databases contain full-text original source data. Currently, full text source data is preferred over reference data. The report reveals how database manufacturers are targeting this preference. Examines five specific types of databases; real-time financial, historical financial, science and technology, company information, and market information. Analyzes the following geographic markets: Western Europe as a whole, the United Kingdom, France, West Germany, Switzerland, and other Western European countries. Forecasts market segments in terms of revenues, the number of competitive factors. Offers strategies for success, based on the need for specialists in the on-line database industry, international marketing, the role of technology, the problems and potential of Eastern Europe, and pricing.
Descriptor: COMPUTER SERVICES & INFORMATION SYSTEMS; DATABASES; WESTERN EUROPE; UNITED KINGDOM; FRANCE; WEST GERMANY; SWITZERLAND; EASTERN EUROPE

Source: FIND/SVP

TABLE 4.2 *Services Offered by FIND/SVP*

QUICK INFORMATION DIVISION	STRATEGIC RESEARCH DIVISION
Consumer Group: Responsible for handling questions on consumer products and services, including cosmetics, toiletries, food, apparel, and home furnishings; also covers agriculture and marketing to the consumer (advertising and direct mail)	*Business Surveys*: Custom-designed surveys using all techniques: personal and telephone interviews, direct mail, focus groups
Industrial-Technical Group: Computers, electronics, telecommunications, energy, chemical, plastics, paper, metal, transportation, materials handling, engineering, construction, and other industrial products and services	*Acquisition Assistance*: Identification and assessment of candidates and due diligence support
Healthcare Group: Products and services manufactured and marketed to healthcare businesses, including pharmaceuticals, medical, and diagnostic equipment, health resources, and clinical information	*Custom Monitoring Services*: Ongoing tracking of current information, news, and trends in markets, products, and technologies, tailored to meet each client's specific needs and frequency
Business-Company-Finance Group: Information on specific companies (excluding credit reports), plus financial services, insurance, trade and international affairs, and economic trends	*General Business Intelligence and Research*: Exhaustive secondary research and information-gathering assignments; extensive on-line database searching
Central Search Group: Biographical information, demographic data, education, politics, the arts, theater, publishing, and other subjects not specifically monitored by the other groups; locates and purchases books, government documents, videos, theater tickets, product samples, catalogs, and price lists, and objects for use as props	*Competitive Intelligence Studies*: Comprehensive assessments of individual companies, business areas, and competitive environments
Document Services Group: Books, photographs, and other documents; photocopies of the full text of articles, patents, proceedings, and SEC documents (such as 10-Ks, proxies); originals or copies of corporate annual reports	*Major Market and Industry Analysis*: Extensive and interpretive studies of all market areas; includes determination of size, trends, segments, structure, competitive situations and opportunities
	Strategic Business Planning and Consulting: Identification and analysis of business opportunities and assistance in the development of strategic business and marketing plans

Source: FIND/SVP

vendor. On-line vendors also provide an index to assist the researcher in determining which databases will most likely meet the researcher's needs. Four of the most popular on-line databases are CompuServe, The Source, Dow Jones News/Retrieval Service, and Dialog. CompuServe is a subsidiary of H&R Block, and The Source is owned by Reader's Digest. Dialog, a subsidiary of Lockheed Company, offers over 200 different databases containing more than 100 million items of information.[12] Selected databases offered by each of the four major on-line vendors are shown in Table 4.3. Database needs of marketers run the gamut from simple mailing lists to detailed consumption patterns broken down by psychographic profiles. Attempting to list every database of interest to marketers would be an encyclopedic task. Moreover, new databases are coming on-line everyday.

Advantages of On-Line Databases

On-line databases provide a number of important advantages. First, the researcher has quick access to a much greater variety of information than ever before. Second, the efficient use of on-line search protocols helps the researcher quickly pinpoint relevant data. (See Figure 4.2 for an example of how to hone your on-line search so

TABLE 4.3   *Selected Offerings of the Four Most Popular On-Line Vendors*

DOW JONES	DIALOG	COMPUSERVE	THE SOURCE
Disclosure II	Disclosure II (business database)	Standard & Poor's General Information File	Management Contents
Dow Jones News	Management Contents	Washington Post	Commodity News Service
Current Quotes	Standard & Poor's Corporate Description	World Book Encyclopedia	Cineman Movie Reviews
Wall Street Journal	Books in Print	Microquote (stock information)	U.S. News Washington Letter
Academic American Encyclopedia	Electronic Yellow Pages	Business Information Wire	Travel Services
Cineman Movie Reviews	Magazine Index	AP News	Employment Service
AP News	AP News	Comp*U*Store	AP News
Comp*U*Store	OAG	OAG	Comp*U*Store
OAG			OAG

the computer finds only what you want.) Third, the large in-house staffs formerly required to research and maintain files can be eliminated. This reduces labor costs and increases productivity. Finally, small firms can gain access to the same secondary data as large organizations and do it just as efficiently. This tends to make small firms competitive with big companies with huge libraries and large staffs.

On-line databases have two layers: individual records that make up the database and search software that picks out the records you want from the thousands or millions in the database. Think of search software as an idiot that works at the speed of light. If you type in a word or phrase, the software will find every occurrence of that word or phrase in the database, exactly as you typed it and regardless of context. The system will respond with the number of records in the database that match your search.[13]

A warehouse club has just opened in Bob's market area. Bob is the regional manager for a chain of grocery stores, and he wants to know how the new store might affect his sales. He logs into a database that contains articles from business publications and does a word search on the name of the wholesaler. Within seconds, he has a list of article abstracts. Perusing these, Bob picks out generic terms for warehouse clubs and does another search to come up with more articles describing the industry, its major players, the target market, and actual customers.

Bob then logs into another database that contains more specialized corporate intelligence. He finds the latest financial reports of his competitors, along with information on how they are planning to expand their markets. He also checks out a survey research database to look at reports on the food retail industry and how different types of merchandisers are targeting markets.

Bob logs off the system, loads up all of the articles and reports he saved while he was on-line, and edits them on his word processor. He produces a first-rate presentation on the ramifications of the new warehouse club on his business. And he never leaves his desk.[14]

MARKETING RESEARCH IN PRACTICE

FIGURE 4.2 *Bermuda not Onion*

Search Statement	Result	Number of Cases
Bermuda	Whoa! Too many cases to search. Let's make sure there are no articles on Bermuda onions.	419
Bermuda Not Onion	This statement will eliminate any cases that mention the word ONION with BERMUDA. So we have eliminated one citation about Bermuda onions, not Bermuda. Still too general. Let's try to reduce the number of citations by being more specific in listing the cases we want.	418
Bermuda and Travel	This statement will note only citations where both the words Bermuda and travel are mentioned. We now have only 19 cases to work with, much more manageable than 418. But what about cruises or vacations in Bermuda? Have we missed any of these by only listing the word travel with Bermuda?	19
Bermuda and (Cruise or Vacations or Travel)	With this statement, we will be sure to capture any citations that mention travel and Bermuda, including cruises and vacations. We have now added 3 cases missed in our previous search statement.	22
4 and 1990	A fast way to eliminate outdated cases from your search is to limit it to a specific time period. This statement will result in any of the citations in the previous search, but from 1990 to present only. Now we have 10 fairly recent citations about travel, cruises, vacations, and Bermuda. This is a very workable number of cases. It's time to look at what we have.	10

Source: Katherine S. Chiang, "How to find online information," *American Demographics* (September 1993), p. 54.

Say you are interested in mentions of the president's home. A search of the phrase *white house* might retrieve forty-five records—fourteen that pertain to 1600 Pennsylvania Avenue, four on the coffee brand, one on Marin County (an area known for the predominantly white color of its houses), and twenty-six from the White House Publishing Company in New Delhi, India.

Disadvantages of On-Line Databases

The immense variety of information available to the marketing researcher could engender a false sense of euphoria. On-line databases are no marketing research panacea. Like all tools of the researcher, this one has its drawbacks.

One potential disadvantage is that a person not skilled at "searching" a database may be deluged with data. The researcher must carefully select the search words used to locate appropriate citations, abstracts, and full text stories. Often this means researchers must familiarize themselves with an industry's terminology to narrow the search.

Most database search techniques use the Boolean operators "and," "or," and "not." These terms help researchers target their needs. For example, a researcher for Kraft General Foods working on a new fruit-flavored frozen dessert containing real fruit might use the "and" operator as follows. Find all documents related to fruit-flavored ice cream and fruit-flavored yogurt. The "or" operator can help eliminate dual listings in a data search. The search command "Find all documents related to fruit-flavored ice cream or fruit-flavored yogurt" would provide a listing of all documents dealing with fruit-flavored ice cream or yogurt and would eliminate duplicate listings by not counting them twice. The "not" operator enables a researcher to eliminate a concept or subset that is not of interest to the researcher. The command "Find all documents related to fruit-flavored ice cream but not dietary ice creams" would eliminate all documents that relate to dietary ice creams.

One novice researcher working for Ogilvy and Mather advertising agency in New York inadvertently punched in a command to call up all stories in their entirety. Once placed, the instruction could not be canceled. The result was a $700 bill for data and telephone time.

Some databases tend to have decision rules for what is included or excluded from the database but do not make this expressly known to the user. For example, one database that indexes news publications includes domestic news and international news but only international news relating to Europe. Thus, a researcher may inadvertently miss important secondary information even when using the proper search operators simply because certain documents were never added to the database.

Another complaint is that some databases do not keep their files up to date. It is not uncommon to find that the most current information is several months old. If current data is of critical importance, the researcher may still end up browsing through current periodicals at a local library.

On-line research is not necessarily cheap. Most vendors charge in fractions of hours. Hourly fees for databases can range from nominal ($20) to expensive ($200 plus). The network through which users call vendors usually charges by the hour, too, and the charge is roughly equivalent to what you might spend if you had to call the vendor's computer long-distance directly. Some vendors also charge for the actual information users retrieve. A bibliographic citation might be free, but the full text of an article might cost a few dollars, and a corporate financial report might run $100 or more. Users must be sure to know what costs they're facing before they request a lot of information.

Computerized Database Packages

A number of companies are now offering computerized database packages for personal computers. For example, the Claritas Corporation has created a package called Compass/Agency designed for advertising agencies and Compass/Newspapers for newspapers to do segmentation and demographic studies and mapping. Claritas recently added Arbitron ratings and data from Simmons Marketing Research Bureau and Mediamark on product usage to Compass/Agency. The Compass/Newspaper system contains more than 200 preformatted reports and maps. Users can also import data on subscribers, readership, or advertisers and display them as reports and maps or export data into other standard software packages, such as spreadsheets, word processing, and graphics applications.[15]

The Department of Commerce has also made 1990 census data available on CD-ROM for use on PCs. Information available includes 1,300 categories of population, education, marital status, number of children in the home, home value or monthly rent, and income. The bureau also offers TIGER files, which provides a digital street map of the entire United States. It includes mapping files that identify the location of streets, highways, railroads, pipelines, power lines, and airports. Boundary files identify counties, municipalities, census tracts, census block groups, congressional districts, voter precincts, rivers, and lakes.[16]

Geo-Visual Databases

The marriage of databases with geographic references, such as census tracts and zip codes, and computer mapping software, has created geo-visual databases. The Census Bureau's TIGER system (Topologically Integrated Geographic Encoding and Referencing) was built to assist census takers. Yet it has been a great help to users of geo-visual database systems. Few businesses would ever go through the time and hassle of digitizing maps themselves. But without a detailed digital map and an equally detailed address coding system, one cannot find customers on a computer screen. Now suppliers are selling mapping and address coding software that uses enhanced TIGER files to meet the needs of market researchers.

Geographers talk about lines, points, and areas, while marketing researchers talk about roads, stores, and sales territories. But thinking in terms of lines, points, and areas is a good way to sort out the business uses of geo-visual databases. Applications involving lines include finding the quickest truck routes for long haul freight companies to calculating the shortest routes for local delivery trucks. Applications involving points include finding the best potential sites for retail bank branches and devising the best strategy for a network of warehouses. Applications involving areas range from finding the best markets for hardware sales or where to

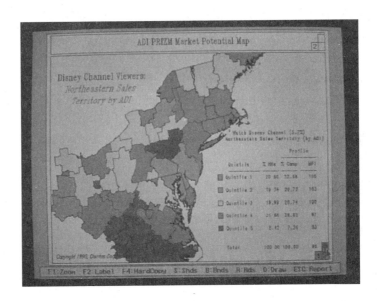

Computerized database packages for personal computers assist researchers with segmentation and demographic studies and mapping. Compass screen courtesy of Claritas/ NPDC, Inc.

locate a new Taco Bell. Geo-visual systems can also answer more detailed marketing questions. If a marketing researcher for Target wanted to know how many of the company's high sales performance stores have trading areas that overlap by at least 50 percent with the trading areas for WalMart, a geo-visual system will perform a function geographers call spatial querying to answer it.

Geo-visual database systems aren't cheap. Also, most systems require an above-average level of computer skills and some mapping training to be used effectively. Therefore, many researchers turn to companies that specialize in geo-visual mapping. A leading company in this field is Intelligent Charting of Mt. Olive, New Jersey.

One of Intelligent Charting's major requests from clients is geo-visual maps for plotting store locations. In addition to population, income, competition, and age statistics, many retailers such as convenience stores and gas stations are concerned with vulnerability to crime. For example, a retailer may know—based on demographic data—that it wants to locate a store in a particular region close to Philadelphia. Yet the retailer wants a specific site with the lowest vulnerability to crime. Figure 4.3 shows an actual retail site that was chosen by a retailer using Intelligent Charting's geo-visual maps. CAP Index, of King of Prussia, Pennsylvania, conducted a crime vulnerability assessment of the general region where the store was to be located. A tabular analysis of the region produced a composite CAP Index score of 223. Based upon this score, the site is considered to be a high crime risk. Figure 4.3 geo-visually displays the Crime Index Score for each individual census tract. The map clearly shows the site itself is located in a low risk area, while the trade area has a composite high risk.

INFORMATION MANAGEMENT

Computerized databases, published secondary data, and internal databases are important parts of an organization's information system. Intelligent decision making is always predicated on having good information.

Everyone who has been faced with a decision immediately comes to realize that information is the single most vital component to the quality of that decision. You need information to define the problem, to determine its scope and magnitude, to generate and evaluate alternatives, and so forth. Poor decisions are principally the result of lack of information, incorrect information, or invalid assumptions.

Today, most managers in large- and medium-size organizations and progressive smaller ones are bombarded with all kinds of information. The concern at firms such as American Airlines, Parke-Davis Pharmaceuticals, and Citicorp has shifted from the generation of information to the shaping and evaluation of information to make it useful to the decision maker.

Information management comes down to the development of a system for procuring, processing, and storing this information so that it can be retrieved when needed for management decision making. In other words, some type of marketing information system is needed. American Airlines foresees in the near future information systems that

> will drive the transition from corporate hierarchies to networks. Companies will become collections of experts who form teams to solve specific business problems and then disband. Information technology will blur distinctions between

FIGURE 4.3   *Geo-Visual Mapping Can Help Retailers Avoid Locating Stores within a High Crime Section of a Trade Area*

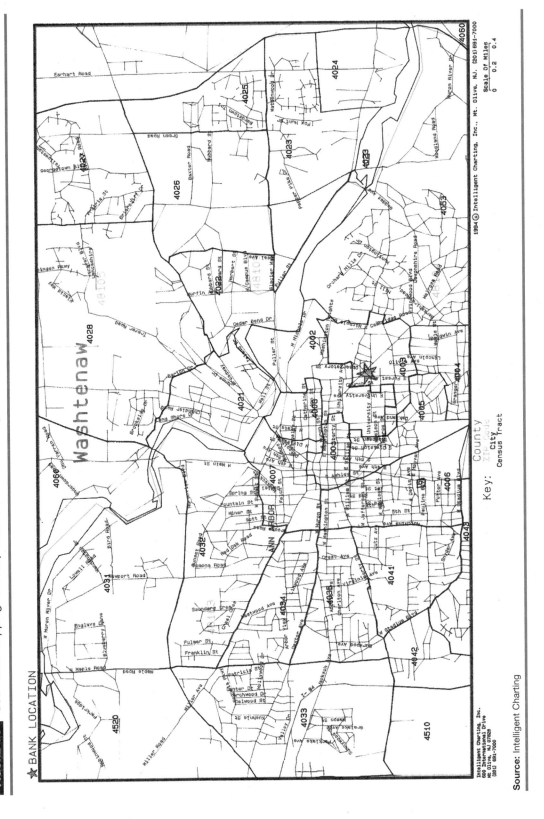

Source: Intelligent Charting

centralization and decentralization; senior managers will be able to contribute expertise without exercising authority.

[Our information system] will allow senior executives to make their presence felt more deeply without requiring more day-to-day control. Eventually, executives should be able to practice selective intervention. The information system, by virtue of its comprehensiveness, will alert senior managers to pockets of excellence or trouble and allow them to take appropriate action more quickly. Over time, the role of management will change from overseeing and control to resolving important problems and transferring the best practices throughout the organization.[17]

Decision Support Systems

Decision support systems (DSS) began coming into vogue during the late 1970s. A DSS is designed from the individual decision maker's perspective. It tends to be relatively unstructured because system use must be initiated and controlled by the individual decision maker. Characteristics of a true DSS system are as follows:

1. *Interactive:* The manager gives simple instructions and sees results generated on the spot. The process is under the manager's direct control; no computer programmer is needed. No need to wait for scheduled reports.
2. *Flexible:* It can sort, regroup, total, average, and manipulate the data in a variety of ways. It will shift gears as the user changes topics, matching information to the problem at hand. For example, the chief executive can see highly aggregated figures, while the marketing analyst can view very detailed breakouts.
3. *Discovery oriented:* It helps managers probe for trends, isolate problems, and ask new questions.
4. *Easy to learn and use:* Managers need not be particularly computer knowledgeable. Novice users should be able to elect a standard, or "default" method of using the system, bypassing optional features to work with the basic system immediately and gradually learning its possibilities. This minimizes the frustration that frequently accompanies new computer software.

Decision support system (DSS)
An interactive, personalized marketing information system (MIS), designed to be initiated and controlled by individual decision makers.

A diagram of a DSS is shown in Figure 4.4. Managers use DSS to conduct sales analyses, forecast sales, evaluate advertising, analyze product lines, and keep tabs on market trends and competitors' actions. A DSS not only allows managers to ask "what if" questions, but enables them to slice the data any way they want (see Figure 4.5).

A hypothetical example of using DSS is provided by Richard Leyh, manager of new products for Central Corporation.

To evaluate sales of a recently introduced new product, Richard can "call up" sales by the week, then by the month, breaking them out at his option by, say, customer segments. As he works at his terminal, his inquiries could go in several directions depending on the decision at hand. If his train of thought raises questions about monthly sales last quarter compared to forecasts, he wants his decision support system to follow along and give him answers immediately.

He might see that his new product's sales were significantly below forecast. Forecasts too optimistic? He compares other products' sales to his forecasts and finds that the targets were very accurate. Something wrong with the product? Maybe his sales department is getting insufficient leads, or is not putting leads to good use? Thinking a minute about how to examine that question, he checks ratios of leads converted to sales—product by product. The results disturb him. Only 5

FIGURE 4.4 *A Decision Support System*

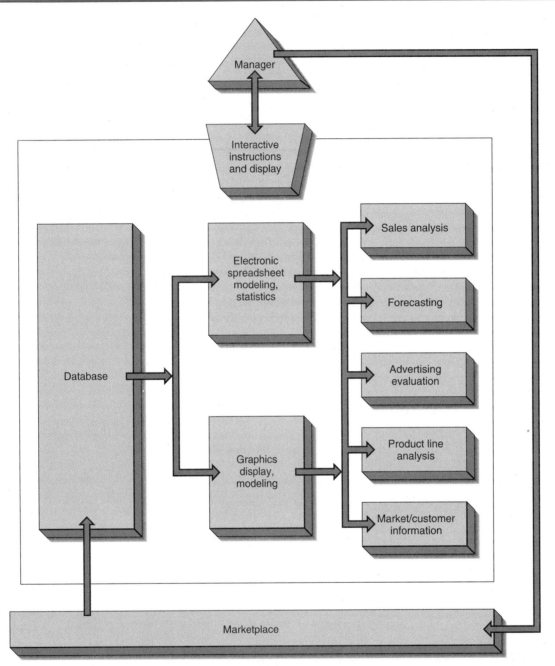

Source: Michael Dressler, Joquin Ives Brant, and Ronald Beall, *Industrial Marketing* (March 1983): 54.

percent of the new product's leads generate orders compared to the company's 12 percent all-product average. Why? He guesses that the sales force is not supporting the new product vigorously enough. Quantitative information from the DSS perhaps could provide more evidence to back that suspicion. But already having enough quantitative knowledge to satisfy himself, the VP acts on his intuition and experience and decides to have a chat with his sales manager.

Decision Support Systems in Practice

More than 400 marketing professionals at Quaker Oats use the DSS daily. System usage can be grouped into three major categories: first, reporting and tracking include running the standard reports; second, marketing planning is how Quaker

FIGURE 4.5   *A DSS Enables a Manager to Slice the Data to Obtain the Specific Information Needed*

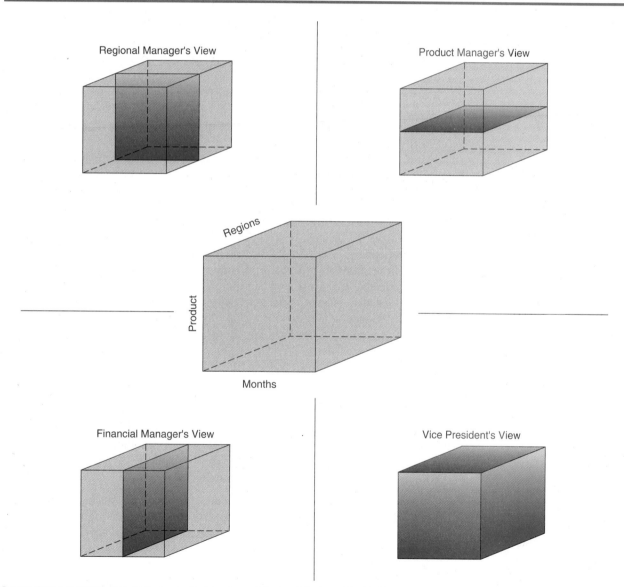

Source: Daniel C. Brown, "The Anatomy of a Decision Support System," *Business Monthly* (June 1985): 82.

**MARKETING
RESEARCH
IN PRACTICE**

Nancy Bydalek, brand manager for Quaker's Van de Camp products, uses the DSS for compiling information needed for brand planning. "By running what-if scenarios and marketing spread-sheets based on such considerations as forecasted volume, prices, and advertising spending," she says, "I get a national view of my business compared to the competition, so I can identify geographical areas that are doing well and not so well."

The system also helps Quaker Sharpen its promotions. "When we plan a specific promotion," explains Greg Peterson, marketing manager of the Cornmeal brand, "we go back in time and see the bottom-line effect that different promotional events had on sales. We then plug in the cost of a planned promotion and see what the final effect is going to be on the brand's volume and profit."[18]

Oats automates the brand planning and budgeting process by adding "what if" analysis and marketing capabilities; third, ad hoc queries elicit people's immediate answers to spontaneous marketing-based questions. Consider the examples in the feature at the top of this page.

Like Quaker Oats, other companies' successful use of DSS has resulted in a growing popularity of the systems. K-mart, Northwestern Mutual Life, and 3M now find that their DSS provide an invaluable competitive advantage. Companies such as Federal Express, Avis, Otis Elevator, and Frito-Lay have increased the efficiency of gathering field reports by providing their employees with hand-held computers.

Frito-Lay for instance, has given hand-held computers to all of its 11,000 delivery people. The data they collect feed a system that helps the company manage production, monitor sales, and guide promotional strategy. A delivery person can enter orders at each store in a minute or two, running through a programmed product list complete with prices. The machine plugs into a printer in the delivery truck to produce an itemized invoice. At day's end, it generates a sales report and, through a hookup in the local warehouse, transmits it in seconds to company headquarters in Dallas.[19]

The Move toward DSS

Today thousands of smaller businesses will also have information systems more sophisticated than those that America's largest corporations had just a decade earlier. A sampling of firms using DSS is shown in Table 4.4. The advantages of an effective DSS are immense, including the following.

1. *Substantial cost savings are realized.* One direct mail insurance company developed a simple method to compare past response rates of various market segments and thereby saved $40,000 that otherwise would have been wasted by mailing to households with a low probability of response. A large industrial products firm, soon after implementation of a decision support system focusing on distribution, reported savings in the hundreds of thousands of dollars. Similarly, other companies can draw direct profitability from their DSS.

TABLE 4.4   *A Sample of Company DSS and How They Are Used*

COMPANY	DSS USE
American Airlines	Price, Route Selection, and Aircraft Maintenance
American Petrofina	Corporate Planning and Forecasting
Central and Southwest Corporation	Corporate Planning and Forecasting
Champlin Petroleum	Corporate Planning and Forecasting
First United Bankcorporation	Investment Evaluation
Frito-Lay, Inc.	Price, Advertising, Distribution, and Promotion Selection
General Dynamics	Price Evaluation
Gifford-Hill and Company	Corporate Planning and Forecasting
Lear Petroleum	Evaluation of Potential Drilling Sites
Mercantile Texas Corporation	Corporate Planning and Forecasting
National Gypsum	Corporate Planning and Forecasting
Southern Railway	Train Dispatching and Routing
New Mexico Power	Corporate Planning and Forecasting
Texas Oil and Gas Corporation	Evaluation of Potential Drilling Sites
Texas Utilities Company	Corporate Planning and Forecasting
The Western Company	Corporate Planning and Forecasting

A DSS developed by Coca Cola enables marketing managers interactively to determine profit and loss by brand, gross margin, and operating profit; it also helps managers examining gross profit changes, and marketing and sales expense fluctuations. This DSS also allows interactive analysis of various profit-and-loss situations with differing performance levels through its interactive interrogation features. As DSS models are built, other areas of Coca Cola are being targeted for support. Company-owned bottlers benefit using models that evaluate financial alternatives for bottler plant expansions. Corporate planning develops models to review company sales, gross profit, and direct marketing expenses, as well as to analyze company and competitor shares of the market and advertising.

2. *Marketer's understanding of the decision environment is increased.* The decision maker is forced to view the decision and information environment within which he or she operates. This perception often leads to facing decision areas too often shoved under the carpet as well as recognizing relationships between decisions and information flows that have never been noticed before.

A sales territory is a dynamic environment, constantly roiled by changes in customers, competitors, products, and sales force turnover. Although this creates imbalanced workloads and potential sales, managers are reluctant to realign their territories to reflect such changes because of the time consumed in tedious calculations. Merrell Dow Pharmaceuticals put an end to such reluctance with a DSS. A manager enters his or her own criteria, such as potential and actual sales, doctor and pharmacy counts, and travel time. The DSS combines this business data with geographic features, road networks, and five-digit zip codes to come up with the optimal territory alignment.

The program was especially helpful when the company replaced its single sales force with two sales forces to get broader product coverage. A Merrell Dow sales force promotes prescription pharmaceuticals, and a Lakeside sales force sells over-the-counter drugs. In all, the United States had to be redrawn to create 400 Merrell Dow sales territories and 250 Lakeside territories.

3. *Decision-making effectiveness is upgraded.* Many companies can now retrieve and utilize information that was never accessible before. This replacement of facts for intuition in decision making has led to more effective and less "seat-of-the-pants" decision making than in the past. Jerome Chazen, executive vice president of Liz Claiborne, Inc., notes that the firm's DSS has improved management decision making. Systematic Updated Retail Feedback (SURF) reports come in daily from sixteen stores that represent a cross section of store sizes and geographical locations. Computer programs take the SURF data and "play with it in dozens of different ways to get a feeling for how the consumer is reacting to the merchandise we're shipping," Chazen says. "Most apparel manufacturers tend to identify the best-selling items in the line with how they're purchased by the retailer. We've discovered that there's often no relationship between what the retailer thinks and what the consumer buys."

4. *Information value is improved.* Tied to decision-making effectiveness, but worthy of its own note, is the improved quantity and quality of information provided to the marketing manager. Managers now have relevant, reliable, and timely information never before available. For example, Chuck Mitchell, district sales manager for Savin Business Machines, used to wade through reams of data and then tenuously suggest, "I think you should try to arrange more product demos." Now, with the flexibility of a new DSS, Chuck can firmly declare to a sales representative, "I know that if you put on more demos you'll write more orders." He points to his terminal and tells the person, "All the information about your activities is there, and it shows that your bookings are down because you're not putting on as many demos as you used to."[20]

Companies use decison support systems to effectively gather and analyze data. A Frito-Lay delivery person enters orders into his computer on-site at a grocery store. An itemized invoice prints out in the delivery truck and a sales report is transmitted at the end of the day to company headquarters. Courtesy of Frito-Lay, Inc.

Problems in Implementing a Decision Support System

With all of the advantages, what seem to be the primary inhibitors to adopt a DSS? In a nutshell, it is a "people" problem. More specifically, the problem involves the following aspects.

1. *Many benefits are intangible.* The tangible benefits from a company's investment in its DSS are few relative to the intangibles. Much of the value of providing accurate, relevant, and timely information to marketing decision makers comes from more effective decision making. But, in some cases, top corporate executives cannot see profits directly attributable to the DSS. This usually lessens commitment by top management and leads to a diversion of funds and interest away from existing and planned computer systems. If a company is going to successfully launch a DSS, it is imperative that high-level managers are involved in developing, implementing, and operating the system. This promotes conceptions of the system's significance and furthers its integration into the organization.[21]

2. *Communication bridges must be built.* To develop an effective DSS, marketing managers and system designers must work closely to identify marketing problems, decision areas, information needs, and information sources. Historically, marketing practitioners and system designers have had great difficulty communicating, which led to sizable gaps in information needed and offered. The result has been an emphasis by system designers on data warehousing instead of matching user needs.

3. *Decision support system users must be trained.* Research has shown that the training of marketing managers as system users has not always been at an acceptable level. Decision makers can hardly be expected to use an information system if they do not understand what it can and cannot do.

4. *Managers are naive or suspicious of computer-based systems.* Closely allied to the preceding problem is the lack of experience and necessary background in many older marketing managers. Such individuals' formal education never provided them with a contemporary computer orientation. Furthermore, much of their on-the-job training has never exposed them to the potential benefits of using a computer, much less how to communicate with one. This lack of training often produced fear, the fear that the computer will make them look foolish or possibly result in the loss of their job. Consequently, they avoid its use and sometimes even express open hostility.

SUMMARY

Secondary data is any information previously gathered but that only might be relevant to the problem at hand. Primary data is survey, observation, or experimental data collected to solve the particular problem under investigation. Secondary data can come from sources internal to the organization or external to it. A database is a collection of related data. The most common type of marketing internal database is founded on customer information. For example, a customer database will have demographic and perhaps psychographic information about existing customers and purchase data such as when the goods and services were bought, the types of merchandise procured, the dollar sales amount, and any promotional information associated with the sales. An internal database also may contain competitive intelligence, such as new products offered by competitors, price changes, and changes in competitors' service policies. A good internal database relies on a database management system. Also, the database users must be trained in how to manipulate the data and retrieve needed information.

There are several advantages to secondary data. First, secondary data may help to clarify or redefine the definition of the problem as part of the exploratory research process. Second, secondary information may actually provide a solution to the problem. Third, secondary information may provide primary data research method alternatives. Fourth, secondary data may alert the marketing researcher to potential problems and difficulties. And finally, secondary information may provide necessary background data and build credibility for the research report.

The disadvantages of secondary data can be the lack of needed information, lack of relevance, inaccurate data, and insufficient information for decision making.

A tremendous growth in on-line databases has made access to secondary information much simpler. An on-line database is a public information database available to anyone with proper communication facilities. Typically, all that is required is a computer terminal and a modem, and of course access to the particular database. There are four major categories of on-line databases: numerical databases, bibliographic databases, directory databases, and full text databases. An on-line database vendor is an intermediary that acquires databases from a variety of database creators. Thus, a user can go to a single on-line vendor and gain access to a variety of databases. The four most popular vendors are Dow Jones, Dialog, The Source, and CompuServe. The advantages of on-line databases are several. First, the researcher has quick access to a tremendous variety of information. Second, the efficient use of on-line search protocols helps quickly pinpoint relevant data. Third, the large in-house staff formally required to research and maintain files can be eliminated. And finally, small firms can gain access to the same secondary data as large organizations and do it just as efficiently. The major disadvantage is that a person not skilled at searching through a database may be inundated with information. Sometimes this information can be very expensive. Decision support systems are designed from the individual decision maker's perspective. A DSS system is interactive, flexible, discovery oriented, and easy to learn. A good DSS offers many benefits to small and large firms alike.

KEY TERMS

Secondary data
Primary data
Internal database
Database management system
Database management software
On-line database
Modem

Numeric database
Bibliographic database
Directory database
Full text database
On-line vendor
Decision support system (DSS)

REVIEW AND DISCUSSION QUESTIONS

1. Why should companies consider creating a marketing internal database? Name some types of information that might be found in this database and sources of this information.
2. What are some of the keys to ensuring the success of an internal database?
3. Why is secondary data often preferred to primary data?
4. What pitfalls might a researcher encounter in using secondary data?
5. What are the major categories of on-line databases? Give examples of each.
6. If your university has access to several on-line vendors, determine the various types of information that can be obtained. If on-line access is not possible, go to the library and determine what information is available in Dialog, CompuServe, and Dow Jones.
7. What are some of the advantages and pitfalls of on-line databases?
8. Assume that you are a brand manager for a line of facial tissues. Your sales have been growing at the rate of 4 percent per year for the last three years. What role might secondary data play in evaluating the market position of your brand?
9. In the absence of company problems, is there any need to conduct marketing research? Develop a decision support system?

CASE

Camp Hyatt

Hyatt Hotels needed more customers, and the first place it looked was in its own lobbies. "We realized that the people who stay with us for business were choosing other hotels when they traveled on vacation with their kids," says Julie Halpern, Hyatt's manager of corporate public relations. "So we came up with a program that combined attractive rates for parents with lots of activities for kids."

Now, Hyatt Hotels' frequent traveler program, Gold Passport, has a young companion called Camp Hyatt Passport. Each stay at a Hyatt Hotel earns a stamp on the passport. After four stays, the child receives a backpack. The program began in May 1989; as of mid 1994, Hyatt had given away over 4,500 backpacks.

Recently, Hyatt checked in with the children to see how they liked the camps. Its survey asked: how many vacations have you taken in the last year? what do you like to eat on vacation? what do you like to do? if you could bring only three things with you on vacation, what would they be? if you could take a vacation with anyone in the world, who would it be? Of the 250 children who responded, 50 percent said their families take more than two vacations a year. Almost one-third (32 percent) of all trips are taken with children, according to the U.S. Travel Data Center. "But family travel has changed," says Halpern. "Families are taking more and shorter vacations, three- or four-day weekends instead of two weeks in the summer."

Kamp Kachina, at the Hyatt resort in Scottsdale, Arizona, caters to these new patterns with a year-round program that varies by season. Up to ten counselors offer a slew of activities, including bolo tie making, sand art, face painting, games, and even ice skating. Kamp Kachina also entertains local children with catered birthday parties, a summer day camp, and pie- or pizza-making lessons in the hotel kitchen. Kamp Kachina sees more than 1,200 kids a year, says recreation director Randy Babick. Back at corporate headquarters, Julie Halpern calls that "drawing new families to Hyatt and creating repeat business."

As far as hotels are concerned, "there are two kinds of parents," says Laura Manske, executive editor of *Child* magazine. "The ones who want private time for themselves are looking for a good child-care program. Other parents want to spend a lot of time with the child, so the program isn't important. Instead, they are looking for wading pools, children's menus, baby-sitters for the evening, and room service to warm up a bottle in the middle of the night."[22]

1. The Camp Hyatt Passport program is an excellent source of information to enter into Hyatt's internal database. As a decision maker, what other type of data would you want in the database for marketing Camp Hyatt?
2. What additional questions would you have asked the Camp Hyatt children besides those asked? Should the questionnaire data be added to the database?
3. Do you see any ethical issues that might be raised from administering a questionnaire to children and adding that information to a database?

CHAPTER 5

Qualitative Research

LEARNING OBJECTIVES

1. To define qualitative research.

2. To explore the popularity of qualitative research.

3. To understand why qualitative research is not held in high esteem by some practitioners and academicians.

4. To learn about focus groups and their tremendous popularity.

5. To gain insight in conducting and analyzing a focus group.

6. To study other forms of qualitative research.

Affluent consumers are more than twice as likely to purchase new products from companies they view as "winners," according to a study released by Brouillard Communications, New York. Other findings of what is being called a "landmark" study, titled "Winning!," were that corporate executives would recommend joint ventures with winners by a more than two-to-one edge; professional investors would invest about 50 percent more money in winning companies; winners would have a three-to-one advantage in employing talent; and building a new plant in a community would be much easier for a top-rated company.

"Everyone wants to be seen as a winner, but what does it take for a company to be seen that way? That was one of the fundamental questions we wanted answered," said James H. Foster, president of Brouillard. "We wanted to go beyond the obvious qualities that people always have talked about to pinpoint key attributes that actually differentiate those with a winning edge."

A qualitative phase preceded more than 1,000 interviews with financial research directors, portfolio managers, corporate executives, and affluent consumers (from households earning $50,000 or more per year). Foster said that "winning" emerged in exploratory research as the term that best described companies having excellent overall reputations. Accordingly, the word "winning" was used throughout the interview process. From a list of fifteen attributes identified in qualitative research, the groups were asked to name the characteristics they considered critically important to the makeup of a winning reputation. Each group cited the seven most critical characteristics to a winning reputation. Five are consensus characteristics across consumer and leadership groups:

- Superior quality in products
- High-quality service to customers
- Flexibility—ability to adapt to changes in the marketplace
- High-caliber management
- Honesty and ethics in business practices[1]

The Brouillard study began with a "qualitative phase." What is qualitative research? How is it conducted? Is one form of qualitative research more popular than others? What makes qualitative research so controversial? These are some of the issues we will explore in Chapter 5.

THE NATURE OF QUALITATIVE RESEARCH

Qualitative Research Defined

Qualitative research is a loosely used term. It means that the research findings are not subject to quantification or quantitative analysis. A quantitative study's findings may determine that a heavy user of a brand of tequila is twenty-one to thirty-five years of age, with an annual income of $18,000 to $25,000. **Quantitative research** can reveal statistically significant differences between heavy and light users. In contrast, qualitative research could be used to examine the attitudes, feelings, and motivations of the heavy user. Advertising agencies planning a campaign for tequila might employ qualitative techniques to learn how the heavy users express themselves, what language they use, and, essentially, how to communicate with them.

Qualitative research
Research data not subject to quantification or quantitative analysis.

Quantitative research
Studies that use mathematical analysis.

The Qualitative versus Quantitative Controversy

Table 5.1 compares qualitative and quantitative research on several levels. Perhaps most significant to managers is that qualitative research typically is characterized by small samples, which has provided a focal point for the criticism of all qualitative techniques. In essence, many managers are reluctant to base important strategy decisions on small sample research because it relies so greatly on the subjectivity and interpretation of the researcher. They strongly prefer a large sample with computer analysis, summarized into tables. Large samples and statistical significance levels are aspects of marketing research with which these managers feel very comfortable because the data is generated in a rigorous and scientific manner.

The Popularity of Qualitative Research

The popularity of qualitative research continues to grow unabated. Several reasons account for its popularity.[2] First, qualitative research is usually much cheaper than

TABLE 5.1   *Qualitative versus Quantitative Research*

COMPARISON DIMENSION	QUALITATIVE RESEARCH	QUANTITATIVE RESEARCH
Types of questions	Probing	Limited probing
Sample size	Small	Large
Information per respondent	Much	Varies
Administration	Requires interviewer with special skills	Fewer special skills required
Type of analysis	Subjective, interpretive	Statistical, summarization
Hardware	Tape recorders, projection devices, video, pictures, discussion guides	Questionnaires, computers, printouts
Ability to replicate	Low	High
Training of the researcher	Psychology, sociology, social psychology, consumer behavior, marketing, marketing research	Statistics, decision models, decision support systems, computer programming, marketing, marketing research
Type of research	Exploratory	Descriptive or causal

quantitative research. Second, there is no better way than qualitative research to understand the in-depth motivations and feelings of consumers. Because product managers often unobtrusively conduct a popular form of qualitative research by observing from behind a one-way mirror, they obtain firsthand experiences with "flesh and blood" consumers. Rather than read a computer printout containing countless tables of numbers or reading a consultant's report that digests reams of numbers, the product manager and other marketing personnel observe the consumer's reactions to concepts, hear consumers discuss the manufacturers' and competitors' products at length using their own language. Sitting behind a one-way mirror can be a humbling experience to a new product development manager when the consumer begins to tear apart product concepts that were months in development in the sterile laboratory environment.

A third reason that qualitative research is popular is that it can improve the efficiency of quantitative research. Volvo of America Corporation was concerned that the U.S. automotive market was undergoing vast changes that could affect its market share. Volvo decided that a major research study was needed to gain an appreciation of the changing marketplace. The project involved both a quantitative and a qualitative phase. The first phase of the project enabled the researchers to conduct a quantitative study that was both more insightful and less expensive due to a shorter questionnaire. Among the insights gained in the qualitative phase were the following. (1) Potential buyers considered Volvo in a number of different ways. Some considered Volvo very seriously and narrowed the choice of cars to Volvo and one other make. Others considered Volvo seriously, but it was not among the cars that survived the final decision. (2) Some considered Volvo seriously without ever visiting a showroom. (3) Despite Volvo's small share of the U.S. market, the qualitative information hinted at several important subsegments within the Volvo market.[3]

As the opening story illustrated, it is becoming more common for marketing researchers to combine qualitative and quantitative research into a single study or a series of studies. The Volvo example shows how qualitative research can be used subsequent to quantitative research; in other research designs the reverse may be used. For instance, the patterns displayed in quantitative research can be enriched with the addition of qualitative information on the reasons and motivations of consumers. Thus, it is not a case of deciding which one is the right research strategy, but of determining where one is more appropriate. Or the situation may require using the two methodologies in conjunction with each other, if possible, to effect a better final research product.

In the final analysis, all research is undertaken to increase the effectiveness of marketing decision making. Qualitative research blends with quantitative measures by providing a more thorough understanding of consumer demand. Qualitative techniques involve open-ended questioning and probing. The data is rich, human, subtle, and often very revealing.

Limitations of Qualitative Research

Qualitative research can, and does, produce helpful and useful information. Yet it is looked down upon by some researchers. One reason is that marketing successes and failures many times are based on small differences in a marketing mix. Qualitative research does not distinguish small differences as well as large-scale quantitative research. Qualitative research sometimes is superior, however, in detecting minor problems that may escape notice in a quantitative study. For example, a major manufacturer of household cleaners conducted a large quantitative study in an effort to learn why its bathroom cleanser had lackluster sales. The manufacturer knew that the chemical compound was more effective than leading competitors. The quantitative study provided no clear-cut answer. The frustrated product manager turned to qualitative research. It was quickly uncovered that the muted pastel colors on the package did not connote "cleansing strength" to the shopper. Also, a number of people were using old toothbrushes to clean between the bathroom tiles. The package was redesigned with brighter colors and included a brush built into the top.

A second limitation of qualitative techniques is that qualitative studies are not necessarily representative of the population of interest to the researcher. One would be hard pressed to demonstrate that a group of ten college students is representative of all college students, of college students at a particular university, of business majors at that university, or even marketing majors! Small sample sizes and free-flowing discussion can lead qualitative research projects down many paths. Also, people who are subjects of qualitative research are often free to tell us what interests them. A dominant individual in a group discussion can lead a group into areas of only tangential interest to the researcher. It takes a highly skilled researcher to get the discussion back on track without stifling the group's interest, enthusiasm, and willingness to speak out.[4]

A final concern about qualitative research is the multitude of individuals who, without formal training, profess to be experts in the field. Because there is no certification body in marketing research, anyone can call himself or herself a qualitative expert. Unfortunately, it is often difficult for the unsuspecting client to discern the researcher's qualifications or the quality of the research. On the other hand, to conduct a sophisticated quantitative study requires extensive training. It is extremely difficult, if not impossible, to bluff one's way through this type of project.

THE GROWING ROLE OF FOCUS GROUPS

Focus Groups Defined

Focus groups had their beginnings in group therapy used by psychiatrists. Today, a **focus group** consists of eight to twelve participants who are led by a moderator in an in-depth discussion on one particular topic or concept. The goal of focus group research is to learn and understand what people have to say and why. The emphasis is on getting people talking at length and in detail about the subject at hand. The intent is to find out how they feel about a product, concept, idea, or organization, how it fits into their lives, and their emotional involvement with it.

Focus groups are much more than merely question and answer interviews. The distinction is made between "group dynamics" and "group interviewing." The interaction provided in **group dynamics** is essential to the success of focus group research; this interaction is the reason for conducting group rather than individual research. One of the essential postulates of group session usage is the idea that a response from one person may become a stimulus for another, thereby generating

Focus groups
Groups of eight to twelve participants who are led by a moderator in an in-depth discussion on one particular topic or concept.

Group dynamics
The interaction among people in a group.

an interplay of responses that may yield more than if the same number of people had contributed independently.

The idea for group dynamics research in marketing came from the field of social psychology, where studies indicated that unknown to themselves, people of all walks of life and in all occupations will tell us more about a topic and do so in greater depth if they are encouraged to act spontaneously instead of reacting to questions. Normally, in group dynamics, direct questions are avoided. In their place are indirect inquiries that stimulate free and spontaneous discussions. The result is a much richer base of information of a kind impossible to obtain by direct interviews.

The Popularity of Focus Groups

Qualitative research and focus groups are often used as synonyms by marketing research practitioners. Popular writings are full of examples of researchers referring to qualitative research in one breath and focus groups in the next even though, as discussed earlier, focus groups are only one type of qualitative research. The overwhelming popularity of the technique has virtually overshadowed other qualitative tools.

How popular are focus groups? Most marketing research firms, advertising agencies, and consumer goods manufacturers use the technique. Today, over $378 million a year is spent on focus group research by client firms.[5] Leo Burnett Company, for example, conducts over 350 focus groups each year for clients. Focus groups tend to be used more extensively by consumer goods companies than by industrial goods organizations. The low incidence of use is understandable as industrial groups pose a host of problems not found in consumer research. For example, it is usually quite easy to assemble a group of twelve homemakers. However, putting together a group of ten engineers, sales managers, or financial analysts is far more costly and time consuming.

TYPES OF FOCUS GROUPS

Bobby Calder, a noted scholar on qualitative research has classified focus groups into three major categories: exploratory, clinical, and experiencing.[6]

Exploratory Groups

Exploratory focus groups
Focus groups that aid in the precise definition of the problem, in pilot testing, or to generate hypotheses for testing or concepts for further research.

Exploratory focus groups are commonly used in the exploratory phase of the market research process to aid in precise definition of the problem (see Chapter 2). They can also be viewed as pilot testing. Groups may be employed to test wording on a questionnaire or product placement instructions. Exploratory groups may have the more lofty goals of attempting to generate hypotheses for testing or concepts for further research. The research director of Time, Inc., says, "We use focus groups for fishing."[7] He then goes on to say that *fishing* means defining problems, generating hypotheses, exploring ideas, and preparing for quantitative research. One focus group came up with 166 new ways to prepare frozen chicken.[8] These ideas became the basis for further research.

Clinical Focus Groups

Clinical focus groups are qualitative research in its purest form. The research is conducted as a scientific endeavor, based upon the premise that a person's true motivations and feelings are subconscious in nature. What consumers say cannot be taken at face value, instead, the researcher must probe beneath the level of consciousness.

Obviously clinical groups require a moderator with expertise in psychology and sociology. It is assumed that a person's real motives must be uncovered using clinical judgment. Thus, the focus group becomes the data input source for clinical judgment. The moderator must be highly skilled to entice participants into revealing inner feelings and thoughts.

Because of the difficulty (if not impossibility) of validating findings from clinical groups and unskilled moderators attempting to conduct clinical groups, their popularity has markedly diminished. Perhaps when new psychoanalytic tools are developed and certification standards are developed for moderators, clinical groups will enjoy a resurgence.

Clinical focus groups
Focus groups that explore subconscious motivation.

Experiencing Focus Groups

A researcher who speaks of "doing a few groups" usually is referring to **experiencing focus groups**. Lewis Stone, former manager of Colgate-Palmolive's Research and Development Division, claims:

> If it weren't for focus groups, Colgate-Palmolive Co. might never know that some women squeeze their bottles of dishwashing soap, others squeeeeze them, and still others squeeeeeeeeeeze out the desired amount. Then there are the ones who use the soap "neat." That is, they put the product directly on a sponge or washcloth and wash the dishes under running water until the suds run out. Then they apply more detergent.
>
> Stone was explaining how body language, exhibited during focus groups, provides insights into a product that are not apparent from reading questionnaires on habits and practices. Focus groups represent a most efficient way of learning how one's products are actually used in the home. By drawing out the panelists to describe in detail how they do certain tasks . . . you can learn a great deal about possible need-gaps that could be filled by new or improved products, and also how a new product might be received.[9]

Thus, an experiencing approach represents an opportunity to "experience" a "flesh-and-blood" consumer. Reality in the kitchen or supermarket differs drastically from that of most corporate offices. It allows the researcher to experience the emotional framework in which the product is being used. In a sense, the researcher can go into a person's life and relive with him or her all of the satisfactions, dissatisfactions, rewards, and frustrations experienced when the product is taken home.

Experiencing focus groups
Focus groups that enable a client to observe and listen to how consumers' think and feel about products and services.

CONDUCTING FOCUS GROUPS

Now that you understand the types of focus groups, we can proceed to the process of conducting focus groups (see Figure 5.1). The space devoted to this topic is

FIGURE 5.1 *Steps in Conducting a Focus Group*

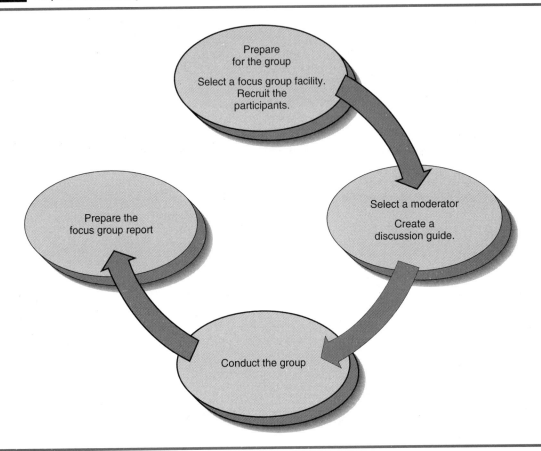

considerable because there is much potential for researcher error in conducting focus groups.

Preparing for a Focus Group

Focus group facility
Facility consisting of conference or living room setting and a separate observation room. Facility also has audio visual recording equipment.

The Setting. Focus groups are usually held in a **focus group facility**. The setting is normally conference room style with a large one-way mirror in one wall. Microphones are placed in an unobtrusive location (usually the ceiling) to record the discussion. Behind the mirror is the viewing room, which consists of chairs and note-taking benches or tables for the clients. The viewing room also houses the recording or videotape equipment. Clients viewing a focus group from behind a one-way mirror are shown in Figure 5.2. Another variation is to not use a one-way mirror, but to televise the proceedings to a remote viewing room. This approach offers the advantage of clients being able to move around and speak in a normal tone of voice without being "heard" through the wall. On more than one occasion a client has lit a cigarette while viewing a group resulting in the flash being seen through the mirror.

FIGURE 5.2   *An Advertisement Illustrating a Focus Group in Progress*

Find out what hundreds of researchers already know...

Focus Suites is like no other facility you've ever tried.

- The expertise of our professional recruiters is unsurpassed in this industry.

- We have three separate, totally private 3-room suites.

- These extraordinary suites are available for the same cost or less than that of an ordinary facility.

Call today for a competitive bid on your next qualitative research project.
Once you've tried us, you'll never be satisfied with an ordinary facility again.

The Right People. . .The Right Price. . .The Right Place

One Bala Plaza, Suite 622, 231 St. Asaphs Road,
Bala Cynwyd, PA 19004 (215) 667-1110

Source: Focus Suites of Philadelphia.

Recruiting Participants.   Participants are recruited for focus groups from a variety of sources. Two common procedures are mall intercept interviews and random telephone screening. (Both methods are described in detail in Chapter 7.) Researchers normally establish criteria for the group participants. For example, if Quaker Oats is researching a new cereal, they might request mothers with children ranging in age from seven to twelve years old who had served cold cereal, perhaps a specific brand, in the past three weeks.

Usually researchers strive to avoid repeat or "professional" respondents in focus groups. Professional respondents are viewed by many researchers as actors or at least persons who provide less than candid answers.[10] Questions may also be raised regarding what type of person will continually come to group sessions. Are they lonely? Do they really need the respondent fee that badly? It is highly unlikely the professional respondents are representative of many, if any, target markets. Unfortunately, field services find it much easier to use repeat respondents rather than recruit a fresh group each time. Most participate simply to get the respondent fee.[11]

A typical group will contain eight to twelve participants. If the group contains more people, there will be little time for the group members to express their opinions. Rarely will a group last over two hours, with an hour and a half more common. The first ten minutes is spent with introductions and an explanation of procedures. This leaves about eighty useful minutes in the session and up to 25 percent of that time is taken by the moderator. With ten people in the group, it leaves an average of only six minutes per individual.

Yet, there is no ideal number of participants. If the topic is quite interesting or of a technical nature, fewer respondents are needed. The type of group will also affect the number recruited. More individuals should be recruited for an experiencing group than for a clinical group.

Selecting the Moderator

Focus group moderator
The person hired by the client to lead the focus group. This person may need a background in psychology or sociology or, at least, marketing.

Having qualified respondents and a good **focus group moderator** are the keys to successful focus groups. Regardless of the type of group conducted, a qualified moderator is essential.

In the past few years there has been an increase in the number of formal moderator training courses offered by manufacturers with large market research departments, advertising agencies, and research firms. Most programs are strictly for employees, but a few are open to anyone. Standardization of moderator training courses and possible certification will be offered by the new Qualitative Research Consultants Association.[12]

A Discussion Guide Is Essential

Discussion guide
A written outline of topics to cover during a focus group discussion.

Regardless of the type of training and personality a moderator possesses, a successful focus group requires a well-planned **discussion guide**. A discussion guide is an outline of the topics to be covered during the session. Usually the guide is generated by the moderator based on the research objectives and client

MARKETING RESEARCH IN PRACTICE

arketing in general and public opinion polling in particular have come into their own in the realm of politics. The results have not always been positive. All media groups have been accused of using polling to distort the political process. James Fishkin, a political science professor at the University of Texas, has developed an innovative idea that will give new meaning to "the voice of the people."

Deliberative polling is a process whereby a sample of respondents are brought together to listen to experts, study research reports, question political leaders, and debate among themselves. After this process they are then surveyed on their attitudes and policy preferences. It is the deliberative process that makes participants different from participants in a typical survey. According to Fishkin, "They become representative of what people would think if the public had a better chance to think about this..." This process will make the voice of the people worth listening to.

Early in 1994, three leading British media organizations plan to sponsor the first deliberative public opinion poll, using a random sample of 400 to 600 British residents. The topic, as yet undecided, will be a national issue. Additional plans are being considered to do a deliberative poll featuring the candidates before Britain's next general election. The project is an attempt to advance the democratic process in Britain.

Other countries have already approached Fishkin about doing deliberative polls. He is, of course, hoping the United States will be interested if the British experiment is successful.[13]

information needs. It serves as a checklist to make certain that all salient topics are covered and in the proper sequence. For example, an outline might begin with attitudes and feelings toward eating out, then move to fast foods, and conclude with a discussion of food and decor of a particular chain. It is very important to get the research director and other client observers, such as a brand manager, to agree that the topics listed on the guide are the most important ones to be covered. It is not uncommon for a "team approach" to be used in generating a discussion guide.

The moderator's guide also tends to flow through three stages. In the first, rapport is established, the rules of group interaction are explained, and objectives are given. The second stage is characterized by the moderator attempting to provoke intensive discussion. The final stage is used for summarizing significant conclusions and testing limits of belief and commitment.

Table 5.2 shows an actual discussion guide (although more detailed than many guides) used by a moderator to explore company benefit managers' reactions to alternative health plans with special emphasis on a new product concept referred to as the *Combo Plan*. The "Combo Plan" offered benefits of both a traditional health maintenance organization (HMO) and a traditional indemnity health insurance plan. Basically, an HMO provides the employee full health care services for a flat monthly rate. The big disadvantage is the patient must go to the HMO facility and has little choice in physicians. An indemnity plan

TABLE 5.2   *Discussion Guide for Health Care Benefit Decision-Maker Focus Groups*

I. Warm-up

   A. Explain focus groups.

   B. No correct answers—only your opinion. You are speaking for many other decision makers like yourself.

   C. Need to hear from everyone.

   D. Some of my associates watching behind mirror. They are very interested in your opinions.

   E. Audio tapes—because I want to concentrate on what you have to say—so I don't have to take notes.

   F. Please—only one person talking at a time. No side discussions—I'm afraid I'll miss some important comments.

   G. Don't ask me questions because what I know and what I think are not important—it's what you think and how you feel that are important. That's why we're here.

   H. Don't feel bad if you don't know much about some of the things we'll be talking about—that's OK and important for us to know. If your view is different from that of others in the group that's important for us to know. Don't be afraid to be different. We're not looking for everyone to agree on something unless they really do.

   I. I will never contact you again.

   J. *Any questions?*

II. What is the first thing that comes to mind when I mention health care coverage for employees?

   A. Likes? Dislikes?

   B. Problems?

   C. Changes you would like to see?

   D. How do you feel about the current health care coverage programs you offer to employees? What do you like or dislike about them? How would you change them?

   E. Do you offer more than one health plan for your employees? What alternatives do you offer? Why did you choose those particular options to offer to your employees?

   F. IF NOT MENTIONED: Do any of you currently offer HMO coverage to your employees? What kind of HMO is that? Staff? IPA? How do your employees like this program? Have you ever offered HMO coverage to your employees?

   G. What factors are important to you in deciding what kinds of health care programs to offer to your employees?

   H. For those of you who currently don't offer HMO coverage, is this something you would consider as an alternative to traditional health insurance?

      1. Why or why not?

      2. What don't you like about HMOs? Like?

      3. How might HMO coverage be changed to make it more attractive to you?

      4. What factors might lead you to consider offering HMO coverage?

   I. Again, for those of you who currently don't have HMO coverage:

      1. Have you considered an HMO? Which HMO did you consider?

      2. Why didn't you choose HMO coverage?

III. Now I would like to show you a description of a new health care program. I am interested in how you feel about this program.

   SHOW COMBO PLAN CONCEPT DESCRIPTION

   A. How many of you would consider offering this plan to your employees?

   B. Why do you say that? What do you like or dislike about it?

   C. Do you see any distinct advantages in this plan over the plans you are currently offering?

   D. How would you expect this plan to be priced?

   E. How would you expect this plan to be priced in comparison to traditional insurance?

IV. Now I would like to present some specific features of this plan (Combo Plan) for your consideration.

   A. First, I would like to discuss the HMO benefits. When you visit one of the HMO doctors from the list of 500 physicians, you pay a copayment of $5 per office visit. All other reasonable charges are covered. If you are admitted to a hospital by one of the HMO doctors or are admitted by any doctor in a true emergency, you are covered 100 percent.
How do you feel about the $5 office visit copayment level? How do you feel if this was raised to $8 or $10 per office visit?

   B. Now, I would like to discuss the *indemnity benefits*. On the flipchart, I have listed different schedules of benefits. Assume that all major medical benefits are subject to a deductible and coinsurance and you have a maximum out-of-pocket expense limit (OPX). Also, assume traditional indemnity benefits—no well care, no physicals, no immunizations.

Schedule A—$250 deductible	75/25 coinsurance	$3,000 OPX
Schedule B—$200 deductible	80/20 coinsurance	$3,000 OPX
Schedule C—$500 deductible	70/30 coinsurance	$3,000 OPX

      1. In terms of the items on this schedule, what would your *optimal plan* look like?

Continued

TABLE 5.2 *Discussion Guide for Health Care Benefit Decision-Maker Focus Groups—Continued*

2. Again, in terms of the items on this list, what would your *minimal plan* look like? What is the highest deductible, highest coinsurance percentage, highest out-of-pocket limit that would be acceptable to you and your employees?
3. How do you feel about the *things the plan covers*?
4. How do you feel about the *deductible, coinsurance,* and *maximum out-of-pocket expense* associated with the indemnity or open portion of this plan?
5. How do you feel about the *premium* associated with this program? Would it be about the same for the Combo Plan as for a stand-alone HMO? Would it be about 5 percent more for the Combo Plan?
6. Which is the most important factor to you in a benefit plan: the deductible, the coinsurance percentage, or the out-of-pocket limit? Why?

V. How likely would you be to consider offering a plan like this to your employees?

A. Why do you say that? What do you like or dislike about it?
B. Do you see any distinct advantages in this plan over the plans you are currently offering? Disadvantages?
C. How would you feel about the pricing of this plan?
D. Would you consider this plan as a possible single choice offering—the only type of health care coverage you would offer to your employees? Why do you say that?

VI. Single choice Combo Plan

Put yourself in the position of an employer that desires to offer the Combo Plan as the single offering to its employees. This product would replace the current indemnity plan.
A. What advantages, if any, do you see to this choice plan?
B. What disadvantages, if any, do you see to this single choice plan?
C. Is it an advantage to you to have single billing and administration through one plan?
D. Would it help to have this product experience rated?
E. Would you expect to pay the same or slightly more for this plan?
F. If the benefits were reasonable, would you pay 5 percent more than your current plan for this product?
G. What indemnity benefits would you recommend? Remember that each covered person may use the HMO system and get virtually everything covered after the small copayments.
Deductible?
Coinsurance?
Maximum out-of-pocket limit?

VII. I am interested in how you see this plan in relation to existing types of health care coverage.

A. First, how do you see it in relation to traditional indemnity insurance? Advantages or disadvantages? Strengths or weaknesses?
B. SAME FOR STAFF HMO
C. SAME FOR IPA HMO

GIVE THEM OPPORTUNITY FOR FINAL QUESTIONS AND COMMENTS

Thanks for your cooperation!

simply reimburses the patient for a percentage of his or her medical bills. The Appendix to this chapter provides a transcript of some of the discussion in the group.

Preparing the Focus Group Report

Typically, after the final group in a series is completed, there will be a moderator debriefing sometimes called an *instant analysis.* There are both pros and cons of this tradition. Arguments for employing instant analysis include (1) it provides a forum for combining the knowledge of the marketing specialists who viewed the group with that of the moderator; (2) getting an initial hearing of and reaction to the moderator's top-of-mind perceptions; and (3) using the heightened awareness and excitement of the moment to generate new ideas and implications in a brainstorming environment.[14]

The shortcomings include (1) biasing future analysis on the part of the moderator; (2) "hipshooting commentary" without leaving time for reflecting on what transpired; (3) recency, selective recall, and other factors associated with limited memory capabilities; and (4) not being able to hear all that was said in a less than highly involved and anxious state. We see nothing wrong with a moderator debriefing as long as the moderator explicitly reserves the right to change his or her opinion after reviewing the tapes.

Formal written reports tend to follow several different patterns, depending upon the client's needs, the researcher's style, and what was formally agreed upon in the research proposal. At one extreme, the investigator can prepare a brief, impressionistic summary of the principal findings, relying mainly on memory. This form of report is most likely to be used when the primary goal is for the clients to "experience flesh-and-blood consumers." The client often retains the tape recordings of the sessions and listens to the groups several additional times to become immersed in what the consumers are saying.

At the other extreme, the researcher listens and relistens to the tapes, copying down salient quotes and fitting the participant's thoughts into a more general scheme derived from the research objectives and the researcher's training.

A method between the two extremes, and the most common, is often called the *cut and paste technique*. The first step is to have the group sessions transcribed. Next, the researcher reviews the transcripts looking for common threads or trends in response patterns. Similar patterns are then cut apart and matched between the groups. The researcher then ends up with folders containing relevant material by subject matter.

The last step is to write the actual report. It normally begins with an introduction describing the purpose of the research, the major questions the researcher sought to answer, the nature and characteristics of the group members, and how they were recruited. Next, it is common to present a two or three page summary of findings and recommendations and follow with the main body of findings. If the group members' conversations have been well segmented and sorted, preparing the main body of the report should not be difficult. The first major topic is introduced, major points of the topic are summarized and then driven home with liberal use of actual respondent's remarks (verbatims). Subsequent topics are then covered in similar fashion.

Advantages and Disadvantages of Focus Groups

The advantages and disadvantages of qualitative research in general also apply to focus groups. Yet, focus groups also have some unique pros and cons that deserve mention.

Advantages of Focus Groups.   The interaction among respondents can stimulate new ideas and thoughts that might not arise during one-on-one interviews. And group pressure can help challenge respondents to keep their thinking more realistic. The energetic interaction among respondents also means that observation of a group generally provides "firsthand" consumer information to the client observers in a shorter amount of time and in a more interesting way than do individual interviews.

MARKETING RESEARCH IN PRACTICE

Power outages typically occur when utility companies have the fewest customer service representatives available to answer calls. This was the situation facing Detroit Edison, a large electric utility company serving 1.9 million customers. It was virtually impossible to reach the company during a power outage. Approximately 60 percent of the customers who called got busy signals.

In an attempt to find a solution to this problem of inaccessibility, Detroit Edison embarked on a comprehensive market research study involving both qualitative and quantitative research. The residential phase of the study began with thirty focus groups designed to define and test issues related to this problem. These groups helped the company to understand that customers were angrier about lack of accessibility than they were about loss of power. This inaccessibility was negatively affecting customers' overall perceptions of the company.

In its effort to improve customer attitudes, Detroit Edison used quantitative research to test a potential solution to their inaccessibility problem and found that there was overwhelming support for an automated telephone system. An interactive voice response unit (VRU) was installed that could handle 42,000 calls per hour and also meet a variety of other customer needs, such as billing arrangements and service calls.

Installing such a system was only the beginning. There was still the critical issue of how to make it user-friendly. In order to insure that the VRU met the needs of its customers, Detroit Edison used focus groups prior to launching the system to test the different scripts customers would hear when they called in. They tested the pace and timing of the scripts, as well as different voices for instructing callers. The company also used focus groups to test and fine-tune various promotional messages and for help in designing the billing and payment aspects of the system.

The end result of this process has been widespread customer acceptance of the VRU and increased customer satisfaction with Detroit Edison's customer service. An unexpected bonus of the focus groups has been increased customer goodwill. While qualitative research cannot be definitive, it can serve as a powerful demonstration of a company's willingness to listen to its customers.[15]

Another advantage focus groups offer is the opportunity to observe customers or prospects from behind a one-way mirror. In fact, there is growing use of focus groups to expose a broader range of employees to the customer comments and views. "We have found that the only way to get people to really understand what customers want is to let them see customers, but there are few people who actually come in contact with customers," says Bonnie Keith, corporate market research manager at Digital Equipment Corporation. "Right now, we are getting people from our manufacturing and engineering operations to attend and observe focus groups," says Keith.

Another advantage focus groups offer is that they often can be executed more quickly than other research approaches. Findings from groups also tend to be easier to understand and have a compelling immediacy and excitement. "I can get up and show a client all the charts and graphs in the world, but it has nowhere near the impact of showing eight or ten customers sitting around a table and saying that the company's service isn't good," says Jean-Anne Mutter, director of marketing research at Ketchum Advertising.[16]

Disadvantages of Focus Groups.   Unfortunately, some of the very strengths of focus groups can also become disadvantages. For example, the immediacy and apparent understandability of focus group findings can mislead instead of inform. Jean-Anne Mutter says, "Even though you're only getting a very small slice, a focus group gives you a sense that you really understand the situation." She adds that focus groups can strongly appeal to "people's desire for quick, simple answers to problems, and I see a decreasing willingness to go with complexity and to put forth the effort needed to really think through the complex data that will be yielded by a quantitative study."[17]

Other disadvantages relate to the focus group process itself. For example, focus group recruiting is a problem if the type of person recruited responds differently to the issues being discussed than other target segments. White middle-class individuals, for example, seem to participate in qualitative research in numbers that are disproportionate to their presence in the marketplace. Also, some focus group facilities create an impersonal feeling, making honest conversation unlikely. Corporate or formal decor with large boardroom tables, unattractive, plain, or gray decor may make it difficult for respondents to relax and share their feelings.

The greatest potential for distorting the focus group research is during the group interview itself. The moderator is part of the social interaction and must take care not to behave in ways that prejudice responses. The moderator's style may contribute to bias. For example, an aggressive, confronting style may systematically lead respondents to say whatever they think the moderator wants them to say, to avoid attack. "Playing dumb" by the moderator may create perceptions that the moderator is insincere or phony, and this may cause respondents to withdraw.[18]

Respondents can also be a problem. Some individuals are simply introverted and do not like to speak out in group settings. Other people may attempt to dominate the discussion. These are people who know it all, or think they do, and who invariably answer every question first and do not give others a chance to speak. A dominating participant may succeed in swaying other group members. If a moderator is abrupt with a respondent it can send the wrong message to other group members. "You'd better be cautious or I will do the same thing to you." Fortunately, a good moderator can stifle a dominant group member and not the rest of the group. Simple techniques used by moderators include avoiding eye contact with a dominant person, reminding the group that "we want to give everyone a chance to talk," saying "let's have someone else go first," or if someone else is speaking and the dominant person interrupts, the moderator should look at the initial speaker and say, "Sorry, I cannot hear you."[19]

TRENDS IN FOCUS GROUPS

A number of fads have come and gone in focus group research in the past decade. No longer do we hear much about replicated groups, mega groups, multivariate groups, video thematic apperception test groups, or sensitivity groups.

What we are seeing is a continued growth in the use of focus groups. Although no reliable data exists, we guestimate that over 50,000 focus groups are conducted in the United States annually. Commensurate with this is the expanding number (over 700) and quality of focus group facilities in the United States. Most cities with over 100,000 in population have at least one group facility. Tiny viewing rooms with small one-way mirrors are rapidly disappearing. Instead, field services are installing plush two-tiered observation areas that wrap around the conference room to provide an unobstructed view of all respondents. Built-in counters for taking notes, padded chairs, and a fully stocked refreshment center are becoming commonplace (the latter can create problems).

Telephone focus groups have recently emerged but may prove to be only a fad. The technique was developed because certain types of respondents, such as doctors, are always difficult to recruit. By using telephone conference calling, the need to travel to a group facility is eliminated. The moderator, who sits in front of a control console, knows who is talking because a light glows under the appropriate name tag when a participant speaks.[20] Visual aids can be mailed to the respondents in advance and opened only when instructed to do so by the moderator.

The disadvantages of this technique are many. The element of face-to-face group interaction is lost and observation of facial expressions, eye movement, glances or gestures toward other participants, and other body language is impossible. Visual aids may not reach the respondents or they may be opened prematurely, thus losing the spontaneous response. In summary, the jury is still out on telephone focus groups.

A second trend is called **two-way focus groups**. The technique was developed by Bozell and Jacobs, Kenyon and Eckhardt, one of America's largest advertising agencies. It allows one target group to listen to and learn from a related group, as the following example shows.

Telephone focus groups
Focus groups that are conducted via conference calling.

Two-way focus groups
A target focus group observes another focus group, then discusses what it learned through observing.

John Houlahan, president of FocusVision Network, uses video transmission to televise a focus group. Courtesy of FocusVision Network, Inc.

Bozell and Jacobs was doing focus groups with physicians and patients related to the management of arthritis. Often, what patients think they are accomplishing by taking a medicine is different from the actual result. And physicians often do not know what their patients are thinking: how they feel about the medicine they are taking and what their emotional needs are, as opposed to physiological needs.

We had the physicians observe a focus group of arthritis patients talking about their physicians and medications. We immediately followed the patient group with a focus group of the physicians who had observed the patients. The effect of the patient group on the physicians was startling. They emerged from behind the viewing room's one-way glass flushed and glassy-eyed. As they talked in their own group, with us observing, it became apparent they had little idea that patients would be taking as many as 10–15 medications at one time.

Nor, it seems, had they really known the desperation their patients felt when their physicians didn't take the time to really talk with them; didn't take the time for them to feel they were being taken seriously. We knew we had a breakthrough technique when, observing the physician's group, we saw the transforming effect the patient group had on the physicians.[21]

Perhaps a third trend is represented by a new focus group television network entitled the FocusVision Network. Instead of flying from city to city, network clients can view the focus groups in their offices. Live focus groups are broadcast by video transmission from a nationwide network of independently owned focus facilities (see Figure 5.3). Clients view all of the action on a 26-inch monitor and control two

FIGURE 5.3   *How the FocusVision Network Functions*

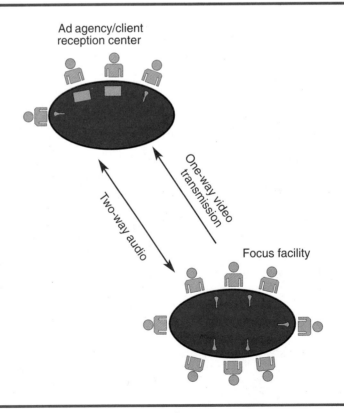

cameras that allow a full group view, close-up, zoom, or pan. They can maintain audio contact with the moderator, videotape highlights or entire sessions, and hold "open mike" postgroup debriefings. Three-way interaction between the client office, a distant ad agency, and the transmitting facility is also available.

The moderator or a colleague behind the one-way mirror wears an earmold for input from the client. A remote control VCR is available for full or selected taping of the group. There is even an on-site fax machine so the client can immediately send new concepts, new copy, and moderator's guide changes. Clients for the new service are heavy focus group users including Ogilvy and Mather Advertising, Seagram Incorporated, Lintas Advertising, Johnson & Johnson, Ortho, and AT&T. Costs will probably prevent smaller firms from joining the network. The transmission fee is $1,450 per group in addition to standard respondent recruiting costs and fees, moderator charges, and written report. A FocusVision Reception Center costs $4,985 monthly plus an installation charge of $6,220.[22]

OTHER QUALITATIVE RESEARCH METHODOLOGIES

Most of this chapter has been devoted to focus groups because of their pervasive use in marketing research. However, several other qualitative techniques are utilized, albeit on a much more limited basis.

Depth Interviews

The term **depth interviews** has historically meant a relatively unstructured one-on-one interview. The interviewer is thoroughly trained in the skill of probing and eliciting detailed answers to each question. Sometimes psychologists are used as depth interviewers. They use clinical nondirective techniques to uncover hidden motivations.

The direction of a depth interview is guided by the responses of the interviewee. As the interview unfolds, the interviewer thoroughly probes each answer and uses the replies as a basis for further questioning. For example, a depth interview might begin with a discussion of snack foods. Each answer might follow with, "Can you tell me more?" "Would you elaborate on that?" "Is that all?" The interview might then move into pros and cons of various ingredients such as corn, wheat, potatoes. The next phase could delve into the sociability of the snack food. Are Fritos, for example, eaten alone or in a crowd? Are Wheat Thins usually reserved for parties? When should you serve Ritz crackers?

The advantages of depth interviews relative to focus groups are as follows:

1. Group pressure is eliminated so that each respondent reveals more honest feelings, not necessarily those considered most acceptable among peers.
2. The personal one-to-one situation gives the respondent the feeling of being the focus of attention, whose personal thoughts and feelings are important and truly wanted.
3. The respondent attains a heightened state of awareness in a personal interview because he or she is in constant rapport with the interviewer and there are no group members to hide behind.

Depth interviews
One-on-one interviews that probe and elicit detailed answers to questions, often using nondirective techniques to uncover hidden motivations.

GLOBAL MARKETING RESEARCH

The Japanese examine American consumers because they believe that the U.S. buyers are the world's trendsetters: what's popular here will soon be popular in the rest of the world. The Japanese track American pop culture to know which hot celebrities will be in demand for advertising. They study the way Americans shop to learn how to design stores. They dig into how buyers view themselves so they can design better-selling cars. Nissan researchers, for example, use qualitative research by asking dozens of consumers to cut out pictures from magazines and make a collage of "who you are."

From that, Nissan gets a snapshot of market segments that traditional surveys cannot touch. People who paste up pictures of lobster dinners, American Express gold cards, and Porsche cars are labeled *showy sophisticates.* They're about 9 percent of the population. People who paste up Victoria's Secret ads and baby food jars are "self-sacrificing escapists"—11 percent of the population. By identifying such segments and learning what objects and images define the people in them, by using qualitative and quantitative techniques, Nissan can design cars to appeal to certain customers.[23]

4. The longer time devoted to individual respondents encourages the revelation of new information.
5. Respondents can be probed at length to reveal the feelings and motivations that underlie statements.
6. Without the restrictions of cultivating a group process, new directions of questioning can be improvised more easily. Individual interviews allow greater flexibility in exploring casual remarks and tangential issues, which may provide critical insights into the main issue.
7. The closeness of the one-to-one relationship allows the interviewer to become more sensitive to nonverbal feedback.
8. Depth interviews may be the only viable technique for certain situations where competitors would otherwise be placed in the same room. For example, it might be very difficult to do a focus group on certain topics (e.g., systems for preventing bad checks) with managers from competing department stores or restaurants.

The disadvantages of depth interviews relative to focus groups are as follows:

1. Depth interviews are much more expensive than groups, particularly when viewed on a per-interview basis.
2. Depth interviews *do not* generally get the same degree of client involvement as focus groups. If one of your objectives is to get the clients to view the research so they benefit firsthand from the information, it is difficult to convince most client personnel to sit through multiple hours of depth interviews.
3. Depth interviews are physically exhausting for the moderator, so it is difficult to cover as much ground in one day as it is with groups. Most moderators will not do more than four or five interviews in a day, yet in two focus groups they will cover twenty people.
4. Focus groups give the moderator an ability to leverage the dynamics of the group to obtain reactions from individuals that might not otherwise be generated in a one-on-one session.[24]

The success of any depth interview depends entirely on the interviewer. Good depth interviewers, whether psychologists or not, are hard to find and expensive. A second factor that determines the success of depth research is proper interpretation. The unstructured nature of the interview and the "clinical" nature of the analysis increases the complexity of the analysis. Small sample sizes, unstructured interviews that make intercomparisons difficult, interpretation that is subject to the nuances and frame of reference of the researcher, and high costs have all contributed to the lack of popularity of depth interviewing.

A few firms have found that depth interviews have an important role to play in qualitative research. N. W. Ayer, one of the nation's largest advertising agencies, had conducted several market segmentation studies of "baby boomers," but still felt that they lacked a good understanding of these consumers. Ayer's research director decided to conduct depth interviews.

> The depth interviews generated four market segments: Satisfied Selves, who are optimistic and achievement-oriented; Contented Traditionalists, who are home-oriented and socially very conservative; Worried Traditionalists, anticipating disaster on all fronts; and '60s in the '90s, people who are aimless, unfulfilled, and have no direction in life.
>
> Behavioral differences translated down to brand use. Using the category of alcohol, for example, Satisfied Selves use upscale brands and are the target for imported wine. Contented Traditionalists consume little alcohol, but when they drink they favor brown liquors, such as whiskey.
>
> Worried Traditionalists drink at an average level, but their consumption levels are very different from the other segments. For each type of liquor there was a dual brand-use pattern; people in this segment reported using an upscale brand as well as a lower-priced one. "Maybe they have one brand on hand for when they entertain guests, the socially visible brands, and a cheaper brand they consume when home alone," the research director said. The members of the '60s in the '90s segment are heavy liquor consumers, especially of vodka and beer.[25]

PROJECTIVE TECHNIQUES

Projective techniques are sometimes incorporated into depth interviews. The origins of projective techniques lie in the field of clinical psychology. In essence, the objective of any projective test is to delve below surface responses to obtain true feelings, meanings, or motivations. The rationale behind projective tests comes from knowledge that people are often reluctant or cannot reveal their deepest feelings. In other instances, they are unaware of those feelings due to psychological defense mechanisms.

Projective tests are techniques for penetrating a person's defense mechanisms and allowing true feelings and attitudes to emerge. In general, a subject is presented with an unstructured and nebulous situation and asked to respond. Because the situation is ill-defined and has no true meaning, the respondent must use his or her own frame of reference to answer the question. In theory, the respondent "projects" his or her feelings into the unstructured stimulus. Because the subjects are not directly talking about themselves, defense mechanisms are purportedly bypassed. The interviewee is talking about something else or someone else, yet revealing his or her inner feelings.

Projective techniques
Ways of tapping respondents' deepest feelings by having them "project" those feelings into an unstructured situation.

Most projective tests are easy to administer and are tabulated like any other open-ended question. They are often used in conjunction with nonprojective open- and closed-ended questions. The projective test serves as a basis for gathering "richer" and perhaps more revealing data than standard questioning techniques. Projective techniques are often intermingled with image questionnaires, concept tests, and occasionally advertising pretests. It is also common to apply several projective techniques during a depth interview.

The most common forms of projective tests used in marketing research are word association, sentence and story completion, cartoon tests, and consumer drawings. Other techniques such as psychodrama and true TAT (Thematic Apperception Test) tests have been popular in treating psychological disorders but have been of less help in marketing research.

Word association tests
Tests where the interviewer says a word and the respondent must mention the first thing that comes to mind.

Word Association Tests.   **Word association tests** are among the most practical and effective projective tools for market researchers. An interviewer reads a word to a respondent and asks him or her to mention the first thing that comes into mind. Usually the consumer will respond with a synonym or an antonym. The list is read in quick succession to avoid time for defense mechanisms to come into play. If the respondent fails to answer within three seconds, some emotional involvement with the word is assumed.

Word association tests are used to select brand names, advertising campaign themes, and slogans. For example, a cosmetic manufacturer might ask consumers to respond to the following potential names for a new perfume:

infinity	flame	precious
encounter	desire	erotic

One of these words or a synonym suggested by the consumers might then be selected as the brand name.

Sentence and story completion tests
Tests in which the respondents complete sentences or stories in their own words.

Sentence and Story Completion.   **Sentence and story completion tests** can be used in conjunction with word association tests. The respondent is furnished with an incomplete story or group of sentences and asked to complete them. A few examples follow:

1. Marshall Fields is . . .
2. The people who shop at Marshall Fields are . . .
3. Marshall Fields should really . . .
4. I don't understand why Marshall Fields doesn't . . .
5. Sally Jones just moved to Chicago from Los Angeles where she had been a salesperson for IBM. She is now a district manager for the Chicago area. Her neighbor, Rhonda Smith, has just come over to Sally's apartment to welcome her to Chicago. A discussion of where to shop ensues. Sally notes, "You know, I've heard some things about Marshall Fields . . ." What is Rhonda's reply?

As you can see, story completion simply provides a more structured and detailed scenario for the respondent. Again, the objective is for the interviewees to project themselves into the imaginary person mentioned in the scenario. Sentence completion and story techniques have been considered by some researchers to be the most useful and reliable of all the projective tests.

FIGURE 5.4   *Cartoon Test*

Hey John, I just received a $500 bonus for a suggestion my company is now using on the production line. I'm thinking about buying a new stereo system at Wal Mart.

Cartoon Tests.   **Cartoon tests** create a highly projective mechanism by means of cartoon figures or strips similar to those seen in comic books. The typical cartoon test consists of two characters—one balloon is filled with dialogue and the other balloon is blank. The respondent is then asked to fill in the blank balloon as in the example in Figure 5.4. Note that the figures are vague and without expression. This is done so that the respondent is not given "clues" regarding a suggested type of response. The ambiguity is designed to make it easier for the respondent to project in the cartoon.

Cartoon tests are extremely versatile. They can be used to obtain differential attitudes toward two types of establishments and the congruity, or lack of congruity, between these establishments and a particular product. They can be used to measure the strength of an attitude toward a particular product or brand. They can also be used to ascertain what function is being performed by a given attitude.

Cartoon tests
Tests in which the respondent fills in the dialogue of one character in a cartoon.

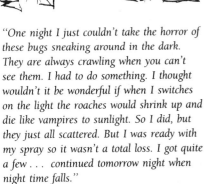

"One night I just couldn't take the horror of these bugs sneaking around in the dark. They are always crawling when you can't see them. I had to do something. I thought wouldn't it be wonderful if when I switches on the light the roaches would shrink up and die like vampires to sunlight. So I did, but they just all scattered. But I was ready with my spray so it wasn't a total loss. I got quite a few . . . continued tomorrow night when night time falls."

"A man likes a free meal you cook for him; as long as there is food he will stay."

"I tiptoed quietly into the kitchen perhaps he wasn't around. I stretched my arm up to open the light. I hoped I'd be alone when the light went on. Perhaps he is sitting on the table I thought. You think that's impossible? Nothing is impossible with that guy. He might not even be alone. He'll run when the light goes on I thought. But what's worse is for him to slip out of sight. No, it would be better to confront him before he takes control and 'invites a companion'."

McCann-Erickson advertising agency asked users of roach spray to create drawings of their prey. From the drawings, the agency determined that roach spray sold better than insecticide disks since the users wanted control and spray allowed them to actively kill the roaches. Courtesy of McCann-Erickson New York.

Consumer drawings
Respondents draw what they are feeling or how they perceive an object.

Consumer Drawings. Researchers sometimes ask consumers to draw what they are feeling or how they perceive an object. Sometimes **consumer drawings** can unlock motivations or express perceptions (see the case at the end of this chapter). For example, McCann-Erickson advertising agency wanted to find out why Raid roach spray outsold Combat insecticide disks in certain markets. In interviews, most users agreed that Combat is a better product because it kills roaches without any effort on the user's part. So the agency asked the heaviest users of roach spray—low-income southern women—to draw pictures of their prey. The goal was to get at their underlying feelings about this dirty job.

All of the 100 women who participated in the agency's interviews portrayed roaches as men. "A lot of their feelings about the roach were very similar to the feelings that they had about the men in their lives," said Paula Drillman, executive vice-president at McCann-Erickson. Many of the women were in common-law relationships. They said that the roach, like the man in their life, "only comes around when he wants food." The act of spraying roaches and seeing them die was satisfying to this frustrated, powerless group. Setting out Combat disks may have been less trouble, but it just didn't give them the same feeling. "These women wanted control," Drillman said. "They used the spray because it allowed them to participate in the kill."[26]

SUMMARY

Qualitative research refers to research findings not subject to quantification or quantitative analysis. It is often used to examine attitudes, feelings, and motivations. Qualitative research, particularly focus groups, continues to grow in popularity for several reasons. First, qualitative research is usually cheaper than quantitative studies. Second, it is an excellent means to understand the in-depth motivation and feelings of consumers. Third, it can improve the efficiency of quantitative research.

Qualitative research is not without its disadvantages. One problem is that qualitative research sometimes will not distinguish small differences in attitudes or opinions as well as large-scale quantitative studies. Also, the respondents in qualitative studies are not necessarily representative of the population of interest to the researcher. Third, a number of individuals lack formal training yet profess to be experts in the field.

Focus groups typically consist of eight to twelve participants who are led by a moderator in an in-depth discussion on a particular topic or concept. The goal of the focus group is to learn and understand what people have to say and why. The emphasis is on getting people talking at length and in detail about the subject at hand. The interaction provided by group dynamics is essential to the success of focus group research. The idea is that a response from one person may become a stimulus for another, thereby generating an interplay of responses that may yield more information than if the same number of people had contributed independently to the discussion. Focus groups are the most popular type of qualitative research.

Focus groups can be divided into three major categories: exploratory, clinical, and experiencing. Exploratory focus groups are used at the exploratory phase of the market research process. They may attempt to clarify the problem or generate hypotheses for testing. A clinical focus group is based on the premise that a person's true motivations and feelings are subconscious in nature. Thus, such a group should be conducted by a moderator with expertise in psychology and sociology. It is assumed that a person's real motives must be uncovered using clinical judgment. Thus, the focus group data becomes the data input source for the clinical judgment. Experiencing focus groups are conducted to experience a so-called flesh-and-blood consumer. They are used by the researcher to experience the emotional framework in which a product is bought and consumed.

Most focus groups are held in a "group facility," which is typically set up in conference room style with a large one-way mirror in one wall. Microphones are placed in unobtrusive locations to record the discussion. Behind the mirror is a viewing room. Respondents are paid to participate. The moderator plays the critical role in determining the success or failure of the group.

A number of other qualitative research methodologies are used, but on a much more infrequent basis. One technique is depth interviews. Depth interviews historically are unstructured interviews. The interviewer is thoroughly trained in the skill of probing and eliciting detailed answers to each question. They often use clinical nondirective techniques to uncover hidden motivations. Projective techniques are another form of qualitative research. The objective of any projective test is to delve below the surface responses to obtain true feelings, meanings, or motivations. Some common forms of projective tests are word association tests, sentence and story completion tests, cartoon tests, and consumer drawings.

KEY TERMS

Qualitative research
Quantitative research
Focus groups
Group dynamics
Exploratory focus groups
Clinical focus groups
Experiencing focus groups
Focus group facility
Focus group moderator

Discussion guide
Telephone focus groups
Two-way focus groups
Depth interviews
Projective techniques
Word association tests
Sentence and story completion tests
Cartoon tests
Consumer drawings

REVIEW AND DISCUSSION QUESTIONS

1. What are the major differences between quantitative and qualitative research?
2. What are some of the possible disadvantages of using focus groups?
3. What differentiates exploratory, clinical, and experiencing groups from one another? Give examples of each.
4. What are some of the trends in focus group research? Why do you think these trends have evolved?
5. What is the purpose of projective techniques? What major factors are to be considered in conducting a projective test?
6. Conduct a focus group in your class on one of the following three topics:
   a. Student experiences at your Student Union.
   b. Quality of frozen dinners and snacks and new items that would be desired.
   c. How students spend their entertainment dollars and what additional items of entertainment they would like to see offered.
7. Consumer drawing tests may ask study participants to draw the kind of person that would be consuming a particular product. Accordingly, assign three individuals to go to the blackboard and draw a typical Pepsi drinker versus a typical Coke drinker. What do the drawn images tell you about the participants' perceptions of Coke and Pepsi drinkers?
8. Write an obituary notice for a Milky Way bar, Dr. Pepper, Pepperidge Farm cookies, and Tony's frozen pizza.

CASE

Pillsbury Cake Mixes

To learn more about their client's product, McCann-Erickson Advertising Agency decided to conduct some qualitative research. They brought fifty consumers into the agency and asked them to sketch likely buyers of two different brands of cake mixes. One cake mix was Pillsbury and the other was Duncan Hines. Examples of the sketches are shown in Figure 5.5. Consistently, the group portrayed Pillsbury customers as

FIGURE 5.5   *Who Baked the Cake?*

apron-clad, grandmotherly types, whereas they pictured Duncan Hines customers as svelte, contemporary women.

1. You are the account executive for Pillsbury. What kind of changes in its advertising program for cake mixes would you recommend? Why?
2. What other projective tests could have been used to ascertain consumers' perceptions of these two products? Pick at least one additional projective test and administer it to the class for Pillsbury and Duncan Hines cake mixes.
3. How might quantitative studies be used to confirm or disconfirm the findings of the qualitative research?

A P P E N D I X A

Selected Excerpts from a Focus Group Conducted with Company Benefit Managers on Health Care Plans

Q. Moderator. What's the first thing that comes into your mind when I mention health care coverage for employees?

A. Cost. Keeping the costs down and the best available.

A. Options—different plans.

A. Administration. Who is going to do it.

Q. Moderator. Who would you like to do it?

A. Somebody else!

Q. Moderator. Effectiveness? How would you describe that?

A. Taking care of the needs of the people that you are serving, and employees are the main people you are serving.

Q. Moderator. How do you assess that?

A. I am not really sure how you assess it. Through feedback from the employees.

A. Another area is through communication. Without communication you haven't got anything. You can have quality, effectiveness, you can have lack of quality. Unfortunately you can have lack of quality that is well communicated.

A. I think turn-around time is very important. How quickly people get paid on their claim, instead of having 200 disgruntled employees calling you and saying, "My goodness I sent in my claim three months ago, I have not heard from that insurance company."

A. Another point concerning a PPO, the option as far as the physicians in the group, where they are located.

A. I think one of the things that has to be irritating to the employee is the terminology, the PPOs, the HMOs, they don't know what you are talking about.

A. That comes back to communication. The quality of the health care and the services are the most important thing. The other things go with it. I think those of us who work in this field are responsible for making sure they do understand and communicate it properly. That means we have to know what that outfit is, so to speak, and so we have an educated group of employees. It is very hard. They are on the phone taking care of a claim—we only had thirty or forty employees—but always somebody had a complaint.

Q. Moderator. Which of the following three are the most important factors in a benefit plan: Deductible amount? Coinsurance percentage? Maximum out-of-pocket expense? Is one of those more important?

A. That would depend on how sick or well you were. If you were ill, or spent a lot of time going then it would be the out of pocket, you would reach that quickly.

A. I would have to say the deductible. In the last twenty years, we have had two children, knock on wood there were some years we never used it, but then again there were years I kept thinking, "Gosh, aren't we going to get this deductible pretty soon?" But then once you hit it you go to the 80/20 which was better than nothing.

. . . End of first side of tape.

A. Right now our coverage is excellent, they pay in a week and a half and just about everything is 100 percent paid, and the premiums aren't that bad, but she [employer] doesn't see it that way because she has friends that have told her that they have $1,000 deductible. What they are probably not telling her is that they cover some of that deductible.

A. That's a very high deductible. I don't think the average person would ever use that high an insurance. We have $200 for a person, $400 for a family. We have just switched from $100 to $200. The $200 deductible for a lot of our single people is a lot—looking from their standpoint, the deductible is the most important. If you really have a major illness you are going to go way over $3,000, it doesn't take very much. If, like in our company, you are looking I'd say the deductible—we have more well people who need the smaller deductible.

A. The deductible is important, because if you just go to the doctor that's where it comes in. Our outpatient coverage is 100 percent. If you go to the emergency room it is 100 percent, so if you go into the hospital you are going to reach the maximum deduction in two days time.

A. My mother had a triple bypass a year ago, it was $35,000. Until you have experienced someone having a hospital bill, you have no idea how lucky you are to have it.

A. To the company, and our employees both its the deductible. It is a pretty hard decision to make—we get more griping from our employees as a result of the deductible. Once you go on a copay something is better than nothing. Our out of pocket is not that high. Most of our employees have come to realize the insurance is there to pay for the major or minor catastrophe, whatever, so they are willing to eat some dollars on the out of pocket. We are absorbing that anyway—I think the most important is the deductible.

A. I went with the out of pocket—I was the first one to respond. It is very difficult to look as the employer and look as the rest of the employees. I am looking personally. I can stand $250, but I can't stand $3,000. For a younger person, probably they let somebody else pay for my deductible.

Q. Moderator. Who isn't offering HMO coverage?

A. I am kinda stuck with Blue Cross/Blue Shield—we tried to move into something else—a couple of the people, we are a small family-held company, and they just like Blue Cross/Blue Shield. I think now that we have some cost figures they will probably change. We periodically get another offering, but they are just reluctant to move from Blue Cross/Blue Shield.

A. No special reason. We have not been mandated. The time I talked to several HMO programs here and I am sure that by the time 1995 arrives and our contract is up—they will have to serve notice on me and mandate me that they will. I would much prefer to select my own HMO.

A. We have a large number of employees who are under twenty-five. People my age, people over thirty-five, who are established with a physician, they are not interested in an HMO. I would like to see an HMO come to town that says you can use practically any doctor that you want. But we have a large number of young people who have no physician. I myself have three sons—they don't go to a doctor—they have a bigger mustache than their pediatrician did—they can't run back to him. So, it would be good for them to join an HMO and get established with someone.

CHAPTER 6

Primary Data Collection: Observation

LEARNING OBJECTIVES

1. To develop a basic understanding of observation research.

2. To learn the approaches to observation research.

3. To understand the advantages and disadvantages of observation research.

4. To explore the types of human observation.

5. To describe the types of machine observation and their advantages and disadvantages.

6. To define the concept of single-source research.

7. To explore the tremendous impact scanner research has had on the marketing research industry in the past few years.

Tracking consumers' every move is giving retailers both revealing statistical detail and new insights. The research efforts have also turned up some surprises:

- By peering from the catwalks at 1,600 shoppers, researchers for Marsh Supermarkets unearthed a troubling trend. People heavily shopped the periphery of the store—the produce, dairy, and meat sections—but frequently circumvented the core dry-goods section that takes up the bulk of store space. The Indiana store chain's inner aisles drew only 13 to 30 percent of the traffic, while the periphery accounted for as much as 80 percent.

- VideOcart, Inc., a Chicago company that uses infrared sensors in store ceilings to track shopping carts, has spotted a lot of "dippers." These shoppers park their carts at the ends of aisles and then walk down, filling their arms with items from the shelves as they go. Retailers figure such shoppers probably buy less because they are limited by what they can carry.

- Certain departments draw huge numbers of people, but that doesn't guarantee proportionate sales, a study by the Food Marketing Institute trade group shows. By retracing the steps of 2,400 shoppers and checking what ended up in their grocery carts, the institute learned, for instance, that 77 percent of people walked through the bakery department, but only a third actually bought anything there.

- A study of Procter & Gamble products in K Mart stores found that sales rose sharply when items like coffee and toothpaste were placed outside their normal aisles on display racks. With no coupons or price cuts, sales of the newly located toothpaste rose as much as 119 percent over a three-week test period, while coffee sales soared more than 500 percent.[1]

The opening story describes several forms of observation research. What is observation research? What are its advantages and limitations? Are other mechanical devices used in observation research? These are some of the questions we will answer in Chapter 6.

THE NATURE OF OBSERVATION RESEARCH

Observation Research Defined

Instead of asking people questions as in the case of a survey, observation depends on watching what people do. Specifically, **observation research** can be defined as the systematic process of recording the behavioral patterns of people, objects, and occurrences without questioning or communicating with them. A market researcher using the observation technique witnesses and records information as events occur or compiles evidence from records of past events. Carried a step further, observation may involve watching people or phenomena and may be conducted by human observers or machines. Examples of these various observational situations are shown in Table 6.1.

Observation research
Recording behavioral patterns without verbal communication.

Conditions for Using Observation

Three conditions must be met before observation can be successfully used as a data collection tool for marketing research. First, the needed information must be observable or inferable from behavior that can be observed. For example, if a researcher wants to know why an individual purchased a new Jeep rather than a Bronco, observation research will not provide the answer. Second, the behavior of interest must be repetitive, frequent, or predictable in some manner. Otherwise, the costs of observation make the approach prohibitively expensive. Finally, the behavior of interest must be of relatively short duration. Observation of the entire decision-making process for purchasing a new home, which might take several weeks or months, is not feasible.

Approaches to Observation Research

The researcher has a variety of observational approaches to choose from. The question is one of choosing the most effective approach from the standpoint of cost and data quality for a particular research problem. The five dimensions along which observational approaches vary are (1) natural versus contrived situations, (2) open

TABLE 6.1   *Observational Situations*

SITUATION	EXAMPLE
People watching people	Observers stationed in supermarkets watch consumers select frozen Mexican dinners. The purpose is to see how much comparison shopping people do at the point of purchase.
People watching phenomena	Observer stationed at an intersection counts traffic moving in various directions.
Machines watching people	Movie or videotape cameras record behavior as in people watching people example.
Machines watching phenomena	Traffic counting machines monitor traffic flow.

versus disguised situations, (3) structured versus unstructured observation, (4) human versus machine observers, and (5) direct versus indirect observation.

Natural versus Contrived Situations. Counting how many people use the drive-in window at a particular bank during certain hours is a good example of a completely natural situation. The observer is playing no role in the behavior of interest. Those being observed should have no idea they are under observation. At the other extreme we might recruit people to do their shopping in a simulated supermarket (rows of stocked shelves set up in a market research field service's mall facility is commonly used) so that we can carefully observe their behavior. In this case, it is necessary that the recruited people have at least some idea that they are participating in a study. The participants might be given grocery carts and told to browse the shelves and pick out items that they might normally use. The researchers might use alternative point-of-purchase displays for several products under study. The observers would note how long the shopper poised in front of the test displays and how often the product was actually selected, thus getting an idea of the effectiveness of the various displays.

A contrived environment better enables the researcher to control extraneous influencers that might have an impact on a person's behavior or the interpretation of that behavior. Also, a simulated environment tends to speed up the observation data gathering process. The researcher does not have to wait for natural events to occur but instead instructs the participants to perform certain actions. Because more observations can be collected in the same length of time, the result will be either a larger sample or a target sample size collected faster. The latter should lower the costs of the project.

The primary disadvantage of a contrived setting is that it is artificial and the observed behavior may be different from what would occur in a real-world situation. The more natural the setting, the more likely the behavior will be normal for the individual being observed.

Open versus Disguised Observation. Does the person being observed know that he or she is being observed? It is well known that the presence of an observer may have an influence on the phenomena being observed.[2] Two general mechanisms work to bias the data. First, if people know they are being observed (as in **open observation**), they may behave differently. Second, the appearance and behavior of the observer offers a potential for bias similar to that associated with the presence of an interviewer in survey research.

A common form of **disguised observation** is the "mystery shopper." Department stores and chains, such as Sears, will send employees to competitors' stores and ask them to pretend to be shopping. The disguised observers check prices, point-of-purchase displays, and other factors.

Structured versus Unstructured Observation. Observation can be structured or unstructured much in the same manner as surveys. In the **structured observation** the observer fills out a questionnairelike form on each person observed. In the totally **unstructured observation** the observer simply makes notes on the behavior being observed. In general, the same considerations that determine whether a survey should be structured or unstructured determine whether an observation should be structured or unstructured. If you already know a good deal about the

Open observation
The process of monitoring people who know they are being watched.

Disguised observation
The process of monitoring people, objects, or occurrences that do not know they are being watched.

Structured observation
A study in which the observer fills out a questionnaire-like form or counts the number of times an activity occurs.

Unstructured observation
A study in which the observer simply makes notes on the behavior being observed.

behavior of interest, it probably makes more sense to do structured observations. If you know very little, unstructured observation is the proper approach, or at least an appropriate preliminary approach.

Structured observation often consists of simply counting the number of times a particular activity occurs. For example, the researcher may be interested in testing two sets of instructions on a new cake mix recipe. To develop a baseline of behavior the researcher could have the homemakers prepare their own favorite recipes using the cake mix. One half of the group would get one set of instructions and the remainder the other set. Activities counted might be things such as number of times the instructions were read, number of trips to the cabinet to retrieve bowls and other instruments, number of strokes that the mix is beaten, oven temperatures, and so forth.

A device that can facilitate structured observation is the Data Myte 801 Performance Analyzer, manufactured by Data Myte Corp., Minnetonka, Minnesota. It enables the researcher to assign up to twenty different behaviors to various keys (e.g., smiled, frowned, tasted the product). The summary calculations provided by the Data Myte include the sequencing of the behaviors, the total number of occurrences for each, and the time taken for those behaviors. The result is a stream of data that effectively measures a behavioral process. Of course, to increase the reliability of the procedure, it is reasonable to use more than one observer.[3]

Human versus Machine Observers.   In some situations it may be possible and even desirable to replace human observers with machines. In certain situations machines may do the job less expensively, more accurately, or more readily. Traffic counting devices are probably more accurate, definitely cheaper, and certainly more willing than human observers. It would not be feasible, for example, for A. C. Nielsen to have human observers in people's homes to record television viewing habits. Movie cameras and audiovisual equipment record behavior much more objectively and in greater detail than human observers ever could. Finally, the electronic scanners found in a growing number of retail stores provide more accurate and timely data on product movement than human observers ever could.

Direct versus Indirect Observation.   Most of the observation done in marketing research is direct observation; that is, directly observing current behavior. However, in some cases past behavior must be observed. To do this, it is necessary to turn to some record of the behavior. Archeologists dig up sites of old settlements and attempt to determine the nature of life in old civilizations from the physical evidence they find. Garbologists sort through people's garbage to analyze household consumption patterns. Marketing research is usually much more mundane. In a product prototype test it may be important for us to know how much of the test product was actually used. The most accurate way to find this out is to have the respondent return the unused product so that the researcher can observe how much was actually used. If a laundry soil and stain remover was placed for in-home use, it would be important to know how much of the product each respondent actually used. All of their answers to other questions would be considered from this usage perspective.

Advantages of Observation Research

The idea of watching what people actually do rather than depending on their reports of what they did has one very significant and obvious advantage: we see what people actually do rather than having to rely on what they say they did.[4] This approach can avoid much of the biasing factors caused by the interviewer and question structure associated with the survey approach. The researcher is not subject to problems associated with the willingness and ability of respondents to answer questions. Finally, some forms of data are gathered more quickly and accurately by observation. Rather than ask people to enumerate every item in their grocery bags, it is much more efficient to let a scanner record it. Alternatively, rather than asking young children which toys they like, the major toy manufacturers invite target groups of children into a large playroom and observe via a one-way mirror which toys are chosen and how long each holds the child's attention.

Disadvantages of Observation Research

The primary disadvantage of observation research is that only behavior and physical personal characteristics can usually be examined. The researcher does not learn about motives, attitudes, intentions, or feelings. Also, only public behavior is observed; private behavior, such as dressing for work, committee decisions of a company, and family activities at home, is beyond the scope of the researcher. A second problem is that present observed behavior may not be projectable to the future. Purchasing a certain brand of milk after examining several alternatives may hold in time period one, but not in the future.

Observation research can be time consuming and costly if the observed behavior occurs rather infrequently. For example, if an observer in a supermarket is waiting to observe purchase behavior of persons selecting Lava soap, it may be a long wait. If the consumers chosen to be observed are selected in a biased pattern, for example, shoppers who go grocery shopping after 5:00 P.M., distorted data may be obtained.

HUMAN OBSERVATION

As noted in Table 6.1, people can be used to watch other people or certain phenomena. For example, people can be used as mystery shoppers, observers behind one-way mirrors, or to record shopper traffic and behavior patterns. Researchers also conduct retail and wholesale audits and do content analysis, which are other types of observation research.

Mystery Shoppers

Mystery shoppers
People employed to pose as consumers and shop at the employer's competitors to compare prices, displays, and the like.

As mentioned earlier, retailers send employees out to shop at competitive stores or company stores. Sears personnel, for example, regularly visit Penney's and other large retailers to observe fixture layouts, merchandise displays, store traffic, and special promotions. McDonald's sends specially trained employees to its various stores to pose as customers. The **mystery shoppers** observe how long it takes to receive their order, courtesy of the counter clerks, whether the food was properly prepared, and cleanliness of the stores. Sometimes mystery shoppers are used not only to evaluate the quality of service but to motivate employees. RCA's Consumer Electronics Division used mystery shoppers to evaluate sales performance and point-of-purchase assistance. A salesperson who asks the mystery shopper the "right questions" and behaves according to a checklist of criteria is rewarded on the spot with a check for $50. Subway Sandwiches also uses mystery shoppers as a motivational tool. One franchisee installed signs behind the counter where only employees could see them. The signs read: "Is this the mystery shopper?"

We helped pay for our college education by working as a mystery shopper for Hallmark Card Shops, Woolworths, and American Express. A mystery shopper not only observes a shopping environment, but also how employees react and behave based upon the shopper's action. For American Express, we would travel to a distant city (sometimes outside the United States), go to the local American Express Office, and tell them our card had been lost or stolen. We then asked for emergency cash and made a variety of other requests. The largest mystery shopper organization in the United States is the Atlanta-based Shop'n Chek Incorporated. It has 16,000 part-time mystery shoppers with clients such as Sears, Wendy's, United Airlines, RCA, and General Motors. Fees range from $20 to $1,000 for each shopping trip, depending on how much information is gathered.[5]

One-Way Mirror Observations

Our discussion of focus groups in Chapter 5 noted that focus group facilities almost always include an observation room with a one-way mirror. This allowed clients to observe the group discussion as it unfolds. New product development managers, for

Child psychologists and toy designers can observe children from behind a one-way mirror at Fisher Price's Play Laboratory to determine what toys the children choose and how they play with them. (Courtesy of Fisher-Price, Inc.)

One-way mirror observations
The practice of watching unseen from behind a one-way mirror.

example, can note consumers' reactions to various package prototypes as they are demonstrated by the moderator. The clients can also observe the degree of emotion exhibited by the consumer as he or she speaks. As mentioned earlier, **one-way mirror observations** are sometimes used by child psychologists and toy designers to watch children at play. One researcher spent 200 hours watching mothers change diapers to help with redesign of disposable diapers.

To properly utilize an observation room, the lighting level must be very dim relative to the actual focus group room. Otherwise, the focus group participants can see into the observation room. Several years ago, we were conducting a focus group using orthopedic surgeons in St. Louis. One physician arrived approximately twenty minutes early and was ushered into the group room. A young assistant product manager for the pharmaceutical manufacturer was already seated in the observation room. The physician, being alone in the group room, decided to take advantage of the large framed mirror on the wall for some last-minute grooming. He walked over to the mirror and began combing his hair . . . at the same time the assistant product manager, sitting about a foot away on the other side of the mirror, decided to light a cigarette. As the doctor combed his hair, there was suddenly a bright flash of light and another face appearing through the mirror. What happened next goes beyond the scope of this text.

Shopper Patterns

Shopper patterns
Drawings that record the footsteps of a shopper through a store.

As the opening story described, **shopper pattern** studies are used by retailers to trace the flow of shoppers through a store. Normally, the researcher uses a diagram of the aisles and uses a pen to trace the footsteps of the shopper. By comparing the flows of a representative sample of shoppers, the store managers can determine where best to place such items as impulse goods. Alternatively, the store can change layouts over time and see how this modifies shopping patterns. Generally speaking, retailers want shoppers to be exposed to as much merchandise as possible while in the store. Supermarkets, for example, typically place necessities toward the rear of the store hoping that shoppers will place more items in their basket on impulse as they move down the aisle to reach the milk, bread, or other necessities.

A variant of shopper patterns studies have been conducted on how music influences shopping behavior. One study found that slow tempo music slowed the pace of shopping in a grocery store and significantly increased the size of the grocery bill.[6] In a study conducted in a restaurant, a researcher observed patrons consuming more alcoholic beverages and staying longer, but consuming about the same amount of food when slow tempo music was played rather than tunes with a fast tempo.[7]

Content Analysis

Content analysis
A technique used to study written material (usually advertising copy) by breaking it into meaningful units, using carefully applied rules.

Content analysis is an observation technique used to analyze written material (usually advertising copy) into meaningful units using carefully applied rules.[8] It is an objective, systematic description of the communication's content. These communications can be analyzed at many levels such as image, words, or roles depicted. Thus, a researcher using content analysis attempts to determine what is being communicated to a target audience.

One study, for example, noted that the Federal Trade Commission adopted an advertising substantiation program.[9] The goal of the program was to provide information that might aid consumers in making rational choices, as well as evidence that would enhance competition by encouraging competitors to challenge advertising claims. Content analysis was used to measure the change in the content of advertisements before and after the substantiation program. In this case, the researchers looked at product attributes and claims, the level of verification in the ads, and how informative the ads were. The study found that the number of claims had declined and the level of verification had increased. The general level of informativeness did not change.

Another study hypothesized that due to the growing number of elderly Americans, advertisers would use more elderly models in their promotions. The researchers found there was, in fact, a significant increase in the use of the elderly in advertisements over the past three decades. The research also found that the elderly were often portrayed in relatively prestigious work situations, and that older men were used much more frequently in ads than older women.[10]

Humanistic Inquiry

A new to marketing and controversial research method that relies heavily on observation is **humanistic inquiry**.[11] The humanistic approach advocates immersing the researcher in the system under study rather than the traditional scientific method, in which the researcher stands apart from the system being studied. Thus, the traditional researcher might conduct a large-scale survey or experiment to test a hypothesis, whereas the humanist engages in "investigator immersion." That is, the researcher becomes part of the group he or she is studying.

Humanistic inquiry
A research method in which the researcher is immersed in the system or group under study.

One humanist researcher was interested in interpreting the consumption values and lifestyles of old-line white, Anglo-Saxon Protestant (WASP) consumers. For eighteen months the researcher engaged in field visits to Richmond, Virginia; Charleston, South Carolina; Wilton, Connecticut; and Kennebunkport, Maine. She participated in organizations and observed WASP consumers at work, at play, eating dinner, attending church, discussing politics, and shopping in department stores and supermarkets.

Throughout the immersion process, the humanist researcher maintains two diaries or logs. One is a **theory-construction diary** that documents in detail the thoughts, premises, hypotheses, and revisions in thinking developed by the researcher. The theory-construction diary is vital to humanist inquiry because it shows the process by which the researcher has come to understand the phenomenon.

Theory-construction diary
A journal that documents in detail the thoughts, premises, hypotheses, and revisions in thinking of a humanistic researcher.

The second set of notes maintained by the humanist researcher is a **methodological log**. In it are kept detailed and time-sequenced notes on the investigative techniques used during the inquiry, with special attention to biases or distortions a given technique may have introduced. The investigative techniques almost always include participant observation and may be supplemented by audiotape or videotape recordings, artifacts (e.g., shopping lists, garbage), and supplemental

Methodological log
A journal of detailed and time-sequenced notes on the investigative techniques used during a humanistic inquiry, with special attention to biases or distortions a given technique may have introduced.

documentation (e.g., magazine articles, health records, survey data, census reports).

To assess whether the interpretation is drawn in a logical and unprejudiced manner from the data gathered and the rationale employed, humanistic inquiry relies on the judgment of an outside auditor or auditors. These individuals should be researchers themselves, familiar with the phenomena under study. Their task is to review the documentation, field notes, methodological diary, and other supportive evidence gathered by the investigator to confirm (or disconfirm) that the conclusions reached do flow from the information collected.

Audits

Audit
The examination and verification of the sale of a product.

Audits are another category of human observation research. An audit is examination and verification of the sale of a product. Audits generally fall into two categories: retail audits that measure sales to final consumers, and wholesale audits that determine the amount of product movement from warehouses to retailers. Wholesalers and retailers allow auditors into their stores and stockrooms and allow them to examine the company's sales and order records to verify product flows. In turn, the retailers and wholesalers receive cash compensation and basic reports about their operations from the audit firms.

Because of the availability of scanner-based data (discussed later in the chapter), physical audits at the retail level may someday all but disappear. Already the largest nonscanner-based wholesale audit company, SAMI, is out of business. Its client list was sold to Information Resources Incorporated (IRI), a company that specializes in providing scanner data. Also, A. C. Nielsen, the largest retail audit organization, no longer uses auditors in grocery stores. The data is entirely scanner based. Nielsen uses both auditors and scanner data for other types of retail outlets. This will probably shift to scanner only when a large majority of retailers within a store category (e.g., hardware stores, drug stores) install scanners.

A. C. Nielsen Retail Index

A. C. Nielsen conducts its audits at the retail, rather than the wholesale level. Nielsen claims the following disadvantages for wholesale auditing:

- Obviously such records do not measure *sales:* they report only movement of goods from one point in the distribution chain to another.
- They do not cover the entire *range* of movement; overlooked completely are goods shipped directly from manufacturers to retailers.
- They cannot possibly reflect product movement to the thousands of stores buying from warehouses that are unwilling or unable to provide information.
- They cannot contain the breadth of information available through on-the-scene, in-store measurements: price, distribution, out-of-stock, store promotion, display, and the like; information so important in evaluating the performance of new or existing products in national, regional, or test markets.[12]

A. C. Nielsen Retail Index
Audit of food, household supplies, beauty aids, etc. at the retail level.

Nielsen divides the forty-eight contiguous states into strata based on geography, population, and store type, and sales volume. The following types of data are provided in the **A. C. Nielsen Retail Index.**

- *Sales to Consumers.* Company sales and sales' share, the same for competitors and total product class sales; reported nationally, by region, sales area, and store type.
- *Retailer Purchases.* Total merchandise purchased by retailers is reported in the same form as sales; that is, by brand, product class, major market divisions, and so on.
- *Retail Inventories.* Inventories are reported in the same manner as sales, but volume and share totals refer to the projected amount of unsold merchandise held by retailers. To complement volume information, Nielsen computes maximum distribution and out-of-stock for each brand on a store count basis, average inventories per store in stock, average monthly sales per store handling, and an index of a month's supply. These retail inventory data may enable management to assess retailer (sales) intentions toward a brand (and competitors') and evaluate inventory sufficiency relative to current and future sales rates.
- *Prices and Retailers' Gross Profit.* Provides the average price charged consumers for each brand, by size, type, and area, as well as the retailers' average margin of profit on each item for large independents. An analysis of the retail price structure of a brand (and its competitors) enables a manager to assess the impact of pricing policies on brand progress.
- *Distribution and Out-of-Stock.* Reflects the extent to which each major brand is exposed to all grocery activity based on the total sales of the stores handling each brand. Out-of-stock figures reveal the relative importance of stores without the item on the date of audit but handling the item during the two month period between audits. These data, reported nationally and by market divisions, provide a revealing picture of sales success in getting distribution among important retail outlets.

TABLE 6.2   *Nielsen Retail Index Auditing*

"Alpha" brand of Spot Remover—3 oz. in Super X Market

INVENTORY		FOR JUNE-JULY PKGS. VALUE	
May 30	114 Pkgs.		
July 30	93 Pkgs.		
Change		21	
PURCHASES			
From manufacturer (1 order)		12	$ 3.72
From wholesalers (4 orders)		48	15.00
Total		60	$18.72
CONSUMER SALES			
Packages		81	
Price, per pkg.			$ .39
Dollars, total			$31.59
ADV. 1 2 3 4 5			
6 7 8 9			
DISPLAY X		SELLING PRICE 39¢	
		SPECIAL PRICE 35¢	

Source: A.C. Nielsen Company.

- *Special Factory Packs.* Cents-off merchandise, banded combinations reflecting price reductions, and 1¢ deals, for example, are reported separately for each listed brand to appraise their sales influence and impact.
- *Retailer Support.* Local advertising, in-store displays, and special prices are reported for each brand in terms of exposure to all-commodity sales nationally and by Nielsen territory. These data give a picture of the cooperation and support provided by retailers in response to trade deals, advertising allowances, and so on.[13]

Table 6.2 illustrates how a Nielsen auditor computes sales and inventories for each item audited. In the example, total sales of the item during the period amounted to eighty-one units (a twenty-one unit change in inventory plus purchases of sixty units during the period). The brand was on display, and had been advertised six separate times, by the retailer, during the period covered. The item was selling for 39¢ on the date of audit, but had been advertised at a special price of 35¢ during the period, as noted. The Nielsen auditor, in recording inventories, separates the inventory of each item on a reserve versus forward basis. As a result, it is possible to break down the store inventories as to percentage in the selling area of the store (visible to customers) versus inventory in the reserve or storage areas.

The Importance of Audits to the Japanese

When Sony researched the market for a lightweight portable cassette player, results showed that consumers would not buy a tape player that did not record. Company chairman Akio Morita decided to introduce the Walkman anyway, and the rest is history. Today it is one of Sony's most successful products. Morita's disdain for large-scale consumer surveys and other scientific research tools is not unique in Japan. Matsushita, Toyota, and other well-known Japanese consumer goods companies are just as skeptical about the Western style of market research.

MACHINE OBSERVATION

The observation methods discussed so far have involved people observing things (audits) or consumers. Now we turn our attention to machines observing people and things.

Traffic Counters

Traffic counters
Machines used to measure vehicular flow over a particular stretch of roadway.

Perhaps the most common and popular form of machine-based observation research (other than scanners) is **traffic counters**. As the name implies, the machines are used to measure the vehicular flow over a particular stretch of roadway. Outdoor advertisers rely on traffic counts to determine the number of exposures per day to a specific billboard. Retailers use the information to ascertain where to place a particular type of store. Convenience stores, for example, require a moderately high traffic volume to reach target levels of profitability.

GLOBAL
MARKETING
RESEARCH

Japanese-style market research relies heavily on two kinds of information: "soft data" obtained from visits to dealers and other channel members and "hard data" about shipments, inventory levels, and retail sales. Japanese managers believe that these data better reflect the behavior and intentions of flesh-and-blood consumers. When Japanese managers want hard data to compare their products to competitors', they look at inventory, sales, and other information that show the items' actual movement through the channels. Then they visit channel members at both the retail and wholesale levels to analyze sales and distribution coverage reports, monthly product movement records (weekly for some key stores), plant-to-wholesaler shipment figures, and syndicated turnover and shipment statistics on competitors.

Japanese managers routinely monitor their markets at home and abroad this way. Consider how Matsushita dealt with the weak performance of its Panasonic distributor in South Africa. The sales figures he reported were reasonable, but he could not produce reliable data on sales and shares for the various types of stores or on inventory levels in the distribution chain.

A few years ago, three managers from the company's household electronics division paid a call on the South African distributor. Then they dropped in on the distributor's retail stores and wholesale facilities. After exchanging greetings and presenting a token gift from headquarters, they got right down to business. They asked to see inventory, shipment, and sales records as part of a complete store audit covering Matsushita and competitive products. Six weeks later, after analyzing all the data, they gave the incredulous distributor a complete picture of Panasonic's product movement and market share through the entire South African channel. They also told the distributor what figures he should collect and report to the home office in the future.[14]

Physiological Measurement

When an individual is aroused, feels inner tension, or alertness, it is referred to as *activation*.[15] Activation is stimulated via a subcortical unit, called the *reticular activation system* (RAS), located in the human brain stem. The sight of a product or advertisement, for example, can activate the RAS. As a result of directly provoking arousal processes in the RAS, there is an increase in the processing of information. Researchers have used a number of devices to measure the level of a person's activation.

EEG. The **electroencephalogram (EEG)** is a machine that measures rhythmic fluctuations in the electric potential in the brain. It is probably the most versatile and sensitive procedure for detecting arousal, but involves expensive equipment, a laboratory environment, and complex data analysis using special software programs. Researchers claim that EEG measures can be used to assess, among other effects, viewers' attention to an advertisement at specific points in time, the intensity of the emotional reactions elicited by specific aspects of the ad, and their

Electroencephalogram (EEG)
A machine that measures the rhythmic fluctuations in electrical potential of the brain.

comprehension and attention to the ad.[16] Other researchers have disputed the value of EEG for marketing research because of the cost of equipment and the special environment required.[17]

Galvanic skin response (GSR)
The measurement of changes in the electric resistance of the skin associated with activation responses.

GSR. The **galvanic skin response (GSR)**, also known as the *electrodermal response*, measures changes in the electric resistance of the skin associated with activation responses. A small electric current of constant intensity is sent into the skin through electrodes attached to the palmar side of the fingers. The changes in voltage observed between the electrodes indicate the level of stimulation. Because the equipment is portable and not expensive, the GSR is the most popular device for measuring activation. The GSR is used primarily to measure stimulus response to advertisements, but is sometimes used in packaging research.

Inner Response Incorporated uses the GSR to evaluate commercials. In one Eastman Kodak Company film-processing ad, Inner Response determined that the viewers' interest level built slowly in the opening scenes, rose when a snapshot of an attractive young woman was shown, but spiked highest when a picture appeared of a smiling, pigtailed girl. Kodak then knew which scenes had the highest impact, and could retain them when making changes in the spot or cutting it to fifteen seconds from thirty.[18]

Pupilometer
A machine that measures changes in pupil dilation.

Pupilometer. The **pupilometer** measures changes in pupil dilation. The basic assumption is that increased pupil size reflects positive attitudes, interest, and arousal in an advertisement. The subjects view an advertisement while brightness and distance from the screen are held constant. The pupilometer has fallen from favor among many researchers because pupil dilation appears to measure some combination of arousal, mental effort, processing load, and anxiety.[19] Arousal alone is much better measured by means of GSR.

Voice pitch analysis
The study of changes in the relative vibration frequency of the human voice to measure emotion.

Voice Pitch Analysis. **Voice pitch analysis** examines changes in the relative vibration frequency of the human voice to measure emotion. In voice analysis, the normal or baseline pitch of an individual's speaking voice is charted by engaging the subject in an unemotional conversation. The greater the deviation from the baseline, the greater is said to be the emotional intensity of the person's reaction to a stimulus, such as a question. There are several advantages of voice pitch analysis over other forms of physiological measurement:

- It records without physically connecting wires and sensors to the subject.
- The subject need not be aware of the record and analysis.
- The nonlaboratory setting overcomes the weaknesses of an artificial environment.
- It provides instantaneous evaluation of answers and comments.[20]

Voice pitch analysis has been used in package research, to predict consumer brand preference for dog food, and to determine which consumers from a target group would be most predisposed to try a new product.[21] Other research has applied voice analyses to measure consumers' emotional responses to advertising.[22] Validity of the studies to date have been subject to serious question.[23]

The devices just discussed are used to measure involuntary changes in an individual's physiological makeup. Arousal produces adrenaline, which enhances the activation process via a faster heart rate, increased blood flow, an increase in skin temperature and perspiration, pupil dilation, and an increase in brain wave frequency. Researchers often impute information about attitudes and feelings based on these measures.

Opinion and Behavior Measurement

People Reader.   The Pretesting Company has invented a device called the **People Reader.** The machine looks like a lamp and is designed so that when respondents sit in front of it they are not aware it is simultaneously recording both the reading material and their eyes. The self-contained unit is totally automatic and can record any respondent—with or without glasses—without the use of attachments, chin rests, helmets, or special optics. It allows respondents to read any size magazine or newspaper and lets them spend as much time as they need to go back and forth through the publication. Through the use of the People Reader and specially designed hidden cameras, the Pretesting Company has been able to document a number of pieces of information concerning both reading habits and the results of different size ads in terms of stopping power and brand-name recall. The company's research has found the following:

People Reader
A machine that simultaneously records the respondent's reading material and eye reactions.

- Nearly 40 percent of all readers start from either the back of a magazine or "fan" a magazine for interesting articles and ads. Less than half of the readers start from the very first page of a magazine.
- Rarely does a double-page ad provide more than 15 percent additional top-of-mind awareness than a single-page ad. Usually, the benefits of a double-page spread are additional involvement and communication, not top-of-mind awareness.
- In the typical magazine, nearly 35 percent of each of the ads receive less than two seconds' worth of voluntary examination.
- The strongest involvement power recorded for ads has been three or more successive single-page ads on the right-hand side of a magazine.

The People Reader lamp system inconspicuously records the reading habits of test subjects and measures the effectiveness of print advertisements. (Courtesy of The Pretesting Company, Inc.)

Remote control cameras and a camera which fits into a product or package are also used to observe consumer's actions. (Courtesy of The Pretesting Company, Inc.)

■ Because most ads "hide" the name of the advertisers and do not show a close-up view of the product package, brand-name confusion is greater than 50 percent on many products such as cosmetics and clothing.

■ A strong ad that is above average in stopping power and communication will work regardless of which section of the magazine it is placed. It will also work well in any type of ad or editorial environment. However, an ad that is below average in stopping power and involvement will be seriously affected by the surrounding environment.[24]

People meter
A microwave computerized rating system that transmits demographic information overnight to measure national TV audiences.

People Meters. In 1987, A. C. Nielsen announced that it would use its **people meter** to measure the size of television audiences. The system is a microwave computerized rating system that transmits demographic information overnight to measure national TV audiences. It replaces the thirty-year-old National Audience Composition (NAC) diary system used to record this information. The people meter provides information on what TV shows are being watched, the number of households watching, and which family members are watching. The type of activity is recorded automatically; household members merely have to indicate their presence by pressing a button.

The introduction of people meters caused considerable concern among networks, ad agencies, and advertisers who requested caution by Nielsen in the implementation of the device. The people meters, network research officials contend, gives younger viewers, who are less resistant to technology, a greater voice; older people, less patient with new devices and reluctant to press buttons, would be underrepresented. It is also contended that children under ten years old will be especially unreliable button pushers. A recent study has shown that "button pushing fatigue" sets in before the end of two years.[25]

To offset the problems of the people meter, a new system has been made available to monitor viewers' faces with a cameralike device. The passive system uses a recorder programmed to recognize faces and note electronically when specific members of a family watch TV. The system notes when viewers leave the room and even when they avert their eyes from the screen.

Nielsen Media Research, the Dun & Bradstreet Corporation unit that compiles national TV ratings, worked jointly with the David Sarnoff Research Center of Princeton, New Jersey, to develop the system. Advertisers are demanding more proof of viewership, and the networks are under more pressure to show that advertising is reaching its intended targets. Ratings are used to help set prices for commercial time.

A Nielsen executive has said that a passive system should yield "even higher quality, more accurate data because the respondents don't have to do anything" other than "be themselves." The sensory equipment can be packaged to resemble a VCR and placed on top of the TV. It will electronically record the names of those it recognizes and the periods during which they watched TV. Strangers would be listed simply as visitors.[26] Already, however, the networks and advertisers are criticizing the passive people meter. One executive noted, "Who would want or allow one of those things in their bedroom?" Others claim that the system requires bright light to operate properly. Also, the box has limited peripheral vision, so it might not sense all of the people in a given room.

Nielsen rival Arbitron Company thinks it has developed a better device to measure television ratings. Arbitron has created a portable, personal, passive people meter. The Arbitron device won't be commercially available for several years and design plans are not yet final. However, it will be small enough to be carried or worn by each member of a household, perhaps in beeper, pin, or pendant form. More importantly, it would use a computer chip to measure both TV viewing and radio listening by a single consumer—offering advertisers, for the first time, an intimate peek into someone's combined media habits. Radio ratings today rely mostly on hand-scrawled diaries.

The new gadget would pick up audio signals encoded in the programs being watched or listened to, eliminating the risk that a lazy viewer would slack off and ignore punching in. Another prime advantage: it could stay with the roving viewer to measure radio habits in the car, TV habits at the local bar, and other out-of-home viewing that the people meter fails to pick up.[27]

Single-Source Research

E. D. Russell, director, Market Research Services of Campbell Soup Company, claims that **single-source research** is bringing ever closer "the Holy Grail" of market research: an accurate, objective picture of the direct causal relationship between different kinds of sales and marketing efforts and actual sales.[28]

A single-source supplier is capable of providing the client an integrated measurement system of key marketing inputs (or variables) that drive product sales. By definition, a single-source system gathers its information from a single panel of respondents by continuously monitoring the advertising and promotion the panel is exposed to and what it subsequently buys. The variables measured are advertising campaigns, coupons, displays, and product prices. This creates a huge database of marketing efforts and resultant consumer behavior.

Two electronic monitoring tools create the single-source system: television meters and laser **scanners**, which "read" the UPC codes on products and produce instantaneous information on sales. Separately, each monitoring device provides marketers with current information on the advertising audience and on sales and inventories of products. Together, television meters and scanners measure the impact of marketing.

The development of single-source research has been slow for several reasons. One problem has been cost. An estimated $100 million has been spent on developing single-source systems, not easily justified in the market research industry obsessed with the bottom line. Cost justification, in terms of profit potential, has made the builders of these systems spread the risk by stretching out the development time. Technology is another problem. Hard technology adaptation to single-source use has been slower than expected. Some of the technology is the nonpassive type, such as home scanners and people meters. This raises questions of bias, requiring validation, a time-consuming process. The soft technology development has also been slower than expected. The enormous computer capacity required to collect, process, and store the information databases has been consistently underestimated. Moreover, users of scanner data have been overwhelmed with the massive amounts of data. Marketing decision makers need information only if it can help them make decisions. Management needs decision-making information, not data. Therefore, suppliers of scanner data have created expert systems to give the data more utility for the managers (examples of these systems will be described later).

Single-source research
A single database, derived from scanner data, containing all relevant data on manipulation of the marketing mix at the household level of aggregation.

Scanners
Devices that read the UPC codes on products and produce instantaneous information on sales.

The marriage of scanners, database management, telecommunications, artificial intelligence, and computing gives hope for a "brave new world" of marketing.

The two major single source suppliers are Information Resources Incorporated (IRI) and the A. C. Nielsen Company; each has about half of the market.[29] To gain an appreciation of the single-source concept, we will examine IRI in more detail.

BehaviorScan.   IRI is the founder of scanner-based research. Its first product is called **BehaviorScan.**[30] A proprietary household panel of some 3,000 households has been recruited and maintained in each BehaviorScan minimarket. Panel members shop with an ID card, which is presented at checkout in scanner-equipped grocery and drug stores, allowing IRI to electronically track each household's purchasing, item by item, over time. With such a measure of household purchasing it is possible to manipulate marketing variables, such as TV advertising or consumer promotions or introduce a new product and analyze real changes in consumer buying behavior.

For strategic tests of alternative marketing plans, the BehaviorScan household panels are split into two or more subgroups, perfectly balanced on past purchasing, demographics, and stores shopped. For advertising issues, commercials can be substituted at the individual household level, allowing one subgroup to view a test commercial, the other a control ad. This makes BehaviorScan the most effective means to evaluate changes in advertising weight, copy, and time of day the ad ran. In each market, IRI maintains permanent warehouse facilities and has an in-market staff to control distribution, price, and promotions. Competitive activity in all categories is monitored and a complete record of pricing, displays, and features permits an assessment of the promotion responsiveness to a brand.

The BehaviorScan markets are geographically dispersed cities: Pittsfield, Massachusetts; Marion, Indiana; Eau Claire, Wisconsin; Midland, Texas; Grand Junction, Colorado; and Cedar Rapids, Iowa. For testing consumer promotions such as coupons, sampling, or refund offers, balanced panel subsamples are created within each market. Then through direct mail or split newspaper-route targeting, a different treatment is delivered to each group. Both sales and profit are analyzed.

In-store variables may also be tested. Within the markets, split groups of stores are used to read the effect on sales of a change in packaging, shelf placement, or pricing. Tests are analyzed primarily on a store movement basis, but analysis of purchasing by panel shoppers in the test and control stores is also possible. With the BehaviorScan system, it is possible to test alternative advertising levels while simultaneously varying in-store prices or consumer promotions, thereby testing a completely integrated marketing plan.

In summary, BehaviorScan allows marketing managers to answer critical marketing questions such as

- How many consumers try my brand and how many buy again?
- What volume level will my brand achieve in one year? In two years?
- Will my line extension "steal" share from its parent brand?
- What flavor mix will maximize trial?
- Does increased advertising or new copy increase sales?
- What are the implications of a change in price, package, or shelf placement?
- Who are my brand's buyers and what else do they buy?

BehaviorScan
A single source system that maintains a 3,000 household panel to record consumer purchases based upon manipulation of the marketing mix.

InfoScan.   IRI's most successful product, with sales of over $120 million per year, is **InfoScan**.[31] InfoScan is a scanner-based, national and local market tracking service for the consumer packaged goods industry. Retail sales, detailed consumer purchasing information (including measurement of store loyalty and total grocery basket expenditures), and promotional activity (trade and consumer) are monitored and evaluated for all UPC-coded products (see Figures 6.1 and 6.2). InfoScan collects weekly purchase data from 2,700 supermarkets, 500 drug stores, and 250 mass merchandisers. This results in a household panel of approximately 60,000 households. Over time, this has created a huge secondary database. IRI has taken the database and examined 780 brands in 116 different packaged goods product categories. In such a database, IRI has what it refers to as thousands and thousands of "naturally occurring experiments." That is to say, hundreds of thousands of data points relating weekly sales to price reductions and merchandising activity. Using the database, the IRI researchers were able to look at a variety of marketing mixes and competitive situations and determine the results of managerial decision

InfoScan
A scanner-based tracking service for consumer packaged goods.

FIGURE 6.1   *How InfoScan Works*

 UPC's for each grocery item are scanned at checkout. Information is sent from store to chain and on to IRI via telecommunication systems.

 Household panel members present an identification card at checkout which identifies and assigns items purchased to that household. Coupons are collected and matched to the appropriate UPC. Information is electronically communicated to IRI computers.

 IRI field personnel visually survey stores and all print media to record retailers' merchandising efforts, displays and ad features. Field personnel also survey retail stores for a variety of custom applications, e.g. average number of units per display, space allocated to specific sections, and number of facings. Results are electronically communicated to IRI computers.

 Household panel members are selected for television monitoring and equipped with meters which automatically record the set's status every five seconds. Information is relayed back to IRI's computers.

Information is received at IRI and processed through the Neural Network (Artificial Intelligence) Quality Control System. The system approves the over 35 million records obtained weekly for further data processing and identifies records that require further verification.

 Completed data bases are converted to the required client format, transferred to appropriate recording mediums... hard copy, mag tape, pc diskette, etc.... and sent to the subscriber.

Source: Information Resources, Inc.

FIGURE 6.2 *Sources of Data to InfoScan*

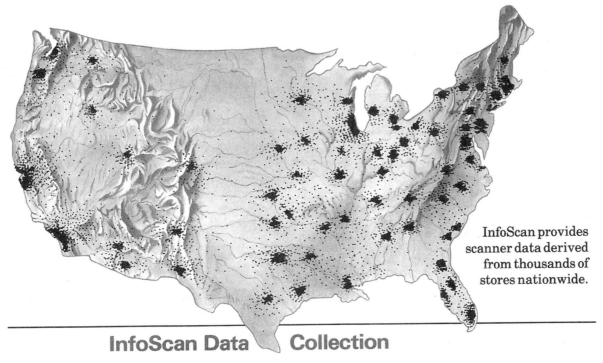

InfoScan provides
scanner data derived
from thousands of
stores nationwide.

InfoScan Data   Collection

Source: Information Resources, Inc.

making. For example, using thousands of data points, IRI looked at the weekly sales response of an average brand to trade promotions (see Figure 6.3). The numbers are all expressed as a percentage over base sales (i.e., the sales level that one would observe with no trade support). IRI found that a 10 percent price reduction, on average, led to a 20 percent sales increase during the week of the price reduction. Adding a feature ad to the price reduction generated a 78 percent sales increase during the promoted week. An in-store display with a 10 percent price reduction doubled sales. An in-store display, coupled with a feature ad and a 10 percent price reduction, tripled sales. Further examination of the database produced other interesting results. These included the following:

1. *Advertising Weight Testing.* The traditional view of the impact of ad weight (advertising expenditures) would hold that increased weight could be expected to result in a sales increase, if one had good copy. In at least 50 percent of the tests involving increased weight, IRI found a significant sales increase. Not surprisingly, the absolute success levels were higher for new brands than for established brands. Presumably, this was because the job of advertising in generating sales increases is somewhat easier for new brands, where simply building awareness is often the key objective.

2. *Copy Testing.* The traditional view is that good copy can be expected to have a relatively immediate impact on sales. IRI completed a detailed analysis of all the copy tests that had been conducted in BehaviorScan with the objective of

understanding the speed with which the effect of copy on sales could be measured. Over two-thirds of the tests conducted in BehaviorScan revealed sales differences of at least 10 percent between the copy alternatives being tested within a three-month period. Approximately 75 percent of the tests showed at least a 10 percent sales difference within four months. And if a sales difference was generated initially, it almost invariably continued through the end of the test. This confirmed that a good creative effort could generate a sales increase— and maintain it.[32]

IRI's Software.   As mentioned previously, managers want decision-making information, not data. The key to IRI's success is not the 35 million new scanner records it obtains each week, but the useful information derived from those records. Useful information for management is gleaned from powerful software. For example, IRI's Apollo Space Management Software helps answer one of the most fundamental questions faced by manufacturers and retailers, What is the most optimal use of retail shelf space—the most valuable asset in any store? Apollo analyzes scanner data from the InfoScan database to review the amount of shelf space, price, and profit components of product category shelf sets such as dishwashing soaps or

FIGURE 6.3   *Topical Report on Trade Promotions: Average Category Response to Trade Promotions*

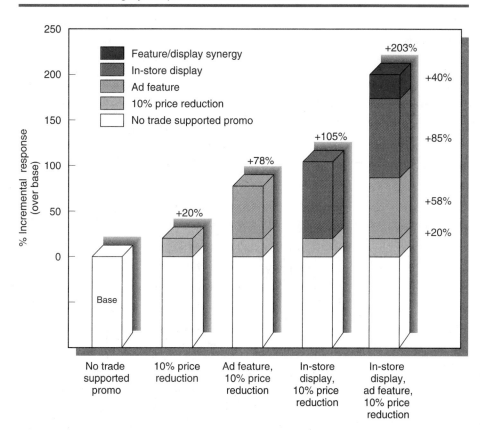

Source: Information Resources Inc.

CoverStory
An expert software system for analyzing massive scanner databases and to prepare a cover memo of the findings.

Sales Partner
Software designed for manufacturers for selling their products to retailers using the retailers' own scanner data.

cereals. It then provides actionable suggestions for optimizing shelf allocations for each item in the section. Apollo also can produce photo-quality schematics using its library of 120,000 product images and dimensions. Thus, the retailer gets a visual picture of what the shelf reallocation will look like (see Figure 6.4).

CoverStory is an IRI expert software system designed to cut the mass of scanner data down to actionable pieces of information. The goal of CoverStory is to provide a cover memo, like the one a marketing researcher would write, to describe the key events reflected in a database. The system locates the important "news" and writes a memo for managers complete with charts, tables, and graphs (see Figure 6.5). Other IRI software available to its clients include Express, used to analyze large databases, and Data Server, which provides PC decision support access to databases maintained on a mainframe. **Sales Partner** is designed to help manufacturers selling to retailers by using the retailers' own scanner data. The Sales Partner software sorts through the data to provide the most convincing arguments a sales representative can use on the retailer. The argument may be increasing promotional support for the manufacturer's brand, replacing a competitive brand with the manufacturer's brands not currently stocked, or some other point.[33]

The Scanner Wars—IRI versus Nielsen.   Like two heavyweight boxers, IRI and A. C. Nielsen are continually punching and counterpunching each other in the large and rapidly growing scanner data market. Each is seeking a competitive advantage

FIGURE 6.4   *IRI's Apollo Space Management Software with Advanced Digitized Imaging Can Produce Photo Quality Schematics of Optimal Shelf Allocations of Products*

Source: Information Resources, Inc.

FIGURE 6.5   *The First Page of a CoverStory Memorandum*

To:	**Director of Marketing**
From:	**CoverStory v1.3**
Date:	**October 24, 1991**
Subject:	**Maxwell House Caf Summary for Four Weeks Ending August 4, 1991 in Total US - Food - Evaluating share vs Year Ago**

Maxwell House Caf's share in Total US - Food was 13.2 share points in the Ground Coffee category for the four weeks ending 8/4/91. This is a decrease of -1.1 share points from a year earlier and a decrease of -0.7 from last period (4 Week Ending Jul 7, 91). This reflects volume sales of 6.5 million Equivalent Units - down -11.6 percent since last year.

Maxwell House Caf's share is 13.2 - down -1.1 share points from the same period last year.

Category volume (currently 49.1 million Equivalent Units) declined -4.3% from a year earlier.

Display activity and unsupported price cuts rose over the past year -unsupported price cuts from 61 points to 85. Price fell during the year by -9.1% to 2.78 dollars. Featuring (51 points of ACV), distribution (100 percent of ACV) remained at about the same level as a year earlier.

Components of Maxwell House Caf Volume

Among components of Maxwell House Caf, the principal gainer is:

Maxwell House OthPkg Caf: up +0.1 share points from last year to 0.8 pts

Losses occurred for:

Maxwell House Can Caf: down -0.6 to 10.2 pts

Maxwell House Bag Caf: down -0.6 to 2.3 pts

Maxwell House Bag Caf's share decrease coincides with a decrease in distribution of -8.9 percent of ACV versus a year ago and occurred despite a fall in price of -8.6% since last year. **Maxwell House Can Caf's** decrease happened even though there was also a decrease in price of -13.1% vs yr ago. **Maxwell House OthPkg Caf's** increase coincides with an increase in featuring of +20.8 points of ACV since last year and occurred despite a decrease in distribution of -1.7 percent of ACV since last year and an increase in price of +5.5% vs yr ago.

Competitor Summary

Among Maxwell House Caf's major competitors, the principal gainers are:

Folgers Caf: up +2.2 share points from last year to 24.7 pts

Savarin Caf: up +0.8 to 2.1 pts

Source: Information Resources Inc.

that will sway purchasers of scanner data (the most rapidly growing area of the marketing research industry). Scanner data revenues were over $500 million in 1993.[34] Kraft General Foods alone spends over $30 million a year for scanner data.[35]

A major difference between IRI and Nielsen is how the household level data is gathered. IRI scanner panel members present an ID card to the retailer, which is bar coded to identify the household making the purchase. Thus the data is captured at retail sites. Nielsen used a similar system consisting of 15,000 households until 1991. Nielsen phased out its in-store panel and substituted an in-home scanner panel (a photo of the household scanner is shown on page 69 in chapter 3). Nielsen households use a hand scanner, after shopping, to manually scan each purchase. In contrast, IRI's bar-coded identification card, which is used to scan the buyer's purchases, is a method of "passive collection." In 1992, Nielsen increased its panel size to 40,000 households and IRI to 60,000. Approximately 4,500 panel members will be connected to Nielsen's Monitor Plus TV program for tracking viewing using the people meter. Nielsen claims its panel will measure all geographic locations. Also, by scanning at home the system is not dependent on retailers that happen to be cooperating. Nielsen's panel covers some 1,147 counties, whereas IRI covers only 30 counties. Andy Tarshis, president of NPD/Nielsen says, "Can households in 30 counties be representative of the total United States?"[36] IRI executives counter Tarshis by asking, "How typical are households who agree to manually scan every item purchased after every shopping trip and then enter the price paid, coupon usage, and store name?" Tarshis also notes:

> "By increasing nearly threefold, our ability to do additional analysis increases maybe tenfold," he said. "For example, warehouse clubs are becoming popular, but not everyone is a member. But by expanding to 40,000, the number of households buying at the clubs may be 5,000, which is a much more usable number than we get from 15,000 households."
>
> The same is true for marketers interested in data from minorities. For example, 6 percent of the panel is Hispanic households; as the panel expands, that percentage becomes "a base large enough for us to do dramatically more analysis. We can compare Hispanic household trends on the East Coast vs. the West Coast or even look at a single market," Mr. Tarshis said. Nielsen intends to maintain at least 12 percent of the panel as black households, also enabling expanded analysis of that group.[37]

IRI's InfoScan was historically based upon cooperating supermarkets to supply scanner data. To counter Nielsen, IRI added 500 drug stores such as Walgreen's, Eckerd, and Drug Emporium. The company also added 250 mass merchandisers including Walmart, K Mart, and Target. This move was made because only 40 percent of health and beauty aid sales are realized in supermarkets. Another 40 percent is sold through drug stores, with the remaining 20 percent in mass merchandise outlets.[38] The new IRI sample, therefore, fills out the consumer package goods universe. In 1992 IRI provided its InfoScan panel members with a "keychain scanner," a portable, pocket-sized wand to register any product purchases made at nonscanner stores.[39]

And so the battle continues. Some scanner data users give Nielsen the edge in data capture and IRI the software advantage. To complicate matters, a third research company, Arbitron, entered the fray with ScanAmerica service. Arbitron, however, folded ScanAmerica in September 1992 because of a lack of sales.[40]

Retailers Are Also Conducting Scanning Research

Retailers are not only purchasing scanner-based research from marketing researchers, they are also conducting their own tests.[41] With a better knowledge of what to stock, how to display it, and how to price and promote the brand for maximum profit, retailers can improve their profit margins and become less dependent on price-cutting promotions. Scanner-based research will help retailers kill off slow moving brands and brands with poor profit margins.

Safeway Stores tests the effect of end-of-aisle displays on sales, even if such displays are not accompanied by price reductions or advertising. Scanner data can show, for example, whether multiproduct or single-product displays yield the most sales. Price elasticity also is tested. Safeway varies prices and display support and analyzes the results. "Although retailers are generally not fond of lowering prices drastically, we found that in some cases the volume of sales associated with the lower price ended up providing both the producer and the retailer with more profits than the 'normal' price," according to Louise Booth, manager of scanner research, Safeway Stores.[42]

Safeway used scanner data to test alternative placements of products within a store. Results showed, for example, that foil-packaged sauce mixes should not be displayed together but spread around the store according to their contents (spaghetti sauce mix near bottled spaghetti sauce, gravy mix near canned gravy, etc.). Another scanner test showed that sales increase 80 percent when candy bars are put on front-end racks near checkout stands. The finding led to a divisional policy change, Booth said.[43]

In 1990, Safeway created Safeway Scanner Marketing Research (SSMRS). Its first product is called StoreLab. Clients can test the effectiveness of off-shelf displays, shelf extenders, in-store signs, new package designs or sizes, and consumer bonus packages. Twenty Safeway stores, all equipped with scanners and all in the Denver metropolitan area, serve as StoreLab sites. SSMRS can match stores on category sales and provide aggregated data for clients in a customized format.[44]

The Future of Scanning

The next generation of scanners, to be known as Scanner Plus, will have abilities far beyond those of today's machines. These scanners will be able to communicate with personal computers in homes. One function could be to analyze an individual household's consumption based on its prior purchase patterns and offer menu projections or product use suggestions with an associated shopping list. To encourage the use of that shopping list, special offers may be made on certain listed items. These special offers can be designed for each household, rather than offering everyone the same promotion.

Scanner Plus may also keep track of each household's coupons and other special offers received directly from advertisers. These offers will simply be entered into the household's electronic account in both the household's personal computer as well as its "promotion" bank in Scanner Plus.

An example of a similar system already in use is the Vision Value card offered by Big Bear Supermarkets in Ohio. They combine scanning with the computerized equivalent of "green stamps" to provide consumers with coupons for products they actually use.

How will this new development affect marketing research? Advertisers will want to test the previously untestable, namely, how is a product's acceptance affected by a household's menu, or what is the optimum menu scenario for a product's particular set of attributes? Advertisers will want to test promotion values as a function of menu mix and repeat consumption, rather than today's criteria of covering the cost of the promotion.[45]

SUMMARY

Observation research is the systematic process of recording the behavioral patterns of people, objects, and occurrences without questioning or communicating with them. To be successful, the needed information must be observable and the behavior of interest must be repetitive, frequent, or predictable in some manner. The behavior of interest should also be of a relatively short duration. There are five dimensions along which observational approaches vary: (1) natural versus contrived situations, (2) open versus disguised situations, (3) structured versus unstructured observation, (4) human versus machine observers, and (5) direct versus indirect observation.

The biggest advantage of observation research is that we can see what people actually do rather than having to rely on what they say they did. Also some forms of data are more quickly and accurately gathered by observation. The primary disadvantage of this type of research is that the researcher learns nothing about motives, attitudes, intentions, or feelings.

People watching people can take the form of mystery shoppers; one-way mirror observations, such as child psychologists watching children play with toys; shopper patterns; content analysis; humanistic inquiry; and audits.

Machine observation includes traffic counters, physiological measurement devices, the People Reader, people meters, and scanners. The use of scanners in carefully controlled experimental settings enables the market researcher to accurately and objectively measure the direct causal relationship between different kinds of marketing efforts and actual sales. The leaders in this so-called single-source type of research are Information Resources and A. C. Nielsen.

Retailers, such as Safeway, are now offering their stores as testing laboratories for manufacturers. Packaged goods producers can vary prices, promotion techniques, and package design and capture sales results via scanners. In the future scanners will be able to communicate with personal computers in homes. One function may be to offer menu and product use suggestions.

KEY TERMS

Observation research
Open observation
Disguised observation
Structured observation
Unstructured observation
Mystery shoppers
One-way mirror observations
Shopper patterns

Content analysis
Humanistic inquiry
Theory-construction diary
Methodological log
Audit
A. C. Nielsen Retail Index
Traffic counters
Electroencephalogram (EEG)

Galvanic skin response (GSR)
Pupilometer
Voice pitch analysis
People Reader
People meter
Single-source research

Scanners
BehaviorScan
InfoScan
CoverStory
Sales Partner

REVIEW AND DISCUSSION QUESTIONS

1. You are charged with the responsibility of determining whether men are brand conscious when shopping for racquetball equipment. Outline an observation research procedure for making that determination.

2. Fisher-Price has asked you to develop a research procedure for determining which of their prototype toys is most appealing to 4- and 5-year-olds. Suggest a methodology for making this determination.

3. What are the biggest drawbacks of observation research?

4. Compare and contrast the advantages and disadvantages of observation research versus survey research.

5. It has been said that, "People buy things not for what they will do, but for what they mean." Discuss this statement in relation to observation research.

6. You are a manufacturer of a premium brand of ice cream. You want to know more about your market share, competitors' pricing, and types of outlets where your product is selling best. What kind of observational research data would you purchase? Why?

7. How might a mystery shopper be valuable to the following organizations: (a) Delta Airlines, (b)Marshall Field's, (c) H & R Block.

8. Why do you think that the research method of humanistic inquiry has caused such a controversy among social scientists? How does it differ from the traditional scientific method?

9. Compare and contrast people meters and the traditional diary approach to measuring audience sizes. What sources of bias might be found in people meter data?

10. Why has single-source research been seen as "the ultimate answer?" Do you see any disadvantages of this methodology?

11. If you were going to purchase scanner data, would you prefer IRI or Nielsen's methodology? Why?

12. Explain the attitudinal versus behavioralist controversy in the marketing research industry. Where do you stand?

CASE

Sara Lee

Anita Scott has just been promoted to brand manager of frozen bakery products for Sara Lee. Her first new product introductions will be a line of frozen pastries. Currently, the company plans to introduce three flavors: chocolate, strawberry, and apricot. The pastries can be heated in a conventional oven or microwaved for quick preparation. Anita is considering using coupons in coordination with the introduction of the pastries. She has recently acquired some scanner data on coupon usage for new products. That information is presented in Tables 6.3–6.5 and Figures 6.6–6.9.

TABLE 6.3   *Coupon Usage on New Product Introductions*

Issues
  Values versus Established Brands
  Use of Coupons on Trial versus Repeat Purchase
  Coupon-Related Purchases versus Other Purchases

The Database

Markets: Evansville, IN
         Portland, ME

Time Period: 39 Weeks from Introduction

Categories, brands:

Ready-to-Eat Cereal	Cookies
Sun Flakes	Soft Batch
S'Mores	Duncan Hines
Fiber One	Puddin Creme
OJ's	Almost Home
Bran Muffin Crisp	Cereal Meal Bars
Almond Delight	S'Mores Chewy
Soluble Coffee	Dandy Bran
Classic	Rice Krispies
Silka	Whipps
Brava	Crackers
Decaf	Great Crisps
	Stone Creek

Sample Size: 3,912 Households

TABLE 6.4   *Index of Coupon Triers to Noncoupon Triers*

CATEGORY	VOLUME	PURCHASE OCCASIONS
Cereal	93%	91%
Soluble coffee	76	77
Cookies	83	82
Cereal meal bars	97	95
Crackers	84	88
Average	87*	87*

Note: The buyer attracted by a coupon did not purchase as much or as often as a buyer that tried without a coupon. This is particularly true for the coffee brands studied.
*"The households that initially tried with a coupon purchased only 87 percent as much as the households that tried without a coupon. This is linked to the fact that triers with coupons purchased only on 87 percent as many occasions."

TABLE 6.5 *Summation*

Coupon values on new brands are slightly higher in absolute face value than coupons on established brands. The percentage discount spread is greater since the average dollar transaction on new products purchased when a coupon is lower.

● Average coupon value

ESTABLISHED BRANDS		NEW BRANDS	
Value	*% Redeemed*	*Value*	*% Redeemed*
$.346	17.6%	$.380	22.0%

● Average retail price

ESTABLISHED	NEW/COUPON REDEMPTION PURCHASE
$1.96	$1.73

FIGURE 6.6 *The Effect of Face Value on Speed of Redemption*

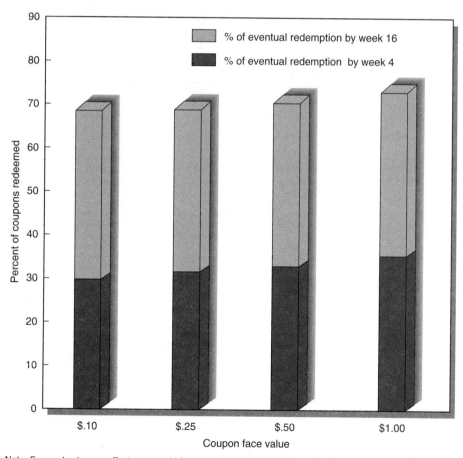

Note: Face value has no effect on speed of redemption at sixteen weeks after the coupon drop. At four weeks post, higher value coupons have achieved only a slightly higher percentage of eventual redemption than do lower value coupons.

FIGURE 6.7   *Percent of Volume with Coupon Redemption*

CATEGORY	ALL BRANDS	NEW BRANDS
Cereal	16.2%	24.8%
Soluble coffee	30.5	17.8
Cookies	6.7	17.6
Cereal meal bars	13.0	18.1
Crackers	7.1	14.8
Average	14.7%	18.6%

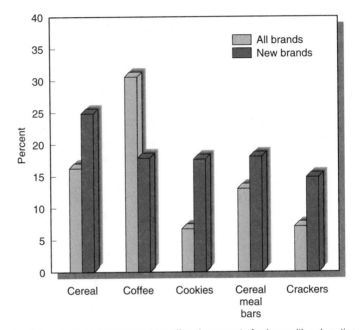

Note: For all new brands studied except soluble coffee, the percent of volume with redemption for new brands substantially exceeded existing brands. The relative difference is greatest in the cookie category.

FIGURE 6.8   *Percent of Buying Households Redeeming Coupons*

CATEGORY	ALL BRANDS	NEW BRANDS
Cereal	73.2%	45.8%
Soluble coffee	57.4	37.1
Cookies	42.0	49.0
Cereal meal bars	41.8	38.8
Crackers	46.3	26.8
Average	52.1%	39.5%

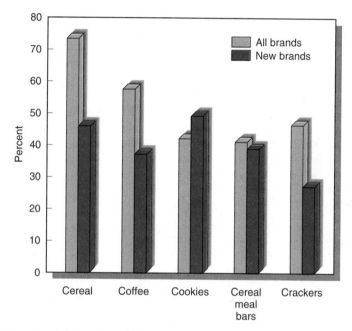

Note: For all new brands but cookies, a higher percentage of households buying on existing brands redeem coupons. This seeming discrepancy in cookies was probably caused by the coupon activity associated with the "Soft Cookie Wars."

FIGURE 6.9 *All Brands*

	OUNCES (000)	PERCENT OF TOTAL VOLUME	PERCENT OF TRIAL OR REPEAT VOLUME
Total volume	414.7	100.0%	
Trial volume	145.8	35.1	
With coupon	29.6	7.1	20.2
Without coupon	116.2	28.0	79.8
Repeat volume	268.9	64.9	
With coupon	46.7	11.3	17.4
Without coupon	222.2	53.6	82.6

Note: When all brands are combined, coupon trial was 20 percent of total trial and peaked in period 2. Coupon repeat equals 17 percent of total repeat volume and grew consistently as a percent of total volume.

1. After examining the scanner data, what kind of couponing strategy, including price, would you recommend for the pastry line?
2. What additional data would be useful to Anita in planning her couponing strategy?
3. What are some limitations that Anita should be aware of in utilizing the scanner data?

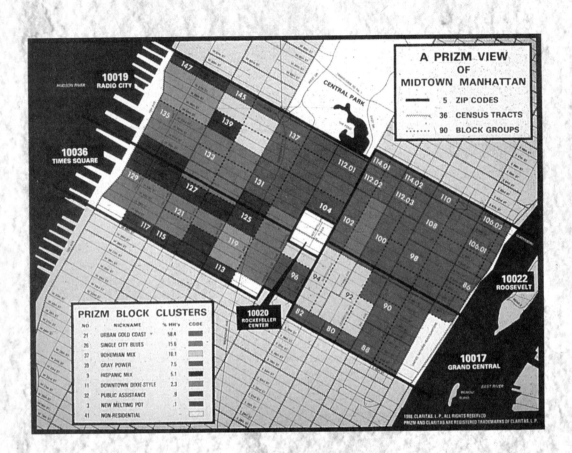

CHAPTER 7

Primary Data Collection: Survey Research

LEARNING OBJECTIVES

1. To understand the reasons for the popularity of surveys.

2. To learn the types of error in survey research.

3. To describe the types of surveys.

4. To gain insight into the factors that determine the choice of particular survey methods.

5. To realize the importance of the marketing research interviewer.

6. To appreciate the differences between domestic and international survey research.

f a researcher is looking for eager participants for a door-to-door survey, talk to western ranchers and southern country folk. But if you need to poll the rich or childless suburbanites, get ready for some hard work. Door-to-door surveys may yield an overall response rate of 70 percent, but the rate drops to 60 percent or less in these neighborhoods.

Knowing who will talk and who will refuse helps researchers design more accurate surveys. That's why Valentine Appel, senior vice president of Backer Spielvogel Bates, and Julian Baim, director of research for Mediamark Research, Inc., analyzed the response rates of different socioeconomic groups. Their tool was PRIZM, a data product from Claritas that divides all Americans into forty geodemographic clusters (with associated names). The four clusters most responsive to personal interviews were: Tobacco Roads (92 percent response rate), Share Croppers (88 percent), Norma-Rae-Ville (83 percent), and Back Country Folks (82 percent). All are characterized as blue-collar and farm workers living in small towns or rural areas of the South. The fifth-ranked cluster, Agri-Business (81 percent), is the wealthiest of this group and is the only one outside the South. This cluster is found in ranching, farming, lumbering, and mining areas of the Great Plains and Mountain states.

The least responsive clusters tend to be wealthy, childless metropolitan residents. They include Urban Gold Coast (62 percent), Money and Brains (60 percent), Blue Blood Estates (59 percent), Gray Power (58 percent), and Bohemian Mix (56 percent). Urban Gold Coast has the highest concentration of one-person households living in high-rise apartment buildings. Money and Brains people tend to live in swank townhouses. Blue Blood Estates are CEOs and heirs to "old money." Gray Power includes nearly 2 million affluent retired people. Bohemian Mix is an integrated, singles-dominated, high-rise hodgepodge of white-collar workers, students, divorced persons, and artists.

Baim and Appel analyzed their list for demographic characteristics such as income, education, home value, household type, and race. They found only one significant correlation: responsiveness increases as median home values decrease. A higher proportion of retired and relatively well-off householders will lower a neighborhood's response rates.

Researchers at J. D. Power and Associates, a firm who specializes in measuring automobile purchaser satisfaction, have found that cluster responsiveness varies greatly for surveys taken by mail. Tobacco Road residents are among the least likely to respond to a mail survey, for example, while Gray Power residents are far more likely to participate by mail.[1]

Survey research is the use of a questionnaire to gather facts, opinions, and attitudes. It is the most popular way to gather primary data. What are the various types of survey research? Why are some more popular than others? As noted previously, not everyone is willing to participate in a survey. What kind of error problems does that create? What are the other types of error in survey research? These questions will be answered in Chapter 7.

REASONS FOR THE POPULARITY OF SURVEYS

Some 126 million Americans have been interviewed at some point in their lives. Almost 72 million people were interviewed in 1990, which was 33 million more than in 1980. Americans spent 50 million hours responding to surveys in 1992. This is the equivalent of over 15 minutes per adult per year.[2] Surveys have a high rate of usage in marketing research compared to other means of collecting primary data for some very good reasons.

1. *The need to know why.* In marketing research there is generally a critical need to have some idea about why people do or do not do something. For example, why did they buy or not buy our brand? What did they like or dislike about it? Who or what influenced them? We do not mean to imply that surveys can prove causation. Only that they can be used to develop some idea of the causal forces at work.
2. *The need to know how.* At the same time, the marketing researcher often finds it necessary to understand the process consumers go through before taking some action. How did they make the decision? What time period passed? What did they examine or consider? When and where was the decision made? What do they plan to do next?
3. *The need to know who.* The marketing researcher also needs to know who the person is from a demographic or lifestyle perspective. Information on age, income, occupation, marital status, stage in the family life cycle, education, and other factors is necessary to the identification and definition of market segments.

TYPES OF ERROR IN SURVEY RESEARCH

When assessing the quality of information obtained from survey research, the manager must make some determination of the accuracy of those results. This requires careful consideration of the research methodology employed in relation to the various types of error that might result. The various types of error that might be encountered in a survey are shown in Figure 7.1.

Sampling Error

Two major types of error may be encountered in connection with the sampling process. They are random error and systematic error, sometimes referred to as *bias*.

FIGURE 7.1 *Total Survey Error and Its Components*

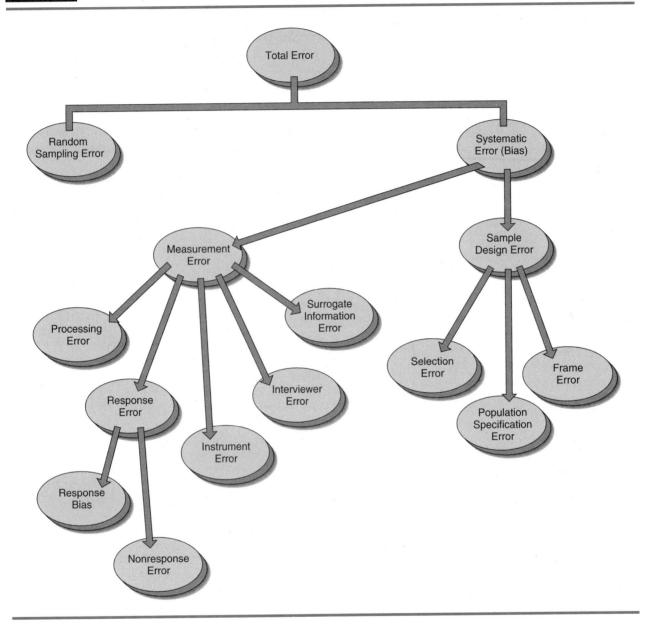

Surveys often attempt to obtain information from a representative cross section of a target population. The goal is to make inferences about the total population based on the responses given by respondents sampled. Even if all aspects of the sample are executed properly, the results will still be subject to a certain amount of error (**random error** or **random sampling error**) because of chance variation. It is the difference between the sample value and the true value of the population mean. This error cannot be avoided, only reduced by increasing the sample size. It is possible to estimate the range of random error at a particular level of confidence.

Random error or random sampling error
Error that results from chance variation.

Random error and the procedures for estimating it are discussed in detail in Chapters 11 and 12.

Systematic Error

Systematic error, or bias, results from mistakes or problems in the research design or from flaws in the execution of the sample design. Systematic error, or bias, exists in the results of a sample if those results show a consistent tendency to vary in one direction (consistently higher or consistently lower) from the true value of the population parameter being estimated. Systematic error includes all sources of error except those introduced by the random sampling process. Therefore, systematic errors or bias are sometimes called *nonsampling errors*. The types of nonsampling error that can systematically influence survey answers can be categorized as sample design error and measurement error. Sample design error is systematic error that results from an error in the sample design or sampling procedures.

Sample design results may be biased for a number of reasons:

■ *Frame error.* The sampling frame is the list of population elements or members from which units to be sampled are selected. **Frame error** results from using an incomplete or inaccurate sampling frame. The problem is that a sample drawn from a list that includes frame error may not be a true cross section of the target population. A common example of a situation that is likely to include frame error in marketing research involves the use of a published telephone directory as a sample frame for a telephone survey. Many households are not listed or not listed accurately in the current telephone book because they do not want to be listed or because they have recently moved or changed their telephone number. Research has shown that those people who are listed in telephone directories are systematically different from those who are not listed in certain important ways.[3] This means that any study purporting to represent the opinions of all households in a particular area that is drawn from the current telephone directory will be subject to frame error.

■ *Population specification error.* **Population specification error** results from an incorrect definition of the universe or population from which the sample is to be selected. For example, we might define the population or universe for a study as people over the age of thirty-five. It might later be determined that younger individuals should have been included and that the population should have been defined as those people twenty years of age or older. If those younger people who were excluded are significantly different in regard to the variables of interest, then the sample results will be biased.

■ *Selection error.* **Selection error** can occur even when the analyst has a proper sample frame and has defined the population correctly. It occurs due to the use of incomplete or improper sampling procedures or when appropriate selection procedures are not properly followed. For example, door-to-door interviewers might decide to avoid houses that do not look neat and tidy because they think the people who live there will not be "pleasant." If people who live in houses that are not neat and tidy are systematically different from those in tidy houses, then selection error will be introduced into the results of the survey. Selection error is a much more serious problem in connection with nonprobability samples discussed in Chapter 11.

Systematic error
Error that results from the research design or execution.

Frame error
Error resulting from an inaccurate or incomplete sample frame.

Population specification error
Error that results from an incorrect definition of the universe, or population, from which the sample is chosen.

Selection error
Error that results from following incomplete or improper sampling procedures or not following proper ones.

Measurement Error

Measurement error is often a much more serious threat to survey accuracy than random error. Frequently in the media, when the results of public opinion polls are quoted, and in professional marketing research reports, an error figure is reported (e.g., plus or minus 5 percent). The television viewer or the user of a marketing research study is left with the impression that this figure refers to total survey error. Unfortunately, this is not the case. This figure refers only to random sampling error. It does not include sample design error and speaks in no way to the measurement error that may exist in the research results. **Measurement error** occurs when there is a variation between the information being sought (true value) and the information obtained by the measurement process. For the most part, we are concerned with systematic measurement error. A number of types of error may be caused by various deficiencies in the measurement process.

- *Surrogate information error.* **Surrogate information error** occurs when there is a discrepancy between the information actually required to solve a problem and the information being sought by the researcher. It is related to general problems in the research design, particularly failure to properly define the problem. A classic and well-known situation that involved surrogate information error relates to the New Coke fiasco. It has been reported that the research for New Coke focused on the taste of the product and failed to consider the attitudes of consumers toward a change in the product. The resulting failure of New Coke strongly suggests, as the producers of Coke should understand, that people purchase Coke for many reasons other than taste.
- *Interviewer error.* **Interviewer error**, or interviewer bias, is due to interactions between the interviewer and the respondent. The interviewer may, consciously or unconsciously, influence respondents to give untrue or inaccurate answers. The interviewer's dress, age, sex, facial expressions, body language, or tone of voice may influence the answers given by some or all respondents. This type of error is caused by problems in the selection and training of interviewers or by the failure of interviewers to follow instructions. Interviewers must be properly trained and supervised to appear neutral at all times. Another type of interviewer error is the problem of deliberate cheating. This can be a particular problem in connection with door-to-door interviewing, where interviewers may be tempted to falsify interviews and get paid for work they did not actually do. The procedures developed by the researcher must include safeguards to make sure this problem will be detected (Chapter 15).
- *Measurement instrument bias.* **Measurement instrument bias** is the result of problems with the measurement instrument or questionnaire (see Chapter 9). It can occur due to such problems as leading questions or by elements of the questionnaire design that make the recording of responses difficult and prone to recording errors (see Chapter 10). Errors of this type are avoided by careful attention to detail in the questionnaire design phase of the research and by the use of questionnaire pretests prior to the start of field interviewing.
- *Processing error.* **Processing errors** are primarily due to mistakes in the transfer of information from survey documents to the computer. For example, a data entry operator might enter the wrong response to a particular question. Errors of this type are avoided by the development and strict adherence to quality control

Measurement error Error that results from a variation between the information being sought and that actually obtained by the measurement process.

Surrogate information error Error that results from a discrepancy between the information needed to solve a problem and that sought by the researcher.

Interviewer error Error that results from conscious or unconscious bias in the interviewer's interaction with the respondent.

Measurement instrument bias Error that results from the design of the questionnaire or measurement instrument.

Processing error Error that results from incorrect transfer of information from the document to the computer.

procedures in the processing of survey results. This process is discussed in detail in Chapter 13.

■ *Nonresponse bias.* Ideally, if we select a sample of 400 people from a particular population, all 400 of those individuals should be interviewed. As a practical matter, this will never happen. Response rates of 5 percent or less are not uncommon in mail surveys. The question is, "Are those who did respond to the survey systematically different in some important way than those who did not respond?" Such differences are called **nonresponse bias.**

Nonresponse error occurs (a) when a person cannot be reached at a particular time, (b) when a potential respondent is reached but cannot or will not participate at that time, for example, receiving a telephone request to participate in a survey just as the family sits down to dinner, and (c) when a person is reached but refuses to participate in a survey. The latter is the most serious problem because it may be possible to achieve future participation in the first two circumstances. In 1990, the refusal to participate rate rose to its highest level ever. Specifically, 36 percent of the respondents in the Walker Research Industry Image Study refused to participate in a research study.[4] Fortunately, most of those people do not refuse 100 percent of the time. In fact, 84 percent of those who refused to participate in at least one study did participate in another study or studies. The three main reasons people refused to participate were[5]

inconvenience	64%
uninteresting subject matter	22%
fear of a sales pitch	13%

Other research on refusal rates suggests that the type of survey may influence whether the individual would participate. For example, consumers had a more favorable attitude toward participating in a door-to-door survey or mall interviews than other types of surveys.[6]

Julian Baim, vice-president of research, Mediamark Research, agrees that nonresponse may be due more to the types of survey than basic changes in consumers' attitudes. Baim feels that this is true throughout the world (see the Global Marketing Research box).

■ *Response bias.* If there is a tendency for people to answer a particular question in a certain way, then we have **response bias.** Response bias can occur in two basic forms: deliberate falsification or unconscious misrepresentation. Deliberate falsification occurs when people deliberately give untrue answers to questions. There are many reasons why people might knowingly misrepresent information in a survey. They may wish to appear intelligent, not reveal information they feel is embarrassing, or conceal information that they consider to be personal. For example, in a survey regarding fast food behavior, the respondent may have a fairly good idea of how many times he or she visited a fast food restaurant in the past month. However, they may not remember which fast food restaurants they visited or how many times they visited each restaurant. Rather than answering "Don't Know" in response to the question regarding which restaurants were visited, the respondent may simply guess.

Unconscious misrepresentation occurs when the respondent is legitimately trying to be truthful and accurate but gives an inaccurate response. This type of bias may occur because of question format, question content, or various other

Nonresponse bias
Error that results from a systematic difference between those who do and do not respond to the measurement instrument.

Response bias
Error that results from the tendency of people to answer a question falsely, through deliberate misrepresentation or unconscious falsification

reasons. Types of error and strategies for minimizing error are summarized in Table 7.1.

TYPES OF SURVEYS

Asking people questions, of course, is the essence of the survey approach. But what type of survey will be "best" in a given situation? The survey alternatives discussed in this chapter are summarized in Table 7.2.

GLOBAL MARKETING RESEARCH

In comparing response rates around the world with personal interviews, Julian Baim did not find a correlation between response rates and number of attempts or length of interview. There were substantial variations in response rates between countries, but no clear-cut culturally based explanation, Baim said.

The perception is that response rates are down in all countries except Norway, but that perception is not completely supported. The biggest drop is in the U.K., leading to the conclusion that something is happening there, he said. Baim concluded that multinational nonresponse is not that different from the U.S. experience. Central cities pose the biggest nonresponse problem, he said, probably because of the inaccessibility of private residences (doormen, etc.), interviewers' fear of crime in some areas, and the demographics of urban areas in general. There are more mail and phone interviews in the U.S., and the problems associated with these methods are not yet being experienced by European researchers, who mainly conducted home and work personal interviews, he said.

In theory, nonresponse rates are higher in international marketing research for several reasons. First, cultural habits in many countries virtually prohibit communication with a stranger, particularly for women. For example, a researcher simply may not be able to speak on the phone with a housewife in an Islamic country to find out what she thinks of a particular brand. Second, in many societies such matters as preferences for hygienic products and food products are too personal to be shared with an outsider. In many Latin American countries, a woman may feel ashamed to talk with a researcher about her choice of a brand of sanitary pad, hair shampoo, or perfume. Third, respondents in many cases may be unwilling to share their true feelings with interviewers because they suspect the interviewers may be agents of the government, for example, seeking information for imposition of additional taxes. Fourth, middle-class people, in developing countries in particular, are reluctant to accept their status and may make false claims in order to reflect the lifestyle of wealthier people. For example, in a study on the consumption of tea in India, over 70 percent of the respondents from middle-income families claimed they used one of the several national brands of tea. This finding could not be substantiated since over 60 percent of the tea sold nationally in India is unbranded, generic tea sold unpackaged. Fifth, many respondents, willing to cooperate, may be illiterate, so that even oral communication may be difficult.[7]

| **TABLE 7.1** | *Types of Error and Strategies for Minimizing Error* |

I. RANDOM ERROR—Random error can be reduced only by increasing sample size.

II. SYSTEMATIC ERROR—Minimize sample design and measurement error.

   A. SAMPLE DESIGN ERROR

Frame Error	This error can be minimized by getting the best frame possible and doing preliminary quality control checks to evaluate the accuracy and completeness of the frame.
Population Specification Error	This error results from flaws in research design (e.g., incorrect definition of population of interest). It can be reduced or minimized only by means of more careful consideration and definition of the population of interest.
Selection Error	This error results from the use of incomplete or improper sampling procedures or when appropriate procedures are not followed. It can occur even if we have a good sample frame and an appropriate specification of the population. It is minimized by developing selection procedures that will ensure randomness and developing quality control checks to make sure that these procedures are being followed in the field.

   B. MEASUREMENT ERROR

Surrogate Information Error	This error results from seeking and basing decisions on the wrong information. (The New Coke example was cited in the text.) It results from poor design and can be minimized only by paying more careful attention to specification of the types of information required to fulfill the objectives of the research.
Interviewer Error	This error occurs due to interactions between the interviewer and respondent that affect the responses given. It is minimized by more careful interviewer selection and training. In addition, quality control checks that involve unobtrusive monitoring of interviewers to ascertain whether prescribed behavior is being adhered to should be employed.
Measurement Instrument Bias	Also referred to as *questionnaire bias*, it is minimized only by careful questionnaire design and pretesting.
Nonresponse Bias	This error results from the fact that people chosen for the sample who actually respond are systematically different from those who are chosen and do not respond. It is particularly serious in connection with mail surveys. It is minimized by doing everything possible (e.g., shorten questionnaire, make questionnaire more respondent friendly, callbacks, incentives, contacting people when they are most likely to be at home, etc.) to encourage those chosen for the sample to respond.
Response Bias	Response bias occurs when something about a question leads people to answer it in a particular way. This type of error can be minimized by paying special attention to questionnaire design. In particular we must be sensitive to questions that are hard to answer, might make respondent look uninformed if they cannot answer, or deal with sensitive issues. Questions should be modified to deal with these problems (see Chapter 10).
Processing Error	These errors can occur in the process of transferring data from the questionnaires to the computer. This error is minimized by developing and following rigid procedures for transferring data and supporting quality control checks.

Door-to-Door Interviewing

Door-to-door interviewing, where consumers are interviewed in person in their homes, has traditionally been thought of as the best survey method. This conclusion was based on a number of factors. First, the door-to-door interview is a personal, face-to-face interview with all the attendant advantages—feedback from the respondent, the ability to explain complicated tasks, the ability to use special questionnaire techniques that require visual contact to speed up the interview or improve data quality, the ability to show the respondent product concepts and other stimuli for evaluation, and so on. Second, the consumer is seen as being at ease in a familiar, comfortable, secure environment.

Door-to-door interviewing
Consumers are interviewed face to face in their homes.

TABLE 7.2 *Different Survey Approaches Commonly Used in Marketing Research*

TYPE OF INTERVIEW	DESCRIPTION
Door to Door	Interviewer interviews consumer in consumer's home.
Executive Interview	Interview industrial product user (e.g., engineer, architect, doctor, executive) or decision maker at place of business regarding industrial product.
Mall Intercept	Interviewer interviews consumer in shopping mall or other high-traffic location. Interviews may be done in public areas of the mall or the respondent may be taken to a private test area.
From-Home Telephone	Interviewers use their home phones to interview consumers and, in some cases, industrial users.
Central Location Telephone	Interviewing is conducted from a telephone facility set up for that purpose. These facilities typically have equipment that permits the supervisor to unobtrusively monitor the interviewing while it is taking place. Some of these facilities have Wide Area Telephone Service (WATS) to permit national sampling from a single location. An increasing number have computer-assisted interviewing capabilities. At these locations the interviewer sits in front of a computer terminal attached to a mainframe or a personal computer. The questionnaire is programmed into the computer. The interviewer enters responses directly.
Direct Computer Interview	Used increasingly, particularly in the mall environment. The consumer is seated at a computer terminal or personal computer. The questionnaire is programmed into the computer and the consumer is, in essence, interviewed by the computer.
Self-Administered Questionnaires	Most frequently employed at high-traffic locations such as shopping malls or in captive audience situations such as classrooms and airplanes. Respondents are given general information on how to fill out the questionnaire and are left to fill it out on their own. Computers are being used in this area by sending software driven questionnaires on diskettes to individuals who have personal computers.
Ad Hoc (one-shot) Mail Surveys	Questionnaires are mailed to a sample of consumers or industrial users. Instructions are included. Respondents are asked to fill out the questionnaire and return it via mail. Sometimes a gift or monetary incentive is provided. The same comment regarding computers under self-administered questionnaires applies here. We have not heard of questionnaires sent by FAX, but why not?
Mail Panels	Several companies, including Market Facts, NPD Research, and National Family Opinion Research operate large (more than 100,000 households) consumer panels. There are several important differences between mail panels and ad hoc mail surveys. First, people in the panel have been precontacted. The panel concept has been explained to them. They have agreed to participate for some period of time. In addition, participants are offered gratuities to participate in mail panels. Mail panels typically generate much higher response rates than ad hoc mail surveys.

The door-to-door interview remains the only viable way to do long depth interviews and certain in-home product tests. In addition, the door-to-door survey is the only way currently available to obtain anything approaching a probability sample in a study that involves showing concepts or other stimuli to consumers.

However, this approach to interviewing has a number of drawbacks that explain its declining use by commercial marketing researchers. Jerry Rosenkranz, chairman of Data Development, a large New York–based custom research firm, lists the disadvantages of door-to-door interviewing:

- The growth of the two-adult working family and other changes in family composition means less availability of potential respondents.
- While traditionally in-home cooperation rates were historically higher than for other approaches, they gradually are deteriorating.
- Unsafe (high crime) areas, distance, and lack of accessibility sometimes negated reaching the desired sample.
- The drop in qualified interviewing personnel—whether due to a drop in education, or the increase in other options, with better pay, all have become a factor over time.

- The requirement of a field interviewer, that is, the "chutzpah to make a cold call" limits the potential pool of interviews.
- The client and field service's unease emanating from the lack of "hands on" control of a field force that was out there somewhere (in direct comparison to a permanent work force in a centralized location under supervision—clocking in 9–5, etc.).
- The lack of communication between the home office, the field office, and the interviewing staff (except at the end of day) is a serious handicap if one wishes to execute questionnaire change, examine incidence rate, or hasten data retrieval.

MARKETING RESEARCH IN PRACTICE

One of the most significant demographic changes in recent years has been the shift from a youth-oriented population to one oriented to people middle-age or older. Not only are more Americans living longer, they are also living better. The 65+ population controls 50 percent of the discretionary income in the United States. This segment of the market is being courted increasingly by marketers. Marketing research plays an important role in understanding the desires, life-styles, and values of this group. However, the research methods, tasks, and techniques must be carefully adapted to accommodate the characteristics of this market.

There are numerous physiological, cognitive, and social changes that take place during the aging process, which have marketing research implications. Farsightedness and other vision changes mean larger type on printed materials, additional lighting, or perhaps the use of contrasting colors. Diminished hearing means that special adjustments must be made for telephone and personal interviews: training interviewers to speak clearly and slowly, using interviewers with deep voices, or paying special attention to the delivery of the questions. In order to compensate for the diminished perception, learning, and information processing, questionnaire design should be simple and parsimonious. Visual aids should be used when possible. Mail questionnaires may be better because respondents can control the pace. If a telephone survey is selected, it could be used in conjunction with a paper questionnaire.

Interviewer training for personal interviews and telephone surveys is important. Data collection takes longer and involves more social interaction so interviewers must be patient and as helpful as possible without biasing the results.

Changes in data collection methods may be necessary. In particular, pretesting is extremely important. Personal interviews are less stressful for older respondents and have higher response rates but also higher costs. Because of the abuses of direct marketers, older people are more likely to refuse to participate. Mail surveys are appropriate because they rely only on vision and they allow self-pacing. However, due to low response rates it is necessary to use a precontact letter, a personalized cover letter, a self-addressed and stamped return envelope, and a reminder card. Mall intercepts have many advantages but the special needs of older respondents must be taken into consideration. If focus groups are used, times as well as special transportation needs must be factored into the research design.[8]

- The effects of such old bugaboos as weather (too good or too bad), car problems, broken-in cars, sickness, etc.
- Cheating, fudging, or shortcutting by the interviewers, interviewing the wrong respondent, etc., prompting high levels of validation. This post-field check may, on occasion, be too late to replace the necessary data or very costly to go back for.[9]

The door-to-door approach to survey data collection is not likely to disappear from the marketing research scene. As noted earlier, it is the only viable data collection alternative in a number of situations. On the other hand, it is also unlikely that we will see this type of interviewing reassume the prominence it once enjoyed. Recent estimates (see Table 7.3) suggest that only about 15 percent of all persons interviewed in 1992 participated in a door-to-door interview.

Mall Intercept

Mall intercept interviewing Shoppers are intercepted in public areas of malls and interviewed face to face.

As the data in Table 7.3 indicate, **mall intercept interviewing** is a popular survey method. This survey approach is relatively simple. Shoppers are intercepted in the public areas of shopping malls and either interviewed on the mall or asked to come to a permanent interviewing facility in the mall. In 1992, approximately 200 malls throughout the country had permanent survey facilities operated by marketing research firms. An equal or greater number of malls permit market research firms to interview on a day-to-day basis. Many malls do not permit marketing research interviewing because they view it as an unnecessary nuisance to shoppers.

Mall interviewing is of relatively recent origin. The earliest permanent facilities date back less than thirty years with the real growth in use of this technique coming during the 1970s. In general, the mall intercept interview is a low-cost substitute for the door-to-door interview. In fact, this approach has probably grown primarily at the expense of door-to-door interviewing.

Mall surveys are less expensive than door-to-door interviews because respondents are coming to the interviewer rather than the other way around. Interviewers spend more of their time actually interviewing and less time hunting for someone to interview. Also, mall interviewers do not have the substantial travel time and mileage expenses associated with door-to-door interviewing. In addition to low

TABLE 7.3 *Participation by Survey Type*

TYPE	PERCENTAGE PARTICIPATION*		
	1980	*1986*	*1990*
Mall	56	54	69
Telephone	75	76	68
Mall intercept**	36	30	32
Door-to-door	18	11	15

* Percentages are greater than 100 because of multiple responses
** Always a nonprobability sample whereas the other methods can be either a probability or nonprobability sample.
Source: 1990 Walker Industry Image Study.

cost, mall interviews have many of the advantages associated with door-to-door interviewing in that respondents can be shown various stimuli for their reactions and special questionnaire techniques can be used.[10]

However, a number of serious disadvantages are associated with mall interviewing. First, it is virtually impossible to get a sample representative of a large metropolitan area from shoppers at a particular mall. Though they may be large, most malls draw from a relatively small area in proximity to the mall. In addition, a mall tends to attract a certain type of person based on the stores it contains. Studies also show that some people shop more frequently and therefore have a greater chance of being selected than others. Finally, many people refuse mall interviews. One study found that over half of those approached refused either on initial contact or after they had been qualified.[11] By *qualified* we mean that responses to screening questions have indicated that the individual falls into a group in which the researcher is interested. In summary, mall interviewing cannot produce a good or representative sample except in the rare case where the population of interest is coincident with or a subset of the population of people who shop at the mall.

Second, the mall environment is not the comfortable home environment associated with the door-to-door interview. The respondent may be ill at ease, in a hurry, or preoccupied by various distractions outside the researcher's control. These factors may adversely affect the quality of the data obtained. The popularity of mall intercept interviews has held steady in recent years (see Table 7.3).

Executive Interviewing

Executive interviewing is used by marketing researchers to refer to the industrial equivalent of door-to-door interviewing. This type of survey involves interviewing business people, at their offices, concerning industrial products or services. For example, if Hewlett-Packard wanted information regarding user preferences for different features that might be offered in a new line of computer printers, it would need to interview prospective user-purchasers of the printers. It is appropriate to locate and interview these people at their offices.

This type of interviewing is very expensive. First, individuals involved in the purchase decision for the product in question must be identified and located. Sometimes lists can be obtained from various sources, but more frequently screening must be conducted over the telephone. It may be likely that a particular company has individuals of the type being sought. However, locating those people within a large organization can be expensive and time consuming. Once a qualified person is located, the next step is to get that person to agree to be interviewed and to set a time for the interview. This is not as hard as it might seem, because most professionals seem to enjoy talking about topics related to their work.

Finally, an interviewer must go to the particular place at the appointed time. Long waits are frequently encountered; cancellations are not uncommon. This type of survey requires the very best interviewers because they are frequently interviewing on topics that they know very little about. Executive interviewing has essentially the same advantages and disadvantages as door-to-door interviewing.

Executive interviewing
The industrial equivalent of door-to-door interviewing.

From-Home Telephone Interviewing

From-home telephone interviewing
Interviewers use their own phones to reach and interview respondents.

Until recent years **from-home telephone interviewing** was the predominant form of telephone interviewing. Under this approach, interviewers come to the office of a field service firm for a training session and then go home and use their home phones to do the interviewing.

As noted earlier, telephone surveys (from home plus central location) were until 1990 the most popular single form of survey. The advantages of telephone interviewing are compelling. First, the telephone is a relatively inexpensive way to collect survey data. The major reason is that interviewer travel time and mileage are eliminated. A second advantage of the telephone interview is that it has the potential to produce a very high-quality sample. If proper sampling and callback procedures are employed, the telephone approach can probably produce a better sample than any other survey procedure.[12] Random digit sampling or random digit dialing is a frequently used sampling approach (see Chapter 11). The basic idea is very simple. Instead of drawing the sample from the phone book or other directory, telephone numbers are generated via a random number procedure. This approach ensures that people with unlisted numbers and those who have moved or otherwise changed their telephone numbers since the last published phone book are included in the sample in their correct proportion.

The telephone survey approach has several inherent disadvantages. First, in the typical telephone interview of today, the respondent cannot be shown anything. Advanced cable TV systems and picture phones, which are expected to be in widespread use in the future, have the potential to overcome this limitation. This shortcoming ordinarily eliminates the telephone survey as an alternative in situations that require that the respondent be shown something—product concepts, advertisements, and the like.

Some have suggested that the telephone interview does not permit the interviewer to make various judgments and evaluations that can be made by the in-home interviewer—judgments regarding respondent income based on the home lived in and other outward signs of economic status. Granted, the interviewer does not have these cues in the telephone situation. However, in reality, the market research interviewer is almost never called upon to make such judgments. The reasons are spelled out in the section on marketing research interviewers.

A third disadvantage of the telephone interview is that it is more limited in regard to the quantity and types of information that can be obtained than is the door-to-door interview. First, some evidence suggests that the telephone interview must be shorter than the door-to-door interview. Respondent patience wears thin more easily, and it is easier to hang up a phone than throw an interviewer out of your living room. Second, the telephone is a poor choice for conducting the depth interview or the long interview with many open-end questions.

A fourth disadvantage of telephone interviewing is the increased use of screening devices, such as CALLER ID, and screening via an answering machine. Approximately 32 million U.S. households are equipped with telephone answering machines.[13] Over half of these households screen their calls at least some of the time. Call screening, of course, increases the nonresponse rate. Nonresponse rates are rising for telephone interviewing primarily because of telemarketing. A major survey recently found that 86 percent of the respondents would be more likely to participate in a telephone survey if they knew the call was to conduct a legitimate telephone survey, rather than to sell them something.[14]

Call display telephones, such as this phone from AT&T, display the area code and telephone number of the person calling. Such devices pose a disadvantage to telephone interviewing, since some people may screen all incoming calls from an unfamiliar number. Courtesy AT&T.

In addition to the problems or disadvantages of telephone interviewing in general, the from-home telephone interview suffers from some special problems of its own. As with the door-to-door interview, the process cannot be monitored at a reasonable cost. Quality control is limited during the interviewing process. Second, actual hours worked by the interviewers cannot be ascertained.

Central Location Telephone Interviews

Central location telephone interviewing is the logical extension of the from-home approach. Under this approach, interviewing is conducted from a facility set up for that specific purpose. Unfortunately, there are no statistics on the proportion of telephone interviews conducted on a from-home and central-location basis. However, it is safe to assume that central location work is growing in importance and accounts for the majority of all telephone interviews at this time.

> **Central location telephone interviewing**
> Interviewers make calls from a centrally located marketing research facility to reach and interview respondents.

The reasons for the growing prominence of the central location phone interview are fairly straightforward. Summarized in a single word, the main reason would be "control." First, the actual interviewing process can be monitored. Most central location telephone interviewing facilities have unobtrusive monitoring equipment that permits supervisors to listen in on interviews as they are actually being conducted. Interviewers who are not doing the interview properly can be corrected. Those who are incapable of conducting a proper interview can be eliminated. One supervisor may monitor anywhere from ten to twenty interviewers. Ordinarily each interviewer will be monitored at least once per shift. Second, completed interviews are edited on the spot as a further quality control check. Interviewers can be immediately informed of any deficiencies in their work. Finally, there is control over the hours that interviewers work. Interviewers report in and out and work regular hours.

Recent developments have expanded the capabilities of central location telephone interviewing. The costs of long distance calling have been dramatically reduced for high volume marketing research operations. This makes it possible for marketing researchers to conduct national surveys from a single location with a

TABLE 7.4   *Data from a Three-City Product Concept Test*

	TOTAL	DALLAS	SACRAMENTO	WASHINGTON
Total	151 (100%)	50 (100%)	51 (100%)	50 (100%)
Definitely Purchase	39 (26%)	11 (22%)	15 (29%)	13 (26%)
Probably Purchase	40 (26%)	8 (16%)	15 (29%)	17 (34%)
Uncertain About	37 (25%)	13 (26%)	9 (18%)	15 (30%)
Probably not Purchase	19 (13%)	10 (20%)	5 (10%)	4 (8%)
Definitely not Purchase	16 (11%)	8 (16%)	7 (14%)	1 (8%)

Note: All percentages are computed with the column total as the base.

single set of supervisors and interviewers. Without this capability, a study requiring, for example, 150 central location telephone interviews in Dallas, 150 in Washington, D.C., and 150 in Sacramento, California, would require the use of a field service firm in each of the three cities to conduct the interviewing. Sample data from such a study are shown in Table 7.4. The researcher faced with analyzing the data is confronted with the question of deciding whether differences in results for the three cities represent real differences or differences in the way the survey was administered in the three cities. If the interviewing had been conducted from a single WATS facility, there would be no question. The analyst could feel relatively certain that consumers in Sacramento and Washington really liked the product better than did consumers in Dallas.

Computer-assisted telephone interviewing
Central location telephone interviewing in which the interviewer enters answers directly into a computer.

Computer-Assisted Telephone Interviewing (CATI)

Today, many companies have computerized the central location telephone interviewing process. Each interviewer is seated in front of a computer terminal or, more likely, a personal computer. When a qualified respondent gets on the line, the

GLOBAL MARKETING RESEARCH

In the United States, telephone interviewing is a well-established information-gathering methodology of survey research. However, the use of the technique to gather information in foreign markets is still relatively new, especially in terms of telephone interviews originating in the U.S. but taking place with foreign consumers. To help researchers overcome residual language barriers, AT&T Co., New York, markets a service that features on-line interpreters fluent in 143 languages and dialects. Those specialists translate conversations into or out of English. Likewise, on a broader scale, the growth of global markets and the trend toward English as the international language of business are breaking down cultural resistance Americans have met when conducting primary research in offshore markets.[15]

interviewer starts the interview by pressing a key or series of keys on the terminal or personal computer keyboard. The questions and multiple choice answers appear on the screen one at a time. The interviewer reads the question, enters the response, and the computer skips ahead to the appropriate next question. For example, we might ask if the person has a dog. If the answer is "yes," there might be a series of questions regarding what type of dog food the person buys. If the answer is "no," these questions would be inappropriate. The computer takes into account the answer to the dog ownership question and skips ahead to the next appropriate question.

In addition, the computer can help customize questionnaires. For example, in the early part of a long interview we might ask respondents the years, makes, and models of all the cars they own. Later in the interview questions might be asked about each specific car owned. The question might come up on the interviewer's screen as follows: "You said you owned a 1992 Ford Taurus. Which family member drives this car most often?" Other questions about this car and others owned would appear in similar fashion. Questions like this can be handled in a traditional pencil and paper interview, but they are handled much more efficiently in the computerized version.

This approach eliminates the need for separate editing and data entry steps. There is no editing because there are no questionnaires. More to the point, in most computer systems it is not possible to enter an "impossible" answer. For example, if a question has three possible answers with codes A, B, C and the interviewer enters D, the computer will not accept it. It will ask that the answer be reentered. If a combination or pattern of answers is impossible, the computer will not accept the answer, and so on. Keypunching of completed questionnaires is eliminated because data are entered into the computer as the interviewing is completed.

Another advantage of computer interviewing is that computer tabulations can be run at any point in the study—after 200 people have been interviewed, after 400, or after any number. This luxury is not available with the pencil and paper interview. With the traditional interview, there may be a wait of a week or more after completion of all interviewing before detailed tabulations of the results are available. Instantaneous results available with computer-assisted telephone interviewing systems provide some real advantages.

Direct Computer Interview

Direct computer interviewing differs from the type of computerized interviewing discussed previously in that instead of seating the interviewer at a terminal or personal computer, the respondent is seated in this position. This approach is currently being used in the mall environment by a number of firms. Consumers are intercepted and qualified in the mall and then brought to a test facility in the mall. They are seated at a computer terminal or personal computer, given some basic instruction on what to do, and the sequence to start the interview is entered by the administrator. The interview then proceeds in much the same way as the on-line telephone interview described earlier. The difference is that answers are being entered by the respondent rather than the interviewer.

Research conducted by us indicates that most individuals have no trouble with the direct computer interview.[16] To respond, they simply enter the letter or number

> **Direct computer interviewing** Consumers are intercepted in a mall and interviewed by a computer that asks questions and accepts responses.

next to their choice. Most seem to find the process interesting. In a recent study of computer interviewing conducted by the authors, 100 interviews were conducted face-to-face by interviewers and 100 of the same interviews were administered by computer. The data produced by the two survey approaches were virtually identical. Respondents were equally likely to provide sensitive information whether interviewed in person or by computer. However, those interviewed by computer had a somewhat higher rate of nonresponse to individual questions. The level of validity (the degree to which a measurement accurately represents or measures what it purports to measure), to the degree that it could be ascertained, was essentially the same for the two data collection approaches.

Because we are substituting machines (computers), which are becoming less expensive, for labor (interviewers), which is becoming more expensive, it is likely that in the future computers will be more widely used to collect survey data. Hardware and software developments continue to make this form of interviewing more feasible.

Self-Administered Interview

The self-administered and mail survey methods discussed in this section have one thing in common. They differ from the other survey methods discussed in that no interviewer—human or computer—is involved.

Self-administered questionnaire
A questionnaire filled out by the respondent with no interviewer.

The major disadvantage of the **self-administered questionnaire** approach is that no one is present to explain things to the respondent and clarify responses to open-end questions. For example, if we ask people why they do not buy a particular brand of soft drink via an open-end question, a typical answer would be something like "because I don't like it." From a managerial perspective this answer is totally useless. It provides no information that can be used by management to alter the marketing mix and thereby make the product more attractive. If the survey were being conducted by an interviewer he or she would be trained to "probe" for a response. This would mean that after receiving and recording the useless response, the interviewer would ask the respondent what it was he or she did not like about the product. The person being interviewed might then indicate a dislike for the taste. The interviewer would then ask what it was about the taste that the person did not like. Here we might finally get something useful with the respondent indicating that the product in question was, for example, too sweet. If many people gave a similar response, management might elect to reduce the sweetness of the drink. The point is that without probing, you would have only the useless first response.

Some have argued that the absence of an interviewer is an advantage in that it eliminates one course of bias. There is no interviewer whose appearance, dress, manner of speaking, failure to follow instructions, and so on may influence answers to questions given by the respondent.

Self-administered interviews are often used in mall or other central locations, where the researcher has access to a captive audience. Airlines, for example, often have programs where questionnaires are administered in flight. Passengers are asked to rate various aspects of the airline's services. The results are used to track passenger perceptions of service over time. Many hotels, restaurants, and other service businesses provide brief questionnaires to patrons to find out how they feel about the quality of service provided.

Mail Surveys

There are two general types of mail surveys used in marketing research: ad hoc or one-shot mail surveys, and mail panels. In the case of **ad hoc** or one-project **mail surveys**, the researcher selects a sample of names and addresses from an appropriate source and mails a questionnaire to the people selected. Ordinarily there is no prior contact, and the sample is used only for the single project. However, the same questionnaire may be sent to nonrespondents several times to increase the overall response rate. In contrast, **mail panels** operate in the following manner:

1. A sample of people is precontacted by letter. In this initial contact the purpose of their participation in the panel is explained. People are usually offered a gratuity for participating in the panel for a period of time.
2. As part of the initial contact, consumers are asked to fill out a background data questionnaire on number of family members, ages, education, income, types of pets, types of vehicles and ages, types of appliances, and so forth.
3. After the initial contact, panel participants are sent questionnaires from time to time. The background data collected on initial contact enables researchers to send questionnaires only to appropriate households. For example, a survey regarding dog food usage and preferences would be sent only to dog owners.

A mail panel is a type of longitudinal study. A **longitudinal study** is one that questions the same respondents at different points in time.

On first consideration, mail appears to be an attractive way to collect survey data. There are no interviewers to recruit, train, monitor, and pay. The entire study can be sent out and administered from a single location. Hard-to-reach respondents can be readily surveyed. Mail surveys appear to be convenient, efficient, and inexpensive.

Mail surveys of both types have the problems associated with not having an interviewer present, which was discussed in the section on self-administered questionnaires. No one is there to assist the respondent. In particular, no one can probe for responses to open-end questions, a real constraint on the types of information that can be sought and the interviewing techniques that can be employed. As a general rule, the length of the interview and consequently the quantity of information is more limited in the case of the mail survey than with survey methods involving interviewers.

The ad hoc mail survey suffers from the additional problem of a high rate of nonresponse and the attendant systematic error. Nonresponse in mail surveys would not be a problem as long as everyone had an equal probability of not responding. However, numerous studies have shown that certain types of people—people with more education, higher-level occupations, women, those less interested in the topic, students, and others—have a greater probability of not responding.[17] Other types of people—generally the opposite of those just named—have a greater probability of responding. Response rates in ad hoc mail surveys may run anywhere from less than 10 percent to nearly 100 percent depending on length of questionnaire, content, group surveyed, incentives employed, and other factors.[18] Those who operate mail panels claim response rates as high as 70 percent.

In response to the problem of low-response rates to mail surveys, many strategies designed to enhance response rate have been developed. Some of the more common

Ad hoc mail surveys
Questionnaires sent to selected names and addresses with no prior contact by the researcher.

Mail panels
Participants are precontacted and screened, then periodically sent

Longitudinal study
The same respondents are re-sampled over time.

Dear Panel Member,

This is a very important survey and you have been selected to participate. I am excited about it and I hope it will be fun for you.

My questionnaire includes a wide range of questions about you—what you do, think, and feel. It's longer and more interesting than most of my questionnaires so it can be answered in more than one sitting, but as soon as possible, please.

Please carefully read the instructions at the beginning of each section. You will find that most of my questions can be answered by placing a circle around a number or an "X" in the box that best expresses your answer.

> AS A TOKEN OF MY APPRECIATION, I WILL SEND YOU A NICE GIFT AFTER I RECEIVE YOUR COMPLETED QUESTIONNAIRE.
>
> IN ADDITION TO THE GIFT, THOSE WHO RETURN A COMPLETED QUESTIONNAIRE POSTMARKED BY **FEBRUARY 16,** 1992 WILL ALSO HAVE A CHANCE TO WIN CASH! THERE WILL BE 10 WINNERS:
>
> TWO FIRST PRIZES OF $150
> EIGHT SECOND PRIZES OF $25
>
> ALL YOU HAVE TO DO TO BECOME ELIGIBLE FOR THE CASH DRAWING IS RETURN YOUR COMPLETED QUESTIONNAIRE POSTMARKED BY THE DATE SHOWN ABOVE.

The bar-code that appears on the questionnaire will be used to enter your name in a drawing to win one of the prizes.

This drawing is open to all participating members of the Consumer Mail Panel. No purchase is necessary to enter. The odds for winning will be determined by the number of entrants.

Winners will be selected by a random drawing conducted by Market Facts, Inc. They will be notified by mail on or before March 31, 1992.

This drawing is void where probibited by law and is subject to state and federal regulation.

Thank you so much for helping with this important survey. I hope you'll be able to return the questionnaire to me as soon as possible. I'm looking forward to receiving your answers. A postage-paid envelope is provided for your convenience.

Cordially,

P.S. REMEMBER: Shortly after I receive and process your questionnaire I will send you a nice gift.

Cover letter for a mail survey. Courtesy of DDB Needham Worldwide.

ones are summarized in Table 7.5. The question always must be, Is the cost of the particular strategy worth the increased response rate generated? Unfortunately, there is no clear answer to this question that can be applied to all procedures in all situations.

Even with all its shortcomings, mail remains a popular survey data collection technique in commercial marketing research. In fact, more people participated in mail surveys than any other type of survey research (see Table 7.3).

FACTORS DETERMINING CHOICE OF PARTICULAR SURVEY METHODS

A number of factors or considerations may affect the choice of a survey method in a given situation. The researcher should choose the survey method that will provide data of the desired types, quality, and quantity at the lowest cost. The major considerations in the selection of a survey method are summarized in Table 7.6 and discussed here.

SECTION I: INTERESTS AND OPINIONS

1. In this section, I have listed a number of statements about interests and opinions. For each statement listed, I'd like to know whether you personally agree or disagree with this statement.

After each statement, there are six numbers from 1-6. The higher the number, the more you tend to *agree* with the statement. The lower the number, the more you tend to *disagree* with the statement. The numbers from 1-6 may be described as follows:

1   I *definitely* disagree with the statement
2   I *generally* disagree with the statement
3   I *moderately* disagree with the statement
4   I *moderately* agree with the statement
5   I *generally* agree with the statement
6   I *definitely* agree with the statement

For each statement, please circle the number that best describes your feelings about that statement. You may think many items are similar. Actually, no two items are exactly alike so be sure to circle *ONE NUMBER FOR EACH STATEMENT*.

CIRCLE ONLY ONE NUMBER FOR EACH STATEMENT	DEFINITELY DISAGREE					DEFINITELY AGREE	
I have more self-confidence than most of my friends	1	2	3	4	5	6	(14)
Our family is too heavily in debt today	1	2	3	4	5	6	
I like to be sure to see the movies everybody is talking about	1	2	3	4	5	6	
I am careful about what I eat in order to keep my weight under control	1	2	3	4	5	6	
I never know how much to tip	1	2	3	4	5	6	5
I would rather spend a quiet evening at home than go out to a party	1	2	3	4	5	6	
Physical strength makes a man more of a man	1	2	3	4	5	6	
Magazines are more interesting than television	1	2	3	4	5	6	
When I see a full ashtray or wastebasket, I want it emptied immediately	1	2	3	4	5	6	
I like to pay cash for everything I buy	1	2	3	4	5	6	10
All men should be clean shaven every day	1	2	3	4	5	6	
I am concerned about getting enough calcium in my diet	1	2	3	4	5	6	
At noontime, I often skip lunch or just have a light snack	1	2	3	4	5	6	
I pretty much spend for today and let tomorrow bring what it will	1	2	3	4	5	6	
I am a homebody	1	2	3	4	5	6	15
I am in favor of legalized abortions	1	2	3	4	5	6	
Women don't need more than a minimum amount of life insurance	1	2	3	4	5	6	
Television is my primary form of entertainment	1	2	3	4	5	6	
It's important for men to "spend time with the boys"	1	2	3	4	5	6	
Before going shopping, I sit down and make out a complete shopping list	1	2	3	4	5	6	20
I like to be considered a leader	1	2	3	4	5	6	
It seems as though everyone in our family is always on the run	1	2	3	4	5	6	
No matter how fast our income goes up we never seem to get ahead	1	2	3	4	5	6	
I try to avoid foods that are high in cholesterol	1	2	3	4	5	6	
I would feel lost if I were alone in a foreign country	1	2	3	4	5	6	25
When I have a favorite brand I buy it—no matter what else is on sale	1	2	3	4	5	6	
I wish I could leave my present life and do something entirely different	1	2	3	4	5	6	
I always check prices even on small items	1	2	3	4	5	6	
Men are better at investing money than women	1	2	3	4	5	6	
I am concerned about the use of pesticides on fruits and vegetables	1	2	3	4	5	6	30
Most big companies are just out for themselves	1	2	3	4	5	6	
People who play state lotteries are not really gambling	1	2	3	4	5	6	
There is too much violence on prime time television	1	2	3	4	5	6	
I dread the future	1	2	3	4	5	6	
I love taking pictures	1	2	3	4	5	6	(48)35

First page of lifestyle profile survey. Courtesy of DDB Needham Worldwide.

TABLE 7.5   *Tactics Employed to Increase Mail Survey Response Rates*

Advance postcard or telephone call alerting respondent of survey

Follow-up postcard or phone call

Monetary incentives (nickel, dime, quarter, half-dollar)

Premiums (pencil, pen, keychain, etc.)

Postage stamps rather than metered envelopes

Self-addressed, stamped return envelope

Personalized address and well-written cover letter

Promise of contributions to favorite charity

Entry into drawings for prizes

Emotional appeals

Affiliation with universities or research institutions

Personally signed cover letter

Multiple mailings of the questionnaire

Bids for sympathy

Reminder that respondent participated in previous studies

Sampling Precision Required

The required level of sampling precision is an important factor in determining which survey method is appropriate in a given situation. Some projects by their very nature require a high level of sampling accuracy, whereas in others this may not be a critical consideration. If sampling accuracy were the only criterion, the appropriate data collection technique would probably be central location telephone interviewing. The appropriate survey method for a project not requiring a high level of sampling accuracy might be the mail approach.

TABLE 7.6   *Factors That Determine the Selection of a Particular Survey Method*

FACTOR	COMMENT
Sampling Precision	How accurate do the study results need to be? If the need for accuracy is not great, less rigorous and less expensive sampling procedures may be appropriate.
Budget Available	How much money is available for the interviewing portion of the study?
Need to Expose Respondent to Various Stimuli	Taste tests, product concept and prototype tests, ad tests and the like, require face-to-face contact, etc.
Quality of Data Required	How accurate do the results of the study need to be?
Length of Questionnaire	Long questionnaires are difficult to do by mail, over the phone, in a mall, etc.
Necessity of Having Respondent Perform Certain Specialized Tasks	Card sorts, certain visual scaling methods, and the like, require face-to-face contact.
Incidence Rate	Are you looking for people who make up 1 percent of the total population or 50 percent of the population? If you are looking for a needle in a haystack, you need an inexpensive way to find it.
Degree of Structure of Questionnaire	Highly unstructured questionnaires may require data collection by the door-to-door approach.
Time Available to Complete Survey	Might not be able to use mail because you do not have time to wait for response.

The trade-off between these two methods in regard to sampling precision is one of cost versus accuracy. The central location telephone survey method employing a random digit dialing sampling procedure will likely produce a better sample than the mail survey method. However, the mail survey will most likely cost less.

Mall surveys, as noted earlier, often produce poor samples. Other methods, such as door-to-door interviewing, have the potential to produce good samples if the interviewing process is carefully monitored and controlled.

Budget Available

The commercial marketing researcher frequently encounters situations where the budget available for a study has a strong influence on the survey method used. Actually, budget usually is not the only impact on the choice of a survey method, but rather budget in combination with other considerations. For example, assume that for a particular study the budgetary constraint for interviewing is $10,000 and the sample size required for the necessary accuracy is 1,000. If we estimate that administering the questionnaire on a door-to-door basis would be $27.50 per interview and the cost of administering it via central location telephone interview would be $9.50 per interview, the choice is fairly clear. This, of course, assumes that nothing about the survey would absolutely require face-to-face contact.

The Need to Expose the Respondent to Various Stimuli

In many studies the marketing researcher needs to get respondent reactions to various marketing stimuli—product concepts, product components, and advertisements. In most cases the need to get respondent reactions to stimuli implies personal contact between interviewer and respondent.

Non-face-to-face interviewing methods are generally out of the question for studies of this type. There are exceptions to this general rule that highlight the creativity of some researchers. Belden and Associates of Dallas developed a procedure built around sending respondents an envelope inside an envelope. The outer envelope contains an explanation of the study and a request that the inner envelope not be opened until the respondent is called on the phone by an interviewer. Researchers want to control respondent access to stimuli so that they can be sure of getting top-of-mind responses and be sure that all respondents have spent an equal amount of time examining materials. People who received envelopes are called on the telephone and told to open the inner envelope. They are then interviewed and their reactions to the stimuli (e.g., product concepts, ads, etc.) are sought.

The options are more limited in regard to taste tests, TV ad tests, and other similar types of tests. Taste tests typically require food preparation. This preparation must be done under controlled conditions so that the researcher can be certain that each person interviewed is responding to the same stimulus. The only viable survey alternative for tests of this type is the mall intercept approach or some variant. Variants include recruiting people to come to properly equipped central locations such as church community centers to sample products and be interviewed. For similar reasons, much TV ad testing is done via mall intercept. TV ad testing depends on use of videotaped prototypes of commercials. The equipment needed to show these tapes is expensive and not readily portable. Interviewing, therefore, must be conducted at malls and other central locations where the equipment can be set up.

Quality of Data Required

The quality of data required is an important determinant of which survey method to use. Data quality refers to the validity and reliability of the resulting data. These two concepts are discussed in greater detail in Chapter 9. However, validity is normally considered to refer to the degree to which a measure reflects only the characteristic of interest. In other words, a valid measure provides an accurate reading of the thing the researcher is trying to measure. Reliability refers to the consistency with which a measure produces the same results with the same or comparable populations.

Many factors other than the interviewing method affect data quality. Sampling methods used, questionnaire design, specific scaling methods employed, and interviewer training are a few of these factors. However, the various interviewing methods each have certain inherent strengths and weaknesses in regard to producing quality data. These strengths and weaknesses are summarized in Table 7.7.

The point is that the issue of data quality may override other considerations such as cost. For example, the researcher might estimate that it would be cheaper to conduct a long questionnaire with many open-end questions via mall intercept. However, the data obtained by conducting the study by this method might be so biased due to respondent fatigue, distraction, carelessness, and so on as to be

TABLE 7.7   *Strengths and Weaknesses of Various Data Collection Techniques in Terms of Quality of Data Produced*

METHOD	STRENGTH	WEAKNESS
Door-to-Door, Executive	Respondent is at ease and secure in home; face-to-face contact; can observe respondent's home, etc.; interviewer can show, explain, probe, etc.	Cannot readily monitor interviewing process; may have distractions from other family members, telephone, etc., greater chance for interviewer bias; sampling problems
Mall Intercept	Interviewer can show, explain, probe like in door-to-door	May have many distractions inherent in mall environment; respondent may be in a hurry—not in proper frame of mind; more chance for interviewer bias; nonprobability sampling problems
From-Home Telephone	Potential for a "good" sample; interviewer can explain and probe	Cannot readily monitor; respondent or interviewer may be distracted by happenings in their separate homes; long interviews and interviews with many open-end questions are a problem
Central Location Telephone	Can monitor the interviewing process readily; can have excellent sample; interviewers can explain and probe	Respondent may be distracted by things going on at the location; problems in long interviews and interviews with many open-end questions
Self-Administered	Elimination of interviewer and associated biases; respondent can complete the questionnaire when convenient; respondent can also look up certain information and work at own pace	No interviewer to show, explain, or probe; poor sample due to nonresponse; no control of who actually completes the questionnaire
Mail Questionnaire	Same as for self-administered	Same as for self-administered questionnaire; sample quality is better with mail panel

worthless at best and misleading at worst. From a quality of information perspective, the study should have been conducted door to door.

Length of Questionnaire

As noted earlier, the length of the questionnaire—the amount of time that it takes the average respondent to complete the survey—is an important determinant of the appropriate survey method to use. If the questionnaire for a particular study takes an hour to complete, the choices of survey method are extremely limited. Telephone, mall intercept, and just about all other types of surveys except door-to-door interviews will not work. People shopping at a mall ordinarily do not have an hour to spend being interviewed. Terminations increase and tempers flare when you try to keep respondents on the phone for an hour. Response rates plummet when you send people questionnaires through the mail that take an hour or more to complete. The trick is to match the survey technique to the length of the questionnaire.

Necessity of Having Respondent Perform Certain Specialized Tasks

Some surveys require face-to-face interviewing because of the use of special measurement techniques or the need for specialized forms of information as input to quantitative techniques. They require face-to-face interviewing because the tasks are so complex that someone must be available to explain the task and to ascertain whether the respondent understands what is required.

Incidence Rate

Incidence rate refers to the percentage of persons or households out of the general population that fit the qualifications of people to be interviewed in a particular study. For example, assume you are doing a taste test for a new Stovetop Stuffing mix. It has been decided that only those who have purchased a Stovetop Stuffing mix in the last thirty days should be interviewed. It is estimated that out of the general population, only 5 percent of all adults fall into this category. The incidence rate for this study is 5 percent. It is not unusual to seek people with a 5 percent or lower incidence rate in marketing research.

Search costs, which are a function of the time spent trying to locate qualified respondents, frequently exceed interviewing costs (time spent actually interviewing). In those situations where the researcher expects incidence rates to be low and search costs high it is important that an interviewing method or combination of methods be employed that will provide the desired survey results at a reasonable cost.

Doing a low-incidence rate study on a door-to-door basis would, of course, be very expensive. This approach should be taken only if there is some compelling reason for using this approach, a long depth interview for example. The lowest-cost survey alternative for the low-incidence study is probably the mail panel. This assumes that the mail panel approach meets the other data collection requirements of the study. This is particularly true if the panel can be prescreened. As noted

Incidence rate
The percentage of people or households in the general population that fit the qualifications to be sampled.

The incidence rate for adult travel in the U.S. is quite high. A market researcher should not have trouble locating qualified respondents for a survey about travelling in the U.S. (Ted Thai/Sygma)

Art collecting has a very low incidence rate. Door-to-door interviewing to locate art collectors for a survey would yield minimal results. A mail panel would be a lower cost alternative. (D. Hudson/Sygma)

earlier, panel members are asked a number of questions, usually including some on product usage, when the panel is set up. If panel members had been asked if anyone in their household participated in downhill or Alpine snow skiing, the mail panel operator could pull out only those households with one or more skiers for a survey of Alpine skiers at very low cost.

Telephone interviewing offers the next most efficient device to screen for the low-incidence consumer. Sometimes two or more survey methods may be combined to deal more efficiently with the problem of locating low-incidence consumers. For example, we might screen for people who meet our qualifications over the telephone and then send someone out to interview them in person. This approach can dramatically reduce costs in comparison to doing the study totally on a door-to-door basis.

Degree of Structure of the Questionnaire

In addition to length of questionnaire, degree of structure of the questionnaire may be a factor in determining which survey method is most appropriate for a given study. By structure we mean the extent to which the questionnaire follows a set sequence or order, set wording of questions, and relies primarily on closed-end (multiple choice) questions. A questionnaire that does all these things would be a "structured" questionnaire. One that deviates from these set patterns would be considered "unstructured." A questionnaire with little structure is likely to require a face-to-face interview. Very brief, highly structured questionnaires do not ordinarily require face-to-face contact between interviewer and respondent. For studies of this type, mail, telephone, and self-administered questionnaires become viable options.

THE MARKETING RESEARCH INTERVIEWER

No discussion of survey research in marketing can be considered complete without at least taking a look at the person who actually does the interviewing. As noted in Chapter 3, most marketing research interviewing is done under the direct supervision of field service firms. The actual interviewing is conducted, to a large extent, by individuals who work on a part-time basis for relatively low wages. The brand new, totally inexperienced interviewer works at a rate somewhere between minimum wage and minimum wage plus 20 percent. It is unusual to find even the most experienced interviewers earning more than minimum wage plus 50 percent. The pay is not good, and fringe benefits are usually nonexistent—no retirement benefits, no insurance, no extras.

Prospective interviewers are ordinarily sent on assignment with only a minimum of training. There is a high failure rate among first-time interviewers. It is strictly a

MARKETING RESEARCH IN PRACTICE

Survey research methods are becoming more creative, making them more adaptable to companies' specific needs. After tracking fashion trends in the youth market for a period of time, the Youthwear Division of Levi Strauss & Company found that the interview was becoming more comprehensive and time consuming. The problem was how to administer a thirty to forty-five minute interview and still maintain the accuracy and integrity of the data as well as the attention and involvement of the boys who were ages nine to fourteen. Additionally, the company wanted to do the interviews in mall facilities across the country.

In conjunction with Touchstone Research Brandon Connecticut and Analytical Computer Software (ACS), Levi Strauss designed a system involving an interviewer and a child. The interview format had a segment in which an interviewer entered data and a segment in which the children interacted with the computer. The system also included a videotape with explanations and instructions. Colors, sounds, and practice questions were included in the system to make it "kid friendly." There were also brief entertainment sections to give the boys a break during the questioning.

The computer-assisted interviewing was successful for several reasons. The boys seemed to be more comfortable interacting with the computer and were, therefore, more open and honest about their feelings. When interviews are done in several different markets, there is a risk that the differences in the quality of interviewing at the different locations will affect the accuracy of the data. The computer-assisted system provided continuity across markets.

The system simplified the interviewing process for the interviewers as well. A handbook was developed, which made the system relatively failsafe for the interviewers. The software greatly reduced the number of tasks and the amount of paperwork interviewers had to handle.

This new technology is certainly not appropriate for all research situations, but it does have many applications. In particular, it seems to have many benefits in children's research, especially in tracking situations, concept testing, and similar situations where complex information must be presented to the respondent and the measurements will be repeated.[19]

"survival of the fittest" system. Somehow, this system produces a core of competent and dedicated interviewers. Questionnaires should be designed with the presumption that the capabilities of those who will administer them are limited. In general, the interviewer is treated as an automaton—ask questions exactly as written, record exactly what the respondent said, and so on. In general, questionnaires and interviewer instructions are set up with this principle in mind. Little or no discretion is left to the interviewer. The sample interviewer instructions and questionnaire shown in Chapter 10 illustrate these points.

Ordinarily, an interviewer's involvement with an interviewing assignment begins when he or she is asked to work on the particular job by a supervisor at a field service firm. If the interviewer accepts the assignment, he or she will be given a date and time for a briefing or training session on the job. At the briefing, the questionnaire for the study and all deadlines and requirements for the job will be discussed. Interviewers may be asked to bring in their first day's work (if interviewing is being conducted off-premises) to be checked to make sure there have been no misunderstandings and that everything is being done correctly. Ultimately, all interviews will be checked and a certain percentage, usually 10–20 percent, of the people interviewed by each interviewer will be recontacted to make certain they were actually interviewed before the completed questionnaires are sent to the client.

SURVEY RESEARCH IN THE INTERNATIONAL MARKET

The total marketing research expenditures for the world are estimated at $5.4 billion. Of the research, 40 percent is conducted in Western Europe and 39 percent in the United States. Japan accounts for only 9 percent of the research expenditures. In Europe, most of the research is done in Germany, France, Italy, the United Kingdom, and Spain. Approximately 40 million interviews a year are carried out in all of Europe. Data collection methods vary substantially from country to country as shown in Table 7.8.

European Marketing Research

In terms of cost, European countries can be examined by quantitative and qualitative methods. In quantitative studies, the five most expensive countries are Germany, Switzerland, Italy, France, and Norway; Greece is the cheapest. For qualitative research, Norway is the most expensive, followed by France, Italy, Germany, and the Netherlands. About 25,000 people are employed professionally in European market research, with well over 100,000 interviewers.

Asian Marketing Research

In Asia, many countries have the capability of conducting some kinds of Western-style marketing research. Japan, Hong Kong, Singapore, and the Philippines have fairly advanced research industries. Japan has its own unique methodology in gathering secondary information. On the basis of highly developed networks of industry contacts, some Japanese research companies use "groupthink" technique

TABLE 7.8 *European Data Collection Methods (percent of use)*

	FRANCE	THE NETHERLANDS	SWEDEN	SWITZERLAND	UNITED KINGDOM
Mail	4	33	23	8	9
Telephone	15	18	44	21	16
Central location/streets	52	37	—	—	—
Home/work	—	—	8	44	54
Groups	13	—	5	6	11
Depth interviews	12	12	2	8	—
Secondary	4	—	4	8	—
Other	0	0	14	5	10

Source: ESOMAR, Amsterdam, The Netherlands.

studies to develop accurate market share estimates and competitive assessment information.

The governments in some Asian countries such as Taiwan and Japan release enough census data on individuals to make sample building easier and more accurate than it is in most Western countries. When a household moves in these countries, it is required to submit up-to-date information to a centralized government agency before any family member can use communal services like water, gas, electricity, and education.

Other countries in Asia such as China, Korea, Indonesia, and India have research capabilities, but they are so underdeveloped as to require special supervision. Asia also has fewer marketing research firms that can act as data "translators," people who can transform computer tables and research results into specific marketing directions.

Marketing Research in the Independent Federation of States (formerly USSR)

Opinion and market research in the Soviet Union dates back to the 1960s, during a brief thaw in the political and economic climate under Khrushchev.[20] For instance, large-scale youth surveys were conducted under the direction of Dr. Boris Grushin, then head of the Soviet Institute of Public Opinion at the *Komsomolskaya Pravda* newspaper. VNIIKS, All-Union Institute for Market Research, attached to the Ministry of Home Trade, also started doing research on issues of supply and demand around the same time. Much of VNIIKS's early work was "industrial research," in which it utilized a network of expert correspondents and informants throughout the Soviet Union.

With a few exceptions, most of the opinion surveys conducted before 1985 were designed to bolster the party line, not to determine truth. Usually, only positive and favorable findings were published. In addition, little concern was given to proper sampling procedures and interview techniques. Most of this early research was based on self-administered questionnaires distributed at respondents' places of work, which provided respondents little faith in the promise of anonymity.

Glasnost and the disintegration of the Russian state has proven to be a boon for the marketing research industry as the independent states struggle for capitalism. Today, there are basically three types of research organizations in the Soviet Union.

The first type conducts marketing research projects almost exclusively. It includes groups that at one time or another were affiliated with government industry and trade agencies, new joint ventures with foreign partners, such as VNIIKS (affiliated with a Finnish research institute) and INFOMARKET (owned by the Russian Ministry of Metallurgy and a Dutch research company).

The second type has a more scholarly orientation, concentrating on public opinion research and social trends. Examples are the Institute of Sociology and the Institute of Applied Social Research, both of the Academy of Sciences. Universities such as Moscow State University and the University of Vilnius, have also started centers of public opinion research.

The third type of research organization seeks to combine marketing and opinion research. Their clientele is diverse, ranging from independent news agencies to government and legislative branches, Western media, government agencies, research institutes, advertising agencies, and corporations. The Center for Public Opinion and Market Research and Vox Populi (VP), headed by Boris Grushin, are typical, and two of the best known, of this kind.

Taken together, currently available research services include individual-republic omnibuses, consumer panels, opinion leader panels, and ad hoc studies covering a wide range of social, economic, political, and marketing or business-related topics. Data collection techniques include face-to-face interviewing, surveys by mail, and even telephone interviewing among elites or opinion leaders.

Random sampling can be carried out using relatively accurate and comprehensive address lists. Largely due to the government's rigid control of society and the lack of population mobility, household rosters and voter registration lists are fairly up-to-date and comprehensive, covering about 95 percent of the population. Reputable survey organizations usually have no difficulty gaining access to these lists. As private housing and employment in the private sector become more commonplace, however, it may be increasingly difficult to update these lists, which, for now, provide an excellent source of sampling.

Much of the personal-interview research carried out to date has focused on key states; that is, Russia, the Ukraine, and the Baltic States—and these studies are generally considered to be more accurate and reliable than those purporting to cover the entire former Russian nation. Typically, field work is carefully controlled. For a new custom research study, supervisors from the various areas to be sampled assemble in Moscow for a briefing session, going over the questionnaire and sampling specifications in great detail. These supervisors, or "team leaders," are responsible for recruiting and training interviewers. The supervisors are often highly educated and usually have other professional jobs. For example, one study included a teacher of Russian literature, who could recite Pushkin forward and backward, and a professor of engineering from a local college. Regional offices validate 10 percent of all interviews. The level of participation in these surveys can make any Western researcher envious. Refusal rates are commonly less than 10 percent and the number of unsuccessful contacts and inaccessible locations (e.g., upscale apartment buildings) is also fairly low.

Conducting International Survey Research

Before conducting survey research, an international market researcher should first examine relevant secondary data. Secondary data have the same advantages and disadvantages in the international market as they do at home. They are relatively inexpensive and can usually be obtained more rapidly than primary data. National economic statistics and industry analyses published by the U.S. Department of Commerce are excellent sources of secondary information.

A number of countries gather census data much as in the United States. European countries such as Switzerland and West Germany print a good deal of information on noncitizens. Canada collects data on religion. Both of these topics are ignored in U.S. censuses.

A marketing researcher cannot expect to find the same range of data topics from one country to the next, and this can complicate research enormously. Consider income data, the lifeblood of most U.S. segmentation studies. Most nations do not include an income question in their censuses. Britain does not, Japan does not, nor do France, Spain, and Italy. Among the few countries that have asked about income are Canada, Australia, New Zealand, Mexico, Sweden, and Finland.

Willingness to Participate.   International marketing research utilizes the same tools, techniques, and theory as domestic research. Yet it is done in vastly different environments. In some countries, a woman would never consider being interviewed by a man. A French-Canadian woman does not like to be questioned and is likely to be reticent; she prefers privacy for herself and her family. In some societies, a man would consider it beneath his dignity to discuss shaving habits or brand preference in personal clothing with anyone— and certainly not with a woman. In Korea, for example, business people are reluctant to answer any survey questions about their companies—it is considered disloyal to divulge any type of information to "outsiders." And most Japanese businesspeople are hesitant to take part in surveys during business hours—taking time away from your work for a survey is like "stealing" from your employer.[21] The growing resistance to surveys everywhere is a result of the misuse of interviewing by door-to-door salespeople claiming to be doing marketing research when, in fact, they are selling household items.

Although cultural differences may make survey research more difficult to conduct, it is possible. In some communities, it is necessary to enlist the aid of locally prominent people to open otherwise closed doors; in other situations, professional people and local students have been used as interviewers because of their knowledge of the market. As with most of the problems of collecting primary data, the difficulties are not insurmountable to a researcher aware of their existence.

Language and Comprehension.   The most universal survey sampling problem in foreign countries is the language barrier.[22] Differences in idiom and the difficulty of exact translation create problems in eliciting the specific information desired and interpreting respondents' answers. Equivalent concepts may not exist in all languages. *Family*, for example, has different connotations in different countries. In the United States, it generally means only the parents and children. In Italy and many Latin countries it could mean the parents, children, grandparents, uncles, aunts, cousins, and so forth. The meaning of names for family members can have different meanings depending on the context within which they are used. In the Indian culture, uncle and aunt are different for the maternal and paternal sides of the family. Also, in India, for example, fourteen official languages are spoken in different parts of the country, and most government and business affairs are conducted in English. Similarly, in Switzerland, German is used in some areas and French in others. In the Republic of Congo, the official language is French, but only a small part of the population is fluent in French. Unfortunately, translating a questionnaire from one language to another is far from easy. Translating "out of sight, out of mind" from English to Danish became "invisible things are insane."

Resolving the Problems.   There are no foolproof methods to take care of all the problems just discussed. The following suggestions, however, may help to eliminate some of the problems.[23]

The international marketing research should be undertaken in conjunction with a reputable local firm. Such a firm may be a foreign office of a U.S. advertising firm like J. Walter Thompson, a U.S. accounting firm like Price Waterhouse, or a locally owned firm belonging to a third country like a Japanese advertising agency in Italy. The resources of the cooperating firm will be invaluable; for example, its knowledge of local customs, including things like the feasibility of interviewing housewives while husbands are at work; its familiarity with local environment, including modes of transportation available for personal interviews in smaller towns; and its contact in different parts of the country as sources for drawing a sample.

From the beginning, a person who has a grasp of both sound marketing research procedures and the local culture should be involved in all phases of the research design. Such a person can recommend the number of languages in which the questionnaire should be printed and the cultural traits, habits, customs, and rituals to keep in mind in different phases of the research.

The questionnaire may first be written in English, and then a native fluent in English can translate it into the local language(s). A third person should retranslate it into English. This retranslated version can then be compared with the original English version. The three people involved should work together to eliminate differences in the three versions of the questionnaire by changing phrases, idioms, and words. Ultimately, the questionnaire in the local language should accurately reflect the questions in the original English questionnaire.

Despite the difficulties often faced in conducting international research, some information is always better than none. Sunbeam, for example, failed to do research and only after lack of sales of its toaster in Italy found that although most Europeans eat toast, Italians do not. Sunbeam also was first in the Italian market with a ladies electric shaver. Again no research was done (after all, it was a high-quality product and sold well in the United States). The shaver bombed. Sunbeam later learned that Italian men like women with hair on their legs.

SUMMARY

Surveys are popular for several reasons. First is the need by managers to know why people do or do not do something. Second, managers need to know how decisions are made. Third, managers need to know what kind of person, from a demographic or lifestyle perspective, is making the decision to buy or not buy a product.

There are two major categories of error in survey research: random sampling error and systematic error or bias. Systematic error can be further broken down into measurement error and sample design error. Sample design error is composed of selection, population specification, and frame error. Frame error results from the use of an incomplete or inaccurate sampling frame. Population specification error results from an incorrect definition of the universe or population from which the sample is to be selected. Selection error results from using incomplete or improper sampling procedures or when appropriate selection procedures are not properly followed.

The second major category of systematic error is measurement error. Measurement error occurs when there is a discrepancy between the information being sought (the true value) and the information obtained by the measurement process. Measurement error can be created by a number of factors, including surrogate information error, interviewer error, measurement instrument bias, processing error, nonresponse bias, or response bias. Surrogate information error results from a discrepancy between the information actually required to solve a problem and the information sought by the researcher. Interviewer error occurs due to interactions between the interviewer and the respondent. Measurement instrument bias is caused by problems within the questionnaire itself. Processing error results from mistakes in the transfer of information from survey documents to the computer. Nonresponse error occurs when a particular individual in a sample cannot be reached or refuses to participate in the survey. Response bias means that interviewees answer questions in a particular way. It may be deliberate falsification or unconscious misrepresentation.

There are several popular types of surveys. Door-to-door interviewing is the traditional method of interviewing individuals in their homes or apartments. Mall intercept interviewing contacts shoppers in public areas of shopping malls, either interviewing them on the mall or asking them to come to a permanent interviewing facility within the mall. Executive interviewing is the industrial equivalent of door-to-door interviewing; it involves interviewing professional people at their offices, typically concerning industrial products or services. From-home telephone interviewing is a process by which interviewers come to the office of a field service firm for a training session and then use their home phones to do the interviewing. Central location telephone interviewing is interviewing from a facility set up for the specific purpose of conducting telephone survey research. Computer-assisted telephone interviewing is associated with the central location interviewing process. Each interviewer is seated in front of a computer terminal or personal computer. The computer guides the interviewer and the interviewing process by having the questionnaire on the computer screen. The data are entered into the computer as the interview takes place. Direct computer interviewing takes place when the respondent sits at a computer terminal and responds to questions using a keyboard. This type of interviewing is limited to mall facilities. A self-administered interview is a survey questionnaire filled out by the respondent. The big disadvantage of this approach is that probes cannot be used to clarify responses. Mail surveys can be divided into ad hoc, or one-shot, surveys and mail panels. In an ad hoc mail survey, questionnaires are mailed to potential respondents without prior contact. The sample is used only for the single survey project. In a mail panel, consumers are precontacted by letter and are offered an incentive for participating in the panel for a period of time. If they agree, they fill out a background data questionnaire. Then periodically panel participants are sent questionnaires.

The factors that determine which survey method will be used include sampling precision, budget availability, the need to expose respondents to various stimuli, quality of data required, length of questionnaire, the necessity of having the respondent perform certain specialized tasks, the incident rate sought, the degree of structure of the questionnaire, and the time available to complete the survey.

The key individual in survey research is the marketing research interviewer. For the most part, interviewing is conducted by individuals who work on a part-time basis for relatively low wages. The pay is not only low, but devoid of fringe benefits. Interviewers are often provided only a minimum of training. Also, because of the high failure rate, it is a survival of the fittest system. Yet, somehow this system tends to produce a core of competent and dedicated interviewers.

International survey research faces many of the same problems and opportunities as domestic research. In addition, international research faces cultural differences that may lower the participation rate and language and comprehension problems. In spite of these barriers, the cost of conducting international survey research is usually less than the benefits.

KEY TERMS

Random sampling error
Systematic error
Frame error
Population specification error
Selection error
Measurement error
Surrogate information error
Interviewer error
Measurement instrument bias
Processing error
Nonresponse bias
Response bias
Door-to-door interviewing

Mall intercept interviewing
Executive interviewing
From-home telephone interviewing
Central location telephone interviewing
Computer-assisted telephone
  interviewing (CATI)
Direct computer interviewing
Self-administered questionnaire
Ad hoc mail surveys
Mail panels
Longitudinal study
Incidence rate

REVIEW AND DISCUSSION QUESTIONS

1. The owner of a hardware store in Eureka, California, is interested in determining demographic characteristics of people who shop at his store versus competing stores. He also wants to know what his image is relative to competing hardware stores. He would like to have the information within three weeks and is working on a limited budget. Which survey method would you recommend? Why?
2. From-home telephone surveys are almost always cheaper to conduct than central location telephone surveys. Why is this true?
3. Your supervisor has asked you to recommend which type of telephone interviewing your company should purchase from a survey research organization. Which would you recommend? Why?
4. The critical function within the survey research process is performed by the interviewer. Yet interviewers are typically paid minimum wage. If interviewers are so important, why is this true? What do you think should be done to raise the quality of survey research?
5. "A mall intercept interview is representative only of persons who shop in that particular mall. Therefore, only surveys that relate to shopping patterns of consumers within that mall should be conducted in a mall intercept interview." Discuss.
6. A colleague is arguing that the best way to conduct a study of attitudes toward city government in your community is through a mail survey because it is cheapest. How would you respond to your colleague? Assume that time is not a critical factor in your decision. Would this change your response? Why?
7. Discuss the various sources of sample design error and give examples of each.
8. Why is it important to consider measurement error in survey research? Why is this typically not discussed in professional market research reports?
9. What types of error might be associated with the following situations?
   (a) Conducting a survey about attitudes toward city government using the telephone directory as a sample frame.

(b) Interviewing respondents only between 8:00 A.M. and 5:00 P.M. on features they would like to see in a new condominium development.

(c) Asking people if they have visited the public library in the past two months.

(d) Asking people how many tubes of toothpaste they used in the past year.

(e) Telling interviewers they can probe using any particular example they wish to make up.

10. Discuss some of the unique problems a researcher faces in conducting international survey research.

CASE

J. C. Penney's

J. C. Penney traditionally positioned itself as a mass merchandiser serving the needs of middle-class Americans. Its major competitors were other mass merchandisers such as Sears Roebuck. However, two decades ago, prompted in large part by demographic change as increasing numbers of women entered the work force, J. C. Penney decided to change its positioning. Penney's mission statement no longer places it in competition with such mass merchandisers as Sears Roebuck; its new competitors are upscale department stores such as Macy's.

Because J. C. Penney has been positioned as a mass merchandiser to middle America for many more decades than it has been positioned as an upscale department store, Penney's perception of its repositioning and new competitors may not mirror the consumers' perception of Penney. Possibly consumers do not yet totally perceive Penney as an upscale department store. A study therefore was conducted to determine Penney's progress toward its repositioning strategy. How do consumers view J. C. Penney? Do consumers perceive Penney as an upscale department store or does the traditional positioning still dominate?

A J. C. Penney store in Florin Mall, a major shopping mall in Sacramento, California, was selected for the study. Sears Roebuck and Mervyn's were selected to represent Penney's previous mass merchandiser positioning. Macy's of California and Weinstock's were selected to represent Penney's current repositioning as an upscale department store. The Sears Roebuck, Weinstock's, and Penney stores are all in the same mall; and the other two stores, Mervyn's and Macy's, are located in the same geoeconomic area. Thus all five stores were equally accessible to the geographic customer base.

A visual display of women's clothing was selected to represent the position of the five stores selected for study, in large part because J. C. Penney has made a major effort to target professional working women. Pictures were taken of the five stores' displays of women's clothing. Managers at the stores identified the displays they believed were most representative of their store. From the initial set of pictures, the researchers selected one display to represent each store.

On a Saturday, 165 women consumers participated in a survey taken at Florin Mall. To obtain a representative sample, the researchers were stationed at three different mall entry locations, which coincidentally were also the locations of the Penney, Sears, and Weinstock's stores. Participants were asked to complete a matching task and a sorting task. The same pictures were used in both tasks.

In the matching task, participants were shown pictures of five displays of women's clothing, labeled P, Q, R, S, and T, and were asked to match the pictures with the list of stores on the survey form: Sears, Mervyn's, Macy's, Penney, and Weinstock's. In the sorting task, participants were given a stack of the five pictures of the displays and were instructed to sort them into piles according to their similarity. They were told that they were free to establish as many or as few piles as they wanted. After the matching and sorting tasks each participant answered a brief questionnaire that provided store patronage patterns and demographic information.

Results

The demographic characteristics of the sample are representative of J. C. Penney's target market, professional working women. Of the sample of women, 48 percent were between the ages of 22 and 35, 58 percent reported household income between $15,001 and $50,000, 56 percent were married, 68 percent were employed in the professions, and 61 percent were Caucasian.

Figure 7.2 shows the results of the sorting task. Customers perceived Penney's display as similar to those of the upscale department stores, Macy's of California and Weinstock's. They did not perceive Penney's display as similar to those of the mass merchandisers, Sears and Mervyn's.

FIGURE 7.2   *Number of Consumers Who Grouped Penney with Other Stores*

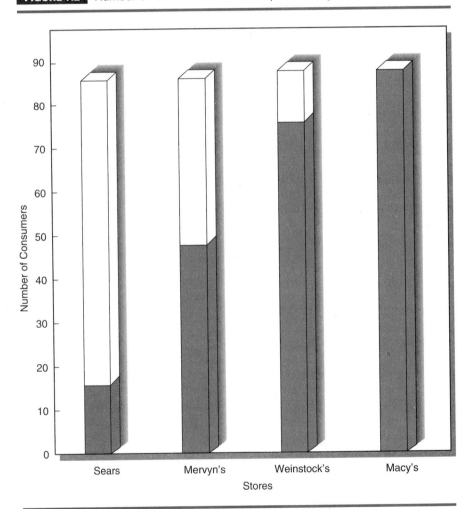

FIGURE 7.3   *Number of Consumers Who Identified the Store Displays as Belonging to Penney*

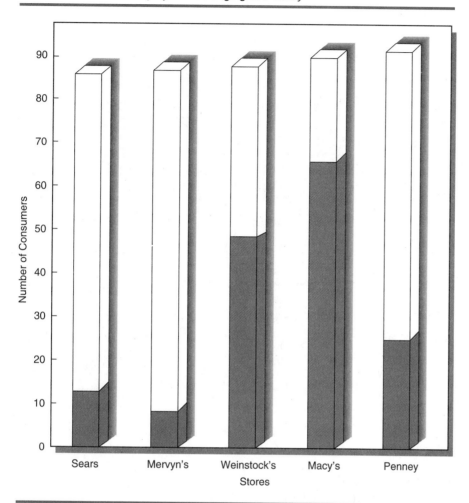

Figure 7.3 shows the results of the matching task. Customers identified Penney's display as belonging to Macy's or Weinstock's. They did not identify Penney's display as belonging to Sears or Mervyn's. Interestingly, consumers did not identify Penney's display as belonging to Penney.[24]

1. What type of survey research was conducted? What are the advantages and disadvantages of the method?
2. What other types of survey research could have been used to accomplish the research objective?
3. Discuss the potential sources of error with the methodology used.
4. What conclusions could be drawn from the research?

CHAPTER 8

Primary Data Collection: Experimentation

LEARNING OBJECTIVES

1. To understand the nature of experiments.
2. To gain insight into proving causation.
3. To learn about the experimental setting.
4. To examine experimental validity and the threats to validity.
5. To learn the disadvantages of experiments that limit their use in marketing research.
6. To compare preexperimental designs, true experimental designs, and quasi-experimental designs.
7. To gain insight into test marketing.

J ane Helstrom is director of advertising for Taco Casita, a Mexican fast-food restarurant chain with over 400 outlets in Texas, New Mexico, Utah, Colorado, Louisiana, and Arkansas. The company has been in business for twelve years and experienced rapid growth over the first ten years of that period. Sales for last year exceeded $350 million. But the company has encountered a slowing in its growth over the last two years, and is considering major changes in its marketing strategy.

Taco City was Taco Casita's major competition in all markets. Taco City has 1,500 outlets throughout the United States and is a subsidiary of a major soft drink marketer. Taco Casita recently conducted a comprehensive marketing strategy evaluation that included focus groups and a large-scale telephone survey with Mexican fast-foot users throughout its market area. This evaluation and research pointed to a number of potential problems, but the one that Jane is most concerned with is the finding that Mexican fast-food users feel that Taco Casita's prices are too high. Taco Casita has positioned itself as the authentic Mexican fast-food restaurant and has supported this position with the use of fresher, higher quality ingredients than those used by its rivals. Jane is very concerned about the pricing issue because she knows that for Taco Casita to reduce its prices, the firm would have to make some reduction in the quality of the food it serves. She does not want to take this action unless she is very sure that the results for Taco Casita will be positive. She does not feel that this question can be definitively answered by surveys, focus groups, or observation-based primary data collection. Jane is considering the possibility of testing a strategy change in the actual marketplace. However, she does not want to take the risk of testing a new "lower-price, somewhat lower quality" strategy throughout the entire area served by Taco Casita. Taco Casita has four restaurants in the isolated market of Lubbock, Texas, and Jane is considering the possibility of testing the new strategy in Lubbock for one year. At the end of this one-year test, she will evaluate the results of the new strategy and make a recommendation to top management regarding a possible change in the marketing strategy for Taco Casita.

Jane is concerned about a number of factors. First of all, is Lubbock a good place to conduct the test? Second, is one year long enough, or longer than necessary? Finally, what factors should she consider when evaluating the results of the Lubbock test?

The issues confronting Jane Helstrom are related to the main topic of this chapter, which pertains to experimental research. When is experimental research appropriate? How does one go about evaluating the results of an experiment? What are the inherent advantages and disadvantages of the experimental approach? Why conduct a field experiment rather than a laboratory experiment? These and a number of other questions will be considered in this chapter. After you have had an opportunity to read it, reconsider the questions raised by Jane's predicament to see whether you can make recommendations to her.

WHAT IS AN EXPERIMENT?

Research based on experimentation is fundamentally different than research based on survey or observation.[1] In the case of both survey and observation, the researcher is, in essence, a passive assembler of data. The researcher asks people questions or observes what they do. In the case of experiments, the situation is very different. The researcher becomes an active participant in the process.

In concept, an **experiment** is straightforward. The researcher changes or manipulates one thing, called an *explanatory, independent,* or *experimental variable,* to observe what effect this change has on something else, referred to as a *dependent variable.* In marketing experiments, the dependent variable is frequently some measure of sales, such as total sales, market share, or the like, and the explanatory or experimental variables are typically marketing mix variables, such as price, amount or type of advertising, changes in product features, or the like.

Experiment
Research approach where one variable is manipulated and the effect on another variable observed.

DEMONSTRATING CAUSATION

Experimental research is often referred to as *causal* (not *casual*) *research.* It is called **causal research** because it is the only type of research that has the potential to demonstrate that a change in one variable causes some predictable change in another variable. In order to demonstrate causation, that *A* likely caused *B,* we must be able to show three things:

Causal research
Research designed to determine whether a change in one variable likely caused an observed change in another.

1. Concomitant variation
2. Appropriate time order of occurrence
3. Elimination of other possible causal factors

Concomitant Variation

To provide evidence that a change in *A* caused a particular change in *B,* we must first show that there is **concomitant variation** or correlation between *A* and *B.* In other words, that they vary together in some predictable fashion. This relationship might be positive or inverse. An example of two variables that are related in a positive manner might be advertising and sales. They would be positively related if sales increased by some predictable amount when advertising increased. An example of two variables that are related in an inverse manner might be price and sales. They would be inversely (negatively) related if sales increased when price decreased and decreased when price increased. The researcher can test for the existence and direction of statistical relationships by means of a number of statistical procedures.

Concomitant variation
A predictable statistical relationship between two variables.

These procedures include chi-square analysis, correlation analysis, regression analysis, and analysis of variance.

However, concomitant variation by itself does not prove causation. Simply because two variables happen to vary together in some predictable fashion does not prove that one causes the other.

Appropriate Time Order of Occurrence

Appropriate time order of occurrence
To be considered a likely cause of a dependent variable, a change in an independent variable must occur before an observed change in the dependent variable.

The second thing that you must show to demonstrate that a causal relationship likely exists between two variables is that there is an **appropriate time order of occurrence**. To demonstrate that A caused B, the researcher must be able to show that A occurred before B occurred. For example, to demonstrate that a price change had an effect on sales, you must be able to show that the price change occurred before the change in sales was observed. However, showing that A and B vary concomitantly and that A occurred before B, still does not provide evidence that is strong enough to permit us to conclude that A is the likely cause of an observed change in B.

Elimination of Other Possible Causal Factors

To infer that a causal relationship likely exists between A and B, the most difficult thing to demonstrate in many marketing experiments is that the change in B was not caused by some factor other than A. For example, we might increase our advertising expenditures and observe a particular increase in the sales of our product. Correlation and appropriate time order of occurrence are present. But has a likely causal relationship been demonstrated? The answer is clearly "No." It is possible that the observed change in sales is due to some factor other than the increase in advertising. For example, at the same time advertising expenditures were increased, a major competitor might have decreased advertising expenditures, or increased price, or pulled out of the market. Even if the competitive environment did not change, one or a combination of other factors may have influenced sales. For example, the economy in the area might have received a major boost for some reason that has nothing to do with the experiment. For any of these reasons or for many other possible reasons, the observed increase in sales might have been caused by some other factor or some combination of factors rather than or in addition to the increase in advertising expenditures. Much of the discussion in this chapter is related to the question of designing experiments that enable us to eliminate or adjust for the effects of other possible causal factors.

THE EXPERIMENTAL SETTING—LABORATORY OR FIELD

Experiments can be conducted in a laboratory or in a field setting.[2] Most experiments in the physical sciences are conducted in a laboratory setting. The major advantage of conducting experiments in a laboratory is the ability to control many other causal factors—temperature, light, humidity, and so on—and focus on the effect of a change in A on B. In the lab, the researcher can more effectively deal with the third element of proving causation (elimination of other possible causal factors) and focus on the first two (concomitant variation and appropriate time order of occurrence).

Laboratory experiments provide a number of important advantages.[3] The major advantage, referred to earlier, relates to the ability to control all variables other than the experimental variable in the laboratory setting. This means that our ability to infer that an observed change in the dependent variable was caused by a change in the experimental or treatment variable is much stronger. As a result, laboratory experiments are generally viewed as having greater internal validity (internal validity is discussed in greater detail later). On the other hand, the controlled and possibly sterile environment of the laboratory may not be a good analog of the marketplace. Because of this, the findings of laboratory experiments sometimes do not hold up when we transfer them to the actual marketplace. Therefore, laboratory experiments are often seen as having greater problems with external validity (discussed in greater detail later). However, laboratory experiments have many advantages and are probably being used to a greater extent today than in the past.

Many marketing experiments are conducted as **field experiments**. This means that they are conducted outside the laboratory in an actual market environment. Test markets, discussed later in this chapter, are a frequently used type of field experiment. Field experiments solve the problem of the realism of the environment, but open up a whole new set of problems. The major problem is that in the field the researcher cannot control all spurious factors that might influence the dependent variable. In the field, the researcher cannot control the actions of competitors, the weather, the economy, societal trends, the political climate, and the like. Therefore, field experiments have more problems related to internal validity, whereas lab experiments have more problems related to external validity.

> **Laboratory experiments**
> Experiments conducted in a controlled setting.

> **Field experiments**
> Tests conducted outside the laboratory in an actual market environment.

Experimental Validity

Validity is defined in Chapter 9 as actually measuring what we attempt to measure. The validity of a measure refers to the extent to which the measure is free from both systematic and random error. In addition to the general concept of validity, in experimentation, we are also interested in two specific kinds of validity: internal validity and external validity.

Internal and External Validity

In an experimental design, any extraneous variable that may interfere with our ability to make causal inferences is considered a threat to validity.

Internal validity refers to the extent to which competing explanations for the experimental results observed can be avoided. If the researcher can show that the experimental or treatment variable actually produced the differences observed in the dependent variable, then the experiment can be said to be internally valid. This kind of validity requires evidence to demonstrate that variation in the dependent variable was caused by exposure to the treatment conditions and not by other causal factors.

External validity refers to the extent to which the causal relationships measured in an experiment can be generalized to outside persons, settings, and times.[4] The issue here is, How representative are the subjects and the setting used in the experiment of other populations and settings to which we would like to project

> **Internal validity**
> The extent to which competing explanations for the experimental results observed can be avoided.

> **External validity**
> The extent to which causal relationships measured in an experiment can be generalized to outside persons, settings, and times.

MARKETING RESEARCH IN PRACTICE

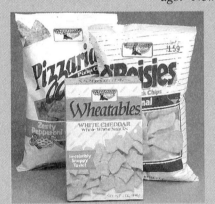

Pizzarias are just one of the new products that are turning what was once a small biscuit and cookie company into a formidable competitor in the salty snack business. Keebler has become a case study of how to flank the competition by creating new products that offer consumers truly unique features. Last year, Keebler sold $1.5 billion worth of cookies, crackers, salty snacks, and other related products. Roughly half of this amount is from products that did not exist ten years ago. New lines such as Pizzarias, Wheatables, and O'Boisies potato chips have distinctive flavors, textures, and appeal.

Keebler learned the advantages of a strong new-product strategy during the cookie wars of the mid-1980s. Procter & Gamble and Frito-Lay tried to break into the cookie business with soft cookies, and Keebler was forced to respond quickly with new formulations of its own.

Since then, Keebler has used new technology and management techniques to reduce the time required for new product development. In 1986 Keebler opened an $11 million pilot plant and laboratory testing center called the Product and Process Development Center or PPDC. This facility includes a new product testing laboratory and a scale replica of a Keebler factory production line. New product ideas are tested with consumers in the testing laboratory. Once these new product ideas have passed consumer screening, new product teams can work out kinks in mixing, baking, frying, and packaging on an assembly line before the product moves into full production. Keebler executives say the production line has enabled it to eliminate 65–70 percent of the disappointments in factory line start-ups. This also means that Keebler can get a new product concept from the laboratory to the retail store with tremendous efficiency. Once management approves a new product, Keebler can get 90 percent national distribution within four weeks.

Another benefit of the laboratory testing and pilot plant is secrecy. Keebler has not needed a real, live test market in ten years. Because of the PPDC, it does not have to do a factory dry run. Taste tests can be done in-house. The benefit: "we don't have to tip off our competition to what we are doing."[5]

the results? In general, field experiments offer a higher degree of external validity and a lower degree of internal validity than laboratory experiments.

Experimental Notation

Further discussion of experiments will be facilitated by using the following standard system of notation to describe experiments:[6]

■ *X* is used to indicate the exposure of an individual or a group to an experimental treatment. The experimental treatment is the factor whose effects we want to measure and compare. Experimental treatments may be factors such as different prices, package designs, point-of-purchase displays, advertising approaches, or product forms. Possible experimental treatments would include all possible elements of the marketing mix.

- O (for observation) is used to refer to the process of taking measurements on the test units. Test units are individuals or groups of individuals or entities (retail stores) whose response to the experimental treatments is being tested. Test units might include individual consumers, groups of consumers, retail stores, total markets, or any other entities that might be the targets of a firm's marketing program.
- Different time periods are represented by the horizontal arrangement of the Xs and Os. For example,

$$O_1 \quad X \quad O_2$$

would describe an experiment where a preliminary measurement was taken on one or more test units O_1, the one or more test units were exposed to the treatment or experimental variable X, and a measurement of the test units was taken after the exposure O_2. The Xs and Os can also be arranged vertically to show simultaneous exposure and measurement of different test units. For example, we might have the following design

$$X_1 \quad O_1$$
$$X_2 \quad O_2$$

This design shows two different groups of test units. It also shows that each group of test units received a different experimental treatment at the same time (X_1 and X_2). Finally, the design shows that the two groups were measured simultaneously (O_1 and O_2).

Extraneous Variables: Threats to Experimental Validity

In interpreting experimental results, we would like to be able to conclude that the observed response is due to the effect of the experimental or treatment variable. However, many things stand in the way of our ability to reach this conclusion. In anticipation of possible problems in interpretation we need to design our experiment so that we can eliminate extraneous factors as possible causes of the observed effect. Examples of extraneous factors or variables follow.[7]

History.   **History** refers to any variable or event other than those manipulated by the researcher (experimental or treatment variable) that takes place between the beginning and end of the experiment and that might affect the value of the dependent variable. Early tests of Prego Spaghetti Sauce by the Campbell Soup Company provide an example of the possible problems with this type of extraneous variable. Campbell executives claim that Ragu greatly increased its advertising levels and use of cents-off deals during their test. They believe that this increased marketing activity was designed to get shoppers to increase their inventories of Ragu and make it impossible for Campbell to get an accurate reading of potential sales for their Prego product.

Maturation.   **Maturation** refers to changes in subjects throughout the course of the experiment that are a function of time and include such things as getting older,

History
Things that happen or outside variables that change between the beginning and end of an experiment.

Maturation
Changes in subjects that take place during the experiment that are not related to the experiment, but may affect their response to the experimental factor.

Campbell Soup Company executives believed that Ragu increased advertising and coupon offers to encourage consumers to stock up on Ragu spaghetti sauce in order to deter the market testing of Prego spaghetti sauce.

hungrier, tired, and the like. As a result, the responses of people to a treatment variable throughout the course of an experiment may change due to these maturation factors rather than to the treatment or experimental variable. The likelihood that maturation will be a serious problem in a particular experiment depends on the length of the experiment. The longer the experiment runs, the more likely it is that maturation will present problems for interpreting the results.

Instrument variation
Differences or changes in measurement instruments (e.g., interviewers or observers) that explain differences in measurements.

Instrument Variation. **Instrument variation** refers to any changes in measurement instruments that might explain differences in the measurements taken. This is a serious problem in many marketing experiments, where people are used as interviewers or observers to measure the dependent variable. Measurements on the same subject may be taken by different interviewers or observers at different points in time. Any differences between these measurements may reflect differences in the way the interviewing or observation was done by different interviewers or observers. On the other hand, the same interviewer or observer may be used to take measurements on the same subject over time. In this case, differences may reflect the fact that the particular observer or interviewer has become less interested and is doing a sloppier job over time.

Selection bias
Systematic differences between the test group and control group due to a biased selection process.

Selection Bias. The threat to validity of **selection bias** is encountered in situations where the experimental or test group is systematically different from the population to which we would like to project the experimental results or from a control group to which we would like to compare results.

In projecting the results to a population that is systematically different than the test group, we may get results very different from those we got in the test because of differences in the makeup of the two groups. In a similar manner, an observed difference between a test group and an untreated control group (not exposed to the experimental or treatment variable) may be due to differences in the two groups and not to the effect of the experimental or treatment variable. We can ensure equality of groups by either matching or randomization. Randomization involves assigning subjects to test groups and control groups at random. Matching involves what the name suggests—we make sure that there is a one-to-one match between people or other units (stores) in the test and control groups in regard to key characteristics (e.g., age).

Mortality.   **Mortality** refers to the loss of test units during the course of an experiment. This is a problem because there is no easy way to know if the test units that we lost would have responded to the experimental or treatment variable in the same way as those units that continued throughout the entire experiment. An experimental group that was representative of the population or the same as a control group may become nonrepresentative because of the systematic loss of the subjects with certain characteristics. For example, in a study of music preferences of the population, if we lost nearly all of the subjects under the age of 25 during the course of the experiment, then we are very likely to get a biased picture of music preferences at the end of the experiment. In this case, our results would probably lack external validity.

Mortality
Loss of test units or subjects during the course of an experiment. The problem is that those lost may be systematically different than those who stay.

Testing Effect.   **Testing effects** result from the fact that the process of experimentation may produce its own effect on the responses we observe. For example, measuring attitude toward a product before exposing subjects to an ad may act as a treatment and influence perception of the ad. Testing effects come in two forms:

Testing effect
An effect that is a by-product of the research process and not the experimental variable.

- Main testing effects are the possible effects of earlier observations on later observations. For example, students taking the GMAT for the second time tend to do better than those taking the test for the first time. This is true even though students have no information about the items they actually missed on the first test. This effect can also be reactive in the sense that responses to the first

Students taking the GMAT exam usually improve on their second try even though they aren't given information about the items they missed on the first test. This is an example of the testing effect. (Stephen Collins/Photo Researchers, Inc.)

administration of an attitude test have some actual effect on the attitudes of subjects, which is reflected in subsequent applications of the same test.

■ Interactive testing effect refers to the effect of a prior measurement on a subject's response to a later measurement. For example, if we ask subjects about their awareness of advertising for various products (preexposure measurement) and then expose them to advertising for one or more of these products (treatment variable), then postmeasurements are likely to reflect the joint effect of the preexposure and the treatment condition.

Regression to the mean
Tendency for behavior of subjects to move toward the average for that behavior during the course of an experiment.

Regression to the Mean. **Regression to the mean** refers to the observed tendency of subjects with extreme behavior to move toward the average for that behavior during the course of an experiment. Test units may exhibit extreme behavior due to chance, or in some cases, they may have been specifically chosen because of their extreme behavior. You may, for example, have chosen people for an experimental group because they are extremely heavy users of a particular product or service. It has been observed that in these situations it is likely for these extreme cases to move toward the average during the course of an experiment. The problem is that this movement toward the average, which has nothing to do with the treatment or experimental variable, may be interpreted to have been caused by the experimental or treatment variable.

EXPERIMENTATION: SUMMARY OF BASIC ISSUES

Experimental Design and Treatment

Experimental design
A test in which the researcher has control over one or more independent variables and manipulates them.

In an **experimental design**, the researcher has control over one or more independent variables and manipulates them. In the experiments we discuss, typically only one independent variable is manipulated. Nonexperimental designs involve no manipulation and typically are referred to as *ex post facto* (after the fact) *research*. In this type of research, an effect is observed and then some attempt is made to attribute this effect to some causal factor. An experimental design includes four factors:

1. The *treatment* or experimental variable (independent variable) to be manipulated
2. The *subjects* to participate in the experiment
3. A *dependent variable* to measure
4. Some *plan or procedure* for dealing with extraneous causal factors.

Treatment
The independent variable that is manipulated in an experiment.

The **treatment** is the independent variable that is manipulated. *Manipulation* refers to the process in which the researcher sets the levels of the independent variable to test a particular causal relationship. To test the relationship between price (independent variable) and sales of a product (dependent variable), a researcher might expose subjects to three different levels of price and record the level of purchases under each level. Price is the variable that will be manipulated; price is the single treatment factor, with three treatment conditions or levels of price.

An experiment may include a test or treatment group and a control group. A *control group* is a group in which the independent variable is not changed during the course of the experiment. A *test group* is a group that is exposed to a manipulation (change) of the independent variable.

Experimental Effects

The term **experimental effect** refers to the effect of the treatment variables on the dependent variable. The goal is to determine the effect of each treatment condition (level of treatment variable) on the dependent variable. For example, suppose that three different markets are selected to test three different prices or treatment conditions. Each price will be tested in each market for a period of three months. In market one, a price 2 percent lower than existing prices for the product is tested, in market two a price 4 percent lower is tested, and in market three a price 6 percent lower is tested. At the end of the three-month test, sales in market one are observed to have increased by less than 1 percent over sales for the preceding three-month period. In market two, sales increased by 3 percent; and in market three sales increased by 5 percent. The change in sales observed in each market would be the experimental effect.

Experimental effect
The effect of the treatment variable on the dependent variable.

The Control of Other (Extraneous) Causal Factors

Other (extraneous) causal factors are variables that can effect the dependent variable and should be controlled in some manner to establish a clear picture of the effect of the manipulated variable on the dependent variable. Extraneous causal factors are ordinarily referred to as *confounding variables* because they confound the treatment condition, making it impossible to determine whether changes in the dependent variable are due solely to the treatment conditions.

Four basic approaches are used to control extraneous factors: randomization, actual physical control, experimental design control, and statistical control.

Randomization involves randomly assigning subjects to treatment conditions, so that we can reasonably assume that extraneous causal factors related to subject characteristics will be represented equally in each treatment condition, thus cancelling out extraneous effects.

Physical control of extraneous causal factors involves somehow holding the value or level of the extraneous variable constant throughout the experiment. Another approach to physical control is *matching*. Under this approach, respondents are matched in regard to important personal characteristics (e.g., age, income, lifestyle) before being assigned to different treatment conditions. The goal is to make sure there are no important differences between characteristics of respondents in the test and control groups. Specific matching procedures are discussed later in this chapter.

Design control refers to the control of extraneous causal factors by means of specific types of experimental designs developed for this purpose. These designs will be discussed later in this chapter.

Finally, **statistical control** procedures can account for extraneous causal factors if they can be identified and measured throughout the course of the experiment. These procedures (e.g., analysis of covariance) can be used to adjust for the effects of

Randomization
The random assignment of subjects to treatment conditions to ensure equal representation of subject characteristics in all groups.

Physical control
Holding the value or level of extraneous variables constant throughout the course of an experiment.

Design control
Use of the experimental design to control extraneous causal factors.

Statistical control
Adjusting for the effects of confounded variables by statistically adjusting the value of the dependent variable for each treatment condition.

a confounded variable on the dependent variable by statistically adjusting the value of the dependent variable within each treatment condition.

Implementation Problems

A number of problems may be encountered that will hamper the implementation of experiments. These include the following: the difficulty of gaining cooperation within the organization, contamination problems, differences between test markets and the total population, and the lack of a group of people or geographic area available as a control group.

It may be extremely *difficult to obtain cooperation* within the organization in regard to executing certain types of experiments. For example, a regional marketing manager might be very reluctant to permit his or her market area to be used as a test market for a reduced level of advertising or a higher price. Quite naturally, there would be concern that the experiment might lower sales for the area.

Contamination refers to the fact that buyers from outside the test area may come into the area to purchase the product because of the experiment. These purchases by outsiders will distort the results of the experiment. Outside buyers might live on the fringes of the test market area and receive TV advertisements intended only for those in the test area that offer a lower price, a special rebate, or some other incentive to buy a product. Their purchases would tend to indicate that the particular sales stimulating factor being tested was more effective than was actually the case.

A third problem relates to the fact that in some cases *test markets may be so different* and the behavior of consumers in those markets so different that it is difficult to detect a relatively small experimental effect. This problem can be dealt with by careful matching of test markets and other strategies designed to ensure a higher degree of equivalency of test units.

Finally, in some situations no geographic area or group of people may be available to serve as a control group. This may be the case when dealing with industrial products, where a very small number of purchasers are concentrated geographically. An attempt to test a new product among a subset of such purchasers would almost certainly be doomed to failure.

Contamination
The inclusion of a group of respondents in a test who are not normally there; for example, outside buyers who see an advertisement intended only for those in the test area and enter the area to purchase the product being tested.

SELECTED EXPERIMENTAL DESIGNS

In the following section, examples of preexperimental, true experimental, and quasi-experimental designs are discussed.[8] In outlining these experimental designs, we use the system of notation introduced earlier.

Three Preexperimental Designs

Studies using **preexperimental designs** are generally difficult to interpret. This is because they offer little or no control over the influence of extraneous factors and, as a result, often are not much better than descriptive studies when it comes to making

Preexperimental designs
Designs that offer little or no control over extraneous factors.

causal inferences. With these designs the researcher has little control over aspects of exposure to the treatment variable and measurements such as to whom and when. However, these designs are frequently used in commercial marketing research because they are simple and inexpensive. They are useful for suggesting new hypotheses but do not offer strong tests of hypotheses. The reasons for this will be clear after you review the discussion that follows.

The One-Shot Case Study.

The **one-shot case study** involves exposing test units (people or test market) to the treatment or experimental variable for some period of time and then taking a measurement of the dependent variable. Symbolically, the design is shown as

$$X \quad O_1$$

There are two basic weaknesses in this design. No pretest observations are made of the test units that will receive the treatment, and no control group of test units that did not receive the treatment is observed. As a result of these deficiencies, the design does not deal with the effects of any of the extraneous variables discussed previously. Therefore, the design lacks internal validity and, most likely, external validity as well. This design is useful for suggesting causal hypotheses, but does not provide a strong test of these hypotheses. Many test markets for new products (not previously on the market) are based on this design. Examples of this and other preexperimental designs are shown in Table 8.1.

One-shot case study
Preexperimental design with no control group and an after measurement only.

The One-Group Pretest-Posttest Design.

The **one-group pretest-posttest design** is the design employed most frequently for test markets that involve testing changes in established products or marketing strategies. The fact that the product was on the market prior to the change provides the basis for the pretest measurement (O_1). The design is shown symbolically as

$$O_1 \quad X \quad O_2$$

Pretest observations are made on a single group of subjects or a single test unit (O_1) that later receives the treatment. Finally, a posttest observation is made (O_2). The treatment effect is estimated by $O_2 - O_1$.

One-group pretest-posttest design
Preexperimental design with pre and post measurements but no control group.

History is a threat to the internal validity of this design because an observed change in the dependent variable might be due to an event outside the experiment that took place between the pretest and posttest measurements. In laboratory experiments this threat can be controlled by insulating respondents from outside influences. Unfortunately, this type of control is impossible in field experiments.

Maturation is another threat to this type of design. An observed effect might be due to the fact that subjects have grown older, smarter, or more experienced between the pretest and the posttest.

This design has only one pretest observation. As a result, we know nothing of the pretest trend in the dependent variable. The posttest score may be higher because of the increasing trend of the dependent variable in a situation where this effect is not the treatment of research interest.

The Static-Group Comparison.

The **static-group comparison** design uses two treatment groups, one (experimental group) is exposed to the treatment and one (control group) is not. The two groups must be considered as nonequivalent

Static-group comparison
Preexperimental design that utilizes an experimental and a control group. However, subjects or test units are not randomly assigned to the two groups and no premeasurements are taken.

TABLE 8.1 *Examples of Preexperimental Designs*

SITUATION

Blue Cross/Blue Shield is in the process of instituting a new sales training program for its existing sales force. The program is designed to increase the productivity of individual salespersons and, thus, the entire sales force.

Butler Moore, vice-president in charge of sales, wants to do a small-scale research project to determine whether the course is producing the desired results.

Billy Marion, director of marketing research, has proposed three preexperimental designs as outlined in the following.

ONE-SHOT CASE STUDY DESIGN

This design would have the following features:

Basic design: $X\ O_1$

Sample: Ask for volunteers from among those who have taken the course.

Treatment (X): Taking the course.

Measurement (O_1): Actual sales performance for the six-month period after the course.

Weaknesses: No conclusive inferences can be drawn from the results.

The posttest measurement of sales may be the result of many uncontrolled factors. It cannot be judged better or worse in the absence of a pretreatment of observation of sales performance.

There is no control group of salespersons who did not receive the treatment (take the course).

STATIC GROUP COMPARISON

This design has the following features:

Basic design:

Experimental group $X\ O_1$

Control group O_2

Sample: Volunteers for both test and control groups.

Treatment: Same as previous.

Measurements (O_1, O_2): O_1 actual sales performance of experimental group for six months after the course;

O_2 same for control group that did not take course (treatment).

Weaknesses:

No pretest measure to help us deal with threats such as history and maturation discussed earlier. Because subjects were not assigned to the two groups at random, differences in performance between the two groups may be attributed to differences in the groups (one group had more good salespersons to begin with), rather than the sales training course.

ONE-GROUP PRETEST-POSTTEST DESIGN

This is a somewhat better design.

Basic design: $O_1\ X\ O_2$

Sample: Same as previous.

Treatment: Same as previous.

Measurement (O_1, O_2): O_1 actual sales performance for the six months prior to course; O_2 actual sales performance for the six months after the course.

Comparison: Same as the previous design except at pretest measure of sales performance (O_2) is taken.

Weaknesses: Better than one-shot case study design, but still has many serious problems.

Difference between pretest and posttest measures may be attributable to a number of things other than the sales training course. These other things (extraneous factors) include

Economic conditions: better or worse conditions may have contributed to the observed change in the dependent variable (history threat).

Salesperson may have matured over the period (gotten better) in ways that had nothing to do with the course (maturation).

The pretest measure and the fact that the sales force knew their performance was being monitored may have affected their performance (testing effect).

Some salespersons may have dropped out (left the company) over the period (mortality).

because subjects are not randomly assigned to the groups. The design can be shown symbolically as follows:

Experimental Group X O_1
Control Group O_2

The treatment effect is estimated as $O_1 - O_2$. The most obvious flaws in this design are the absence of pretests and the fact that any posttest differences between the groups may be due to the treatment effect, selection differences between the nonequivalent groups, or many other reasons.

Two True Experimental Designs

In a **true experimental design**, the experimenter randomly assigns treatments to randomly selected test units. The random assignment of test units to treatments is denoted by (R) in our notation system. Randomization is an important mechanism that makes the results of true experimental designs better (more valid) than the results from preexperimental designs. True experimental designs are superior to preexperimental designs because randomization takes care of many extraneous variables. The principal reason for choosing to conduct randomized experiments over other types of research design is that they make causal inference clearer.[9] Two true experimental designs are discussed in this section.

True experimental design
Research using an experimental group and a control group, and assignment of test units to both groups is randomized.

Before and After with Control Group.   The **before and after with control group** can be presented symbolically as

Experimental Group (R) O_1 X O_2
Control Group (R) O_3 O_4

Because the test units in this design are randomly assigned to the experimental and the control groups, the two groups can be considered equivalent. Therefore, they are likely to be subject to the same extraneous factors except for the treatment of research interest in the experimental group. For this reason, the difference between the pre- and postmeasurements of the control group ($O_4 - O_3$) should provide a good estimate of the effect of all the extraneous influences experienced by each group. To get the true impact of the treatment variable X, the extraneous influences must be removed from the difference between the pre- and postmeasurements of the experimental group. Thus, the true impact of X is estimated by $(O_2 - O_1) - (O_4 - O_3)$. This design generally controls for all but two major threats to validity: mortality and history.

Before and after with control group
True experimental design that includes random assignment of subjects or test units to experimental and control groups and premeasurement of both groups.

Mortality will be a problem if certain units drop out during the study and if the units dropping out differ systematically from the ones that remain. This results in a selection bias, because the experimental and control groups are composed of different subjects at the posttest than they were at the pretest. History will be a problem in those situations where events other than the treatment variable affect the experimental group but not the control group, or vice versa. Examples of this and other true experimental designs are provided in Table 8.2.

The After-Only with Control Group.   The **after-only with control group** design differs from the static-group comparison design (with nonequivalent groups) discussed earlier in regard to the assignment of the test units. In the earlier design,

After-only with control group
True experimental design that involves random assignment of subjects or test units to experimental and control groups, but no premeasurement of the dependent variable.

TABLE 8.2 *Examples of True Experimental Designs*

SITUATION

A shampoo marketer wants to measure the sales effect of a point-of-purchase display. The firm is considering two true experimental designs.

AFTER-ONLY WITH CONTROL GROUP DESIGN

This design would have the following features.

Basic design:

Experimental Group (R) X O_1
Control group (R) O_2

Sample: Random sample of stores that sell shampoo. Stores are randomly assigned to test and control groups. Groups can be considered equivalent.

Treatment (X): Placing the point-of-purchase display in stores in the experimental group for one month.

Measurements (O_1, O_2): Actual sales of company's brand during the period that the point-of-purchase displays are in the test stores.

Comments:

Because of random assignment of stores to groups, the test group and control group can be considered equivalent. Measure of the treatment effect of X is $O_1 - O_2$. If $O_1 = 113{,}000$ units and $O_2 = 125{,}000$ units, then the treatment effect = 12,000 units.

BEFORE AND AFTER WITH CONTROL GROUP DESIGN

This design would have the following features.

Basic design:

Experimental Group (R) O_1 X O_2
Control Group (R) O_3 O_4

Sample: Same as previous.

Treatment (X): Same as previous.

Measurements $(O_1$ to $O_4)$: O_1 and O_2 pre- and postmeasurements for the experimental group; O_3 and O_4 same for control group.

Results:

$O_1 = 113{,}000$ units
$O_2 = 125{,}000$ units
$O_3 = 111{,}000$ units
$O_4 = 118{,}000$ units

Comments:

Random assignment to groups means that they can be considered equivalent.

Because groups are equivalent, it is reasonable to assume that they will be equally affected by the same extraneous factors. The difference between the pre- and postmeasurements for the control group $(O_4 - O_3)$ provides a good estimate of the effects of all extraneous factors on both groups. Based on these results, $O_4 - O_3 = 7{,}000$ units.

The estimated treatment effect is $(O_2 - O_1) - (O_4 - O_3)$ or $(125{,}000 - 113{,}000) - (118{,}000 - 111{,}000) = 5{,}000$ units.

---

the test units were not randomly assigned to treatment groups. As a result, it was possible for the groups to differ in regard to the dependent variable prior to presentation of the treatment. This design deals with this shortcoming and can be shown symbolically as

$$\text{Experimental Group: } (R) \ X \quad O_1$$
$$\text{Control Group: } (R) \qquad O_2$$

You will notice that the test units are randomly (R) assigned to experimental and control groups. This random assignment of test units to the groups should produce experimental and control groups that are approximately equal in regard to the dependent variable prior to presentation of the treatment to the experimental group. In addition, you can also reasonably assume that test unit mortality (one of the threats to internal validity) will affect each group in the same way.

Considering this design in the context of the shampoo example described in Table 8.2 we can see a number of problems. Events other than the treatment may have occurred during the experimental period in one or a few stores in the experimental group. If a particular store in the experimental group ran a sale on certain other products and, as a result, had a larger (more than average) number of customers in the store, shampoo sales might be increased due to the heavier traffic. Events such as these, which are store specific (history), may distort the overall treatment effect. Also, there is a possibility that a few stores may drop out during the experiment (mortality threat) resulting in a selection bias because the stores in the experimental group will be different at the posttest.

If the experimenter added second experimental and control groups, and the stores in the second experimental group were subjected to the new point-of-sale advertising campaign, then posttest measures of shampoo sales for stores in the second experimental and control group would be taken (O_5 and O_6).

If the marketer observed an agreement between the measures $[(O_2 - O_1) - (O_4 - O_2)]$, $(O_6 - O_5)$, and $(O_2 - O_4)$, then the inference about the effects of point-of-sale advertising campaign would be much more conclusive.

Quasi-Experiments

When designing a true experiment, the researcher often must create artificial environments to control independent and extraneous variables. Because of this artificiality, questions are raised about the external validity of the experimental findings. **Quasi-experimental designs** have been developed to deal with this problem. They are generally more feasible in field settings than are true experiments.

In quasi-experiments the researcher lacks complete control over the scheduling of treatments or must assign respondents to treatments in a *nonrandom* fashion. These designs are frequently used in marketing research studies because cost and field constraints often do not permit the researcher to exert direct control over the scheduling of treatments and the *randomization* of respondents. Selected examples of these types of designs follow.

Quasi-experiments
Studies in which the researcher lacks complete control over the scheduling of treatment or must assign respondents to treatment in a nonrandom manner.

Interrupted Time-Series Designs. **Interrupted time-series designs** involve repeated measurement of an effect both before and after a treatment is introduced and "interrupts" previous data patterns. Interrupted time-series experimental designs can be shown symbolically as

$$O_1 \, O_2 \, O_3 \, O_4 \qquad X \qquad O_5 \, O_6 \, O_7 \, O_8$$

Interrupted time-series designs
Research in which the treatment "interrupts" ongoing repeated measurements.

A common example of this type of design in marketing research involves the use of consumer purchase panels. You might use a panel to make periodic measures of consumer purchase activity (the Os). We might introduce a new promotional campaign (the X) and examine the panel data for an effect. The researcher has control over the timing of the promotional campaign but cannot be sure when the panel members were exposed to the campaign or if they were exposed at all.

This design is very similar to the one-group pretest-posttest design, $O_1 \, X \, O_2$. However, time-series experimental designs have greater interpretability than the one-group pretest-posttest design because the many pretest-posttest measurements taken provide more understanding of extraneous variables. If, for example, sales of a product were on the rise and a new promotional campaign was introduced, the true effect of this campaign could not be estimated if a pretest and posttest design was used. However, the rising trend in sales would be obvious if a number of pretest and posttest observations had been made. The time-series design helps in determining the underlying trend of the dependent variable and provides better interpretability in regard to the treatment effect.

There are two fundamental weaknesses of this design. The primary weakness is the experimenter's *inability to control history*. Although maintaining a careful log of all possible relevant external happenings can reduce this problem, the experimenter has no way of determining the appropriate number and timing of pretest and posttest observations.

The other weakness of this design comes from the possibility of *interactive effects of testing* and evaluation apprehension resulting from the repeated measurements taken on test units. For example, panel members may become "expert" shoppers or become more conscious of their shopping habits. Under these circumstances, it may be inappropriate to make generalizations to other populations.

Multiple time-series design
An interrupted time-series design with a control group.

Multiple Time-Series Designs.   In some studies, based on time-series designs, we are able to find a group of test units to serve as a control group. If a control group can be added to the straight time-series design, then we can be more certain in our interpretation of the treatment effect. This design, called the **multiple time-series design**, can be shown symbolically as

$$\text{Experimental Group: } O_1\, O_2\, O_3 \quad X \quad O_4\, O_5\, O_6$$
$$\text{Control Group: } O_1\, O_2\, O_3 \qquad\quad O_4\, O_5\, O_6$$

The researcher must take care in selecting the control group. For example, an advertiser might test a new advertising campaign in a test city. That city would constitute the experimental group, and another city that was not exposed to the new campaign would be chosen as the control group. It is important that the test and control cities be roughly equivalent in regard to characteristics related to the sale of the product (e.g., competitive brands available).

TEST MARKETS

Test market
Testing of a new product or some element of the marketing mix using experimental or quasi-experimental designs.

The term **test market** is used by marketing researchers rather loosely to refer to any research that[10]

- Involves testing a new product or any change in an existing marketing strategy (e.g., product, price, place promotion) in a single market, a group of markets, or a region of the country.
- Involves the use of experimental procedures.

Test Market Usage and Objectives

New product introductions play a key role in shaping a firm's financial success or failure. The conventional wisdom in the corporate world is that new products will have to contribute more profits in the future than in the past due to higher levels of competition and a faster pace of change. However, according to various published sources, 70–80 percent of all new packaged goods fail. In addition, data reported by Burke Marketing Research Services indicates that 65 percent of all new product dollars are spent on marginal or losing brands. To make up for the failures and maintain corporate profitability at necessary levels, those products that succeed must produce a return on investment averaging greater than 30 percent.

As you probably already recognize, test market studies have the goal of helping marketing managers make better decisions about new products and additions or changes to existing products or marketing strategies. Test market studies do this by providing a real-world test for evaluating products and marketing programs. Marketing managers use test markets to evaluate proposed national programs with all of their separate elements on a smaller, less-costly scale. The basic idea is to make a determination of whether the estimated profits that will result if the product is rolled out on a national basis justify the potential risks. Test market studies are designed to provide information in regard to following issues:

- Estimates of market share and volume that can be projected to the total market.
- The effect that the new product will have on the sales of similar products (if any) already marketed by the company. The extent to which the new product takes business away from the company's existing products is referred to as the *cannibalization rate*.
- Characteristics of consumers who buy the product. Demographic data will almost surely be collected, and lifestyle, psychographic, and other types of classification data may be collected. This information will be useful in helping the firm refine the marketing strategy for the product. For example, knowing the demographic characteristics of likely purchasers will help in developing a media plan that will more effectively and efficiently reach target customers. Knowing

Thousands of new consumer package goods products are test marketed in the United States each year. (Courtesy of MarketSource, a college marketing company, Cranberry, N. J.)

MARKETING RESEARCH IN PRACTICE

Although it wasn't developed with marketing applications in mind, Virtual Reality (VR) is one of the latest technologies to be applied as a tool in experimentation. VR users are able to participate directly in real-time 3-D environments generated by computers. Market Ware Simulation Services in Norcross, Georgia, has used VR in the development of a system called Visionary Shopper, which provides a simulated shopping environment and an experience as close to the real thing as possible.

In place of the helmet, gloves, and bodysuit associated with VR, Visionary Shopper uses a video screen to display very sharp 3-D color images of a simulated retail shelf. On the shelf is a complete set of products within a product category, arranged as they would be in a grocery store, with prices below the brands and promotions highlighted by shelf markers. As consumers use a trackball to "walk down" the aisle of a store, they can observe the brands on the shelf. They can touch a product on the screen and it will become larger and cover most of the

screen. The consumer can then examine it on all sides as its price and other characteristics are displayed on the screen. Another touch of the screen returns it to the shelf or puts it into a shopping basket.

Visionary Shopper tests any marketing product variable that can be changed at the shelf. It also has applications for product concept testing because it shows a product in the midst of competitive products as it would appear on the shelf.

The system can be found at various mall locations geographically dispersed throughout the United States. Once recruited, shoppers participate in a twenty minute session. When needed, additional questions can be displayed on the screen. Multiple shopping trips are compressed into one setting.

The goal of a simulation is realism, and it is the realism of both the shelf environment and the shopping scenario that makes Visonary Shopper so promising. The real power of the system is generating data for input into models for forecasting, including concept tests and concept/product tests.[11]

the psychographic and lifestyle characteristics of target customers will provide valuable insights into how to position the product and the types of promotional messages that will appeal to them.

- The behavior of competitors during the test may provide some indication of what they will do if the product is introduced nationally.

In addition to traditional test markets, we will also discuss the growing area of simulated test markets (STM) as an alternative. STMs use survey data and mathematical models to simulate test market results at a much lower cost. Details of how STMs are actually conducted are provided later.

Test markets are, of course, discussed in this chapter because they employ experimental designs. Traditional test markets, by definition, are field experiments whereas STMs tend to rely on a laboratory approach. Traditional test markets rely almost exclusively on preexperimental and time-series designs. STMs use preexperimental, time-series, and in some cases, true experimental designs.

Costs of Test Marketing

Test marketing is expensive. It is estimated that a simple two-market test can cost $300,000–400,000 and that a long-running, complex test in four or more markets can cost more than $1 million. These estimates refer only to *direct costs*, which can include[12]

- Production of commercials
- Payments to advertising agency for services
- Media time at a higher rate because of low volume
- Syndicated research information
- Customized research information and associated data analysis
- Point-of-purchase materials
- Coupons and sampling
- Higher trade allowances to obtain distribution.

Also many possible *indirect costs* are associated with test marketing, including the following:

- Cost of management time spent on the test market
- Diversion of sales activity from existing products
- Possible negative impact of a test market failure on other products with the same family brand
- Possible negative trade reactions to your products if you develop a reputation of not doing well
- Cost of letting your competitors know what you are doing, allowing them to develop a better strategy or beat you to the national market.

The costs of test markets are high, and as a result, they should be used only as the last step in a research process that has already shown the new product or strategy to have considerable potential. In some situations, it may be cheaper to go ahead and launch the product, even if it fails.

Deciding Whether to Conduct a Test Market

Based on the preceding discussion, you can see that test markets offer at least two important benefits to the firm conducting the test:[13]

- First and foremost, the test market provides a vehicle by which the firm can obtain a good estimate of a product's sales potential under realistic market conditions. On the basis of these test results, the researcher can develop estimates of the product's national market share and use this figure to develop estimates of financial performance for the product.
- Second, the test should identify weaknesses of the product and the proposed marketing strategy for the product and give management an opportunity to correct any weaknesses. It will be much easier and less expensive to correct these problems at the test market stage than to correct them after the product has gone into national distribution.

On the other hand, these benefits must be weighed against a number of costs and other negatives associated with test markets.[14] The financial costs of test markets were discussed previously and are not insignificant. Another problem with test markets is that they give competitors an early indication of what you are planning to do. This gives them an opportunity to make adjustments in their marketing strategy, or if your idea is easily copied and not legally protected, they may be able to emulate your idea and move into national distribution faster than you can. It has been suggested that four major factors should be taken into account in determining whether to conduct a test market:[15]

- First, you should weigh the cost and risk of failure against the probability of success and associated profits. If estimated costs are high and you are very uncertain about the likelihood of success, then you should lean toward doing a test market. On the other hand, if expected costs are low and the risk of product failure is also low, then an immediate national rollout without a test market may be the appropriate strategy.
- As suggested earlier, the likelihood and speed with which your competitors can copy your product and introduce it on a national basis must also be considered. If it can be easily copied, then it may be appropriate to go ahead and introduce the product without a test market.
- Consider the investment required to produce the product for the test market versus the investment required to produce the product in the quantities necessary for a national rollout. In some cases, the difference in investment required may be very small. In these cases, it may make sense to introduce the product nationally without a test market. However, in those cases where there is a very large difference between the investment required to produce the product for test market and the investment required to produce the product for a national rollout, conducting a test market before making a decision to introduce the product nationally makes good sense.
- The final consideration relates to the damage that an unsuccessful new product launch can inflict on a company's reputation. Failure may hurt the company's reputation with other members of the channel of distribution (retailers) and damage the company's ability to gain their cooperation in future product launches. In those cases where this is a particular concern, test marketing is called for.

Steps in a Test Market Study

Once you have decided to conduct a test market, you must carry out a number of steps if you are to achieve a satisfactory result.

Define the Objective. As always with these kinds of lists, the first step in the process is to define the objectives of the test. Typical test market objectives are to

- Develop share and volume estimates
- Determine the characteristics of people who are purchasing the product
- Determine frequency and purpose of purchase
- Determine where (retail outlets) purchases are made
- Measure effect of sales of the new product on sales of the similar existing products in your line.

Select a Basic Approach.   After you have specified the objectives of the test market exercise, the next step is to decide on the type of test market method that is appropriate given the stated objectives. Three basic approaches are available.

- *Simulated test market:* As noted earlier, STMs do not involve actual testing in the marketplace. Under this approach, we expose a sample of individuals, representative of the target group, to various stimuli (new product concepts) and have them make simulated purchase choices between this stimuli. These results are used as input to mathematical models to make projections of how the new product will sell if available nationally.
- *Standard test market:* As noted earlier, this approach involves an actual market test on a limited basis.
- *Controlled test market:* Under this approach the test market will be handled by an outside research company such as Information Resources (see Chapter 6 for a more detailed discussion). This approach uses minimarkets operated by the testing company as well as controlled store panels. The companies handling the test typically guarantee the distribution of the new product in stores that cover some percentage of the minimarkets. They typically provide warehouse facilities and have their own field representatives to sell the product to retailers. They are also typically responsible for stocking shelves and tracking sales either manually or electronically.

Develop Detailed Procedures for the Test.   After we have developed the objectives and a basic approach for the test, then it is a question of developing a detailed plan for conducting the test. Manufacturing and distribution decisions must be made to ensure adequate product is available and it is available in most stores of the type that sell the particular product. In addition, the detailed marketing plan to be used for the test must be specified. The basic positioning approach must be selected, the execution of that approach in terms of actual commercials must be developed, a pricing strategy must be chosen, a media plan must be developed, and various promotional activities must be specified.

Select Markets for the Test.   The selection of markets for the test is an important decision. A number of factors must be taken into account when making this decision:[16]

- The market should not be overtested. Markets that have been used extensively by other companies for testing purposes may not respond in the same way as if they have not been used.
- The market should have normal development in the particular class. Sales in the market of the particular product should be typical, not unusually high or unusually low.
- Markets with unusual demographic profiles should be avoided. For example, college towns and retirement areas are not particularly good areas for testing most new products.
- Cities selected should reflect significant regional differences. If we find that sales of the product type vary significantly by region, then all of the major regions should be represented by at least one city in the test.
- The markets chosen should have little media spillover into other markets and receive relatively little media from outside the area. For example, if the television

stations in a particular market reach a very large area outside that market, the advertising used for the test product may pull in a large number of consumers from outside the market. This eventuality will make the product appear to be more successful than it really is.

■ Media usage patterns for the market should be similar to national norms. For example, television viewership should not differ significantly from national patterns. This might bias the estimates that you make for the national market.

■ The markets chosen should be big enough to provide meaningful results but not so big that testing becomes too expensive.

■ Distribution channels in the chosen markets should reflect national patterns. For example, all of the types of stores that sell the particular product should be present in the market and in their approximate national proportions.

■ The competitive situation in the markets chosen should be similar to the national situation for the product category. For example, you would not want to use a market in which one or more of your national competitors are not present.

■ The demographic profiles of the cities used should be similar to each other and similar to the national demographic profile.

As you can see by examining this list, many of the criteria relate to using cities that are microcosms of the country or a region of the country where the product will ultimately be sold. The basic motivation for taking this approach is to make sure that the test market results can be projected to the total area where the product will be sold. This is critical if you are to meet one of your important objectives, the objective of developing reliable estimates of sales of the new product from the test market. A list of the most typical metropolitan areas in the United States prepared by *American Demographics* is provided in Table 8.3.[17] The cumulative index in the table is an index of similarity to the national market considering housing value, age, and race characteristics of the market simultaneously. A value of 0.0 indicates a perfect match to the national market on these characteristics.

Execute the Plan. Now that you have a plan in place, you can begin the execution of that plan. As you begin the test, you will have to decide how long the test should run. The average test runs for six to twelve months. However, shorter and longer tests are not uncommon. The test must run long enough for an adequate number of repeat purchase cycles to be observed. This provides a measure of the "staying power" of a new product or marketing program. The shorter the average period is, the shorter the test needs to be. Cigarettes, soft drinks, and packaged goods are purchased every few days, whereas shaving cream, toothpaste, and so on are purchased only every few months. The latter types of products would require a longer test. Regardless of the product type, you need to continue your test until the repeat purchase rate stabilizes. There is a tendency for the percentage of people making repeat purchases to drop for some period of time before reaching a level that remains relatively constant. Repeat purchase rate is very critical to the process of estimating ultimate sales of the project. If you end your test too soon, then you will overestimate sales.

Two other considerations relate to the expected speed of competitor reaction and the costs of running the test. If you have reason to expect that competitors will react quickly to what you are doing (introduce their own version of the new product), then the test should be as short as possible. By minimizing the length of the test, you reduce the amount of time they have to react. Finally, you must consider the

TABLE 8.3 *Most Typical Metropolitan Areas*

RANK	METROPOLITAN AREA	1990 POPULATION	CUMULATIVE INDEX	HOUSING VALUE INDEX	AGE INDEX	RACE INDEX
1	Detroit, MI	4,382,000	22.8	11.8	1.5	9.5
2	St. Louis, MO-IL	2,444,000	22.8	15.1	1.6	6.2
3	Charlotte-Gastonia-Rock Hill, NC-SC	1,162,000	24.1	13.5	2.7	7.9
4	Fort Worth-Arlington, TX	1,332,000	25.0	17.0	5.9	2.2
5	Kansas City, MO-KS	1,566,000	25.4	17.9	2.7	4.8
6	Indianapolis, IN	1,250,000	25.5	16.7	2.4	6.3
7	Philadelphia, PA-NJ	4,857,000	26.7	18.0	1.7	7.1
8	Wilmington, NC	120,000	27.2	15.1	4.1	8.0
9	Cincinnati, OH-KY-IN	1,453,000	27.2	19.1	1.6	6.6
10	Nashville, TN	985,000	27.6	18.5	2.9	6.2
11	Dayton-Springfield, OH	951,000	27.6	19.5	1.9	6.2
12	Jacksonville, FL	907,000	27.6	17.2	2.5	7.9
13	Toledo, OH	614,000	27.8	20.0	2.4	5.5
14	Greensboro-Winston-Salem-High Point, NC	942,000	27.8	17.6	2.9	7.3
15	Columbus, OH	1,377,000	28.4	19.0	3.8	5.7
16	Charlottesville, VA	131,000	28.5	16.9	6.3	5.2
17	Panama City, FL	127,000	28.6	20.1	2.6	6.0
18	Pensacola, FL	344,000	28.7	21.8	2.2	4.7
19	Milwaukee, WI	1,432,000	28.8	23.4	1.4	4.1
20	Cleveland, OH	1,831,000	28.9	18.2	3.4	7.4

Source: Judith Waldrop, "All American Markets," *American Demographics* (January 1992): 27.

value of additional information to be gained from the test against the cost of continuing to run the test. At some point, the value of additional information will be outweighed by its cost.

Analyze the Test Results.   Though you should have been evaluating the data produced by your experiment as you went along, after completion of the experiment you must make a more careful and thorough evaluation of the data. This analysis will focus on four areas:

- *Purchase data:* This is often the most important data produced by the experiment. The levels of initial purchase (trial) throughout the course of the experiment provide an indication of how well your advertising and promotion program worked. The repeat rate (percentage of initial triers who made second and subsequent purchases) provides an indication of how well the product met the expectations created through advertising and promotion. Of course, the trial and repeat purchase results provide the basis for estimating sales and market share for the product if it were distributed nationally.
- *Awareness data:* How effective was the media weight and media plan in creating awareness of the product? Do consumers know how much your product costs? Do they know its key features?
- *Competitive response:* Ideally, you monitored the response of competitors during the period of the test market. For example, competitors may try to distort your test results by offering special promotions, price deals, quantity discounts, and

the like. This may provide some indication of what they will do when you move into national distribution and will provide some basis for estimating the effect of these actions on their part.

- *Source of sales:* Assuming this is a new entry in an existing product category, it is important to determine where your sales are coming from. In other words, which brands did the people who purchased your test product previously purchase. This gives you a true indication of real competitors and, if you have an existing brand in the market, tells you to what extent your new product will take business from your existing brands and from the competition.

Based on your evaluation, you will decide to go back and improve the product or marketing program, decide to drop the product, or decide to move into national or regional distribution.

Simulated Test Markets. We briefly mentioned simulated test markets (sometimes referred to as *pretest markets*) earlier. STMs do not involve an actual market test. Rather than use the field experiment approach of actual test markets, they rely on laboratory approaches. The typical STM includes the following steps:

- Intercept consumers at shopping malls (the mall intercept approach discussed in Chapter 7).
- Screen them for category use or target market membership. This is achieved via screening questions on a separate questionnaire or as the initial questions on the main questionnaire.
- Those who qualify are exposed to the new product concept or prototype and, in many cases, prototype advertising for the new product.
- Participants are given an opportunity to buy the new product in a real or laboratory setting.
- Interview those who purchased the new product after an appropriate time interval to determine their assessment of it and their likelihood to make further purchases.
- The trial and repeat purchase estimates, developed previously, provide the input for a mathematical model that is used to project share or volume for the product if it were distributed on a national basis. In addition, management must supply information regarding proposed advertising, distribution, and other elements of the proposed marketing strategy for the new product.

Several STM systems are currently in widespread use. The foremost popular STMs and the companies offering them are LTM (Yankelovich/Clancy/Shulman), ASSESSOR (M/A/R/C), BASES (Burke Marketing Services), and COMP (Elrick and Lavidge).

There are three major reasons for the growing popularity of STMs. First, they are relatively surreptitious. Given the fact that laboratory designs are employed, competitors are unlikely to know you are conducting the test or to know any of the details of the test or the nature of the new product you are testing. Second, they can be done more quickly than standard test markets. STMs can usually be completed in a maximum of three to four months. Standard test markets almost always take longer. Third, STMs are much cheaper than standard test markets. A typical STM can be conducted for $50,000–$100,000. Cost of a typical standard test market may approach $1 million. Finally, and perhaps most important, evidence has been provided to show that STMs can be very accurate. For example, on the basis of a published validation study, ASSESSOR has been shown to produce predictions of market share that are, on average, within 0.8 share points of the actual shares achieved for the products.[18] In terms of the variance of the estimates produced by ASSESSOR, this study shows that 70 percent of the predictions fell within 1.1 share points of actual results.

SUMMARY

Experimental research provides evidence whether the change in an independent variable causes some predictable change in a dependent variable. In order to show that a change in *A* likely caused an observed change in *B,* we must show three things: correlation, appropriate time order of occurrence, and the elimination of other possible causal factors. Experiments can be conducted in a laboratory or in a field setting. The major advantage of conducting experiments in a laboratory is that in this environment the researcher can control extraneous factors. However, in market research, laboratory settings often do not appropriately replicate the marketplace. Experiments conducted in the marketplace are called *field experiments*. The major difficulty with field experiments is that the researcher cannot control all the other factors that might influence the dependent variable.

In experimentation, we are concerned with internal and external validity. *Internal validity* refers to the extent to which competing explanations of the experimental results observed can be avoided. *External validity* refers to whether the causal relationships measured in an experiment can be generalized to other settings. *Extraneous variables* are other independent variables that may effect the dependent variable. They stand in the way of our ability of being able to conclude that an observed change in the dependent variable was due to the effect of the experimental or treatment variable. Extraneous factors discussed include history, maturation, instrument variation, selection bias, mortality, testing effects, and statistical regression.

In an experimental design, the researcher has control over one or more independent variables and manipulates one or more independent variables. Nonexperimental designs involve no manipulation and are referred to as *ex post facto research*. An experimental design includes four elements: the treatment, subjects, a dependent variable that will be measured, and a plan or procedure for dealing with extraneous causal factors. An experimental or treatment effect refers to the effect of a treatment variable on the dependent variable. Four basic approaches are used to control extraneous factors: randomization, actual physical control, experimental design control, and statistical control.

Experiments have an obvious advantage in that they are the only type of research that can demonstrate the existence and nature of causal relationships between variables of interest. Yet the amount of actual experimentation done in marketing research is limited because of the high cost of experiments, security issues, and implementation problems. There is evidence to suggest that the use of experiments in marketing research is growing.

Preexperimental designs offer little or no control over the influence of extraneous factors and are thus generally difficult to interpret. Examples include the one-shot case study, the one-group pretest-posttest design, and the static-group comparison. In a true experimental design, the researcher is able to eliminate all extraneous variables as competitive hypotheses to the treatment. Examples of true experimental design are the before and after with control group design and after-only with control group design.

In quasi-experimental designs, the researcher has control over data collection procedures but lacks complete control over the scheduling of treatments. The treatment groups in a quasi-experiment are normally formed by assigning respondents to treatments in a nonrandom fashion. Examples of quasi-experimental designs are the interrupted time-series design and multiple time-series design.

Test marketing involves testing a new product or some element of the marketing mix by using experimental or quasi-experimental designs. Test markets are field experiments, and they are extremely expensive to conduct. The steps in conducting a test market study include defining the objectives for the study, selecting a basic approach to be used, developing detailed procedures for the test, selecting markets for the test, and analyzing the test results.

KEY TERMS

Experiment
Causal research
Concomitant variation
Appropriate time order of
  occurrence
Laboratory experiments
Field experiments
Internal validity
External validity
History
Maturation
Instrument variation
Selection bias
Mortality
Testing effect
Regression to the mean
Experimental design
Treatment

Experimental effect
Randomization
Physical control
Design control
Statistical control
Contamination
Preexperimental designs
One-shot case study
One-group pretest-posttest design
Static-group comparison
True experimental design
Before and after with control group
After-only with control group
Quasi-experiments
Interrupted time-series designs
Multiple time-series design
Test market

REVIEW AND DISCUSSION QUESTIONS

1. Ralston-Purina has developed a new frozen dog food. One simply heats it and serves it in the tray to the dog. Ralston-Purina is considering skipping test marketing and going directly into a national rollout. What are the advantages of doing so, given that Ralston-Purina is a major marketer of dog food? What are the disadvantages of not test marketing?

2. You are getting ready to test market a new shampoo for elderly consumers. How might you select test cities for this product? What are some cities that you would choose?

3. Why is experimentation best suited for determining causation?

4. Describe some independent and dependent variables that could be used in consumer goods experiments.

5. The student center at your university is considering three alternative brands of hot dogs to be offered on the menu. Design an experiment to determine which brand of hot dogs the students prefer.

6. The night students at the university are much older than day students. Introduce an explicit control for day versus night students in the preceding experiment.
7. Why are quasi-experiments much more popular in marketing research than true experiments?
8. How does the history effect differ from the maturation effect?
9. The manufacturer of microwave ovens has designed an improved model that will reduce energy cost and cook food evenly throughout. However, this new model will increase the product's price by 30 percent because of extra components and engineering design changes. The company wants to ascertain whether and to what extent the new model will affect sales of its microwave ovens. Propose an appropriate experimental design that can provide the information for management. Why did you select this design?
10. Discuss various methods by which extraneous causal factors can be controlled.

CASE

Market Analyst and Promotional Specialists, Inc.

Market Analyst and Promotional Specialists, Inc., (M.A.P.S.) is a marketing consulting firm that specializes in the development of promotional campaigns. The firm was formed five years ago by two young marketing graduate students, David Roth and Lisa Ryan. The students soon overcame their initial lack of experience and since have become known for their innovativeness and creativity. Their clients now include industrial wholesalers, retail product manufacturers, food brokers, and distributors as well as retail outlets.

In 1989, Dixie Brewing Company enlisted M.A.P.S. to develop a new promotional campaign for its line of beers. At the time, Dixie was the last of the microbreweries in New Orleans and distributed its products within a 200 mile radius of the city. The company had enjoyed a good reputation for a number of years but recently tarnished its image by accidentally distributing a shipment of bad beer. Dixie was also losing market share due to increased competition from national brewers. Recently Miller High Life purchased Crescent Distributors, a large liquor distributor in the New Orleans area, and was beginning to implement aggressive promotional tactics in the local market.

Dixie was concerned primarily with its retail merchandising methods. M.A.P.S. immediately began to study Dixie's product line and the present shelf-space allocations in various stores throughout the market area. Due to its previous experience with food brokers, M.A.P.S. realized that proper shelf placement was extremely important in supermarket merchandising.

The company's product line consisted of two beers, Dixie and Dixie Light. Both beers were sold in 32-ounce glass bottles, 12-ounce glass bottle six-packs, and 12-ounce can six-packs.

In New Orleans, beer may be purchased in supermarkets and convenience stores. Also, in most stores beer can be purchased either warm or cold. In studying the refrigerated closets holding beverages, M.A.P.S. noticed that most were small, eight to twelve feet in length, and usually had glass doors on the front. Because of the relatively small size of the entire cold beer display, David and Lisa believed that the typical consumer would view the case from left to right. As such, they believed Dixie should place their products on the extreme left side of all cold beer cases.

Warm beer was displayed in a much different manner. Most stores displayed beverage products in bulk and usually devoted an entire aisle for such displays. David and Lisa reasoned that the normal consumer could not view all the brands at once and would thus have to "shop" or walk into the aisle. For this reason, they recommended that Dixie place its beer in the middle of the other brands.

Because Dixie Light was produced in response to Miller Lite, David and Lisa recommended that it be placed to the left of Miller Lite in both warm and cold beer displays. Traditionally, Dixie Light had been placed next to their standard beer brand. Dixie had noticed a significant decrease in their regular brand's market share on the introduction of Dixie Light.

To test its theories, M.A.P.S. selected a convenience store located in a suburb of New Orleans. The store contained both warm and cold beer displays. This store was then used in an experiment to measure the effect of shelf placement on beer sales. One treatment consisted of setting up the displays as they were currently being used in stores across town. The second treatment arranged the displays according to the new M.A.P.S. plan. All other factors such as price, number of bottles, and so forth, were held constant throughout the experiment. The first version of the setup was used for the first two weeks in April, and the second treatment was run for the last two weeks.

The following statistics show the percentage of beer purchased by brand for each treatment:

	Treatment #1	Treatment #2
Dixie	18%	23%
Miller	18%	15%
Bud	19%	18%
Coors	13%	13%
Dixie Light	10%	8%
Miller Lite	13%	14%
Coors Light	9%	9%

1. Critique the research design with respect to internal and external validity considerations.
2. Discuss the advantages and disadvantages of using the convenience store in this experiment.
3. Based on the information given, what conclusions can be made regarding the M.A.P.S. plan?
4. Recommend a research design that would produce more interpretable results.

Ethical Dilemma——PART TWO

Mission Bell Field Services

Mission Bell Field Services, of Marina Del Rey, California, is like no other marketing research field service in the nation. Founded by Mary Ann Stubbs in 1984, its purpose is not to earn a profit, but to provide funding for two charities. The organization provides all of the financing for the Marina Del Rey Home for Battered Women and 25 percent of the budget for a local homeless shelter. Stubbs founded the home for abused women after a close friend was killed by an abusive husband. Currently, the home provides meals, a place to stay, and counseling for an average of three women a week plus their children. Stubbs has used her country club and junior league connections to recruit volunteer interviewers. These women, and a few men, conduct marketing research interviews but donate their salaries to the company. Thus, Mission Bell not only earns a profit but keeps the interviewers' salaries as well.

Despite this unique situation, Stubbs is not meeting her budget projections. The home for battered women is facing an $80,000 shortfall for the final quarter of the year, and the homeless shelter is expecting a $25,000 contribution from Mission Bell Field Services yet no funds are available.

Stubbs is desperate. She is strongly considering "puffing up" the number of hours worked by 20 percent. Some marketing research companies pay field services based on hours worked, travel time, and mileage, plus a commission. Stubbs justifies her actions to herself by claiming that the big New York marketing research firms will not notice a small increase in reported hours worked, and they can afford it. Also, rather than all the money going into a rich New Yorker's pocket (the marketing research company's owners), a small amount of the potential profit will go to two worthwhile California charities.

Stubbs currently has three people in her office that do nothing but validate interviewers' work. Fifteen percent validation is an industry standard. Stubbs has recruited only socially prominent people to be her volunteer interviewers. They are doing the interviewing strictly for charity and certainly would not cheat. Stubbs decides that she will put the validators to work as interviewers to help increase total revenues.

Recently, Mission Bell conducted a major central location telephone study of 10,000 interviews on planned durable goods purchases within the next two years. The survey was conducted for the California Department of Economic Affairs to use as input in their econometrics forecasting model. The department is responsible for forecasting economic activity for the state government that, in turn, uses the data for revenue and spending projections for state agencies. Stubbs realized that she had a gold mine of information. She had a huge list of the names, addresses, and telephone numbers of Californians who planned to purchase automobiles, homes, major appliances, and electronics over the next two years. A Japanese automobile manufacturer had already approached her about buying the names of potential new car buyers. A quick financial projection by Stubbs showed that by selling the names to ten different manufacturers of various consumer durable goods, she could cover her financial shortfall for the homeless shelter and reduce the deficit of the home for battered women. Selling people's names is a harmless act and the introductory remarks of the survey never mentioned confidentiality. Besides, a person does not have to buy something from the manufacturer.

1. Would you advise Stubbs not to "puff" the interviewers' hours? Are her actions nothing more than a small, involuntary contribution to her charities by some rich New Yorkers?
2. As Stubbs uses unpaid volunteers as interviewers, is it not rather ridiculous to validate their work? Is this not particularly true as the validators could be bringing in additional revenue as interviewers?
3. Is it unethical for Stubbs to sell the names of the respondents? Is the "greater good" not being served by keeping the two charities in full operation? No one is going to be hurt by Stubbs's actions, and the respondents were not explicitly promised confidentiality.
4. Identify any unethical practices you feel Mary Ann is committing.
5. Which level of moral development do you think Mary Ann has achieved as a marketing researcher?
6. Which practice do you feel is Mary Ann's worst breach of research supplier ethics? Defend your answer.

PART 3

Data Acquisition

CHAPTER 9

The Concept of Measurement and Attitude Scales

LEARNING OBJECTIVES

1. To understand the concept of measurement.
2. To understand the four levels of scales and their typical usage.
3. To become aware of the concepts of reliability and validity.
4. To become familiar with the concept of scaling.
5. To learn about the various types of attitude scales.
6. To realize the importance of purchase intent scales in marketing research.
7. To examine some basic considerations when selecting a type of scale.

ampbell Soup Company sells a lot of food products for children. Segmenting a market when the customer who is buying the product isn't necessarily the one eating it is not always easy. Campbell does a lot of within-household segmentations to explore the constant food fight between parents and kids. Kids would be perfectly happy to live on Twinkies, Coke, and Gummi Worms if parents let them. But the parents' role is to be a gatekeeper and role model for their children's food choices. And as marketers, Campbell's role is to develop nutritious food that children will enjoy eating but parents won't feel bad about buying. Luckily for Campbell's, and for parents, kids do like stuff that comes in cans.

When researching a children's product, the company must ask both parents and kids to determine purchase interest, preferences, and attribute ratings. Often, there is a lot of variation. Campbell tested a canned pasta and sauce product and found that 56 percent of kids rated the product high on the liking scale, but only 11 or 12 percent of mothers agreed. Fewer than half of moms indicated definite purchase intent, while over 70 percent of kids wanted their mothers to buy the product for them. Campbell also found that these products appeal most to the under six age group, and that interest declined with age. This kind of research indicates how to market the product. In this case, it shows that the ads must assure moms of quality while appealing to children's positive purchase desire.[1]

Campbell's segmentation research is based on the concept of measurement, for example, product attribute ratings. What are the roles of reliability and validity in the measurement process? Campbell's research also encompassed several types of attitude scales. What tools are available for measuring attitudes? What factors should be considered when selecting an attitude scale? These are the topics of Chapter 9.

THE CONCEPT OF MEASUREMENT AND MEASUREMENT SCALES

Measurement
Process of assigning numbers or labels to things in accordance with specific rules to represent quantities or qualities of attributes.

Measurement is the process of assigning numbers or labels to objects, persons, states, or events in accordance with specific rules to represent quantities or qualities of attributes. Measurement, then, is a procedure used to assign numbers that reflect the amount of an attribute possessed by an event, person, or object. Note that the event, person, or object is not being measured, but rather its attributes. A researcher, for example, does not measure a consumer but measures attitudes, income, brand loyalty, age, and other relevant factors.

Another key aspect of measurement is the concept of rules. A **rule** is a guide, a method, or a command that tells a researcher what to do. For example, a rule might say "assign the numbers 1 through 5 to people according to their disposition to do household chores. If they are extremely willing to do any and all household chores, assign them a *1*. If they are not willing to do any household chores, assign them a *5*." Equally specific rules would be stated for assigning a *2, 3,* or *4.*

A problem often encountered with rules is a lack of clarity or specificity. Some things are easy to measure because rules are easy to create and follow. The measurement of gender, for example, is quite simple, and concrete criteria can be offered to determine sex. The researcher is then told to assign a 1 for male and a 2 for female. Unfortunately, many characteristics of interest to a market researcher such as brand loyalty and purchase intent are much more difficult to measure because it is difficult to devise rules to measure the true value of these consumer attributes. Researchers rely on measurement scales to understand these difficult consumer attributes.

Measurement Scales

A **scale** is a set of symbols or numbers so constructed that the symbols or numbers can be assigned by a rule to the individuals (or their behaviors or attitudes) to whom the scale is applied. The assignment on the scale is indicated by the individual's possession of whatever the scale is supposed to measure.

Creating a measurement scale begins with determining the level of measurement desirable or possible. Table 9.1 describes the four basic levels of measurement, which are nominal, ordinal, interval, and ratio. These four levels lead to the four kinds of scales discussed in the following paragraphs.

Nominal Scales   **Nominal scales** are one of the most common in marketing research. A nominal scale partitions data into categories that are mutually exclusive and collectively exhaustive. This implies that every bit of data will fit into one and only one category and all data will fit somewhere in the scale. The term *nominal* means "namelike," implying that the numbers assigned to objects or phenomena are naming or classifying but have no true number meaning; the numbers cannot be ordered, added, or divided. The numbers are simply labels or identification numbers and nothing else. Examples of nominal scales are

Sex   (1) Male   (2) Female
Geographic area (1) Urban   (2) Rural   (3) Suburban

The only quantification in nominal scales are the number and percentages of objects in each category; for example, fifty males (48.5 percent) and fifty-three females (51.5 percent). Computing a mean, for example, of 2.4 for geographic area would be meaningless; only the mode, the value that appears most often, would be appropriate.

Ordinal Scales   **Ordinal scales** maintain the labeling characteristics of nominal scales plus an ability to order data. Ordinal measurement is possible when the transitivity postulate can be applied. A postulate is an assumption that is an essential prerequisite to carrying out an operation or line of thinking. The

Rule
A guide, a method, or a command that tells a researcher what to do.

Scale
A set of symbols or numbers so constructed that the symbols or numbers can be assigned by a rule to the individuals (or their behaviors or attitudes) to whom the scale is applied.

Nominal scales
Scales that partition data into mutually exclusive and collectively exhaustive categories

Ordinal scales
Nominal scales that can order data.

TABLE 9.1   *The Four Major Levels of Measurement*

LEVEL	DESCRIPTION*	BASIC EMPIRICAL OPERATIONS	TYPICAL USAGE	TYPICAL DESCRIPTIVE STATISTICS
Nominal	Uses numerals to identify objects, individuals, events, or groups	Determination of equality/inequality	Classification (male/female; buyer/nonbuyer)	Frequency counts, percentages/modes
Ordinal	In addition to identification, the numerals provide information about the relative amount of some characteristic posed by an event, object, etc.	Determination of greater or less	Rankings/ratings (preferences for hotels, banks, etc., social class; ratings of foods based upon fat content, cholesterol)	Median (mean and variance metric)
Interval	Possesses all the properties of nominal and ordinal scales plus the intervals between consecutive points are equal	Determination of equality of intervals	Preferred measure of complex concepts/constructs (temperature scale; air pressure scale; level of knowledge about brands)	Mean/variance
Ratio	Incorporates all the properties of nominal, ordinal, and interval scales plus it includes an absolute zero point	Determination of equality of ratios	When precision instruments are available (sales; number of on-time arrivals; age)	Geometric mean/harmonic mean

*Because higher levels of measurement contain all the properties of lower levels, we can convert higher level scales into lower level ones (i.e., ratio to interval or ordinal or nominal; or interval to ordinal or nominal; or ordinal to nominal).

Source: Adapted from S. S. Stevens, "On the Theory of Scales of Measurement," *Science* 103 (June 7, 1946), pp. 677–680.

transitivity postulate may be described by the notion that "if *a* is greater than *b*, and *b* is greater than *c*, then *a* is greater than *c*." Other terms that can be substituted are *is preferred to, is stronger than,* or *precedes.* An example of an ordinal scale is

Please rank the following airlines from *1* to *5* with *1* being the most preferred and *5* the least preferred.

Delta	3
American	1
United	4
USAir	2
Northwest	5

Ordinal numbers are used strictly to indicate rank order. The numbers do not indicate absolute quantities, nor do they imply that the intervals between the numbers are equal. For example, the person ranking the airlines might like American only slightly more than USAir and perceive Northwest as totally unacceptable. Such information would not be obtained from an ordinal scale.

Because ranking is the objective of an ordinal scale, any rule prescribing a series of numbers that preserves the ordered relationship is satisfactory. In other words, American could have been assigned a value of 12, USAir 17, Delta 20, United 25, and Northwest 26, or any other series of numbers as long as the basic ordering is preserved. Common arithmetical operations such as addition or multiplication cannot be used with ordinal scales. The appropriate measure of central tendency is the mode and the median. A percentile or quartile measure is used for measuring disperson.

A controversial (yet rather common) use of ordinal scales is to rate various characteristics. In this case, the researcher assigns numbers to reflect the relative ratings of a series of statements, then uses these numbers to interpret relative distance. Recall that our market researchers examining role ambiguity used a scale ranging from *very certain* to *very uncertain*. Note that the following values had been assigned:

(1)	(2)	(3)	(4)	(5)
Very Certain	Certain	Neutral	Uncertain	Very Uncertain

If a researcher can justify the assumption that the intervals are equal within the scale, then the more powerful parametric statistical tests can be applied. Parametric statistical tests will be discussed in Chapter 14. Indeed, some measurement scholars argue that we should normally assume equal intervals.

> The best procedure would seem to be to treat ordinal measurements as though they were interval measurements, but to be constantly alert to the possibility of *gross* inequality of intervals. As much as possible about the characteristics of the measuring tools should be learned. Much useful information has been obtained by this

Ordinal scales can be used to rank airline preferences. (Kevin Horan/ Stock, Boston)

approach, with resulting scientific advances in psychology, sociology, and education. In short, it is unlikely that researchers will be led seriously astray by heeding this advice, if they are careful in applying it.[2]

Interval scales

Ordinal scales with equal intervals between points to show relative amounts; may include an arbitrary zero point.

Interval Scales.   **Interval scales** contain all the features of ordinal scales with the added dimension that the intervals between the points on the scale are equal. The concept of temperature is based upon equal intervals. Market researchers often prefer to use interval scales over ordinal scales because they can measure how much of a trait one consumer has (or does not have) over another. Interval scales enable a researcher to discuss differences separating two objects. The scale possesses properties of order and difference but with an arbitrary zero point; for example, Fahrenheit and centigrade scales. Thus, the freezing point of water is zero on one scale and 32 degrees on the other.

The arbitrary zero point of interval scales restricts the statements that a researcher can make about the scale points. One can say that 80°F is hotter than 32°F or that 64°F is 16° cooler than 80°F. However, one cannot say that 64°F is twice as warm as 32°F. Why? Because the zero point on the Fahrenheit scale is arbitrary. To prove our point, consider the transformation of the two temperatures to Celsius using the formula Celsius = (F − 32)(5/9). Thus, 32° F equals 0°C and 64°F equals 17.8°C. Our previous statement for Fahrenheit (64° is twice as warm as 32°) does not hold for Celsius. The same would be true if we were evaluating airlines on which factors were liked the most on an interval scale. If American Airlines is given a 20 and Piedmont a 10, we cannot say that American is liked twice as much as Piedmont. This is because a zero point defining the absence of liking has not been identified and assigned a value of 0 on the scale.

Interval scales are amenable to computation of an arithmetic mean, standard deviation, and correlation coefficients. The more powerful parametric statistical tests such as t-tests and F-tests can be applied. In addition, researchers can take a

These family members might give different answers to a McDonald's service quality questionnaire if they were surveyed with friends, alone, or by phone. (Sybil Shackman/ Monkmeyer Press)

more conservative approach and use nonparametric tests if there is concern about the equal intervals assumption.

Ratio Scales.   **Ratio scales** have all the powers of those previously discussed as well as a meaningful absolute zero or origin. Because there is universal agreement as to the location of the zero point, comparisons among the magnitudes of ratio-scaled values is acceptable. Thus, a ratio scale reflects the actual amount of a variable. Physical characteristics of a respondent such as age, weight, or height are examples of ratio-scaled variables. Other ratio scales are based on area, distance, money values, return rates, population counts, and lapsed periods of time.

Because some objects have none of the property being measured, a ratio scale originates at zero, thus having an absolute empirical meaning. For example, an investment (albeit a poor one) can have no rate of return, or a census tract in New Mexico could be devoid of any persons. Also, an absolute zero implies that all arithmetic operations are possible, including multiplication and division. Numbers on the scale indicate the actual amounts of the property being measured; that is, a large bag of McDonald's french fries weighs 8 ounces and a regular bag at Burger King weighs 4 ounces. Thus, a large McDonald's bag of fries weighs twice as much as a regular Burger King bag.

Ratio scales
Interval scales with a meaningful zero point so that magnitudes can be compared arithmetically.

SOURCES OF MEASUREMENT DIFFERENCES

An ideal market research study would provide information that is accurate, precise, lucid, and timely. Accurate data implies accurate measurement, or $M = A$, where M refers to measurement and A stands for complete accuracy. In market research, this ideal is rarely, if ever, obtained. Instead we have

$$M = A + E, \text{ where } E = \text{errors}$$

Errors can be either random or systematic, as noted in Chapter 7. **Systematic error** is error that results in a constant bias in the measurements. The bias results from faults in the measurement instrument or process. For example, if we are using a faulty ruler (1″ is actually 1½″) in Pillsbury's test kitchens to measure the height of chocolate cakes using alternative recipes, all cakes will be recorded below their actual height. **Random error** also influences the measurements but not systematically. Thus, random error is transient in nature and does not occur in a consistent manner. A person may not answer a question truthfully because he or she is in a bad mood that day.

Systematic error
Error that results in a constant bias in the measurements.

Random error
Error that affects measurement in a transient, inconsistent manner.

Reliability

A measurement scale that provides consistent results over time is reliable. If a ruler consistently measures a chocolate cake as 9″ high, then the rule is said to be reliable. Reliable scales, gauges, and other measurement devices can be used with confidence and the knowledge that transient and situational factors are not interfering with the measurement process. Reliable instruments provide stable measures at different times under different conditions. A key question regarding reliability is, If we measure some phenomenon over and over again with the same measurement

TABLE 9.2	*Assessing the Reliability of a Measurement Instrument*
Test-retest reliability	Use the same instrument a second time under nearly the same conditions as possible.
Equivalent form reliability	Use two instruments that are as similar as possible to measure the same object during the same time period.
Internal consistency reliability	Compare different samples of items being used to measure a phenomenon during the same time period.

Reliability
Measures that are consistent from one administration to the next.

device, will we get the same or highly similar results? If the answer is affirmative, the device is reliable.

Therefore, **reliability** is the degree to which measures are free from random error and, therefore, provide consistent data. The less error there is, the more reliable the observation, so that a measurement that is free of error is a correct measure. Therefore a measurement is reliable if the measurement does not change when the concept being measured remains constant in value. However, if the concept being measured does change in value, the reliable measure will indicate that change. How can a measuring instrument be unreliable? If your weight stays constant at 150 pounds but repeated measurements on your bathroom scale show your weight to fluctuate, the lack of reliability may be due to a weak spring inside the scale.

There are three ways to assess reliability: test-retest, equivalent forms, and internal consistency (see Table 9.2).

Test-retest reliability
The ability of the same instrument to produce consistent results when used a second time under conditions as nearly the same as possible.

Test-Retest Reliability. **Test-retest reliability** is obtained by repeating the measurement using the same instrument under as nearly the same conditions as possible. The theory behind test-retest is that, if random variations are present, they will be revealed by variations in the scores between the two tests. **Stability** means that very few differences in scores are found between the first and second administration of the tests; the measuring instrument is said to be stable. For example, assume that a thirty-item department store image measurement scale was administered to the same group of shoppers at two points in time. If the correlation between the two measurements was high, the reliability would be assumed to be high.

Stability
Lack of change in results from test to retest.

There are several problems with test-retest reliability. First, it may be very difficult to locate and gain the cooperation of respondents for a second testing. Second, the first measurement may alter the person's response on the second measurement. Third, environmental or personal factors may change, causing the second measurement to change.

Equivalent form reliability
The ability to produce similar results using two instruments as similar as possible to measure the same object.

Equivalent Form Reliability. The problems of the test-retest approach can be avoided by creating equivalent forms of a measurement instrument. For example, assume that researcher is interested in identifying inner-directed versus outer-directed lifestyles. Two questionnaires can be created containing measures of inner-directed behavior and outer-directed behavior. Further, these measures should receive about the same emphasis on each questionnaire. Thus, although the questions used to ascertain the lifestyles are different on each questionnaire, the same number of questions used to measure each lifestyle should be approximately equal. The recommended interval for administering the second equivalent form is two weeks, although in some cases they are given one after the other or simultaneously. **Equivalent form reliability** is determined by measuring the correlation of the scores on the two instruments.

There are two problems with equivalent forms that should be noted. First, it is very difficult and perhaps impossible to create two totally equivalent forms. Second, if equivalence can be achieved it may not be worth the time, trouble, and expense involved. The theory behind the equivalent forms approach to reliability assessment is the same as test-retest. The primary difference between the test-retest and the equivalent forms methods is the testing instrument itself. Test-retest uses the same instrument, whereas equivalent form uses a different, but highly similar, measuring instrument.

Internal Consistency Reliability.   The **internal consistency** measure of **reliability** assesses the ability to produce the similar results using different samples to measure a phenomenon during the same time period. The theory of internal consistency rests on the notion of equivalence. Equivalence is concerned with how much error may be introduced by different samples of items being used to measure a phenomenon. It is concerned with variations at one point in time among samples of items. A researcher can test for item equivalence by assessing the homogeniety of a set of items. The total set of items used to measure a phenomenon, such as inner-directed lifestyles, is divided into two halves; the total score of the two halves is then correlated (see Figure 9.1). Use of the **split-half technique** typically calls for scale items to be randomly assigned to one half or the other. The problem with this

Internal consistency reliability
Ability to produce the similar results using different samples to measure a phenomenon during the same time period.

Split-half technique
A method of assessing the reliability of a scale by dividing into two the total set of measurement items, and correlating the results.

FIGURE 9.1   *Statements Used to Measure Inner-Directed Lifestyles*

I often don't get the credit I deserve for things I do well.

I try to get my own way regardless of others.

My greatest achievements are ahead of me.

I have a number of ideas that some day I would like to put into a book.

I am quick to accept new ideas.

I often think about how I look and what impression I am making on others.

I am a competitive person.

I feel upset when I hear that people are criticizing or blaming me.

I'd like to be a celebrity.

I get a real thrill out of doing dangerous things.

I feel that almost nothing in life can substitute for great achievement.

It's important for me to be noticed.

I keep in close touch with my friends.

I spend a good deal of time trying to decide how I feel about things.

I often think I can feel my way into the innermost being of another person.

I feel that ideals are powerful motivating forces in people.

I think someone can be a good person without believing in God.

The Eastern religions are more appealing to me than Christianity.

I feel satisfied with my life.

I enjoy getting involved in new and unusual situations.

Overall, I'd say I'm happy.

I feel I understand where my life is going.

I like to think I'm different from other people.

I adopt a common-sense attitude toward life.

method, however, is that the estimate of the coefficient of reliability is totally dependent upon how the items were split. Different splits result in different correlations, but should not.

To overcome the split-halves problems, many researchers now use the Cronbach-Alpha. This technique computes the mean reliability coefficient estimates for all possible ways of splitting a set of items in half. A lack of correlation of an item with other items in the scale is evidence that the item does not belong in the scale and should be omitted. One limitation of the Cronbach-Alpha is that the scale items require equal intervals. If this criteria cannot be met, another test called the *KR-20* can be used. The KR-20 technique is applicable for all dichotomous or nominally scaled items.

Validity

Validity
Whether what we tried to measure was actually measured.

Recall that the second characteristic of a good measurement device is validity. **Validity** addresses the issue of whether what we tried to measure was actually measured. When Coke first brought out "new Coke," it had conducted over 5,000 interviews that purported to show new Coke was favored over original Coke. Unfortunately, its measurement instrument was not valid. This led to one of the greatest marketing debacles of all time! The validity of a measure refers to the extent to which the measurement instrument and procedure are free from both systematic and random error. Thus, a measuring device is valid if differences in scores solely reflect true differences on the characteristic we seek to measure rather than systematic or random error. You should realize that a necessary precondition for validity is that the measuring instrument is reliable. An instrument that is not reliable will not yield consistent results when measuring the same phenomenon over time.

A scale or other measuring device is basically worthless to a researcher if it lacks validity, because it is not measuring what it is supposed to. On the surface, this seems like a rather simple notion, yet validity often is based on subtle distinctions. Assume that your teacher gives an exam that he has constructed to measure marketing research knowledge, and the test consists strictly of applying a number of formulas to simple case problems. A friend receives a low score on the test and protests to the teacher that she "really understands marketing research." Her position, in essence, is that the test was not valid. Rather than measuring knowledge of marketing research, it measured memorization of formulas and the ability to use simple math to find solutions. The teacher could repeat the exam only to find that student scores still fall in the same order. Does this mean that the protesting student was incorrect? Not necessarily; the teacher may be systematically measuring the ability to memorize rather than a true understanding of marketing research.

Unlike the teacher, who was attempting to measure market research knowledge, a brand manager is more interested in successful prediction. The manager, for example, wants to know if a purchase intent scale successfully predicts trial purchase of a new product. Thus, validity can be examined from a number of different perspectives, including face, content, criterion-related, and construct (see Table 9.3).

Face validity
A measurement seems to measure what it is supposed to measure.

Face Validity.   **Face validity** is the weakest form of validity. It is concerned with the degree to which a measurement "looks like" it measures what it is supposed to. It is

TABLE 9.3 *Assessing the Validity of a Measurement Instrument*

Face validity	Researchers judge the degree to which a measurement instrument seems to measure what it is supposed to.
Content validity	The degree to which the instrument items represent the universe of the concept under study.
Criterion-related validity	The degree to which a measurement instrument can predict a variable that is designated a criterion. (a) Predictive ability: The extent to which a future level of a criterion variable can be predicted by a current measurement on a scale. (b) Concurrent validity: The extent to which a criteria variable measured at the same point in time as the variable of interest can be predicted by the measurement instrument.
Construct validity	The degree to which a measure confirms a hypothesis created from a theory based upon the concepts under study. (a) Convergent validity: The degree of association among different measurement instruments that purport to measure the same concept. (b) Discriminant validity: The lack of association among constructs that are supposed to be different.

a judgment call by the researcher, made as the questions are designed. Thus as each question is scrutinized, there is an implicit assessment of its face validity. Revisions enhance the face validity of the question until it passes the researcher's subjective evaluation. Alternatively, *face validity* can refer to the subjective agreement of researchers, experts, or people familiar with the market, product, or industry that a scale logically appears to be accurately reflecting what it is supposed to measure. A straightforward question such as, What is your age? followed by a series of age categories, is generally agreed to have face validity. Most scales used in market research attempt to measure attitudes or behavioral intentions, which are much more elusive.

Content Validity. **Content validity** is the representativeness or sampling adequacy of the content of the measurement instrument. In other words, does the scale provide adequate coverage of the topic under study? Say that McDonald's has hired you to measure the image of the company among adults eighteen to thirty years of age who eat fast food hamburgers at least once a month. You devise a scale that asks consumers to rate the following:

modern building	1	2	3	4	5	old fashioned building
beautiful landscaping	1	2	3	4	5	poor landscaping
clean parking lots	1	2	3	4	5	dirty parking lots
attractive signs	1	2	3	4	5	unattractive signs

Content validity
The degree to which the instrument items represent the universe of the concept under study.

A McDonald's executive would quickly take issue with this scale, claiming that a person could evaluate McDonald's on this scale either good or bad and never have eaten a McDonald's burger. In fact, the evaluation can be made simply by driving past a McDonald's. The executive could further argue that the scale lacks content validity because many important components of image such as the quality of the food, cleanliness of the eating area and restrooms, and promptness and courtesy of service had been omitted.

The determination of content validity is not always a simple matter. It is very difficult and perhaps impossible to identify all the facets of McDonald's image. Content validity ultimately becomes a judgmental matter. One can approach content validity by first carefully defining precisely what is to be measured. Second, an exhaustive literature search and focus groups can be conducted to identify all possible items for inclusion on the scale. Third, a panel of experts can be asked their opinions on whether an item should be included. Finally, the scale could be pretested and an open-ended question could be asked that might identify other items to be included. For example, after a more refined image scale for McDonald's has been administered, a follow-up question could be, Do you have any other thoughts about McDonald's that you would like to express? Answers to this pretest question may provide clues for other image dimensions not previously covered.

Criterion-Related Validity. **Criterion-related validity** examines the ability of a measuring instrument to predict a variable that is designated a criterion. To illustrate, assume that we wish to devise a test to identify marketing researchers who are exceptional at moderating focus groups. We begin by having impartial marketing research experts determine from a directory of marketing researchers who they judge to be best at moderating focus groups. We then construct 300 items to which group moderators are asked to reply yes or no, such as "I believe it is important to compel shy group participants to speak out" and "I like to interact with small groups of people." We then go through the responses and select the items that the good focus group moderators answered one way and the remainder the other way. Assume that this process produces eighty-four items, which we put together to form what we shall call the Test of Effectiveness in Focus Group Moderating (TEFGM). We feel that this test will identify good focus group moderators. The criterion of interest here is the ability to conduct a good focus group. We might explore further the criterion-related validity of TEFGM by administering it to a new group of moderators that has been previously divided into those who are good moderators and those who are not. Then we could determine how well the test identifies the group to which each marketing researcher is assigned. Thus criterion-related validity is concerned with detecting the presence or absence of one or more criteria considered to represent constructs of interest.

Two subcategories of criterion-related validity are predictive validity and concurrent validity. **Predictive validity** is the extent to which a future level of a criterion variable can be predicted by a current measurement on a scale. A voter-motivation scale, for example, is used to predict the likelihood of a person voting in the next election. A savvy politician is not interested in what the community as a whole perceives are important problems, but only what persons who are likely to vote perceive as important problems. These are the issues that the politician would address in speeches and advertising. Another example of predictive validity is the extent to which a purchase intent scale for a new Pepperidge Farm pastry predicts actual trial of the product.

Concurrent validity is concerned with the relationship between the predictor variable and the criterion variable, both of which are assessed at the same point in time; for example, the ability of a home pregnancy test to accurately determine whether a woman is pregnant right now. Such a test with low concurrent validity could cause a lot of undue stress.

Construct Validity. **Construct validity**, although often not consciously addressed by many market researchers on a day-to-day basis, is extremely important to marketing scientists. It involves understanding the theoretical foundations underlying the obtained measurements. A measure has construct validity if it

---

Criterion-related validity
The degree to which a measurement instrument can predict a variable that is designated a criterion.

Predictive validity
The degree to which the future level of a criterion can be forecast by a current measurement scale.

Concurrent validity
The degree to which a variable, measured at the same point in time as the variable of interest, can be predicted by the measurement instrument.

Construct validity
The degree to which a measurement instrument represents and logically connects, via the underlying theory, the observed phenomenon to the construct.

behaves according to the underlying theory. Instead of addressing the major issue of interest to the brand manager (e.g., whether the scale adequately predicts whether a consumer will try my new brand), construct validity is concerned with the theory behind the prediction. Purchase behavior is something we can observe directly; someone either buys product A or does not. Yet scientists have developed constructs on lifestyles, involvement, attitude, and personality that help explain why someone purchases something or does not. These constructs are largely unobservable. We can observe behavior related to the constructs—that is, buying a product—but not the constructs themselves—such as an attitude. Constructs help scientists communicate and build theories to explain phenomena.

Two statistical approaches for assessing construct validity are convergent and discriminant validity. **Convergent validity** is the degree of correlation among different measures that purport to measure the same construct. **Discriminant validity** is the lack of or low correlation among constructs that are supposed to be different. Assume that we develop a multi-item scale that measures the propensity to shop at discount stores. Our theory suggests that this propensity is caused by four personality variables: high level of self confidence, low need for status, low need for distinctiveness, and high level of adaptability. Further, our theory suggests that propensity to shop at discount stores is not related to brand loyalty or high-level aggressiveness.

Convergent validity
The degree of association among different measurement instruments that purport to measure the same concept.

Discriminant validity
The lack of association among constructs that are supposed to be different.

Evidence of construct validity would exist if our scale

- Correlates highly with other measures of propensity to shop at discount stores, such as reported stores patronized and social class (convergent validity)
- Has a low correlation with the unrelated constructs of brand loyalty and a high level of aggressiveness (discriminant validity).

Relating the Measures to Assess Validity.   All of the types of validity discussed here are somewhat interrelated in both theory and practice. Predictive validity is obviously very important on a scale to predict whether a person will shop at a discount store. A researcher developing a discount store patronage scale would probably first attempt to understand the constructs that provide the basis for prediction. The researcher would put forth a theory about discount store patronage that, of course, is the foundation of construct validity. Next, the researcher would be concerned with which specific items to include on the discount store patronage scale and whether these items relate to the full range of the construct. Thus, the researcher would ascertain the degree of content validity. The issue of criterion-related validity can be addressed in a pretest by measuring scores on the discount store patronage scale and actual store patronage.

Reliability and Validity—A Concluding Comment

The concepts of reliability and validity are illustrated conceptually in Figure 9.2. Situation 1 shows holes all over the target. It could be due to the use of an old rifle, being a poor shot, or many other factors. This complete lack of consistency means there is no reliability. Because the instrument lacks reliability, thus creating huge errors, it cannot be valid. Measurement reliability is a necessary condition for validity.

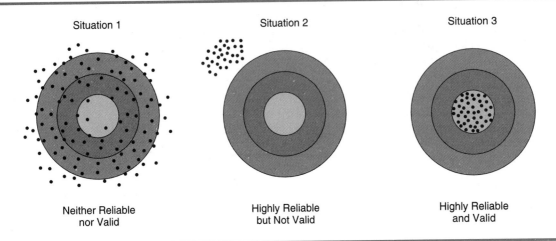

Situation 1

Situation 2

Situation 3

Neither Reliable
nor Valid

Highly Reliable
but Not Valid

Highly Reliable
and Valid

The second target denotes a very tight pattern (consistency) but is far removed from the bull's-eye. This illustrates that we can have a high level of reliability in an instrument (little variance) that lacks validity. The instrument is consistent, but it does not measure what it is supposed to measure. The shooter has a steady eye, but the sights are not adjusted properly. Situation 3 shows the criteria that researchers strive to achieve in a measurement instrument that is reliable, consistent, and valid (on target with what we are attempting to measure).

Despite the critical importance of assessing the reliability and validity of measurement instruments, most research articles written by marketing academics avoid the issue. Of all articles published from 1980 to 1990 in the *Journal of Marketing, Journal of Marketing Research,* and the *Journal of Consumer Research* that utilized survey research measures, only 40 percent reported reliability and validity estimates.[3] Although an improvement over the previous decade, more researchers and practitioners must address measurement issues. This is a necessary requirement to improve the decision-making information provided to management and to advance the science of marketing. If, for example, companies utilize measurement scales that lack reliability and/or validity they may spend millions of dollars bringing out the wrong product.

ATTITUDE SCALES

Measurement of attitudes is much more difficult and uses less precise scales than those found in the physical sciences. An attitude is a construct that exists in the minds of the consumer and is not directly observable unlike, for example, weight in the physical sciences. Attitude scaling is based on various operational definitions created to measure the attitude construct. In many cases, attitudes are measured at the nominal or ordinal level. Some more sophisticated scales enable the market researcher to measure at the interval level. One must be careful not to attribute the more powerful properties of an interval scale to the lower level nominal or ordinal scales.

Scaling Defined

The term **scaling** refers to procedures for attempting to determine quantitative measures of subjective and sometimes abstract concepts. It is defined as a procedure for the assignment of numbers (or other symbols) to a property of objects in order to impart some of the characteristics of numbers to the properties in question. A scale is a measurement tool. Thus, we assign a number scale to the various levels of heat and cold and call it a thermometer. Actually, we assign numbers to indicants of the properties of objects. The rise and fall of mercury in a glass tube is an indicant of temperature variations.

Scales are either unidimensional or multidimensional. **Unidimensional scaling** is designed to measure only one attribute of a respondent or object. Thus, we may create a scale to measure consumers' price sensitivity. We may use several items to measure price sensitivity, but we will combine them into a single measure and place all interviewees along a linear continuum, called *degree of price sensitivity*. **Multidimensional scaling** recognizes that a concept or object might be better described using several dimensions rather than one. For example, target customers for Jaguar automobiles may be defined in three dimensions: level of wealth, degree of price sensitivity, and appreciation of fine motor cars.

Scaling
Procedures for assignment of numbers (or other symbols) to a property of objects in order to impart some of the characteristics of numbers to the properties in question.

Unidimensional scaling
Procedures designed to measure only one attribute of a respondent or object.

Multidimensional scaling
Procedures designed to measure several dimensions of a concept or object.

Graphic Rating Scales

Graphic rating scales present respondents with a graphic continuum typically anchored by two extremes. Figure 9.3 depicts three types of graphic rating scales that might be used to evaluate La-Z-Boy recliners. Scale A represents the simplest form of a graphic scale. Respondents are instructed to check their response along the continuum. After a check mark is made, a score is assigned by dividing the line into as many categories as desired and assigning the score based upon the category into which the mark has been placed. For example, if the line is 6 inches long, every inch could represent a category. Scale B offers the respondent slightly more structure by assigning numbers along the scale.

Graphic rating scales are not limited to simply placing a check mark along a continuum, as illustrated by scale C. Scale C has been used successfully by many researchers to speed up the interviewing process. The interviewer has the scale mounted on a card that is held in front of the respondent. Respondents are asked to touch the thermometer that best depicts their feelings.

Graphic ratings scales can be constructed easily and are simple to use. They also enable a researcher to discern fine distinctions, assuming that the rater has adequate discriminatory abilities. Numerical data obtained from the scales is typically treated as interval data.

One disadvantage of the scale is that if the anchors are too extreme they tend to force respondents toward the middle of the scale. Also, one study has suggested that graphic rating scales are not as reliable as itemized rating scales.

Graphic rating scales
Graphic continuums anchored by two extremes presented to respondents for evaluation of a concept or object.

Itemized Rating Scales

Itemized rating scales are very similar to graphic rating scales, except that respondents must select from a limited number of ordered categories rather than placing a check mark on a continuous scale (purists would argue that scale C in

Itemized rating scales
Scales in which the respondent selects an answer from a limited number of ordered categories.

FIGURE 9.3   *Three Types of Graphic Rating Scales*

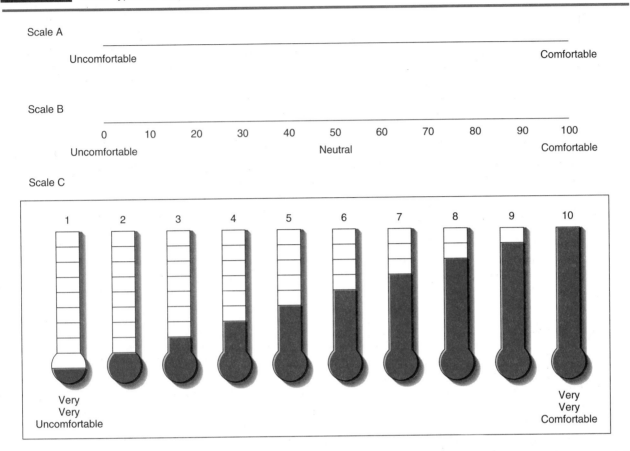

Scale A

Uncomfortable   Comfortable

Scale B

     0   10   20   30   40   50   60   70   80   90   100
   Uncomfortable   Neutral   Comfortable

Scale C

  1   2   3   4   5   6   7   8   9   10

Very   Very
Very   Very
Uncomfortable   Comfortable

Figure 9.3 is an itemized ratings scale). Figure 9.4 illustrates itemized ratings scales taken from nationwide market research surveys. As you can see, researchers often hand a copy of the basic scale to the respondent and ask for a rating after the interviewer reads off a characteristic. Starting points are rotated on each questionnaire to eliminate order bias. That is, starting with the same characteristic each time may act as a source of bias.

Scale A was part of a questionnaire used to evaluate watches with a Sears logo. Scale B was on a screening questionnaire used for in-home placements of a new shampoo concept. The manufacturer wanted an equal number of users in each hair condition category. Scale C was also part of an in-home product test. It was administered after the teenager had used the sample product for two weeks. Scale D was used in a study of children's TV ads. Examples of other itemized rating categories are shown in Table 9.4.

Itemized ratings scales are easy to construct and administer, but do not allow for the fine distinctions that can be achieved in a graphics rating scale. Yet the definitive categories found in itemized ratings scales usually produce more reliable ratings. We will examine several special itemized rating scales later in the chapter.

FIGURE 9.4   *Itemized Rating Scales Used in National Survey*

SCALE A

Now, I'd like to ask you about just two watches specifically. The first one is the SEARS watch. I'm going to mention some characteristics of watches and as I mention each one please tell me whether you think the SEARS watch is (HAND RESPONDENT RATING CARD) excellent, very good, good, fair, or poor

. . . for the particular characteristic.

The first characteristic is (READ CHARACTERISTIC CIRCLED BELOW). Do you feel that the SEARS watch is excellent, very good, good, fair or poor for (CHARACTERISTIC)?

(CONTINUE FOR *ALL* CHARACTERISTICS BELOW)

Starting Point		Excellent	Very Good	Good	Fair	Poor
X	Value for the money	□ 5	□ 4	□ 3	□ 2	□ 1
X	Brand name	□ 5	□ 4	□ 3	□ 2	□ 1
X	Accuracy	□ 5	□ 4	□ 3	□ 2	□ 1
X	Durability	□ 5	□ 4	□ 3	□ 2	□ 1
X	Manufacturer's reputation	□ 5	□ 4	□ 3	□ 2	□ 1
X	After-sales service	□ 5	□ 4	□ 3	□ 2	□ 1
X	Styling	□ 5	□ 4	□ 3	□ 2	□ 1

SCALE B

9. Which statement on this card (HAND RESPONDENT CARD B) best describes the present condition of your hair?

1 ( ) Very damaged

2 ( ) Somewhat damaged

3 ( ) Slightly damaged

4 ( ) Not at all damaged

SCALE C

Now, I would like to get your opinion on Stridex Cleansing Pads on some characteristics. (HAND RATING CARD) Using the phrases on this card, please tell me which one best indicates how much you agree or disagree that Stridex Cleansing Pads . . . (START WITH CHECKED CHARACTERISTIC AND CONTINUE UNTIL ALL ARE ASKED)

Start		Agree Strongly	Agree Somewhat	Disagree Somewhat	Disagree Strongly
( )	Help prevent blemishes	___ 9-4	___ –3	___ –2	___ –1
( )	Help to clear up blemishes	___ 10-4	___ –3	___ –2	___ –1
( )	Are convenient to use	___ 11-4	___ –3	___ –2	___ –1
(✔)	Are not irritating	___ 12-4	___ –3	___ –2	___ –1
( )	Leave face feeling fresh	___ 13-4	___ –3	___ –2	___ –1
( )	Make you feel confident you are doing everything you can to help your skin look good	___ 14-4	___ –3	___ –2	___ –1

Continued

FIGURE 9.4   *Itemized Rating Scales Used in National Survey—(Continued)*

Scale D

Very
Very
Good

Very
Very
Poor

Source: Scale D is adapted from Fred Cutler, "To Meet Criticisms of TV Ads Researchers Find New Ways to Measure Children's Attitudes," *Marketing News* (January 27, 1978), p. 16, published by the American Marketing Association.

TABLE 9.4   *Selected Itemized Rating Scales*

		PURCHASE INTENT		
Definitely will buy	Probably will buy	Probably will not buy		Definitely will not buy
		LEVEL OF AGREEMENT		
Strongly agree	Somewhat agree	Neither agree nor disagree	Somewhat disagree	Strongly disagree
		QUALITY		
Very good	Good	Neither good nor bad	Fair	Poor
		DEPENDABILITY		
Completely dependable	Somewhat dependable	Not very dependable		Not dependable at all
		STYLE		
Very stylish	Somewhat stylish	Not very stylish		Completely unstylish
		SATISFACTION		
Completely satisfied	Somewhat satisfied	Neither satisfied nor dissatisfied	Somewhat dissatisfied	Completely dissatisfied
		COST		
Extremely expensive	Expensive	Neither expensive nor inexpensive	Slightly inexpensive	Very inexpensive
		EASE OF USE		
Very easy to use	Somewhat easy to use	Not very easy to use		Difficult to use
		COLOR BRIGHTNESS		
Extremely bright	Very bright	Somewhat bright	Slightly bright	Not bright at all
		MODERNITY		
Very modern	Somewhat modern	Neither modern nor old-fashioned	Somewhat old-fashioned	Very old-fashioned

Rank-Order Scale

Itemized and graphic scales are **noncomparative** because the respondent makes a judgment without reference to another object, concept, or person. **Rank-order scales**, on the other hand, are **comparative** because the respondent is asked to judge one item against another. Rank-order scales are widely used in market research for several reasons. They are easy to use and form an ordinal scale of the items evaluated. Instructions are easy to understand and the process typically moves at a steady pace. Some researchers claim that it forces respondents to evaluate concepts in a realistic manner. For example, Figure 9.5 illustrates a series of rank-order scales taken from a study on eye shadows.

Rank-order scales also possess several disadvantages. If all of the alternatives in a respondent's choice set are not included, the results could be misleading. For example, a respondent's first choice on all dimensions in the eye shadow study might have been Max Factor, which was not included. A second problem is that the concept being ranked may be completely outside a person's choice set, thus producing meaningless data. Perhaps a respondent doesn't use eye shadow and feels that the product isn't appropriate for any woman. A final limitation is that the scale gives the researcher only ordinal data. Nothing is learned about how far apart the items stand or how intense a person feels about the ranking of an item. Finally, we don't know why the items were ranked as they were.

> **Noncomparative scales**
> Scales using a judgment made without reference to another object, concept, or person.
>
> **Rank-order scales**
> Scales in which the respondent compares one item with another or a group of items against each other and ranks them.
>
> **Comparative scales**
> A judgment comparing one object, concept, or person against another on a scale.

Q-Sorting

Q-sorting is basically a sophisticated form of rank ordering. A set of objects—verbal statements, slogans, product features, potential customer services, and so forth—is given to an individual to sort into piles according to specified rating categories (see Table 9.4). For example, the cards may each have a feature in them that can be designed into a new automobile. The respondents could then be asked to sort the cards according to how well they like the potential feature. With a large number of cards—Q sorts usually contain between 60 and 120 cards—it would be very difficult to rank-order them. For statistical convenience, the sorter is instructed to put varying numbers of cards in several piles, the whole making up a normal statistical distribution.

Here is a Q-sort distribution of 90 items:

> **Q-sorting**
> A sophisticated form of rank-ordering using card sorts.

Excellent Feature									Poor Feature	
3	4	7	10	13	16	13	10	7	4	3
10	9	8	7	6	5	4	3	2	1	0

This is a rank-order continuum from *Excellent Feature* to *Poor Feature,* with varying degrees of approval and disapproval between the extremes.

The numbers 3, 4, 7, . . ., 7, 4, 3 are the numbers of cards to be placed in each pile. The numbers below the line are the values assigned to the cards in each pile. That is, the three cards at the left, *Excellent Feature,* are each assigned 10, the four cards in the next pile are assigned 9, and so on through the distribution to the three cards at the extreme right, which are assigned 0. The center pile is a neutral pile. The

FIGURE 9.5	A Series of Rank-Order Scales Used to Evaluate Eye Shadows

Please rank the following eye shadows with 1 being the brand that best meets the characteristic being evaluated and 6 the worst brand on the characteristic being evaluated. The six brands are listed on card C. (HAND RESPONDENT CARD C.) Let's begin with the idea of having high-quality compacts or containers. Which brand would rank as having the highest quality compacts or containers? Which is second? (RECORD BELOW.)

	Q.48	HAVING HIGH-QUALITY CONTAINER	Q.49	HAVING A HIGH-QUALITY APPLICATOR	Q.50	HAVING A HIGH-QUALITY EYE SHADOW
Avon		_____		_____		_____
Cover Girl		_____		_____		_____
Estee Lauder		_____		_____		_____
Maybelline		_____		_____		_____
Natural Wonder		_____		_____		_____
Revlon		_____		_____		_____

Card C

Avon	Cover Girl	Estee Lauder
Maybelline	Natural Wonder	Revlon

respondent is told to put cards into the neutral pile that are left over after other choices have been made, cards that seem ambiguous or about which he or she cannot make a decision. In brief, this Q-distribution has eleven piles with varying numbers of cards in each pile, the cards in the piles being assigned values from 0 through 10. A Q-sort scale can be used to determine the relative ranking of items by individuals and to derive clusters of individuals who exhibit the same preferences.

Using rank-order scales to evaluate eye shadow brands is comparative because the respondent is asked to judge one item against another.

These clusters of people may then be analyzed as a potential basis for market segmentation.

Paired Comparisons

Paired comparison scales ask a respondent to pick one of two objects from a set based upon some stated criteria. The respondent, therefore, makes a series of paired judgments between objects. Figure 9.6 shows a paired comparison scale used in a national study for suntan products. Only part of the scale is shown, as the data collection procedure typically requires the respondent to compare all possible pairs of objects.

Paired comparison scales
Scales that ask the respondent to pick one of two objects in a set based on some stated criteria.

GLOBAL MARKETING RESEARCH

abra Brock, vice-president of Citicorp, notes that devising scales and other types of questions requires careful planning when conducting marketing research in Asia. In Asia, many countries have the capability of conducting some kinds of Western-style marketing research. Japan, Hong Kong, Singapore, and the Philippines have fairly advanced research industries. Other countries in Asia such as China, Korea, Indonesia, and India have research capabilities, but they are so underdeveloped as to require special supervision. Asia also has fewer research and marketing firms that can act as data "translators," people who can transform computer tables and research results into specific marketing directions.

Attitudes toward research vary from country to country in Asia, as do reactions to pricing, distribution, and promotion strategies. Most Asians respond differently to being interviewed than Americans. They frequently have less patience with the abstract and rational phrasing commonly used in questionnaires, particularly where literacy rates are low.

The interpretation of research tools like scales is different among educated Asians. The Japanese desire not to contradict, for example, makes for more yea-saying and upward scale bias than in a Western culture.

Apart from the varying reactions to research, there are also design implications to the distinct pricing and distribution strategies employed in Asia. For example, when querying Asians about pricing, the researcher must realize that they are especially prone to equating high price with high quality. In countries where imports are restricted or highly taxed, like Korea and the Philippines, "imported" and especially "made in USA" are strong product claims.

Among the Chinese countries in Asia, many distinct dialects are spoken. A Hong Kong native speaks the Cantonese dialect and must study Mandarin to communicate easily in Taiwan. These language dissimilarities are critical in questionnaire development. In Hong Kong, written and oral Cantonese are different enough to necessitate rewriting a questionnaire when the methodology changes from self-administered to interviewer-read.[4]

FIGURE 9.6   *A Paired Comparison Test for Suntan Products*

14. Thinking about sun products in general, here are some characteristics used to describe them. Please tell me which characteristic in each pair is more important to you when selecting a sun care product.

a. Tans evenly	b. Tans without burning
a. Prevents burning	b. Protects against burning and tanning
a. Good value for the money	b. Goes on evenly
a. Not greasy	b. Does not stain clothing
a. Tans without burning	b. Prevents burning
a. Protects against burning and tanning	b. Good value for the money
a. Goes on evenly	b. Tans evenly
a. Prevents burning	b. Not greasy

Paired comparisons overcome several problems of traditional rank-order scales. First, it is easier for people to select one item from a set of two than to rank a large set of data. Second, the problem of order bias is overcome. That is, a pattern in the ordering of items or questions may create a source of bias. On the negative side, because all possible pairs are evaluated, as the number of objects to be evaluated increases arithmetically, the number of paired comparisons increases geometrically. Thus, the number of objects to be evaluated should remain fairly small to prevent interviewee fatigue.

Constant Sum Scales

Constant sum scales
Scales that ask the respondent to divide a given number of points, typically 100, among two or more attributes based on their importance to the person.

Constant sum scales are used more often by market researchers than paired comparisons because the long list of paired items is avoided. This technique requires the respondent to divide a given number of points, typically 100, among two or more attributes based on their importance to the person. This scale requires that respondents value each individual item relative to all other items. The number of points allocated to each alternative indicates the ranks assigned to them by the respondent. The values assigned are also indicative of the relative magnitudes of each alternative as perceived by the respondent. A constant sum scale used in a national study of tennis sportswear is shown in Figure 9.7. An additional advantage of the constant sum scale over a rank-order or paired comparison scale is that if two characteristics are perceived to have equal value, it can be so indicated.

A major disadvantage of this scale is that as the number of characteristics or items increases, it may confuse the respondent. That is, the respondent may have difficulty allocating the points to total 100. Most researchers feel that ten items is the outer limit on a constant sum scale.

The Semantic Differential

The semantic differential was developed by Charles Osgood, George Suci, and Percy Tannenbaum.[5] The focus of the original research was on the measurement of meaning of an object to a person. Thus, the object might be a savings and

---

FIGURE 9.7   *A Constant Sum Scale Used in a Tennis Sportswear Study*

Below are seven characteristics of women's tennis sportswear. Please allocate 100 points among the characteristics such that the allocation represents the importance of each characteristic to you. The more points that you assign to a characteristic, the more important it is. If the characteristic is totally unimportant, you should not allocate any points to it. When you've finished, please double-check to make sure that your total adds to 100.

CHARACTERISTICS OF TENNIS SPORTSWEAR	NUMBER OF POINTS
Is comfortable to wear	_____
Is durable	_____
Is made by well-known brand or sports manufacturers	_____
Is made in the U.S.A.	_____
Has up-to-date styling	_____
Gives freedom of movement	_____
Is a good value for the money	_____
	100 points

---

loan association and the meaning the image of the association to a certain group.

The construction of a **semantic differential** scale begins with the determination of a concept to be rated, such as a company, brand, or store image. The researcher selects dichotomous (opposite) pairs of words or phrases that could be used to describe the concept. Respondents then rate the concept on a scale (usually 1–7). The mean of these responses for each pair of adjectives is computed and plotted as a "profile" or image.

Figure 9.8 is an actual image profile of an Arizona Savings and Loan Association as perceived by noncustomers with family incomes of $45,000 and above. A quick glance shows that the firm is viewed as somewhat old-fashioned with rather plain facilities. It is viewed as well-established, reliable, successful, and probably very nice to deal with. The institution has parking problems and perhaps entry and egress difficulties. Its advertising is viewed as dismal.

The semantic differential is a quick and efficient means of examining the strengths and weaknesses of a product or company image versus the competition. More important, however, the semantic differential has been shown to be sufficiently reliable and valid for decision making and prediction in marketing and the behavioral sciences.[6] Also, the semantic differential has proven to be statistically robust (applicable) from one group of subjects to another when applied to corporate image research.[7] This makes possible the measurement and comparison of images held by interviewees with diverse backgrounds.

Although these advantages have led many researchers to use the semantic differential as an image measurement tool, it is not without disadvantages. First, there is a lack of standardization. The semantic differential is a highly generalized technique that must be adapted for each research problem. There is no single set of standard scales, and hence the development of these becomes an integral part of the research.

The number of divisions on the semantic differential scale also presents a problem. If too few divisions are used, the scale is crude and lacks meaning; if too many are used the scale goes beyond the ability of most people to discriminate. Researchers have found the seven-point scale to be the most satisfactory.

Semantic differential
A method of examining the strengths and weaknesses of a product or company versus the competition by having respondents rank it between dichotomous pairs of words or phrases that could be used to describe it; the mean of the responses is then plotted in a profile or image.

Another disadvantage of the semantic differential is the "halo effect." The rating of a specific image component may be dominated by the interviewee's overall impression of the concept being rated. This may be a significant bias if the image is hazy in the respondent's mind. To partially counteract the halo effect, the scale adjectives should be randomly reversed so all of the "good" phrases are not placed on one side of the scale and the "bad" on the other. This forces the interviewee to evaluate the adjectives before responding. To facilitate analysis after the data has been gathered, all of the "good adjectives" are placed on one side and the negative ones on the other.

Another problem occurs when analyzing a seven-point semantic differential scale in that care must be taken in interpreting a score of 4. A response of 4 will indicate one of two things—the respondent is either unable to relate the given pair of adjectives to the concept (they do not know) or simply may be neutral or indifferent. In many image studies, there frequently will be a large number of 4 responses. This phenomena tends to pull the profiles toward the neutral position. Thus, the profiles lack clarity and little distinction appears.

FIGURE 9.8   A Semantic Differential Profile of an Arizona Savings and Loan Association

ADJECTIVE 1	MEAN OF EACH ADJECTIVE PAIR	ADJECTIVE 2
	1 2 3 4 5 6 7	
Modern		Old-fashioned
Aggressive		Defensive
Friendly		Unfriendly
Well-established		Not well-established
Attractive exterior		Unattractive exterior
Reliable		Unreliable
Appeal to small companies		Appeal to big companies
Makes you feel at home		Makes you feel uneasy
Helpful services		Indifferent to customers
Nice to deal with		Hard to deal with
No parking or transportation problems		Parking or transportaion problems
My kind of people		Not my kind of people
Successful		Unsuccessful
Ads attract a lot of attention		Haven't noticed ads
Interesting ads		Uninteresting ads
Influential ads		Not influential

FIGURE 9.9   *Example of a Stapel Scale*

+5	+5
+4	+4
+3	+3
+2	+2
+1	+1
Friendly Personnel	Competitive Loan Rates
−1	−1
−2	−2
−3	−3
−4	−4
−5	−5

Select a *plus* number for words that you think describe the savings and loan accurately. The more accurately you think the word describes the company, the larger the plus number you should choose. Select a *minus* number for words you think do not describe the savings and loan accurately. The less accurately you think the word describes the institution, the larger the minus number you should choose; therefore, you can select any number from +5 for words that you think are very accurate all the way to −5 for words that you think are very inaccurate.

Stapel Scale

The **Stapel scale** is a modification of the semantic differential. A single adjective is placed in the center of the scale. Typically it is designed as a ten point scale ranging from +5 to −5. The technique is designed to measure both the direction and intensity of attitudes simultaneously. The semantic differential, on the other hand, reflects how close the descriptor adjective fits the concept being evaluated. An example of a Stapel scale is shown in Figure 9.9.

The primary advantage of the Stapel scale is that it enables the researcher to avoid the arduous task of creating bipolar adjective pairs. It is also claimed that the scale permits finer discrimination in measuring attitudes. On the negative side is the problem that descriptor adjectives can be phrased in a positive, neutral, or a negative vein. The choice of phrasing has been shown to affect the scale results and the person's ability to respond.[8] The popularity of the semantic differential has declined extensively in the 1980s and 1990s, primarily due to the increase in telephone interviewing. The Stapel scale has never had much popularity in commercial research and is used less than the semantic differential.

Stapel scale
A scale, ranging from +5 to −5, that requires the respondent to rate how close and in what direction a descriptor adjective fits a given concept.

Likert Scales

The **Likert scale** also avoids the problem of developing pairs of dichotomous adjectives. The scale consists of a series of statements that express either a favorable or unfavorable attitude toward the concept under study. The respondent is asked the level of agreement or disagreement with each statement. Each respondent is then given a numerical score to reflect how favorable or unfavorable their attitude is toward each statement. The scores are then totaled to measure the respondent's attitude.

Likert scale
A scale in which the respondent specifies a level of agreement or disagreement with statements that express a favorable or unfavorable attitude toward the concept under study.

Table 9.5 shows a Likert scale for persons who have admitted on a screening questionnaire that they have a foot odor problem but have not tried Johnson's Odor Eater Insoles. The scale is taken from a national study on the product.

The Likert scale only requires the respondent to consider one statement at a time with the scale running from one extreme to another. A series of statements (attitudes) can be examined, yet there is only a single set of uniform replies for the respondent to give.

Rensis Likert created his scale to measure a person's attitude toward concepts (i.e., unions), activities (i.e., swimming), and so forth. He recommended the following steps in building the scale:

1. The researcher identifies the concept to be scaled. Let us assume that it is snow skiing.

TABLE 9.5   *A Likert Scale for Persons with Foot Odor Problems Who Have Not Tried Johnson's Odor Eaters*

(SHOW CARD J) Now I would like to find out your impressions about Johnson's Odor Eaters, which you said you were familiar with but had not tried. As I read each characteristic, please tell me, using the statements on this card, if you strongly agree, agree, neither agree nor disagree, or strongly disagree.

	STRONGLY AGREE	AGREE	NEITHER AGREE NOR DISAGREE	DISAGREE	STRONGLY DISAGREE
They might make my feet feel hot	5	4	3	2	1
I am satisfied with what I am using	5	4	3	2	1
My problem is not serious enough	5	4	3	2	1
Too much trouble to cut them to fit to size	5	4	3	2	1
Price is too expensive	5	4	3	2	1
Might make my shoes too tight	5	4	3	2	1
I'm embarrassed to buy them	5	4	3	2	1
The advertising has not convinced me that the product is effective	5	4	3	2	1
Other insoles I've tried didn't work	5	4	3	2	1
Foot sprays work better	5	4	3	2	1
Foot powders work better	5	4	3	2	1
I've never used an insole	5	4	3	2	1
Wouldn't last more than a couple of weeks	5	4	3	2	1
Would look unattractive in my shoes	5	4	3	2	1
Would have to buy more than one pair	5	4	3	2	1
Would have to move them from one pair of shoes to another	5	4	3	2	1
No product for foot odor works completely	5	4	3	2	1
They might get too wet from perspiration	5	4	3	2	1
Don't know what an insole would feel like in shoe	5	4	3	2	1

	CARD J			
Strongly Agree	Agree	Neither Agree nor Disagree	Disagree	Strongly Disagree

2. The researcher assembles a large number (e.g., 75 to 100) of statements concerning the public's sentiments toward snow skiing.

3. Each test item is classified by the researcher as generally "favorable" or "unfavorable" with regard to the attitude under study. No attempt is made to scale the items; however, a pretest is conducted that involves the full set of statements and a limited sample of respondents.

4. In the pretest the respondent indicates agreement (or not) with *every* item, checking one of the following direction-intensity descriptors:
   a. Strongly agree
   b. Agree
   c. Undecided
   d. Disagree
   e. Strongly disagree

5. Each response is given a numerical weight (e.g., 5, 4, 3, 2, 1).

6. The individual's *total-attitude score* is represented by the algebraic summation of weights associated with the items checked. In the scoring process, weights are assigned so that the direction of attitude—favorable to unfavorable—is consistent over items. For example, if 5 were assigned to "strongly approve" for favorable items, 5 should be assigned to "strongly disapprove" for unfavorable items.

7. After seeing the results of the pretest, the analyst selects only those items that appear to discriminate well between high and low *total* scorers. This may be done by first finding the highest and lowest quartiles of subjects on the basis of *total* score. Then, the mean differences on each *specific* item are compared between these high and low groups (excluding the middle 50 percent of subjects).

8. The twenty to twenty-five items finally selected are those that have discriminated "best" (i.e., exhibited the greatest differences in mean values) between high versus low total scorers in the pretest.
9. Steps 3 through 5 are then repeated in the main study.[9]

Likert created his scale so that a researcher could look at a summed score and tell if a person's attitude toward a concept is positive or negative. For example, the maximum favorable score on a twenty-item scale would be 100, therefore a person scoring 92 would be presumed to have a favorable attitude. Of course two people could both score 92 and yet have rated various statements differently. Thus, specific attitudes toward components of their overall attitude could differ markedly. For example, respondent A might strongly agree (5) that a bank has good parking and strongly disagree (1) that their loan programs are the best in town. Respondent B could have the exact opposite attitude, yet both summed scores would be 6.

In the world of commercial market research, Likert-like scales are very popular. They are quick and easy to construct and can be administered over the phone or a respondent can be given a "reply category" card and be asked to call out an answer. Commercial researchers rarely follow the textbooklike process just outlined. Instead the scales are usually developed jointly by a client project manager and a researcher. Many times the scales are created after a focus group.

Most important, the commercial researcher usually has a totally different motivation for using the scale. Instead of trying to discern positive and negative attitudes of individual respondents, they are more interested in attitudes toward the various components of the scale! Thus, referring back to the Odor Eater scale, the company was interested in determining what factors were causing target customers not to purchase Odor Eaters. They were not really concerned whether respondent A had a positive or negative attitude toward Odor Eaters. This notion is also often true for the semantic differential.

Purchase Intent Scales

Purchase intent scale
A scale used to measure a respondent's intention to buy or not buy a product.

Perhaps the single scale used most often in commercial market research is the **purchase intent scale**. The ultimate issue for marketing managers is, Will they buy the product, or not? If so, what percentage of the market can I expect to obtain? The purchase intent question is normally asked for all new products and services, product modifications, new services or service modifications by a retailer, and even by nonprofit organizations.

During new product development, the purchase intent question is asked during concept testing to get a rough idea of demand. The manager wants to quickly eliminate potential turkeys, take a careful look at those where purchase intent is moderate, and push forward the projects that seem to have star potential. At this stage, investment is minimal and product modification or repositioning the concept is an easy task. As the product moves through development, the product itself, promotion strategy, price levels, and distribution channels become more concrete and focused. Purchase intent is evaluated at each stage of development and demand estimates are refined. The crucial go–no go decision for national or regional rollout typically comes after test marketing. Immediately prior to test marketing, commercial researchers have another critical stage of evaluation. Here the final, or near final, version of the product is placed in consumers' homes in test cities around the country. After a period of in-home use (usually two to six weeks), a follow-up survey is conducted among participants to find out their likes, dislikes, how the product compares to what they use now, and what they would pay for it. The critical question, near the end of the questionnaire is purchase intent.

Figure 9.10, question 21, is a purchase intent question taken from a follow-up study on in-home placement of a fly trap. The trap consisted of two 3-inch discs held about ¼-inch apart by three plastic pillars looking somewhat like a large, thin yo-yo. The trap worked on the same principle as the Roach Motel. It contained a pheramone to attract the flies and a glue that would remain sticky for six months. Supposedly, the flies flew in but never out! Centered on the backside of one of the discs was an adhesive tab so that the disc could be attached to a kitchen window. The concept was to eliminate flies in the kitchen area without resorting to a pesticide. Question 22 in Figure 9.10 was designed to aid in positioning the product, and question 23 was traditionally used by the manufacturer as a double check on purchase intent. That is, if 60 percent of the respondents claimed that they would definitely buy the product and 90 percent said they would definitely not recommend the product to their friends, the researcher would question the validity of the purchase intent.

The purchase intent scale has been found to be a good predictor of consumer choice of frequently purchased and durable consumer products.[10] The scale is very easy to construct and consumers are simply asked to make a subjective judgment on their likelihood of buying a new product. From past experience in the product category, a marketing manager can translate consumer responses on the scale to estimates of purchase probability. Obviously, everyone who claims that they "definitely will buy" the product will not do so; in fact, a few who state that they definitely would not buy, will buy the product. The manufacturer of the fly trap is a major producer of both pesticide and nonpesticide pest control products. Assume

---

FIGURE 9.10 *Purchase Intent Scale and Related Questions for an In-Home Product Placement of Fly Traps*

21. If a set of three traps sold for approximately $1.00 and was available in the stores where you normally shop, would you:

	(51)
definitely buy the set of traps	1
probably buy	2
probably not buy—SKIP TO Q23	3
definitely not buy—SKIP TO Q23	4

22. Would you use the traps (a) instead of or (b) in addition to existing products?

	(52)
instead of	1
in addition to	2

23. Would you recommend this product to your friends?

	(53)
definitely	1
probably	2
probably not	3
definitely not	4

that, based upon historical follow-up studies, the manufacturer has learned the following about purchase intent of nonpesticide home-use pest control products:

- 63 percent of the "definitely will buy" actually purchase within twelve months
- 28 percent of the "probably will buy" actually purchase within twelve months
- 12 percent of the "probably will not buy" actually purchase within twelve months
- 3 percent of the "definitely will not buy" actually purchase within twelve months.

Suppose that the fly trap study resulted in the following:

- 40 percent—definitely will buy
- 20 percent—probably will buy
- 30 percent—probably will not buy
- 10 percent—definitely will not buy

Assuming that the sample is representative of the target market, then:

$$(.4)(63\%) + (.2)(28\%) + (.3)(12\%) + (.1)(3\%) = 34.7 \text{ percent market share.}$$

Most marketing managers would be deliriously happy at a market share prediction this high for a new product. Unfortunately, the fly trap prediction was not nearly this high and the product was killed after the in-home placement.

It is not uncommon for market research firms to conduct studies containing a purchase intent scale, but the client does not have historical data to use as a basis for weighing the data. A reasonable but conservative estimate would be 70 percent of the "definitely will buy," 35 percent of the "probably will buy," 10 percent of the "probably will not buy," and 0 for the "definitely will not buy."[11] Higher weights are common in the industrial market.

Some companies use the purchase intent scale to make go–no go decisions in product development without reference to market share. Typically, the managers simply add the "definitely will buy" and "probably will buy" and use that against a predetermined go–no go threshold. One consumer goods manufacturer, for example, requires a combined score of 80 percent or higher at the concept testing stage and 65 percent for a product to move from in-home placement tests to test marketing.

Some Basic Considerations When Selecting a Scale

With the exception of purchase intent, for most nonimage studies, the question arises as to which scale to use. We have presented the most commonly used scales and the advantages and disadvantages of each.

Selecting a Rating, Ranking, Sorting, or Purchase Intent Scale.   Most commercial researchers lean toward scales that can be administered over the telephone to save interviewing expense. Ease of administration and development are also important considerations. For example, a rank-order scale can be quickly created, whereas a semantic differential (rating scale) is often a long and tedious process. Decision-making needs of the client are always of paramount importance. Can the decision be made using ordinal data, or must we have interval information? Researchers must also consider the respondents who usually prefer nominal and ordinal scales because of their simplicity. Ultimately, the choice of which type of scale to use will depend upon the problem at hand and the questions that must be answered. It is not uncommon to find several types of scales in one research study. For example, an image study for a grocery chain might have a ranking scale of competing chains and a semantic differential to examine components of the chain's image.

Balanced versus Nonbalanced Alternatives. A **balanced scale** has the same number of positive and negative categories; a **nonbalanced scale** is weighted toward one end or the other. If the researcher expects a wide range of opinions, then a balanced scale is probably in order. If past research or a preliminary study has determined that most opinions are positive, then the scale should contain more positive gradients than negative. This would enable the researcher to ascertain the degree of positiveness toward the concept being researched. We have conducted a series of studies for the YMCA and know that the overall image of the institution is positive. In tracking the YMCA's image, the following categories are used: (1) outstanding, (2) very good, (3) good, (4) fair, (5) poor.

Balanced scale
A scale with the same number of positive and negative categories.

Nonbalanced scale
A scale weighted toward one end or the other.

Number of Categories. The number of categories to be included in a scale is another question that must be resolved by the market researcher. If the number of categories is too small—for example, good, fair, poor—the scale is crude and lacks richness. A three-category scale does not reveal the intensity of feeling that, say, a ten-category scale offers. Yet, a ten-category scale may go beyond a person's ability to accurately discriminate from one category to another. Research has shown that rating scales should typically have between five and nine categories.[12] When a scale is being administered over the telephone, five categories seems to be the most that respondents can adequately handle.

Odd or Even Number of Scale Categories. An even number of scale categories means that there is no neutral point. Without a neutral point, respondents are forced to indicate some degree of positive or negative feelings on an issue. Persons who are truly neutral are not allowed to express this feeling. On the other hand, some commercial market researchers say that putting a neutral point on a scale gives the respondent an easy way out. Assuming that he or she has no really strong opinion, the person does not have to concentrate on his or her actual feelings and can easily say that he or she is neutral. However, researchers also point out that it is rather unusual to be highly emotional about a new flavor salad dressing, a package design, or a test commercial for a Ford pickup truck.

Forced versus Nonforced Choice. A consideration, mentioned in our discussion of the semantic differential, is that if a neutral category is included it will typically contain those who are neutral and those who lack knowledge to answer the question. Some researchers have resolved this issue by adding a "don't know" response as an additional category. For example, a semantic differential might be set up as follows:

Friendly	1	2	3	4	5	6	7	Unfriendly	Don't Know
Unexciting	1	2	3	4	5	6	7	Exciting	Don't Know

Adding a *don't know* option, however, can be an easy out for the lazy respondent.

A neutral point on a scale without a *don't know* option does not force a respondent to give a positive or negative opinion. A scale without a neutral point or a *don't know* forces even those persons with no information about an object to state an opinion. The argument for forced choice is the same as for a scale with an even number of categories. The arguments against forced choice are that inaccurate data are recorded or respondents refuse to answer the question. A questionnaire that continues to require respondents to provide an opinion when, in fact, they lack information to make a decision can create ill will and result in termination of the interview.

SUMMARY

Measurement consists of using rules to assign numbers to objects in such a way as to represent quantities of attributes. Thus, it is a procedure used to assign numbers that reflect the amount of attributes possessed by an event, person, or object. A measurement rule is a guide, a method, or command that tells the researcher what to do. Accurate measurement requires rules that are both clear and specific. This rule includes order, distance, and origin.

There are four basic levels of measurement: nominal, ordinal, interval, and ratio. A nominal scale partitions data into categories that are mutually exclusive and collectively exhaustive. The numbers assigned to objects or phenomena are numerical but have no number meaning; they are simply labels. Ordinal scales maintain the identification characteristics of nominal scales plus an ability to order data. Interval scales contain all the features of ordinal scales with the added dimension that the invervals between the points on the scale are equal. Interval scales enable the researcher to discuss differences separating two objects. They are amenable to computation of an arithmetic mean, standard deviation, and correlation coefficients. Ratio scales have all the powers of those previously discussed scales plus the concept of an absolute zero or origin, which enables comparison of the absolute magnitude of the numbers and reflects the actual amount of the variable.

Measurement data consists of accurate information and errors. Systematic errors result in a constant bias in the measurements. Random errors also influence the measurements but are not systematic; they are transient in nature and do not occur in a consistent manner. Reliability is the degree to which measures are free from random error and therefore provide consistent data. There are three ways to assess reliability: test-retest, internal consistency, and use of equivalent forms. Validity refers to the notion of actually measuring what you are attempting to measure. The validity of a measure refers to the extent to which the measurement device or process is free from both systematic and random error. Concepts of validity include face, content, criterion, and construct validity.

Scaling refers to procedures for attempting to determine quantitative measures of subjective and sometimes abstract concepts. It is a procedure for the assignment of numbers or other symbols to a property of objects to impart some of the characteristics of the numbers to the properties in question. Scales are either unidimensional or multidimensional. A unidimensional scale is designed to measure only one attribute of a respondent or object. Multidimensional scaling recognizes that a concept or object might be better described using several dimensions rather than one.

One type of scale is called a graphic rating scale. Respondents are presented with a graphic continuum typically anchored by two extremes. Itemized rating scales are very similar to graphic rating scales except that respondents must select from a limited number of categories rather than placing a check mark on a continuous scale. A rank-order scale is comparative because respondents are asked to judge one item against another. A Q-sort is a sophisticated form of rank ordering. Respondents are asked to sort a large number of cards into piles of predetermined size. Paired comparison scales present two objects from a set and ask the respondent to pick one based on some stated criteria. Constant sum scales ask the respondent to divide a given number of points, typically 100, among two or more attributes based upon their importance to the person. This scale requires the respondent to value each individual item relative to all other items. The number of points allocated to each alternative indicates the ranks assigned them by the respondent.

The semantic differential was developed to measure the meaning of an object to a person. The construction of a semantic differential scale begins with a determination of the concept to be rated, such as a brand, and then the researcher selects dichotomous pairs of words or phrases that could be used to describe the concept. Respondents then rate the concept on a scale, usually 1–7. The mean of these responses for each pair of adjectives is computed and plotted as a profile or image. The Stapel scale is one in which a single adjective is placed in the center of the scale. Typically, it is designed to simultaneously measure both the direction and intensity of attitudes. The Likert scale also avoids the problem of developing pairs of dichotomous adjectives. The scale consists of a series of statements that express either a favorable or unfavorable attitude toward the concept under study. The respondent is asked the level of agreement or disagreement with each statement. Each respondent is then given a numerical score to reflect how favorable or unfavorable their attitude is toward each statement. Scores are then totaled to measure the respondent's attitude.

The scale used most often and perhaps most important to market researchers is the purchase intent scale. The purchase intent scale is used to measure a respondent's intention to buy or not buy a product. The purchase intent question usually asks a person to state whether he or she would: definitely buy, probably buy, probably not buy, or definitely not buy the product under study. The purchase intent scale has been found to be a good predictor of consumer choice of frequently purchased consumer durable goods.

When attempting to select a particular scale for a study, several factors should be considered. The first is whether to use a rating, ranking, or choice scale. Next, consideration must be given to the use of a balanced scale versus nonbalanced scale. The number of categories also must be determined. Another factor is whether to use an odd or even number of scale categories. Finally, the researcher must consider whether to use force versus nonforce choice sets.

KEY TERMS

Measurement	Random error
Rule	Reliability
Scale	Test-retest relability
Nominal scales	Stability
Ordinal scales	Equivalent form reliability
Interval scales	Internal consistency reliability
Ratio scales	Split-half technique
Systematic error	Validity

Face validity
Content validity
Criterion-related validity
Predictive validity
Concurrent validity
Construct validity
Convergent validity
Discriminant validity
Scaling
Unidimensional scaling
Multidimensional scaling
Graphic rating scales
Itemized rating scales

Noncomparative scales
Rank-order scales
Comparative scales
Q-sorting
Paired comparison scales
Constant sum scales
Semantic differential
Stapel scale
Likert scale
Purchase intent scale
Balanced scale
Nonbalanced scale

REVIEW AND DISCUSSION QUESTIONS

1. What is measurement?
2. Differentiate among the four types of measurement scales, and discuss the types of information contained in each.
3. How does reliability differ from validity? Give examples of each.
4. Give an example of a scale that would be reliable but not valid. Also give an example of a scale that would be valid but not reliable.
5. What are three methods of assessing reliability?
6. What are three methods of assessing validity?
7. Discuss some of the considerations in selecting a rating, ranking, or purchase intent scale.
8. What are some of the arguments for and against having a neutral point on a scale?
9. Compare and contrast the semantic differential, Stapel scale, and Likert scale. Under what conditions would a researcher use each one?
10. Develop a Likert scale to evaluate the parks and recreation department in your city.
11. Develop a purchase intent scale for students eating at the university's cafeteria. How might the reliability and validity of this scale be measured? Why do you think purchase intent scales are so popular in commercial marketing research?
12. What are the disadvantages of a graphic rating scale?
13. Develop a rank-order scale for beer preferences of college students. What are the advantages and disadvantages of this type of scale?
14. What are some adjective pairs or phrases that could be used in a semantic differential to measure the image of your university?

CASE

Frigidaire Refrigerators

Frigidaire was interested in comparing its image with a number of other appliance corporations. Some of the questions used on the questionnaire follow.

1. What types of scales are represented in the questionnaire? What is the purpose of each scale? What other scales could have been substituted to obtain the same data?
2. Could a semantic differential have been used in this questionnaire? If so, what are some of the adjective pairs that might have been used?
3. Do you think the managers of Frigidaire have the necessary information now to evaluate their competitive position as perceived by consumers? If not, what additional questions should be asked?

Q.1 We are interested in your overall opinion of five companies that manufacture refrigerators. Please rank them from 1 to 5 with 1 being the best and 5 the worst (READ LIST. BEGIN WITH COMPANY (   ) AND WRITE IN NUMBER GIVEN FOR *EACH* COMPANY LISTED. BE SURE *ONE* ANSWER IS RECORDED FOR EACH COMPANY.)

COMPANIES	RANK
General Electric	_____
Westinghouse	_____
Frigidaire	_____
Sears	_____
Whirlpool	_____

Q.2 Now, I would like to have your opinion on a few statements that could be used to describe Frigidaire and the refrigerators it makes.

For each statement I read, please tell me how much you *agree* or *disagree* with the statement about Frigidaire. If you *agree completely* with the statement made, you should give it a *10* rating. If you *disagree completely* with the statement made, you should give it a *0* rating. Or, you can use any number in between which best expresses your opinion on each statement about Frigidaire. (READ LIST. BEGIN WITH STATEMENT CHECKED AND WRITE IN NUMBER GIVEN FOR *EACH* STATEMENT LISTED. BE SURE ONE ANSWER IS RECORDED FOR EACH.)

STATEMENTS	RATING
( ) It is a modern up-to-date company	_____
( ) Its refrigerators offer better value than those made by other companies	_____
( ) Its refrigerators last longer than those made by other companies	_____
( ) It is a company that stands behind its products	_____
(✔) Its refrigerators have more special features than those made by other companies	_____
( ) It is a well-established, reliable company	_____
( ) Its refrigerators are more dependable than those made by other companies	_____
( ) Its refrigerators offer higher quality construction than those made by other companies	_____
( ) Its refrigerators have a better guarantee or warranty than those made by other companies	_____

Q.3 If you were buying a (READ APPLIANCE) today, what make would be your first choice? Your second choice? Your third choice? (DO *NOT* READ LIST. CIRCLE NUMBER BELOW APPROPRIATE APPLIANCE.)

(Begin with appliance checked)

| | ( ) Refrigerator | | | (✔) Electric Range | | |
BRANDS	FIRST CHOICE	SECOND CHOICE	THIRD CHOICE	FIRST CHOICE	SECOND CHOICE	THIRD CHOICE
General Electric	1	1	1	1	1	1
Westinghouse	2	2	2	2	2	2
Frigidaire	3	3	3	3	3	3
Sears	4	4	4	4	4	4
Whirlpool	5	5	5	5	5	5
Other (SPECIFY)						

Q.4 If you were in the market for a refrigerator today, how interested would you be in having the 199> Frigidaire refrigerator that was described in the commercial in your home?

Would you say you would be . . . (READ LIST)

	Very interested	1
(CIRCLE	Somewhat interested	2
ONE	Neither interested or disinterested	3
NUMBER)	Somewhat disinterested, or	4
	Very disinterested	5

Q.5 Why do you feel that way? (PROBE FOR COMPLETE AND MEANINGFUL ANSWERS.)

_____

_____

_____

_____

Q.6 Now, I would like to ask you a few questions for statistical purposes only:

(A) Do you currently own any major appliances made by Frigidaire?

(CIRCLE ONE NUMBER)	Yes	1
	No	2

(B) Is the head of household male or female?

(CIRCLE ONE NUMBER)	Male	1
	Female	2

(C) Which letter on this card corresponds to your age group?

	A. Under 25	1
(CIRCLE	B. 25 to 34	2
ONE	C. 35 to 44	3
NUMBER)	D. 45 to 54	4
	E. 55 and Over	5

Michael Douglas voiceover with *America the Beautiful* under: For future generations, our country is leaving behind our knowledge, our technologies, our values…

and 190 million tons of garbage every year! Recycling alone just can't do it. Keep America Beautiful is an organization that can do something.

We have solutions that have worked in cities and towns across the country.

What can you do?

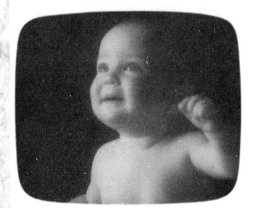

More than you think!

Write to Keep America Beautiful for your free brochure and find out!
("800#" version has "1-600-USA-4-KAB")

CHAPTER 10

Questionnaire Design

LEARNING OBJECTIVES

1. To learn the objectives of questionnaire design.

2. To understand the role of the questionnaire in the data collection process.

3. To become familiar with the criteria for a good questionnaire.

4. To learn the process for questionnaire development.

5. To become knowledgeable of the three basic forms of questions.

6. To learn the necessary procedures for successful implementation of a survey.

I f they ever build a TV commercial Hall of Fame there will surely be a space reserved for Iron Eyes Cody. Cody—you may remember him as the "Crying Indian"—was the "star" of the long-running public service announcement for Keep America Beautiful, Inc., (KAB) that ran on TV stations across the country during the past decade. Few who saw the commercial could forget its image of a single tear crawling down Cody's face as he reacted to the actions of litterbugs.

Effective though the spot was, it became outdated as the larger issue of waste management eclipsed littering in the public consciousness as the nation's top garbage-related problem. When Keep America Beautiful—a national nonprofit organization dedicated to improving waste handling practices in American communities—decided to develop a new PSA (public service announcement) to address the problem of waste management, it had to answer the question: How do you duplicate the impact of the "Crying Indian" spot? With the help of research, KAB and the Stamford, Connecticut–based ad agency Rotando Partners developed a spot that just might do that.

The central image of the new KAB spot is a shot of a baby surrounded by mounds of garbage. The commercial begins with a close-up of the baby and pulls back to a wide shot as actor Michael Douglas narrates over the strains of "America the Beautiful": "For future generations, our country is leaving behind our knowledge, our technologies, our values . . . and 190 million tons of garbage every year. Recycling alone just can't do it. Keep America Beautiful is an organization that can do something. We have solutions that have worked in cities and towns across the country. What can you do? More than you think!" Viewers are then invited to contact KAB for a free booklet. One version asks them to write to the address on the screen, the other flashes a toll-free number.

Using a detailed questionnaire to test the ad concept, KAB found that the image had broad appeal, says Jeff Francis, director of communications, Keep America Beautiful. "We showed them a tape of the idea and then conducted an interview. We found that the baby appealed to everyone. It was an image that, no matter what your age, your sex, if you have children or not, no matter what category you fall into, there was an emotional attachment to that child; which was good because we wanted this ad to be very broad based and hit as many constituency groups as possible. The interviews helped make up our minds about using the baby and the fact that it did appeal to everybody." The interviews lasted about thirty minutes and included discussion of the ad concept and the issue of waste management. Since the ad was targeted at a broad cross section of people, the respondents came from a variety of backgrounds.[1]

The heart and soul of an advertising research study, or any form of survey research, is the questionnaire. If the questions are poorly worded, the information gathered will be misleading. A faulty questionnaire design can lead to interviewer frustration and a confused respondent. This, in turn, leads to interviews terminated by the respondent. What is required for a good questionnaire? What steps are involved in questionnaire development? We will explore these and other issues in Chapter 10.

You will learn the vital role played by the questionnaire and the primary considerations to be held in mind when a researcher develops a questionnaire. Next, a step-by-step procedure for designing a questionnaire is presented. Within this procedure are descriptions of guidelines for evaluating individual questions for appropriateness as well as an overview of alternative questions forms. We then describe the instructions for supervisors and interviewers that must accompany the questionnaire. Finally, the differences between observation forms and question-naires are explained.

THE ROLE OF A QUESTIONNAIRE

Every form of survey research relies on the use of a questionnaire. The questionnaire is the common thread for almost all data collection methods. A **questionnaire** is a set of questions designed to generate the data necessary for accomplishing the objectives of the research project. It is a formalized schedule for collecting information from respondents. Probably you have seen one or even filled one out recently. Creating the "right questionnaire" requires both hard work and creativity.

A questionnaire provides standardization and uniformity in the data gathering process. It standardizes the wording and sequencing of the questions. Every respondent sees or hears the same words and questions; every interviewer asks identical questions. Without such, every interviewer could ask whatever he or she felt at the moment, and the researcher would be left with the question of whether respondents' answers were a consequence of interviewer influence, prompting, or interpretation. A valid basis for comparing respondents' answers would not exist. The jumbled mass of data would be unmanageable from a tabulation standpoint. In a very real sense, then, the questionnaire is a control device, but it is a very unique device as you will see.

The questionnaire (sometimes referred to as an *interview schedule* or *survey instrument*) plays a critical role in the data collection process. An elaborate sampling plan, well-trained interviewers, proper statistical analysis techniques, and good editing and coding are all for naught if the questionnaire is poorly designed. Improper design can lead to incomplete information, inaccurate data, and of course higher costs. The questionnaire and the interviewer are the production line of marketing research. It is here that the product, be it good or bad, is created. The questionnaire is the workers' (interviewers') tool that creates the basic product (respondent information).

Questionnaire
A set of questions designed to generate the data necessary for accomplishing the objectives of the research project.

CRITERIA FOR A GOOD QUESTIONNAIRE

To design a good questionnaire, a number of considerations must be kept in mind: Does it provide the necessary decision-making information for management and does it consider the respondent.

Does It Provide the Necessary Decision-Making Information?

The primary role of any questionnaire is to provide the required information for management decision making. Any questionnaire that fails to provide important insights for management or decision-making information should be discarded or revised. This means that managers who will be using the data should always approve the questionnaire. By signing off on the questionnaire the manager is implying, "Yes, this instrument will supply the data I need to reach a decision." If the manager does not sign off, then the marketing researcher will continue to make revisions to the questionnaire.

Consider the Respondent

As companies have recognized the importance of marketing research, the number of surveys taken annually has mushroomed. Poorly designed, confusing, lengthy surveys have literally "turned off" thousands of potential respondents. It is estimated that over 40 percent of all persons contacted refuse to participate in surveys.

To gather completed interviews a questionnaire should be concise, interesting, and flow in a logical, clear-cut manner. Although a questionnaire is constructed at a person's desk or in a conference room, it is administered in a variety of situations and environments. Busy, or otherwise preoccupied, respondents will terminate uninteresting interviews. Some are conducted while a person is anxious to get back to the television; others are done with a shopper who is in a hurry to finish his or her chores; and still others are conducted while the respondent's child is clinging to the harried parent. Length alone can create a dull interview. One New York company administers a social attitudes study that typically takes three to four and one-half hours to complete. The researcher who is designing the questionnaire must not only consider the type of respondent but the interviewing environment and questionnaire length as well.

Sometimes brand managers engage in "as long as you're out there asking questions, it would be nice to know" false logic. "Nice to know" questions are those that seem interesting, but convey no managerially useful information. By tacking on additional questions not related to the original purpose of the survey, two problems emerge. First, the interview becomes disjointed. A homemaker is being questioned about soap purchase habits and suddenly the interviewer is asking about wine consumption. This destroys the flow and continuity of the questionnaire. The second problem is additional questionnaire length. Generally the longer the interview, the more difficult it is to find cooperative survey participants, and terminations also rise. Usually an interview that is only partially completed (a termination) is worthless to the researcher. It is also time consuming, costly, and frustrating to the interviewer.

A questionnaire should be designed explicitly for the intended respondent. Although a parent is typically the purchaser of cold cereals, the child, either directly or indirectly, often makes the decision as to which brand. Thus, a taste test questionnaire for children should be formulated in children's language. On the other hand, an interview schedule for the adult purchaser would be worded in language suitable for the adult interviewee. One of the most important tasks of questionnaire design is to "fit" the questions to the prospective respondent. The questionnaire designer must strip away the marketing jargon and business termi-nology that may be misunderstood by the respondent. In fact, it is best to use simple, everyday language, as long as the result is not insulting or demeaning to the respondent.

A Questionnaire Serves Many Masters

In summary, a questionnaire serves many masters. First, it must accommodate all the research objectives in sufficient depth and breadth to satisfy the information requirements of the manager. Next, it must "speak" to the respondent in under-standable language and at the appropriate intellectual level. Furthermore, it must be convenient for the interviewer to administer, and it must allow the interviewer to quickly record the respondent's answers. At the same time, it must be easy and fast to check for completeness. Finally, the questionnaire must be translatable back into findings that respond to the manager's original questions.

THE QUESTIONNAIRE DEVELOPMENT PROCESS

Designing a questionnaire involves a logical series of steps, as shown in Figure 10.1. The steps may vary slightly from researcher to researcher, but all researchers tend to follow the same general sequence. Committees and lines of authority can complicate the questionnaire design process. It is often wise to clear each step of the design process with the individual who has the ultimate project authority. This is particularly true for step one, determining the decision-making information needed. We have seen many work-hours wasted on questionnaire design where a researcher developed a questionnaire to answer one type of question and the "real" decision maker wanted something entirely different.

It should also be noted that the design process itself, such as question wording and format, can raise additional issues or unanswered questions. This, in turn, can send the researcher back to stage one for a clearer delineation of information sought.

Step One: Determine Survey Objectives, Resources, and Constraints

The research process often begins when a marketing manager, brand manager, or new product development specialist has a need for decision-making information that is not available. In some firms it is the responsibility of the manager to evaluate all secondary sources to make certain that the needed information has not already been gathered. In other companies, the manager leaves all research activities, primary and secondary, to the research department. The discussion of the research process in Chapter 2 covers this issue in more detail.

Although a brand manager may initiate the research request, everyone affected by the project, such as the assistant brand manager, group product manager, and even the marketing manager, should provide input into exactly what data are needed. **Survey** (information) **objectives** should be spelled out as clearly and precisely as possible. If this step is completed in a thorough fashion, the rest of the process will follow more smoothly and efficiently.

Survey objectives
The decision-making information sought through the questionnaire.

FIGURE 10.1   *The Questionnaire Development Process*

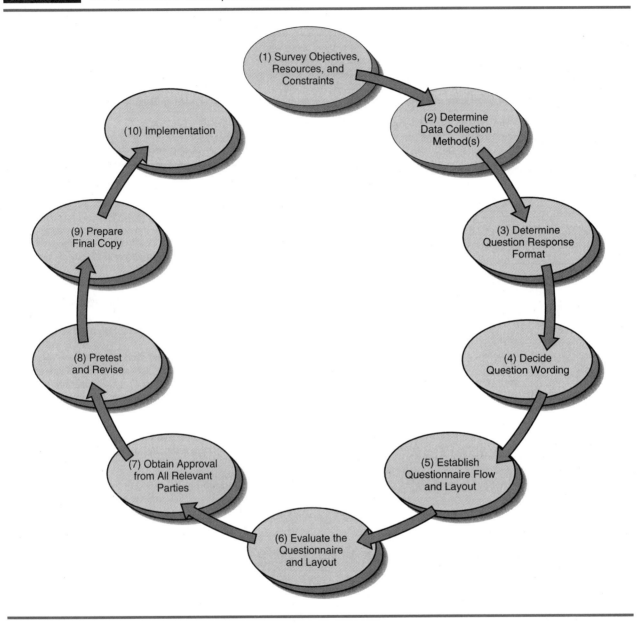

Too much emphasis cannot be placed upon having empathy with the respondent. This is the place to make sure that other projects are not "tagged on" to the study objectives. It is also the point to "hash out" budget constraints versus information needs. If, for example, a consumer needs to be shown several package styles and logos, a personal interview is mandatory. Given a limited budget it probably means that a mall intercept study is dictated. A mall intercept interview should almost always be kept to fifteen minutes or less. Thus, the brand manager (or project initiator) is quite limited in the quantity of data that can be gathered.

Picture yourself standing in a mall or sitting at an interview station for twenty minutes or more. Tempers and terminations begin to rise. If the interview is completed, the quality of data toward the end of the interview is often suspect.

Step Two: Determine the Data Collection Method

Chapter 7 discussed the variety of ways that survey data can be gathered, such as in-person, telephone, mail, self-administration, or CRT. Each method will have an impact on questionnaire design. In fact, an in-person questionnaire in a mall will have constraints not found in an in-home interview. A mall interview, for example, faces the time limitation just discussed. A self-administered questionnaire must be very explicit and usually rather short. Because no interviewer will be present, opportunities to clarify a question will be lacking. A telephone interview often requires a rich verbal description of a concept to make certain the respondent understands the idea being discussed. In contrast, in a personal interview an interviewer can show the respondent a picture or demonstrate the concept.

Step Three: Determine the Question Response Format

Once the data collection method has been determined, the actual questionnaire design process begins. The first phase in the process concerns itself with the types of questions to be used in the survey. Three major types of question response formats are used in marketing research: open-ended, closed-ended, and scale-response questions.

Open-Ended Questions.   **Open-ended questions** are those where the respondent can reply in his or her own words. In other words, the researcher does not limit the response choices.

> Open-ended questions
> Questions that ask the respondent to reply in his or her own words.

Often open-ended questions require "probes" from the interviewer. A *probe* is encouragement from the interviewer for the respondent to elaborate or continue the discussion. The interviewer may say, "Is there anything else?" or "Would you elaborate on that?" Probes aid in clarifying the respondent's interest, attitudes, and feelings. Today computers are playing an increasingly important role in analyzing and recording probes to open-ended questions.

Open-ended questions offer several advantages to the researcher. They enable respondents to give their general reactions to questions like

1. What advantages, if any, do you think ordering from a mail-order catalog company offers compared to local retail outlets? (*probe:* What else?)
2. Why do you have one or more of your rugs or carpets professionally cleaned rather than you cleaning them yourself or having someone else in the household clean them?
3. What is there about the *color* of Product _____ that makes you like it the best? (*probe with:* What color is that?)
4. Why do you say that brand (you use most often) is better?

Each of these were taken from a different nationwide survey covering four products and services. Note that in questions 2 and 4, the open-ended question is part of a skip pattern. In question 2, for example, the respondents have already indicated that they use a professional carpet cleaning service and do not depend on members of the household.

Another advantage of open-ended responses is that they can provide the researcher with a rich array of information. The respondent is answering from his or her own frame of reference. Advantages are described in "real world" terminology rather than laboratory or marketing jargon. Often this is helpful in designing promotion themes and campaigns. It enables copywriters to use the consumer's language. This rich array of information can now be captured even in computer-assisted interviews.

The inspection of open-ended data can also serve as a means of interpreting closed-ended questions. This analysis often sheds additional light on the motivations or attitudes behind the closed-ended response patterns. It is one thing to know that color ranks second in importance out of five product attributes. But it might be much more valuable to know why color is important. For example, a recent study on mobile home park residents uncovered a great deal of dissatisfaction with the trash pick-up service, but further inspection of the open-ended responses uncovered the reason: neighbors' dogs were allowed to run free and overturned the receptacles.

Similarly, open-ended questions may suggest additional alternatives not listed in a closed-ended question. For example, a previously unrecognized advantage of using a mail-order catalog might be uncovered from question 1. This advantage would have been omitted from a closed-ended question on the same subject.

One manufacturer that we consult with always ends a product placement questionnaire with the following, "Is there anything else that you would like to tell us about the product that you have tried during the past three weeks?" This seeks any final tidbit of information that might provide additional insight for the researcher.

Open-ended questions are not without their problems. One factor is the time-and-money-consuming process of editing and coding. Editing open-ended responses requires collapsing the many response alternatives into some reasonable number. If too many categories are utilized, data patterns and response frequencies may be difficult for the researcher to interpret. If the categories are too broad, the data are too general and important meaning may be lost. Even if a proper number of categories are used, editors may have to interpret what the interviewer has recorded and force the data into a category. Assume that the question was asked in a food study, "What, if anything, do you normally add to a taco that you have prepared at home, besides meat?" The question, of course, is open-ended and the coding categories might be as follows:

RESPONSE	CODE
Avocado	1
Cheese (Monterey Jack, Cheddar)	2
Guacamole	3
Lettuce	4
Mexican hot sauce	5
Olives (black or green)	6
Onion (red or white)	7
Peppers (red or green)	8
Pimento	9
Sour cream	0
Other	X

MARKETING RESEARCH IN PRACTICE

Audits and Surveys has developed a system called A&S Voice/ CATI. When an open-ended question comes up on the screen, the interviewer has the capability to record the entire response in the respondent's own voice onto PC disk rather than a tape recorder. The assumption is that the interview is taking place via PC rather than a dumb terminal. The system affords some important new benefits for analysts of open-ended responses:

- By recording the entire open-ended response, the interviewer does not break spontaneity by interrupting to clarify and write or type the response.
- How a thing is said is captured along with what is said.
- It's even possible to record how the interviewers ask the questions and the give and take between the interviewer and the respondent.

The system stores the response on a computer as a digital file on hard disk or floppies. Hence, the verbatim response can be sorted like any other computer file. The data can be transmitted via telephone lines like any other data or the floppies can be mailed to researchers at the client firm.

In analyzing a customer satisfaction study, for example, the analyst can sort respondents who are satisfied and those who are dissatisfied and listen to each group's actual comments as to "why." During analysis and report presentation or preparation, actual-voice, open-ended responses can be sorted by answers to any other question in the questionnaire and by traditional classification questions (sex, age, income, etc.).[2]

What if an editor finds the following response, "I usually add a green, avocado-tasting hot sauce." How would you code it? Or, "I cut up a mixture of lettuce and spinach." Or, "I'm a vegetarian; I don't use meat at all, my taco is filled only with guacamole."

Thus, a basic problem with open-ended questions lies in the interpretation-processing area. In fact, a two-phase judgment must be made. First, the researcher must decide on the proper set of categories and then each response must be evaluated as to which category it falls into.

A related problem of open-ended questions is interviewer bias. Although training sessions continually stress the importance of verbatim recording of open-ended questions, it is often not practiced in the field. Also, slow writers may unintentionally miss important comments. Good probers that ask, "Can you tell me a little more?" or "Is there anything else?" generally have better quality answers than poor probers.

These problems can be partially overcome by precoding open-ended questions. For example, possible answers to the taco question could have been listed on the questionnaire. A space would have been provided to write in any nonconforming reply in the "other" category. In a telephone interview, the question would still qualify as open-ended because the respondent would not see the categories, and the interviewer would be instructed not to divulge them. Precoding necessitates sufficient familiarity with previous studies of a similar nature to anticipate respondents' answers. Otherwise, a pretest with a fairly large sample is needed.

Open-ended questions may also be biased toward the articulate interviewee. A person with elaborate opinions and the ability to express them may have much greater input than a shy, inarticulate, or withdrawn respondent. Yet, they could be equally likely prospects for a product.

A final difficulty with open-ended questions is their inappropriateness on some self-administered questionnaires. If no interviewer is there to probe, a shallow, incomplete, or unclear answer may be recorded. If the taco question had appeared on a self-administered interview schedule without precoded choices, answers might read, "I use a little bit of everything," or "the same things they use in restaurants." These answers would have virtually no value to a researcher.

Closed-ended question
A question that asks the respondent to choose from a list of answers.

Closed-Ended Questions.   A **closed-ended question** is one that requires the respondent to make a selection from a list of responses. The primary advantage of closed-ended questions is simply the avoidance of many of the problems of open-ended questions. Interviewer and coder bias are removed because the interviewer is simply checking a box, circling a category, recording a number, or punching a key. Reading response alternatives may jog a person's memory and provide a more realistic response. Also, because the option of expounding on a topic is not given to a respondent, there is no bias toward the articulate. Finally, the coding and data entry process is greatly simplified.

One should realize the difference between a precoded open-ended question and a multiple-choice question. An open-ended question allows the respondent to answer in a freewheeling format. The interviewer simply checks the points on the prerecorded answers as they are given. Probing is used, but a list is *never* read. If an answer is given that is not precoded, it is written verbatim in the "other" column. In contrast, the closed-ended question *requires* that alternatives are read or shown to the respondent.

Traditionally, marketing researchers have separated the two-item response option from the many-item type. A two-choice question is called *dichotomous* and the many-item type is often called *multiple-choice* or *multichotomous*. With the dichotomous closed-ended question, the response categories are sometimes implicit. For instance, how would you respond to the following question: "Did you buy gasoline for your automobile in the last week?" Obviously, the implicit options are "Yes" or "No." Regardless of the fact that a respondent may say, "I rented a car last week, and they filled it up for me. Does that count?" the questions would still be classified as dichotomous closed-ended.

Dichotomous Questions.   The simplest form of a closed-ended question is the dichotomous choice. A few examples are

1. Did you heat the Danish roll before serving it?

    Yes   1
    No   2

2. The federal government doesn't care what people like me think.

    Agree   1
    Disagree   2

3. Do you think that inflation will be greater or less than last year?

    Greater than   1

    Less than   2

Note that the respondent is limited to two fixed alternatives. It is easy to administer and usually evokes rapid response. Many times a neutral or no opinion—don't know option is added to dichotomous questions to take care of those situations. Sometimes interviewers will jot down DK for "Don't know" or NR for "No response" if the neutral option is omitted from the questionnaire.

Dichotomous questions are prone to a large amount of measurement error. Because alternatives are polarized, the wide range of possible choices between the poles is omitted. Thus, question wording is very critical to obtain accurate responses. Questions phrased in a positive form may well result in answers opposite from those expressed in a negative format. In the third question, response may vary depending upon whether *greater than* or *less than* is listed first. These problems can be overcome using a split ballot technique. One-half of the questionnaires are worded with *greater than* listed first and the other half with *less than* first. This procedure will aid in reducing potential bias.

> **Dichotomous questions**
> Questions that ask the respondent to choose between two answers.

Multiple-Choice Questions.   **Multiple-choice questions** have about the same advantages and disadvantages as those given in the general discussion of closed-ended questions. Replies do not have to be coded like an open-ended question but limited information is provided. The interviewee is asked to give one alternative that correctly expresses his or her opinion, or, in some instances, to indicate all that apply. Some examples of multiple-choice questions follow:

> **Multiple choice questions**
> Questions that ask a respondent to choose among a list of more than two answers.

1. I'd like you to think back to the last footwear of any kind that you bought. I'll read you a list of descriptions and would like for you to tell me which category they fall into. (READ LIST AND CHECK THE PROPER CATEGORY)

    Dress and/or Formal   1

    Casual   2

    Canvas-Trainer-Gym Shoes   3

    Specialized Athletic Shoes   4

    Boots   5

2. (HAND RESPONDENT CARD) Please look at this card and tell me the letter which indicates the age group you belong to:

    A. Under 17   1

    B. 17–24 Years   2

    C. 25–34 Years   3

    D. 35–49 Years   4

    E. 50–64 Years   5

    F. 65 and Over   6

3. In the *last three months*, have you used Noxzema Skin Cream: (CHECK ALL THAT APPLY)

    as a facial wash   1

    for moisturizing the skin   2

    for treating blemishes   3

    for cleansing the skin   4

    for treating dry skin   5

    for softening skin   6

    for sunburn   7

    for making the facial skin smooth 8

Question 1 may not cover all possible alternatives and thus, would not capture a true response.[3] Where, for example, would an interviewer record work shoes? The same thing can be said for question three. Not only are all possible alternatives not included, but there is no possibility for respondents to elaborate or qualify their answers. Part of the problem can be easily overcome by adding an "Any other use?—RECORD VERBATIM" alternative to the questions.

Disadvantages of Closed-Ended Questions.   Each type of closed-ended question represents unique disadvantages. For the dichotomous question form, the researcher finds that frequently the responses fail to communicate any intensity of feeling from the respondent. In some cases, the matter of intensity does not apply, as for the previous example on gasoline purchasing. But instances do arise where the respondent feels very strongly about an issue but the intensity is lost in the dichotomous response form. If that interview had continued with this question, "Would you purchase gasoline priced 50¢ above current prices, but which would guarantee twice the miles per gallon?" there is a high likelihood that the responses might range in intensity as observed in the following quotes: "No. Absolutely not"; "Gee, I doubt it"; "Well, I might try it"; or "You bet!"

The multiple response close-ended question has two additional disadvantages. First, the researcher must spend time generating the list of possible responses. This phase may require intensive analysis of focus group tapes, brainstorming, or secondary data investigation. In any case, it requires more time and effort than the open-ended alternative or the dichotomous form. Another problem with closed-ended multiple response questions is the range of possible answers. If the list is too long, the respondent may become confused or disinterested. One way to help overcome this problem is to show the interviewee a card and read down the list with him or her. A related problem with any list is position bias. Respondents typically will choose from among the first and last alternatives all other things being equal.[4] Position bias can be overcome by marking an alternative with an X and instructing the interviewer to begin reading the list at the X'ed alternative instead of at the beginning of the list. The first question is marked with an X at alternative one, the second question at alternative two, and so forth.

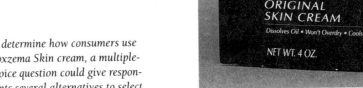

To determine how consumers use Noxzema Skin cream, a multiple-choice question could give respondents several alternatives to select.

MARKETING RESEARCH IN PRACTICE

Recently, a study was conducted (the results below are disguised) in which 200 respondents were asked to rate a product on ten attributes using a 10-point scale—the type of thing market researchers request people to do every day. The results looked something like this:

SCALE	MEAN
Easy to open	3.62
Tastes good	6.54
For children	5.62
For adults	5.89
Good value	7.77
Easy to prepare	9.21
Attractive packaging	5.18
Sweetness	7.21
Reputable manufacturer	8.94
Nutritious	4.85

Now, in a vacuum, there's nothing at all unsettling about these results. But this particular test was actually a pretest of a new product evaluation system that was under consideration. In fact, since these scales were a small portion of a much larger, more elaborate questionnaire and the pretest was of an entirely new methodology, the scales weren't rotated—intentionally so, not as an indication of bad research design. When the order of asking is tacked on to the above results, we see something a little different.

SCALE	MEAN	ORDER
Easy to prepare	9.21	First
Reputable manufacturer	8.94	Second
Good value	7.77	Third
Sweetness	7.21	Fourth
Tastes good	6.54	Fifth
For children	5.62	Sixth
For adults	5.89	Seventh
Attractive packaging	5.18	Eighth
Nutritious	4.85	Ninth
Easy to open	3.62	Tenth

These results were, as you might imagine, quite unnerving. With one exception, the means decrease uniformly by question order. So these data illustrate yet again the necessity of rotating items to control for position bias.[5]

Scaled-Response Questions.   The last response format to be considered is **scaled-response questions**. Consider the following two question forms:

1. Now that you have used the product, would you say that you would buy it or not? (CHECK ONE)

   _____ Yes, would buy it
   _____ No, would not buy it

2. Now that you have used the product, would you say that you would . . . (CHECK ONE)

   _____ Definitely buy it
   _____ Probably buy it
   _____ Might or might not buy it
   _____ Probably would not buy it
   _____ Definitely would not buy it

The first question fails to capture intensity. It determines the direction (Yes versus No), but it cannot compare to the second one for completeness or sensitivity of response. The latter is also ordinal in nature.

A primary advantage of scaled-response questions is that scaling permits the measurement of the intensity of respondents' answers. Another advantage is that many scaled-response forms incorporate numbers, and these numbers may be used

FIGURE 10.2 *Sample Telephone Interviewer Instructions for a Scaled-Response Question Form*

EXAMPLE #1:

I have some statements which I will read to you. For each one, please indicate whether you "strongly agree," "agree," "disagree," "strongly disagree," or have no opinion. I will read the statement, and you indicate *your* opinion as accurately as possible. Are the instructions clear?

(IF THE RESPONDENT DOES NOT UNDERSTAND, REPEAT RESPONSE CATEGORIES. GO ON TO READ STATEMENTS AND RECORD RESPONSES. CIRCLE RESPONDENT'S OPINION IN EACH CASE.)

EXAMPLE #2:

---

4. Now I'm going to read you a list of statements that may or may not be important to you in deciding where to shop for stereo equipment. Let's use your telephone dial as a scale. #1 would mean "definitely disagree" and #6 would mean "definitely agree." Or you can pick any number in between that best expresses your feelings.

Let's begin. To what extent do you agree or disagree that (INSERT STATEMENT) is an important aspect when deciding where to shop for stereo equipment?

EXAMPLE #3:

Now I shall read a list of statements about automotive servicing which may or may not be *important* to you when servicing your car.

Let's use your telephone dial as a scale. . . .

Number 1 would mean you *disagree completely* with the statement.
Number 2 would mean you *disagree* with the statement.
Number 3 would mean you *somewhat disagree* with the statement.
Number 4 would mean you *somewhat agree* with the statement.
Number 5 would mean you *agree* with the statement.
Number 6 would mean you *agree completely* with the statement.

Do you have any questions about the scale?

I) To what extent do you agree or disagree that   1
   (FILL IN THE STATEMENT) is a feature you consider   2
   when selecting a place to have your car serviced?   3

---

directly as codes. Finally, the marketing researcher is allowed to use much more powerful statistical tools with some scaled-response questions as discussed in Chapter 14.

The most significant problems of scaled-response questions evolve from respondent misunderstanding. Scaled questions sometimes tax respondents' abilities to remember and answer. First, the questionnaire must explain the response category options, then the respondent must translate these into his or her own frame of reference. To overcome the first problem, interviewers are usually provided with a detailed description of the response categories allowed, and even instructed to elicit a "Yes" as to understanding the scale from the respondent before asking the questions. Take a look at Figure 10.2 for examples of a telephone interviewer's instructions for scaled response questions. In the case of self-administered questionnaires, the researcher often presents an example of responding to a scale as part of the instructions.

Step Four: Decide the Question Wording

Once the marketing researcher has decided on the specific types of questions and the response formats, the next task is the actual writing of the questions. The wording of specific questions always poses significant time investment for the marketing researcher. It is a skill developed over time and subject to constant improvement. Four general guidelines are useful to bear in mind during the wording and sequencing of each question.

1. *The wording must be clear.* If the researcher decides that a question is absolutely necessary, that question must be stated so that it means the same thing to all respondents. Ambiguous terminology should be avoided, such as "Do you live within five minutes of here?" or "Where do you usually shop for clothes?" The first example depends on mode of transportation (maybe the respondent walks),

GLOBAL MARKETING RESEARCH

Question context is very important when conducting Asian marketing research. Asian respondents often need to understand the context of a question before they can fully respond. The respondents use context as a filter through which they structure their "reality." If researchers don't provide a recognizable context, the respondents will either redirect the question, answer in ways that give no real information, or create a context in order to respond. The obvious danger is that researchers may get information that reflects issues other than those sought.

Short and abrupt answers in themselves do not necessarily mean respondents are unwilling to engage in discussion. The respondents may, in fact, be signaling you that they can't relate to the framework as presented. The researcher needs to be perceptive enough to realize when his or her cultural construct or template has no meaning—or a significantly different meaning—for the respondents. Furthermore, the same cultural template may have different meanings among subsegments of the same ethnic group.

Let's say you are preparing research on behavioral patterns of parents' leisure time with children. One widespread American assumption is that people value spending time with their families on their days off from work. The interpretation of "spending time

with family" means passing time with one's spouse and children. Another assumption is that "good" parents are involved in their children's extracurricular activities. A common scenario has the parents taking their kids to a Little League game, then barbecuing at home with a few friends and their children.

This American cultural construct has different degrees of relevance to various subgroups of the Asian segment. While the more acculturated Asian-American families can relate comfortably to this concept, it's quite unfamiliar to many Asian families. If your target audience is Asian but your research design is based on the aforementioned assumptions, you would be presenting a cultural construct that's not relevant to your intended audience. "Spending time with the family" holds a very different meaning for many Chinese. They would more likely interpret this concept as getting together socially with members of their extended families (parents, siblings, aunts, uncles, cousins, etc.) than doing things with just their spouse and children. Moreover, the concept of "good parenting" for many Chinese parents does not include involvement in their children's sports activities. Many of them regard children's play and adult leisure as distinct activities, to be done separately or in parallel, rather than together.[6]

driving speed, perceived elapsed time, and other factors. It would normally be prudent to show the respondents a map with certain areas delineated and ask if they live within the area. The second question depends on the type of clothing, the occasion, the member of the family, and the meaning of the word *where*.

Clarity also implies the use of reasonable terminology. A questionnaire is not a vocabulary test. Jargon should be avoided and verbiage should be geared to the target audience. A question such as "State the level of efficacy of your proponderant dishwasher liquid" would probably be greeted by a lot of blank stares. It would be much simpler to say "Are you (1) very satisfied, (2) somewhat satisfied, or (3) not satisfied with your current brand of dishwasher liquid?" It is best to use words that have precise meanings, universal usage, and minimal connotative confusion. When respondents are uncertain of what a question means, the incidence of "no response" increases.[7]

Every prospective respondent represents a separate frame of reference. That is, each person is unique in personality, mental ability, experiences, education, and views of the world. The marketing manager's and the marketing researcher's frames of reference have much compatability, but they may differ from those of consumer-respondents. Consequently, the questionnaire designer must use terminology native to the target respondent group and not research jargon. The first task of wording questions, then, is to translate questions into everyday language.

A further complication of this translation is to custom-tailor the wording to the target respondent group. If, for example, lawyers are to be interviewed, the wording should be appropriate. If construction laborers are to be questioned, the terminology must be modified appropriately. This advice is painfully obvious, but there are instances where the failure to relate to respondents' frames of reference has been disastrous. A case in point is the use of the word *bottles* (or *cans*) in this question, "How many bottles of beer do you drink in a normal week?" In some southern states, beer is sold in 32, 12, 8, 7, 6, and even 4 ounce bottles. So a "heavy" drinker of eight bottles may consume only 32 ounces per week (8 × 4 oz.); in contrast a "light" drinker might only consume three bottles but 96 ounces (3 × 32 oz.).

Clarity can also be improved at the beginning of the interview by stating the purpose of the survey. Usually, the respondent should understand the nature of the study and what is expected but not necessarily who is sponsoring the project. This aids the interviewee in placing the questions in the proper perspective.

A final aspect of clarity is the avoidance of two questions in one, sometimes called a *double-barreled question*. For example, "How did you like the taste and texture of the coffee cake?" This should be broken into two questions: one concerning taste and the other texture. Each question should address only one aspect of evaluation.

2. *Select words so as to avoid biasing the respondent.* A question such as, "Do you often shop at lower-class stores like K Mart?" evokes an obvious response. Similarly, "Have you purchased any high-quality Black and Decker tools in the past six months?" also biases respondents. Questions can be leading such as, "Weren't you pleased with the good service you received last night at the Holiday Inn?" These examples are quite obvious. Unfortunately, bias may be much more subtle than is illustrated in these examples.

Sponsor identification too early in the interviewing process can also distort answers.[8] It does not take long, for example, for a person to recognize that a survey is being conducted for Miller beer if, after the third question, every question is related to this product. Or an opening statement such as "We are conducting a study on the quality of banking for Northeast National Bank and would like to ask you a few questions." Sometimes, of course, the true purpose of the study must be disguised to obtain an unbiased response. For example, a major food processor developed a package that would enable liquids, such as milk, to be kept without refrigeration for several weeks as long as the carton was unopened. This new process would save untold millions in refrigeration expenses, yet it goes against everything Americans were ever taught about food sanitation and refrigeration. Thus, the study was disguised as an orange juice taste test. One-half of the consumers were given cartons of the product to take home and told that refrigeration was unnecessary; the other half were told to refrigerate the product. Subsequent call-back interviews revealed a significant difference in the perceived quality of the identical product. The manufacturer concluded that cultural taboos were too strong at that time to overcome.

3. *Consider the ability of the respondent to answer the question.* In some cases a respondent may have never acquired the information to answer the question. Asking a man which brand of sewing thread is most preferred by his wife would often fall into this category. Asking respondents about a brand or store that they have never encountered creates the same problem. When a question is worded in such a manner that it implies that the respondent should be able to answer it, then often a reply will be forthcoming, but it will be nothing more than a wild guess. This creates measurement error, since uninformed opinions are being recorded.

A second problem is forgetfulness. For example, "What was the name of the last movie you saw in a theater?" "Who were the stars?" "Did you have popcorn?" "How many ounces were in the container?" "What price did you pay for the popcorn?" "Did you purchase any other snack items?" "Why or why not?" You

Beer is sold in bottles and cans of varying sizes. In classifying respondents by the number of bottles they drink in a week, an inaccurate reading of the market may result.

probably cannot remember the answers to all of these questions. The same is true for the typical respondent. Yet a brand manager for Mars, Incorporated, wants to know what brand of candy you purchased last; what alternative brands were considered; and what factors led to the brand selected. Because brand managers want answers to these questions, market researchers ask them. This, in turn, also creates measurement error. Often respondents will give the name of a well-known brand, like Milky Way or Hershey. In other cases, respondents will mention a brand that they often purchase, but it may not be the last brand purchased.

To avoid the problem of a respondent's inability to recall, time periods should be kept relatively short. For example, "Did you purchase a candy bar within the past seven days?" If the reply is "yes" then brand and purchase motivation questions can be asked. Alternatively, a poor question would be, "How many movies have you rented in the past year to view at home on your VCR?" Instead, the researcher might ask:

(1) How many movies have you rented in the past month to view on your VCR?

(2) Would you say that in the last month, you rented more movies, less movies, or about the average number of movies you rent per month? IF "MORE" OR "LESS" ASK:

(3) What would you say is the typical number of movies you rent per month?

4. *Consider the willingness of the respondent to answer the question.* The memory of a respondent may be totally clear, yet the respondent may not be willing to give a truthful reply. Reporting of an event is likely to be distorted in a socially desirable direction. If the event is perceived as embarrassing, sensitive in nature, threatening, or divergent from one's self-image, it is likely either not to be reported at all or to be distorted in a desirable direction.[9]

Perhaps the question that interviewers dislike asking more than others and researchers are most dubious of is the income question. One study on savings revealed that small account balances were overreported and large savings balances were underreported.[10]

Embarrassing topics that deal with things such as borrowing money, personal hygiene, sexual activities, and criminal records must be phrased in a careful manner to minimize measurement error. One technique is to ask the question in the third person. For example, "Do you think that most people charge more on their credit cards than they should? Why?" By asking about "most people" rather than themselves, researchers may be able to learn more about the individual's attitude about credit and debt.

A third method for soliciting embarrassing information is to state that the behavior or attitude is not unusual prior to asking the question. For example, "Millions of Americans suffer from hemorrhoids; do you or any member of your family suffer from this problem?" This technique is called using counterbiasing statements and makes it less intimidating for the respondent to discuss embarrassing topics.

Step Five: Establish Questionnaire Flow and Layout

After the questions have been properly formulated, the next step is to sequence them and develop a layout for the questionnaire. Questionnaires are not constructed haphazardly. There is a logic to the positioning of each section of the

TABLE 10.1 *How a Questionnaire Should Be Organized*

LOCATION	TYPE	EXAMPLES	RATIONALE
Screeners	Qualifying questions	"Have you been snow skiing in the past twelve months?" "Do you own a pair of skis?"	To identify target respondents. Survey of ski owners who have skied in the past year.
First few questions	Warm-ups	"What brand of skis do you own?" "How many years have you owned them?"	Easy to answer shows respondent that survey is simple.
First third of questions	Transitions	"What features do you like best about the skis?"	Relate to research objectives, slightly more effort needed to answer.
Middle half to second third	Difficult and complicated	Following are ten characteristics of snow skis. Please rate your skis on each characteristic using the scale below.	Respondent has committed to completing questionnaire and can see that just a few questions are left.
Last section	Classification and demographic	"What is the highest level of education you have attained?"	Some questions may be considered "personal" and respondent may leave them blank, but they are at the end of the survey.

questionnaire, and this logic is depicted in Table 10.1. Experienced marketing researchers are well aware that questionnaire development is the key to obtaining interviewer-interviewee rapport. The greater the rapport, the more likely the interviewer will obtain a completed interview. Also, the respondent's answers will probably be more carefully thought out and detailed. Researcher wisdom has developed the following general guidelines concerning questionnaire flow.

1. *Use the screener questions to identify qualified respondents.* Most market research today employs some variation of quota sampling. Only qualified respondents are interviewed, and specific minimum numbers (quotas) of various types of qualified respondents may be desired. A study on food products generally has quotas of users of specific brands, a magazine study screens for readers, a cosmetic study screens for brand awareness, and so forth.

The **screeners** (screen questions) may be on the questionnaire or, in many cases, a "screening questionnaire" is provided. In this instance, a screener is filled out for everyone interviewed. Thus, any demographics obtained provide a basis for comparison against persons who qualify for the full study. A long screener can significantly increase the cost of the study. It means that you are obtaining more information from every contact with a respondent. Short screeners such as the one in Figure 10.3 quickly eliminate unqualified persons and enable the interviewer to move immediately to the next potential respondent. Yet a longer screener can provide important information on the nature of nonusers, nontriers, or persons unaware of the product or service being researched.[11]

Most important, screeners provide a basis for estimating the costs of a survey. A survey for which everyone qualified to be interviewed is going to be much cheaper than one with a 5 percent incidence rate, all else being equal. Many surveys are placed with field services at a flat rate per completed questionnaire. The rate is based on a stated "average interview time" and

Screeners
Questions used to screen for appropriate respondents.

FIGURE 10.3   *A Screening Questionnaire That Seeks Men Fifteen Years of Age and Older That Shave at Least Three Times a Week with a Blade Razor*

Hello. I'm from Data Facts Research. We are conducting a survey among men and I'd like to ask you a few questions.

1. Do you or does any member of your family work for an advertising agency, market research firm, or a company that manufactures or sells shaving products?

   (TERMINATE AND RECORD ON CONTACT RECORD SHEET)   Yes ( )
                                    (CONTINUE WITH Q. 2)   No ( )

2. How old are you? Are you . . . (READ LIST)

   (TERMINATE AND RECORD ON CONTACT RECORD SHEET)   Under 15 Yrs Old ( )
   CHECK QUOTA CONTROL FORM—IF QUOTA GROUP FOR   15 to 34 Yrs. Old ( )
   WHICH THE RESPONDENT QUALIFIES *IS NOT* FILLED CONTINUE—IF   Over 34 Yrs. Old ( )
   QUOTA GROUP *IS* FILLED THEN—TERMINATE AND RECORD)

3. The last time you shaved, did you use an electric razor or a razor that uses blades?

   (TERMINATE AND RECORD ON CONTACT RECORD SHEET)   Electric Razor ( )
                                    (CONTINUE WITH Q. 4)   Blade Razor ( )

4. How many times have you shaved in the past seven days?

   (IF LESS THAN THREE TIMES, TERMINATE AND RECORD ON
   CONTACT RECORD SHEET. IF THREE OR MORE TIMES CONTINUE).

incidence rate. The screener is used to determine if, in fact, the incidence rate holds true in a particular city. If it does not, the flat rate is adjusted accordingly.

2. *After obtaining a qualified respondent, begin with a question that obtains a respondent's interest.* After introductory comments and screens to find a qualified respondent, the initial questions should be simple, interesting, and nonthreatening. To open a questionnaire with an income or age question might be disastrous. These are often considered threatening and immediately put the respondent on the defensive. The initial question should be easy to answer without much forethought.

3. *Ask general questions first.* Once the interview proceeds beyond the opening "warm-up" questions, the questionnaire should proceed in a logical fashion. General questions are covered first to get the person thinking about a concept, company, or type of product and then to the specifics. For example, a questionnaire on shampoo might begin with "Have you purchased a hair spray, hair conditioner, or hair shampoo within the past six weeks?" Then it would ask about the frequency of shampooing, brands purchased in the last three months, satisfaction and dissatisfaction with brands purchased, repurchase intent, characteristics of an "ideal" shampoo, respondent's hair characteristics, and finally demographics.

   The flow in the preceding example is logical. It initiates consumer thoughts on shampooing as it moves through the questionnaire and concludes with personal data. The shampoo format was taken from an actual questionnaire by a leading manufacturer. The interview lasted approximately twenty minutes. By the time the interviewer reached the personal data, the respondent was conditioned to answering questions. That is, a question-answer dialogue had been in progress for approximately seventeen minutes; thus, the respondent continued to answer partially due to conditioning. Also, rapport had been established. By this time the respondent realized that it was definitely a legitimate request for information and not a sales pitch. Trust had been established and the interviewee was less reluctant to offer personal information.

4. *Ask questions that require "work" in the middle of the questionnaire.* Initially, the respondent is only vaguely interested and understanding of the nature of the survey. As the interest-building questions transpire, the interview process builds momentum and commitment to the interview. When the interviewer shifts to questions with scaled-response formats, the respondent must be motivated to understand the response categories and options. Alternatively, there might be questions that necessitate some recall or opinion formation on the part of the respondent. The interest, commitment, and rapport built up sustain the respondent in this part of the interview. Even if the self-administered method is used, the approach is the same: build interest and commitment early to motivate the respondent to finish the rest of the questionnaire.

5. *Insert "prompters" at strategic points.* Good interviewers can sense when a respondent's interest and motivation sag and will attempt to build them back up. However, it is always worthwhile for the questionnaire designer to insert short encouragements at strategic locations in the questionnaire. These may be simple statements such as, "I only have a few more questions to go," or "This next section will be easier." On the other hand, they may be inserted as part of an introduction to a section, "Now that you have helped us with those comments, we would like to ask a few more questions."

6. *Position sensitive, threatening, and demographic questions at the end.* As mentioned earlier, occasions sometimes arise when the objectives of the study necessitate questions on topics about which respondents may feel uneasy. Embarrassing topics should be covered near the end of the questionnaire. Placing these questions at the end of the survey ensures that most of the questions will be answered before the respondent becomes defensive or breaks off the interview. Moreover, rapport has been established between the respondent and the interviewer by this time, increasing the likelihood of obtaining an answer. Another argument for placing sensitive questions toward the end is that by the time sensitive questions are asked, interviewees have been conditioned to respond. In other words, a pattern has been repeated many times. The interviewer asks a question and the respondent gives an answer. By the time embarrassing questions are asked, the respondent has become conditioned to reply.

Step Six: Evaluate the Questionnaire

Once a rough draft of the questionnaire has been designed, the marketing researcher is obligated to take a step back and critically evaluate it. This phase may seem redundant, given all the careful thought that went into each question. But recall the crucial role played by the questionnaire. At this point in the questionnaire development, the following items should be considered: (1) is the question necessary? (2) is the survey too long? and (3) will the questions provide the answers to the survey objectives?

Is the Question Necessary?   Perhaps the most important criterion for this phase of questionnaire development is ascertaining the necessity for a given question. Sometimes researchers and brand managers want to ask questions because "they

MARKETING RESEARCH IN PRACTICE

The ideal questionnaire doesn't exist. What suits the purpose of one study often proves wrong for another.

The first three dos are basic rules that can provide a solid foundation on which to build your questionnaire.

1. A questionnaire must be written as a conversation *with*—*not an interrogation of*—a respondent.
2. It must be arranged in a logical sequence, not in a maze apt to confuse and puzzle respondents, embarrassing them in efforts to extricate themselves, or to say anything to the researchers just to get out.
3. At the beginning of each questionnaire, briefly, do provide respondents with the purpose of being asked for information. Respondents are entitled to know. Put additional explanations in parentheses to use when needed.
4. Do use proper punctuation marks. They separate sentences, independent clauses, and parenthetical phrases. They may be used to make meanings more clearly understood, to emphasize, or to give pause for absorption of one part of your communication before moving to the next. Also of help are all capitalized letters, underlining, etc.
5. Do allow for "don't knows." Many authors leave "don't knows" off a questionnaire. If respondents have never seen or heard of "Whatchamacallit," why force them into a "cooperative," friendly, but meaningless reply? Also, remember that too many "don't knows" can be a problem because you don't obtain meaningful information.
6. Do provide pronunciations in brackets for words that differ in various parts of the country. If you've been met anywhere with "Oh, we call that . . .," then you

were on the last survey we did like this," or because "it would be nice to know." Excessive demographics questions are very common. Education data, number of children in multiple age categories, and extensive demographics on the spouse are simply not warranted by the nature of many studies.

Each and every question must serve a purpose. Either it must be a screener, an interest generator, a required transition, or it must be directly and explicitly related to the stated objectives of this particular survey. Any question that fails to satisfy at least one of these criteria should be omitted.

Is the Questionnaire Too Long?   At this point the researcher should role-play the questionnaire with volunteers acting as respondents. Although there is no magic number of iterations, the length of time it takes to complete the questionnaire should be averaged over a minimum of five trials. Any questionnaire to be administered in a mall or over the telephone that averages longer than twenty minutes should be a candidate for cutting. Sometimes mall interviews can run slightly longer if an incentive is provided to the respondent. In-home interviews that last more than forty-five minutes should also offer the respondent some incentive.

know already that proper research prior to writing a questionnaire will help in preventing embarrassment on all sides.

Now for the don'ts:

1. Don't begin with, "I would like to ask you . . ." Who are you? Speaking on what authority? Far better to say, "We," and even that shouldn't be overdone. On a five-page questionnaire, it was found eleven times. A bit overwhelming, right? Why not simply say, "Now the next question . . ." and say it quickly. They know you didn't come to play bridge.

2. Don't say, "Would you mind . . ." Why should they? Why enter a negative thought? In the same vein, rule out "Can you" and "Could you." Why deflate a respondent's ego and self-confidence.

3. Don't use lengthy, unfamiliar words unless really justified by the topic of study. Why use "conversely," rather than "on the contrary?" Why use "noxious" rather than "hurtful"? Why use "pernicious" rather than "harmful"? There's always the danger a respondent might pretend, or honestly believe, to understand and offer completely irrelevant answers.

4. Don't use words that could sound like something else.

5. Don't preface sentences with "You might want to . . ." or "You might not want to . . ." These might influence respondents in having to make a certain choice. If a respondent doesn't like the flow of the copy—or the interviewer—the outcome may differ radically from expectations due to such negative influences. Watch behavioral attitudes.[12]

Common incentives are movie tickets, pen and pencil sets, and cash or checks. The use of incentives often actually lowers the survey costs because response rates increase and terminations during the interview fall. If checks are used instead of cash, the canceled checks can be used to create a list of survey participants for follow-up purposes.

Will the Questions Provide the Desired Information to Accomplish the Research Objectives? The researcher must make certain that a sufficient number and type of questions are contained within the questionnaire to meet the decision-making needs of management. A suggested procedure is to carefully review the written objectives for the research project. Next, the researcher should go down the questionnaire and write each question number next to the objective that the particular question will help accomplish. For example, question 1 applies to objective 3, question 2 to objective 2, and so forth. If a question cannot be tied to an objective, the researcher should determine whether the list of objectives is complete. If the list is sufficient, the question should be omitted. Also, if after going through the entire questionnaire there is an objective with no questions listed beside it, appropriate questions should be added to the questionnaire.

Some very good advice on evaluating questionnaires comes from a woman who has evaluated thousands over the years. Joan Fredericks, president of Joan Fredericks Field Service, offers "dos" and "don'ts" in the Marketing Research feature on page 298.

The objective of a good questionnaire layout is to make the tasks of the interviewer and respondent as clear, logical, and simple as possible. Several key considerations of layout and design follow.

Appearances of Mail and Self-Administered Questionnaires. The appearance of a questionnaire that will be filled in by the respondent is a major determinant of the response rate. The questionnaire should be as professional looking as possible. It should be printed on high-quality paper and have a "typeset" appearance. If the questionnaire is four pages or longer, the researcher should consider putting it in a booklet format. Booklets are easy to use, look professional, and when stapled, minimize the problems of lost pages.

Avoid a Cluttered Look. The questionnaire should allow for plenty of open space. Rows and columns of answers should be spread far enough apart so that the interviewer or respondent can easily pick the proper row or column. A questionnaire that attempts to cram as much material on a page as possible appears busy, complex, and difficult. Crowded questionnaires lead to more incorrect replies being recorded. Naturally, if a questionnaire looks difficult and foreboding, it will have a negative effect on a person's willingness to participate in the study.

A mistake that is often made by novice questionnaire designers is to try to reduce the numbers of pages of a questionnaire by cramming material together. It is preferable by far to have a questionnaire that runs one or two pages longer and has an open, inviting format than a shorter, cluttered appearance.

Allow Plenty of Space for Open-Ended Responses. An open-ended question that allows half a line for a reply will usually receive a reply of that length and nothing more. Generally speaking, three to five lines (using $8\frac{1}{2}''$ wide paper) are deemed sufficient for open-ended replies. The researcher must use his or her judgment on how much detail is desirable for an open-ended reply. Answer space for "Which department store did you visit most recently?" requires much less space. However, a follow-up question that asks, "What factors were most important in your decision to go to (Name of department store)?" requires substantially more lines for the response.

Consider Color-Coding the Questionnaires. If the research project is based upon interviewing specific groups of respondents, it is desirable to color-code the questionnaires. For example, a racquet manufacturer has placed a prototype racquet (made of a new alloy) with 300 people who play racquet sports at least twice a week. The sample consists of three groups of 100 each: racquetball players, tennis players, and squash players. Although the questionnaire focuses on the prototype racquet, the questions vary somewhat depending upon the sport being played. To avoid confusion among the interviewers, the tennis questionnaires are green, the racquetball questionnaires are blue, and the squash questionnaires are white.

Instructions Printed within the Questionnaire Should Be in Capital Letters. To avoid confusion and to clarify what is a question and what is an instruction, all instructions should be in capital letters. Capitalizing helps bring the instructions to the interviewers' or respondents' attention. For example, "IF 'YES' TO QUESTION 13, SKIP TO QUESTION 17."

Step Seven: Obtain Approval of All Relevant Parties

At this point in the questionnaire design process, the first draft of the questionnaire has been completed. Copies of it should be distributed to all parties that have direct authority over the project. Practically speaking, managers may step in at any time in the design process with new information, requests, or concerns. Wherever this arises, revisions are often necessitated. It is still important to get final approval of the first draft even if managers have already interceded in the development process.

Managerial approval commits management to obtaining a body of information via a specific instrument (questionnaire). If the question is not asked, the data will not be gathered. Thus, questionnaire approval tacitly reaffirms what decision-making information is needed and how it will be obtained. For example, assume that a new product questionnaire asks about shape, material, end use, and packaging. Once the form is approved, the new product development manager is implying that "I know what color the product will be" or "It is not important to determine color at this time."

Step Eight: Pretest and Revise

When final managerial approval has been obtained, the questionnaire must be pretested. No survey should be taken without a pretest. Moreover, a **pretest** does not mean that one researcher should administer the questionnaire to another re-searcher. Ideally, a pretest is done by the best interviewers who will ultimately be working on the job and administered to target respondents for the study. They are told to look for misinterpretations by respondents, lack of continuity, poor skip patterns, additional alternatives for precoded and closed-ended questions, and general respondent reaction to the interview. The pretest should also be conducted in the same mode as the final interview. If the study is to be door to door, then the pretest should be the same.

Pretest
A trial run of a questionnaire.

Researchers should consider coding and tabulating the pretest data. The data should be put into tabular form and simple cross-tabulations and other statistical routines carried out where possible. This will give the researcher a rough notion of the type of output that will be generated from the study and its adequacy to answer the study objectives. Also, the hypothetical tables will confirm the need for various sets of data. If there is no place to put the responses to a question, either the data are superfluous or some contemplated analysis was omitted. If some part of a table remains empty, a necessary question may have been omitted. Trial tabulations show, as no previous method can, that all data collected will be put to use, and that all necessary data will be obtained.[13]

After completion of the pretest, any necessary changes should be made. Approval should then be reobtained before going into the field. If the pretest resulted in extensive design and question alterations, a second pretest would be in order.

Step Nine: Prepare Final Questionnaire Copy

Even the final copy phase does not allow the researcher to relax. Precise typing instructions, spacing, numbering, and precoding must be set up, monitored, and proofread. In some instances the questionnaire may be photoreduced to save space, or it even may be specially folded and stapled. Duplication may require typesetting, although this instance is rare. In general, the quality of copying and the paper used is a function of who will see the questionnaire. In a mail survey, compliance and subsequent response rates may be affected positively by a professional appearance. For telephone interviews, in contrast, the quality is of much less importance; the copy simply must be readable.

STEP TEN: IMPLEMENTING THE SURVEY

The completion of the questionnaire establishes the basis for obtaining the desired decision-making information from the marketplace. A series of forms and procedures must also be issued with the questionnaire to make certain that the data are gathered correctly, efficiently, and at a reasonable cost. Depending on the data collection method, these include supervisor's instructions, interviewer instructions, screeners, call record sheets, and visual aids.

TABLE 10.2 *A Sample Page of Supervisor's Instructions for a Diet Soft Drink Taste Test*

Purpose:	To determine from diet soft drink users their ability to discriminate among three samples of Diet Dr. Pepper and give opinions and preferences between two of the samples.
Staff:	3–4 experienced interviewers per shift.
Location:	One busy shopping center in a middle to upper-middle socioeconomic area. The center's busiest hours are to be worked by a double shift of interviewers.
	In the center, 3–4 private interviewing stations are to be set up and a refrigerator and good counter space made available for product storage and preparation.
Quota:	192 completed interviews broken down as follows:
	A minimum of 70 Diet Dr. Pepper users A maximum of 122 other diet brand users
Project Materials:	For this study, you are supplied the following:
	250 Screening Questionnaires 192 Study Questionnaires 4 Card A's
Product/Preparation:	For this study, our client shipped to your refrigerated facility 26 cases of soft drink product. Each case contains 24 10-oz. bottles—312 coded with an *F* on the cap, 312 with an *S*.
	Each day, you are to obtain from the refrigerated facility approximately 2–4 cases of product—1–2 of each code. Product must be transported in coolers and kept refrigerated at the location. It should remain at approximately 42°F.
	In the center, you are to take one-half of the product coded *F* and place the #23 stickers on the bottles. The other half of the *F* product should receive #46 stickers.
	The same should be done for product *S*—one-half should be coded #34, the other half #68. A supervisor should do this task before interviewing begins. Interviewers will select product by *code number*. Code number stickers are enclosed for this effort.
	Each respondent will be initially testing three product samples as designated on the questionnaire. Interviewers will come to the kitchen, select the three designated bottles, open and pour 4 oz. of each product into its corresponding coded cup. The interviewer should cap and *refrigerate* leftover product when finished pouring and take only the three *cups* of product on a tray to respondent.

TABLE 10.3   *A Sample Page of Interviewer Instructions for a Magazine Readership Study*

Purpose:	The purpose of this study is to determine a relationship between people's attitudes and the magazines they read regularly.
Method:	All interviewing is to be conducted by telephone with your local dialing area. We will neither use nor pay for any work not conducted in exact accordance with our job instructions.
When to Interview:	Begin interviewing immediately. All interviewing is to be conducted from 5:30 P.M. to 9:30 P.M. weekdays and all day Saturday. You may also interview on Sunday. All work is to be completed by Sunday, November 5.
Sample Lists:	You have been provided with Sample Lists. You are to interview the person in the household who reads the magazine and is a qualified respondent.
	Use all the Sample Lists and try to complete interviews with subscribers or readers of affluent publications.
Eligible Respondents:	A respondent is eligible if
	1. The total annual family income is above $25,000 and
	2. He or she is employed in one of the prelisted categories in Q. B.
Quota:	You are to complete a total of thirteen interviews.
Call Record Sheets:	You are to use the Call Record Sheet to list the name and telephone number of each call you make. All telephone numbers and listings are to be done during the interviewing hours. We *will not* pay for additional time for looking up numbers and listings.
	Record the outcome of each call you make.
Validation Forms:	We have included Validation Forms on which you must list information about completed interviews. A properly filled out Validation Form must accompany each delivery of work you make to your supervisor. Fill in all the information required at the top of the form. Then, fill in the following:
	—Under "Quota Group"—name of magazine.
	—Under "Sex"—sex of respondent.
	—Under "Respondent Name"—write in the full name.
	—Under "Telephone Number"—write in the phone number.

Supervisor's Instructions

As discussed in Chapter 3, most research interviewing is conducted by field services. It is the service's job to complete the interviews and send them back to the researcher. In essence, field services are the production line of the marketing research industry.

Supervisor's instructions inform them of the nature of the study, start and completion dates, quotas, reporting times, equipment and facility requirements, sampling instructions, number of interviewers required, and validation procedures. In addition, detailed instructions are required for any taste test that involves food preparation. Quantities are typically measured and cooked using rigorous measurement techniques and devices.

The supervisor's instructions are a vitally important part of any study. They establish the parameters under which the research is conducted. Without clear instructions the interview may be conducted ten different ways in ten cities. A sample page from a set of supervisor's instructions is shown in Table 10.2.

Supervisor's instructions
Written directions to the field service on how to conduct the survey.

Interviewer's Instructions

Interviewer's instructions cover many of the same points as supervisor's instructions but are geared to the actual interview. The nature of the study is explained, sampling methodology is given, reporting forms and times are given. Often a sample

Interviewer's instructions
Written directions to the interviewer on how to conduct the interview.

interview is included with detailed instructions on skip patterns, probing, and quotas. A sample page of interviewer's instructions is shown in Table 10.3.

Call Record Sheets

Call record sheets
Interviewers' logs listing the number and results of a contact.

Call record sheets are used to measure the efficiency of the interviewers. The form normally indicates the number of contacts and the results of the contact (see Table 10.4). A supervisor can examine calls per hour, contacts per completed interview, average time per interview, and similar measures to analyze an interviewer's efficiency. If, for example, contacts per completed interview are high, the field supervisor should examine the reasons behind it. Perhaps the interviewer is not using a proper approach or the area may be difficult to cover; for example, a ghetto is hard to work.

A researcher can use aggregated data for all interviewers of a field service to measure field service efficiency. A high cost per interview for a field service might be traced to a large number of contacts per completed interview. This, in turn, may be due to poor interviewer selection and training by the field service.

TABLE 10.4 *The Call Record Sheet for a Deodorant Study*

	DATE	DATE	DATE	DATE
Total Completions				
Quota A	_____	_____	_____	_____
Quota B	_____	_____	_____	_____
Terminate at				
Q. A	_____	_____	_____	_____
Q. B	_____	_____	_____	_____
Q. C—No deodorant/antiperspirant	_____	_____	_____	_____
Q. D—No Roll-On	_____	_____	_____	_____
Q. E—Ban full	_____	_____	_____	_____
Q. E—"Other" Full	_____	_____	_____	_____
Q. F—Refusal	_____	_____	_____	_____
Q. G—No Telephone	_____	_____	_____	_____
Total Incomplete Contacts				
No One Home	_____	_____	_____	_____
No Woman Available	_____	_____	_____	_____
Refused	_____	_____	_____	_____
Language/Hearing	_____	_____	_____	_____
Respondent Break-Off	_____	_____	_____	_____
Knows Respondent	_____	_____	_____	_____
Other	_____	_____	_____	_____
Briefing Hours	_____	_____	_____	_____
Interviewing Hours	_____	_____	_____	_____
Travel Hours	_____	_____	_____	_____
Mileage	_____	_____	_____	_____

Visual Aids and Other Supplements

Many studies utilize visual aids to facilitate the interviewing process. These range from simple "show cards" that enumerate alternatives to closed-ended questions to videotape players that show test commercials or a product in use. In product studies, a test product, or products, is often left with the respondent. This can present logistics difficulties if weight or perishability is a problem. Consider, for example, a door-to-door ice cream study in the summer time where each respondent is given a half gallon of three different test products. In this case, the product was packed in styrofoam containers of fifteen half gallons. Each box contained dry ice, thus avoiding the melting problem. However, the boxes were so large that most interviewers could get only one or two in their car. There was a tremendous increase in interviewer mileage and travel time over a typical study due to the continual return to the frozen food locker for additional product. As you can see by now, the researcher's job is just beginning, when the questionnaire design is completed.

SUMMARY

This chapter examines the objectives of the questionnaire as well as its construction and evaluation. After defining a questionnaire and explaining its role in the data collection process, the criteria for a good questionnaire are established. These criteria are categorized into the following topic areas:

1. Achieving the goals of the study
2. Fitting the questionnaire to the respondent

   The bulk of this chapter is devoted to the process of developing a questionnaire. This process is addressed in a sequential format beginning with survey objectives, resources, and constraints. The process continues with

1. Determine data collection method
2. Determine question response format
3. Decide question wording
4. Establish questionnaire flow and layout
5. Evaluate the questionnaire
6. Obtain approval from all relevant parties
7. Pretest and revise questionnaire
8. Prepare final copy
9. Implement questionnaire

   Specific attention is paid to distinguishing among the three different types of questions (open-ended, close-ended, and scaled-response) and the advantages and disadvantages of each. In addition, guidelines are introduced to facilitate the proper wording and positioning of questions within the questionnaire.

   This chapter concludes with special procedures necessary for successful implementation of the survey. These steps are used to ensure that the data is gathered properly. Supervisor's instructions, interviewer's instructions, call record sheet, and visual aids are all discussed within this context.

KEY TERMS

Questionnaire
Survey objectives
Open-ended questions
Closed-ended question
Dichotomous questions
Multiple-choice questions

Scaled-response questions
Screeners
Pretest
Supervisor's instructions
Interviewer's instructions
Call record sheets

REVIEW AND DISCUSSION QUESTIONS

1. Explain the role of the questionnaire in the research process.
2. How do respondents influence the design of a questionnaire? Suggest some examples, such as questionnaires designed for engineers, welfare recipients, baseball players, generals in the army, and finally migrant farm workers.
3. Discuss the advantages and disadvantages of open-ended questions and closed-ended questions.
4. Outline the procedure for developing a questionnaire. Assume that you are developing a questionnaire for a new sandwich for McDonald's. Use this situation to discuss the questionnaire development.
5. Give examples of poor questionnaire wording. What is wrong with each of these questions?
6. Once a questionnaire is developed, what other factors need to be considered prior to putting the questionnaire in the hands of interviewers?
7. Why is pretesting a questionnaire important? Are there some situations where pretesting can be foregone?
8. Design three open-ended and three closed-ended questions to measure consumers' attitudes toward BMW automobiles.
9. What's wrong with the following questions?
   a) How do you like the flavor of this high-quality Maxwell House coffee?
   b) What do you think of the taste and texture of this Sara Lee coffee cake?
   c) We are conducting a study for Bulova watches. What do you think of the quality of Bulova watches?
   d) How far do you live from the closest mall?
   e) Who in your family shops for clothes?
   f) Where do you buy most of your clothes?

CASE

The Maxim Hotel

The Maxim Hotel in Las Vegas, like most service businesses today, is interested in providing quality customer service. Marketing research is a key link in the customer service process. It is the feedback mechanism that allows management to evaluate and control the level of service it is providing. Accordingly, the Maxim has created a questionnaire that is left in the guest rooms. The one-page questionnaire folds so that it forms a prepaid business reply envelope. Also, the following message is printed on the back. (The questionnaires are left in the rooms with the back facing upwards.)

HOW DO WE RATE?

In order to maintain the high standards of service for which we are known at the Maxim Hotel, it is helpful for us to receive constructive comments from our guests. You can help us in this endeavor if you will take a moment to complete this simple form.

Thank you.

The Management

(This form may be left at the front desk or dropped in any mailbox.)

The format of the questionnaire is shown in Figure 10.4 on page 308.

1. Evaluate the sampling plan used to evaluate service quality. Would you do it any differently? If so, how?
2. Critique the questionnaire.
3. Do you think the dichotomous questions are adequate?
4. Are there additional questions that you would add or delete?

FIGURE 10.4 *Maxim Guest Questionnaire: How Do We Rate?*

1. RECEPTION & SERVICE

Were you pleased with the service rendered by:

	(YES)	(NO)
Bellman	_____	_____
Cashiers (Front Desk)	_____	_____
Casino Personnel	_____	_____
Front Desk Personnel	_____	_____
Parking Attendants	_____	_____
Room Service	_____	_____
Telephone Operators	_____	_____

Comments: _____

_____

_____

2. GUEST ROOM

Was your Guest room:

	(YES)	(NO)
Clean	_____	_____
Comfortable	_____	_____
Well Furnished	_____	_____
Adequately Supplied	_____	_____

(Soap, towels, paper supplies, ashtrays, etc.)

Comments: _____

_____

_____

3. RESTAURANTS

While dining in our restaurants, were the following satisfactory?

	FOOD (YES)	(NO)	SERVICE (YES)	(NO)
Treehouse Coffee Shop	___	___	___	___
JB's Sidewalk Cafe	___	___	___	___
DaVinci's Gourmet Dining Room	___	___	___	___
Cabaret Showroom (liq. ser.)	___	___	___	___

Comments: _____

4. We are proud of our employees, and like to give them recognition whenever possible. If you have observed any of our staff who you think worthy of singling out, will you please note the details.

_____

_____

_____

_____

_____

_____

5. If you have enjoyed your stay, what features of the Maxim did you find most appealing or pleasant?

_____

_____

_____

_____

_____

6. Was there anything about the Maxim, its service or personnel that you did not enjoy?

_____

_____

_____

7. How did you learn of the Maxim?

☐ Radio   ☐ T.V.   ☐ Newspapers

☐ Billboards   ☐ Friends

What was your Room Number? _____

Date of Visit _____

—o—o—o—o—o—o—o—o—

OPTIONAL

NAME _____

ADDRESS _____

CITY & STATE _____

ZIP CODE _____

CHAPTER 11

Basic Sampling Issues

LEARNING OBJECTIVES

1. To understand the concept of sampling.
2. To learn the steps in developing a sampling plan.
3. To distinguish between probability samples and nonprobability samples.
4. To understand the concepts of sampling error and nonsampling error.
5. To review the types of probability sampling methods.
6. To gain insight into nonprobability sampling methods.

Adele Johnson is marketing director for Citycell. Citycell provides cellular telephone service in a large California metropolitan area. Based on careful analysis of Citycell subscribers and other marketing research, Johnson has developed a very good profile of her target customer. She is preparing to begin a $2 million advertising campaign for the coming year and is uncertain about two different creative approaches suggested by Citycell's advertising agency. Before selecting one of the approaches and giving the agency approval to go ahead and produce commercials, Johnson feels that she needs to do some marketing research.

She is currently considering a marketing research proposal prepared by a research firm that she has worked with in the past. She has considerable confidence in the competence of the research supplier. The research firm has suggested two alternative approaches for collecting the necessary data. The first approach is built around telephone interviewing. The firm has suggested that telephone numbers be generated at random, that all interviewing be conducted from its central location telephone facility, and that a sample size of 400 be employed for the study. The firm has indicated that a sample of this size will provide estimates of consumer sentiment that are within plus or minus 5 percent of true values with 95 percent confidence. Although they suggested the telephone approach, they have expressed some misgivings about this approach to obtaining consumer reactions to the different advertising concepts.

As an alternative, the supplier suggested that the data be collected via mall intercept interviewing. They reason that the mall intercept approach will provide a better environment in which to expose consumers to the test commercials. Consumers will be exposed to a tape that includes simulated radio spot commercials. The research company is concerned that it will be much more difficult to simulate the commercials over the phone than in the mall environment. On the other hand, the proposal indicates that because the mall intercept sample will be a quota sample, the results will not be projectable to the total market. The firm has also recommended a sample size of 400 for the mall survey.

The bid for the survey based on a telephone approach is $10,500 and the bid for the mall intercept approach is $15,000. The mall approach is more expensive and may well generate a more valid response from individual consumers, but because all the interviewing will be conducted at a single mall location, it cannot produce a sample that is representative of the entire population of target customers in the market. The telephone survey will be cheaper and will involve a truly representative sample of target consumers. However, there is concern that consumer reactions to the ads will not be as valid as those obtained in a mall intercept situation. Johnson is weighing the alternatives and trying to arrive at the best decision.

The issues confronting Adele Johnson are related to the central topic of this chapter. The question is one of choosing the "best" approach, in a given situation, for selecting a sample of people from whom to collect data. As this example suggests, different alternatives have different costs, data quality levels, and levels of sampling accuracy associated with them. The challenge, as always, is to obtain the required information at the appropriate level of quality at the lowest possible cost. These issues are covered in this chapter. After you have had an opportunity to read this chapter, return to Adele Johnson's dilemma, and see what choice you would make between the two alternatives.

DEFINITION OF IMPORTANT TERMS

Population or Universe

In the area of sampling, the terms **population** and **universe** are used interchangeably.[1] In this discussion, we will use the term *population*. The population or population of interest is the total group of people from whom we need to obtain information. One of the first things the analyst must do is to define the population of interest. This often involves defining the target market for the product or service in question.

For example, a researcher conducting a product concept test for a new nonprescription cold symptom relieving product, such as Contac, might take the position that the population of interest includes everyone because everyone suffers from colds from time to time. However, although everyone suffers from colds from time to time, not everyone buys a nonprescription cold symptom relieving product. In this case, the first task would probably be to ask people whether they had purchased or used one or more of a number of competing brands during some time period. Those who had purchased or used one of these brands would be included in the population of interest. Those who had not purchased one of these brands would not be included.

Defining the population of interest is a key step in the sampling process. The issue is, Whose opinions are needed to fulfill the objectives of the research? There are no specific rules to follow in defining the population of interest. It requires the researcher to apply good logic and judgment. Often the definition of the population is based on the characteristics of current or target customers.

Population or universe
The total group of people from whom information is needed.

Sample versus Census

The term **census** is used to refer to those situations where data are obtained from or about every member of the population of interest. Censuses are not often employed in marketing research. In most marketing research situations, the population includes many thousands, hundreds of thousands, or millions of individuals. The cost and time required to take a census of population of this magnitude are so great as to preclude the possibility of their use.

Census
Data obtained from every member of the population of interest.

MARKETING RESEARCH IN PRACTICE

A New Technique for Objective Methods for Measuring Reader Interest in Newspapers" was the title of George Gallup's Ph.D. thesis at the University of Iowa. Working with the *Des Moines Register and Tribune* and the 200-year old statistical theory probabilities of Swiss mathematician Jakob Bernoulli, Gallup developed "sampling" techniques. He showed that you did not have to talk to everybody as long as you randomly selected respondents according to a sampling plan that takes into account whatever diversity was relevant in the universe of potential respondents—geographic, ethnic, economic. Although not everybody understood or believed his ideas then— or now—this intellectual invention was a big deal.

On many occasions Gallup used a particular example to explain what he was talking about and doing. "Suppose there are 7,000 white beans and 3,000 black beans well churned in a barrel. If you scoop out 100 of them, you'll get approximately 70 white beans and 30 black beans in your hand, and the range of your possible error can be computed mathematically. As long as the barrel contains many more beans than your handful, the proportion will remain within that margin of error 997 times out of 1,000."

In the early 1930s George Gallup was in great demand around the country. He became head of the Journalism Department at Drake University and then switched to Northwestern. During this period he was doing readership surveys for newspapers throughout the northeastern United States. In the summer of 1932 a new advertising agency, Young and Rubicam, invited him to New York to create a research department and procedures for evaluating the effectiveness of advertising. In that same year, he used his polling techniques to help his mother-in-law get elected secretary of state of Iowa. Based on this experience, he was confident that his sampling methodology was valid not only for beans and newspaper readers but for voters also. As long as you understood the sampling universe—white, black, male, female, rich, poor, urban, rural, Republican, Democratic—you could predict elections or calculate public attitudes on public opinion questions by interviewing a relatively small number of people as long as that small number of people was representative of that total population from which they were drawn. Gallup proved that population values could be accurately estimated by means of scientific samples and made a fortune in the process.[2]

Sample
A subset of the population of interest.

It has been demonstrated time and time again that a relatively small but carefully chosen **sample** can quite accurately reflect the characteristics of the population from which it is drawn. A sample is nothing more than a subset of the population. Information is obtained from or about a subset of the population to make estimates about various characteristics of the total population. Ideally, the subset of the population from or about which information is obtained should be a representative cross section of the total population.

Though, as we noted earlier, censuses are not often used in marketing research, there are instances where they are appropriate and feasible. For example, censuses may be appropriate and feasible in industrial products settings where a particular firm may have only a small number of customers for the highly specialized products it sells. In these situations it may be possible to obtain information from the entire population of customers.

STEPS IN DEVELOPING A SAMPLING PLAN

The process of developing an operational sampling plan can be separated into seven steps, which are summarized in Figure 11.1. Each step in the process is discussed here.

FIGURE 11.1 *Steps in Developing a Sampling Plan*

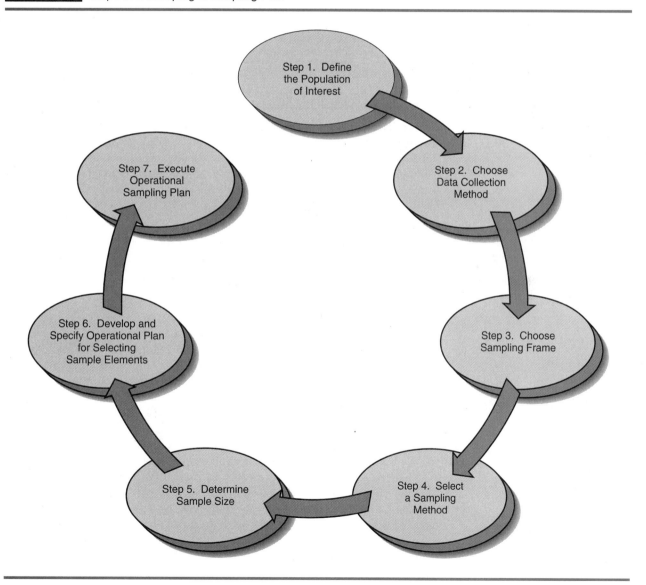

TABLE 11.1   *Some Bases for Defining the Population of Interest*

BASIS	DISCUSSION
Geography	What geographic area is to be sampled? Usually a question of a client's scope of operation. Could be a city, county, metropolitan area, state, group of states, the entire United States, or a number of countries.
Demographics	Given the objectives of the research and the target market for the product, whose opinions, reactions, and so on are relevant? Are we interested in getting information from women over 18; women 18–34; women 18–34 with household incomes over $35,000 per year, who work and have preschool children?
Use	In addition to the preceding, the population of interest frequently is defined in terms of some product or service use requirement. This is usually stated in terms of some use vs. nonuse or use of some quantity of the product or service on some period of time. The following examples of use screening questions illustrate the point: • Do you drink five or more cans, bottles, or glasses of diet soft drinks in a typical week? • Have you traveled to Europe for vacation or business purposes in the last two years? • Have you or has anyone in your immediate family been in a hospital for an overnight or extended stay in the past two years?
Awareness	We may be interested in surveying those individuals who are aware of the company's advertising to explore what the ad communicated to them about the characteristics of the product or service.

Defining the Population of Interest

The basic issue is to specify the characteristics of those individuals or things (e.g., companies, stores, etc.) from whom information is needed to meet the objectives of the research. The population of interest is often specified in terms of some combination of the following characteristics: geography, demographic characteristics, product or service use characteristics or awareness measures. These bases for population definition are discussed in Table 11.1. In surveys, the question of whether a particular individual does or does not belong to the population of interest is often dealt with by means of screening questions at the beginning of the questionnaire. Even if we have a list of the population and sample from that list, screening questions are still used to qualify the potential respondent. A sample sequence of screening questions is provided in Figure 11.2.

In addition to defining who will be included in the population of interest, it is sometimes important also to define who will be excluded. Most commercial marketing research surveys exclude certain individuals for so-called security reasons. Very frequently the first question on a questionnaire will ask whether the individual or anyone in the household works in marketing research, advertising, or in the product or service area dealt with in the survey (see question 5 in Figure 11.2). If the individual indicates that he or she or someone in the household works in one of these industries, the interview is terminated at that point. This is referred to as a security question, because individuals in the industries in question are viewed as security risks. They may be competitors or work for competitors, and we do not want to give them some indication of what we may be planning to do.

There may be other reasons to exclude individuals. For example, Coca Cola might wish to do a survey among individuals who drink five or more cans, bottles, or glasses of soft drink in a typical week but who do not drink Coca Cola because they are interested in developing a better understanding of heavy soft drink users who do not drink Coke. Therefore, they might wish to exclude those individuals who indicate they have drunk one or more cans, bottles, or glasses of Coca Cola in the last week.

Choosing a Data Collection Method

The selection of a data collection method, as indicated in the opening vignette, has considerable impact on the nature of the sampling process. Subsequent steps in the sampling process will be influenced by the data collection method to be used. As noted in the opening vignette, for example, telephone interviewing has certain

---

FIGURE 11.2 *Example of Screening Question Sequence to Determine Population Membership*

Hello. I'm _____ with _____ Research. We're conducting a survey about products used in the home. May I ask you a few questions?

1. Have you been interviewed about any products or advertising in the past *3 months*?

   Yes   TERMINATE AND TALLY
   No   →   *CONTINUE*

2. Which of the following hair care products, if any, have you used in the past month? (HAND PRODUCT CARD TO RESPONDENT. CIRCLE ALL MENTIONS.)

   1   Regular Shampoo

   2   Dandruff Shampoo

3 Creme Rinse/Instant Conditioner
4 "Intensive" Conditioner

   IF NONE OF PRODUCTS IN BOX IS CIRCLED, TERMINATE AND TALLY

   INSTRUCTIONS: IF "4" IS CIRCLED—SKIP TO Q. 4 AND CONTINUE FOR "INTENSIVE" QUOTA
   IF "3" IS CIRCLED BUT NOT 4—ASK Q. 3 AND CONTINUE FOR "INSTANT" QUOTA

3. You said that you have used a creme rinse/instant conditioner in the past month. Have you used either a creme rinse or an instant conditioner in the past week, or not?

   Yes (used in the past week)   →   *CONTINUE FOR "INSTANT" QUOTA*
   No (not used in past week)   →   TERMINATE AND TALLY

4. Into which of the following groups does your age fall? (READ LIST, CIRCLE AGE.)

   X   Under 18   →   CHECK AGE QUOTAS
   1   18–24
   2   25–34
   3   35–44
   X   45 or over

5. Previous surveys have shown that people who work in certain jobs may have different reactions to certain products. Now, do you or does any member of your immediate family work for an advertising agency, a market research firm, a public relations firm, or a company that manufactures or sells personal care products?

   Yes   TERMINATE AND TALLY
   No   →   *CONTINUE*

IF RESPONDENT QUALIFIES, INVITE HER TO PARTICIPATE AND COMPLETE NAME GRID BELOW.

inherent advantages and mall intercept interviewing has certain inherent disadvantages in regard to sampling.

Choosing a Sampling Frame

Sampling frame
List of population elements from which we select units to be sampled.

The third step in the process is to identify the **sampling frame**. Previously, we defined the *sampling frame* as a list of the population elements or members from which we select units to be sampled. In the ideal situation, we have such a list and it is complete and accurate. Unfortunately, all too often, we have no such list. For example, the population for a particular study may be defined to include those individuals who have played three or more rounds of eighteen holes of golf in the last thirty days. There is obviously no list that provides a complete enumeration of these individuals. In these instances, instead of a sample frame in the traditional sense, we will have to reflect the sample frame in some procedure that will produce a representative sample of individuals with the desired characteristics. For example, a telephone book might be the sample frame for a telephone survey sample. This example also illustrates that there seldom is a perfect correspondence between the sampling frame and the population of interest. The population of interest might be all households in the city in question. However, the telephone book would not include those households that do not have telephones and those with unlisted numbers.

Unfortunately, there is substantial evidence that those with listed numbers and those with no listing are significantly different in regard to a number of important characteristics. It has been shown that voluntarily unlisted subscribers are more likely to be renters, live in the central city, have recently moved, have larger families, have younger children, and have lower incomes than their counterparts with listed numbers.[3] There are also significant differences between the two groups in terms of purchase, ownership, and usage patterns of certain products.

Unlisted numbers are more prevalent in the West, in metropolitan areas, and among nonwhites and those in the 18–34 age group.[4] These findings have been confirmed in a number of studies.[5] The implications are clear; if representative samples are to be obtained in telephone surveys, sampling procedures that include an appropriate proportion of households with unlisted numbers must be employed.

The extent of the problem is suggested by the data in Table 11.2. In such cases, a procedure may be used to generate a list of the elements of the population to be sampled. **Random digit dialing**, described in Figure 11.3, involves generating lists of telephone numbers at random. Developing an appropriate sampling frame is often one of the most challenging problems facing the researcher in the area of sampling.[6]

Random digit dialing
Method of generating lists of telephone numbers at random.

Selecting a Sampling Method

The fourth step in the process involves the selection of a sampling method. The selection of a particular sampling method will depend on the objectives of the study, the financial resources available, time limitations, and the nature of the problem under investigation. The major alternative sampling methods can be grouped under two headings: probability sampling methods and nonprobability sampling methods. A number of alternatives are available under each of these headings.

TABLE 11.2   *The 1989 25 Metros with the Highest Incidence of Unlisted Phones among the Top 100*

METRO AREA	TOTAL HOUSEHOLDS	PERCENT HOUSEHOLDS WITH TELEPHONES	PERCENT ESTIMATED TELEPHONE HOUSE-HOLDS UNLISTED
Las Vegas	261,700	90.8	62.3
Los Angeles–Long Beach	3,162,100	93.4	61.2
Oakland	778,100	95.6	59.2
Fresno	219,600	93.0	57.4
San Jose	508,900	97.0	55.5
Sacramento	543,400	94.6	54.3
Anaheim–Santa Ana	808,200	96.6	53.9
Riverside–San Bernardino	816,100	93.6	53.9
San Francisco	675,400	95.5	53.2
Bakersfield	183,400	91.8	52.2
Jersey City	213,000	88.8	51.9
San Diego	867,400	95.0	50.9
Oxnard–Ventura	213,300	95.8	49.5
Miami–Hialeah	710,300	90.8	46.8
Tucson	258,900	91.2	46.5
Denver	671,600	95.1	45.5
Detroit	1,625,700	96.0	44.6
Chicago	2,303,200	94.1	44.4
Phoenix	809,800	91.8	43.4
Tacoma	210,300	93.8	41.7
Houston	1,176,600	91.7	41.4
El Paso	174,100	87.6	40.4
Newark	694,900	94.0	40.1
Portland, OR	469,200	94.5	39.8
San Antonio	442,200	92.2	39.7

NOTE: The unlisted rate is determined by comparing the estimated number of telephone households with the actual number of households found in telephone directories. Estimated telephone households are computed by taking projected household estimates at the county level calculated by Market Statistics for *Sales & Marketing Management* magazine and applying a figure from the U.S. Census that indicates the percent of households with a telephone.
© Copyright Survey Sampling, Inc. 1990. All rights reserved.

Probability samples must be selected in such a way that every element of the population has a known, nonzero probability of selection.[7] The simple random sample is the best known and most widely used probability sampling method. The simple random sample must be selected in such a way that every member or element of the population has a known and equal probability of being selected. Under probability sampling, the researcher must closely adhere to precise selection procedures that avoid arbitrary or biased selection of elements. When these procedures are followed strictly, the laws of probability are in effect. This allows calculation of the extent to which a sample value can be expected to differ from a population value. This difference is referred to as *sampling error.*

Nonprobability samples include the selection of specific elements from the population in a nonrandom manner. Nonrandomness occurs due to accident when population elements are selected on the basis of convenience—because they are easy or inexpensive to reach. Purposeful nonrandomness would involve a sampling plan that systematically excluded or overrepresented certain subsets of the population. For example, a sample designed to represent the opinions of all women over the age of 18 that was based on a telephone survey conducted during the day on weekdays would systematically exclude working women.

Probability samples
Samples in which every element of the population has a known, nonzero probability of selection.

Nonprobability samples
Samples that include the selection of specific elements from the population in a nonrandom manner.

FIGURE 11.3 *Random Digit Dialing Procedure*

The only solution to the problems of unlisted telephone numbers is to generate phone numbers by some random process. This practice, referred to as random-digit dialing (RDD), is simple in theory—phone numbers are generated at random. However, practical considerations complicate the picture greatly. The first and foremost of these is the relatively small proportion of working numbers among all possible ten-digit telephone numbers. Only about 1 in 170 of all possible telephone numbers (9,999,999,999 possible) are actually in use (60,000,000 residential numbers). The proportion of working residential numbers in RDD samples can be increased dramatically by selecting from only the 103 working area codes (first three digits). This approach yields approximately one working residential number for every seventeen randomly generated. From a cost standpoint this rate is still too low, entailing too many unproductive dialings. The question at this point is, what type of RDD system will simultaneously cut the proportion of unproductive dialings while including a proportionate number of unlisted phone homes in the sample? There are three alternative approaches that meet these two objectives to varying degrees: the four-digit approach, three-digit approach, and approaches built around the use of a telephone book.

FOUR-DIGIT APPROACH

Taking the four-digit approach the researcher must, in addition to restricting the sample to the 103 working area codes, select numbers only from working central offices or exchanges. The last four digits of the number are generated via some process that approaches randomness. There are approximately 30,000 working exchanges in the continental United States or about 300 million possible numbers. This approach will, therefore, yield approximately one working number for every five generated randomly. Problems with this approach relate to the fact that all exchanges have an equal probability of being selected while some have a high proportion of all possible numbers in service and others have only a small proportion in service.

THREE-DIGIT APPROACH

The next logical progression in RDD technology is the three-digit approach. The three-digit method increases the proportion of working numbers to better than one in three. This is possible because the phone company does not assign numbers from a particular exchange at random but from within working banks of 1,000 numbers. Consulting the section of a criss-cross directory where phone numbers are listed numerically will show that within a particular exchange certain sequences of 1,000 numbers (000–999) are totally unused while other groups of 1,000 are, for example, 70 percent in use. Employing the three-digit option, the user must specify area codes, exchanges, and "working banks" (fourth digit) of numbers within exchanges. Working banks may be identified from a criss-cross directory or selected via probability sample from the telephone book. A bank with no working listed numbers has no chance of being selected, while a bank with 60 percent of its numbers listed has twice as much chance of being selected as one with only 30 percent listed. The final step of the three-digit approach is to generate the last three digits of each working area code/exchange/bank by means of some random process.

The three-digit method is more efficient in eliminating nonworking numbers, but increases bias due to missing (from the directory) new working banks that have been activated. The four-digit method is safer from the standpoint of avoiding bias, but more expensive due to the greater number of calls that must be made. It is suggested that the three-digit method is most appropriate when the directory or directories for the area of interest are relatively current or when there has been little growth in the area since the publication of the most recent directory. In other cases the four-digit method should be given serious consideration.

USING TELEPHONE BOOKS

RDD samples can also be generated from the telephone book. In general, this is accomplished by selecting numbers at random from the book and adding a random number to the sixth or seventh digits. Somewhere between one in two and one in three of the numbers generated will be working residential numbers. This is a viable approach because all exchanges and banks are proportionately represented in the book. Generally, the phone book is recommended as a RDD sample source only in those cases where the appropriate computer hardware and software are not available. There are two major reasons for making this recommendation. First, the construction of a sample by this approach is fairly time consuming and expensive whether it is done for or by the interviewers. Second, if the interviewers are given directions and left to generate the numbers themselves, the researcher loses all control over the validity of the sample.

Computer programs can incorporate three- or four-digit approaches and generate RDD samples at very low cost. In addition, the printout can be set up to capture additional data and to help the researcher control field costs and proper execution of the sampling plan.

Source: Roger Gates and Bob Brobst, "RANDIAL: A Program for Generating Random Telephone Numbers," *Journal of Marketing Research* 14 (May 1977): 240.

Probability samples offer several advantages, including the following:[8]

- The researcher can be sure of obtaining information from a representative cross section of the population of interest.
- Sampling error can be computed.
- The survey results are projectable to the total population. For example, if 5 percent of the individuals sampled in a research project based on a probability sample gave a particular response, the researcher can project this percentage, plus or minus the sampling error, to the total population.

On the other hand, certain disadvantages are associated with probability samples:

- They are more expensive than nonprobability samples of the same size in most cases. A certain amount of professional time must be spent in developing the sample design.
- Probability samples take more time to design and execute than nonprobability samples. The procedures that must be followed in the execution of the sampling plan will increase the amount of time required to collect data.

Reprinted from Advertising Age.
Courtesy of Bill Whitehead.

The disadvantages of nonprobability samples are essentially the reverse of the advantages of probability samples:

- Sampling error cannot be computed.
- The researcher does not know the degree to which the sample is representative of the population from which it was drawn.
- The results of nonprobability samples cannot be projected to the total population.

Given the disadvantages of nonprobability samples, one may wonder why they are used. In fact they are used frequently by marketing researchers. The reasons for their use relate to their inherent advantages:

- Nonprobability samples cost less than probability samples. This characteristic of nonprobability samples may have considerable appeal in those situations where accuracy is not of the utmost importance. Exploratory research is an example of this type of situation.

MARKETING RESEARCH IN PRACTICE

We have all seen the 900 number telephone polls on CNN and other news programs. These polls violate all of the statistical principles on which legitimate research surveys are based. The responses from self-selection 900 number polls are not projectable to any definable population group because they are biased due to the fact that they are based on responses from only those aware of the poll, interested enough to respond, willing and able to pay to respond, and able to reach the given number. There is also the possibility that a given individual may make multiple calls to such a 900 number poll.

Though these polls are clearly not representative, a recent poll conducted by the R. H. Bruskin Company based on a national telephone probability survey of 1,000 adults indicates that substantial proportions of the general population believe these polls are legitimate and representative in certain respects:

- 45 percent believe that the results of these call-in polls are believable.

- 40 percent believe that the results of these polls should be believed because thousands of people participated in the poll.
- 40 percent believe that those who call in on these kinds of polls have the same opinions as those who do not call in.
- 38 percent believe that those who respond to these kinds of polls are typical of the entire U.S. population.
- 36 percent believe that the results of these polls would not be reported if they were not accurate.
- 34 percent believe that the results of these polls should be believed because they are sponsored by major television, newspaper, or magazine organizations.
- 24 percent believe that these polls are scientific.
- 24 percent believe that the results of these polls accurately represent what the country as a whole thinks.[9]

FIGURE 11.4   *Classification of Sampling Methods*

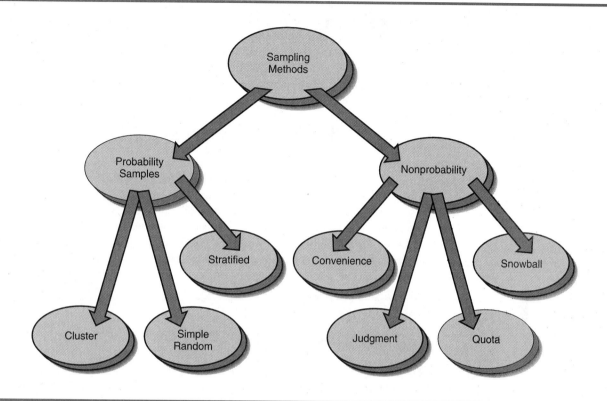

- Nonprobability samples ordinarily can be conducted more quickly than probability samples. The reasons for this were discussed earlier.
- Nonprobability samples can produce samples of the population that are reasonably representative if executed properly.

Issues related to beliefs of the public in regard to sampling issues are summarized in the preceding Marketing Research in Practice box.

In addition to choosing between probability and nonprobability samples, the researcher must choose between a number of types of samples under each of these major categories. These options are summarized in Figure 11.4. and are discussed in greater detail later in the chapter.

Determining Sample Size

Once we have chosen the sampling method, the next step is to determine the appropriate sample size. The issue of sample size determination is covered in detail in the next chapter. In Chapter 12, we discuss the role that available budget, various rules of thumb, the number of subgroups to be analyzed, and traditional statistical methods play in this process. In the case of nonprobability samples, we can rely only on budget available, rules of thumb, and number of subgroups to be analyzed in determining sample size. However, with probability samples formulas are used to calculate the sample size required given target levels of acceptable error (difference between sample result and population value) and levels of confidence (likelihood that the confidence interval, which is the sample result plus or minus the acceptable error, will take in the true population value). As noted earlier, the ability to make statistical inferences about population values based on sample results is a major advantage of probability samples.

Development of Operational Procedures for Selecting Sample Elements

The operational procedures to be used in the selection of sampling elements in the data collection phase of a project should be developed and specified whether a probability or nonprobability sample is being used.[10] The procedures are much more critical to the successful execution of a probability sample. In regard to probability samples, the procedures should be detailed, clear, and unambiguous and should take all discretion regarding the selection of specific sample elements away from the interviewer. Failure to develop a proper operational plan for selecting sample elements can jeopardize the entire sampling process. An example of an operational sampling plan is provided in Figure 11.5.

Execution of the Sampling Plan

The final step in the sampling process involves the execution of the operational sampling plan discussed in the previous step. It is important that this step include adequate checking to make sure that specified procedures are adhered to.

FIGURE 11.5   *Example of Operational Sampling Plan*

In the instructions that follow, reference is made to follow your route around a "block." In cities this will be a city block. In rural areas, a "block" is a segment of land surrounded by roads.

1. If you come to a dead end along your route, proceed down the opposite side of the street, road, or alley, traveling in the other direction. Continue making right turns, where possible, calling at every third occupied dwelling.

2. If you go all the way around a block and return to the starting address without completing four interviews in listed telephone homes, attempt an interview at the starting address. (This should seldom be necessary.)

3. If you work an entire block and do not complete the required interviews, proceed to the dwelling on the opposite side of the street (or rural route) that is *nearest* the starting address. Treat it as the next address on your Area Location Sheet and interview that house only if the address appears next to an "X" on your sheet. If it does not, continue your interviewing to the left of that address. Always follow the right turn rule.

4. If there are no dwellings on the street or road opposite the starting address for an area, circle the block opposite the starting address, following the right turn rule. (This means that you will circle the block following a clockwise direction.) Attempt interviews at every third dwelling along this route.

5. If, after circling the adjacent block opposite the starting address, you do not complete the necessary interviews, take the next block found, *following a clockwise direction.*

6. If the third block does not yield the dwellings necessary to complete your assignment, proceed to as many blocks as necessary to find the required dwellings; these blocks follow a clockwise path around the primary block.

Source: Reprinted from interviewer guide by permission of Belden Associates, Dallas, Texas. The complete guide was over thirty pages long and contained maps and other aids for the interviewer.

SAMPLING AND NONSAMPLING ERRORS

Consider a situation where our goal is to determine the average age of the members of a particular population.[11] If we can obtain accurate information about all members of the population, we can compute the population parameter average age. A population parameter is a value that defines a true characteristic of a total population. Assume that μ (population parameter or average age) is 36.3 years. As already noted, it is almost always impossible to measure the entire population. Instead, the researcher takes a sample and makes inferences about population parameters from sample results. In regard to the problem of computing average age, the analyst might take a sample of 400 from a population of 250,000. An estimate of the average age of the members of the population $(\overline{X})$ would be calculated from the sample values. Assume the average age of the sample members is 35.8 years. A second random sample of 400 might be drawn from the same population and the average again computed. In the second case, the average might be 36.8 years. Additional samples might be chosen and means computed for the various samples. The researcher would find that the means computed for the various samples would in most cases be fairly close but not identical to the true population value.

The accuracy of sample results is affected by two general types of error: sampling error and nonsampling (measurement) error. The following formula portrays the effect of these two types of error on the problem of estimating a population mean:

$$\overline{X} = \mu \pm \epsilon_s \pm \epsilon_{ns}$$

$\overline{X}$ = sample mean

μ = true population mean

ϵ_s = sampling error

ϵ_{ns} = nonsampling or measurement error

Sampling error is the error that results when the sample selected is not perfectly representative of the population. There are two types of sampling error: random and administrative error. Administrative error relates to problems in the administration or execution of the sample. That is, there are flaws in the design or execution of the sample that cause it to be not representative of the population. This type of error can be avoided or minimized by careful attention to the design and execution of the sample. Random sampling error is due to chance and cannot be avoided. This type of error can only be reduced by increasing sample size.

Measurement or nonsampling error includes everything other than sampling error that can cause inaccuracy and bias in the study results.

PROBABILITY SAMPLING METHODS

Simple Random Sampling

Simple random sampling is considered to be the purest form of probability sample. As mentioned earlier, a probability sample is a sample in which every element of the population has a *known* and *equal* probability of being selected into the sample. For a simple random sample that known and equal probability is computed as follows:

$$\text{Probability of selection} = \frac{\text{Sample size}}{\text{Population size}}$$

Simple random sampling
Probability sampling in which the sample is selected in such a way that every element of the population has a known and equal probability of inclusion in the sample.

For example, if the population size is 10,000 and the sample size is 400, then the probability of selection is 4 percent. It is computed as follows:

$$.04 = \frac{400}{10,000}$$

If a sampling frame (listing of all the elements of the population) is available, the researcher can select a simple random sample as follows:

1. Assign a number to each element of the population. A population of 10,000 elements would be numbered from 1 to 10,000.
2. Using a table of random numbers (see Table 1 in the Statistical Appendix), you would begin at some arbitrary point and move up, down or across until 400 (sample size) five-digit numbers between 00001 and 10,000 are chosen.
3. The numbers selected from the table identify specific population elements to be included in the sample.

Simple random sampling is appealing because it seems simple and meets all necessary requirements of a probability sample. It guarantees that every member of the population has a known and equal chance of being selected for the sample. Simple random samples begin with a complete listing of the population. Complete listings that are current are extremely difficult and often impossible to obtain. It can be employed quite successfully in telephone surveys through the use of random digit dialing. Finally, simple random sampling can be used to select respondents from computer files. Computer programs are available or can be readily written to select random samples from computer files such as customer lists.

Systematic Sampling

Systematic sampling
Probability sampling in which the entire population is numbered, and elements are drawn using a skip interval.

Systematic sampling is often used as a substitute for simple random sampling. Its popularity is based on its simplicity. Systematic sampling produces samples that are almost identical to those generated via simple random sampling.

To use this approach, it is necessary to obtain a listing of the population, just as in the case of simple random sampling. The researcher must determine a *skip interval* and select names based on this skip interval. This interval can be computed very simply through the use of the following formula:

$$\text{Skip interval} = \frac{\text{Population size}}{\text{Sample size}}$$

For example, if you were using the local telephone directory and computed a skip interval of 100, every hundredth name would be selected for the sample. The use of this formula ensures that the entire list will be covered.

A random starting point should be used in systematic sampling. For example, if you were using a telephone directory, it would be necessary to draw a random number to determine the page on which to start. Suppose page 53 is drawn. Another random number would be determined to decide the column on that page. Assume the third column is drawn. A final random number would be drawn to determine the actual starting position in that column; say, the seventeenth name. From that beginning point, the skip interval would be employed.

The main advantage of systematic sampling over simple random sampling is economy. It is often simpler, less time consuming, and less expensive to use systematic sampling than simple random sampling. The greatest danger in the use of systematic sampling lies in the listing of the population. Some populations may contain hidden patterns that the researcher may inadvertently pull into the sample. However, this danger is remote when alphabetical listings are used.

Stratified Samples

Stratified samples are probability samples that are distinguished by the following procedural steps:

- First, the original or parent population is divided into two or more mutually exclusive and exhaustive subsets (e.g., male and female).
- Second, simple random samples of elements from the two or more subsets are chosen independently from each other.

Stratified samples
Probability samples that force sample to be more representative.

Though some authors go to great pains to point out that the requirements for a stratified sample do not specify the bases that should be used to separate the original or parent population into subsets, common sense dictates that the population be divided on the basis of factors that can be shown to be related to the characteristic of the population we are really interested in measuring. For example, if you are doing a political poll to predict the outcome of an election and can show that there is a significant difference in the way men are likely to vote and the way women are likely to vote, then gender would be an appropriate basis for stratification. If you do not do stratified sampling in this manner, then you do not get the benefits of stratified sampling, and you have expended additional time, effort, and resources for no benefit. In the preceding example, gender is the basis for stratification, and we will have one stratum made up of men and one stratum made up of women. These strata are mutually exclusive and exhaustive in that every population element can be assigned to one and only one stratum (male or female) and no population elements are unassignable. The second stage in the process involves drawing simple random samples independently from each stratum.

Stratified samples are used rather than simple random samples because of their potential for greater statistical efficiency.[12] This means that if we have two samples from the same population, one a properly stratified sample and the other a simple random sample, the stratified sample will have a smaller sampling error. If, on the other hand, the goal is to attain a certain target level of sampling error, it can be achieved with a smaller stratified sample. Stratified samples are statistically more efficient because one source of variation has been eliminated. How this is achieved is explained in greater detail later.

You might ask the question, "If stratified samples are statistically more efficient, why are they not used all the time?" There are two reasons:

1. Frequently the information necessary to *properly* stratify the sample is not available. For example, little may be known about the demographic characteristics of the consumers of a particular product. Note that we said *properly* stratify the sample. To properly stratify the sample and to get the benefits of stratification you must pick bases for stratification where there are significant differences between the members of the two or more strata in regard to the measurement of interest.

2. Even if the necessary information is available, the time or costs of stratification may not be warranted from a cost versus value of information perspective.

In the case of a simple random sample, the researcher depends entirely on the laws of probability to generate a representative sample of the population. In the case of a stratified sample, the researcher, to some degree, forces the sample to be representative by making sure that important or salient dimensions of the population are represented in the sample in their true population proportions. For example, the researcher may know that, although men and women are equally likely to be users of a particular product, women are much more likely to be heavy users of that product. In a study designed to analyze consumption patterns of the product, failure to properly represent women in the sample will result in a biased view of consumption patterns. Assume that women make up 60 percent of the population of interest and men account for 40 percent of the population. A simple random sample of the population, even if everything were done absolutely correctly, might result in a sample that is made up of 55 percent women and 45 percent men. This would be due to sampling fluctuations. This is the kind of error we get when we flip a coin ten times. The correct result would be five heads and five tails but more than half of the time we would get a result other than five heads and five tails. In similar fashion, even a properly drawn and executed simple random sample will seldom generate a sample made up of 60 percent women and 40 percent men from a population made up of 60 percent women and 40 percent men. However, in the case of a stratified sample, the researcher will force the sample to have 60 percent women and 40 percent men.

As noted, the added precision of a stratified sample comes at some cost. Three steps are involved in implementing a properly stratified sample:

1. Identify salient (important) demographic or classification factors—factors that are correlated with the behavior of interest. For example, in a study of consumption rates for a particular product, there may be reason to believe that men and women have different average consumption rates. To use gender as a basis for meaningful stratification, the researcher must be able to show with actual data that there are significant differences in the consumption levels of men and women. In this manner, various salient factors are identified. Research indicates that after the six most important salient factors have been identified, the identification of additional salient factors adds little in the way of additional sampling efficiency.[13]

2. Next, determine what proportions of the population fall into the various subgroups under each stratum (e.g., if gender has been determined to be a salient factor, what proportion of the population is male and what proportion is female?). Using these proportions you can determine how many respondents are required from each subgroup. However, before making a final determination, a decision must be made as to whether to use proportional allocation or disproportional or optimal allocation.[14]

   - Under **proportional allocation**, the number of elements that would be selected from a stratum is directly proportional to the size of the stratum in relation to the size of the population. With proportional allocation, the proportion of elements to be taken from each stratum is given by the formula n/N, where n = the size of the stratum and N = the size of the population.
   - **Disproportional or optimal allocation** produces the most efficient samples and provides the most precise or reliable estimates for a given sample size. This

Proportional allocation
Sampling in which the number of elements selected from a stratum is directly proportional to the size of the stratum relative to the population.

Disproportional or optimal allocation
Sampling in which the number of elements taken from a given stratum is proportional to the relative size of the stratum and the standard deviation of the characteristic under consideration.

approach requires a *double weighting scheme*. Under this double weighting scheme, the number of sample elements to be taken from a given stratum is proportional to the relative size of the stratum and the standard deviation of the distribution of the characteristic under consideration for all elements in the stratum. This is done for two reasons. First, the size of a stratum is important because those strata with a larger number of elements are more important in determining the population mean. Therefore, these strata are more important in deriving estimates of population parameters. Second, it also makes sense that relatively more elements should be drawn from those strata having larger standard deviations (more variation) and relatively fewer elements should be drawn from those strata having smaller standard deviations. By allocating relatively more of our sample to those strata where the potential for sampling error is greatest (largest standard deviation) we get more bang for our buck and improve the overall accuracy of our estimates. There is no difference between proportional allocation and disproportional allocation if the distributions of the characteristic under consideration have the same standard deviations from stratum to stratum.

3. Finally, the researcher would select separate simple random samples from each strata. Actually, this process will be implemented somewhat differently in reality. Assume that our stratified sampling plan requires that 240 women and 160 men be interviewed. We will sample from the total population including both men and women and keep track of the number of men and women interviewed during the process. Let us say, for example, that at some point in the process we have interviewed 240 women and 127 men. From that point on, we will interview only men until we have reached the target of 160 men. In this manner, the process would generate a sample where the proportion of men and women in the sample is as required by the allocation scheme in Step 2.

Stratified samples are not used as often as one might expect in marketing research. The problem is that the researcher frequently does not have, in advance, the information necessary to properly stratify the sample. Stratification cannot be based on guesses or hunches, but must be based on hard data regarding the characteristics of the population and the relationship between these characteristics and the behavior under investigation. Stratified samples are frequently used in political polling and media audience research. In those areas, the researcher is much more likely to have the information necessary to implement the stratification process just described.

Cluster Samples

The types of samples discussed up until now have all been single unit samples, where each sampling unit is selected separately. In the case of **cluster samples**, the sampling units are selected in groups.[15] There are two basic steps in cluster sampling:

- First, the population of interest is divided into mutually exclusive and exhaustive subsets.
- Second, a random sample of the subsets is selected.

If the researcher samples all of the elements in the subsets selected, the procedure is a one-stage cluster sample. However, if a sample of elements is selected in some

Cluster samples
Sampling approach used with door-to-door interviewing in which the sampling units are selected in groups to reduce data collection costs.

If market researchers chose this area of San Francisco for cluster sampling, would they get a heterogeneous sample typical of the metropolitan area? (Spencer Grant/ Stock, Boston)

probabilistic manner from the selected subsets, then the procedure is a two-stage cluster sample. Both stratified and cluster sampling involve dividing the population into mutually exclusive and exhaustive subgroups. However, the issue that distinguishes the two is that in the case of stratified samples, a sample of elements is selected from each subgroup. In the case of cluster sampling, the researcher selects a sample of subgroups and then either collects data from all the elements in the subgroup (one-stage cluster sample) or from a sample of the elements (two-stage cluster sample).

All of the probability sampling methods discussed up to this point require sample frames that list or provide some organized breakdown of all the elements in the target population. Under cluster sampling, the researcher develops sample frames that include groups or clusters of elements of the population without actually listing individual elements. Sampling is executed with such frames by taking a sample of the clusters in the frame and generating lists or other breakdowns for only those clusters that have been selected for the sample. Finally, a sample is selected from the elements of the clusters selected.

The area sample, where the clusters are units of geography (e.g., city blocks), is the most popular type of cluster sample. A researcher, conducting a door-to-door survey in a particular metropolitan area, might randomly choose a sample of city blocks from that metropolitan area. After selecting a sample of clusters, a sample of consumers would be interviewed from each cluster. All interviews would be conducted in the clusters selected and none in other clusters. By interviewing only within the cluster selected, the researcher would dramatically reduce interviewer travel time and expenses. Cluster sampling is considered to be a probability sampling technique because of the random selection of clusters and the random selection of elements within each cluster selected.

Under cluster sampling it is assumed that the elements in a cluster are just as heterogeneous as the total population. If the characteristics of the elements of a cluster are very similar, then that assumption is violated and the researcher has a problem. In the example just described, there may be little heterogeneity within clusters because the residents of clusters are very similar to each other and different from those in other clusters. Typically, this potential problem is dealt with in the sample design by selecting a large number of clusters into the sample and sampling a relatively small number of elements from each cluster.

This type of cluster sample is a two-stage cluster sample. Stage One involves the selection of clusters, and Stage Two involves the selection of elements from within clusters. Multistage area sampling or multistage area probability samples involve three or more steps.[16] These types of samples are used for national surveys or surveys that cover large regional areas. Under samples of this type the researcher randomly selects geographic areas in progressively smaller units. For example, a statewide door-to-door survey might include the following steps:

1. Choose counties within the state to make sure that different areas are represented in the sample. Counties within the state should be selected with a probability proportional to the number of sampling units (households) within the county. Counties with a larger number of households would have a higher probability of selection than counties with a smaller number of households.
2. Select residential blocks within the selected counties.
3. Select households within the residential blocks selected.

From the standpoint of statistical efficiency, cluster samples are generally less efficient than other types of probability samples. In other words, a cluster sample of a certain size will have a larger sampling error than a simple random sample or a stratified sample of that same size. To illustrate the greater cost efficiency and lower statistical efficiency of a cluster sample, consider the following example. We need to select a sample of 200 households in a particular city for in-home interviews. If these 200 households were selected via a simple random sample, they would be scattered across the city. A cluster sample might be implemented in this situation by selecting twenty residential blocks in the city and randomly selecting ten households within each block to be interviewed. It is easy to see that interviewing costs will be dramatically reduced under the cluster sampling approach. Interviewers would not have to spend as much time traveling and would dramatically reduce their mileage and travel time. In regard to sampling error, we can see that the advantage would go to the simple random sample. Interviewing 200 households scattered across the city would increase the chance of getting a representative cross section of respondents. If all the interviewing is conducted in twenty randomly selected city blocks within the city, it is possible that certain ethnic, social, or economic groups could be missed or over- or underrepresented.

As noted previously, cluster samples are, in nearly all cases, statistically less efficient than simple random samples. It is possible to view a simple random sample as a special type of cluster sample, where the number of clusters is equal to the total sample size, and we select one sample element per cluster. At this point, the statistical efficiency of the cluster sample and the simple random sample are equal.

From this point on, as we decrease the number of clusters and increase the number of sample elements per cluster, the statistical efficiency of the cluster sample declines. At the other extreme, we might select a single cluster and select all the sample elements from that cluster. For example, we might select one relatively small geographic area in the city where you live and interview 200 people from that area. How comfortable would you be that a sample selected in this manner would be representative of the entire metropolitan area where you live?

NONPROBABILITY SAMPLING METHODS

In a general sense, any sample that does not meet the requirements of a probability sample is, by definition, a nonprobability sample. We have already noted that a major disadvantage of nonprobability samples is the inability to calculate sampling error. This suggests the even greater difficulty of evaluating the overall quality of nonprobability samples. We know that they do not meet the standard required of probability samples, but the question is, How far do they deviate from that standard? The user of the data from a nonprobability sample must make this assessment. The assessment must be based on a careful evaluation of the methodology used to generate the nonprobability sample. Is it likely that the methodology employed would generate a reasonable cross section of target population? Or is the sample hopelessly biased in some particular direction? These are the assessments that must be made. Four types of nonprobability samples are frequently used: convenience, judgment, quota, and snowball samples.

Convenience Samples

Convenience samples
Samples used primarily for reasons of convenience.

Convenience samples are samples used, as their name implies, for reasons of convenience. Companies like Frito Lay often do preliminary tests of new product formulations developed by their R&D departments using employees. At first, this may seem to be a highly biased approach to the problem. However, they are not asking employees to evaluate their existing products or to compare their products with competitive products. They are asking employees only to provide gross sensory evaluations of new product formulations (e.g., saltiness, crispiness, greasiness). In situations like this, convenience samples may represent an efficient and effective means of obtaining the required information. This is particularly true if we are dealing with an exploratory situation, where there is a pressing need to get an approximation of the true value inexpensively. The Marketing Research in Practice box provides an example of an appropriate use of convenience sampling.

Judgment Samples

Judgment samples
Samples in which the selection criteria are based on personal judgment that the element is representative of the population under study.

The term **judgment sample** is applied to any situation where the researcher is attempting to draw a representative sample based on judgmental selection criteria. Most test markets and many product tests conducted in shopping malls are essentially judgmental samples. In the case of test markets, one or a few markets are selected based on the judgment that they are representative of the population as a

Ethnic research is becoming more commonplace, given the ethnic diversity in the United States today. The problem is that traditional research methods may not be effective for sampling from ethnic subcultures. Locating ethnic respondents can be problematic because they may not be listed in directories or on mailing lists. Also, they are often suspicious of outsiders, especially those wanting to ask a lot of questions. Accessibility to research facilities can be a hindrance, as well. Likewise, there may be social or cultural barriers in the form of customs or practices.

As consumers of goods and services ethnics are an important part of the marketplace and, therefore, have an important role to play in the marketing research process. This is especially true for neighborhood-based companies such as financial services companies, health care providers, utilities, or retail chains. For ethnic group research, it is the respondent's *convenience* that is important rather than the researcher's.

In conducting research with different ethnic groups, an alternative to traditional methods is to use community-based research, where the researcher goes to the respondents in their own neighborhoods. This is very effective for newcomers, elders, and children—those ethnics who are not assimilated.

There are several points to keep in mind when planning community-based research studies:

- Allow extra lead time during the recruiting phase
- Understand the organization of the ethnic community
- Get the support of the community leaders
- Communicate research objectives clearly and explain how community leaders can help
- Create chains of personal referrals
- Try to match the recruiters and the subjects to facilitate trust
- Choose a meeting space accessible and convenient to the respondents
- Be prepared for contingencies
- Confirm, confirm, and reconfirm
- Leave extra time for data analysis[17]

MARKETING RESEARCH IN PRACTICE

whole. Malls are selected for product taste tests based on the researcher's judgment that the particular mall attracts a reasonable cross section of consumers who fall into the target group for the product being tested.

Quota Samples

Because **quota samples** are typically selected in such a way that demographic characteristics of interest to the researcher are represented in the sample in the same proportions as they are in the population, it is easy to understand how quota samples and stratified samples might be confused. There are, however, two key differences between a quota sample and a stratified sample. First of all, respondents for a quota sample are not selected on a random basis, as they must be for a stratified sample. Second, in a stratified sample, the classification factors used for stratification must be selected on the basis of the existence of correlation between the

Quota samples
Samples in which quotas are established for population subgroups. Selection is by nonprobability means.

classification factor and the behavior of interest. There is no such requirement in the case of a quota sample. The demographic or classification factors of interest in a quota sample are selected on the basis of researcher judgment.

Snowball Sampling

Snowball samples
Samples in which selection of additional respondents is based on referrals from the initial respondents.

Snowball samples use sampling procedures that involve the selection of additional respondents on the basis of referrals from the initial respondents. This procedure is used to sample from low incidence or rare populations.[18] By *low incidence* or *rare populations,* we are referring to populations that make up a very small percentage of the total population. The costs of finding members of these rare populations may be so great as to force the researcher to use a technique like snowball sampling for cost efficiency. For example, an insurance company might be interested in obtaining a national sample of individuals who have switched from the indemnity form of health care coverage to a health maintenance organization in the last six months. It would be necessary to sample an extremely large number of consumers nationally to locate 1,000 consumers who fall into this population. It would be far more economical to conduct an initial sample to identify 200 people who fall into the population of interest and obtain the names of an average of four other people from each of the respondents to the initial survey to complete the sample of 1,000.

The main advantages of snowball sampling relate to the dramatic reduction in search costs. However, this advantage comes at some cost. The total sample is likely to be biased because the individuals whose names were obtained from those sampled in the initial phase are likely to be very similar to those initially sampled. As a result, the resulting sample may not be a good cross section of the total population. There should be some limits on the number of respondents obtained through referral, though there are no specific rules regarding what these limits should be. Finally, this approach may be hampered by the fact that respondents may be reluctant to give referrals.

SUMMARY

The population, or universe, is the total group of people in whose opinions one is interested. A census involves collecting desired information from all the members of the population of interest. A sample is simply a subset of a population. The steps in developing a sampling plan are as follows: define the population of interest, choose the data collection method, choose the sampling frame, select the sampling method, determine sample size, develop and specify an operational plan for selecting sampling elements, and execute the operational sampling plan. The sampling frame is the means of listing the elements of the population from which the sample will be drawn or the specification of a procedure for generating the elements of the population to be sampled.

Probability sampling methods are selected in such a way that every element of the population has a known, nonzero probability of selection. Nonprobability sampling methods include all methods that select specific elements from the population in a nonrandom manner. Probability samples have several advantages over nonprobability samples, including reasonable certainty that information will be obtained from a representative cross section of the population, sampling error that can be computed, and survey results that can be projected to the total population. However, probability samples are more expensive than nonprobability samples and usually take much more time to design and execute.

The accuracy of sample results is affected by sampling error and nonsampling error. Sampling error is the error that results because the sample selected is not perfectly representative of the population. There are two types of sampling error: random and administrative error. Random sampling error is due to chance and cannot be avoided.

Probability sampling methods include simple random samples, systematic sampling, stratified samples, and cluster samples. Nonprobability sampling techniques include convenience samples, judgment samples, quota samples, and snowball samples.

KEY TERMS

Population or universe
Census
Sample
Sampling frame
Random digit dialing
Probability samples
Nonprobability samples
Simple random sampling
Systematic sampling

Stratified samples
Proportional allocation
Disproportional or optimal allocation
Cluster samples
Convenience samples
Judgment samples
Quota samples
Snowball samples

REVIEW AND DISCUSSION QUESTIONS

1. Describe five distinct populations at your university.
2. What are some situations where a census would be better than a sample? Why are samples usually taken rather than censuses?
3. Develop a sampling plan for examining undergraduate business students' attitudes toward children's advertising.
4. Give an example of a perfect sample frame. Why is a telephone directory often not an acceptable sample frame of a particular city?
5. Distinguish between probability and nonprobability samples. What are the advantages and disadvantages of each? Why are nonprobability samples so popular in marketing research?
6. Distinguish among a systematic sample, cluster sample, and stratified sample. Cite examples of each.
7. What is the difference between a stratified sample and a quota sample?
8. American National Bank has 1,000 customers. The manager wishes to draw a sample of 100 customers. How would this be done using systematic sampling? What impact would it have on the technique, if any, if the list were ordered by average size of deposit?
9. Simple random samples are rarely used for door-to-door interviewing. Why do you think this is true?
10. Do you see any problem with drawing a systematic sample from a telephone book, assuming that the telephone book is an acceptable sample frame?
11. Define snowball sampling. Give an example.
12. Name some possible sampling frames for the following: (a) patrons of sushi bars, (b) owners of hamsters, (c) racquetball players, (d) flyrod owners, (e) retailers of

silly putty, (f) immigrants to the United States of less than two years, (g) persons with acne, (h) women wearing size 4 dresses.

13. Identify the following sample designs:
    (a) The names of twenty patrons of a bingo parlor are drawn out of a hat and a questionnaire is administered to them.
    (b) A radio talk show host invites listeners to call in and vote yes or no on banning nuclear weapons.
    (c) A dog food manufacturer wants to test a new dog food. It decides to select 100 dog owners who feed their dog canned food, 100 who feed their dog dry food, and 100 who feed their dog semimoist food.
    (d) All members of Alpha Beta fraternity are questioned regarding their satisfaction with the last Spring Dinner.

CASE

New Mexico National Bank

New Mexico National Bank (NMNB) operates branches in forty-three cities and towns throughout New Mexico. The bank offers a complete range of financial services, including Visa and Mastercard credit cards. NMNB has 62,500 people in the state using its credit cards. From the original application, they have certain information about these individuals, including name, address, zip code, telephone number, income, education, and assets. NMNB is interested in determining whether there is a relationship between the volume of purchases charged on their credit cards and demographic characteristics of the individual card holder. For example, are individuals in certain parts of the state more or less likely to be heavy users of the card? Is there a relationship between the person's income and his or her level of card usage? Is there a relationship between the person's level of education and card usage? Norman Robbins is research director for NMNB, and he is currently in the process of developing a design for the research. If you were Robbins, how would you answer the following questions:

1. How would you define the population of interest for the study?
2. What sample frame would you use for the project?
3. What procedure would you use to select a simple random sample from the sampling frame you chose above?
4. How would you approach the process of drawing a stratified sample from the sampling frame you chose?
5. Could you use your sample frame to draw a cluster sample? How would you go about it?
6. Which of the three probability sampling methods, just covered, would you choose for this study? Why would you choose that particular procedure?

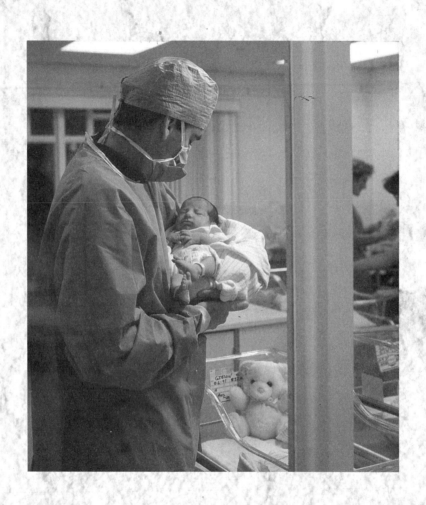

Sample Size Determination

LEARNING OBJECTIVES

1. To learn the financial and statistical issues in the determination of sample size.

2. To discover the methods for determining sample size.

3. To gain an appreciation of a normal distribution.

4. To understand population, sample, and sampling distribution.

5. To distinguish between point and interval estimates.

6. To recognize problems involving sampling means and proportions.

B

ill Boggs is the marketing research director for Allied National Health Plans, an operator of HMOs in forty markets throughout the country. Bill is preparing a request for proposal (RFP) that he is going to send to five potential research suppliers. The subject of the RFP is a member satisfaction study to be conducted in all forty markets where Allied operates HMOs. He is trying to decide on what sample size to specify for each market. Numerous discussions with the managers who will use the results of the research to evaluate the performance of the different health plans operated by Allied have indicated that management would like to make inferences regarding the research results for each plan at a relatively high level of precision. Bill feels that if management is to be satisfied with the results, they must have an error of no greater than plus or minus 5 percent at the 95 percent confidence level.

Bill is in the process of calculating the required sample size for each plan. These and other related issues will be dealt with in this chapter. After reading this chapter, you should know how to approach the sample size problem that Bill is presently considering.[1]

DETERMINING SAMPLE SIZE FOR PROBABILITY SAMPLES

Financial, Statistical, and Managerial Issues

The process of determining sample size for probability samples involves financial, statistical, and managerial issues. Other things equal, the larger the sample, the less the sampling error. However, larger samples cost more money, and the funds available for a particular project are always limited. In addition, though the costs of larger samples tend to increase on a linear basis, the level of sampling error decreases at a rate only equal to the square root of the relative increase in sample size. In other words, if sample size is quadrupled, data collection costs will be quadrupled, but the level of sampling error will be reduced by only one-half. Finally, managerial issues must be reflected in sample size calculations. How accurate do our estimates need to be and how confident do we need to be that true population values are taken in by the chosen confidence interval? As you will see later in the chapter, there are a number of possibilities. In some cases, there is a need to be very precise (small sampling error) and very confident that population values fall in the small range of sampling error (confidence interval). In other cases, you may not need to be as precise or confident. Issues related to these questions are addressed in the Marketing Research in Practice box.

I t is the size of the change or the difference to be measured that determines sample size needs. Even to fit narrow specifications, there is no "one-size-fits-all" sample size.

For example, assume we are testing two products against one another; product A (the current product) and product B (the new version of the product). The new version will be put in place should it score significantly higher than product A. Significance is determined as either 90 or 95 percent confidence level.

To protect against the risk of random sampling error causing an *overstatement* of favorable response—the false conclusion that product B should be adopted—the above action criterion should be enacted. However, the opposite error, *understating* of favorable response, could lead to the false conclusion that product B should be rejected. This conclusion is just as likely and is not protected against by the above action criterion.

Effect size refers to a rough estimate of how small a superiority product B would have to have over product A in order to make the change from A to B worthwhile. Assume a small sample size, say 120, is used and the effect size is determined to be 10 percentage points, as is the actual superiority of product B; the probability of finding a 95 percent significant superiority for B is only 45 percent. Flipping a coin would be a more productive alternative.

In the above example, a sample size of only 120 is lacking in statistical power; a power that would guard against failure to recognize the superiority of product B. Many small sample surveys are misleading and a waste of effort due to initial lack of consideration of statistical power.

When effect size is large, 15 or more percentage points, statistical power is not usually a problem. However, very small effect sizes, like two percentage points, require such large samples sizes that it becomes impractical; surveys cannot measure reliably such small changes or differences.[2]

MARKETING RESEARCH IN PRACTICE

METHODS FOR DETERMINING SAMPLE SIZE

Budget Available

Frequently, the sample size for a project is determined by the budget available. Sample size, in essence, is frequently determined backwards. A brand manager may have $20,000 available in the budget for a particular marketing research project. After deducting other project costs (e.g., research design, questionnaire development, data processing, analysis, etc.), the remainder determines the size of the sample that can be surveyed. There are limits, of course. If the dollars available are enough for only a clearly inadequate sample, a decision must be made. Either additional funds must be found or the project should be cancelled.

Although this approach may seem highly unscientific and arbitrary, it is a fact of life in a corporate environment based on the budgeting of financial resources. Financial constraints challenge the researcher to develop research designs that will generate data of adequate quality for decision-making purposes with limited resources. This "budget available" approach forces the researcher to carefully consider the value of information in relation to its cost.

Rules of Thumb

Potential clients may specify in RFPs that they want a sample of 200, 400, 500, or some other specific size. Sometimes this number is based on some consideration of sampling error, and in other cases it is based on nothing more than past experience and sample sizes used in the past for similar studies. The justification for the specified sample size may boil down to nothing more than the "gut feel" that it is an appropriate sample size.

It may be that the sample size requested is judged to be adequate to support the objectives of the proposed research. In other cases, the researcher may determine that the sample size requested is not adequate. In these instances, the researcher should present arguments for a larger sample size to the client and let the client make the final decision. If the arguments for a larger sample size fall on deaf ears, the researcher may decline to submit a proposal in the belief that the sample size is so inadequate as to fatally cripple the research effort.

Number of Subgroups to Be Analyzed

In any sample size determination problem, serious consideration must be given to the number and anticipated size of various subgroups of the total sample about which there will be a need to make statistical inferences. For example, we might decide that a sample of 400 is quite adequate on an overall basis. However, if male and female respondents must be analyzed separately and the sample is expected to be 50 percent male and 50 percent female, then the expected sample size for each subgroup is only 200. Is this number adequate to permit the analyst to make the desired statistical inferences about the characteristics of the two groups? If, in addition, the results are to be analyzed by both gender and age, the problem gets even more complicated.

Other things equal, the larger the number of subgroups to be analyzed, the larger the required total sample size. It has been suggested that the sample should be large enough so that there will be 100 or more respondents in each major subgroup and a minimum of 20 to 50 respondents in each of the less important subgroups.

Traditional Statistical Methods

You have probably been exposed to traditional approaches for determining sample size for simple random samples. These approaches are reviewed in this chapter. Three pieces of information are required to make the necessary calculations when using a sample result:

- An estimate of the population standard deviation.
- The acceptable level of sampling error.
- The desired level of confidence that the sample result will fall within a certain range (result ± sampling error) of true population values.

MARKETING RESEARCH IN PRACTICE

Benjamin Sackmary, of the Department of Marketing at the University of Hartford says: "For researchers, sample size is always a tough question. Statistics aside, if a sample is seen as undersized, results may not have the impact needed to drive a tough decision; if oversized, the researcher is criticized for being wasteful. The cost of a research project usually is related directly to the sample size. One would assume that in most cases an effort is made to keep sample size to a minimum. But I have seen instances in which samples are larger than needed in statistical terms, and expenses are far greater than called for by the research objectives. The reason for this is simple: Research buyers, like buyers of many other services and supplies, do not always act rationally. There are emotional elements in a research decision, and these can be expensive for a company.

"Obviously, the usual constraints of time, money, and personnel are with us as much in research as in any other enterprise. These set the parameters for a research project and limit sample size, but despite their importance, less tangible factors can override such 'rational' limitations. Therefore, when selecting an appropriate sample size, researchers should take into account not only statistical requirements but also emotional factors and organizational necessity. The latter factors often are very subtle.

"Ignoring the nonstatistical aspect of setting sample size can imperil the value of a research project. The in-house researcher or outside supplier should be sensitive to the expectations of decision makers, as well as to the relative importance of the research results for the organization. Textbooks, handbooks, and journals offer helpful information about the concepts and theories involved in determining sample size. However, these statistical discussions often can be of limited value when dealing with the special aspects of a specific research project. In reality, questionnaire length, budget, schedule, and attitudes and expectations all have a direct impact on sample size decisions. Handbooks offer little help when it comes to balancing these issues.

"Professional research suppliers often prefer to treat sample size as a straightforward technical matter. They may offer a client a table of figures to show the relative confidence that can be placed on the results as the sample size gets larger. Although this is helpful, the client will ask, 'How much confidence is enough?' The research supplier may answer with technical jargon. The research user needs a hard-edged response that takes into account the reality of the organizational environment. When dealing with random samples, we can use statistical measures with accuracy. When dealing with people, we have to become involved in the psychological and, possibly, even political aspects of sample size. In fact, organizational situations or style may require larger and more compelling samples than most researchers would ever recommend to a company."[3]

With these three pieces of information, we can calculate the size of the simple random sample required.

THE NORMAL DISTRIBUTION

General Properties

Normal distribution
A continuous distribution that is bell shaped and symmetrical about the mean—mean, median, and mode are equal. Sixty-eight percent of the observations fall within plus or minus one standard deviation of the mean, approximately 95 percent fall within plus or minus two standard deviations, and approximately 99.5 fall within plus or minus three standard deviations.

Central limit theorem
A distribution of a large number of sample means or sample proportions will approximate a normal distribution regardless of the actual distribution of the population from which they were drawn.

The concept of a **normal distribution** is crucial to classical statistical inference. There are several reasons for its importance. First, many variables encountered by marketers have probability distributions that are close to the normal distribution. Examples include the number of cans, bottles, or glasses of soft drink consumed by soft drink users; the number of times that people who eat at fast food restaurants go to restaurants of thi s type in an average month; the average hours per week spent viewing television. Second, the normal distribution is useful for a number of theoretical reasons, one of the more important of these relates to the central limit theorem. According to the **central limit theorem**, for any population (regardless of its distribution), a distribution of sample means ($\overline{X}$) approaches a normal distribution as the sample size increases. The importance of this factor will become clear later in the chapter. Third, the normal distribution is a useful approximation of many discrete probability distributions.

If, for example, we were to measure the heights of a large sample of men in the United States and plot those values on a graph, a distribution similar to the one shown in Figure 12.1 would result. This distribution is a normal distribution that has a number of important characteristics, including the following:

FIGURE 12.1 *Distribution of the Heights of Men in the United States Based on a Large Sample*

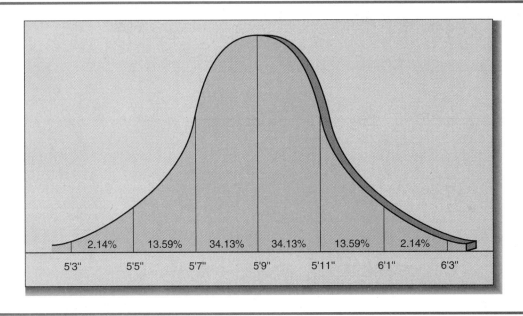

1. The normal distribution is bell-shaped and has only one mode. The mode is a measure of central tendency and is the particular value that occurs most frequently. A bimodal (two modes) distribution would have two peaks or humps.
2. A normal distribution is symmetric about its mean. This is another way of saying that it is not skewed and that the three measures of central tendency (mean, median, and mode) are all equal to the same value.
3. A particular normal distribution is uniquely defined by its mean and standard deviation.
4. The total area under a normal curve is equal to one, meaning that it takes in all observations.
5. The area of a region under the normal distribution curve between any two values of a variable equals the probability of observing a value in that range when randomly selecting an observation from the distribution. For example, on a single draw there is a 34.13 percent chance of selecting a man between 5'7" and 5'9" in height from the distribution shown in Figure 12.1.
6. The normal distribution has the feature that the area between the mean and a given number of standard deviations from the mean is the same for all normal distributions. In other words, the area between the mean and plus or minus one standard deviation takes in 68.26 percent of the area under the curve or 68.26 percent of the observations. This is called the *proportional property* of the normal distribution. This feature provides the basis for much of the statistical inference that we will discuss in this chapter.

The Standard Normal Distribution

Any normal distribution can be transformed into what is known as a **standard normal distribution.** The standard normal distribution has the same features as any normal distribution. However, the mean of the standard normal distribution is always equal to 0 and the standard deviation is always equal to 1. The probabilities provided in Table 2 in the Statistical Appendix are based on a standard normal distribution. A simple transformation formula can be used to transform any value X from any normal distribution to its equivalent value Z for a standard normal distribution. This transformation is based on the proportional property of the normal distribution:

Standard normal distribution
A normal distribution with a mean of zero and a standard deviation of one.

$$Z = \frac{\text{value of variable} - \text{mean of the variable}}{\text{standard deviation of the variable}}$$

TABLE 12.1 Area Under Standard Normal Curve for Z Values (standard deviations) of 1, 2, and 3

Z VALUES (STANDARD DEVIATION)	AREA UNDER STANDARD NORMAL CURVE (%)
1	68.26
2	95.44
3	99.74

FIGURE 12.2   *Standardized Normal Distribution*

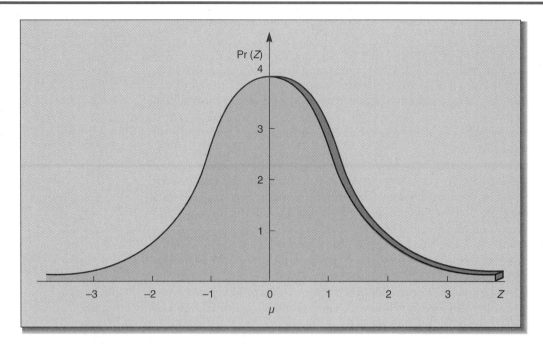

The term *Pr (Z)* is read "the probability of *Z*."

Symbolically, the formula can be stated as

$$Z = \frac{X - \mu}{\sigma}$$

where

X = value of the variable

μ = mean of the variable

σ = standard deviation of the variable

The areas under (percent of all observations) a standard normal distribution for various Z values (**standard deviations**) are shown in Table 12.1. The standardized normal distribution is shown in Figure 12.2.

POPULATION, SAMPLE, AND SAMPLING DISTRIBUTIONS

The purpose of conducting a survey based on a sample is to make inferences about the population, not to describe the sample. The population, as defined earlier, includes all possible individuals or objects from whom or about which we might collect information to meet the objectives of the research. A sample is a subset of the total population.

A **population distribution** is a frequency distribution of all the elements of the population. This frequency distribution has a mean, usually represented by the

Standard deviation
A measure of dispersion calculated by subtracting the mean of a series from each value in a series, squaring each result, summing them, dividing the sum by the number of items minus 1, and taking the square root of this value.

Population distribution
A frequency distribution of all the elements of a population.

Greek letter μ, and a standard deviation, usually represented by the Greek letter σ. A **sample distribution** is a frequency distribution of the elements of an individual (single) sample. In a sample distribution, the mean is usually represented by $\overline{X}$ and the standard deviation is usually represented by S.

At this point, it is necessary to introduce a third distribution, the sampling distribution of the sample mean. Understanding this distribution is crucial to understanding the basis for our ability to compute sampling error in simple random samples. The **sampling distribution of the sample mean** is a conceptual and theoretical probability distribution of the means of all possible samples of a given size drawn from a particular population. Though this distribution is seldom calculated, its known properties have tremendous practical significance. To actually derive a distribution of sample means, a large number of simple random samples (e.g., 25,000) of a certain size are drawn from a particular population. Then, the means for each sample are computed and arranged in a frequency distribution. Because each sample is composed of a different subset of sample elements, the sample means will not all be exactly the same.

If the samples are sufficiently large and random, then the resulting distribution of sample means will approximate a normal distribution. This assertion is based on the central limit theorem. Once again, this theorem states that as the sample size increases, the distribution of the means of a large number of random samples taken from virtually any population approaches a normal distribution with a mean equal to μ and a standard deviation (referred to as *standard error*) equal to

$$S_{\overline{X}} = \frac{\sigma}{\sqrt{n}}$$

where n = sample size

It is important to note that the central limit theorem holds regardless of the shape of the population distribution from which the samples are selected. This means that regardless of the distribution of the population, a distribution of means of samples selected from that distribution will tend to be normally distributed. The notation ordinarily used to refer to the means and standard deviations of population, sample, and sampling distributions is summarized in Table 12.2.

The **standard error of the mean** ($S_{\overline{X}}$) is computed as indicated earlier because the variance or dispersion within a particular distribution of sample means will be smaller if it is based on larger samples. Common sense tells us that individual sample means will, on the average, be closer to the population mean with larger samples. The relationships among the population distribution, sample distribution, and sampling distributions of the mean are shown graphically in Figure 12.3. The sampling distribution of the mean is discussed further and another concept, the sampling distribution of the proportion, is introduced in the following sections.

Sample distribution
A frequency distribution of all the elements of an individual sample.

Sampling distribution of the sample mean
A frequency distribution of the means of many samples drawn from a particular population. It is normally distributed.

Standard error of the mean
The standard deviation of a distribution of sample means.

TABLE 12.2	*Symbols Used for Means and Standard Deviations of Various Distributions*

DISTRIBUTION	MEAN	STANDARD DEVIATION
Population	μ	σ
Sample	$\overline{X}$	S
Sampling	$\mu_{\overline{X}} = \mu$	$S_{\overline{X}}$

FIGURE 12.3   *Relationships of the Three Basic Types of Distribution*

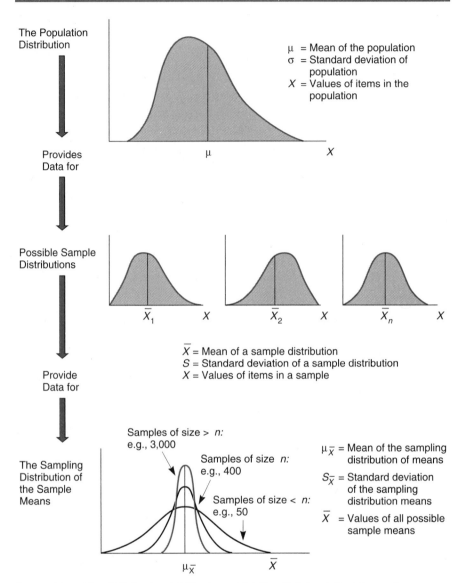

The Population Distribution

Provides Data for

μ = Mean of the population
σ = Standard deviation of population
X = Values of items in the population

Possible Sample Distributions

$\overline{X}$ = Mean of a sample distribution
S = Standard deviation of a sample distribution
X = Values of items in a sample

Provide Data for

The Sampling Distribution of the Sample Means

Samples of size > n:
e.g., 3,000

Samples of size n:
e.g., 400

Samples of size < n:
e.g., 50

$\mu_{\overline{X}}$ = Mean of the sampling distribution of means

$S_{\overline{X}}$ = Standard deviation of the sampling distribution means

$\overline{X}$ = Values of all possible sample means

Source: Adapted from D.H. Sanders, A.F. Murphy, and R.J. Eng, *Statistics: A Fresh Approach,* p. 123, © 1980 McGraw-Hill.

Making Inferences on the Basis of a Single Sample

In practice we are not interested in taking all possible random samples from a particular population. Normally, we want to take one simple random sample and make some statistical inference about the population from which the sample was drawn. The question is, What is the probability that any one simple random sample of a particular size will produce an estimate of the population mean that is within one standard error (plus or minus) of the true population mean? The answer, based on the information provided in Table 12.1, is that there is a 68 percent probability that any one sample from a particular population will produce an estimate of the population mean that is within plus or minus one standard error of the true value, because 68 percent of all sample means will fall in this range. There is a 95 percent probability that any one simple random sample of a particular size from a given population will produce a value that is within plus or minus two standard errors of the true population mean and a 99.7 percent probability that such a sample will produce an estimate of the mean that is within plus or minus three standard errors of the population mean.

Point and Interval Estimates

When using the results of a sample to make estimates of a population mean, two kinds of estimates can be generated: point and interval estimates. In **point estimates**, the sample mean is the best estimate of the population mean. It is likely that a particular sample result will produce a mean that is relatively close to the population mean. However, the mean of a particular sample could be any one of the sample means shown in the distribution. A small percentage of these sample means are a considerable distance from the true population mean. The distance between the sample mean and the true population mean is called the *sampling error.*

Given that point estimates based on sample results are exactly correct in only a small percentage of all possible cases, **interval estimates** are generally preferred to point estimates. An interval estimate is an estimate regarding an interval or range of values of the variable, such as a population mean, that the researcher is attempting to estimate. In addition to stating the size of the interval, it is customary to state the probability that the interval will take in the true value of the population mean. This probability is normally referred to as the *confidence coefficient* or **confidence level** while we refer to the interval as the *confidence interval.*

Interval estimates of the mean are derived as follows. A random sample of a given size is drawn from the population of interest and the mean of that sample is calculated. This particular sample mean is known to lie somewhere within the sampling distribution of all possible sample means but exactly where this particular mean falls in that distribution is not known. In addition, there is a 68 percent probability that this particular sample mean lies within one standard error (plus or minus) of the true population mean. Based on this information, the statement can be made that the researcher is 68 percent confident that the true population value is equal to the sample value plus or minus one standard error. Symbolically, this statement would be stated as follows:

$$\overline{X} - 1\sigma_{\overline{X}} \leq \mu \leq \overline{X} + 1\sigma_{\overline{X}}$$

Using this same logic, the statement can be made that the researcher is 95 percent confident that the true population value is equal to the sample estimate plus or minus two standard errors (technically 1.96, but 2 is often used for convenience in calculation); and 99.7 percent confident that the true population value falls within the interval defined by the sample value plus or minus three standard errors.

All of this assumes that the standard deviation of the population is known. In most situations, this is not the case. If the standard deviation of the population were known, by definition the mean of the population also would be known, and there would be no need to take a sample in the first place. Lacking information on the

Point estimates
Inferences regarding the sampling error associated with a particular estimate of a population value.

Interval estimates
Inferences regarding the likelihood that a population value will fall within a certain range.

Confidence level
The probability that a particular confidence interval will include the true population value.

standard deviation of the population, its value is estimated based on the standard deviation of the sample.

SAMPLING DISTRIBUTION OF THE PROPORTION

Marketing researchers are frequently interested in estimating proportions or percentages rather than or in addition to estimating means. Common examples include the following:

- The percent of the population that are aware of a particular ad.
- The percent of the population who will buy a new product.
- The percent of the population of all individuals who have visited a fast-food restaurant in the last thirty days, who have visited a fast-food restaurant four or more times during that period.
- The percent of the population who subscribe to a particular newspaper.

In situations like these, where a population proportion or percentage is of interest, we shift to the sampling distribution of the proportion.

The **sampling distribution of the proportion** is a relative frequency distribution of the sample proportions of a large number of random samples of a given size drawn from a particular population. The sampling distribution of a proportion has the following characteristics:

1. It approximates a normal distribution.
2. The mean proportion for all possible samples is equal to the population proportion.
3. The standard error of a sampling distribution of proportions can be computed with the following formula:

$$S_p = \sqrt{\frac{P(1-P)}{n}}$$

where

S_p = standard error of sampling distribution of proportions

P = estimate of population proportion

n = sample size

Sampling distribution of the proportion
A frequency distribution of the proportions of many samples drawn from a particular population. It is normally distributed.

Consider the need to estimate the percentage of all fast-food users who have visited a fast-food restaurant four or more times in the last thirty days. As when generating a sampling distribution of the mean, 1,000 random samples of size 200 might be selected from the population of all fast-food users, and the proportion of users who have visited a fast-food restaurant four or more times in the last month for all 1,000 samples computed. These values can then be plotted in a frequency distribution, and this frequency distribution will approximate a normal distribution. The estimated standard error of the proportion for this distribution is computed using the formula for the standard error of a proportion provided earlier.

For reasons that, we hope, will be clear after you read the next section, marketing researchers have a tendency to cast sample size problems as problems of estimating proportions rather than means.

A distribution of sample means for average number of visits to fast-food restaurants will be normally distributed. (J. Gerard Smith/ Monkmeyer)

SAMPLE SIZE DETERMINATION

Problems Involving Means

Consider the previous example that involved estimating how many times the average fast-food restaurant user visits a fast-food restaurant in an average month. Management needs an estimate of the average number of visits to make a decision regarding a new promotional campaign currently under consideration. To make this estimate, the marketing research manager for the firm intends to survey a simple random sample of all fast-food users. The question is, What information is necessary to determine the appropriate sample size for the project? First of all, the formula for calculating the required sample size for problems that involve the estimation of a mean is as follows:

$$n = \frac{Z^2 \sigma^2}{E^2}$$

where

Z = level of confidence expressed in standard errors

σ = population standard deviation

E = acceptable amount of sampling error

Three pieces of information are needed to compute the sample size required.

1. Specification of the acceptable or **allowable** level of **sampling error** (E).
2. Specification of the acceptable level of confidence in standard errors or Z values. In other words, how confident do you want to be that the specified confidence interval takes in the population mean.
3. Finally, an estimate of the **population standard deviation** (σ) is required.

The level of confidence (Z) and the amount of error (E) to be used must be set by the researcher. As noted earlier, the level of confidence and amount of error are set based not only on statistical criteria, but also financial and managerial criteria.

Allowable sampling error
The amount of sampling error the researcher is willing to accept.

Population standard deviation
The standard deviation of a variable for the entire population.

In an ideal world, we would like to always set the level of confidence at a very high level and the amount of error at a very small level. However, because this is a business decision, cost must be considered. An acceptable trade-off between accuracy, level of confidence, and cost must be determined. In some situations, the need for precision and a high level of confidence may be less than in others. For example, in an exploratory study you may be interested in developing a basic sense of whether attitudes toward your product are generally positive or negative. Precision may not be critical. However, in a product concept test you may need to make a much more precise estimate of sales for a new product in order to make a potentially costly and risky decision to introduce a new product.

The third item on the list of required information, an estimate of the population standard deviation, presents a more serious problem. As noted earlier, if the population standard deviation were known, the population mean also would be known (the population mean is needed to compute the population standard deviation). There would be no need to draw a sample. The question is, How can the researcher estimate the population standard deviation before selecting the sample? One or some combination of four approaches can be used to deal with this problem:

1. *Use results from a prior survey.* In many cases, the firm may have conducted a prior survey dealing with the same or a similar issue. In this situation, the most obvious solution to the problem would be to use the results of the prior survey as an estimate of the population standard deviation in this situation.

2. *Conduct a pilot survey.* If this is to be a large scale project, it may be possible to devote some time and some resources to a small scale pilot survey of the population. The results of this pilot survey can be used to develop an estimate of the population standard deviation that can be used in the sample size determination formula.

3. *Use secondary data.* In some cases, secondary data may be available that can be used to develop an estimate of the population standard deviation.

4. *Use judgment.* If all else fails, an estimate of the population standard deviation can be developed based solely on judgment. This process may be implemented by seeking judgments from a variety of managers who would be in a position to make educated guesses regarding the required population parameters.

It should be noted that after the survey has been conducted and the sample mean and sample standard deviation have been calculated, the researcher is in a position to assess the accuracy of the estimate of the population standard deviation used to calculate the required sample size. At this time, if it is deemed appropriate, adjustments can be made in the initial estimates of sampling error.

Consider the problem involving estimation of the average number of fast-food visits made in an average month by users of fast-food restaurants. The values to be substituted into the formula follow:

■ After consultation with managers in the company, the marketing research manager determines that it is necessary to produce an estimate of the average number of times that fast-food users visit fast-food restaurants. She further determines that managers believe that a high degree of accuracy is needed and translates this to mean that the estimate should be within 0.10 (one-tenth) of a visit of the true population value. This value (0.10) should be substituted into the formula for the value of E.

■ In addition, the marketing research manager has decided that, all things considered, she needs to be 95 percent confident that the true population mean falls into the interval defined by the sample mean plus or minus E (as just defined). Two standard errors (technically 1.96) are required to take in 95 percent of the area under a normal curve; therefore, a value of 2 would be substituted into the equation for Z.

■ Finally, there is the question of what value to insert into the formula for σ. Fortunately, the company had previously conducted a very similar study, and in that study the standard deviation for the variable, average number of times visiting a fast-food restaurant in the last thirty days, was 1.39 times. This is the best estimate of σ available. Therefore, a value of 1.39 would be substituted into the formula for the value of σ. The calculation follows.

$$n = \frac{Z^2 \sigma^2}{E^2}$$

$$n = \frac{2^2 \, (1.39)^2}{(0.10)^2}$$

$$n = \frac{4 \, (1.93)}{0.01}$$

$$n = \frac{7.72}{0.01}$$

$$n = 772$$

Based on this calculation, a simple random sample of 772 is necessary to meet the requirements outlined.

Problems Involving Proportions

Consider the problem of estimating the proportion of all fast-food users who visit a fast-food restaurant four or more times in an average month. The goal is to take a simple random sample from the population of all fast-food users to estimate this proportion. A discussion of the determination of the appropriate values to substitute into the formula follows.

■ As in the previous problem, involving the estimation of a population mean on the basis of sample results, the first task is to decide on an acceptable value for E. If, for example, it is decided that an error level of plus or minus 4 percent is acceptable, a value of .04 will be substituted into the formula for E.

■ Next, assume that the researcher has determined a need to be 95 percent confident that the sample estimate is within plus or minus 4 percent of the true population proportion. As in the previous example, we would substitute a value of 2 into the equation for Z.

■ Finally, in a study of the same issue conducted one year ago, the researcher found that 30 percent of all respondents indicated they had visited a fast-food restaurant four or more times in the previous month. We would substitute a value of .30 into the equation for P.

■ The resulting calculations are as follows:

$$n = \frac{Z^2 [P(1 - P)]}{E^2}$$

$$n = \frac{2^2 [.30(1 - .30)]}{.04^2}$$

$$n = \frac{4 (.21)}{.0016}$$

$$n = \frac{.84}{.0016}$$

$$n = 525$$

Given the requirements, a random sample of 525 respondents is needed. It should be noted, that in comparison to the process of determining the sample size necessary to estimate a mean, the researcher has one major advantage when determining sample size necessary to estimate a proportion: if there is no basis for estimating P, you can make what is sometimes referred to as the *most pessimistic* or *worst case* assumption regarding the value of P. What value of P, given values of Z and E, will require the largest possible sample? A value of 0.50 will make the value of the expressions $P (1 - P)$ larger than any other possible value of P. There is no corresponding most pessimistic assumption that the researcher can make regarding the value of σ in problems that involve determining sample size necessary to estimate a mean with given levels of Z and E.

Population Size and Sample Size

You may have noticed that none of the formulas for determining sample size takes into account in any way the size of the population. Students (and managers) frequently find this troubling. It seems to make sense that we should take a larger sample from a larger population. However, this is not true. Generally, there is no direct relationship between the size of the population and the size of the sample required to estimate a particular population parameter with a particular level of error and a particular level of confidence. In fact, the size of the population is of interest only in those situations where the size of the sample is large in relation to the size of the population. One rule of thumb suggests that we need to make an adjustment in the sample size if the sample size is more than 5 percent of the size of the total population. The normal presumption is that sample elements are drawn independent of one another (independence assumption). This assumption is justified when the sample is small relative to the population. However, it is not appropriate when the sample is a relatively large (5 percent or more) proportion of the population. As a result, we must adjust the results obtained with the standard formulas. For example, the formula for the standard error of the mean, presented earlier, is

$$\sigma_{\bar{x}} = \frac{\sigma}{\sqrt{n}}$$

Adjusting for a sample that is 5 percent or more of the population and dropping the independence assumption, the correct formula is

$$\sigma_{\bar{x}} = \frac{\sigma}{\sqrt{n}} \sqrt{\frac{N-n}{N-1}}$$

The factor $(N - n)/(N - 1)$ is referred to as the **finite population correction factor** (FPC).

Finite population correction factor
An adjustment to the required sample size that is made in those cases where the sample is expected to be equal to 5 percent or more of the total population.

In those situations where the sample is large (5 percent or more) in relation to the population, the researcher can appropriately reduce the required sample size using the FPC. This calculation is made using the following formula:

$$n' = \frac{nN}{N + n - 1}$$

where

n' = revised sample size
n = original sample size
N = population size

If the population has 2,000 elements and the original sample size is 400, then

$$n' = \frac{400(2{,}000)}{2{,}000 + 400 - 1} = \frac{800{,}000}{2{,}399}$$

$$n' = 333$$

Based on the FPC adjustment, we need a sample of only 333 rather than the original 400.

The key is not the size of the sample in relation to the size of the population, but whether the sample selected is truly representative of the population. Empirical evidence shows that relatively small but carefully chosen samples can quite accurately reflect characteristics of the population. Many well-known national surveys and opinion polls are based on samples of less than 2,000. The Gallup Poll, the Harris Poll, and the Nielsen Television Ratings are examples. These polls have shown that the behavior of tens of millions of people can be predicted quite accurately on the basis of samples that are minuscule in relation to the size of the population.

Determining Sample Size for Stratified and Cluster Samples

The formulas for sample size determination presented in this chapter apply only to simple random samples. There are also formulas for determining required sample size and sampling error for other types of probability samples such as stratified and cluster samples. Though many of the general concepts presented in this chapter apply to these other types of probability samples, the specific formulas are much more complicated.[4] In addition, these formulas require information that frequently is not available or difficult to obtain. For these reasons, sample size determination for other types of probability samples is beyond the scope of this introductory text. Those interested in pursuing the question of sample size determination for stratified and cluster samples are referred to advanced texts on the topic of sampling.

SUMMARY

Determining sample size involves financial, statistical, and managerial considerations. Other things being equal, the larger the sample the less the sampling error. In turn, the cost of the research grows with the size of the sample.

There are several methods for determining sample size. One is the funds that are available. In essence, sample size is determined by the budget. Although seemingly unscientific, this is often a very real factor in the world of corporate marketing research. The second technique is the so-called rule of thumb approach. It is basically a determination of the sample size by a "gut feel" or common practice. Often samples of 300, 400, or 500 are listed in requests for proposals. Yet another technique for determining sample size is based on the number of subgroups to be analyzed. Generally speaking, the more subgroups that need to be analyzed, the larger is the required total sample size.

In addition to these factors, there are a number of traditional statistical techniques for determining sample size. Three pieces of data are required to make sample size calculations: an estimate of a population standard deviation, the level of sampling error that the researcher or client is willing to accept, and the desired level of confidence that the population value will fall within the acceptable limits. Crucial to statistical sampling theory is the concept of the normal distribution. The normal distribution is bell-shaped and has only one mode. It is also symmetric about the mean. The standard normal distribution has the features of a normal distribution, however, the mean of the standard normal distribution is always equal to zero and the standard deviation is always equal to one. The transformation formula is used to transform any value X from any normal distribution to its equivalent value Z from a standard normal distribution. The central limit theorem states that the distribution of the means of a large number of random samples taken from virtually any population approaches a normal distribution with a mean equal to μ and a standard deviation equal to

$$S_{\bar{X}} = \frac{\sigma}{\sqrt{n}}$$

The standard deviation of a distribution of sample means is called the *standard error of the mean.*

When using the results of a sample to estimate a population mean, two kinds of estimates can be generated: point and interval estimates. For point estimates, the sample mean is the best estimate of the population mean. An interval estimate is an estimate regarding an interval or range of values of a variable that the researcher is attempting to estimate. Along with the magnitude of the interval, we also state the probability that the interval will take in the true value of the population mean; that is, the confidence level. The interval is the confidence interval.

The researcher who is interested in estimating proportions rather than means utilizes the sampling distribution of the proportion. The sampling distribution of the proportion is a relative frequency distribution of the sample proportions of a large number of samples of a given size drawn from a particular population. The standard error of a sampling distribution of proportions is computed as follows:

$$S_p = \sqrt{\frac{P(1 - P)}{n}}$$

The formula for calculating the required sample size for situations that involve the estimation of a mean is as follows:

$$n = \frac{Z^2 \sigma^2}{E^2}$$

To calculate sample size the following are required: specification of the acceptable level of sampling error (E), specification of the acceptable level of confidence in standard errors or Z values, and an estimate of the population standard deviation. To calculate the required sample size for problems involving proportions we use the following formula:

$$n = \frac{Z^2 [P(1-P)]}{E_2}$$

KEY TERMS

Normal distribution
Central limit theorem
Standard normal distribution
Standard deviation
Population distribution
Sample distribution
Sampling distribution of the sample
  mean
Standard error of the mean

Point estimates
Interval estimates
Confidence level
Sampling distribution of the
  proportion
Allowable sampling error
Population standard deviation
Finite population correction factor

REVIEW AND DISCUSSION QUESTIONS

1. Explain why the determination of sample size is a financial, statistical, and managerial issue.
2. Discuss and give examples of three methods for determining sample size.
3. A market researcher analyzing the fast-food industry noticed the following. The average amount spent at a fast-food restaurant in California was $3.30, and the standard deviation was $.40. Yet in Georgia, the average amount spent was $3.25 with a standard deviation of $.10. What do these statistics tell us about fast-food consumption expenditures in these two states?
4. Distinguish between population, sample, and sampling distributions.
5. What is the finite population correction factor? Why is it used? When should it be used?
6. Assume that previous fast-food research has shown that 80 percent of the consumers like curlicue french fries. The researcher wishes to have an error of 6 percent or less and be 95 percent confident of an estimate to be made about curlicue french fry consumption from a survey. What sample size is necessary?
7. A researcher at Disney World knows that 60 percent of the patrons like rollercoaster rides. The researcher wishes to have an error of no more than 2 percent and to be 90 percent confident about attitudes toward a new rollercoaster ride. What sample size is required?
8. You are in charge of planning a chili cook-off. You must make sure that there are plenty of samples for the patrons of the cook-off. The following standards have been set: a confidence level of 99 percent and an error of less than 4 ounces per cooking team. Last year's cook-off had a standard deviation in amount of chili cooked of 3 ounces. What would be the necessary sample size?

9. You are doing a survey of beer prices during spring break at Daytona Beach. Last year the average price per six-pack for premium beer was $3.00 with a standard deviation of $.20. Your survey requires a 95 percent confidence level with an acceptable level of error of $.10 per six-pack. Calculate the required sample size.

10. Based on a client's requirements of a confidence interval of 99 percent and acceptable sampling error of 2 percent, a sample size of 500 was calculated. The cost to the client would be $20,000. The client replies that the budget for this project is $17,000. What are the alternatives?

CASE

Baldweiner's Department Store

Baldweiner's target market is the middle- and upper-middle-income consumer, and the store is known primarily for having good, serviceable, yet not too fashionable lines of men's and women's clothing. It also carries popular names of perfumes, colognes, and so forth. Other departments in Baldweiner's include carpeting, china, custom draperies, fashion jewelry, fine jewelry, a fur salon, glassware, and housewares. Several years ago Baldweiner's gave up its major appliance business because of competition from the discounters.

Last year Baldweiner's management noticed a significant decrease in sales, much of which was in the areas of men's and women's apparel. Management was concerned that its target market customers were interested in more high-fashion merchandise. Thus, a market research study was commissioned to determine if Baldweiner's should attempt to stock more designer clothing in the men's, women's, and children's departments.

The interviews were going to be conducted in the consumers' homes and would probably be rather lengthy, lasting over an hour and thirty minutes. Baldweiner's planned to show respondents a number of potential lines that could be added, including examples of the clothing and information about the designers themselves, thus accounting for the lengthy interview. The cost of the marketing research project was also of concern to management because of a relatively tight budget due to declining overall sales. Thus, management was concerned with the number of interviews to be taken, because this naturally would affect the total cost of the project. Several scenarios were proposed to the market research service.

1. The estimated percentage of consumers who had shopped at Baldweiner's in the past six months is 75 percent, the allowable error is ± 10 percent, and the confidence level is 95 percent.

2. The estimated percentage of consumers who have shopped at Baldweiner's in the past six months is 80 percent, the allowable error is ± 10 percent, and the confidence level is 95 percent.

3. The estimated percentage of consumers who have shopped at Baldweiner's in the past six months is 85 percent, the allowable error is ± 10 percent, and the confidence level is 95 percent.

Management was also interested in the inferences that could be drawn from the sample after it had been taken. Management, therefore, asked for calculations of allowable errors under the following situations:

4. Given the sample size calculated in situation 2, a confidence level of 95 percent, and a sample percentage of consumers who have shopped at Baldweiner's in the past six months is found to be 75 percent.

5. Given the sample size calculated in situation 3, a confidence level of 95 percent, and a sample percentage of consumers who have shopped at Baldweiner's in the past six months is found to be 80 percent.

After receiving the calculations, management planned to decide what sample size to take based on its budgetary restrictions and other information presented.

1. What sample sizes should have been calculated for situations 1, 2, and 3?
2. What allowable errors should have been calculated for situations 4 and 5?

Ethical Dilemma——PART THREE

Dickson Research, Inc.

Dickson Research is a small, full-service custom marketing research firm located in Burlington, Vermont. Last year Dickson's total revenues were only $85,000. This was barely enough for Richard Dickson, his secretary, and one assistant to survive and pay all the bills. It is now late September and this year has been kinder to the organization than last. Total revenue to date is $95,000. The company is completing a major research project for a national consumer goods manufacturer. Dickson conducted a total of 800 interviews in ten different locations in enclosed malls. The company charged the client $40 per interview for a total of $32,000. This will be paid on completion and presentation of the final report, which is due next week. The data has now been cleaned and tabulated and Richard has just glanced at the first printout. To his horror, he notes that only 760 questionnaires were completed. Further checking reveals that two field services did not complete their quotas. One service in San Francisco was twenty-five interviews short and a second firm in Albuquerque, New Mexico, was fifteen interviews short. Because of the tight deadline, there is no time to return to the respective cities and get the 40 interviews required for the contract sample size of 800.

Richard's assistant notes that this is only about a 5 percent shortage from the total quota. He suggests that 40 questionnaires be randomly selected from the 760 interviews and simply replicated. He claims that replicating 40 interviews from a total of 760 is not going to have much impact on the total results. Besides, the responses are likely to be similar to what is already in the database. The client has demanded a full 800 interviews. Chances are that if the contract is not fully met, the firm will not pay for any of the survey. Not only will Dickson Research lose the $32,000 revenue, but it will be out the expense to all of the field services.

1. You are Richard Dickson. Would you replicate the forty interviews? Why or why not?
2. Given the time constraints, do you see any other alternatives that Richard might pursue?

PART 4

Data Analysis

_____

_____

_____

CHAPTER 13

Data Processing, Basic Data Analysis, and Statistical Testing of Differences

LEARNING OBJECTIVES

1. To develop an understanding of the importance and nature of quality control checks.

2. To understand the data entry process and data entry alternatives.

3. To learn how surveys are tabulated and crosstabulated.

4. To understand how to state and test hypotheses.

5. To describe several common statistical tests of differences.

R

ita Alvarez graduated from the University of Nebraska in June of 1994. She accepted a job with Transworld Insurance in July and started in its management training program at that time. She spent three months working in the human resources department and was assigned to the newly formed customer satisfaction measurement department in October 1994. Her boss, Janet Washington, was previously the director of customer service at the company and has no prior research experience. In September, the previous director of the customer satisfaction measurement department, who later left the company in a dispute over compensation, sent out mail surveys to 10,000 Transworld customers. Transworld has received 3,305 responses. Senior management is very anxious to see the results of these surveys so that it can assess customer satisfaction and make some key decisions about its customer service programs.

Rita's boss has been told that senior management wants tabulations of all the surveys and that it is very interested in crosstabulations of the customer satisfaction results by age of the customer. There is a general belief that the customer service programs have not been providing adequate service to older customers (over age sixty). In addition, Janet has been instructed to make extensive use of graphics in the management presentation that is scheduled in one month. She has assigned to Rita the task of preparing the tabulations, doing any necessary statistical analysis, and preparing the graphs for the report. Rita has consulted the marketing research text that she used in her college course in an attempt to figure out how to perform all the tasks necessary to complete the assignment. She is not totally comfortable with her knowledge in these areas.

The material in this chapter answers these and other questions. Consider the problems faced by Rita after you have completed the chapter. At this point, all data collection has been completed and all completed questionnaires have been returned from the field to the marketing research firm. The researcher is now confronted with a large stack of anywhere from a few hundred to several thousand interviews, and each interview may range from a few pages to twenty or more. A recent study completed by the authors involved 1,300 ten-page questionnaires. This amounted to a stack of paper nearly 3 feet high including 13,000 pages. How does the researcher transform all the information contained on the 13,000 pages of completed questionnaires into a form that will permit the summarization necessary for detailed analysis? At one extreme, the researcher could read all of the interviews, make notes while reading them, and draw some kind of conclusions from this review of the questionnaires. The folly of this approach is fairly obvious. Instead of this haphazard and inefficient approach, professional researchers follow a five-step procedure in regard to data analysis.

1. Validation and editing (quality control)
2. Coding
3. Data entry
4. Machine cleaning
5. Tabulation and statistical analysis

Each of these five steps is discussed in detail in subsequent sections of this chapter.

VALIDATION AND EDITING

The purpose of this step is to make sure that all of the interviews were actually conducted as specified (**validation**) and that the questionnaires have been filled out properly and completely (**editing**).

Validation

The first step is to determine, to the extent possible, that each of the questionnaires to be processed represents a valid interview. Here we are using the term *valid* in a different sense than in Chapter 9. In Chapter 9 *validity* was defined as the extent to which a measurement measures what it is supposed to measure. A valid interview in this case is one that was actually conducted in the appropriate manner. The goal is to detect interviewer fraud or failure to follow key instructions.[1] In the various questionnaire examples presented throughout the text, you may have noticed that there is almost always a place to record the respondent's name, address, and telephone number. This information is ordinarily not used in any way in the analysis of the data. It is collected only to provide a basis for *validation*.

Professional researchers know that interviewer cheating is not uncommon.[2] Various studies have documented the existence and prevalence of interviewer falsification of various types. For this reason, validation is an integral and necessary step in the data processing stage of a marketing research project.

After all of the interviews are completed, the research firm recontacts by telephone a certain percentage of the respondents surveyed by each interviewer. This applies to door-to-door, mall intercept, and telephone surveys. Normally this percentage ranges from 10 to 20 percent. Telephone validation typically covers five areas:

1. Was the person actually interviewed?
2. Did the person who was interviewed actually qualify to be interviewed according to the screening questions on the survey?
3. Was the interview conducted in the required manner? For example, a mall survey should have been conducted in the designated mall. Was this particular respondent actually interviewed in the mall, or was he or she interviewed at some other place such as a restaurant or a social gathering?
4. Did the interviewer cover the entire survey? Respondents for the particular survey may be very difficult to find, so the interviewer may be motivated to ask

Validation
The process of ascertaining that interviews actually were conducted as specified.

Editing
The process of ascertaining that questionnaires were filled out properly and completely.

this respondent a few questions at the beginning, a few questions at the end, and then fill out the rest of the interview himself or herself.

5. Finally, validation normally involves checking for other kinds of problems. Was the interviewer courteous? Was the interviewer neat in appearance? Does the respondent have any other negative comments about the interviewer or the interview experience?

The purpose of the validation process, as noted earlier, is to make sure that interviews were administered properly and in their entirety. Researchers must be sure that the research results on which they are basing their recommendations reflect the true responses of target consumers.

Editing

Whereas validation involves checking for interviewer cheating and failure to follow instructions, editing involves checking for interviewer mistakes. Questionnaires are normally edited at least twice before being submitted for data entry. First, they are edited by the field service firm that conducted the interviews, and then they are edited by the marketing research firm that hired the field service firm to do the interviewing. The editing process involves manual checking for a number of problems including the following:

1. *Determining whether the interviewer failed to ask or record answers for certain questions.* The purpose of the first edit—the field edit—is to identify these types of problems at a point when there is still time to recontact the respondent and determine the appropriate answer for the question that was not asked.[3]

Skip pattern
Requirement to pass over certain questions in response to the respondent's answer to a previous question.

2. *Questionnaires are checked to make sure that **skip patterns** were followed.* Sometimes, particularly during the first few interviews that they conduct on a particular study, interviewers may get mixed up and skip when they actually should not or fail to skip when they should.

3. *Responses to open-end questions are checked.* Marketing researchers and their clients are usually very interested in the responses to open-end questions. The quality of the response, or at least what was recorded, is an excellent indicator of the competence of the interviewer who recorded the response. Interviewers are normally trained to record responses verbatim and not paraphrase or insert their own language in any way.

The editing process is extremely tedious and time consuming. Imagine for a moment, reading through the 13,000 pages of interviews in the example cited earlier. However, editing is an important step in the data processing stage.

CODING

Coding Defined

Coding
The process of grouping and assigning numeric codes to the various responses to a question.

Coding refers to the process of grouping and assigning numeric codes to the various responses to a particular question.[4] Most questions on most surveys are closed-end and precoded. This means that numeric codes have been assigned to the various responses on the questionnaire itself. All closed-end questions should be precoded.

Open-end questions are another matter. They were stated as open-end questions because the researcher either had no idea what answers to expect or wanted a richer response than is possible with a closed-end question. As with editing, the process of coding responses to open-end questions is tedious and time consuming. In addition, the procedure is, to some degree, subjective. For these reasons there is some tendency to avoid open-end questions if at all possible.

The Coding Process

There are four steps in the process of coding responses to open-end questions:

1. *Listing responses.* Coders at the research firm prepare lists of the actual responses to each open-end question on a particular survey.
2. *Consolidating responses.* A sample list of responses to an open-end question is provided in Figure 13.1. Examination of this list indicates that a number of the responses can be interpreted to mean essentially the same thing; for example, the first three responses and probably the fourth. Therefore, they can be appropriately consolidated into a single category. After going through this process of consolidation, we end up with the list shown in Table 13.1. This is the final consolidated list of responses.

FIGURE 13.1   *Sample of Responses to Open-end Question*

Question: Why do you drink that brand of beer (BRAND MENTIONED IN PREVIOUS QUESTION) most often?

Sample Responses:

1. Because it tastes better.
2. It has the best taste.
3. I like the way it tastes.
4. I don't like the heavy taste of other beers.
5. It is the cheapest.
6. I buy whatever beer is on sale. It is on sale most of the time.
7. It doesn't upset my stomach the way other brands do.
8. Other brands give me headaches. This one doesn't.
9. It has always been my brand.
10. I have been drinking it for over 20 years.
11. It is the brand that most of the guys at work drink.
12. All my friends drink it.
13. It is the brand my wife buys at the grocery store.
14. It is my wife's/husband's favorite brand.
15. I have no idea.
16. Don't know.
17. No particular reason.

TABLE 13.1 *Consolidated Response Categories and Codes for Open-End Responses from Beer Study Introduced in Figure 13.1*

RESPONSE CATEGORY DESCRIPTOR	RESPONSE ITEMS FROM FIGURE 13.1 INCLUDED	ASSIGNED NUMERIC CODE
Tastes better/like taste/tastes better than others	1, 2, 3, 4	1
Low/lower price	5, 6	2
Does not cause headache, stomach problems	7, 8	3
Long-term use, habit	9, 10	4
Friends drink it/influence of friends	11, 12	5
Wife/husband drinks/buys it	13, 14	6
Don't know	15, 16, 17	7

3. *Setting codes.* This is done after the final consolidated list of responses has been derived. Numeric codes are assigned to each of the categories on the final consolidated list of responses. Code assignment for the sample beer study question is shown in Table 13.1.
4. *Entering codes.* After listing responses, consolidating responses, and setting codes, the final step involves the actual entry of codes. This involves several substeps:
   a. Read responses to individual open-end questions on questionnaires.
   b. Match individual responses with consolidated list of response categories developed in step 2.
   c. Get the numeric code for the category into which you classified the particular response.
   d. Write the numeric code in the appropriate place on the questionnaire for the response to the particular question (see Table 13.2).

DATA ENTRY

The questionnaires have now been validated, edited, and coded. We are ready for the next step in the process, data entry. The term *data entry* is used to refer to the process of converting information from a form that cannot be read by a computer to a form that can be read by a computer.[5] This process requires a data entry device and a storage medium. Data entry devices in use today include computer terminals and personal computers. Storage media used in connection

TABLE 13.2 *Example Questionnaire Setup for Open-End Questions*

37. Why do you drink that brand of beer (BRAND MENTIONED IN PREVIOUS QUESTION)?

(48) 2

Because it's cheaper. (P) Nothing. (AE) Nothing.

with the data entry include magnetic tape, floppy disks, and hard (magnetic) disks.

The Data Entry Process

The validated, edited, and coded questionnaires are given to a data entry operator seated in front of a personal computer or computer terminal and the actual data entry process is ready to begin. Normally, the data will be entered directly from the questionnaires. Data are normally not transferred from questionnaires to computer coding sheets by professional marketing researchers, because experience has shown that a large number of errors are made in the process of transposing data from the questionnaires to coding sheets. The process of going directly from the question- naire to the data entry device and the associated storage medium has proven to be more accurate and efficient.

Scanning

Scanning is another data collection approach that is becoming increasingly attractive. You are probably familiar with scanning in connection with some of the multiple-choice tests that you have taken. The traditional approach to scanning often used for college testing has been unacceptable for most marketing research applications because it requires a separate scoring sheet and the use of a number two pencil. However, recent developments in scanning technology have permitted the development of more respondent friendly approaches that integrate the questions and the answer sheet in a single document and do not require the use of a number two pencil.[6] Ball point pen, ink pen, felt tip pen, pencil, or virtually any other writing implement can be used and sucessfully scanned. In addition, the new technology does not require the respondent to shade the entire answer block. The block can be shaded, checked, x'd, or marked in any way and successfully scanned. This makes scanning an attractive option in almost any situation involving large numbers of questionnaires (more than 1,000).

Scanning
Using machines, called scanners, to read and record respondent answers from paper questionnaires.

MACHINE CLEANING OF DATA

At this point, the data from all questionnaires have been entered and stored in the computer that will be used to process them. It is time to do final error checking before proceeding to the tabulation and statistical analysis of the survey results. Most colleges have one or more statistical packages available for the tabulation and statistical analysis of data. You probably have access to SAS (Statistical Analysis System), SPSS (Statistical Package for the Social Sciences), or BMDP on a mainframe or minicomputer at your university. SAS, SPSS, SYSTAT, and many other statistical packages are also available for PCs in DOS and, more recently, Windows versions.[7]

Regardless of which computer package is used to tabulate the data, the first step is to do final error checking or what is sometimes referred to as **machine cleaning of data**. This may be done in one or both of two ways: error checking routines and marginal reports.

Machine cleaning of data
A final computerized error check of data.

TABLE 13.3 *Sample Marginal Report (Marginal Counts of 300 Records)*

COL	1	2	3	4	5	6	7	8	9	10	11	12	BL	TOT
1!1	100	100	1	0	0	0	0	0	0	99	0	0	0	300
1!2	30	30	30	30	30	30	30	30	30	0	0	0	0	300
1!3	30	30	30	30	30	30	30	30	30	30	0	0	0	300
1!4	67	233	0	0	0	0	0	0	0	0	0	0	0	300
1!5	192	108	0	0	0	0	0	0	0	0	0	0	0	300
1!6	108	190	0	0	0	0	0	0	0	0	0	2	0	300
1!7	13	35	8	0	2	136	95	7	2	0	0	0	2	298
1!8	0	0	0	0	0	0	0	0	0	0	0	2	298	2
1!9	29	43	12	1	2	48	50	6	4	1	0	0	104	196
1!11	6	16	6	1	1	10	18	4	2	0	0	0	236	64
1!13	3	4	1	1	0	1	2	0	1	0	0	0	288	12
1!15	0	0	0	1	1	0	0	2	0	0	0	0	296	4
1!17	24	2	22	0	1	239	9	2	0	0	0	0	1	299
1!18	0	0	0	0	0	0	0	0	0	0	0	1	299	1
1!19	4	49	6	0	0	81	117	5	2	0	0	0	36	264
1!20	0	0	0	0	0	0	0	0	0	0	0	36	264	36
1!21	5	60	6	0	0	84	116	4	3	1	0	0	21	279
1!22	0	0	0	0	0	0	0	0	0	0	0	21	279	21
1!23	118	182	0	0	0	0	0	0	0	0	0	0	0	300
1!24	112	187	0	0	0	0	0	0	0	0	0	0	1	299
1!25	47	252	0	0	0	0	0	0	0	0	0	1	0	300
1!26	102	198	0	0	0	0	0	0	0	0	0	0	0	300
1!27	5	31	5	1	0	33	31	9	1	0	0	0	184	116
1!28	0	0	0	0	0	0	0	0	0	0	0	2	298	2
1!29	0	3	1	0	0	4	8	2	1	0	0	0	281	19
1!31	7	16	3	0	2	60	21	3	0	0	0	0	188	112
1!33	1	3	1	0	0	2	3	1	0	0	0	0	289	11

Error checking routines
Computer programs that accept instructions from the user to check for logical errors in the data.

Some computer programs permit the user to write **error checking routines**. These routines include statements to check for various conditions. For example, if a particular field on the data records for a particular study should only have a 1 or a 2 code, a logical statement can be written to check for the presence of any other code in that field. Some of the more sophisticated packages generate reports indicating how many times a particular condition was violated and list the data records on which it was violated. With this list the user can refer to the original questionnaires and determine the appropriate values.

Another approach to machine cleaning often used for error checking is the **marginal report** or one-way frequency table. A sample marginal report is shown in Table 13.3. The rows of this report are the fields of the data record. The columns show the frequencies with which each possible value was encountered in each field. For example, the first row in Table 13.3 shows that in field 1 (column 1) of the data records for this study there are 100 "1" punches, 100 "2" punches, 1 "3" punch, and 99 "10" punches. This report permits the user to determine whether invalid codes were entered and whether skip patterns were followed properly. If all the numbers are consistent, there is no need for further cleaning. However, if logical errors are detected, then the appropriate original questionnaires must be located and the corrections must be made in the computer data file.

Marginal report
A computer-generated table of the frequencies of the responses to each question to monitor entry of valid codes and correct use of skip patterns.

This is the final error check in the process. When this step is completed, the computer data file should be "clean" and ready for tabulation and statistical analysis.

TABULATION OF SURVEY RESULTS

At this point the survey results are stored in a computer file and should be free of all logical data entry and interviewer recording error. By *logical errors* we mean violated skip patterns and impossible codes (a *3* was entered when *1* and *2* are the only possible codes). The procedures, described previously, cannot identify situations where an interviewer or data entry operator entered a *2* for a "no" response instead of the correct *1* for a "yes" response.[8] The next step is to tabulate the survey results.

One-Way Frequency Tables

The most basic tabulation is the **one-way frequency table**. An example of this type of table is shown in Table 13.4. A one-way frequency table shows the number of respondents who gave each possible answer to each question. Table 13.4 shows that 144 consumers (48 percent) said they would choose a hospital in Fort Worth, 146 (48.7 percent) said they would choose a hospital in Dallas, and 10 people (3.3 percent) said they didn't know which one they would choose. A computer printout will be generated showing one-way frequency tables for every question on the survey. In most instances, this will be the first summary of survey results seen by the research analyst.

In addition to frequencies, one-way frequency tables typically indicate the percentage of those responding to a question that gave each possible response.

One-way frequency table
A table showing the number of responses to each answer of a survey question.

Base for Percentages.   Another issue that must be dealt with at the time one-way frequency tables are run is the question of the bases to be used for the percentages for each table. There are three choices:

1. *Total respondents.* If 300 people are interviewed in a particular study, and the decision is to use total respondents as the base for calculating percentages, then the percentages in each one-way frequency table will be based on 300 respondents.

TABLE 13.4   *One-Way Frequency Table*

Q.30 If you or a member of your family were to require hospitalization in the future, and the procedure could be performed in Fort Worth or Dallas, where would you choose to go?

	TOTAL
Total	300
	100%
To a hospital in Fort Worth	144
	48.0%
To a hospital in Dallas	146
	48.7%
Don't know/No response	10
	3.3%

TABLE 13.5 *One-Way Frequency Table with Percents Shown for Total Respondents, Total Respondents Who Were Asked the Question, and Total Respondents Answering (gave response other than "don't know")*

Q.35 Why would you not consider going to Fort Worth for hospitalization?

	TOTAL* RESPONDENTS	TOTAL ASKED	TOTAL ANSWERING
Total	300 100%	60 100%	52 100%
They aren't good/poor service	18 6.0%	18 30.0%	18 34.6%
Fort Worth doesn't have the services/ equipment that Dallas does	17 5.7%	17 28.3%	17 32.7%
Fort Worth is too small	6 2.0%	6 10.0%	6 11.6%
Bad publicity	4 1.3%	4 6.7%	4 7.7%
Other	11 3.7%	11 18.3%	11 21.2%
Don't know/no response	8 2.7%	8 13.3%	

*A total of 300 respondents were surveyed. Only sixty answered this question because in the previous question they said they would not consider going to Fort Worth for hospitalization.

2. *Number of people asked the particular question.* Because most questionnaires have skip patterns, not all respondents will be asked all questions. For example, question 4 on a particular survey might have asked whether the person owned a dog or cat. Assume that 200 respondents indicated they owned a dog or a cat. If questions 5 and 6 on that same survey should have been asked only of those individuals who own a dog or a cat, then question 5 and question 6 should have been asked of only 200 respondents. In most instances, it is appropriate to use 200 as the base for percentages associated with the one-way frequency tables for questions 5 and 6.

3. *Number answering.* Another alternative base for computing percentages in one-way frequency tables is the number of people who actually answered a particular question. Under this approach, if 300 people were asked a particular question but 28 indicated "don't know," or gave no response to the particular question, then the base for the percentages would be 272.

Ordinarily, the number of people who were asked a particular question is used as the base for all percentages throughout the tabulations, but there may be special cases where other bases are judged appropriate. One-way frequency tables using the three different bases for calculating percentages are shown in Table 13.5.

Selecting the Base for One-Way Frequency Tables Showing Results from Multiple Response Questions. Some questions, by their nature, solicit more than one response from respondents. For example, consumers might be asked to name all the hospitals that come to mind. Most people will be able to name more than one hospital. Therefore, when these answers are tabulated there will be more responses than people. If 200 consumers are surveyed and the average consumer names three hospitals, then the 200 respondents will have given 600 answers. The question is, Should percentages in frequency tables showing the results to these questions be based on the number of respondents, or the number of responses? Common practice among marketing researchers is to compute percentages for multiple response questions on the basis of the number of respondents. This is based on the logic that we are primarily interested in the proportion of people that gave a particular answer.

Crosstabulations

Crosstabulations are likely to be the next step in analysis. They represent a simple to understand, yet powerful analytical tool. Many marketing research studies, possibly most, go no further than crosstabulations in terms of analysis. The idea is to look at the responses to one question in relation to the responses to one or more other questions. Table 13.6 shows a simple crosstabulation. Here we are examining the relationship between cities consumers are willing to consider for hospitalization and their age. This crosstabulation shows frequencies and percentages, and the percentages are based on column totals. This table shows an interesting relationship between age and likelihood of choosing Fort Worth or Dallas for hospitalization. Consumers in successively older age groups are increasingly likely to choose Fort Worth and increasingly less likely to choose Dallas.

Crosstabulation
Examination of the responses to one question relative to responses to one or more other questions.

There are a number of considerations regarding the setup and percentaging of crosstabulation tables.[9] Some of the more important ones are summarized:

- The previous discussion regarding the selection of the appropriate base for percentages, and the appropriate base for the percentaging of tables with multiple responses apply to crosstabulation tables as well.
- Three different percentages may be calculated for each cell in a crosstabulation table: column, row, and total percentages. Column percentages are computed on the basis of the column total, row percentages are based on the row total, and total

---

TABLE 13.6 *Simple Crosstabulation*

Q.30. If you or a member of your family were to require hospitalization in the future, and the procedure could be performed in Fort Worth or Dallas, where would you choose to go?

	TOTAL	AGE 18–34	35–54	55–64	65 or OVER
Total	300 100%	65 100%	83 100%	51 100%	100 100%
To a hospital in Fort Worth	144 48.0%	21 32.3%	40 48.2%	25 49.0%	57 57.0%
To a hospital in Dallas	146 48.7%	43 66.2%	40 48.2%	23 45.1%	40 40.0%
Don't know/no response	10 3.3%	1 1.5%	3 3.6%	3 5.9%	3 3.0%

percentages are based on the total for the table. Table 13.7 shows a crosstabulation table with frequencies and all three of the percents shown for each cell in the table.

■ A common way of setting up crosstabulation tables is to create a table where the columns represent various factors such as demographics and lifestyle characteristics that are expected to be predictors of the state of mind, behavior, or intentions data shown as rows of the table. In such tables, percentages are normally calculated on the basis of column totals. This approach permits easy comparisons of the relationship between the state of mind, behavior, or intentions data and expected predictors such as sex or age. The question might be, How do people in different age groups differ in regard to the particular factor under examination? An example of this type of table is shown in Table 13.6.

Crosstabulations provide a powerful and easily understood approach to the summarization and analysis of survey research results. However, it is easy to become swamped by the sheer volume of computer printouts if a careful tabulation plan has not been developed. The crosstabulation plan should be developed with the research objectives and hypotheses in mind. The results to a particular survey might be crosstabulated in an almost endless number of ways. This is why it is important for the analyst to exercise some judgment and select from all possibilities those crosstabulations truly responsive to the research objectives of the project. SAS, SPSS, BMDP, and most other statistical packages can generate crosstabulations. Later in this chapter we will discuss the chi-square test. This test can be used to determine whether the results in a particular crosstabulation table are significantly

TABLE 13.7 *Crosstabulation Table with Row, Column, and Total Percentages**

Q.34 To which of the following towns and cities would you consider going for hospitalization?

	TOTAL	MALE	FEMALE
Total	300	67	233
	100%	100%	100%
	100%	22.3%	77.7%
	100%	22.3%	77.7%
Fort Worth	265	63	202
	88.3%	94.0%	86.7%
	100%	23.6%	76.2%
	88.3%	21.0%	67.3%
Dallas	240	53	187
	80.0%	79.1%	80.3%
	100%	22.1%	77.9%
	80.0%	17.7%	62.3%
Waco	112	22	90
	37.3%	32.8%	38.6%
	100%	19.6%	80.4%
	37.3%	7.3%	30.0%

*Percentages listed are column, row, and total percentages, respectively.

TABLE 13.8 *A More Complex Crosstabulation Table (sometimes referred to as a stub and banner table)*

North Community College—Anywhere, U.S.A.
Q.1c. Are you currently single, married, or formerly married?

	Total	ZONES			GENDER		AGE			RACE			FAMILY PROFILE		VOTE HISTORY		REGISTERED VOTER	
		1	*2*	*3*	*M*	*F*	*18-34*	*35-54*	*55 and Over*	*White*	*Black*	*Other*	*Child <18*	*Child >18*	*2×-3×*	*4× or more*	*Yes*	*No*
Total	300	142	103	55	169	131	48	122	130	268	28	4	101	53	104	196	72	228
	100%	100%	100%	100%	100%	100%	100%	100%	100%	100%	100%	100%	100%	100%	100%	100%	100%	100%
Married	228	105	87	36	131	97	36	97	95	207	18	3	82	39	80	148	58	170
	76%	74%	84%	65%	78%	74%	75%	80%	73%	77%	64%	75%	81%	74%	77%	76%	81%	75%
Single	5	1	2	2	4	1	2	1	2	5	—	—	—	—	2	3	1	4
	2%	1%	2%	4%	2%	1%	4%	1%	2%	2%					2%	2%	1%	2%
Formerly married	24	11	10	3	12	12	3	9	12	18	6	—	5	6	10	14	3	21
	8%	8%	10%	5%	7%	9%	6%	7%	9%	7%	21%		5%	11%	10%	7%	4%	9%
Refused to answer	43	25	4	14	22	21	7	15	21	38	4	1	14	8	12	31	10	33
	14%	18%	4%	25%	13%	16%	15%	12%	16%	14%	14%	25%	14%	15%	12%	16%	14%	14%

different from what we would expect. In other words, for example, are the response patterns of men significantly different than those of women. This statistical procedure enables us to determine whether the differences between two groups likely occurred due to chance or likely reflect real differences between the groups.

A more complex crosstabulation is shown in Table 13.8. It was generated using the UNCLE software package. UNCLE was designed with the special needs of marketing researchers in mind and is widely used in the marketing research industry. As indicated, this more complex table is sometimes referred to as a *stub and banner table*. The column headings are referred to as the *banner* and the row titles are referred to as the *stub*. In this table, the relationship between marital status and seven other variables is explored.

GRAPHIC REPRESENTATIONS OF DATA

You have heard the saying, "one picture is worth a thousand words." Graphic presentation involves the use of "pictures" rather than tables to present research results. Results, particularly key results, can be presented more powerfully and efficiently by means of graphs. Crosstabulations and statistical analyses help us identify important findings. Graphs are the best way to present those findings to the users of our research.

Marketing researchers have probably always known that results could be best presented graphically. However, until recent years the preparation of graphs was tedious, difficult, and time consuming. The advent of personal computers, coupled with graphics software and graphics printers has changed all of this. Nearly all spreadsheet programs, such as Lotus 1-2-3, have a graphics capability. In addition, many programs designed specifically to produce high-quality graphics, such as Power Point and Harvard Graphics, are available. With these programs, it is possible to

- Quickly produce graphs
- Display those graphs on the computer screen
- Make desired changes and redisplay
- Print final copies on a laser or dot matrix graphics printer

All the graphs shown in this section were produced using a personal computer, laser printer, and a graphics software package.[10]

Line Charts

Line charts are perhaps the simplest form of graphs. They are particularly useful for presenting measurements taken at a number of points over time. Top-of-mind awareness measurements for Sound City are shown in Figure 13.2. The data are taken from tracking research conducted for Sound City during 1993 and 1994.

The results show an upward trend in top-of-mind awareness with annual peaks in July followed by declines. This is consistent with the scheduling of Sound City advertising. In each year they spent approximately two-thirds of their budget in the April through June period.

FIGURE 13.2   *Top of Mind Awareness of Sound City*

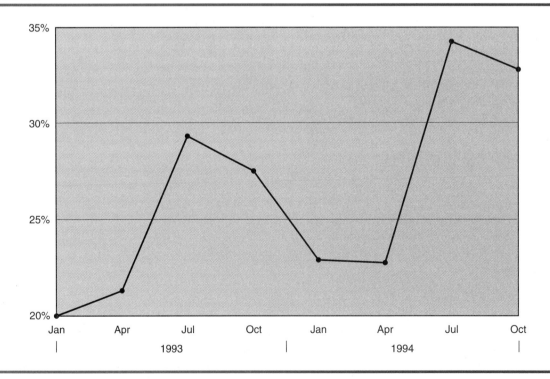

FIGURE 13.3   *City-Hospital Preference*

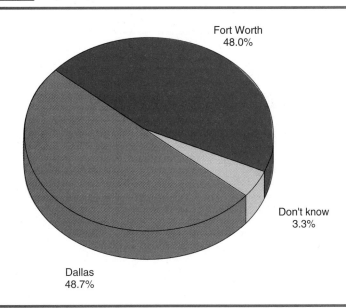

Pie Charts

Pie charts are another frequently used type of graph. They are appropriate for the display of marketing research results in a wide range of situations. Data from the first column of Table 13.6 are shown in Figure 13.3. Note the three-dimensional effect produced by the software.

Bar Charts

Bar charts are the most flexible of the three types of graphs discussed in this section. Anything that can be shown in a line graph or a pie chart can also be shown in a bar chart. In addition, many things that cannot be shown or effectively shown with other types of graphs can readily be shown with bar charts. Four types of bar charts are discussed here.

1. *Plain bar chart.* As the name suggests, plain bar charts are the simplest form of bar chart. The same information displayed in the previous section in a pie chart is shown in a bar chart in Figure 13.4. Draw your own conclusions regarding whether the pie chart or the bar chart is the most effective way to present this information. Figure 13.4 is shown as a traditional two-dimensional chart. Many of the software packages available today can take the same information and present it with a three-dimensional effect. The same information is shown with this effect in Figure 13.5. Again, decide which approach is visually most appealing and interesting.
2. *Clustered bar charts.* Clustered bar charts represent the first of three types of bar charts that are useful for showing the results of cross-tabulations. Total results

FIGURE 13.4 *City-Hospital Preference*

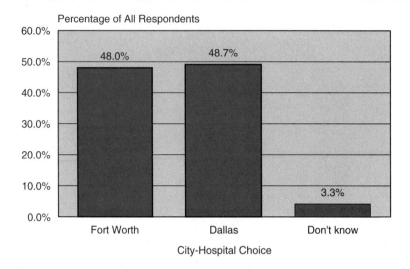

and results for different age groups for Table 13.6 are presented in Figure 13.6. For purposes of simplicity, the four age groups presented in the table (18–34, 35–54, 55–64, and 65 or over) have been reduced to two age groups (18–54 and 55 or over).

3. *Stacked bar charts.* The same information presented in Figure 13.6 is presented in the form of a stacked bar chart in Figure 13.7.

4. *Multiple row, three-dimensional bar charts.* This approach provides what we believe to be the most visually appealing way of presenting cross-table information. The same information displayed in Figures 13.6 and 13.7 is presented in a multiple row, three-dimensional bar chart in Figure 13.8.

FIGURE 13.5 *City-Hospital Preference (three-dimensional effect)*

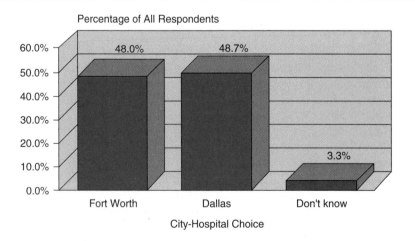

FIGURE 13.6   *Relationship Between Age and City-Hospital Preference (clustered bar)*

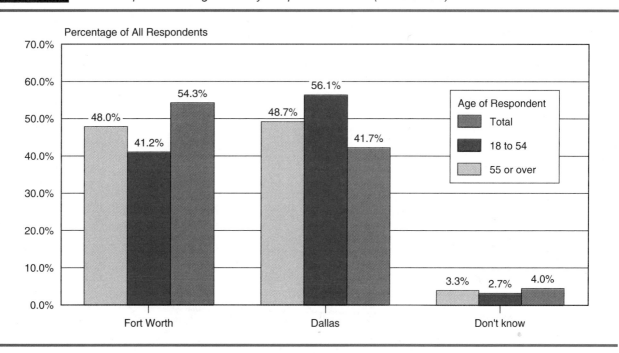

FIGURE 13.7   *Relationship between Age and City-Hospital Preference (stacked bar)*

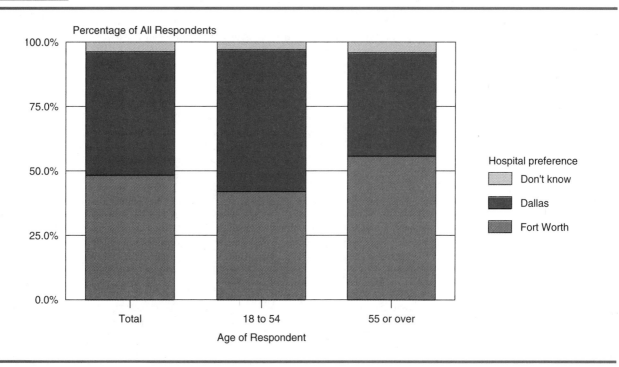

FIGURE 13.8 *Relationship between Age and City-Hospital Preference (multirow, three-dimensional bar)*

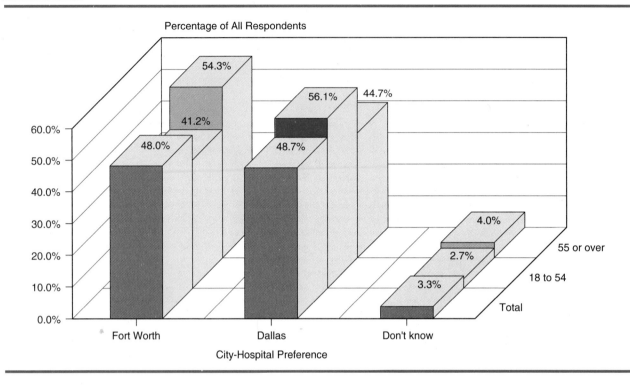

DESCRIPTIVE STATISTICS

Statistical measures represent even more powerful ways of summarizing the characteristics of large sets of data. In the case of statistical analysis, the analyst calculates one number or a few numbers that reveal something about the characteristics of large sets of data.

Measures of Central Tendency

There are three measures of central tendency: the arithmetic mean, median, and mode. Before beginning this section, it would be a good idea to review the types of data scales presented in Chapter 9. There are four basic types of scales: nominal, ordinal, interval, and ratio. Nominal and ordinal scales are sometimes referred to as *nonmetric data scales,* whereas interval and ratio scales are referred to as *metric scales.* Many of the statistical procedures discussed in this section and in following sections require metric data, and others are designed for nonmetric data.

The arithmetic **mean** is properly computed only from interval or ratio scale (metric) data. It is computed by adding the values for all observations for a particular variable such as age and dividing the resulting sum by the number of observations. When working with survey data, the exact value of the variable may not be known but it may be known that the particular case falls in a particular category. For example, an age category on a survey might be 18–34 years of age. If

Mean
The sum of the values for all observations of a variable divided by the number of observations.

a person falls in this particular category, we do not know the person's exact age only that it is somewhere between 18 and 34. In group data, the midpoint of each category is multiplied by the number of observations in that category, the resulting totals are summed, and the total is divided by the total number of observations. This process is summarized in the following formula:

$$\overline{X} = \frac{\sum\limits_{i=1}^{h} f_i X_i}{n}$$

where

f_i = the frequency of the ith class

X_i = the midpoint of that class

h = the number of classes

n = the total number of observations

The **median** can be computed for all types of data except nominal data. It is calculated by finding the value below which 50 percent of the observations fall. If all of the values for a particular variable were put in an array in either ascending or descending order, the median would be the middle value in that array. The median is often used for variables such as income where the researcher is concerned that the arithmetic mean will be affected by a few extreme values and not accurately reflect the predominant central tendency for that variable for that group.

The **mode** can be computed with any type of data (nominal, ordinal, interval, ratio). It is determined by finding the value that occurs most frequently. In a frequency distribution, the mode is the value of the variable that has the highest frequency. One problem with the mode is that a particular data set may have more than one mode. If three different values occur with the same level of frequency and that frequency is higher than for any other value, then that data set has three modes. The mean, median, and mode for sample data on beer consumption are shown in Table 13.9.

Median
The observation below which 50 percent of the observations fall.

Mode
The value that occurs most frequently.

Measures of Dispersion

Frequently used measures of dispersion include the standard deviation, variance, and range. Whereas measures of central tendency indicate typical values for a particular variable, measures of dispersion indicate how "spread out" the data are. The dangers associated with relying only on measures of central tendency are suggested by the example shown in Table 13.10.

The formula for computing the **standard deviation** for a sample of observations is as follows:

$$S = \sqrt{\frac{\sum\limits_{i=1}^{n} (X_i - \overline{X})^2}{n-1}}$$

S = sample standard deviation

X_i = the value of the ith observation

Standard deviation
The square root of the sum of the squared deviations from the mean divided by the number of observations minus 1.

TABLE 13.9   *Mean, Median, and Mode*

A total of ten beer drinkers (drink one or more cans, bottles, or glasses of beer per day on the average) were interviewed in a mall intercept study. They were asked how many cans, bottles, or glasses of beer they drink in an average day. Their responses are summarized.

RESPONDENT	NUMBER OF CANS/ BOTTLES/GLASSES PER DAY
1	2
2	2
3	3
4	2
5	5
6	1
7	2
8	2
9	10
10	1

Mode = 2 cans/bottles/glasses

Median = 2 cans/bottles/glasses

Mean = 3 cans/bottles/glasses

TABLE 13.10   *Measures of Dispersion and Measures of Central Tendency*

Consider the beer drinker example presented in Table 13.9. Assume that interviewing was conducted in two markets. The results for both markets are shown.

RESPONDENT	NUMBER OF CANS/ BOTTLES/GLASSES MARKET ONE	NUMBER OF CANS/ BOTTLES/GLASSES MARKET TWO
1	2	1
2	2	1
3	3	1
4	2	1
5	5	1
6	1	1
7	2	1
8	2	3
9	10	10
10	1	10
Mean	3	3
Standard deviation	2.7	3.7

Average beer consumption is the same in both markets—3 cans/bottles/glasses. However, the standard deviation is larger in Market Two, indicating more dispersion in the data. Whereas the mean suggests the two markets are the same, the added information provided by the standard deviation tells us they are different.

$\overline{X}$ = the sample mean

n = the sample size

The **variance** is calculated by using the same formula as for the standard deviation with the exception that the square-root sign is removed. Finally, the **range** is equal to the maximum value for a particular variable minus the minimum value for that variable.

STATISTICAL SIGNIFICANCE

The basic motive for making statistical inferences is to be able to generalize from sample results to population characteristics. A basic tenet of statistical inference is that it is possible for numbers to be different in a mathematical sense but not significantly different in a statistical sense. For example, a sample of cola drinkers is asked to try two cola drinks in a blind taste test and indicate which they prefer. The results show that 51 percent prefer one test product and 49 percent prefer the other. There is a mathematical difference in the results, but the difference would appear to be minor and unimportant. The difference is probably well within the range of accuracy of our ability to measure taste preference, and the difference is probably not significant in a statistical sense. Three different concepts can be applied to the notion of differences.

■ *Mathematical differences.* By definition, if numbers are not exactly the same, they are different. This does not, however, suggest that the difference is either important or statistically significant.

Variance

The sums of the squared deviations from the mean divided by the number of observations minus 1.

Range

The maximum value for a variable minus the minimum value for that variable.

If 51 percent of cola testers prefer one test product and 49 percent prefer the other, the difference is probably not statistically significant. (Jim Richardson/Woodfin Camp & Associates, Inc.)

- *Statistical significance.* If a particular difference is large enough to be unlikely to have occurred due to chance or sampling error, then the difference is statistically significant.
- *Managerially important differences.* If results or numbers are different to the extent that the difference would matter from a managerial perspective, we can argue that the difference is important. For example, the difference in consumer response to two different packages in a test market might be statistically significant but yet so small as to have little practical or managerial significance.[11]

Different approaches for testing whether results are statistically significant will be discussed below.

HYPOTHESIS TESTING

Hypotheses
Assumptions or theories that a researcher or manager makes about some characteristic of the population under study.

A **hypothesis** can be defined as an assumption or guess that a researcher or manager makes about some characteristic of the population being investigated. The marketing researcher is often faced with the question of whether research results are different enough from the norm to conclude that some element of the firm's marketing strategy should be changed. Consider the following situations.

- The results of a tracking survey show that awareness of the product is lower than it was in a similar survey conducted six months ago. Is the result significantly lower? Is the result sufficiently lower to call for a change in advertising strategy?
- A product manager believes that the average purchaser of his product is 35 years of age. A survey is conducted to test this hypothesis, and the survey shows that the average purchaser of the product is 38.5 years of age. Is the survey result enough different from the product manager's belief to conclude that the belief is incorrect?
- The marketing director of a fast-food chain believes that 60 percent of her customers are female and 40 percent are male. She does a survey to test this hypothesis and finds that, according to the survey, 55 percent are female and 45 percent are male. Is this result sufficiently different from her original theory to permit her to conclude that her original theory was incorrect?

All these questions can be evaluated with some kind of statistical test. In hypothesis testing, the researcher determines whether a hypothesis concerning some characteristic of the population is likely given the evidence. A statistical hypothesis test allows us to calculate the probability of observing a particular result if the stated hypothesis is actually true.

There are two basic explanations for observing a difference between a hypothesized value and a particular research result: either the hypothesis is true and the observed difference is quite likely due to sampling error; or the hypothesis is most likely false and the true value is some other value.

Five basic steps are involved in testing a hypothesis.

Stating the Hypothesis. Hypotheses are stated using two basic forms: the null hypothesis H_0 and the alternative hypothesis H_a. The null hypothesis H_0 (sometimes called the *hypothesis of the status quo*) is the hypothesis that is tested against its complement, the alternative hypothesis, H_a (sometimes called the *research hypothesis of interest*). For example, the manager of Burger City believes that his operational procedures will guarantee that the average customer will have to wait two minutes in the drive-in window line. He conducts research based on the observation of 1,000 customers at randomly selected stores at randomly selected times. The average customer observed in this study spent 2.4 minutes in the drive-in window line. The null hypothesis and the alternative hypothesis might be stated as follows:

Null hypothesis H_0: Mean waiting time $= 2$ minutes.
Alternative hypothesis H_a: Mean waiting time $\neq 2$ minutes.

It should be noted that the null hypothesis and the alternative hypothesis must be stated in such a way that both cannot be true. The idea is to use the available evidence to ascertain which hypothesis is more likely to be true.

Choosing the Appropriate Test Statistic. As you will see in the following sections of this chapter, the analyst must choose the appropriate statistical test given the characteristics of the situation under investigation. A number of different statistical tests and the situations where they are appropriate are discussed in this chapter. Table 13.11 provides a guide to selecting the appropriate test for various situations.

Developing a Decision Rule. Based on our previous discussions of distributions of sample means, you may recognize that it is very unlikely to get a sample result that is exactly equal to the value of the population parameter. The problem is one of determining whether the difference or deviation between the value of the actual sample mean and its expected value based on the hypothesis could have occurred by chance 5 times out of 100, for example, if the statistical hypothesis is true. A decision rule or standard is needed to determine whether to reject or fail to reject the null hypothesis. Statisticians state such decision rules in terms of significance levels.

The significance level (α) is critical in the process of choosing between the null and alternative hypotheses. The level of significance is the probability that is considered too low—.10, .05 or .01, for example—to justify acceptance of the null hypothesis.

Consider a situation where we have decided that we want to test a hypothesis at the .05 level of significance. This means that we will reject the null hypothesis if the test indicates that the probability of occurrence of the observed result (e.g., difference between the sample mean and its expected value) due to chance or sampling error is less than 5 percent. Rejection of the null hypothesis is equivalent to supporting the alternative hypothesis.

Calculating the Value of the Test Statistic. In this step we

- Use the appropriate formula to calculate the value of the statistic for the test chosen.
- Compare the value calculated (previously) to the critical value of the statistic (from the appropriate table) based on the decision rule chosen.
- Based on your comparison, state the result in terms of either rejecting or failing to reject the null hypothesis (H_0).

Stating the Conclusion. Make a statement of your conclusion that summarizes the results of your test. State your conclusion from the perspective of the original research question.

TABLE 13.11   *Statistical Tests and Their Uses*

AREA OF APPLICATION	SUBGROUPS OR SAMPLES	LEVEL OF SCALING	TEST	SPECIAL REQUIREMENTS	EXAMPLE
Hypotheses about frequency distributions	One	Nominal	X^2	Random sample	Are observed differences in the numbers responding to three different promotions likely/not likely due to chance?
	Two or more	Nominal	X^2	Random sample, independent samples	Are differences in the numbers of men and women responding to a promotion likely/not likely due to chance?
	One	Ordinal	K–S	Random sample, natural order in data	Is the observed distribution of women preferring an ordered set of make-up colors (light to dark) likely/not likely due to chance?
Hypotheses about means	One (large sample)	Metric (interval or ratio)	Z-test for one mean	Random sample, $n \geqslant 30$	Is the observed difference between a sample estimate of the mean and some set standard or expected value of the mean likely/not likely due to chance?
	One (small sample)	Metric (interval or ratio)	t-test for one mean	Random sample, $n < 30$	Sample as for small sample
	Two (large sample)	Metric (interval or ratio)	Z-test for two means	Random sample, $n \geqslant 30$	Is the observed difference between the means for two subgroups (mean income for men and women) likely/not likely due to chance?
	Two (small sample)	Metric (interval or ratio)	One-way ANOVA	Random sample	Is the observed variation between means for three or more subgroups (mean expenditures on entertainment for high, moderate, and low-income people) likely/not likely due to chance?
Hypotheses about proportions	One (large sample)	Metric (interval or ratio)	Z-test for one proportion	Random sample, $n \geqslant 30$	Is the observed difference between a sample estimate of proportion (percentage who say they will buy) and some set standard or expected value likely/not likely due to chance?
	Two (large sample)	Metric (interval or ratio)	Z-test for two proportions	Random sample, $n \geqslant 30$	Is the observed difference between estimated percentages for two subgroups (percentage of men and women who have college degrees) likely/not likely due to chance?

HYPOTHESIS TESTS

Three commonly used statistical hypothesis tests of differences are presented in the following section. Many other statistical tests have been developed and are used, but a full discussion of all of them is beyond the scope of this text.

The distributions used in the following section for comparing the computed and tabular values of the statistics are the Z-distribution, the t-distribution, and the chi-square (X^2) distribution. The tabular values for these distributions appear in Tables 2, 3, and 4 of the statistical appendix.

Independent versus Related Samples

In some cases one may need to test the hypothesis that the value of a variable in one population is equal to the value of that same variable in another population. The selection of the appropriate test statistic requires the researcher to consider whether the samples are independent or related. **Independent samples** involve situations where measurement of the variable of interest in one sample has no effect on the measurement of the variable in the other sample. It is not necessary that there be two different surveys, only that the measurement of the variable in one population has no effect on the measurement of the variable in the other population. In the case of **related samples**, the measurement of the variable of interest in one sample may influence the measurement of the parameter of interest in another sample.

If, for example, men and women were interviewed in a particular survey regarding their frequency of eating out, there is no way that a man's response could affect or change the way a woman would respond to the question in this survey. This would be an example of independent samples. On the other hand, consider a situation where the researcher needed to determine the effect of a new advertising campaign on consumer awareness of a particular brand. To do this, the researcher might survey a random sample of consumers before introducing the new campaign and survey the same sample of consumers ninety days after the new campaign was introduced. These samples are not independent. The measurement of awareness ninety days after the start of the campaign may be affected by the first measurement.

Independent samples
Samples in which measurement of a variable in one population has no effect on the measurement of the variable in the other.

Related samples
Samples in which the measurement of a variable in one population may influence the measurement of the variable in the other.

Degrees of Freedom

As you will see, many of the statistical tests discussed in this chapter require the researcher to specify degrees of freedom in order to find the critical value of the test statistic from the table for that statistic. Degrees of freedom are the number of observations in a statistical problem that are not restricted or are free to vary.

The number of degrees of freedom (d.f.) is equal to the number of observations minus the number of assumptions or constraints necessary to calculate a statistic. For example, consider the problem of adding five numbers when, for example, the mean of the five numbers is known to be 20. In this situation, only four of the five numbers are free to vary because once four of the numbers are known, the last value is also known (can be calculated) because the mean value must be 20. If we knew that four of the five numbers were 14, 23, 24, and 18, then the fifth number must be 21 to produce a mean of 20. We would say that the sample has $n - 1$ degrees of freedom. It is as if the sample had one less observation. The inclusion of degrees of freedom in this calculation adjusts for this fact.

GOODNESS OF FIT

Chi-Square

Chi-square test
Test of the goodness of fit between the observed distribution and the expected distribution of a variable.

Data collected in surveys, as noted earlier in the text, are often analyzed by means of one-way frequency counts and crosstabulations. The purpose of crosstabulation is to study relationships among variables. The question is, Does the number of responses that fall into different categories differ from what one would expect? This could involve partitioning users into groups such as gender (male, female), age (under 18, 18–35, over 35), or income level (low, middle, high) and crosstabulating by the results to questions such as preferred brand or level of use. The **chi-square** (χ^2) **test** enables the research analyst to determine whether an observed pattern of frequencies corresponds to or fits an "expected" pattern.[12] It tests the "goodness of fit" of the observed distribution in relation to an expected distribution. In the following section, we will describe the application of this technique to test distributions of crosstabulated categorical data for two independent samples.

Chi-Square Test of Two Independent Samples

Marketing researchers often need to determine whether there is any association between two or more variables. Questions such as, Are men and women equally divided into heavy, medium, and light user categories? or, Are purchasers and nonpurchasers equally divided into low, middle, and high income groups? may need to be answered prior to formulation of a marketing strategy. The chi-square (χ^2) test for two independent samples is the appropriate test in this situation.

This technique is illustrated using the data from Table 13.12. A convenience store chain wants to determine the nature of the relationship, if any, between gender of customer and frequency of visiting stores in the chain. Frequency of visits has been divided into three categories: 1–5 visits per month (light user), 6–14 visits per month (medium user), and 15 and above visits per month (heavy user). The steps necessary for conducting this test follow.

1. State the null and alternative hypotheses.
    Null hypothesis H_0: There is no relationship between gender and frequency of visit.
    Alternative hypothesis H_a: There is a significant relationship between gender and frequency of visit.
2. Place the observed (sample) frequencies in a $k \times r$ table (crosstabulation or contingency table) using the k columns for the sample groups and the r rows for the conditions or treatments. Calculate the sum of each row and each column. Record those totals at the margins of the table (they are called *marginal totals*). Also, calculate the total for the entire table (N).

Frequency of Visits	Male	Female	Totals
1–5	14	26	40
6–14	16	34	50
15 and Above	15	11	26
Totals	45	71	116

TABLE 13.12   *Data for χ^2 Two Independent Sample Test*

	VISITS TO CONVENIENCE STORE BY MALES			VISITS TO CONVENIENCE STORE BY FEMALES			
X_m	Frequency f_m	Percent	Cumulative Percent	Number X_{1f}	Frequency f_{1f}	Cumulative Percent	Percent
2	2	4.4	4.4	2	5	7.0	7.0
3	5	11.1	15.6	3	4	5.6	12.7
5	7	15.6	31.1	4	7	9.9	22.5
6	2	4.4	35.6	5	10	14.1	36.6
7	1	2.2	37.8	6	6	8.5	45.1
8	2	4.4	42.2	7	3	4.2	49.3
9	1	2.2	44.4	8	6	8.5	57.7
10	7	15.6	60.0	9	2	2.8	60.6
12	3	6.7	66.7	10	13	18.3	78.9
15	5	11.1	77.8	12	4	5.6	84.5
20	6	13.3	91.1	15	3	4.2	88.7
23	1	2.2	93.3	16	2	2.8	91.5
25	1	2.2	95.6	20	4	5.6	97.2
30	1	2.2	97.8	21	1	1.4	98.6
40	1	2.2	100.0	25	1	1.4	100.0

Total $n_m = 45$ $n_f = 71$

$$\text{Mean number of visits by males, } \bar{X}_m = \frac{\sum X_m f_m}{45} = 11.49$$

$$\text{Mean number of visits by females, } \bar{X}_1 = \frac{\sum X_f f_f}{71} = 8.51$$

3. Determine the expected frequency for each cell in the contingency table by calculating the product of the two marginal totals common to that cell and dividing that value by N.

	Male	Female
1–5	$\dfrac{45 \times 40}{116} = 15.52$	$\dfrac{71 \times 40}{116} = 24.48$
6–14	$\dfrac{45 \times 50}{116} = 19.40$	$\dfrac{71 \times 50}{116} = 30.60$
15 and Above	$\dfrac{45 \times 26}{116} = 10.09$	$\dfrac{71 \times 26}{116} = 15.91$

The χ^2 value will be distorted if more than 20 percent of the cells have an expected frequency of less than 5 or if any cell has an expected frequency of less than 1. The test should not be used under these conditions.

4. Calculate the value of χ^2 using

$$X^2 = \sum_{i=1}^{r} \sum_{j=1}^{k} \frac{(O_{ij} - E_{ij})^2}{E_{ij}}$$

where

$$O_{ij} = \text{observed number in the } i\text{th row of the } j\text{th column}$$
$$E_{ij} = \text{expected number in the } i\text{th row of the } j\text{th column}$$

For our example,

$$\chi^2 = \frac{(14 - 15.52)^2}{15.52} + \frac{(26 - 24.48)^2}{24.48} + \frac{(16 - 19.4)^2}{19.4}$$
$$+ \frac{(34 - 30.6)^2}{30.6} + \frac{(15 - 10.09)^2}{10.09} + \frac{(11 - 15.91)^2}{15.91}$$
$$\chi^2 = 5.12$$

5. The tabular χ^2 value at a .05 level of significance, and $(r - 1)(k - 1) = 2$ degrees of freedom is 5.99 (see Table 4 of the statistical appendix). Because the calculated $\chi^2 = 5.12$ is less than the tabular value, we *fail to reject the null (FTR) hypothesis* and conclude that there is no significant difference between males and females in terms of frequency of their visits.

HYPOTHESES ABOUT PROPORTIONS

In many situations researchers are concerned with phenomena that are expressed as percentages.[13] For example, marketers might be interested in testing for the proportion of respondents who "prefer brand A" versus those who "prefer brand B"; or those who are "brand loyal" versus those who are not.

Bank managers want to know the value of offering a special services package for customers with annual incomes over $50,000. They need to know the percentage of their customers with that income level. (Charles Gupton/Stock, Boston)

Test of Differences between Two Proportions, Independent Samples

In many instances management is interested in the difference between the proportions of people in two different groups that engage in a certain activity or have a certain characteristic. For example, management of a convenience store chain had reason to believe, on the basis of a research study, that the percentage of men who visit convenience stores nine or more times per month (heavy users) was larger than the percentage of women. The specifications required and the procedure for testing this hypothesis are as follows.

1. The null and alternative hypotheses are formally stated as follows:
   Null hypothesis H_0: $P_m - P_f \leq 0$, the proportion of men (P_m) reporting nine or more visits per month is the same or less than the proportion of women (P_f) reporting nine or more visits per month.
   Alternative hypothesis H_a: $P_m - P_f > 0$, the proportion of men (P_m) reporting nine or more visits per month is greater than the proportion of women (P_f) reporting nine or more visits per month.
   The sample proportions and the difference can be calculated from Table 13.12 as follows:

$$P_m = 26/45 = .58$$

$$P_f = 30/71 = .42$$

$$P_m - P_f = .58 - .42$$

$$= .16$$

2. Set the level of sampling error α at .10 (management decision). For $\alpha = .10$, the table value of Z (critical) $= 1.28$. (See Table 3 in the statistical appendix—d.f. $= \infty$, .10 significance, one-tail. The table for t is used because $t = Z$ for samples greater than 30.)

3. The estimated standard error of the differences between the two proportions is calculated as follows:

$$S_{Pm-f} = \sqrt{P(1-P)\left(\frac{1}{n_m} + \frac{1}{n_f}\right)}$$

where

$$P = \frac{n_m P_m + n_f P_f}{n_m + n_f}$$

P_m = proportion in sample m (men)
P_f = proportion in sample f (women)
n_m = size of sample m
n_f = size of sample f

Therefore,

$$P = \frac{45\,(.58) + 71\,(.41)}{45 + 71}$$

$$= .48$$

and

$$S_{Pm-f} = \sqrt{.48(1-.48)\left[\frac{1}{45}+\frac{1}{71}\right]}$$

$$= .10$$

4. Calculate the test statistic.

$$Z = \frac{\left(\begin{array}{c}\text{difference between}\\\text{observed proportions}\end{array}\right) - \left(\begin{array}{c}\text{difference between proportions}\\\text{under the null hypothesis}\end{array}\right)}{\begin{array}{c}\text{estimated standard error of differences}\\\text{between two proportions}\end{array}}$$

$$Z\text{ (calculated)} = \frac{(.58 - .42) - (0)}{.10}$$

$$Z = 1.60$$

5. *The null hypothesis is rejected* because the calculated Z-value (1.60) is larger than the critical Z = value (1.28 for α = .10). Management can conclude with 90 percent confidence $(1 - \alpha = .90)$ that the proportion of men that visit convenience stores nine or more times per month is larger than the proportion of women.

It should be noted that if the level of sampling error α had been set at .05, the critical Z-value would equal 1.64. In this case, we would fail to reject (FTR) the null hypothesis because Z (calculated) is smaller than Z (critical).

P-VALUES AND SIGNIFICANCE TESTING

In the various tests discussed in this chapter, we established a standard—level of significance and associated critical value of the statistic—then calculated the value of the statistic to see whether it beat that standard. If the calculated value of the statistic exceeded the critical value, then the result being tested was said to be statistically significant at that level.

However, this approach did not tell us the exact probability of getting a computed test statistic that large due to chance. The calculations necessary to compute this probability are tedious. Fortunately, they are easy for computers. This probability is commonly referred to as the *P-value*. The *P*-value is the most demanding level of statistical (not managerial) significance that can be met based on the calculated value of the statistic. You may see one of the following in output from various computer statistical packages:

- *P*-Value
- $\leq$ PROB
- PROB =

These labels are used by various computer programs to identify the probability that such a large distance between the hypothesized population parameter and the observed test statistic could have occurred due to chance. The smaller the *P*-value, the smaller is the probability that the observed result occurred due to chance (sampling error).

SUMMARY

Once the questionnaires have been returned from the field, a five-step process takes place. These steps are (1) quality control checks, (2) coding, (3) data entry, (4) machine cleaning, and (5) tabulation and statistical analysis. The first step in the process is very critical. It is important to make sure that the data has integrity; otherwise the age-old adage is true, "garbage in, garbage out." Within the quality control process, the first step is called *validation;* that is, determining as closely as possible that each questionnaire is, in fact, a valid interview. A valid interview in this sense is one that was conducted in an appropriate manner. The objective of validation is to detect interviewer fraud or failure to follow key instructions. Validation is accomplished by recontacting a certain percentage of the respondents surveyed by each interviewer.

After the validation process is completed, editing begins. Editing involves checking for interviewer mistakes. This entails making certain that all questions that should be answered were, that skip patterns were followed properly, and that open-ended questions were recorded properly. Upon completion of editing, the next step is to code the data. Most questions on surveys are closed-ended and precoded. This means that numeric codes have already been assigned to the various responses on the questionnaire. With open-ended questions, the researcher has no idea in advance what the responses will be. Therefore, the coder must go back and establish numeric codes for response categories.

After validation, editing, and coding, the next step is data entry. The data typically is entered directly from the questionnaires.

The final step in the process is tabulation of the data. The most basic tabulation is a one-way frequency table. A one-way frequency table indicates the number of respondents who give each possible answer to each question. The next step in the analysis process is often crosstabulation: examination of the responses to one question in relation to the responses to one or more other questions. Crosstabulations are a very powerful and easily understood approach to the summarization and analysis of survey research results.

Statistical measures are an even more powerful way to analyze data sets. Perhaps the most common statistical measures are those of central tendency: the arithmetic mean, the median, and the mode. The arithmetic mean is computed only from interval or ratio data by adding the values for all observations for a particular variable and dividing the resulting sum by the number of observations. The median can be computed for all types of data except nominal data by finding the value below which 50 percent of the observations fall. The mode can be computed with any type of data by simply finding the value that occurs most frequently. The arithmetic mean is, by far, the most commonly used measure of central tendency.

In addition to central tendency, researchers often want to have an indication of the dispersion of the data. Measures of dispersion include the standard deviation, variance, and range. The range is equal to the maximum value for a particular variable minus the minimum value for that variable.

The purpose of making statistical inferences is to generalize from sample results to population characteristics. Three important concepts relate to the notion of differences: mathematical differences, managerially important differences, and statistical significance.

A hypothesis is an assumption, or theory, that a researcher or manager makes about some characteristic of the population being investigated. By testing, the researcher determines whether a hypothesis concerning some characteristic of the population is valid. A statistical hypothesis test permits the researcher to calculate the probability of observing the particular result if the stated hypothesis were actually true. In hypothesis testing, the first step is to specify the hypothesis. Next, an appropriate statistical technique should be selected to test the hypothesis. Finally, a decision rule must be specified as the basis for determining whether to accept or reject the hypothesis.

KEY TERMS

Validation	Mean
Editing	Median
Skip pattern	Mode
Coding	Standard deviation
Scanning	Variance
Machine cleaning of data	Range
Error checking routines	Hypotheses
Marginal report	Independent samples
One-way frequency table	Related samples
Crosstabulation	Chi-square test

REVIEW AND DISCUSSION QUESTIONS

1. Assume that Sally Smith, an interviewer, completed fifty questionnaires. Ten of the questionnaires were validated by calling the respondents and asking them one opinion question and two demographic questions over again. On one questionnaire, the respondent claimed that his age category was 30–40, and the age category marked on the questionnaire was 20–30. On a second questionnaire, the respondent was asked, "What is the most important problem facing our city government?" and the interviewer had written down, "The city council is too eager to raise taxes." When the interview was validated, the respondent said, "The city tax rate is too high." As a validator, would you assume that these were honest mistakes that were made and accept the entire lot of fifty interviews as valid? If not, what would you do?

2. Give an example of a skip pattern on a questionnaire. Why is it important to always follow the skip patterns correctly?

3. What is the purpose of machine cleaning the data? Give some examples of how data can be machine cleaned. Do you think that machine cleaning is an expensive and unnecessary step in the data tabulation process? Why or why not?

4. It has been said that a crosstabulation of two variables gives the researcher much richer information than simply two one-way frequency tables. Why is this true? Give an example.

5. Calculate the mean, median, mode, and standard deviation from the data set that appears at the top of page 395.

6. Using data from a newspaper or magazine article, create the following types of graphs:
   a. Line graph
   b. Pie chart
   c. Bar chart

7. Explain the notions of mathematical differences, managerially important differences, and statistical significance. Can results be statistically significant and yet lack managerial importance? Explain your answer.

8. Describe the procedure for testing hypotheses. Discuss the difference between a null hypothesis and an alternative hypothesis.

RESPONDENT	TIMES VISITED WHITEHALL MALL IN PAST SIX MONTHS	TIMES VISITED NORTHPARK MALL IN PAST SIX MONTHS	TIMES VISITED SAMPSON MALL IN PAST SIX MONTHS
A	4	7	2
B	5	11	16
C	13	21	3
D	6	0	1
E	9	18	14
F	3	6	8
G	2	0	1
H	21	3	7
I	4	11	9
J	14	13	5
K	7	7	12
L	8	3	25
M	8	3	9

9. A market researcher has completed a study of pain relievers. The following table depicts the brand purchased most often broken down by men versus women. Perform a chi-square test on the data and determine what can be said regarding the crosstabulation.

PAIN RELIEVERS	MEN	WOMEN
Anacin	40	55
Bayer	60	28
Bufferin	70	97
Cope	14	21
Empirin	82	107
Excedrin	72	84
Excedrin PM	15	11
Vanquish	20	26

CASE

Tan It All

Tan It All is a chain of twenty-two tanning salons in the Chicago metropolitan area. Business has been fairly flat for the last two years and the company believes that it needs a change in its pricing plan. Shannon Kelly, marketing director for Tan It All, met the marketing director for a chain of tanning salons in Cincinnati at an industry trade convention. The person she met told her about a new pricing plan her company was using in Cincinnati that had proven, in her opinion, to be very effective. Shannon has just completed a survey of 500 target customers in the Chicago area. In that survey, she described their current pricing (Plan A) plan and the pricing plan being used in Cincinnati (Plan B) and asked respondents which plan they preferred. In addition to the overall preference, Shannon is interested in adopting a plan that will be equally attractive to men and women and to those with incomes over $50,000 per year and those with incomes of $50,000 per year and less. Results, overall and by gender and income are shown in Table 13.13.

TABLE 13.13 *Preference for Pricing Plans by Gender and Income*

	TOTAL	GENDER		INCOME	
		Male	*Female*	≤*$50K*	>*$50K*
Total	500	239	261	289	211
	100.0%	100.0%	100.0%	100.0%	100.0%
Prefer Plan A	201	112	89	147	54
	40.2%	46.9%	34.1%	50.9%	25.6%
Prefer Plan B	299	127	172	142	157
	59.8%	53.1%	65.9%	49.1%	74.4%

1. Which plan appears to be most popular overall?
2. Is the plan preferred overall equally attractive to men and women?
3. What is the nature of the relationship between preference for pricing plans and income portrayed in the table?

Correlation and Regression Analysis

1. To understand regression analysis.
2. To become aware of the coefficient of determination R^2.
3. To comprehend the nature of correlation analysis.

S

andi Amarini is responsible for making store location decisions for the Pak A Sak convenience store chain. The company and other convenience store companies have long believed that the higher the traffic vehicle counts on streets adjacent to a location, the higher the expected sales for that location. Sandi has identified several instances where sales at locations with extremely high vehicle traffic counts are lower than at other stores with lower traffic counts. She is interested in determining whether the long-held belief that there is a close correlation or association between higher traffic counts and higher sales is actually true.

In order to test the theory, she has obtained sales and vehicle traffic count data for 100 randomly selected Pak A Sak locations. Visual inspection of the data indicates that the relationship between traffic counts and sales does not appear to be as close as one might expect. She is interested in exploring two issues in greater detail. First, she would like to have some statistical measure of the degree of association or correlation between sales and vehicle traffic counts. One of her associates has suggested that correlation analysis is the appropriate technique for use in addressing this issue. Second, she is interested in developing a model that could be used to predict sales volume based on traffic counts for prospective locations. The same co-worker recommended that she use regression analysis to develop a model to predict sales based on traffic counts. This same person also warned her that her model should contain other variables besides traffic count data because he believes that many other factors affect sales for a given location.

When you finish this chapter you should be able to answer the questions facing Sandi.

BIVARIATE ANALYSIS OF ASSOCIATION

Bivariate Analysis Defined

Bivariate techniques
Statistical methods of determining the relationship between two variables.

In many marketing research studies, the interests of the researcher and manager go beyond issues that can be addressed by the statistical testing of differences discussed in the previous chapter. They may be interested in the degree of association between two variables. Statistical techniques appropriate for this type of analysis are referred to as **bivariate techniques**.[1] When more than two variables are involved, the techniques employed are known as *multivariate techniques*. Multivariate techniques are discussed later in the chapter.

When analyzing the degree of association between two variables, the variables are classified as the **independent** (predictor) **variable** or the **dependent** (criterion) **variable**. Independent variables are those that we believe affect the value of the dependent variable. Independent variables such as price, advertising expenditures, or number of retail outlets are often used to predict and explain sales or market share of a brand—the dependent variable. Bivariate analysis can help provide answers to questions such as, How does the price of our product affect sales? and What is the relationship between household income and expenditures on entertainment?

It must be noted that none of the techniques we will present can be used to prove that one variable caused some change in another variable. They can be used only to describe the nature of statistical relationships between variables.

Independent variable
The variable believed to affect the value of the dependent variable.

Dependent variable
The variable whose value is believed to change in response to the independent variable.

Types of Bivariate Procedures

The analyst has a large number of bivariate techniques from which to choose. In this chapter we discuss three procedures that are appropriate for metric (ratio or interval) data, bivariate regression, Pearson product moment correlation, and multivariate regression. Other statistical procedures that can be used for analyzing the statistical relationship between two variables include

■ Two group *t*-test.
■ Chi-square analysis of crosstab or contingency tables.
■ ANOVA (analysis of variance) for two groups.

BIVARIATE REGRESSION

Bivariate Regression Defined

Bivariate regression analysis is a statistical procedure appropriate for analyzing the relationship between two variables when one is considered the dependent variable and the other the independent variable. For example, we might be interested in analyzing the relationship between sales (dependent variable) and advertising (independent variable). If the relationship between advertising expenditures and sales can be estimated by regression analysis, the researcher can predict sales for different levels of advertising. When the problem involves using two or more independent variables (e.g., advertising and price) to predict the dependent variable of interest, multiple regression analysis is appropriate.

Bivariate regression analysis
Analysis of the strength of the linear relationship between two variables when one is considered the independent variable and the other the dependent variable.

Nature of the Relationship

To study the nature of the relationship between the dependent and the independent variables, the data can be plotted in a scatter diagram. The dependent variable Y is plotted on the vertical axis, while the independent variable X is plotted on the horizontal axis. By examining the scatter diagram we can determine whether the relationship between the two variables, if any, is linear or curvilinear. If the relationship appears to be linear or close to linear, linear regression is appropriate.

If a nonlinear relationship is shown in the scatter diagram, curve-fitting nonlinear regression techniques are appropriate. These techniques are beyond the scope of this discussion.[2]

Figure 14.1 depicts several kinds of underlying relationships between the X and Y variables. Scatter diagrams A and B suggest a positive linear relationship between X and Y. However, the linear relationship shown in B is not as strong as that portrayed in A; there is more scatter in the data shown in B. Diagram C shows a perfect negative or inverse relationship between variables X and Y. Diagrams D and E show nonlinear relationships between the variables, and appropriate curve-fitting techniques should be used to mathematically describe these relationships. The scatter diagram in F shows no relationship between X and Y.

Bivariate Regression Example

Vicki Cole is the sales manager for Arena Services, Inc. (ASI). ASI has a contract with the Dallas Mavericks to handle all concession and souvenir sales during Dallas Mavericks home games at Reunion Arena.

ASI has followed the practice of staffing all concession stands and sales booths first and then assigning any excess personnel to the job of selling Maverick pennants to the crowd in the arena. Vicki's boss does not believe that there is any relationship between the number of employees assigned to pennant sales and the number of pennants sold. Vicki is not so sure. She has requested data on number of pennants sold and number of employees assigned to pennant sales for the eighteen 1992–1993 home games played up to this point (provided in Table 14.1). It should be noted that all games were sell-outs and there was very little variation in actual attendance for the eighteen games.

A scatter plot of the data is shown in Figure 14.2. A visual examination of this scatter plot suggests that the total number of pennants sold increases as the number of salespersons increases. How can we mathematically describe this relationship?

Least Squares Estimation Procedure

The least squares procedure is a fairly simple mathematical technique that can be used to fit a line to data for X and Y (see Figure 14.2) that best represents the relationship between the two variables. No straight line can perfectly represent every observation in the scatter plot. This is reflected in discrepancies between the actual values (dots on scatter diagram) and predicted values (value indicated by the line). Any straight line fitted to the data in the scatter plot will be subject to error. A number of lines could be drawn that would seem to fit the observations in Figure 14.2.

The least squares procedure results in a straight line that fits the actual observations (dots) better than any other line that could be fitted to the observations. Put another way, the sum of the squared deviations from this line (squared differences between dots and the line) will be less than for any other line that can be fitted to the observations.

FIGURE 14.1 *Types of Relationships Found in Scatter Diagrams*

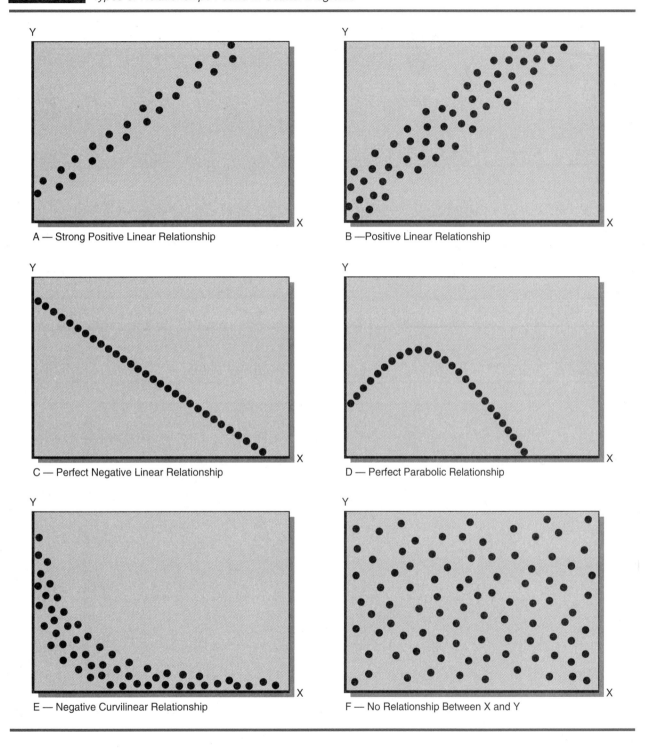

A — Strong Positive Linear Relationship

B —Positive Linear Relationship

C — Perfect Negative Linear Relationship

D — Perfect Parabolic Relationship

E — Negative Curvilinear Relationship

F — No Relationship Between X and Y

TABLE 14.1   *Pennants Sold and Employees Assigned*

GAME NUMBER (i)	NUMBER OF SALESPEOPLE (X_i)	TOTAL NUMBER OF PENNANTS SOLD (Y_i)
1	7	97
2	6	86
3	5	78
4	1	10
5	5	75
6	4	62
7	7	101
8	3	39
9	4	53
10	2	33
11	8	118
12	5	65
13	2	25
14	5	71
15	7	105
16	1	17
17	4	49
18	5	68

FIGURE 14.2   *Scatter Plot of Number of Pennants Sold by Number of Salespeople*

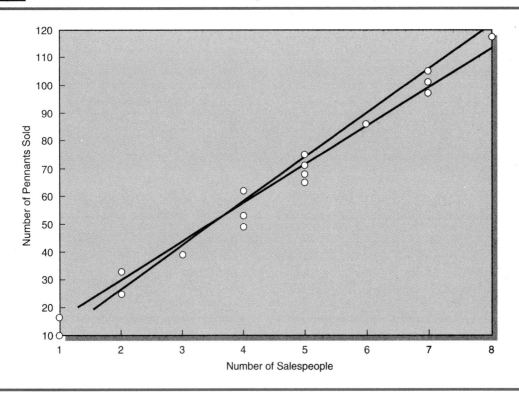

The general equation for the line is $Y = a + bX$. The estimating equation for regression analysis is

$$Y = \hat{a} + \hat{b}X + e$$

where

Y = dependent variable—number of pennants sold
$\hat{a}$ = estimated Y intercept for regression line
$\hat{b}$ = estimated slope of the regression line—regression coefficient
X = independent variable—number of salespeople
e = error—difference between actual value and value predicted by regression line

Values for $\hat{b}$ and $\hat{a}$ can be calculated as follows:

$$\hat{b} = \frac{\sum X_i Y_i - n\overline{X}\,\overline{Y}}{\sum X^2_{\,i} - n(\overline{X})^2}$$

$$\hat{a} = \overline{Y} - \hat{b}\overline{X}$$

Arena Services, Inc. wants to know the relationship between the number of employees assigned to pennant sales at Dallas Mavericks home game and the number of pennants sold per game. (Courtesy Dallas Mavericks. Photo by Layne Murdoch)

where

$$\overline{X} = \text{mean value of } X$$
$$\overline{Y} = \text{mean value of } Y$$
$$n = \text{sample size (number of units in the sample)}$$

Using the data from Table 14.2, $\hat{b}$ is calculated as follows:

$$\hat{b} = \frac{6282 - 18(4.5)(64)}{439 - 18(4.5)^2}$$

$$= 14.74$$

The value of $\hat{a}$ is calculated as follows:

$$\hat{a} = \overline{Y} - \hat{b}\overline{X}$$

$$= 64 - (14.74)4.5$$

$$= -2.32$$

Thus, our estimated regression function is given by

$$\hat{Y} = \hat{a} + \hat{b}X$$

$$\hat{Y} = -2.32 + 14.74X$$

where $\hat{Y}$ (Y hat) is the value of the estimated regression function for a given value of X.

According to this equation, for every additional salesperson (X), the total number of pennants sold will increase by nearly fifteen (estimated value of b). The value of a in our example is negative and is equal to -2.32. Technically, $\hat{a}$ is our estimate of value of the dependent variable (Y) when the value of the independent variable (X) is zero.

TABLE 14.2 *Least Squares Computation*

GAME	X	Y	X²	Y²	XY
1	7	97	49	9,409	679
2	6	86	36	7,396	516
3	5	78	25	6,084	390
4	1	10	1	100	10
5	5	75	25	5,625	375
6	4	62	16	3,844	248
7	7	101	49	10,201	707
8	3	39	9	1,521	117
9	4	53	16	2,809	212
10	2	33	4	1,089	66
11	8	118	64	13,924	944
12	5	65	25	4,225	325
13	2	25	4	625	50
14	5	71	25	5,041	355
15	7	105	49	11,025	735
16	1	17	1	289	17
17	4	49	16	2,401	196
18	5	68	25	4,624	340
Σ (sum)	= 81	1,152	439	90,232	6,282
	Mean = 4.5	64			

TABLE 14.3   *Predicted Values and Errors for Each Observation*

GAME	X	Y	$\hat{Y}$	$Y - \hat{Y}$	$\hat{Y} - \overline{Y}$	$(Y - \hat{Y})^2$	$(\hat{Y} - \overline{Y})^2$
1	7	97	100.9	-3.9	36.9	15.21	1361.61
2	6	86	86.1	-0.1	22.1	0.01	488.41
3	5	78	71.4	6.6	7.4	43.56	54.76
4	1	10	12.4	-2.4	-51.6	5.76	2662.56
5	5	75	71.4	3.6	7.4	12.96	54.76
6	4	62	56.6	5.4	-7.4	29.16	54.76
7	7	101	100.9	0.1	36.9	0.01	1361.61
8	3	39	41.9	-2.9	-22.1	8.41	488.41
9	4	53	56.6	-3.6	-7.4	12.96	54.76
10	2	33	27.2	5.8	-36.8	33.64	1354.24
11	8	118	115.6	2.4	51.6	5.76	2662.56
12	5	65	71.4	-6.4	7.4	40.96	54.76
13	2	25	27.2	-2.2	-36.8	4.84	1354.24
14	5	71	71.4	-0.4	7.4	0.16	54.76
15	7	105	100.9	4.1	36.9	16.81	1361.61
16	1	17	12.4	4.6	-51.6	21.16	2662.56
17	4	49	56.6	-7.6	-7.4	57.76	54.76
18	5	68	71.4	-3.4	7.4	11.56	54.76
Σ (sum)	= 81	1152	1152.3			320.69	16195.89
	Mean = 4.50	64.00					

Regression Line

Predicted values for Y, based on calculated values for $\hat{a}$ and $\hat{b}$, are shown in Table 14.3. In addition, errors for each observation $(Y - \hat{Y})$ are shown. The regression line resulting from the $\hat{Y}$ values is shown in Figure 14.3.

Strength of Association—R^2

The estimated regression function describes the nature of the relationship between X and Y. In addition, we are interested in the strength of the relationship between the variables. How widely do the actual values of Y differ from the values predicted by our model?

The **coefficient of determination**, denoted by R^2, is the measure of the strength of the linear relationship between X and Y. The coefficient of determination measures the percent of the total variation in Y that is "explained" by the variation in X. The R^2 statistic ranges from 0 to 1. If there is a perfect linear relationship between X and Y, all the variation in Y is explained by the variation in X, then R^2 equals 1. At the other extreme, if there is no relationship between X and Y, then none of the variation in Y is explained by the variation in X and R^2 equals 0.

> Coefficient of determination (R^2)
> The percent of the total variation in the dependent variable explained by the independent variable.

The coefficient of determination for our example would be computed as follows (see Table 14.3 for calculation of $(Y - \hat{Y})^2$ and $(Y - \overline{Y})^2$):

$$R^2 = \frac{\text{explained variance}}{\text{total variance}}$$

$$\text{explained variance} = \text{total variance} - \text{unexplained variance}$$

$$R^2 = \frac{\text{total variance} - \text{unexplained variance}}{\text{total variance}}$$

FIGURE 14.3 *Least Squares Regression Line Fitted to Sample Data*

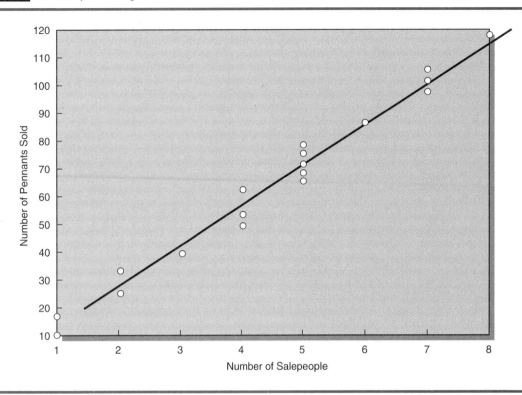

$$R^2 = 1 - \frac{\text{unexplained variance}}{\text{total variance}}$$

$$R^2 = 1 - \frac{\sum\limits_{i=1}^{n} (Y_i - \hat{Y}_i)^2}{\sum\limits_{i=1}^{n} (Y_i - \overline{Y})^2}$$

$$R^2 = 1 - \frac{321}{16,196} = .98$$

Of the variation in Y (total number of pennants sold), 98 percent is explained by the variation in X (total number of salespeople). There is a very strong linear relationship between X and Y.

Statistical Significance of Regression Results

In computing R^2, the total variation in Y was partitioned into two component sums of squares:

Total variation = explained variation + unexplained variation

The total variation is a measure of variation of the observed Y values around their mean Y. It measures the variation in the Y values without any consideration of the X values.

Total variation, known as the *total sum of squares* (SST), is given by

$$\text{SST} = \sum_{i=1}^{n} (Y_i - \overline{Y})^2 = \sum_{i=1}^{n} Y_i^2 - \left(\frac{\sum_{i=1}^{n} Y_i^2}{n} \right)$$

The explained variation or the **sum of squares due to regression (SSR)** is given by

Sum of squares due to regression (SSR)
The variation explained by the regression.

$$\text{SSR} = \sum_{i=1}^{n} (\hat{Y}_i - \overline{Y})^2 = a \sum_{i=1}^{n} Y_i + b \sum_{i=1}^{n} X_i Y_i - \left(\frac{\sum_{i=1}^{n} Y_i}{n} \right)^2$$

Figure 14.4 shows the various measures of variation (i.e., sum of squares) in a regression. SSR represents the differences between the $\hat{Y}_i$ (the values of Y predicted by the estimated regression equation) and Y (the average value of Y). In a well-fitting regression equation, the variation explained by regression (SSR) will represent a

FIGURE 14.4 *Measures of Variation in a Regression*

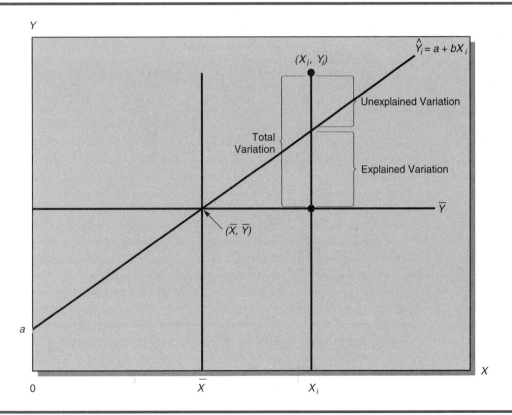

large portion of the total variation (SST). If $Y_i \equiv \hat{Y}_i$ at each value of X_i, then a perfect fit has been achieved. All the observed values of Y would then be on the computed regression line. Of course, in that case SSR $\equiv$ SST.

The unexplained variation or **error sum of squares (SSE)** is obtained from

Error sum of squares (SSE)
The variation not explained by the regression.

$$SSE = \sum_{i=1}^{n} (Y_i - \hat{Y})^2 = \sum_{i=1}^{n} Y_i^2 - a \sum_{i=1}^{n} Y_i - b \sum_{i=1}^{n} X_i Y_i$$

From Figure 14.4 note that SSE represents the residual differences (error) between the observed and predicted Y values. Therefore, the unexplained variation is a measure of scatter around the regression line. If the fit were perfect, there would be no scatter around the regression line and SSE would be zero.

Hypotheses Concerning the Overall Regression. Here we are interested in hypotheses regarding the computed R^2 value for our problem. Is the amount of variance explained in our result (by our model) significantly greater than we would expect due to chance or, as in the various statistical tests discussed in Chapter 13, to what extent can we rule out sampling error as an explanation of our results? Analysis of variance (F-test) is used to test the significance of the results.

The analysis of variance table would be set up as shown in Table 14.4. The computer output for our example is shown in Table 14.5. The breakdowns of the total sum of squares and associated degrees of freedom are displayed in the form of an analysis of variance table. We use the information in this table to test the significance of the linear relationship between Y and X. As noted previously, an F-test will be used for this purpose. Our hypotheses are

TABLE 14.4 *Analysis of Variance*

SOURCE OF VARIATION	DEGREES OF FREEDOM	SUM OF SQUARES	MEAN SQUARE	F-STATISTIC
Due to Regression (explained)	1	SSR	$MSR = \dfrac{SSR}{1}$	$F = \dfrac{MSR}{MSE}$
Error (unexplained)	$n-2$	SSE	$MSE = \dfrac{SSE}{n-2}$	
Total	$n-1$	SST		

TABLE 14.5 *Analysis of Variance Computer Output*

DEPENDENT VARIABLE: TOTAL SALES OF PENNANTS

SOURCE	DF	SUM OF SQUARES	MEAN SQUARE
MODEL	1	16182.60	16182.60
ERROR	16	321.40	20.09
CORRECTED TOTAL	17	16504.00	

PARAMETER	ESTIMATE	T FOR HO: PARAMETER = 0	PR > |T|
INTERCEPT	-2.32	-0.91	0.38
SALESPER	14.74	28.38	0.0001

Null hypothesis H_0: There is no linear relationship between X (number of salespeople) and Y (total number of pennants sold)

Alternative hypothesis H_a: There is a linear relationship between X and Y

As in other statistical tests, we must choose α. This is the likelihood that the observed result occurred due to chance or the probability of incorrectly rejecting the null hypothesis. In this case we decided on a rather standard level of significance or $\alpha = .05$. This means that if the calculated value of F exceeds the tabular value we are willing to accept a 5 percent chance of incorrectly rejecting the null hypothesis. The value of F or the F-ratio is computed as follows (see Table 14.5):

$$F = \frac{MSR}{MSE}$$
$$= \frac{16182.60}{20.09}$$
$$= 805.5$$

We will reject the null hypothesis if the calculated F-statistic is greater than or equal to the table or critical F-value. The numerator and denominator degrees of freedom for this F-ratio are 1 and 16, respectively. As noted earlier, it was decided that an alpha level of .05 ($\alpha = .05$) should be used.

The table or critical value of F with 1 (numerator) and 16 (denominator) degrees of freedom at $\alpha = .05$ is 4.49 (see Table 5 in the statistical appendix). Because the calculated value of F is greater than the critical value, we can reject the null hypothesis and conclude that there is a significant linear relationship between the number of salespeople (X) and the total number of pennants sold (Y). This result is consistent with the high coefficient of determination R^2 discussed earlier.

Hypotheses about the Regression Coefficient (b). Finally, we may be interested in making hypotheses about b, the regression coefficient. As you may recall, b is the estimate of the effect of a one unit change in X on Y. The hypotheses are

Null hypothesis $\qquad H_0: b = 0$
Alternative hypothesis $\qquad H_a: b \neq 0$

The appropriate test is a t-test, and as you can see from the last line of Table 14.5, the computer program calculates the t-value (28.38) and the p-value (probability of incorrectly rejecting the null hypotheses of .0001). See Chapter 13 for a more detailed discussion of p-values. Given our α criterion of .05, we would reject the null hypothesis in this case.

CORRELATION ANALYSIS

Correlation for Metric Data—Pearson's Product Moment Correlation

Correlation is the measurement of the degree to which changes in one variable (the dependent variable) are associated with changes in another. If we are analyzing the relationship between two variables, the analysis is called simple or bivariate

Correlation analysis
Analysis of the degree to which changes in one variable are associated with changes in another.

Pearson's product moment correlation
Correlation analysis technique for use with metric data.

correlation analysis. The **Pearson's product moment** approach is used if metric data are involved.

In bivariate regression, we discussed the coefficient of determination R^2 as a measure of the strength of the linear relationship between X and Y. Another descriptive measure, called the *coefficient of correlation (R)*, is a measure of the degree of association between X and Y. It is the square root of the coefficient of determination with the appropriate sign (+ or −):

$$R = \pm \sqrt{R^2}$$

The value of R can range from −1 (perfect negative correlation) to +1 (perfect positive correlation). The closer R is to ± 1, the stronger is the degree of association between X and Y. If R is equal to zero, then there is no association between X and Y.

If we are not interested in estimating the regression function, R can be computed directly, with the data from our Dallas Mavericks example, using this formula:

$$R = \frac{n\Sigma XY - (\Sigma X)(\Sigma Y)}{\sqrt{[n\Sigma X^2 - (\Sigma X)^2][n\Sigma Y^2 - (\Sigma Y)^2]}}$$

The correlation coefficient

$$R = \frac{18(6282) - (81)(1152)}{\sqrt{[18(439) - (81)^2][18(90232) - (1152)^2]}}$$

This value of R indicates a positive correlation between the number of salespeople and the total number of pennants sold.

MULTIVARIATE ANALYSIS

Developments in computer technology, both hardware and software, have provided the basis for remarkable advances in the use of powerful statistical procedures for the analysis of marketing research data. These developments have made it possible to analyze large amounts of complex data with relative ease. In particular, developments related to a group of analytical techniques known as *multivariate analysis* have been extremely significant in this data analysis revolution.

Multivariate analysis
Statistical procedures that simultaneously analyze multiple measurements on each individual or object under study.

The term **multivariate analysis** is used to refer to a group of statistical procedures that simultaneously analyze multiple measurements on each individual or object being studied.[3] Some experts consider any simultaneous statistical analysis of more than two variables to be multivariate analysis. Multivariate procedures are extensions of the univariate and bivariate statistical procedures discussed earlier in this chapter.

A number of techniques fall under the heading of multivariate analysis procedures:

- Multiple regression analysis
- Multiple discriminant analysis
- Cluster analysis
- Factor analysis

FIGURE 14.5   *Brief Description of Multivariate Statistical Techniques Covered*

Multiple regression enables the researcher to predict the level or magnitude of a dependent variable based on the levels of more than one independent variable.

Multiple discriminant analysis enables the researcher to predict group membership on the basis of two or more independent variables.

Cluster analysis is a procedure for identifying subgroups of individuals or items that are homogeneous within subgroups and different from other subgroups.

Factor analysis permits the analyst to reduce a set of variables to a smaller set of factors or composite variables by identifying dimensions under the data.

Perceptual mapping is appropriate when the goal is to analyze consumer perception of companies, products, brands, and so on.

Conjoint analysis provides a basis to estimate the utility that consumers associate with different product features or attributes.

- Perceptual mapping
- Conjoint analysis

Multiple regression analysis is discussed in this section. Discussion of the other techniques is beyond the scope of this text. Students interested in the other techniques are referred to several references. See Figure 14.5 for a summary of various other techniques.

MULTIPLE REGRESSION ANALYSIS

Multiple regression analysis is the appropriate multivariate technique if the researcher's goal is to examine the relationship between two or more metric predictor (independent) variables and one metric dependent (criterion) variable.[4] Under certain circumstances, described later in this section, nominal predictor variables can be used if they are recoded as binary variables.

Multiple regression analysis is an extension of bivariate regression discussed earlier. Instead of fitting a straight line to observations in a two-dimensional space, multiple regression analysis fits a plane to observations in a multidimensional space. The output obtained and the interpretation of multiple regression are essentially the same as for bivariate regression. The general equation for multiple regression is as follows:

$$Y = a + b_1X_1 + b_2X_2 + b_3X_3 + \ldots + b_nX_n$$

where

Y = dependent or criterion variable

a = estimated constant

b_{1-n} = coefficients associated with the predictor variables so that a change of one unit in X will cause a change of b_1 units in Y; the values for the coefficients are estimated from the regression analysis

X_{1-n} = predictor (independent) variables that influence the dependent variable

> **Multiple regression analysis**
> A procedure for predicting the level or magnitude of a dependent variable based on the levels of more than one independent variable.

For example, consider the following regression equation (note that values for a, b_1, and b_2 have been estimated by means of regression analysis):

$$\hat{Y} = 200 + 17X_1 + 22X_2$$

where

$\hat{Y}$ = estimated sales in units
X_1 = advertising expenditures
X_2 = number of salespersons

This equation indicates that sales increase by 17 units for every one dollar increase in advertising and 22 units for every one unit increase in the number of salespersons.

Possible Applications of Multiple Regression

There are many possible applications of multiple regression analysis in marketing research:

- Determining what effects various marketing mix variables have on sales or market share.
- Determining the relationship between various demographic or psychographic factors and frequency of visiting fast-food restaurants or other service businesses.
- Quantifying the relationship between various classification variables, such as age and income, and overall attitude toward a product or service.
- Determining which variables are predictive of sales of a particular product or service.

As just shown, multiple regression analysis can serve one or a combination of two basic purposes: prediction of the level of the dependent variable based on given levels of the predictor variables; or understanding the relationship between the independent variables and the dependent variable.

Multiple Regression Analysis Measures

In the earlier discussion of bivariate regression, a statistic referred to as the coefficient of determination, or R^2, was noted as one of the outputs of regression analysis. This statistic can assume values from 0 to 1 and provides a measure of the percentage of the variation in the dependent variable explained by variation in the independent variables. For example, if the R^2 in a given regression analysis was calculated to be .75, that means that 75 percent of the variation in the dependent variable is explained by variation in the independent variables. The analyst would prefer to have a calculated R^2 of close to 1. Frequently, variables are added to a regression model to see what effect they have on the R^2 value.

The b values, or **regression coefficients**, indicate the effect of the individual independent variables on the dependent variable. It is appropriate to determine the

Regression coefficients
Values that indicate the effect of the individual independent variables on the dependent variable.

likelihood that each individual b value is the result of chance. This calculation is part of the output provided by virtually all statistical software packages. Normally, these packages compute the probability of incorrectly rejecting the null hypothesis of $b_n = 0$.

Dummy Variables

In some situations, the analyst would like to include nominally scaled independent variables such as gender, marital status, occupation, or race in a multiple regression analysis. For this purpose, dummy variables can be created. Dichotomous nominally scaled independent variables can be transformed into dummy variables by coding one value (e.g., female) as 0 and the other (e.g., male) as 1. For nominally scaled independent variables that can assume more than two values, a slightly different approach is required. Consider a question regarding racial group with three possible answers: black, Hispanic, or white. Binary or dummy variable coding of responses will require the use of two dummy variables, X_1 and X_2, that might be coded as follows:

	X_1	X_2
If person is black	1	0
If person is Hispanic	0	1
If person is white	0	0

Potential Problems in Using and Interpreting Multiple Regression Analysis

We must be sensitive to certain problems that may be encountered in the use and interpretation of multiple regression analysis results. These problems are summarized in the following sections.

Collinearity.   One of the key assumptions of multiple regression analysis is that the independent variables are not correlated with each other.[5] If the independent variables are correlated, then the estimated b values (regression coefficients) will be biased and unstable. Conventional wisdom says that this is not a problem if the regression model is developed strictly for purposes of prediction. However, when the goal of the analysis is to determine how each of the predictor variables influences the dependent variable, the fact that the b values are biased due to **collinearity** is a serious problem.

The simplest way to check for collinearity is to examine the matrix showing the correlations between each variable in the analysis. One rule of thumb is to look for correlations between independent variables of .30 or greater. If correlations of this magnitude exist, then the analyst should check for distortions of the b values. One way to do this is to run regressions with the collinear variables and with each variable separately. The b values in the regression with all variables in the equation should be similar to the b values computed for the variables run separately.

Collinearity
The correlation of independent variables with each other. Can bias estimates of regression coefficients.

There are a number of strategies for dealing with collinearity. Two common approaches follow. First, if two variables are heavily correlated with each other, one of the variables can be dropped from the analysis. Second, the correlated variables can be combined in some fashion (e.g., an index) to form a new composite independent variable and this variable can be used in subsequent regression analyses.

Causation. Although regression analysis can show that variables are associated or correlated with each other, it cannot prove **causation**. Causal relationships can be confirmed only by other means (see Chapter 8). A strong, logical, or theoretical basis must be developed to support the idea that there is a causal relationship between the independent variables and the dependent variable. However, even a strong logical base coupled with statistical results demonstrating correlation are only indicators of causation.

Causation
The inference that a change in one variable is responsible for, or caused, an observed change in another variable.

Scaling of Coefficients. The magnitude of the regression coefficients associated with the various independent variables can be compared directly only if they are scaled in the same units or if the data have been standardized. This point is illustrated in the following example:

$$\hat{Y} = 50 + 20X_1 + 20X_2$$

where

$\hat{Y}$ = estimated sales volume
X_1 = advertising expenditure in thousands of dollars
X_2 = number of salespersons

On initial examination it would appear that a dollar spent on advertising and an additional salesperson would have an equal effect on sales. However, on further consideration, this is false because X_1 and X_2 are measured in different kinds of units. If we want to make direct comparisons of regression coefficients, all independent variables must be measured in the same units (e.g., dollars or thousands of dollars) or the data must be standardized. Standardization is achieved by taking each number in a series, subtracting the mean of the series from the number, and dividing the result by the standard deviation of the series. The formula for this process is as follows:

$$\frac{X_i - \overline{X}}{\sigma}$$

where

X_i = individual number from a series of numbers
$\overline{X}$ = mean of the series
σ = standard deviation of the series

Sample Size. The value of R^2 is influenced by the number of predictor variables relative to sample size.[6] A number of rules of thumb have been proposed and suggest that the number of observations should be equal to at least ten to fifteen times the number of predictor variables. This means that for the preceding example (sales volume is a function of advertising expenditures and number of salespersons) with two predictor variables, twenty to thirty observations are required as a minimum.

SUMMARY

This chapter discusses the relationship between variables taken two at a time. The techniques used for this analysis are called *bivariate analyses*. Bivariate regression analysis is used so that a single dependent variable can be predicted from the knowledge about a single independent variable. One way to examine the underlying relationship between a dependent and an independent variable is to plot them on a scatter diagram. If the relationship appears to be linear, then linear regression analysis may be used. If it is curvilinear, then curve-fitting techniques should be applied. The general equation for a straight line fitted to two variables is given by the equation

$$Y = a + bX$$

where

Y = the dependent variable
X = the independent variable
a = Y intercept
b = the amount of Y increases with each unit increase in X

Both a and b are unknown and must be estimated. This is known as *simple linear regression analysis*. Bivariate least squares regression analysis is a mathematical technique for fitting a line to measurements of the two variables X and Y. The line is fitted so that the algebraic sum of deviations of the actual observations from the line are zero and the sum of the squared deviations is less than they would be for any other line that might be fitted to the data.

The estimated regression function describes the nature of the relationship between X and Y. In addition, researchers want to know the strength of the relationship between the variables. This is measured by the coefficient of determination, denoted by R^2. The coefficient of determination measures the percent of the total variation in Y that is "explained" by the variation in X. The R^2 statistic ranges from 0 to 1.

Correlation analysis is the measurement of the degree to which changes in one variable are associated with changes in another. Correlation analysis will tell the researcher whether the variables are positively correlated, negatively correlated, or independent.

Multivariate analysis refers to a group of statistical procedures that are used to simultaneously analyze multiple measurements on each individual or object being studied. Some of the more popular multivariate techniques include multiple regression analysis, multiple discriminant analysis, factor analysis, cluster analysis, perceptual mapping, and conjoint analysis.

Multiple regression enables the researcher to predict the magnitude of a dependent variable based upon the levels of more than one independent variable. Multiple regression fits a plane to observations in a multidimensional space. One statistic that results from multiple regression analysis is called the *coefficient of determination* or R^2. The value of this statistic ranges from 0 to 1. It provides a measure of the percentage of the variation in the dependent variable that is explained by variation in the independent variables. The b values, or regression coefficients, indicate the effect of the individual independent variable on the dependent variable.

KEY TERMS

Bivariate techniques
Independent variable
Dependent variable
Bivariate regression analysis
Coefficient of determination (R^2)
Sum of squares due to regression (SSR)
Error sum of squares (SSE)
Correlation analysis

Pearson's product moment correlation
Multivariate analysis
Multiple regression analysis
Regression coefficients
Collinearity
Causation

REVIEW AND DISCUSSION QUESTIONS

1. What are the primary differences between simple regression and correlation analysis?
2. A sales manager of a firm administered a standard multiple-item job satisfaction scale to a random sample of the firm's sales force. The manager then correlated the satisfaction scores with the years of school the salespeople had completed. The Pearson correlation between satisfaction and years of school turned out to be .15. On the basis of this evidence, the sales manager came to the following conclusions: "A salesperson's level of education has little to do with his or her job satisfaction. Furthermore, as education level rises, they continue to have the same average levels of job satisfaction." Would you agree or disagree with the sales manager's conclusions? Explain your answer.
3. What is the purpose of a scatter diagram?
4. Explain how a marketing researcher can use the coefficient of determination.
5. Comment on the following: "When the AFC team has won the Super Bowl, the stock market has always risen in the first quarter of the year in every case except one; when the NFC has won the Super Bowl, the stock market has fallen in the first quarter in all cases except two."
6. The following table gives data collected for a convenience store chain for twenty of its stores. The data are

   - Column 1—ID number for each store.
   - Column 2—Annual sales for the store for the previous year in thousands of dollars.
   - Column 3—Average daily numbers of vehicles that pass the store each day based on actual traffic counts for one month.
   - Column 4—Total population that lives within a two mile radius of the store based on 1990 census data.
   - Column 5—Median family income for households within a two mile radius of the store based on 1990 census data.

Store ID#	Annual Sales ($000)	Average Daily Traffic	Population in 2 Mile Radius	Average Income in Area
1	$1,121	61,655	17,880	$28,991
2	$ 766	35,236	13,742	$14,731
3	$ 595	35,403	19,471	$ 8,114
4	$ 899	52,832	23,246	$15,324
5	$ 915	40,809	24,485	$11,438
6	$ 782	40,820	20,410	$11,730
7	$ 833	49,147	28,997	$10,589
8	$ 571	24,953	9,981	$10,706
9	$ 692	40,828	8,982	$23,591
10	$1,005	39,195	18,814	$15,703
11	$ 589	34,574	16,941	$ 9,015
12	$ 671	26,639	13,319	$10,065
13	$ 903	55,083	21,482	$17,365
14	$ 703	37,892	26,524	$ 7,532
15	$ 556	24,019	14,412	$ 6,950
16	$ 657	27,791	13,896	$ 9,855
17	$1,209	53,438	22,444	$21,589
18	$ 997	54,835	18,096	$22,659
19	$ 844	32,916	16,458	$12,660
20	$ 883	29,139	16,609	$11,618

Answer the following:

a. Which of the other three variables is the best predictor of sales? Compute correlation coefficients to answer the question.

b. Do the following regressions:
  1. Sales as a function of average daily traffic.
  2. Sales as a function of population in two mile radius.

c. Interpret the results of the two regressions.

7. Interpret the following:

a. $Y = .11 + .009X$, where Y is the likelihood of sending children to college and X is family income in thousands of dollars. Remember, it is family income in thousands.
  1. According to our model, how likely is a family with an income of $30,000 to send their children to college?
  2. What is the likelihood for a family with an income of $50,000?
  3. What is the likelihood for a family with an income of $17,500?
  4. Is there some logic to the estimates? Explain.

b. $Y = .25 - .0039X$, where Y is the likelihood of going to a skateboard park and X is age.
  1. According to our model, how likely is a 10-year-old to go to a skateboard park?
  2. What is the likelihood for a 60 year-old?
  3. What is the likelihood for a 40 year-old?
  4. Is there some logic to the estimates? Explain.

8. What purpose does multiple regression serve? Give an example of how it might be used in marketing research. How is the strength of multiple regression measures of association determined?

9. A sales manager examined age data, education level, a personality measure that indicated introvertedness versus extrovertedness, and levels of sales attained by the company's 120-person sales force. The technique used was multiple regression analysis. After analyzing the data, the sales manager said, "It is apparent to me that the higher level of education and the greater the degree of extrovertedness a salesperson has, the higher will be an individual's level of sales. In other words, a

good education and being extroverted cause a person to sell more." Would you agree or disagree with the sales manager's conclusions? Why?

10. The following table shows regression coefficients for two dependent variables. The first dependent variable is consumers' willingness to spend money for cable TV. The independent variables are responses to attitudinal statements. The second dependent variable is persons who would never allow cable TV in their homes. By examining the regression coefficients, what can you say about persons willing to spend money for cable TV and those who would not allow cable TV in their home?

	Regression Coefficients
Willing to Spend Money for Cable TV	
Easy-going on cable repairs	−3.04
Cable movie watcher	2.81
Comedy watcher	2.73
Early to bed	−2.62
Breakdown complainer	2.25
Lovelorn	2.18
Burned out on repeats	−2.06
Never Allow Cable TV in Home	
Antisports	+1.37
Object to sex	+ .47
Too many choices	+ .88

CASE

Selling Chevrolets to Female Car Buyers

Women are becoming increasingly important in America's car lots. Today they buy about 45 percent of all new cars sold in the United States, up from 23 percent in 1970. In addition, they influence 80 percent of all new car purchases. Most important for American manufacturers, among women car buyers, 76 percent bought domestic cars. If they choose an import, women are more likely to buy Japanese cars than men, whereas men are more likely to buy European models. The most popular domestic line of cars among women is the Chevrolet; about 14 percent of female new-car buyers purchased Chevrolets in the late 1980s.

Chevrolet has been targeting the women's market since about 1985, making it the leader in this area among divisions of General Motors. Recently, Chevrolet launched an extensive direct mail and print campaign aimed exclusively at women. Secondary research by Chevrolet's market researchers has noted that women could account for up to 60 percent of new car purchases by the year 2000. Additional secondary research has uncovered some interesting facets of the female automobile purchaser. Women are less comfortable than men when dealing with the financial aspects of purchasing their car. Thus, it is likely that manufacturers and car dealerships that make women feel more comfortable with financial aspects can build a dominant market share among female purchasers. Also, women tend to be more brand loyal in car buying than men. Women pick up on showroom details that men usually ignore. For example, they notice whether a showroom or service area is dirty or noisy. They are more aware of smells, decorative details, and the overall environment.

The company decided to test these theories by means of empirical research:

■ They randomly selected twenty-five dealerships from the population of all Chevrolet dealerships.

TABLE 14.6   *Results of Chevrolet Survey of Female Car Shoppers*

DEALER ID#	PERCENT WHO PURCHASED	AVERAGE DECOR RATING	AVERAGE CLEANLINESS RATING	AVERAGE AGE
1	11%	6.2	8.7	39
2	30	9.2	9.4	44
3	20	8.4	7.3	22
4	9	5.9	6.9	29
5	5	5.2	5.5	34
6	6	6.0	8.8	45
7	5	6.6	6.8	53
8	14	7.1	8.2	21
9	12	6.8	6.9	26
10	7	5.9	4.9	35
11	3	5.1	6.6	27
12	4	8.3	6.3	72
13	5	6.3	7.3	44
14	14	7.8	7.1	39
15	12	7.0	9.1	47
16	4	4.9	7.0	44
17	3	5.2	5.4	34
18	9	6.7	7.3	44
19	8	6.5	8.2	58
20	4	5.9	6.2	62
21	6	6.1	6.3	37
22	11	7.0	7.9	48
23	19	8.8	8.9	41
24	21	9.1	9.4	22
25	22	8.8	8.3	55

■ During a one week period, 100 randomly selected women were interviewed at each dealership. Results of that study are summarized in Table 14.6.

The data includes

■ Column 1—ID number assigned to each dealership.
■ Column 2—Percent of women who purchased a car from the particular dealership (they were tracked for thirty days after the interview).
■ Column 3—Average rating assigned to overall decor of the dealership on a 10 point scale (10 = excellent and 1 = poor).
■ Column 4—Average rating assigned to cleanliness of dealership (10 = extremely clean and 1 = extremely dirty).
■ Column 5—Average age of the women interviewed in years.

1. Which of the other three variables is the best predictor of the percent who purchased? Use correlation analysis.
2. Do the following regressions:
   a. Percent who purchased as a function of decor rating.
   b. Percent who purchased as a function of cleanliness rating.
3. Interpret the results of the two regressions. Which rating has the largest effect on purchasing? Explain.
4. What do your results suggest that the effect of a one unit increase in decor rating on percent purchasing would be?
5. If you were a marketing manager for Chevrolet, what would you be inclined to do based on the statistical results? Explain.

Ethical Dilemma——PART FOUR

General Electric's Americom Satellite Division

Barry Cook, director of marketing research for the NBC division of General Electric, was asked to conduct a market research study to provide a quantitative estimate of the market potential of a direct broadcast satellite business for GE's Americom satellite division, using Ku-band transmissions. (Ku band uses much higher frequencies than C band and requires a three-foot diameter dish-shaped antenna rather than the eight- to ten-foot dish for C band.) This technology could be used as either an adjunct to cable or an alternative to cable, where subscribers throughout the United States could acquire the three-foot receiving dish and decoder, which would allow them to receive a number of channels of programming. Several programming and pricing options were under consideration. A study had already been conducted, using conjoint analysis to test a vast number of programming packages at various pricing options—and this study yielded estimates of high penetration rates for some of the packages (15–20 percent adoption).

This venture involved a large long-term investment, and management asked NBC's research department to design a study that would provide a valid estimate of the number of subscribers such a service would achieve. They did not believe the conjoint study's estimates, and they wanted the researchers to conduct a study that they could believe.

Initially, Barry had two concerns: was it possible to do a study that produced estimates that he would believe of a future market for a nonexistent product? And even if he believed it, why should management believe it? The researchers who had conducted the conjoint analysis believed in what they were doing, but management doubted them.

To do a believable study, the method had to be based on clear reasoning and direct evidence. The logic of the method was shared with management prior to doing the study, and they were committed to a belief in the outcome before the study was even done.

But how can you estimate the market potential for a product that would not be available for years? The last refuge of a market researcher is consumer opinion. However, consumer opinion could be misused in so many ways in the service of predicting a market. Barry felt a lot more confident about measuring consumer *behavior* to predict consumer behavior than measuring consumer *behavior* to predict consumer behavior than measuring consumer *opinion* to predict consumer behavior. How could he test consumer behavior relative to a product that does not exist?

You can describe the three-foot satellite dish to people, you can describe what kind of programming is available on the channels it receives—and people should be able to imagine what the product is. You can also describe the price to them and people can certainly imagine a multi-hundred-dollar price tag. If you ask them if that dish is worth the money (plus the monthly charge for the decoder box), a certain percentage of people are going to say it is worth the money and the balance are not. Is this the percentage of people who will buy it?

When you ask consumers to help you predict a market for a product or service, they tell you what they think the market is going to be, or what they think other people will do, or what they think they will do. None of these pieces of information give you a market estimate. What you need to know is what consumers will actually do. Do not ask them to help predict a market; ask them to be a market.

What Barry really wanted to do was to test market the dish and service. In a test market, you are not asking people to play what-if. You are telling them what, and they are telling you if. The percent who say yes *are* willing to spend their money on the product. That is the number GE needs to know. But GE did not have the dish and service yet, so Barry could not test market it. Also, he needed to make an estimate for a very large geographical universe: those parts of the continental United States that are covered by a strong enough satellite signal for the three-foot dish to work (about 85 percent of the country). The cost of installing and servicing the dishes across the entire country is not a test market, it is the market. And GE wanted to test about ten different options for pricing and programming. So those constraints pointed to a simulated test market with a telephone sampling frame.

What could be simulated? Telemarketing the sign ups for this service, that is what. Here is the concept: a random sample of people throughout the potential coverage area of the satellite signal get a telephone call in which the interviewer gives them a sales pitch for the satellite dish, the channels it receives, what it costs, how they could finance it with Visa or MasterCard—and then the interviewer pops the question: can we count on you to buy it? The percentage of people who say "yes" is an estimate of the percentage of people who would say "yes" if the product were available today and it were marketed this way. That is not quite the same as the percentage of people who would say "yes" three years from now, especially if some unforeseen technology were also available to them that met similar needs.

So the approach is simulated test marketing through telemarketing. To tighten the estimate, Barry needed to find out who were the qualified prospects. Therefore, he also planned to collect qualification data from the respondents who said they would sign up in the interview. It was important to identify respondents who say yes but who already own the big dishes—because there may be a separate market for converters from big dishes. Also, he wanted to disqualify those with very low income—he did not expect many low-income people to say "yes," but those who did might be poor risks. Barry also disqualified people who lived in apartments where the landlord would not let them put a TV aerial on the roof—in the end, they would not be able to put up a dish.

One more point, it is important to distinguish between people who can get cable and those who live in what are called nonpassed areas—places where cable is not available. The prime market for this device is probably in nonpassed areas—but no one had a list of people in nonpassed areas—cable is available in 90 percent of the country, but there are all these little pockets where cable is not available. Barry wanted to test different options in passed versus nonpassed areas, so he needed to oversample nonpassed areas. He planned to start the interview with a screening question to identify people who could not get cable even if they wanted to, but it was going to be very expensive to screen for the required number of interviews in nonpassed areas, given the low incidence. Barry decided to use a clustering approach rather than pure RDD: when he found a person who claimed to live in a nonpassed area, he made many more dialings in the same telephone exchange (with four digit random suffixes)—and found that he could triple the yield of nonpassed homes over pure RDD using this enrichment technique.

So if GE did a research interview that sounds like a telemarketing sales pitch—but is really a research interview because nothing was being sold at the time, then Barry would get what he needs—real consumer behavior because they think they are buying when they answer the "can we count on you to buy" question.

The researchers start off by telling them that they are not selling anything, but are doing a research study. This is the truth, although it happens to be the same wording that telemarketers use when they engage in deceptive practices. The researcher then asks them a couple of questions about their cable status and the availability of cable in their neighborhood if they are nonsubscribers. Then the interviewers launch into a big pitch about how wonderful this new dish is and all the great things you can receive on it and it costs only X hundred dollars to purchase the dish plus Y tens of dollars a month for the decoder box. When this dish and service become available in your neighborhood, can we count on you to buy? At this point, respondents are placed in a situation that they are likely to perceive as a real purchase decision. The percent who say "yes" is the estimate of market penetration (less the disqualifications noted previously for low income, large dish ownership, and inability to install a dish).

Notice that the researcher is not asking them how likely they think they would be to purchase (definitely purchase, probably purchase, probably not purchase, or definitely not purchase). When you ask that kind of question, you then have to apply weights to the obtained percentages to discount some of the intended purchasers because this method produces estimates that past experience has shown to be too high. The past experience is with the question, not with the particular product or service. Do researchers really believe that a fixed percentage of people who hold an attitude will act on it—no matter what the attitude? And when you analyze the characteristics of those who hold the attitude, most of whom will not exhibit the behavior of interest, what are you learning about the characteristics of those who will exhibit the behavior? Certainly, you have a larger sample size of intended purchasers than purchasers, so you can attribute greater statistical significance to the analyses you do on the wrong people. The fundamental problem is that you have not asked people to make a purchase decision, you have asked them to sing the praises of your concept. Then, without the use of data from the market research, you, the market researcher, through your expertise alone, decide how many of the people who are gushing over the concept would actually purchase and how many of the people who are mildly interested in it will actually purchase. Why ask the wrong question and guess what percentage of the answer to believe, when you could have the information GE needs simply by asking the right question in the right context?

Recall that the key here was to produce an estimate that management could believe. To the extent that the respondents in the study believed that they were purchasing the dish, the clients for the study could believe the estimates of potential market.*

*This case was developed from Barry Cook, "Simulation of Purchase Decisions: Is It Unethical to be Too Realistic?" *CASRO Journal 1991:* 105–112.

1. Was Barry's research methodology unethical? Remember, respondents were told at the outset that it was not a sales call.
2. A pretest of twenty interviews was completed; sixteen out of the twenty people thought that they were making a commitment to purchase the dish. Does this information change your feelings about the ethical nature of the research?
3. Do you think that it is important to tell the respondents at the end of the interview that they didn't purchase anything and they could not have purchased anything because it is a research study? Why or why not?

PART 5

Marketing Research in Action

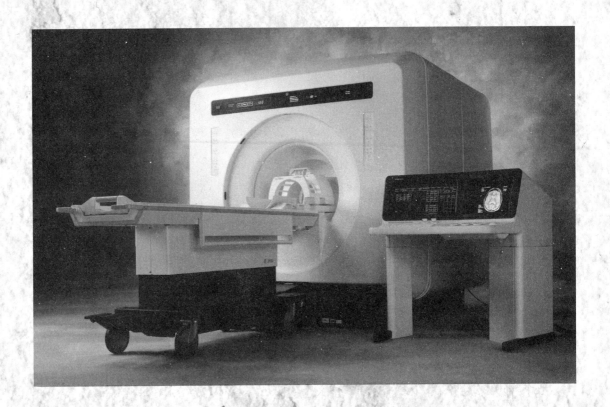

CHAPTER 15

Communicating the Research Results

LEARNING OBJECTIVES

1. To gain an understanding of barriers to communication.

2. To become aware of the primary roles of a research report.

3. To understand how to organize a research report.

4. To learn how to prepare a research report.

5. To review pitfalls in marketing research reports.

6. To become acquainted with evaluating report drafts.

7. To learn about oral presentations.

8. To understand the obstacles to the effective use of marketing research information.

W ith a core market of radiology departments in approximately 7,500 hospitals and clinics in the United States, GE Medical Systems Group has a small customer base relative to many industries. Soliciting the opinions of these customers who have made six- (or even seven-) figure investments in GE diagnostic imaging equipment is a high priority for GE Medical Systems.

Milwaukee-based GE Medical, a business group of General Electric, uses two types of mailed surveys to encourage customers to voice their opinions. The first survey is called the postinstallation tracking study, which asks for the customer's opinion of the sales process, preinstallation, delivery, installation, training, and product performance for his or her recent purchase. The second survey is the sales and service tracking study, which asks the customer to evaluate GE Medical's total account management and service delivery performance. This survey is mailed to every GE medical customer annually.

The surveys achieved their initial goal—obtaining customer feedback—but GE Medical did not have an ongoing process to resolve the issues the surveys uncovered. In late 1991, GE Medical created a customer satisfaction department for this purpose, with the additional mission of raising overall customer satisfaction. The new department took on responsibility for the surveys.

Study results were distilled a variety of ways. Since the findings addressed the performance of several different departments at GE Medical, Kennedy Research tailored a potpourri of written reports to the specific needs of various departments, including a monthly one-page summary of key findings from each individual survey, and a quarterly overview of the top five sources of satisfaction. "But as the study matured, it mushroomed in terms of the type of information we wanted from it," Dennis Cook, GE Medical customer satisfaction process manager, noted. "Each department was interested in a different aspect of the study, which meant that reporting the results became a fairly complicated process."[1]

W hat is the role of the research report? How can marketing researchers communicate more effectively? What constitutes a "good" report? What pitfalls should be avoided in writing a research report? We will address these questions in this chapter.

It should almost go without saying that no matter how appropriate the research design, how proper the statistical analyses, how representative the sample, how carefully worded the questionn aire, how stringent the quality control checks for field collection of the data, or how well-matched the research was to the original research objectives, everything will be for naught if the researcher cannot communicate with the decision makers. Chapter 15 begins with a discussion of the communication process. Next, the roles of the research report are presented. From here, the chapter delves into the organization of the report and points out how findings are interpreted into conclusions and how conclusions are then formulated into recommendations. Next, the chapter turns to the actual writing of the report. Because oral presentations are common in marketing research, the chapter includes discussion of this aspect of reporting the results. We conclude with suggestions for getting managers to use the research recommendations.

EFFECTIVE COMMUNICATION

Good **communication** is the result of any action, physical, written, or verbal, that conveys accurate meanings between two individuals. The essence of communication is shared meaning and mutual understanding. In other words, communication results in two or more individuals sharing the meaning of some concept such as an action, a word, or a symbol.

Perfect communication probably never occurs. Nonetheless, it is the goal of every marketing researcher writing a research report to present the information in as lucid a manner as possible. A number of factors have been identified to be deterrents or barriers to communication. Most of these factors are relevant to the marketing researcher attempting to communicate the research results to the decision makers.

Communication
The result of any action, physical, written, or verbal, that conveys meanings between two individuals.

Noise

In communication theory, anything that interferes with the audience receiving a message is considered **noise**. This noise can be physical such as other people talking, a machine operating in the background, coughing, shuffling of the feet, or any other physical distraction that can be identified. Noise can also be of a psychological origin such as a distracting thought, some emotional turmoil in the mind of the receiver, or even a faulty mental process. The executive who listens to a marketing research presentation but is thinking about other company problems, such as how to improve production efficiency, is experiencing noise that interferes with the communication process.

Noise
Anything that interferes with the audience receiving a message.

Attention Span

Every person has a limited **attention span**. Each individual's attention span is different, and it may be long or short, depending upon the person's interest or ego involvement with the topic, physical state, and mental capabilities. Marketing researchers are constantly encountering problems with the attention span of the decision makers in attempts to communicate the results of research. The marketing researcher is accustomed to working with large data sets, leafing through pages and pages of computer output, and compiling large tabular presentations of information. In other words, the marketing researcher has a very long attention span for a

Attention span
The length of time a particular individual will concentrate on a particular subject at a particular time.

particular research study. However, the decision maker is much more accustomed to short periods of intense attention on a problem. Consequently, although the researcher must provide the findings, summaries, and whatever else is included in the research report, he or she constantly fights the battle of holding or restimulating the attention of the reader or listener.

Selective Perception

Selective perception
The ability of the listener or reader to filter out some information for conscious or subconscious reasons.

Research report writers must always be cognizant of **selective perception**. Managers and other users of research data tend to "see what they want to see." A new product manager may rejoice over a high rate of initial trial on a test market and ignore the low repurchase rate. Or, a manager may make an equivocal statement regarding a research project but ignore sampling limitations that greatly hamper the generalizability of the results. Subconsciously, individuals also filter out messages of low interest or for which they have preconceived notions. There is a human tendency to avoid opposing, disagreeable, and dissonant information. Alternatively, there exists a tendency to select specific pieces of information that support a preconceived opinion or lend credence to a particular argument while ignoring or discounting information that does not support it.

How does the marketing researcher overcome barriers of selective perception, attention span, and noise? Unfortunately, there are no easy answers to this question. There is no guaranteed way or combination of ways to effect complete and perfect communication. But, a number of guidelines can help overcome various parts of these communication barriers. These will be discussed after we describe the research report.

THE RESEARCH REPORT

The marketing research report has three primary roles: to communicate findings, to serve as a reference document, and to provide credibility for the work accomplished.

1. *The marketing research report must communicate the study's specifics.* The marketing research report has the critical function of containing a complete and accurate description of the relevant findings of the marketing research project undertaken. That is, it must be detailed and communicate to the reader the following items:
   - The research objectives
   - Central background information
   - An overview of the research methods used
   - The findings displayed in tabular or visual format
   - Summary of the findings
   - Conclusions
   - Recommendations
2. *The research report must act as a reference document.* Once the research report has been duplicated and distributed to the relevant decision makers, it begins to live a life of its own. From that point on it serves as a valuable reference document. Most studies cover several objectives and contain a significant amount of

information. Normally, it is impossible for a decision maker to retain this information in his or her memory for any length of time. Consequently, the marketing researcher will find that decision makers and others, perhaps those performing a secondary information search, will turn back to the report, rereading it to reacquaint themselves with the findings of the study. The findings may even serve as a baseline for a follow-up study. For example, a company's image may be measured yearly and changes in the strengths and weakness of the image can be examined by the decision makers.

3. *The research report must build and sustain the credibility of the study.* This third and final role of the marketing research report cannot be overemphasized. The marketing research report must communicate to the reader the degree of care and quality control that went into the marketing research project. The attention span and selective perception barriers operate against the marketing researcher in this capacity. In fact, it is not unusual for a manager to completely skip over the description of the research method and go directly to the findings, conclusions, or recommendations. Because this may be the case, the marketing researcher will find that the credibility of the study is greatly affected by the physical appearance of the research report itself. In other words, items such as typographical errors, poorly documented tables or figures, inconsistent margins, heading arrangements, or even the cover and binding of the report will affect the reader's evaluation of the credibility of the study. Such a situation is unfortunate, but it is a reality. The perceived quality of the research report by managers is a primary determinant of whether the managers will use the research findings.[2]

ORGANIZING THE RESEARCH REPORT

Physical Organization of the Report

Sometimes corporate policy or other factors may dictate the precise format of the research report. Nonetheless, every research report should have certain topics regardless of its specific format or physical appearance. The report must be structured and written in a manner that communicates timely, relevant, and succinct information to management decision makers. An important premise to recall in report writing is that middle and upper management often have extreme demands on their time. To help key people read the report, the writer must avoid jargon and structure the data presentation properly. We recommend the following basic components be included:

1. Table of Contents
2. Objectives of the Research
3. Concise Statement of the Methodology ⎫
4. Brief Summary of the Findings   ⎬ Management Summary
5. Conclusions and Recommendations   ⎭
6. Detailed Introduction
7. Detailed Analysis and Findings
8. Detailed Conclusions
9. Detailed Methodology
10. Limitations
11. Appendices (if necessary)

Management summary
The portion of a research report that explains why the research was done, what was found and what those findings mean, and what action, if any, management should undertake.

Because a number of managers may be reading the report (many of whom were not present during the research request stage or the oral presentation), a management summary is needed. The **management summary** explains why and how the research was undertaken, what was found and what it means, and what action, if any, management should undertake. It is important to begin the summary with a statement of objectives. Why did the company spend the time and money and what was it trying to accomplish? This section places the remainder of the report in the proper prospective. It also allows management to review the findings and recommendations with a common frame of reference—the problem statement.

The objectives should be as explicit as possible, yet confined to one or two pages at most. The summary of findings should also be confined to one or two pages. Again, if the researcher wants management to read the work, the essential elements of the report (items 2–5) must be kept short. The conclusions and recommendations should also remain as brief as possible. Depending on circumstances, this section may run a few pages longer than the other essential elements.

Obviously some managers, such as product managers, the director of marketing research, or others, want more information about the research. They will delve into the body of the report to examine the logic of the conclusions, to obtain a better understanding of key findings, to find nuances overlooked by the report writer, and to accept or reject the recommendations. The body of the report is written for these readers. But, it should not be a foregone conclusion that the detailed findings section of the report must be dull and boring. Proper use of summary tables and visual aids such as pie charts, bar graphs, and other tools will illustrate key points and provide additional clarity to the data. In the past, graphic displays of data were time consuming and expensive to prepare. Personal computers and graphics software packages have solved this problem by providing a quick and low-cost means of preparing graphics of all types, from simple bar charts in black and white, to sophisticated full-color graphics (see Figure 15.1).

The appendix should be reserved for tables not included in the detailed findings section, a sample questionnaire, maps, and other material that is too complex, too specialized, or not directly relevant to the main body of the report. A suggested format for the research report is shown in Figure 15.2.

Richard Kitaeff, manager of marketing research and quality measurements for AT&T, claims it is crucial that a transmittal letter addressed to the client should accompany each report. The transmittal letter should include a short summary of the findings (sort of a highlight of the highlights) and the report's key recommendations. Often, Kitaeff notes, "even if the report is never read by the decision makers—the transmittal letter will be."[3]

Interpreting the Findings and Formulating Recommendations

Among the greatest difficulties faced by individuals who are writing a research report for the first time occurs in the interpretation of the findings to arrive at conclusions and using these conclusions to formulate recommendations. This difficulty is completely understandable given that the marketing researcher is often inundated with mounds of computer printouts, stacks of questionnaires, bundles of respondent contact and recontact sheets, and a scratch pad full of notes on the project. There is, however, a systematic method that the researcher can follow to

FIGURE 15.1   *Black-and-White Bar Graph and Pie Chart Prepared on a Personal Computer with Graphics Software*

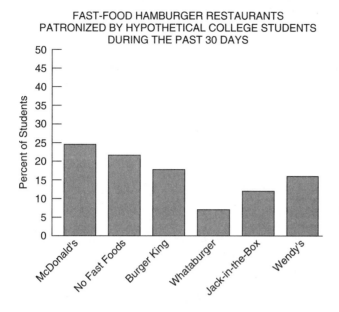

FAST-FOOD HAMBURGER RESTAURANTS
PATRONIZED BY HYPOTHETICAL COLLEGE STUDENTS
DURING THE PAST 30 DAYS

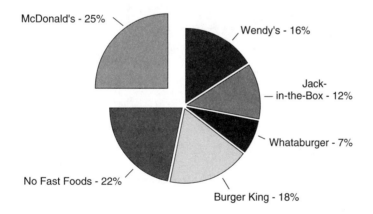

FAST-FOOD HAMBURGER RESTAURANTS
PATRONIZED BY HYPOTHETICAL COLLEGE STUDENTS
DURING THE PAST 30 DAYS

draw conclusions. The overall guide comes from the research objectives stated very early in the marketing research process. These research objectives are stated as specifically as possible and perhaps even with an explicit priority rank for each objective. Also, the questionnaire was designed to touch facets of the objectives, but the specific bits of information for any one objective were spread across the questionnaire. The computer printouts often contain information in a statistical order rather than in the order in which managers will use the data. Consequently, the researcher's first task is to pull together all the printouts and results pertaining to each of the various objectives. By focusing attention on the objectives one at a time, a system will evolve.

For example, assume that Burger King is considering its breakfast menu. An objective of its breakfast research study is "to determine the feasibility of adding

---

FIGURE 15.2 *Contents of Marketing Research Report*

Title page
1. Title
2. Client
3. Research company
4. Date

Table of Contents
1. Section titles and subheadings with page numbers
2. Table of tables; titles and pages
3. Table of figures; titles and pages
4. Appendices; titles and pages

Management Summary
1. Concise statement of objectives
2. Concise statement of methodology
3. Concise statement of major finding(s)
4. Concise statement of conclusions and recommendations
5. Other pertinent information as required (e.g., special techniques, limitations, or background information)

Introduction
1. Background of the research undertaken
2. People involved and positions held
3. Acknowledgments

Analysis and Findings
1. Types of analysis described in general terms
2. Tables and figures
3. Explanatory text

Conclusions and Recommendations

Research Methodology
1. Type of study
2. Intent of study
3. Definition of population
4. Sample design and technique
    a. Definition of sampled unit
    b. Type of design (probability versus nonprobability; specific)
5. Data collection method (e.g., telephone, personal, mail, self-administered)
6. Questionnaire
    a. General description
    b. Discussion of "special" types of questions used
7. Special problems or considerations

Limitations
1. Sample size limitations
2. Sample selection limitations
3. Other limitations (frame error, timing, analysis, etc.)

Appendices
1. Questionnaire
2. Technical appendix (e.g., detailed explanation of a statistical tool such as conjoint analysis)
3. Other appendices as necessary (e.g., a map of the area in which the survey took place)

(a) bagels and cream cheese, (b) a western omelette, or (c) French toast." All crosstabulations and one-dimensional tables referring to these food items should be brought together. Generally, the researcher first examines the one-dimensional tables to get the overall picture; that is, which of the three breakfast items was most preferred. Next, crosstabulations are analyzed to obtain a better understanding of the overall data; that is, which age group was most likely to prefer French toast.

Conclusions are generalizations that answer the questions raised by the research objectives or otherwise satisfy the objectives. These conclusions are derived through the process of induction, which is the process of generalizing from small pieces of information. The researcher should try to combine the information and to paraphrase it in a few descriptive statements that generalize the results. In short, the conclusion or generalization would be a statement or series of statements that would communicate the results of the study to the reader but would not necessarily indicate the numbers derived from the statistical analysis.

Recommendations are gained from the process of deduction. The marketing researcher takes the conclusions to be specific areas of application for marketing strategy or tactics. A recommendation should normally focus on how the client can gain a differential advantage. A differential advantage is the true benefit offered by a potential marketing mix that the target market cannot obtain anywhere else, such as United Airlines having exclusive U.S. carrier landing rights at a foreign airport.

In some instances, a marketing researcher must refrain from making specific recommendations and fall back on general recommendations. These are cases in which the marketing researcher either does not have sufficient information about the resource and experience base of the company or decision maker to whom the report is being directed or the researcher has been notified that the recommendations will be determined by the decision maker. Under these circumstances, the researcher offers conclusions and stops at that point.

PREPARING THE REPORT

The final report, whether written, oral, or both, represents the culmination of the research effort. The quality of the report and its recommendations often determine whether a research user will return to a supplier. Within a corporation, an internal report prepared by a research department may have a similar impact. If you want to think on a more selfish level, a history of excellent reports prepared by a research staff member may lead to merit salary increases and ultimately promotion.

Pitfalls in Marketing Research Reports

A number of common faults are encountered in writing research reports, and it is wise to keep them in mind throughout the report writing process.

Length Does Not Mean Quality.   One of the common misconceptions in marketing research is "the longer the report, the better it is."[4] Often after working months on a project, a researcher is highly involved in a problem and wants to tell the reader everything known about the issue. All qualifications, implications, and hundreds of pages of computer printouts are included resulting in noise sometimes referred to as "information overload." It is often difficult to convince a young researcher that

MARKETING RESEARCH IN PRACTICE

Verbatims
Use of the respondent's own words.

Howard Gordon, a principal of George R. Fredricks and Associates, a Chicago-based market research company, offers the following advice on preparing a good research report.

1. *Present tense works better.* Use present tense. Results and observations expressed in *now* terms sound better and are easier to read.

   Don't say: "The test panel liked the taste of the juice." Say: "People like the taste of the juice."

   We do studies for clients to help them make decisions today and tomorrow—not yesterday.

2. *Use active voice.* Use active voice where possible—which is in most cases. Passive voice doesn't swing. There is nothing wrong with saying: "We believe . . ." rather than, "It is believed that . . ."

   Passive voice is stilted. Use first person plural—not third person singular.

   Present tense and active voice make reports sound action oriented—businesslike.

3. *Use informative headlines—not label headlines.* Your reader will welcome this headline: "Convenience is the packaging's major benefit." Your reader will not generally welcome this headline: "Analysis of packaging." Nor this: "How people feel about packaging."

4. *Let your tables and charts work. Help them with words when needed.* Don't take a paragraph or a page to describe what a table already says. If there is nothing to say about a table or a chart, don't say it.

The purpose of a table or a chart is to simplify. Use your words to point out significant items in the table—something that is not readily clear. Or use your words to offer interpretive comments. Use verbatims from sample respondents to support a point. But if you're simply going to repeat what's already in the chart, don't bother.

5. *Use the double-sided presentation whenever possible.* This format will reduce the verbiage in your report. It simply presents the table on the left side of the open report. Your informative headline and interpretive comments are on the right-hand page.

   Most people don't like research reports because they're wordy. Wordy reports offer little reader reward. They're right. Avoid wordy reports. Thin reports get taken home on weekends—and slide easily into brief cases for airplane and train reading.

6. *Make liberal use of verbatims.* Great nuggets of marketing wisdom have come from people's comments. Use **verbatims** if you have them.

   Sprinkle the verbatims throughout your report in appropriate places.

   Bulova Accutron was born from verbatims. So was man-size from Kleenex, Libby's bite-size fruit, United's friendly skies. They did not come from tables.

   Besides, verbatims help make research reports interesting and readable.

   People who think research reports are readable, interesting, rewarding, and useful usually ask for more research.[5]

most management people will not read the entire report. In fact, they may not read any of it if the report is not properly structured. Research is not bought by the pound. Rather, quality, conciseness, and validity count.

Insufficient Explanation.   Some researchers simply repeat numbers from the tables without any attempt at interpretation. Although most people can read a table, it is normally the function of the writer to impart meaning to the data. Moreover, few things will "turn off" a reader more than page after page of statistics without an attempt at interpretation or explanation as to why the tables are there.

Failure to Relate to Objectives or Reality.   Reporting mounds of data without referring to the research objectives is another common pitfall of report writing. The reader wants to know what the survey results mean in terms of marketing goals. Are the goals now unattainable? Are additional resources needed? Should the product or service be repositioned?

Perhaps just as bad as failing to relate results to objectives is the unrealistic recommendation. Increasing promotional expenditures $10,000 per market may be beyond the financial capabilities of the firm. Or, if a product placement reveals that items "A" and "B" are perceived as parity products, a recommendation to produce both may be imprudent. A bank image study that recommends wholesale firing of loan officers would undoubtedly be considered impractical.

Indiscriminate Use of Quantitative Techniques.   Some report writers are guilty of the "snow job"; that is, writing a report in highly technical terms and using quantitative overkill. Sometimes extensive use of multivariate and other statistical techniques is a cover-up for ill-defined objectives and methodology. Little will cause a report to be rejected faster than writing not understandable by a nontechnical marketing manager. Overuse of statistics often raises legitimate questions of the quality of the research in the mind of the research user.

False Accuracy.   Quoting statistics to two decimal places with a relatively small sample gives an unwarranted illusion of accuracy, or **false accuracy**. For example, a statement that our product was preferred by 68.47 percent of survey respondents tends to legitimize the statistic 68 percent. A reader may think that if the researcher can quote a number to .47 percent, then the 68 percent must be cast in concrete.

False accuracy
An unwarranted illusion of accuracy provided by details, such as statistics quoted to two decimal places.

The Fallacy of Single-Number Research.   Some researchers place far too much emphasis on a single statistic to provide an answer to a client's decision. This tendency is prevalent in concept tests and product placements. The key question is purchase intent. If the "definitely will buy" and "probably will buy" do not add up to a predetermined standard, say, 75 percent, the concept or test product is dropped. But, a product placement questionnaire may contain fifty questions designed to ferret out positioning information, segmentation data, perceived strengths and weaknesses; yet all of this is totally subordinate to the purchase intent question. There is no magic in any one question or predetermined cut-off standard. Overreliance on **single-number research** may result in missed opportunities or, in other situations, marketing the wrong product.

Single-number research
Placing too much emphasis on a single statistic.

Inaccurate Data Interpretation.   It is the researcher's obligation to render objective interpretations; however, it is sometimes easy to slip into inaccurate interpretation. For example, scaling is a very common candidate for inaccurate data analysis. A researcher conducted a call back on a test coffee product placement with a Stapel scale devised to measure bitterness of coffees "A" and "B." The scale runs from "very bitter" to "no bitterness" with values of −2, −1, 0, +1, and +2. The average rating for "A" is 1.2 and, for "B," 0.8. Subtracting one from another and calculating a simple percentage leads to the conclusion that "B" is perceived at 50 percent more bitter than "A."

But what if a different set of weights had been used? Assume a 1 to 5 scale of "very bitter" to "no bitterness" had been applied. "A" is rated 4.2, and "B" receives an average of 3.8. Using the same respondents, the same coffees, the same questionnaire, and a different rating scale yields a percentage difference of only 11.5 percent. Now test coffee "B" does not look so bad.

Now, take a third look at the same data. In this case, the researcher uses the 1 to 5 scale but reverses the adjectives. "No bitterness" is now 1 and "very bitter" equals 5. The mean ratings of 2.2 for coffee "B" and 1.8 for coffee "A," a percentage difference of 18.2 percent.

Accurate interpretation requires that the report writer have intimate knowledge of scaling assumptions, statistical methods, and the study's limitations.

The Gee Whiz Chart.   A good picture is worth a thousand words, but a bad picture (chart) is not simply worthless, it is misleading. It may be artistic, colorful, and eye-catching but fail to fulfill its function. A chart dramatizes the facts, but many charts overdramatize them. These are called "gee-whiz" charts.[6]

FIGURE 15.3   *The Gee Whiz Chart Versus Reality*

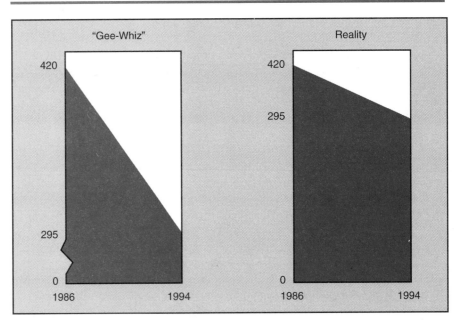

Source: Adapted from Thomas T. Semon, "A Bad Picture Is Worth Very Few Words," *Marketing News* (May 24, 1993): 11.

MARKETING RESEARCH IN PRACTICE

n determining the quality of a marketing research report, use these guidelines.

1. Does the report contain data from the pertinent survey exclusively, or does it also rely on other data, data from previous reports or external data in order to gain more perspective and to control the validity of survey data through external data?

2. Does the report rely on the direct statements of respondents, taking them at face value? This could be called passing the investigation task on to the respondent. Or has more knowledge been brought to light by translating them into new questions, ideas, and new tests, as well as by applying mathematical-statistical analysis, than would have been obtained by direct questioning of the respondents and simply tallying up their responses?

3. Does the report contain surprising findings for you? Are these findings numerically established, crucial in providing an answer to the investigation task, and do they have an impact on the concrete conclusions you draw? Especially important, does the report contain results that common sense would not have expected?

4. Check the linguistic quality of both report and tables, and check in particular whether specific technical terms of your trade and your market are used, and used correctly. And conversely, how much superfluous jargon is used, befogging the text? Linguistic quality of text and tables (and particularly of tables) is like the tip of an iceberg. It reveals the overall quality of the work you receive.

5. Check whether the questions you want to find answered are clearly worded and answered in the report. Or is the report rather written in a fortune-telling style; that is, the assertions of one sentence nullify that of the other?

6. Check whether the report contains hints toward the practical significance of the results and consequences for their application. How well has the author of the report been able to immerse himself or herself in your problems? And even if you draw your own conclusions, never leave out the opportunity of hearing the view of the report author.[7]

Making a gee-whiz chart is simple. You draw a correct chart and cut off the bottom part, show a little jog in the vertical scale on the left to indicate that the scale is incomplete, and voila! Any trend, up or down, will look much more impressive.

A gee-whiz chart similar to one in Figure 15.3 ran in a respected business publication recently, depicting sales of an imported car. Compare that to the real chart showing the same data. A drop from 420 to 295 is a 30 percent decline. When charted, it should look like a 30 percent decline, not 90 percent as in the gee-whiz chart. Sure, when we look at the numbers we realize that the decline is not 90 percent, but the whole point of a chart is to get away from looking at the numbers and to represent their impact pictorially.

EVALUATING THE REPORT DRAFTS

The writing process is an art enhanced with communication effectiveness guidelines. With each written draft, the report writer should evaluate the quality of the work. The draft should be reviewed from the perspective of the client. Will he or she fully understand what this means? The writer should also become his or her own devil's advocate. If possible, a third party should critique the draft.

During the review process, the writer should refer to the research proposal. Did the report meet the objectives established in the proposal? Was the methodology outlined in the proposal followed? Are the conclusions based upon logical deductions from the data analysis? Do the recommendations seem prudent given the research conclusions?

Is the writing style crisp and lucid? The report should be as concise as possible. It should follow the format outlined earlier in the chapter so that salient findings and recommendations can be determined quickly and easily.

Although checklists often "overmechanize" an evaluation process, the points offered by Elizabeth Noelle-Neumann of the Institut fur Demoskopie Allensbach, Frankfurt, Germany, in the Marketing Research in Practice box can be helpful in determining the quality of a marketing research report.

THE ORAL PRESENTATION

Most clients expect an oral presentation of the research findings. This activity serves many purposes. It assembles the several interested parties together. It reacquaints them with the research objectives and method. Also, an oral presentation brings to light any unexpected events or findings. Most of all, it highlights the research conclusions. In fact, it is safe to say that for some decision makers in the company, the oral presentation will be their *only* exposure to the findings: they will never read the report. Other managers may only skim the written report, using it as a memory

A good oral presentation requires that the speaker uses terminology to which the audience can relate. (Charles Gupton/Stock, Boston)

An American executive conducted an extensive marketing research study concerning the prospect of his company entering a strategic alliance with a Malaysian counterpart to market consumer products in Malaysia. Upon completing the study he wrote a report that he would later present orally in Malaysia. The research results looked very promising, and the report was full of enthusiasm for the possibility of future success. Upon arriving in Malaysia to present the report to a Malaysian "top decision maker," the American was introduced to several Malaysian individuals, all with rather long and difficult names to pronounce. However, one distinguished looking fellow had a name he could remember, namely—Rodger (or so he thought). Throughout his oral presentation, he addressed his finding to this man and electing to take on an air of informality that often prevails in the United States, called him "Rog." Near the middle of his presentation, "Rodger" got up and left the room, apparently in a huff. The American's research presentation was immediately suspended, and the strategic alliance postponed. What had happened? Unfortunately, this well-meaning American did not know that in Malaysia, while many states are headed by sultans, one is controlled by rajahs. Rajah is a title of nobility, not a personal name. The American not only insulted the "top decision maker" but sacrificed his joint venture.

GLOBAL MARKETING RESEARCH

recall trigger for points made in the oral presentation. In short, effective communication in the oral presentation is absolutely critical.

Materials for the Oral Presentation

We recommend four aids to be used in the oral presentation:

1. *Presentation outline.* Every audience member should be supplied a presentation outline that very briefly details the presentation flow (major parts) and significant findings. The outline should not contain statistics or tables, but it should have ample "white space" for the person to jot down notes or comments.
2. *Visuals.* The most commonly used visual device is a projector. Either a slide projector or an overhead projector can be used. The presentation should rely heavily on visual portrayals of the findings. Graphs, charts, and figures should be used whenever possible. If tables are used, color highlights can enhance the presentation or otherwise focus attention on the specific parts of interest. Summaries, conclusions, and recommendations should be made with visuals.
3. *Management (or executive) summary.* Each audience member should have a copy of the management summary (preferably several days in advance). This allows for a more fruitful discussion. It also enables managers to contemplate questions to ask in advance of the presentation.
4. *Copies of the final report.* The report serves as physical evidence of the research and should make clear that much detail has been omitted in the oral presentation. It should be made available to interested parties at the end of the presentation.

Making an Oral Presentation

Philip H. Abelson, a distinguished scientist and editor of *Science,* recently wrote a very blunt statement about the problem of communication in science and business: "when it comes to communicating, few researchers are skillful. The majority cannot even effectively convey scientific information to each other. This is true of verbal presentations, in which decade after decade most scientists use slides that cannot be read beyond the front row of the audience."[8] Some marketing researchers are guilty of inadequate oral presentations. Perhaps one reason for this is a lack of understanding of the barriers to effective communication outlined at the beginning of this chapter. A second factor is failure to recognize or admit that the purpose of many research reports is persuasion. This does not mean stretching or bending the truth but rather using research findings to reinforce the conclusions and recommendations of the researcher.

An effective oral presentation recognizes the nature of the audience. It is cognizant of the receiver's frame of reference, attitudes, prejudices, educational background, and time constraints. The speaker must select words, concepts, and illustrative figures to which an audience can relate. A good presentation also leaves time at the end for questions and discussion.

In preparing an oral presentation, the researcher should keep the following questions in mind:

- What do the data really mean?
- What impact do they have?
- What have we learned from the data?
- What do we need to do, given the information we now have?
- How can future studies of this nature be enhanced?
- What can make information such as this more useful?[9]

Figure 15.4 provides a few helpful hints that can increase the effectiveness of an oral presentation.

Getting Managers to Use the Research Information

Marketing managers today are faced with the significant task of making more effective use of marketing research information. Failure to use appropriate information or use it effectively can hinder productivity and increase the time it takes to go to the marketplace with new ideas and products. All companies can make more effective use of marketing research information. Even firms that currently use research information very effectively, such as AMOCO, Citicorp, Kraft General Foods, and Eastman Kodak, still feel they can do a better job. The task is complicated by the fact that marketing managers use research information differently and value information differently.

A research study was conducted recently of Fortune 500 companies in the chemical, consumer packaged-goods, and telecommunications industries and of forty executives of large and medium-sized companies who are members of The Strategic Planning Institute, an international business think tank. The purpose of the research was to identify the key factors in the effective use of marketing research.[10] Those factors are

---

FIGURE 15.4   *Eighteen Ways to Communicate Better*

---

1. Prepare yourself by organizing primary and secondary data for your presentation.

2. Get to know your audience members and their interests before you make the presentation.

3. Know your objectives. Ask yourself: Why am I making the presentation? Develop a communicative strategy of how to combine the interest of your audience with your own goal. Practice the communication concept.

4. Use notes. Memorize the opening if you must.

5. Just be yourself. Nobody expects you to be Jay Leno, Bob Hope, or Billy Graham.

6. Start by outlining the entire presentation in the form of four or five key topics on the screen. It helps your audience see where things fit together and where the presentation is going.

7. Begin with your most dramatic and convincing point or quickly build up to a climax so that you receive the full attention of the audience from the start.

8. Think of your presentation as a service. Look at it from your audience members' viewpoints. Continuously ask yourself: How does the presentation help the audience? The organization? My own operation? What is in it for all? Establish mutual benefits. Think of the plus-plus relationship in transactional analysis.

9. Keep it simple and easy to understand. Use short sentences: subject, verb, object.

10. Do not discuss too many points and details; the main mission of your presentation may get lost.

11. Anticipate objections. Recognize them if you cannot fight them. Stating an objection calmly takes the emotion out of it. You also show that you are aware of it.

12. End with a positive note. Summarize what the listeners might lose and what they will gain.

13. Remember, a presentation is not a sermon. It is sharing ideas with your audience—ideas that may affect their jobs, their future.

14. Don't talk down to your audience. Use "we" instead of "I."

15. Talk directly to your audience. Don't lose personal contact by looking out of the window or at your shoes. Look people straight in the eyes.

16. Use charts and figures. Don't overload them. Keep them simple. A chart or figure shouldn't say all there is to say. It can later be distributed.

17. When you use charts or figures, talk to the audience, not to the chart or figure.

18. Look at your watch. Finish your presentation on time.

Source: Adapted from: Hugh Kramer, "Communication Concept Would Offer Idea in Recipient's Terms," *Marketing News* (December 29, 1978): 4.

---

1. *The perceived credibility and usefulness of the report to the users.* A good study "has recommendations that can be used to formulate a strategy." It "redirects activities, accentuates the positive, and corrects weaknesses." A good study also has a clearly defined scope, shows how the quantitative analysis meshes with the qualitative information, contains no "big surprises," or radical recommendations. At the least, a good study "provides an understanding that wasn't there before."

2. *The degree of client/researcher interaction.* Managers often assess a study's credibility or value even before the final presentation of findings. And this assessment is often based on their involvement (or lack thereof) with the study design and its conduct. "If involvement is low . . . then the lack of communication can cause surprises and the quality of the study becomes a moot point . . . because the study is likely to be shelved."

3. *The organizational climate for research.* Managers have to perceive top management's approval for the use of research studies and consultants. One manager noted, "It's crucial to have signals from the top that encourage the use of outside help and openness to new ideas."

4. *The personality and job tenure of key users.* Some managers have a pro-innovation bias and are willing to try almost anything. Other managers view outside information as threatening to their decision-making authority. Also, other research has shown that senior (longer tenured) managers value more sources of marketing research information and tend to use more "soft information" than younger managers. Senior managers also tend to make more conservative decisions.[11] When managers have been in the same business for a long time, they naturally believe they "know the markets and customers in depth" and that marketing researchers are unlikely to offer any new information.

Obstacles to the Effective Use of Marketing Research Information

There are seven serious obstacles to the effective use of survey research findings.[12] The marketing researcher must take the lead in removing the barriers. The barriers to information use and the means for overcoming them are as follows:

1. *Post-survey regret.* This obstacle refers to the regret, following the collection of information, that certain questions were not asked or were not asked differently. It is reflected in such statements as, "I wish we had asked . . ." "Why wasn't 'X' included as a question?" "It's too bad we didn't include . . ." "Why did we bother asking this?" Some **post-survey regret** is unavoidable. It can, in fact, be a positive sign that some learning has occurred as a result of the study. More often, however, it reflects a failure to think about the use of information early enough in the research process. One way to eliminate many sources of post-survey regret is to simulate the use of information before doing the field work. This prompts thinking about the actual use of information and leads to changes in research methods and instruments that will produce more usable results.

2. *Data-poor thinking.* There is a tendency to think differently and more richly about an issue when it is illustrated with relevant data. This is true even when the "relevant" data are hypothetical or simulated. Thinking about outcomes without data, real or contrived is called **data-poor thinking**. The stimulus to thinking that simulated data provide helps identify important differences in perspectives among managers. By thinking about specific empirical outcomes well in advance of actual findings, managers and researchers are better prepared to interpret final results and can do so more quickly, perhaps shortening the decision time.

3. *Pseudo-clairvoyance.* The phenomenon of **pseudo-clairvoyance** is reflected in such statements as, "I could have told you that," "I already knew that," or "That's pretty obvious." The dynamics of pseudo-clairvoyance work something like this: (a) a particular result (e.g., the number of people expressing satisfaction with a product attribute) triggers thinking about what might have caused the result; (b) with the benefit of hindsight, causal factors become more obvious; (c) managers conclude that they would have given these factors much greater weight relative to factors producing other outcomes; and (d) from this they conclude that had they been asked to predict an outcome, they would have correctly given special attention to the factors causing the actual outcome and hence would have

Post-survey regret
The regret, following data collection, that certain questions were not asked or were not asked differently.

Data-poor thinking
Thinking about potential outcomes without data either real or contrived.

Pseudo-clairvoyance
The impression by managers that they could have predicted the empirical outcome of a survey research project.

correctly predicted it. One way of addressing pseudo-clairvoyance is by asking managers to predict important data outcomes. This serves two related purposes. The first is to document for the individual manager the difference between what he or she predicted and the actual outcome, thereby providing a better sense of the value of the research. The second purpose is to be able to calculate the value of individual questions and of the overall project to managers. The higher the discrepancy among managers' expectations and predictions for a given questionnaire item and the more important that item is, the more valuable are the findings for that particular question to the individual or the group.

4. *Misunderstanding comfort zones.* **Comfort zones** are the expected and acceptable ranges for research findings. For example, a manager might expect that about 50 percent of all respondents will like a certain product feature. If many more than half the respondents dislike the feature, a manager might not feel comfortable with the research results. Such a finding does not ring true with his or her knowledge and experience. The manager's discomfort with these findings calls the research into question. The tendency in such cases is to find out what the source of the error is, for example, an improper wording of the question, a biased sampling plan, and so forth, and to dismiss the result because of the error. Knowing whether managers have broad or narrow comfort zones helps researchers decide how to present results. For instance, if a finding falls outside the comfort zone of a key decision maker, the researcher should verify and be prepared to discuss the technical validity of the result. The researcher might also present other evidence supporting the finding.

    One of the many bases for establishing personal trust between researchers and managers is a manager's knowing that the researcher will not come up with an embarrassing surprise. That is, if there is an unexpected result, the manager knows he or she will be informed privately in advance of any open discussion among other managers. By knowing who might find what to be an uncomfortable surprise, the researcher is better prepared to extend the courtesy of forewarning.

5. *Failure to perform action audits.* One of the most common sources of post-survey regret is when research results suggest a novel decision or action but do not provide sufficient data for its evaluation because it had not been anticipated. For example, interviews with hospital purchasing agents suggested a particular shipping container design that management had not contemplated, even though the stimulus for the study was dissatisfaction with delivery problems and the high incidence of damaged goods. Had more thought been given to what might be done with answers to the single question about the containers, more helpful information about improving them might have been obtained. Instead, a follow-up study was required. Thus, it is important to enumerate alternative actions or decisions prior to the design of a questionnaire; this is what is meant by an **action audit**. A wide array of possible actions and better information about those possibilities are obtained when managers explicitly consider: (a) the importance of a question, (b) the question's utility in developing an action, and (c) what else is needed in choosing or implementing a decision for a given question to be useful.

6. *Unequal-opportunity methodologies.* An equal-opportunity research methodology is one that gives a bad news answer the same opportunity to show up as a good news answer. An unequal-opportunity methodology favors the good news

Comfort zones
A manager's expected and accepted ranges for research findings.

Action audit
Managerial enumeration of alternative actions or decisions prior to questionnaire design.

answer. Unequal-opportunity methodologies are seldom the consequence of a deliberate effort to skew results.

The sources of bias toward particular outcomes are many and varied. A sampling procedure may result in a cluster of people being over- or underrepresented, thereby giving incorrect emphasis to their thoughts and practices. Subsequent analyses may not be correct because of this sampling bias. Bias is often found in the design of a questionnaire and particularly in the wording of the individual questions. Rating scales may use unbalanced anchor labels. At one end may be *very likely,* and at the other end, *rather unlikely,* which does not allow for people, whose response would be a much stronger *very unlikely,* to express the intensity of their feelings.

7. *Missing information and uncertainty.* Doing research is like piecing together a jigsaw puzzle. We never have the time or the funds to position all the pieces, only just enough of them to give us a sense of the true picture. The remaining pieces we fill in from our other knowledge—from facts not formally researched. Such facts are derived from experience as well as from related research. Most information used in the decision-making process is usually derived from these experiences. (In a very technical sense, the data that are missing from experience are usually sought out through formal research.)

Managers seem to appreciate those researchers who are willing to join them in absorbing uncertainty. It is important to identify early in the research process the areas where uncertainty will likely persist even after formal research and relevant experiences are brought forth. Decision and risk analyses can be made as to whether resources should be (re)allocated to reducing any of these persistent uncertainties, rather than to reducing those uncertainties already being addressed by the planned research. Also, a common understanding between managers and researchers about what uncertainties will remain reduces certain post-survey regrets and better prepares the researcher to deal with the uncertainties when asked to do so. For example, some issues can be pursued in exploratory research that might help interpret data later on, even though these issues could not be pursued in the more formal project.[13]

As you have seen, there are many obstacles that can stand in the way of managers deciding to use marketing research findings. Doing "good research" per se does not guarantee that the findings will be used. The researcher must understand how managers think and work with them to remove potential bias against using the research findings. Remember, marketing research has value only when it is considered and acted upon by management.

SUMMARY

The essence of communication is shared meaning. There are several barriers to effective communication, including noise, limited attention span, and selective perception.

The primary roles of the marketing research report are to communicate the findings, to serve as a reference document, and to provide credibility for the work that was accomplished. The basic components of a research report include beginning with a management summary, followed by a detailed introduction, analysis of findings, conclusions, methodology, recommendations, and appendices, if necessary.

Typically, a research report should be in the present tense and in the active voice whenever possible. Informative headlines are better than label headlines. Tables and charts should be used liberally in a report rather than several pages of verbiage. Also, the use of verbatims can make a research report come alive.

There are several pitfalls in marketing research reports. Length does not necessarily mean quality. Simply repeating numbers from tables without any attempt at interpretation degrades the quality of the research report. Also, research reports should refer back to the research objectives from time to time. Care must also be taken to ensure adequate data interpretation. A number of factors are given in the chapter to help the reader evaluate the quality of the research report.

Oral presentations should include four aids: the presentation outline, visuals, the management summary, and copies of the final report. An effective oral presentation recognizes the nature of the audience and attempts to meet the needs of that audience.

It is extremely important that marketing managers use marketing research information and use it appropriately. The key determinants of whether marketing research data are used are the perceived credibility and usefulness to the users, the degree of client/researcher interaction, the organizational climate for research, and the personality and job tenure of key users. The seven obstacles to the effective use of marketing research information are post-survey regret, data-poor thinking, pseudo-clairvoyance, misunderstanding comfort zones, failure to perform action audits, unequal-opportunity methodologies, and missing information and uncertainty.

KEY TERMS

Communication
Noise
Attention span
Selective perception
Management summary
Verbatims
False accuracy

Single-number research
Post-survey regret
Data-poor thinking
Pseudo-clairvoyance
Comfort zones
Action audit

REVIEW AND DISCUSSION QUESTIONS

1. What are the roles of the research report? Give examples.
2. What are some of the more common pitfalls in marketing research reports? Give examples of each pitfall.
3. Distinguish among findings, summaries, conclusions, and recommendations.
4. Should research reports contain executive summaries? Why or why not? If so, what should be contained in an executive summary?
5. Discuss the seven basic components of the research report. List several criteria that may be used to evaluate a research report and give examples of each.
6. What should be done to ensure the success of an oral report? Critique the following two paragraphs from a research report:

   The trouble began when the Department of Agriculture published the hot dog ingredients—everything that may legally qualify—because it was asked by the poultry industry to relax the conditions under which the ingredients might also include chicken. In other words, can a chickenfurter find happiness in the land of the frank?

Judging by the 1,066 mainly hostile answers that the department got when it sent out a questionnaire on this point, the very thought is unthinkable. The public mood was most felicitously caught by the woman who replied, "I don't eat feather meat of no kind."

7. Develop one or more visual aids to present the following data. Indicate why you chose your particular form of visual aid.

Candidate	Local # Employees	Revenues (in millions)	Target as Charter or Affiliate Member	Potential Membership Fee
Mary Kay Cosmetics	958	$360	Charter	$ 50,000
Arrow Industries	950	50	Charter	20,000
NCH Corp.	800	427	Charter	50,000
Stratoflex, Inc.	622	81	Charter	25,000
BEI Defense Sys.	150	47	Affiliate	7,500
Atlas Match Corp.	150	82	Affiliate	7,500
Mangren R&D	143	20	Affiliate	7,500
Jet Research Ctr.	157	350	Affiliate	7,500

8. Explain why younger and older marketing managers might use marketing research data differently. Give some examples.
9. Explain each of the seven obstacles to effective use of marketing research information. Show how the obstacles can be overcome using examples.

CASE

Americos Dog Collars

Americos commissioned a market research study to evaluate two prototype dog collars for flea prevention and one existing collar from Hartz Mountain. The study was a mall intercept where dog owners were asked to view and handle the three dog collars. Part of the methodology was asking the respondents to smell the collars. The Executive Summary for the report follows.

Survey Conclusions

1. Most pet owners feel that there is substantial room for improvement in pet collar effectiveness. They generally felt that a collar lasted two to three months.
2. If consumers view collars "R" (Hartz Mountain Rabon), "S" (Sendran), and "E" (Dow's Purified Chlorphyrifos) as parity products, their preferences are as follows: "R"—53 percent; "S"—31 percent; and "E"—16 percent.

    The lack of odor is the major preference factor for "R." Those selecting "E" did so for perceived strength and color. Color and smell were the two most important factors in selecting "S."
3. Most respondents (87 percent) were able to discern an odor difference in the three collars. A majority thought that "E" either smelled bad or had greater strength due to the greater odor.
4. When told that "E" was twice as effective as "R" and "S," 58 percent claimed that they would definitely or probably purchase "E." Purchase intent was significantly higher among owners of outdoor dogs. Both "R" and "S" were shown to be vulnerable to "E." "S" was the most susceptible to penetration by "E."

5. A substantial number of consumers (42 percent) stated that they probably or definitely would not buy "E" even with the long life benefit. The respondents did not like the odor or perceived it as harmful to their pet.

6. Suggested selling price for "E" was under $4.00—51%; $4.01–$5.00—35%; over $5.00—14%.

7. When collar "D" (Ketal's Chlorpyrifos) was introduced into the test it was strongly preferred (81 percent) over "E." The lack of odor was the main reason for selecting "D."

8. Suggested selling price for "D" was under $4.00—47%; $4.01–$5.00—37%; over $5.00—15%.

9. When all four test collars were considered, preferences were as follows: "R"—25%; "E"—15%; "S"—14%; and "D"—45%. Consumers switching from another collar to "D" preferred "R" originally—47%; preferred "E" originally—50%; preferred "S" originally—43%.

10. This data was gathered from a mall intercept study in St. Louis, Missouri, during January, 1992. One hundred fifty dog owners were interviewed.

Recommendations

1. Although "E" is clearly at a disadvantage related to "D," it does have a place in the market. Remember, 18 percent of the respondents did prefer "E" over "D." The market for "E" seems to be among owners of outdoor dogs that really want a strong collar. Many of these people equate smell with collar effectiveness. We recommend an in-home product placement with "E" in the above-mentioned segment.

2. Product "D" seems to have great potential in the marketplace. Its appeal lies with pet owners that want extra strength without a strong chemical odor. Owners of both indoor and outdoor pets are receptive to product "D." We recommend an in-home product placement with "D" to sharpen the marketing strategy in terms of price, packaging, and brand name. It is also very important to determine if consumers actually perceive "D" as more effective than other collars. If they do not, you may achieve significant first-time triers but a low repurchase rate.

1. Critique the Executive Summary. Are all elements present that should be included within an Executive Summary?

2. Based on the survey conclusions, do the recommendations logically follow? Why or why not?

Ethical Dilemma——PART FIVE

KXXX Radio Research

Radio sweeps research is conducted four times per year by Arbitron Research. The ratings, as determined by Arbitron, mean hundreds of thousands of dollars of advertising revenue to the winners and similar losses to the losers.

KXXX decided to improve its ratings by sending out the following letter and questionnaire immediately prior to sweeps week.

Dear Radio Listener:

We are conducting a research study on radio listening preferences in the Dallas–Fort Worth area, and we are requesting your participation. Your opinions will help shape the kind of music presented to the Dallas–Fort Worth radio audience.

You have been carefully selected to represent a specific demographic segment of the general population. To obtain better information, each participant has been assigned a specific radio station. We would greatly appreciate your cooperation by listening to your assigned station for one hour and completing the brief survey card enclosed.

The station you have been assigned is *KXXX*, which can be found at *100.5* on the *FM* dial. Please listen for at least one-half (½) hour, between 6–10 am and another one-half (½) hour at any other time during the week, then at your convenience, complete the enclosed survey card within the next week and return it to us. The postage is prepaid.

Your opinions are very important. Please answer honestly. A donation will be made to a local charity when we receive your completed survey card. Thank you for your cooperation.

Ken Jones
Vice-President, Research

YOUR OPINION COUNTS

Please answer all questions, detach the card and mail it immediately.

Thank you for your help.

I listened to **KXXX** for at least one half hour between 6–10 AM and another half hour at any other time during the week of _____, 1991.

I listened: □ EARLY MORNING (6–10 AM)
  □ MIDDAY (10 AM–2 PM)
  □ LATE AFTERNOON (2–6 PM)
  □ NIGHT (6 PM–6 AM)

(Check as many boxes as you wish)

I listened: □ at home   □ at work
  □ in a car   □ other place

I liked: The music played by **KXXX**
  □ Yes   □ No

  The morning program
  □ Yes   □ No

  The on-air personalities
  □ Yes   □ No

  The uninterrupted music sets
  □ Yes   □ No

Overall I would rate *KXXX*: (circle one)

Really Dislike   Really Like

1   2   3   4   5

My other comments about **KXXX** music, artists, personalities, etc., are:

_____
_____
_____
_____
_____

OPTIONAL

NAME _____

ADDRESS _____

CITY _____

STATE ___ ZIP CODE _____

PHONE (   ) _____

BIRTHDAY _____

1. Is the questionnaire simply a novel way to promote a radio station, or is it unethical?

2. If KXXX actually decided to use the research data, would its actions regarding the questionnaire be unethical?

3. What if the radio station conducted an extensive, in-depth research project immediately prior to the radio sweeps that asked people to listen to KXXX for a week in order to give meaningful replies to the questionnaire? Would management's actions be unethical?

APPENDIX

Statistical Tables

TABLE 1 *Random Digits*

63271	59986	71744	51102	15141	80714	58683	93108	13554	79945
88547	09896	95436	79115	08303	01041	20030	63754	08459	28364
55957	57243	83865	09911	19761	66535	40102	26646	60147	15702
46276	87453	44790	67122	45573	84358	21625	16999	13385	22782
55363	07449	34835	15290	76616	67191	12777	21861	68689	03263
69393	92785	49902	58447	42048	30378	87618	26933	40640	16281
13186	29431	88190	04588	38733	81290	89541	70290	40113	08243
17726	28652	56836	78351	47327	18518	92222	55201	27340	10493
36520	64465	05550	30157	82242	29520	69753	72602	23756	54935
81628	36100	39254	56835	37636	02421	98063	89641	64953	99337
84649	48968	75215	75498	49539	74240	03466	49292	36401	45525
63291	11618	12613	75055	43915	26488	41116	64531	56827	30825
70502	53225	03655	05915	37140	57051	48393	91322	25653	06543
06426	24771	59935	49801	11082	66762	94477	02494	88215	27191
20711	55609	29430	70165	45406	78484	31639	52009	18873	96927
41990	70538	77191	25860	55204	73417	83920	69468	74972	38712
72452	36618	76298	26678	89334	33938	95567	29380	75906	91807
37042	40318	57099	10528	09925	89773	41335	96244	29002	46453
53766	52875	15987	46962	67342	77592	57651	95508	80033	69828
90585	58955	53122	16025	84299	53310	67380	84249	25348	04332
32001	96293	37203	64516	51530	37069	40261	61374	05815	06714
62606	64324	46354	72157	67248	20135	49804	09226	64419	29457
10078	28073	85389	50324	14500	15562	64165	06125	71353	77669
91561	46145	24177	15294	10061	98124	75732	00815	83452	97355
13091	98112	53959	79607	52244	63303	10413	63839	74762	50289
73864	83014	72457	22682	03033	61714	88173	90835	00634	85169
66668	25467	48894	51043	02365	91726	09365	63167	95264	45643
84745	41042	29493	01836	09044	51926	43630	63470	76508	14194
48068	26805	94595	47907	13357	38412	33318	26098	82782	42851
54310	96175	97594	88616	42035	38093	36745	56702	40644	83514
14877	33095	10924	58013	61439	21882	42059	24177	58739	60170
78295	23179	02771	43464	59061	71411	05697	67194	30495	21157
67524	02865	39593	54278	04237	92441	26602	63835	38032	94770
58268	57219	68124	73455	83236	08710	04284	55005	84171	42596
97158	28672	50685	01181	24262	19427	52106	34308	73685	74246
04230	16831	69085	30802	65559	09205	71829	06489	85650	38707
94879	56606	30401	02602	57658	70091	54986	41394	60437	03195
71446	15232	66715	26385	91518	70566	02888	79941	39684	54315
32886	05644	79316	09819	00813	88407	17461	73925	53037	91904
62048	33711	25290	21526	02223	75947	66466	06332	10913	75336
84534	42351	21628	53669	81352	95152	08107	98814	72743	12849
84707	15885	84710	35866	06446	86311	32648	88141	73902	69981
19409	40868	64220	80861	13860	68493	52908	26374	63297	45052
57978	48015	25973	66777	45924	56144	24742	96702	88200	66162
57295	98298	11199	96510	75228	41600	47192	43267	35973	23152
94044	83785	93388	07833	38216	31413	70555	03023	54147	06647
30014	25879	71763	96679	90603	99396	74557	74224	18211	91637
07265	69563	64268	88802	72264	66540	01782	08396	19251	83613
84404	88642	30263	80310	11522	57810	27627	78376	36240	48952
21778	02085	27762	46097	43324	34354	09369	14966	10158	76089

TABLE 2   *Standard Normal Distribution—z Values*

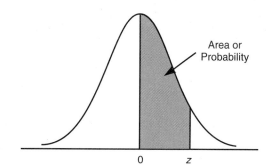

Entries in the table give the area under the curve between the mean and z standard deviations above the mean. For example, for z = 1.25 the area under the curve between the mean and z is .3944.

z	.00	.01	.02	.03	.04	.05	.06	.07	.08	.09
.0	.0000	.0040	.0080	.0120	.0160	.0199	.0239	.0279	.0319	.0359
.1	.0398	.0438	.0478	.0517	.0557	.0596	.0636	.0675	.0714	.0753
.2	.0793	.0832	.0871	.0910	.0948	.0987	.1026	.1064	.1103	.1141
.3	.1179	.1217	.1255	.1293	.1331	.1368	.1406	.1443	.1480	.1517
.4	.1554	.1591	.1628	.1664	.1700	.1736	.1772	.1808	.1844	.1879
.5	.1915	.1950	.1985	.2019	.2054	.2088	.2123	.2157	.2190	.2224
.6	.2257	.2291	.2324	.2357	.2389	.2422	.2454	.2486	.2518	.2549
.7	.2580	.2612	.2642	.2673	.2704	.2734	.2764	.2794	.2823	.2852
.8	.2881	.2910	.2939	.2967	.2995	.3023	.3051	.3078	.3106	.3133
.9	.3159	.3186	.3212	.3238	.3264	.3289	.3315	.3340	.3365	.3389
1.0	.3413	.3438	.3461	.3485	.3508	.3531	.3554	.3577	.3599	.3621
1.1	.3643	.3665	.3686	.3708	.3729	.3749	.3770	.3790	.3810	.3830
1.2	.3849	.3869	.3888	.3907	.3925	.3944	.3962	.3980	.3997	.4015
1.3	.4032	.4049	.4066	.4082	.4099	.4115	.4131	.4147	.4162	.4177
1.4	.4192	.4207	.4222	.4236	.4251	.4265	.4279	.4292	.4306	.4319
1.5	.4332	.4345	.4357	.4370	.4382	.4394	.4406	.4418	.4429	.4441
1.6	.4452	.4463	.4474	.4484	.4495	.4505	.4515	.4525	.4535	.4545
1.7	.4554	.4564	.4573	.4582	.4591	.4599	.4608	.4616	.4625	.4633
1.8	.4641	.4649	.4656	.4664	.4671	.4678	.4686	.4693	.4699	.4706
1.9	.4713	.4719	.4726	.4732	.4738	.4744	.4750	.4756	.4761	.4767
2.0	.4772	.4778	.4783	.4788	.4793	.4798	.4803	.4808	.4812	.4817
2.1	.4821	.4826	.4830	.4834	.4838	.4842	.4846	.4850	.4854	.4857
2.2	.4861	.4864	.4868	.4871	.4875	.4878	.4881	.4884	.4887	.4890
2.3	.4893	.4896	.4898	.4901	.4904	.4906	.4909	.4911	.4913	.4916
2.4	.4918	.4920	.4922	.4925	.4927	.4929	.4931	.4932	.4934	.4936
2.5	.4938	.4940	.4941	.4943	.4945	.4946	.4948	.4949	.4951	.4952
2.6	.4953	.4955	.4956	.4957	.4959	.4960	.4961	.4962	.4963	.4964
2.7	.4965	.4966	.4967	.4968	.4969	.4970	.4971	.4972	.4973	.4974
2.8	.4974	.4975	.4976	.4977	.4977	.4978	.4979	.4979	.4980	.4981
2.9	.4981	.4982	.4982	.4983	.4984	.4984	.4985	.4985	.4986	.4986
3.0	.4986	.4987	.4987	.4988	.4988	.4989	.4989	.4989	.4990	.4990

TABLE 3   *t Distribution*

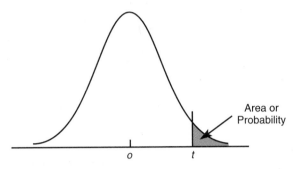

Area or
Probability

Entries in the table give *t* values for an area or probability in the upper tail of the *t* distribution. For example, with 10 degrees of freedom and a .05 area in the upper tail, $t_{.05} = 1.812$.

DEGREES OF FREEDOM	AREA IN UPPER TAIL				
	.10	.05	.025	.01	.005
1	3.078	6.314	12.706	31.821	63.657
2	1.886	2.920	4.303	6.965	9.925
3	1.638	2.353	3.182	4.541	5.841
4	1.533	2.132	2.776	3.747	4.604
5	1.476	2.015	2.571	3.365	4.032
6	1.440	1.943	2.447	3.143	3.707
7	1.415	1.895	2.365	2.998	3.499
8	1.397	1.860	2.306	2.896	3.355
9	1.383	1.833	2.262	2.821	3.250
10	1.372	1.812	2.228	2.764	3.169
11	1.363	1.796	2.201	2.718	3.106
12	1.356	1.782	2.179	2.681	3.055
13	1.350	1.771	2.160	2.650	3.012
14	1.345	1.761	2.145	2.624	2.977
15	1.341	1.753	2.131	2.602	2.947
16	1.337	1.746	2.120	2.583	2.921
17	1.333	1.740	2.110	2.567	2.898
18	1.330	1.734	2.101	2.552	2.878
19	1.328	1.729	2.093	2.539	2.861
20	1.325	1.725	2.086	2.528	2.845
21	1.323	1.721	2.080	2.518	2.831
22	1.321	1.717	2.074	2.508	2.819
23	1.319	1.714	2.069	2.500	2.807
24	1.318	1.711	2.064	2.492	2.797
25	1.316	1.708	2.060	2.485	2.787
26	1.315	1.706	2.056	2.479	2.779
27	1.314	1.703	2.052	2.473	2.771
28	1.313	1.701	2.048	2.467	2.763
29	1.311	1.699	2.045	2.462	2.756
30	1.310	1.697	2.042	2.457	2.750
40	1.303	1.684	2.021	2.423	2.704
60	1.296	1.671	2.000	2.390	2.660
120	1.289	1.658	1.980	2.358	2.617
∞	1.282	1.645	1.960	2.326	2.576

Reprinted by permission of Biometrika Trustees from Table 12. Percentage Points of the *t* Distribution, 3rd. Edition, 1966. E. S. Pearson and H. O. Hartley, *Biometrika Tables for Statisticians,* Vol. I.

TABLE 4 *Chi-Square Distribution*

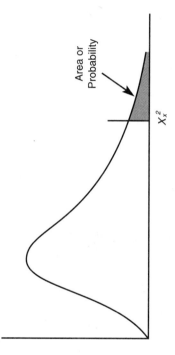

Area or Probability

χ_x^2

Entries in the table give χ_α^2 values, where α is the area or probability in the upper tail of the chi-square distribution. For example, with 10 degrees of freedom and a .01 area in the upper tail, $\chi_\alpha^2 = 23.2093$.

AREA IN UPPER TAIL

DEGREES OF FREEDOM	.995	.99	.975	.95	.90	.10	.05	.025	.01	.005
1	$392,704 \times 10^{-19}$	$157,088 \times 10^{-9}$	$982,069 \times 10^{-9}$	$393,214 \times 10^{-8}$	.01570908	2.70554	3.84146	5.02389	6.63490	7.87944
2	.0100251	.0201007	.0506356	.102587	.210720	4.60517	5.99147	7.37776	9.21034	10.5966
3	.0717212	.114832	.215795	.351846	.584375	6.25139	7.81473	9.34840	11.3449	12.8381
4	.206990	.297110	.484419	.710721	1.063623	7.77944	9.48773	11.1433	13.2767	14.8602
5	.411740	.554300	.831211	1.145476	1.61031	9.23635	11.0705	12.8325	15.0863	16.7496
6	.675727	.872085	1.237347	1.63539	2.20413	10.6446	12.5916	14.4494	16.8119	18.5476
7	.989265	1.239043	1.68987	2.16735	2.83311	12.0170	14.0671	16.0128	18.4753	20.2777
8	1.344419	1.646482	2.17973	2.73264	3.48954	13.3616	15.5073	17.5346	20.0902	21.9550
9	1.734926	2.087912	2.70039	3.32511	4.16816	14.6837	16.9190	19.0228	21.6660	23.5893
10	2.15585	2.55821	3.24697	3.94030	4.86518	15.9871	18.3070	20.4831	23.2093	25.1882
11	2.60321	3.05347	3.81575	4.57481	5.57779	17.2750	19.6751	21.9200	24.7250	26.7569
12	3.07382	3.57056	4.40379	5.22603	6.30380	18.5494	21.0261	23.3367	26.2170	28.2995
13	3.56503	4.10691	5.00874	5.89186	7.04150	19.8119	22.3621	24.7356	27.6883	29.8194
14	4.07468	4.66043	5.62872	6.57063	7.78953	21.0642	23.6848	26.1190	29.1413	31.3193

TABLE 4 (continued)

DEGREES OF FREEDOM	AREA IN UPPER TAIL									
	.995	.99	.975	.95	.90	.10	.05	.025	.01	.005
15	4.60094	5.22935	6.26214	7.26094	8.54675	22.3072	24.9958	27.4884	30.5779	32.8013
16	5.14224	5.81221	6.90766	7.96164	9.31223	23.5418	26.2962	28.8454	31.9999	34.2672
17	5.69724	6.40776	7.56418	8.67176	10.0852	24.7690	27.5871	30.1910	33.4087	35.7185
18	6.26481	7.01491	8.23075	9.39046	10.8649	25.9894	28.8693	31.5264	34.8053	37.1564
19	6.84398	7.63273	8.90655	10.1170	11.6509	27.2036	30.1435	32.8523	36.1908	38.5822
20	7.43386	8.26040	9.59083	10.8508	12.4426	28.4120	31.4104	34.1696	37.5662	39.9968
21	8.03366	8.89720	10.28293	11.5913	13.2396	29.6151	32.6705	35.4789	38.9321	41.4010
22	8.64272	9.54249	10.9823	12.3380	14.0415	30.8133	33.9244	36.7807	40.2894	42.7958
23	9.26042	10.19567	11.6885	13.0905	14.8479	32.0069	35.1725	38.0757	41.6384	44.1813
24	9.88623	10.8564	12.4011	13.8484	15.6587	33.1963	36.4151	39.3641	42.9798	45.5585
25	10.5197	11.5240	13.1197	14.6114	16.4734	34.3816	37.6525	40.6465	44.3141	46.9278
26	11.1603	12.1981	13.8439	15.3791	17.2919	35.5631	38.8852	41.9232	45.6417	48.2899
27	11.8076	12.8786	14.5733	16.1513	18.1138	36.7412	40.1133	43.1944	46.9630	49.6449
28	12.4613	13.5648	15.3079	16.9279	18.9392	37.9159	41.3372	44.4607	48.2782	50.9933
29	13.1211	14.2565	16.0471	17.7083	19.7677	39.0875	42.5569	45.7222	49.5879	52.3356
30	13.7867	14.9535	16.7908	18.4926	20.5992	40.2560	43.7729	46.9792	50.8922	53.6720
40	20.7065	22.1643	24.4331	26.5093	29.0505	51.8050	55.7585	59.3417	63.6907	66.7659
50	27.9907	29.7067	32.3574	34.7642	37.6886	63.1671	67.5048	71.4202	76.1539	79.4900
60	35.5346	37.4848	40.4817	43.1879	46.4589	74.3970	79.0819	83.2976	88.3794	91.9517
70	43.2752	45.4418	48.7576	51.7393	55.3290	85.5271	90.5312	95.0231	100.425	104.215
80	51.1720	53.5400	57.1532	60.3915	64.2778	96.5782	101.879	106.629	112.329	116.321
90	59.1963	61.7541	65.6466	69.1260	73.2912	107.565	113.145	118.136	124.116	128.299
100	67.3276	70.0648	74.2219	77.9295	82.3581	118.498	124.342	129.561	135.807	140.169

Reprinted by permission of Biometrika Trustees from Table 8, Percentage Points of the χ^2 Distribution, by E. S. Pearson and H. O. Hartley, *Biometrika Tables for Statisticians*, Vol. I, 3rd Edition, 1966.

TABLE 5   *F Distribution*

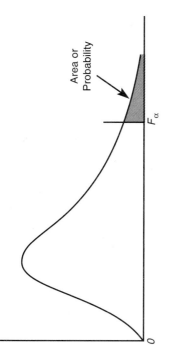

Area or Probability

F_α

0

Entries in the table give F_α values, where α is the area or probability in the upper tail of the F distribution. For example, with 12 numerator degrees of freedom, 15 denominator degrees of freedom, and a .05 area in the upper tail, $F_{.05} = 2.48$.

TABLE OF $F_{.05}$ VALUES

DENOMINATOR DEGREES OF FREEDOM	NUMERATOR DEGREES OF FREEDOM																		
	1	2	3	4	5	6	7	8	9	10	12	15	20	24	30	40	60	120	∞
1	161.4	199.5	215.7	224.6	230.2	234.0	236.8	238.9	240.5	241.9	243.9	245.9	248.0	249.1	250.1	251.1	252.2	253.3	254.3
2	18.51	19.00	19.16	19.25	19.30	19.33	19.35	19.37	19.38	19.40	19.41	19.43	19.45	19.45	19.46	19.47	19.48	19.49	19.50
3	10.13	9.55	9.28	9.12	9.01	8.94	8.89	8.85	8.81	8.79	8.74	8.70	8.66	8.64	8.62	8.59	8.57	8.55	8.53
4	7.71	6.94	6.59	6.39	6.26	6.16	6.09	6.04	6.00	5.96	5.91	5.86	5.80	5.77	5.75	5.72	5.69	5.66	5.63
5	6.61	5.79	5.41	5.19	5.05	4.95	4.88	4.82	4.77	4.74	4.68	4.62	4.56	4.53	4.50	4.46	4.43	4.40	4.36
6	5.99	5.14	4.76	4.53	4.39	4.28	4.21	4.15	4.10	4.06	4.00	3.94	3.87	3.84	3.81	3.77	3.74	3.70	3.67
7	5.59	4.74	4.35	4.12	3.97	3.87	3.79	3.73	3.68	3.64	3.57	3.51	3.44	3.41	3.38	3.34	3.30	3.27	3.23
8	5.32	4.46	4.07	3.84	3.69	3.58	3.50	3.44	3.39	3.35	3.28	3.22	3.15	3.12	3.08	3.04	3.01	2.97	2.93
9	5.12	4.26	3.86	3.63	3.48	3.37	3.29	3.23	3.18	3.14	3.07	3.01	2.94	2.90	2.86	2.83	2.79	2.75	2.71
10	4.96	4.10	3.71	3.48	3.33	3.22	3.14	3.07	3.02	2.98	2.91	2.85	2.77	2.74	2.70	2.66	2.62	2.58	2.54
11	4.84	3.98	3.59	3.36	3.20	3.09	3.01	2.95	2.90	2.85	2.79	2.72	2.65	2.61	2.57	2.53	2.49	2.45	2.40
12	4.75	3.89	3.49	3.26	3.11	3.00	2.91	2.85	2.80	2.75	2.69	2.62	2.54	2.51	2.47	2.43	2.38	2.34	2.30
13	4.67	3.81	3.41	3.18	3.03	2.92	2.83	2.77	2.71	2.67	2.60	2.53	2.46	2.42	2.38	2.34	2.30	2.25	2.21
14	4.60	3.74	3.34	3.11	2.96	2.85	2.76	2.70	2.65	2.60	2.53	2.46	2.39	2.35	2.31	2.27	2.22	2.18	2.13
15	4.54	3.68	3.29	3.06	2.90	2.79	2.71	2.64	2.59	2.54	2.48	2.40	2.33	2.29	2.25	2.20	2.16	2.11	2.07
16	4.49	3.63	3.24	3.01	2.85	2.74	2.66	2.59	2.54	2.49	2.42	2.35	2.28	2.24	2.19	2.15	2.11	2.06	2.01
17	4.45	3.59	3.20	2.96	2.81	2.70	2.61	2.55	2.49	2.45	2.38	2.31	2.23	2.19	2.15	2.10	2.06	2.01	1.96
18	4.41	3.55	3.16	2.93	2.77	2.66	2.58	2.51	2.46	2.41	2.34	2.27	2.19	2.15	2.11	2.06	2.02	1.97	1.92
19	4.38	3.52	3.13	2.90	2.74	2.63	2.54	2.48	2.42	2.38	2.31	2.23	2.16	2.11	2.07	2.03	1.98	1.93	1.88
20	4.35	3.49	3.10	2.87	2.71	2.60	2.51	2.45	2.39	2.35	2.28	2.20	2.12	2.08	2.04	1.99	1.95	1.90	1.84
21	4.32	3.47	3.07	2.84	2.68	2.57	2.49	2.42	2.37	2.32	2.25	2.18	2.10	2.05	2.01	1.96	1.92	1.87	1.81
22	4.30	3.44	3.05	2.82	2.66	2.55	2.46	2.40	2.34	2.30	2.23	2.15	2.07	2.03	1.98	1.94	1.89	1.84	1.78
23	4.28	3.42	3.03	2.80	2.64	2.53	2.44	2.37	2.32	2.27	2.20	2.13	2.05	2.01	1.96	1.91	1.86	1.81	1.76
24	4.26	3.40	3.01	2.78	2.62	2.51	2.42	2.36	2.30	2.25	2.18	2.11	2.03	1.98	1.94	1.89	1.84	1.79	1.73
25	4.24	3.39	2.99	2.76	2.60	2.49	2.40	2.34	2.28	2.24	2.16	2.09	2.01	1.96	1.92	1.87	1.82	1.77	1.71
26	4.23	3.37	2.98	2.74	2.59	2.47	2.39	2.32	2.27	2.22	2.15	2.07	1.99	1.95	1.90	1.85	1.80	1.75	1.69
27	4.21	3.35	2.96	2.73	2.57	2.46	2.37	2.31	2.25	2.20	2.13	2.06	1.97	1.93	1.88	1.84	1.79	1.73	1.67
28	4.20	3.34	2.95	2.71	2.56	2.45	2.36	2.29	2.24	2.19	2.12	2.04	1.96	1.91	1.87	1.82	1.77	1.71	1.65

TABLE 5 *(continued)*

NUMERATOR DEGREES OF FREEDOM

DENOMINATOR DEGREES OF FREEDOM	1	2	3	4	5	6	7	8	9	10	12	15	20	24	30	40	60	120	∞
29	4.18	3.33	2.93	2.70	2.55	2.43	2.35	2.28	2.22	2.18	2.10	2.03	1.94	1.90	1.85	1.81	1.75	1.70	1.64
30	4.17	3.32	2.92	2.69	2.53	2.42	2.33	2.27	2.21	2.16	2.09	2.01	1.93	1.89	1.84	1.79	1.74	1.68	1.62
40	4.08	3.23	2.84	2.61	2.45	2.34	2.25	2.18	2.12	2.08	2.00	1.92	1.84	1.79	1.74	1.69	1.64	1.58	1.51
60	4.00	3.15	2.76	2.53	2.37	2.25	2.17	2.10	2.04	1.99	1.92	1.84	1.75	1.70	1.65	1.53	1.43	1.32	1.39
120	3.92	3.07	2.68	2.45	2.29	2.17	2.09	2.02	1.96	1.91	1.83	1.75	1.66	1.61	1.55	1.50	1.43	1.35	1.25
∞	3.84	3.00	2.60	2.37	2.21	2.10	2.01	1.94	1.88	1.83	1.75	1.67	1.57	1.52	1.46	1.39	1.32	1.22	1.00

TABLE OF $F_{.01}$ VALUES

NUMERATOR DEGREES OF FREEDOM

DENOMINATOR DEGREES OF FREEDOM	1	2	3	4	5	6	7	8	9	10	12	15	20	24	30	40	60	120	∞
1	4,052	4,999.5	5,403	5,625	5,764	5,859	5,928	5,982	6,022	6,056	6,106	6,157	6,209	6,235	6,261	6,287	6,313	6,339	6,366
2	98.50	99.00	99.17	99.25	99.30	99.33	99.36	99.37	99.39	99.40	99.42	99.43	99.45	99.46	99.47	99.47	99.48	99.49	99.50
3	34.12	30.82	29.46	28.71	28.24	27.91	27.67	27.49	27.35	27.23	27.05	26.87	26.69	26.60	26.50	26.41	26.32	26.22	26.13
4	21.20	18.00	16.69	15.98	15.52	51.21	14.98	14.80	14.66	14.55	14.37	14.20	14.02	13.93	13.84	13.75	13.65	13.56	13.46
5	16.26	13.27	12.06	11.39	10.97	10.67	10.46	10.29	10.16	10.05	9.89	9.72	9.55	9.47	9.38	9.29	9.20	9.11	9.06
6	13.75	10.92	9.78	9.15	8.75	8.47	8.26	8.10	7.98	7.87	7.72	7.56	7.40	7.31	7.23	7.14	7.06	6.97	6.88
7	12.25	9.55	8.45	7.85	7.46	7.19	6.99	6.84	6.72	6.62	6.47	6.31	6.16	6.07	5.99	5.91	5.82	5.74	5.65
8	11.26	8.65	7.59	7.01	6.63	6.37	6.18	6.03	5.91	5.81	5.67	5.52	5.36	5.28	5.20	5.12	5.03	4.95	4.86
9	10.56	8.02	6.99	6.42	6.06	5.80	5.61	5.47	5.35	5.26	5.11	4.96	4.81	4.73	4.65	4.57	4.48	4.40	4.31
10	10.04	7.56	6.55	5.99	5.64	5.39	5.20	5.06	4.94	4.85	4.71	4.56	4.41	4.33	4.25	4.17	4.08	4.00	3.91
11	9.65	7.21	6.22	5.67	5.32	5.07	4.89	4.74	4.63	4.54	4.40	4.25	4.10	4.02	3.94	3.86	3.78	3.69	3.60
12	9.33	6.93	5.95	5.41	5.06	4.82	4.64	4.50	4.39	4.30	4.16	4.01	3.86	3.78	3.70	3.62	3.54	3.45	3.36
13	9.07	6.70	5.74	5.21	4.86	4.62	4.44	4.30	4.19	4.10	3.96	3.82	3.66	3.59	3.51	3.43	3.34	3.25	3.17
14	8.86	6.51	5.56	5.04	4.69	4.46	4.28	4.14	4.03	3.94	3.80	3.66	3.51	3.43	3.35	3.27	3.18	3.09	3.00
15	8.68	6.36	5.42	4.89	4.56	4.32	4.14	4.00	3.89	3.80	3.67	3.52	3.37	3.29	3.21	3.13	3.05	2.96	2.87
16	8.53	6.23	5.29	4.77	4.44	4.20	4.03	3.89	3.78	3.69	3.55	3.41	3.26	3.18	3.10	3.02	2.93	2.84	2.75
17	8.40	6.11	5.18	4.67	4.34	4.10	3.93	3.79	3.68	3.59	3.46	3.31	3.16	3.08	3.00	2.92	2.83	2.75	2.65
18	8.29	6.01	5.09	4.58	4.25	4.01	3.84	3.71	3.60	3.51	3.37	3.23	3.08	3.00	2.92	2.84	2.75	2.66	2.57
19	8.18	5.93	5.01	4.50	4.17	3.94	3.77	3.63	3.52	3.43	3.30	3.15	3.00	2.92	2.84	2.76	2.67	2.58	2.49
20	8.10	5.85	4.94	4.43	4.10	3.87	3.70	3.56	3.46	3.37	3.23	3.09	2.94	2.86	2.78	2.69	2.61	2.52	2.42
21	8.02	5.78	4.87	4.37	4.04	3.81	3.64	3.51	3.40	3.31	3.17	3.03	2.88	2.80	2.72	2.64	2.55	2.46	2.36
22	7.95	5.72	4.82	4.31	3.99	3.76	3.59	3.45	3.35	3.26	3.12	2.98	2.83	2.75	2.67	2.58	2.50	2.40	2.31
23	7.88	5.66	4.76	4.26	3.94	3.71	3.54	3.41	3.30	3.21	3.07	2.93	2.78	2.70	2.62	2.54	2.45	2.35	2.26
24	7.82	5.61	4.72	4.22	3.90	3.67	3.50	3.36	3.26	3.17	3.03	2.89	2.74	2.66	2.58	2.49	2.40	2.31	2.21
25	7.77	5.57	4.68	4.18	3.85	3.63	3.46	3.32	3.22	3.13	2.99	2.85	2.70	2.62	2.54	2.45	2.36	2.27	2.17
26	7.72	5.53	4.64	4.14	3.82	3.59	3.42	3.29	3.18	3.09	2.96	2.81	2.66	2.58	2.50	2.42	2.33	2.23	2.13
27	7.68	5.49	4.60	4.11	3.78	3.56	3.39	3.26	3.15	3.06	2.93	2.78	2.63	2.55	2.47	2.38	2.29	2.20	2.10
28	7.64	5.45	4.57	4.07	3.75	3.53	3.36	3.23	3.12	3.03	2.90	2.75	2.60	2.52	2.44	2.35	2.26	2.17	2.06
29	7.60	5.42	4.54	4.04	3.73	3.50	3.33	3.20	3.09	3.00	2.87	2.73	2.57	2.49	2.41	2.33	2.23	2.14	2.03
30	7.56	5.39	4.51	4.02	3.70	3.47	3.30	3.17	3.07	2.98	2.84	2.70	2.55	2.47	2.39	2.30	2.21	2.11	2.01
40	7.31	5.18	4.31	3.83	3.51	3.29	3.12	2.99	2.89	2.80	2.66	2.52	2.37	2.29	2.20	2.11	2.02	1.92	1.80
60	7.08	4.98	4.13	3.65	3.34	3.12	2.95	2.82	2.72	2.63	2.50	2.35	2.20	2.12	2.03	1.94	1.84	1.73	1.60
120	6.85	4.79	3.95	3.48	3.17	2.96	2.79	2.66	2.56	2.47	2.34	2.19	2.03	1.95	1.86	1.76	1.66	1.53	1.38
∞	6.63	4.61	3.78	3.32	3.02	2.80	2.64	2.51	2.41	2.32	2.18	2.04	1.88	1.79	1.70	1.59	1.47	1.32	1.00

GLOSSARY

A. C. Nielsen Retail Index Audit of food, household supplies, beauty aids, etc, at the retail level.

Action audit Managerial enumeration of alternative actions or decisions prior to questionnaire design.

Ad agency marketing research departments Departments of advertising agencies that produce or oversee research to support the development and evaluation of advertising for the agency's clients.

Ad hoc mail surveys Questionnaires sent to selected names and addresses with no prior contact by the researcher.

After-only with control group True experimental design that involves random assignment of subjects or test units to experimental and control groups, but no premeasurement of the dependent variable.

Allowable sampling error The amount of sampling error the researcher is willing to accept.

Applied research Research aimed at solving a specific, pragmatic problem— better understanding of the marketplace, determination of why a strategy or tactic failed, reduction of uncertainty in management decision making.

Appropriate time order of occurrence To be considered a likely cause of a dependent variable, a change in an independent variable must occur before an observed change in the dependent variable.

Attention span The length of time a particular individual will concentrate on a particular subject at a particular time.

Audience data syndicated services Companies that collect, package, and sell general data on media audiences to many firms.

Audit The examination and verification of the sale of a product.

Balanced scales Scales with the same number of positive and negative categories.

Basic research Research aimed at expanding the frontiers of knowledge rather than solving a specific, pragmatic problem.

Before and after with control group True experimental design that includes random assignment of subjects or test units to experimental and control groups and premeasurement of both groups.

BehaviorScan A single source system which maintains a 3000 household panel to record consumer purchases based upon manipulation of the marketing mix.

Bibliographic database An index of published studies and reports, may include explanation and analysis.

Bivariate regression analysis Analysis of the strength of the linear relationship between two variables when one is considered the independent variable and the other the dependent variable.

Bivariate techniques Statistical methods of determining the relationship between two variables.

Call record sheets Interviewers' logs listing the number and results of a contact.

Cartoon tests Tests in which the respondent fills in the dialogue of one character in a cartoon.

Causal research Research designed to determine whether a change in one variable likely caused an observed change in another.

Causal studies These studies examine whether one variable causes or determines the value of another variable.

Causation The inference that a change in one variable is responsible for, or caused, an observed change in another variable.

Census Data obtained from every member of the population of interest.

Central limit theorem A distribution of a large number of sample means or sample proportions will approximate a normal distribution regardless of the actual distribution of the population from which they were drawn.

Central location telephone interviewing Interviewers make calls from a centrally located marketing research facility to reach and interview respondents.

Chi-square test Test of the goodness of fit between the observed distribution and the expected distribution of a variable.

Clinical focus groups Focus groups that explore subconscious motivation.

Closed-ended questions Questions that ask the respondent to choose from a list of answers.

Cluster samples Sampling approach used with door-to-door interviewing in which the sampling units are selected in groups to reduce data collection costs.

Coding The process of grouping and assigning numeric codes to the various responses to a question.

Coefficient of determination (R^2) The percent of the total variation in the dependent variable explained by the independent variable.

Collinearity The correlation of independent variables with each other. Can bias estimates of regression coefficients.

Comfort zones A manager's expected and accepted ranges for research findings.

Communication The result of any action, physical, written, or verbal, that conveys meanings between two individuals.

Comparative scales A judgment comparing one object, concept, or person against another on a scale.

Computer-assisted telephone interviewing Central location telephone interviewing in which the interviewer enters answers directly into a computer.

Concomitant variation A predictable statistical relationship between two variables.

Concurrent validity The degree to which a variable, measured at the same point in time as the variable of interest, can be predicted by the measurement instrument.

Confidence level The probability that a particular confidence interval will include the true population value.

Constant sum scales Scales that ask the respondent to divide a given number of points, typically 100, among two or more attributes based on their importance to the person.

Construct validity The degree to which a measurement instrument represents and logically connects, via the underlying theory, the observed phenomenon to the construct.

Consumer drawings Respondent draws what they are feeling or how they perceive an object.

Consumer orientation Identification of and focus on the group of people or firms most likely to buy a product and production of a good or service that will meet their needs most effectively.

Contamination The inclusion of a group of respondents in a test who are not normally there; for example, outside buyers who see an advertisement intended only for those in the test area and enter the area to purchase the product being tested.

Content analysis A technique used to study written material (usually advertising copy) by breaking it into meaningful units, using carefully applied rules.

Content validity The degree to which the instrument items represent the universe of the concept under study.

Convenience samples Samples used primarily for reasons of convenience.

Convergent validity The degree of association among different measurement instruments that purport to measure the same concept.

Corporate marketing research departments Departments of major firms that produce or oversee collection and analysis of information relevant to marketing the firm's present or future products or services.

Correlation analysis Analysis of the degree to which changes in one variable are associated with changes in another.

Council for Marketing and Opinion Research (CMOR) An umbrella organization for survey research companies designed to protect the research industry against unnecessarily restrictive legislation, deal with reduced respondent cooperation, and fight selling disguised as research.

CoverStory An expert software system for analyzing massive scanner databases and to prepare a cover memo of the findings.

Criterion-related validity The degree to which a measurement instrument can predict a variable that is designated a criterion.

Crosstabulation Examination of the responses to one question relative to responses to one or more other questions.

Custom, or ad hoc, marketing research firms Research companies that carry out customized marketing research to address specific projects of corporate clients.

Database management software Computer programs for the retrieval and manipulation of data.

Database management system The system in which data are captured on the computer, organized for effective use, updated, and maintained to provide information for decision making.

Data-poor thinking Thinking about potential outcomes without data either real or contrived.

Decision support system (DSS) An interactive, personalized MIS, designed to be initiated and controlled by individual decision makers.

Dependent variable A symbol or concept expected to be explained or caused by the independent variable.

Depth interviews One-on-one interviews that probe and elicit detailed answers to questions, often using nondirective techniques to uncover hidden motivations.

Descriptive function The gathering and presentation of statements of fact.

Descriptive studies These studies answer the questions who, what, where, when, and how

Design control Use of the experimental design to control extraneous causal factors.

Diagnostic function The explanation of data or actions.

Dichotomous questions Questions that ask the respondent to choose between two answers.

Direct computer interviewing Consumers are intercepted in a mall and interviewed by a computer that asks questions and accepts responses.

Directory database Data available through directories or indexes of directory-type data.

Discriminant validity The lack of association among constructs that are supposed to be different.

Discussion guide A written outline of topics to cover during a focus group discussion.

Disguised observation The process of monitoring people, objects, or occurrences that do not know they are being watched.

Disproportional or optimal allocation Sampling in which the number of elements taken from a given stratum is proportional to the relative size of the stratum and the standard deviation of the characteristic under consideration.

Door-to-door interviewing Consumers are interviewed face to face in their homes.

Editing The process of ascertaining that questionnaires were filled out properly and completely.

Electroencephalogram (EEG) A machine that measures the rhythmic fluctuations in electrical potential of the brain.

Equivalent form reliability The ability to produce similar results using two instruments as similar as possible to measure the same object.

Error checking routines Computer programs that accept instructions from the user to check for logical errors in the data.

Error sum of squares (SSE) The variation not explained by the regression.

Executive interviewing The industrial equivalent of door-to-door interviewing.

Experiencing focus groups Focus groups that enable a client to observe and listen to how consumers' think and feel about products and services.

Experiment Research to measure causality in which one or more variables are changed while observing the effect of the change on another variable.

Experimental design A test in which the researcher has control over one or more independent variables and manipulates them.

Experimental effect The effect of the treatment variable on the dependent variable.

Exploratory focus groups Focus groups that aid in the precise definition of the problem, in pilot testing, or to generate hypotheses for testing or concepts for further research.

Exploratory research Preliminary research to clarify the exact nature of the problem to be solved.

External validity The extent to which causal relationships measured in an experiment can be generalized to outside persons, settings, and times.

Face validity A measurement seems to measure what it is supposed to measure.

False accuracy An unwarranted illusion of accuracy provided by details, such as statistics quoted to two decimal places.

Field experiments Tests conducted outside the laboratory in an actual market environment.

Field service firms Companies that only collect survey data for corporate clients or research firms.

Finite population correction factor An adjustment to the required sample size that is made in those cases where the sample is expected to be equal to 3 percent or more of the total population.

Focus group facility Facility consisting of conference or living room setting and a separate observation room. Facility also has audio visual recording equipment.

Focus group moderator The person hired by the client to lead the focus group. This person may need a background in psychology or sociology or, at least, marketing.

Focus groups Groups of eight to twelve participants who are led by a moderator in an in-depth discussion on one particular topic or concept.

Frame error Error resulting from an inaccurate or incomplete sampling frame.

From-home telephone interviewing Interviewers use their own phones to reach and interview respondents.

Full text database Index containing the full text of source documents, such as articles.

Galvanic skin response (GSR) The measurement of changes in the electric resistance of the skin associated with activation responses.

Goal orientation A focus on the accomplishments of corporate goals; a limit set on consumer orientation.

Graphic rating scales Graphic continuums anchored by two extremes presented to respondents for evaluation of a concept or object.

Group dynamics The interaction among people in a group.

History Things that happen or outside variables that change between the beginning and end of an experiment.

Humanistic inquiry A research method in which the researcher is immersed in the system or group under study.

Hypotheses Assumptions or theories that a researcher or manager makes about some characteristic of the population under study.

Incidence rate The percentage of people or households in the general population that fit the qualifications to be sampled.

Independent samples Samples in which measurement of a variable in one population has no effect on the measurement of the variable in the other.

Independent variable The symbol or concept over which the researcher has some control or can manipulate to some extent and that is hypothesized to cause or influence the dependent variable.

InfoScan A scanner-based tracking service for consumer packaged goods.

Instrument variation Differences or changes in measurement instruments (e.g., interviewers or observers) that explain differences in measurements.

Internal consistency reliability Ability to produce the similar results using different samples to measure a phenomenon during the same time period.

Internal database Database developed from data within the organization.

Internal validity The extent to which competing explanations for the experimental results observed can be avoided.

Interrupted time-series design Research in which the treatment "interrupts" ongoing repeated measurements.

Interval estimates   Inferences regarding the likelihood that a population value will fall within a certain range.

Interval scales   Ordinal scales with equal intervals between points to show relative amounts; may include an arbitrary zero point.

Interviewer error   Error that results from conscious or unconscious bias in the interviewer's interaction with the respondent.

Interviewer's instructions   Written directions to the interviewer on how to conduct the interview.

Itemized rating scales   Scales in which the respondent selects an answer from a limited number of ordered categories.

Judgment samples   Samples in which the selection criteria are based on personal judgment that the element is representative of the population under study.

Laboratory experiments   Experiments conducted in a controlled setting.

Likert scale   A scale in which the respondent specifies a level of agreement or disagreement with statements that express a favorable or unfavorable attitude toward the concept under study.

Longitudinal study   The same respondents are resampled over time.

Machine cleaning of data   A final computerized error check of data.

Mail panels   Participants are precontacted and screened, then periodically sent questionnaires.

Mall intercept interviewing   Shoppers are intercepted in public areas of malls and interviewed face to face.

Management summary   The portion of a research report that explains why the research was done, what was found and what those findings mean, and what action, if any, management should undertake.

Marginal reports   A computer-generated table of the frequencies of the responses to each question to monitor entry of valid codes and correct use of skip patterns.

Marketing   The process of planning and executing the conception, pricing, promotion, and distribution of ideas, goods, and services that satisfy individual and organizational objectives.

Marketing concept   A business philosophy based on consumer orientation, goal orientation, and systems orientation.

Marketing mix   The unique blend of product pricing, promotion, offerings, and distribution designed to meet the needs of a specific group of consumers.

Marketing research   The planning, collection, and analysis of data relevant to marketing decision making and the communication of the results of this analysis to management.

Marketing strategy   Guiding the long-run use of the firm's resources based on its existing and projected capabilities and on projected changes in the external environment.

Maturation   Changes in subjects that take place during the experiment that are not related to the experiment, but may affect their response to the experimental factor.

Mean   The sum of the values for all observations of a variable divided by the number of observations.

Measurement   Process of assigning numbers or labels to things in accordance with specific rules to represent quantities or qualities of attributes.

Measurement error   Error that results from a variation between the information being sought and that actually obtained by the measurement process.

Measurement instrument bias   Error that results from the design of the questionnaire or measurement instrument.

Median   The observation below which 50 percent of the observations fall.

Methodological log   A journal of detailed and time-sequenced notes on the investigative techniques used during a humanistic inquiry, with special attention to biases or distortions a given technique may have introduced.

Mode   The value that occurs most frequently.

Modem   A modulator-demodulator used to convert digital to analog data so that the data can be transmitted over a telephone system.

Mortality   Loss of test units of subjects during the course of an experiment. The problem is that those lost may be systematically different than those who stay.

Multidimensional scaling   Procedures designed to measure several dimensions of a concept or object.

Multiple choice questions   Questions that ask a respondent to choose among a list of more than two answers.

Multiple regression analysis   A procedure for predicting the level or magnitude of a dependent based on the levels of more than one independent variable.

Multiple time-series design   An interrupted time-series design with a control group.

Multivariate analysis   Statistical procedures that simultaneously analyze multiple measurements on each individual or object under study.

Mystery shoppers   People employed to pose as consumers and shop at the employer's competitors to compare prices, displays, and the like.

Noise   Anything that interferes with the audience receiving a message.

Nominal scales   Scales that partition data into mutually exclusive and collectively exhaustive categories.

Nonbalanced scales   Scales weighted toward one end or the other.

Noncomparative   A judgment made without reference to another object, concept, or person.

Nonprobability samples   Subsets of a population in which little or no attempt is made to ensure a representative cross section.

Nonresponse bias   Error that results from a systematic difference between those who do and do not respond to the measurement instrument.

Normal distribution   A continuous distribution that is bell shaped and symmetrical about the mean—mean, median and mode are equal. Sixty-eight percent of the observations fall within plus or minus one standard deviation of the mean, approximately 95 percent fall within plus or minus two standard deviations, and approximately 99.5 fall within plus or minus three standard deviations.

Numeric database   Database containing original survey data on a wide variety of general topics.

Observation research   Recording behavioral patterns without verbal communication.

One-group pretest-posttest design   Preexperimental design with pre and post measurements, but no control group.

One-shot case study   Preexperimental design with no control group and an after measurement only.

One-way frequency table   A table showing the number of responses to each answer of a survey question.

One-way mirror observations   The practice of watching unseen from behind a one-way mirror.

On-line database   A public information database accessible to anyone with proper communication facilities.

On-line vendor   An intermediary that acquires databases from a variety of database creators.

Open-ended questions   Questions that ask the respondent to reply in his or her own words.

Open observation   The process of monitoring people who know they are being watched.

Ordinal scales   Nominal scales that can order data.

Paired comparison scales   Scales that ask the respondent to pick one of two objects in a set based on some stated criteria.

Pearson's product moment correlation   Correlation analysis technique for use with metric data.

People meter   A microwave computerized rating system that transmits demographic information overnight to measure national TV audiences.

People Reader   A machine that simultaneously records the respondent's reading material and eye reactions.

Physical control   Holding the value or level of extraneous variables constant throughout the course of an experiment.

Point estimates   Inferences regarding the sampling error associated with a particular estimate of a population value.

Population distribution   A frequency distribution of all the elements of a population.

Population or universe   The total group of people from whom information is needed.

Population specification error   Error that results from an incorrect definition of the universe, or population, from which the sample is chosen.

Population standard deviation   The standard deviation of a variable for the entire population.

Post-survey regret   The regret, following data collection, that certain questions were not asked or were not asked differently.

Predictive function   Specification of how to use the descriptive and diagnostic research to predict the results of a planned marketing decision.

Predictive validity   The degree to which the future level of a criterion can be forecast by a current measurement scale.

Preexperimental design   A design that offers little or no control over extraneous factors.

Pretest   A trial run of a questionnaire.

Primary data   New data gathered to help solve the problem at hand.

Probability samples   Subsets of a population that ensure a representative cross section by giving every element in the population a known nonzero chance of being selected.

Processing error   Error that results from incorrect transfer of information from the document to the computer.

Product movement data syndicated services   Companies that collect, package, and sell retail sales data to many firms.

Projective techniques   Ways of tapping respondents' deepest feelings by having them "project" those feelings into an unstructured situation.

Proportional allocation   Sampling in which the number of elements selected from a stratum is directly proportional to the size of the stratum relative to the population.

Pseudo-clairvoyance   The impression by managers that they could have predicted the empirical outcome of a survey research project.

Pupilometer   A machine that measures changes in pupil dilation.

Purchase intent scales   Scales used to measure a respondent's intention to buy or not buy a product.

Q-sorting   A sophisticated form of rank-ordering using card sorts.

Qualitative research   Research data not subject to quantification or quantitative analysis.

Quantitative research   Studies that use mathematical analysis.

Quasi-experiments   Studies in which the researcher lacks complete control over the scheduling of treatment or must assign respondents to treatment in a nonrandom manner.

Questionnaire   A set of questions designed to generate the data necessary for accomplishing the objectives of the research project.

Quota samples   Samples in which quotas are established for population subgroups. Selection is by nonprobability means.

Random digit dialing Method of generating lists of telephone numbers at random.

Random error or random sampling error Error that results from chance variation.

Randomization The random assignment of subjects to treatment conditions to ensure equal representation of subject characteristics in all groups.

Range The maximum value for a variable minus the minimum value for that variable.

Rank-order scales Scales in which the respondent compares one item with another or a group of items against each other and ranks them.

Ratio scales Interval scales with a meaningful zero point so that magnitudes can be compared arithmetically.

Regression coefficients Values that indicate the effect of the individual independent variables on the dependent variable.

Regression to the mean Tendency for behavior of subjects to move toward the average for that behavior during the course of an experiment.

Related samples Samples in which the measurement of a variable in one population may influence the measurement of the variable in the other.

Reliability Measures that are consistent from one administration to the next.

Research design The plan to be followed to answer the research objectives; the structure or framework to solve a specific problem.

Research request Document used in large organizations that describes a potential research project, its benefits to the organization, and estimated costs. A project cannot begin until the research request has been formally approved.

Response bias Error that results from the tendency of people to answer a

question falsely, through deliberate misrepresentation or unconscious falsification.

Rule A guide, a method, or a command that tells a researcher what to do.

Sales Partner Software designed for manufacturers for selling its products to retailers using the retailer's own scanner data.

Sample A subset of the population of interest.

Sample distribution A frequency distribution of all the elements of an individual sample.

Sampling distribution of sample means A frequency distribution of the means of many samples drawn from a particular population. It is normally distributed.

Sampling distribution of the proportion A frequency distribution of the proportions of many samples drawn from a particular population. It is normally distributed.

Sampling frame List of population elements from which we select units to be sampled.

Scale A set of symbols or numbers so constructed that the symbols or numbers can be assigned by a rule to the individuals (or their behaviors or attitudes) to whom the scale is applied.

Scaled-response questions Multiple choice questions where the choices are designed to capture the intensity of the respondent's answer.

Scaling Procedures for assignment of numbers (or other symbols) to a property of objects in order to impart some of the characteristics of numbers to the properties in question.

Scanners Devices that read the UPC codes on products and produce instantaneous information on sales.

Scanning Using machines, called scanners, to read and record respondent answers from paper questionnaires.

Screeners Questions used to screen for appropriate respondents.

Secondary data Data that has been previously gathered.

Selection bias Systematic differences between the test group and control group due to a biased selection process.

Selection error Error that results from following incomplete or improper sampling procedures or not following proper ones.

Selective perception The ability of the listener or reader to filter out some information for conscious or subconscious reasons.

Self-administered questionnaire A questionnaire filled out by the respondent with no interviewer.

Semantic differential A method of examining the strengths and weaknesses of a product or company versus the competition by having respondents rank it between dichotomous pairs of words or phrases that could be used to describe it; the mean of the responses is then plotted in a profile or image.

Sentence and story completion tests Tests in which the respondents complete sentences or stories in their own words.

Shopper patterns Drawings that record the footsteps of a shopper through a store.

Simple random sample Sample selected in such a way that every element of the population has a known and equal probability of inclusion in the sample.

Single-number research Placing too much emphasis on a single statistic.

Single source research A single database, derived from scanner data, containing all relevant data on manipulation of the marketing mix at the household level of aggregation.

Skip pattern Requirement to pass over certain questions in response to the respondent's answer to a previous question.

Snowball samples Samples in which selection of additional respondents is based on referrals from the initial respondents.

Specialized service or support firms Companies that handle a specific facet of research, such as data processing or statistical analysis, for many corporate clients.

Split-half technique A method of assessing the reliability of a scale by dividing into two the total set of measurement items, and correlating the results.

Stability Lack of change in results from test to retest.

Standard deviation The square root of the sum of the squared deviations from the mean divided by the number of observations minus 1.

Standard error of the mean The standard deviation of a distribution of sample means.

Standard normal distribution A normal distribution with a mean of zero and a standard deviation of one.

Stapel scale A scale, ranging form +5 to −5, that requires the respondent to rate how close and in what direction a descriptor adjective fits a given concept.

Static-group comparison Preexperimental design that utilizes an experimental and a control group. However, subjects or test units are not randomly assigned to the two groups and no premeasurements are taken.

Statistical control Adjusting for the effects of confounded variables by statistically adjusting the value of the dependent variable for each treatment condition.

Strategic partnering Two or more marketing research firms with unique skills and resources form an alliance to offer a new service for clients, provide strategic support for each firm, or in some other manner create mutual benefits.

Stratified samples Probability samples that force sample to be more representative.

Structured observation A study in which the observer fills out a questionnaire-like form or counts the number of times an activity occurs.

Sum of squares due to regression (SSR) The variation explained by the regression.

Supervisor's instructions Written directions to the field service on how to conduct the survey.

Surrogate information error Error that results from a discrepancy between the information needed to solve a problem and that sought by the researcher.

Survey objectives The decision-making information sought through the questionnaire.

Survey research Research where an interviewer interacts with respondents to obtain facts, opinions, and attitudes.

Syndicated service research firms Companies that collect, package, and sell the same general market research data to many firms.

Systematic error Error that results in a constant bias in the measurements.

Systematic sampling Probability sampling in which the entire population is numbered, and elements are drawn using a skip interval.

Systems orientation Creation of systems to monitor the external environment and deliver the marketing mix to the target market.

Telephone focus groups Focus groups that are conducted via conference calling.

Temporal sequence Appropriate causal order of events.

Testing effect An effect that is a byproduct of the research process and not the experimental variable.

Test market Testing of a new product or some element of the marketing mix using experimental or quasi-experimental designs.

Test-retest reliability The ability of the same instrument to produce consistent results when used a second time under conditions as nearly the same as possible.

Theory-construct diary A journal that documents in detail the thoughts, premises, hypotheses, and revisions in thinking of a humanistic researcher.

Traffic counters Machines used to measure vehicular flow over a particular stretch of roadway.

Treatment The independent variable that is manipulated in an experiment.

True experimental design Research using an experimental group and a control group, and assignment of test units to both groups is randomized.

Two-way focus groups A target focus group observes another focus group, then discusses what it learned through observing.

Unidimensional scaling Procedures designed to measure only one attribute of a respondent or object.

Unstructured observation A study in which the observer simply makes notes on the behavior being observed.

Validation The process of ascertaining that interviews actually were conducted as specified.

Validity Whether what we tried to measure was actually measured.

Variance The sums of the squared deviations form the mean divided by the number of observations minus 1.

Verbatims Use of the respondent's own words.

Voice pitch analysis The study of changes in the relative vibration frequency of the human voice to measure emotion.

Word association tests Tests where the interviewer says a word and the respondent must mention the first thing that comes to mind.

CHAPTER AND PART OPENING PHOTO CREDITS

ENDNOTES AND ACKNOWLEDGMENTS

CHAPTER 1

1. Wilke, John R., "Beech's Sleekly Styled Starship Fails to Take Off with Corporate Customers," *The Wall Street Journal,* September 29, 1993, pp. B1, B5. Reprinted by permission of *The Wall Street Journal* © 1993, Don Jones & Company, Inc. All Rights Reserved Worldwide.

2. "AMA Board Approves New Marketing Definitions," *Marketing News* (March 1, 1985): 1.

3. "New Marketing Research Definition Approved," *Marketing News* (January 2, 1987): 1, 14.

4. Kevin Higgins, "Root Beer's War over Market Share as U.S. Battle Comes to a Head," *Marketing News* (August 2, 1982): 5.

5. An excellent article on the value of marketing research is J. Walker Smith, "Beyond Anecdotes: Toward a Systematic Model of the Value of Marketing Research," *Marketing Research* (March 1991): 3–14.

6. This case is partially adapted from Faye Rice, "Hotels Fight for Business Guests," *Fortune* (April 23, 1990): 265–74.

7. Theodore Dunn, "How Agencies Use Research," *Advertising Age* 45 (July 15, 1984): 69–70.

8. The 3M story is from Joseph R. Kendall, "Corporate Marketing Research at 3M," *Marketing Research* (June 1991): 4–6.

CHAPTER 2

1. Pare, Terrence P., "How to Find Out What They Want," *Fortune,* © 1993 Time Inc. All Rights Reserved.

2. Diane Schmalensee, "Establishing Objectives with the Client Is Vital to Success of Research Project," *Marketing News* (January 22, 1982): 2–17.

3. "Big Brother Gets a Job in Market Research," *Business Week* (April 8, 1985): 96–97.

4. This list is adapted from Paul Conner, "Research Request Step Can Enhance Use of Results," *Marketing News* (January 4, 1985): 41.

5. Johnny K. Johansson and Ikujiro Nonaka "Market Research the Japanese Way," *Harvard Business Review* (May/June 1987): 16–18, 22.

6. See Sil Seggev, "Listening is Key to Providing Useful Marketing Research," *Marketing News* (January 22, 1982): 6.

7. See "It's a Manager's Job to Be Responsible for Research," *Marketing News* (November 8, 1985): 22; and "Five Suggestions for Positioning a Department," *Marketing News* (January 4, 1988): 39–40.

8. Rohit Deshpande and Scott Jeffries, "Attitude Affecting the Use of Marketing Research in Decision Making: An Empirical Investigation," in *Educators' Conference Proceedings,* series 47, ed. Kenneth L. Bernhardt et al. (Chicago: American Marketing Association, 1981): 1–4.

9. Rohit Deshpande and Gerald Zaltman, "Factors Affecting the Use of Market Research Information: A Path Analysis," *Journal of Marketing Research* 19 (February 1982): 14–31 Rohig Deshpande [1984], "A Comparison of Factors Affecting Researcher and Manager Perceptions of Market Research Use," *Journal of Marketing Research* 21 (February 1989): 32–38; Hanjoon Lee, Frank Acito, and Ralph Day. "Evaluation and Use of Marketing Research by Decision Makers: A Behavioral Simulation," *Journal of Marketing Research* 24 (May 1987): 187–96; and Michael Hu, "An Experimental Study of Managers' and Researchers' Use of Consumer Market Research," *Journal of the Academy of Marketing Science* (Fall 1986): 44–51.

10. Rohit Deshpande and Gerald Zaltman, "A Comparison of Factors Affecting Use of Marketing Information in Consumer and Industrial Firms," *Journal of Marketing Research* 24 (February 1987): 114–18.

CHAPTER 3

1. Joseph Rydholm, "Scanning the Seas," *Quirk's Marketing Research Review* (May 1993): 6–7, 26–27.

2. Jack Honomichl, "Some Final Musings As Jack Writes Off into the Sunset," *Marketing News* (January 3, 1994): 17, 20.

3. Ibid.

4. "Revenues Near $2 Billion, but Stormy Times Ahead," *Advertising Age* (June 3, 1991): 33.

5. Ibid.

6. Jack Honomichl, "Research Cultures Are Different in Mexico, Canada," *Marketing News* (May 10, 1993): 12–13.

7. Jack Honomichl, "Prediction: Traditional Research Firms Will Vanish," *Marketing News* (February 3, 1992): 8.

8. Adapted with permission from "Nielsen Gets Boost in Pan-European Win," *Advertising Age* (March 12, 1990): 58.

9. *Standard Directory of Advertising Agencies* (Skokie, Illinois: National Register Publishing Co., 1989).

10. James Donius, *Marketplace Measurement: Tracking and Testing* (New York: Association of National Advertisers, Inc., 1986): 1–2.

11. Scott Hume, "Research Partnerships Here to Stay," *Advertising Age* (October 14, 1991): 33.

12. Ibid.; also see Laurie Ashcraft, "The Evolving Marketing Research Industry," *Marketing Research* (June 1991): 23–29; and Paul Boughton, "Marketing Research Partnerships: A Strategy for the 90s," *Marketing Research* (December 1992): 8–12.

13. "Dial-in TV Polls Blasted as Junk," *Marketing News* (January 2, 1989): 30; also see Newton Frank, "900-Number Polls and the Marketing Research Community," *Marketing Research* (September 1991): 3–4.

14. Diane Bowers, "New Organization Formed to Face Legislative Challenges and

Public Skepticism," *Marketing News* (August 16, 1993): A1, A8.

15. Ellen Neuborne, "Researchers See Chill from Suit," *Advertising Age* (July 20, 1987): 3, 50; "A Case of Malpractice–In Research," *Business Week* (August 10, 1987): 28–29; and Ted Knutson, "Marketing Malpractice Causes Concern," *Marketing News* (October 10, 1988): 1, 7. Beecham has since sold the Delicare brand to Benckieser Consumer Products.

16. "AMA's Law Firm Drafts Sample Arbitration Clause for Research Contracts," *Marketing News* (January 2, 1989), p. 2.

17. "Self-Regulated Research," *Marketing News* (January 2, 1987): 1, 10.

18. Diane Bowers, "Saga of a Sugger—Part 1," *Marketing Research* (March 1990): 64–67.

19. Diane Bowers, "Promoting a Positive Image," *Marketing Research* (Winter 1993): 40–42.

20. The data from this case is real. See Ashcraft, 27–29.

CHAPTER 4

1. Robert Bengen, "Teamwork: It's in the Bag," *Marketing Research* (Winter 1993): 30–33.

2. Joe Schwartz, "Databases Deliver the Goods," *American Demographics* (September 1989): 24.

3. "Duke Power's Powerful Database," *American Demographics* (© June 1991): 47–48. Excerpted with permission.

4. "KGF Taps Data Base to Target Consumers," *Advertising Age* (October 8, 1990): 3, 83.

5. "Databases Uncover Brands' Biggest Fans," *Advertising Age* (February 19, 1990): 3, 73.

6. Ibid.

7. Kathleen Deveny, "Segments of One," *Wall Street Journal* (Marsh 22, 1991): B4.

8. "The New Stars in Retailing," *Business Week* (December 16, 1991): 122.

9. For a rebuttal to some of the limitations of secondary data, see Tim Powell, "Despite Myths, Secondary Research Is a Valuable Tool," *Marketing News* (September 21, 1991): 28, 33.

10. See David Steward, *Secondary Research: Information Sources and Methods* (Beverly Hills, Calif.: Sage Publications, 1984) 23–33; also see "Prospecting for Marketing Trea-

sures in Your Customer's Database," *Banker's Monthly* (June 1989): 44–48.

11. "Information Brokers: New Breed with Access to Secondary Research," *Marketing News* (February 27, 1987): 14.

12. "Leading Vendors of On-line Information," *Nation's Business* (April 1898): 55; also see "Information Service Can Focus Research Project," *Marketing News* (September 11, 1989): 7, 47, 62; "Many Software Programs Available, but Customizing Often Yields Best Results," *Marketing News* (February 18, 1991): 11, 22.

13. Chiang, "How to Find Online Information," 53.

14. Katherine Chiang, "How to Find Online Information," *American Demographics* (© September 1993): 52–55. Excerpted with permission.

15. "Many Software Programs Available," 11, 22.

16. Ed Campbell, "CD-ROMs Bring Census Data In-House," *Marketing News* (January 6, 1992): 12, 16.

17. Max Hopper, "Rattling SABRE–New Ways to Compete on Information," *Harvard Business Review* (May-June 1990): 125.

18. Trish Baumann, "How Quaker Oats Transforms Information into Market Leadership," *Sales and Marketing Management* (June 1989): 79.

19. "Hand-Held Computers Help Field Staff Cut Paper Work and Harvest More Data," *Wall Street Journal* (January 30, 1990): B1; and "How Software Is Making Food Sales a Piece of Cake," *Business Week* (July 2, 1990): 54–56.

20. "Savin Replaces 'I Think' with 'I Know,'" *Sales and Marketing Management* (December 9, 1985): 74.

21. Neal Pruchansky, "Beware of Mentality that Puts Blame on Computers," *Marketing News* (November 7, 1985): 10; Robert Trippi and Tamer Salameh, "Strategic Information Systems: Current Research Issues," *Journal of Information Systems Management* (Summer 1989): 30–35.

22. This case is taken from "Camp Hyatt," *American Demographics* (© January 1991): 50–51. Reprinted with permission.

CHAPTER 5

1. "To the Winners Belong the Spoils," *Marketing News* (Oct. 10, 1986), p. 1.

2. "The Qualitative vs. Quantitative Conflict Is a Futile One," *Marketing News* (August 29, 1988), p. 22; "Quantitative or Qualitative? That Is the Research Question," *Marketing News* (August 29, 1988), p. 46; Sonia Yuspeh, "Point of View: Dracula and Frankenstein Revisited," *Journal of Advertising Research* (February–March 1988), pp. 53–59.

3. Thomas Dupont, "Exploratory Group Interview in Consumer Research: A Case Example," *Advances in Consumer Research* 4 (1976), pp. 431–433.

4. Wendy Sykes, "Taking Stock: Issues from the Literature on Validity and Reliability in Qualitative Research," *Journal of the Marketing Research Society* (January 1991), pp. 3–12.

5. Lewis Winters, "What's New in Focus Group Research," *Marketing Research* (December 1990), pp. 69–70.

6. Much of this section is taken from Bobby Calder, "Focus Groups and the Nature of Qualitative Marketing Research," *Journal of Marketing Research* 14 (August 1977); pp. 353–364.

7. "Focus Groups Are Used as Bait in Trolling for Ideas," *Marketing News* (August 28, 1987), p. 48.

8. "Two Twists on Focus Groups: Off-the-Wall Respondents, Written Answers Work Best," *Marketing News* (August 29, 1988), p. 31.

9. "Moves Are as Important as Words When Group Describes a Product," *Marketing News* (August 28, 1987), p. 49.

10. Wendy Hayward and John Rose, "We'll Meet Again . . . Repeat Attendance at Group Discussions—Does It Matter?" *Journal of the Market Research Society* (July 1990), pp. 377–407.

11. "Marketing," *The Wall Street Journal* (January 13, 1992), p. B1.

12. Vivian Thonger, "Moderator Training Comes of Age," *Marketing News* (January 2, 1989), pp. 19, 37.

13. Richard Morin, "A New Way to Take People's Pulse," *The Washington Post National Weekly Edition* (Sept. 27, 1993): 3.

14. Martin Lautman, "Focus Groups: Theory and Method," *Advances in Consumer Research* 9 (October 1981), p. 54; "Debriefing Sessions: The Missing Link in Focus Groups," *Marketing News* (January 8, 1990), pp. 20, 22.

15. Mark Carnack, "Restoring Power," *Quirk's Marketing Research* (June/July 1993): 6, 7, 24–26.

16. B. G. Yovovich, "Focusing On Consumers' Needs and Motivations," *Business Marketing* (March 1991), pp. 41–43.

17. Yovovich, op cit

18. Deborah Potts, "Bias Lurks in All Phases of Qualitative Research," *Marketing News* (September 3, 1990), pp. 12, 13.

19. Judith Langer, "18 Ways to Say 'Shut Up!'" *Marketing News* (January 6, 1992), p. FG-2; also, Stephanie Tudor, "Tips on Controlling Focus Group Crosstalk," *Quirk's Marketing Research Review* (December 1991), pp. 30–31.

20. "Feedback on the Phone," *Business Marketing* (March 1991), p. 46.

21. Michael Silverstein, "Two-Way Focus Groups Can Provide Startling Information," *Marketing News* (January 4, 1988), p. 31; also, "What the '90s Will Hold for Focus Group Research," *Advertising Age* (January 22, 1990), p. 267.

22. "Network to Broadcast Live Focus Groups," *Marketing News* (September 3, 1990), pp. 10, 47.

23. "Japanese Companies Import U.S. Trends," *USAToday* (March 21, 1990), p. 2B.

24. Hal Sokolow, "In-Depth Interviews Increasing in Importance," *Marketing News* (September 13, 1985), pp. 26, 31; Pamela Rogers, "One-on-One Don't Get the Credit They Deserve," *Marketing News* (January 2, 1989), pp. 9–10; Hazel Kahan, "On-on-One Should Sparkle Like the Gems They Are," *Marketing News* (September 3, 1990), pp. 8–9; Thomas Greenbaum, "Focus Groups vs. One-on-Ones: The Controversy Continues," *Marketing News* (September 2, 1991), p. 16.

25. "Projective Profiting Helps Reveal Buying Habits of Power Segments," *Marketing News* (August 28, 1987), p. 10.

26. Piirto, "Beyond Mind Games," p. 52.

CHAPTER 6

1. McCarthy, Michael J., "James Bond Hits the Supermarket: Stores Snoop on Shoppers' Habits to Boost Sales," *The Wall Street Journal,* August 25, 1993, pp. B1, B8. Reprinted by permission of *The Wall Street Journal* © 1993, Dow Jones & Company, Inc. All Rights Reserved Worldwide.

2. E. W. Webb, D. T. Campbell, K. D. Schwartz, and L. Sechrest, *Unobtrusive Measures: Nonreaction Research in the Social Sciences* (Chicago: Rand McNally, 1966), 113–114.

3. Daniel Seymour, "Seeing Is Believing with Systematic Observation," *Marketing News* (August 28, 1987): 36.

4. See Henry Krueckeberg, "Customer Observation: Procedures, Results, and Implications," *Quirk's Marketing Research Review* (December 1989): 16–22, 42–43.

5. "The Spy Who Came in from the Cold Cuts," *Business Week* (July 20, 1987); "Who Was that Masked Customer?" *Chain Store Age Executive* (November 1988): 80–82; "Mystery Shoppers," *Restaurant Business* (February 10, 1989): 38, 119; "There's No Mystery in How to Retain Customers," *Marketing News* (February 4, 1991): 10.

6. Ronald Milliman, "Using Background Music to Affect the Behavior of Supermarket Shoppers," *Journal of Marketing* (Summer 1982): 86–91. Another interesting study on shopper research behavior in supermarkets is Cathy Cobb and Wayne Hoyer, "Direct Observation of Search Behavior in the Purchase of Two Nondurable Products," *Psychology and Marketing* (Fall 1985): 161–179.

7. Ronald Milliman, "The Influence of Background Music on the Behavior of Restaurant Patrons," *Journal of Consumer Research* (September 1986): 286–289.

8. Harold Kassarjian, "Content Analysis in Consumer Research," *Journal of Consumer Research* (June 1977): 8–18. An excellent summary article on content analysis is: Richard Kolbe and Melissa Burnet, "Content-Analysis Research: An Examination of Applications with Directives for Improving Research Reliability and Objectivity," *Journal of Consumer Research* (September 1991): 243–250. Other examples of content analysis are Mary Zimmer and Linda Golden, "Impressions of Retail Stores: A Content Analysis of Consumer Images," *Journal of Retailing* (Fall 1988): 265–293; and Terence Shimp, Joel Urbany, and Sakeh Camlin, "The Use of Framing and Characterization for Magazine Advertising of Mass-Marketed Products," *Journal of Advertising* (January 1988): 23–30. Several good reference articles on content analysis are: Hans Kepplinger, "Content Analysis and Reception Analysis," *American Behavioral Scientist* (November/December 1989); Bradley Greenberg, "On Other Perspectives toward Message Analysis," *American Behavioral Scientist* (November/December 1989); Sonia Livingstone, "Audience Reception and the Analysis of Program Meaning," *America's Behavioral Scientist* (November/December 1989): 187–190; and Carl Roberts, "Other than Counting Words: A Linguistic Approach to Content Analysis," *Social Forces* (September 1989): 147–177.

9. John Healy and Harold Kassarjian, "Advertising Substantiation and Advertiser Response: A Content Analysis of Magazine Advertisements," *Journal of Marketing* (Winter 1983): 107–117.

10. Anthony Ursic, Michael Ursic, and Virginia Ursic, "A Longitudinal Study of the Use of the Elderly in Magazine Advertising," *Journal of Consumer Research* (June 1986): 131–133.

11. Much of this section is taken from Elizabeth Hirschman, "Humanistic Inquiry in Marketing Research: Philosophy, Method and Criteria," *Journal of Marketing Research* (August 1986): 237–249. For more detailed information see Yvonna Lincoln and Edward Guba, *Naturalistic Inquiry* (Beverly Hills, CA: Sage Publications, 1985).

12. A. C. Nielsen Retail Index Services (Northbrook, IL: A. C. Nielsen Company).

13. Ibid.

14. Johny Johanson and Ikujiro Nonaka, "Market Research the Japanese Way," *Harvard Business Review* (May–June 1987): 16–22; an excellent article on Japanese observation research is Magoroh Maruyama, "International Proactive Marketing," *Marketing Research* (June 1990): 36–49.

15. Werner Kroeber-Riel, "Activation Research: Psychological Approaches in Consumer Research," *Journal of Consumer Research* (March 1979): 240–250.

16. S. Weinstein, C. Weinstein, and R. Drozdenko, "Brain Wave Analysis in Advertising Research: Validation from Basic Research and Independent Replications," *Psychology and Marketing* (Fall 1984): 17–42.

17. See John Cacioppo and Richard Petty, "Physiological Responses and Advertising Effects," *Psychology and Marketing* (Summer 1985): 115–126.

18. McCarthy, Michael J., "Mind Probe," *The Wall Street Journal* (March 22, 1991): B3. Reprinted by permission of *The Wall Street Journal,* © 1994, Dow Jones & Company, Inc. All Rights Reserved Worldwide.

19. Michael Eysenck, "Arousal, Learning,

and Memory," *Psychological Bulletin* 83 (1976): 389–404.

20. James Grant and Dean Allman, "Voice Stress Analyzer is a Marketing Research Tool," *Marketing News* (Jaunary 4, 1988): 22.

21. Glen Brickman, "Uses of Voice-Pitch Analysis," *Journal of Advertising Research* (April 1980): 69–73.

22. Ronald Nelson and David Schwartz, "Voice-Pitch Analysis," *Journal of Advertising Research* (October 1979): 55–59.

23. Nancy Nighswonger and Claude Martin, Jr., "On Using Voice Analysis in Marketing Research," *Journal of Marketing Research* (August 1981): 350–355.

24. "Real-World Device Sheds New Light on Ad Readership Tests," *Marketing News* (June 5, 1987): 1, 18.

25. "Networks Urge Changes in People Meter System," *Marketing News* (January 22, 1990): 6, 21; and "Nielsen's Magic Lantern Leaves the Networks Seeing Red," *Superbrands 1991: A Supplement of Adweek's Marketing Week,* p. 26.

26. "Nielsen, Samoff to Develop Passive People Meter," *Marketing News* (July 3, 1989): 7; and "People Meter Rerun," *Marketing News* (September 2, 1991): 1, 44.

27. Rebecca Piirto, "Do Not Adjust Your Set," *American Demographics* (March 1993): 6.

28. Robert Levy, "Scanning for Dollars," *Dun's Business Month* (September 1986): 64.

29. "IRI, Nielsen Slug It Out in Scanning Wars," *Marketing News* (September 2, 1991): 1. Three excellent summary articles on single-source systems are David Curry, "Single-Source Systems: Retail Management Present and Future," *Journal of Retailing* (Spring 1989): 1–20; Melvin Prince, "Some Uses and Abuses of Single Source Data for Promotional Decision Making," *Marketing Research* (December 1989): 18–22; and "Futuristic Weaponry," *Advertising Age* (June 11, 1990): 5–12.

30. The information on BehaviorScan is taken from a pamphlet from Information Resources Incorporated entitled, "Behavior-Scan." A good article that compares alternative single-source suppliers and their different methodologies is Leon Winters, "Home Scan vs. Store Scan Panels: Single Source Options for the 1990s," *Marketing Research* (December 1989): 61–65.

31. Information Resources, Incorporated, 1990 Annual Report.

32. Speech given by Olan M. Fulgoni, president and CEO of Information Resources, Incorporated, delivered before the Advertising Research Foundation Annual Conference, March 4, 1987, New York City.

33. Sales Partner brochure provided by Information Resources, Incorporated.

34. "Rivals Duel Bitterly for Job of Supplying Market Information," *Wall Street Journal* (November 15, 1993): A1, A9.

35. "Now It's Down to Two Equal Competitors," *Superbrands 1991: A Supplement to Adweek's Marketing Week,* p. 28.

36. "IRI, Nielsen Slug It Out," p. 47.

37. "Nielsen Weighs Assets," *Advertising Age* (August 12, 1991): 29.

38. "Information Resources Wires the Drugstores," *Adweek's Marketing Week* (May 27, 1991): 34.

39. "Researchers Rev Up" *Advertising Age* (January 13, 1992): 34.

40. "ScanAmerica Rolls With CBS," *Advertising Age* (November 4, 1991): 3.

41. James Sinkula, "Status of Company Usage of Scanner Based Research," *Journal of the Academy of Marketing Science* (Spring 1986): 63–71.

42. "Merchandising Plays Effective? Scanners Know," *Marketing News* (January 4, 1985): 17.

43. Ibid.

44. "Safeway Launches New StoreLab Testing Service," *Marketing News* (January 8, 1990): 45.

45. Undated speech entitled "New Technology Contributions to New Product and Advertising Strategy Testing: The ERIM Testsight System," by Laurence Gold, VP-Marketing, A. C. Nielsen Co.

CHAPTER 7

1. Susan Kraft, "Who Slams the Door on Research," *American Demographics* (September 1991), p. 14. Reprinted with permission.

2. *Walker 1990 Industry Image Study* (Indianapolis: Walker Research, Incorporated), p. 3.

3. Patricia E. Moberg, "Biases in Unlisted Phone Numbers," *Journal of Advertising Research* (August–September 1982), p. 55.

4. *Walker 1990,* p. 3.

5. Ibid.

6. Cynthia Webster, "Consumer's Attitudes Toward Data Collection Methods," in Robert King, ed., *1991 Southern Marketing Association Proceedings* (Richmond, Va.: University of Richmond Press), 1991, pp. 220–223.

7. Lynn Coleman, "Researchers Say Nonresponse Is Single Biggest Problem," *Marketing News* (January 7, 1991), pp. 32–33; and Subhash Jain, *International Marketing Management,* 3rd ed (Boston: PWS-Kent Publishing Company) 1990, pp. 338–339.

8. Thomas Gruca, "Researching Older Consumers," *Marketing Research* (Sept. 1992): 18–23.

9. Jerry Rosenkranz, "Don't Knock Door-to-Door Interviewing," *CASRO Journal 1991,* p. 45.

10. Roger Gates and Paul Solomon, "Changing Patterns in Survey Research—Growth of the Mall Intercept," *Journal of Data Collection* 22 (Spring 1986), pp. 3–8.

11. Cecil Phillips, "A View from All Sides," *Alert* 17 (September 1978), pp. 6–7.

12. Roger Gates and Bob Brobst, "RANDIAL: A Program for Generating Random Telephone Numbers in Interviewer Usable Form," *Journal of Marketing Research* 14 (May 1977), pp. 240–242; also see Dianne Schmidley, "How to Overcome Bias in a Telephone Survey," *American Demographics* (November 1986), pp. 50–51; Lewis Winters, "What's New in Telephone Sampling Technology," *Marketing Research: A Magazine of Management and Applications* (March 1990), pp. 80–82.

13. *Walker 1990,* p. 3.

14. Todd Remington, "Rising Refusal Rates: The Impact of Telemarketing," *Quirk's Marketing Research Review* (May 1992), pp. 8–15.

15. Kate Betrand, "The Global Spyglass," *Business Marketing* (September 1990), pp. 52–56.

16. Carl McDaniel and Roger Gates, "Personal vs. Computer Interviewing: Comparisons of Data Quality," *Journal of Data Collection* 22 (Fall 1982), pp. 15–20.

17. Charles D. Parker and Kevin F. McCrohan, "Increasing Mail Survey Response Rates: A Discussion of Methods and Induced Bias," in *Marketing: Theories and Concepts for an Era of Change,* ed. John Summey, R. Viswanathan, Ronald Taylor, and Karen Glynn (Atlanta: Southern Marketing Association, 1983), pp. 254–256.

18. Douglas Berdie, "Reassessing the Value of High Response Rates to Mail Surveys," *Marketing Research: A Magazine of Management and Applications* (September 1989), pp. 52–64.

19. Joseph Rydholm, "Keep the Kids Interested," *Quirk's Marketing Research* (Feb. 1993): 6, 7, 37.

20. The section on Russian marketing research is from William Wilson and Xiaoyan Zhao, "Perestroika and Research: Ivan's Opinion Counts," *CASRO Journal 1991,* pp. 29–30.

21. Jeffrey Pope, "International Research—It's a Different Game," *CASRO Journal 1991,* pp. 23–26.

22. This section is adapted from Phillip Cateora, *International Marketing,* 7th ed. (Homewood, Ill.: Richard D. Irwin, 1990), pp. 387–391.

23. Ibid.

24. This case was developed from Gail Tom, Michelle Dragics, and Christi Holderegger, "Using Visual Presentation to Assess Store Positioning: A Case Study of J. C. Penney," *Marketing Research* (September 1991), pp. 48–52.

CHAPTER 8

1. T. D. Cook and P. T. Campbell, *Experimentation: Design Analysis Issues for Field Settings* (Chicago: Rand McNally, 1979).

2. A good example of a laboratory experiment is described in Carroll Mohn, "Simulated-Purchase 'Chip' Testing vs. Tradeoff Conjoint Analysis—Coca Cola's Experience," *Marketing Research* (March 1990): 49–54.

3. A. G. Sawyer, "Demand Artifacts in Laboratory Experiments in Consumer Research," *Journal of Consumer Research* (March 1975): 181–201; and N. Giges, "No Miracle in Small Miracle: Story Behind Failure," *Advertising Age* (August 16, 1989), p. 76.

4. John G. Lynch, "On the External Validity of Experiments in Consumer Research," *Journal of Consumer Research* (December 1982): 225–239.

5. John Barry, "Keebler Springs to Life," *Adweek's Marketing Week* (© January 6, 1992), pp. 19–20. Used with permission.

6. For a more detailed discussion of this and other experimental issues, see Thomas D. Cook and Donald T. Campbell. "The Design and Conduct of Quasi-Experiments and True Experiments in Field Settings," in *Handbook of Industrial and Organizational Psychology,* ed. M. Dunnette (Skokie, Ill.: Rand McNally, 1978).

7. Ibid.

8. For a discussion of the characteristics of various types of experimental designs, see Donald T. Campbell and Julian C. Stanley, *Experimental and Quasi-Experimental Design for Research* (Chicago: Rand McNally, 1966); also see Richard Bagozzi and Youjar Yi, "On the Use of Structural Equation Models in Experimental Design," *Journal of Marketing Research* (August 1989): 225–270.

9. Thomas D. Cook and Donald T. Campbell, *Quasi-Experimentation: Design and Analysis Issues for Field Settings* (Boston: Houghton-Mifflin, 1979); p. 56.

10. Alvin Achenbaum, "Market Testing: Using the Marketplace as a Laboratory," in *Handbook of Marketing Research,* ed. Robert Ferber (New York: McGraw-Hill, 1974), pp. 4–32; T. Karger, "Test Marketing as Dress Rehearsals," *Journal of Consumer Marketing* (Fall 1985): 49–55; and Tim Harris, "Marketing Research Passes Toy Marketer Test," *Advertising Age* (August 24, 1987); pp. 1, 8.

11. Lawrence Gold, "Virtual Reality Now a Research Reality," *Marketing Research* (Nov. 1993): 50–51.

12. Jay Klompmaker, G. David Hughes, and Russell I. Haley, "Test Marketing in New Product Development," *Harvard Business Review* (May–June 1976): 129; and N. D. Cadbury, "When, Where and How to Test Market," *Harvard Business Review* (May–June 1985): 97–98.

13. Joseph Rydholm, "To Test or Not to Test," *Quirk's Marketing Research Review* (February 1992): 61–62.

14. "Testing Is Valuable, But It's Often Abused," *Marketing News* (January 2, 1987), p. 40.

15. Joseph Rydholm, "To Test or Not to Test," *Quirk's Marketing Research Review* (February 1992): 61–62.

16. Benjamin Lipstein, "The Design of Test Market Experiments," *Journal of Advertising Research* (December 1965): 2–7.

17. For a discussion of typical American cities and metropolitan areas, see Jane Rippeteau, "Where's Fort Wayne When You Need It?" *The Marketer* (July–August 1990): 46–49; and Judith Waldrop, "All American Markets," *American Demographics* (January 1992): 24–30, © 1992; reprinted with permission.

18. G. L. Urban and G. M. Katz, "Pre-Test Market Models: Validation and Managerial Implications," *Journal of Marketing Research* (August 1983): 221–234.

CHAPTER 9

1. Bickley Townsend, "Marketing Research That Matters," *American Demographics* (© August 1992): 58–60. Reprinted with permission.

2. F. N. Kerlinger, *Foundations of Behavioral Research,* 3rd ed. (New York: Holt, Rinehart & Winston, 1986), 403; also see Mel Crask and R. J. Fox, "An Exploration of the Internal Properties of Three Commonly Used Research scales," *Journal of the Marketing Research Society* (October 1987): 317–319.

3. Raghav Singh, "Reliability and Validity of Survey Research in Marketing: The State of the Art," in *Marketing: Toward the Twenty-First Century, Proceedings of the 1991 Southern Marketing Association,* ed. Robert King (Richmond, Va: University of Richmond, 1991), 210–213; also see Paul Hensel, Gordon Bruner, and Calvin Berkey, "Towards the Compilation and Critical Assessment of Psychometric Scales Reported in Marketing Research," in *Progress in Marketing Thought, Proceedings of the 1990 Southern Marketing Association,* eds. Louis Capella et al. (Houston, Houston Baptist College, 1990), 330–334.

4. Sabra Brock, "Marketing Research in Asia: Problems, Opportunities, and Lessons," *Marketing Research: A Magazine of Management and Applications* (September 1989): 44–51.

5. For an excellent discussion of the semantic differential, see Charles E. Osgood, George Suci, and Percy Tannenbaum, *The

Measurement of Meaning (Urbana: University of Illinois Press, 1957).

6. See ibid., 140–153, 192, 193; also, William D. Barclay, "The Semantic Differential as an Index of Brand Attitude," *Journal of Advertising Research* 4 (March 1964): 30–33.

7. Theodore Clevenger, Jr., and Gilbert A. Lazier, "Measurement of Corporate Images by the Semantic Differential," *Journal of Marketing Research* 2 (February 1965): 80–82.

8. Michael J. Etzel, Terrell G. Williams, John C. Rogers, and Douglas J. Lincoln, "The Comparability of Three Stapel Forms in a Marketing Setting," in *Marketing Theory: Philosophy of Science Perspectives,* ed. Ronald F. Bush and Shelby D. Hunt (Chicago: American Marketing Association, 1982); 303–306.

9. Adapted from Paul Green, Donald Tull, and Gerald Albaum, *Research for Marketing Decisions,* 5th ed. (Englewood Cliffs, N.J.: Prentice Hall, 1988), 305–306.

10. M. V. Kalwani and A. J. Silk, "On the Reliability and Prediction Validity of Purchase Intention Measures," *Marketing Science* 1 (Summer 1982): 243–287.

11. Glen Urban, John Hauser, and Nikhilesh Dholakia, *Essentials of New Product Development* (Englewood Cliffs, N.J.: Prentice Hall, 1987), 145.

12. M. M. Givon and Z. Shapira, "Response to Rating Scalings," *Journal of Marketing Research* (November 1984): 410–419; and D. E. Stem, Jr., and S. Noazin, "The Effects of Number of Objects and Scale Positions on Graphic Position Scale Reliability," in *1985 AMA Educators' Proceedings,* eds. R. F. Lusch et al. (Chicago: American Marketing Association, 1985), 370–372.

CHAPTER 10

1. Joseph Rydholm, "Here's Looking At You, Kid," *Quirk's Marketing Research Review* (March 1993): 27–29.

2. Lewis Winters, "Innovations in Open-Ended Questions," *Marketing Research* (June 1991): 69–70.

3. Thomas Semon, "Asking Questions Is Too Limited," *Marketing News* (October 28, 1991): 19.

4. See S. L. Payne, *The Art of Asking Questions* (Princeton, N.J.: Princeton University Press, 1951). The entire book is highly recommended for any designer of questionnaires; also recommended is Seymour Sudman and Norman Bradburn, *Asking Questions* (San Francisco: Jossey-Bass, 1983).

5. Gary Mullet, "Back to Basics: Remember to Rotate," *Quirk's Marketing Research Review* (January 1993): 10–13.

6. Sandra M. J. Wong, "The Importance of Context in Conducting Asian Research," *Quirk's Marketing Research Review* (December 1993): 24–27.

7. Robert Peterson, Roger Kerin, and Mohammad Sabertehrani, "Question Understanding in Self-Report Data," in *An Assessment of Marketing Thought and Practice—1982 AMA Educators' Conference Proceedings,* ed. Bruce Walker et al. (Chicago: American Marketing Association, 1982): 426–429; also M. C. Macklin, "Do Children Understand TV Ads?" *Journal of Advertising Research* (February–March 1983): 63–70.

8. See Robert Greene and Ann Marie Thompson, "Sequential Position Bias: Is the Phenomenon for Real?" in *Southwestern Marketing Association 1985 Proceedings,* ed. John Crawford and Barbara Garland (Denton: North Texas State University): 99–101.

9. Charles F. Connell, Louis Oksenberg, and Jean M. Converse, "Striving for Response Accuracy: Experiments in New Interviewing Techniques," *Journal of Marketing Research* 14 (August 1977): 306–315; also see K. C. Schneider, "Uniformed Response Rates in Survey Research," *Journal of Business Research* (April 1985): 153–162; G. F. Bishop, A. F. Tuchfarber, and R. W. Oldendick, "Opinions on Fictitious Issues," *Public Opinion Quarterly* (Summer 1986): 240–250; and D. I. Hawkins, K. A. Coney, and D. W. Jackson, Jr., "The Impact of Monetary Inducement on Uninformed Response Error," *Journal of the Academy of Marketing Science* (Summer 1988): 30–35.

10. E. Scott Maynes, "The Anatomy of Response Errors: Consumer Saving," *Journal of Marketing Research* 2 (November 1965): 278–387; also see R. E. Goldsmith, "Personality and Uninformed Response Error," *Journal of Social Psychology* (February 1986): 37–45; R. E. Goldsmith, J. D. White, and H. Walters, "Explanations for Spurious Response in Survey Research," *Business and Economic Review* (Summer 1988): 93–104; and R. E. Goldsmith, "Spurious Response Error in a New Product Survey," *Journal of Business Research* (December 1988): 271–281.

11. Kevin Waters, "Designing Screening Questionnaires to Minimize Dishonest Answers," *Applied Marketing Research* (Spring–Summer 1991): 51–53.

12. Joan Fredricks, "Observe These Rules When Designing Questionnaires," *Marketing News* (January 22, 1982): 2–18.

13. Shelby D. Hunt, Richard D. Sparkman, Jr., and James B. Wilcox, "The Pretest in Survey Research: Issues and Preliminary Findings," *Journal of Marketing Research* 19 (May 1982): 265–275.

CHAPTER 11

1. For excellent discussions of sampling, see Seymour Sudman, *Applied Sampling* (New York: Academic Press, 1976); and L. J. Kish, *Survey Sampling* (New York: John Wiley & Sons, 1965).

2. "George Gallup's Nation of Numbers," *Esquire* (December 1983), pp. 91–92.

3. J. A. Brunner and G. A. Brunner, "Are Voluntary Unlisted Telephone Subscribers Really Different?" *Journal of Marketing Research* 8 (February 1971): 121–124, 395–399.

4. G. J. Glasser and G. D. Metzger, "Random-Digit Dialing as a Method of Telephone Sampling," *Journal of Marketing Research* 9 (February 1972): 59–64.

5. S. Roslow and L. Roslow, "Unlisted Phone Subscribers Are Different," *Journal of Advertising* 12 (August 1972): 25–38.

6. Charles D. Coway, "Using Multiple Sample Frames to Improve Survey Coverage, Quality, and Costs," *Marketing Research* (December 1991): 66–69.

7. James McClove and P. George Benson, *Statistics for Business and Economics* (San Francisco: Dellen Publishing Co., 1988), pp. 184–185.

8. R. J. Jaeger, *Sampling in Education and the Social Sciences,* (New York: Longman, 1984), pp. 28–35.

9. Newton Frank, *CASRO Journal* (January 1991): 113–115.

10. Lewis C. Winters, "What's New in Telephone Sampling Technology?" *Marketing Research,* (March 1990): 80–82.

11. For discussions of related issues, see John E. Swan, Stephen J. O'Connor, and Seuug Doug Lee, "A Framework for Testing Sampling Bias and Methods of Bias Reduction in a Telephone Survey," *Marketing Research* (December 1991): 23–34; and Charles D. Cowan "Coverage Issues in Sample Surveys: A Component of Measurement Error," *Marketing Research* (June 1991): 65–68.

12. For an excellent discussion of stratified sampling, see William G. Cochran, *Sampling Techniques,* 2d ed. (New York: John Wiley and Sons, 1963).

13. Sudman, *Applied Sampling,* pp. 110–121.

14. Ibid., pp. 110–112.

15. Earl R. Babbie, *The Practice of Social Research,* 2d ed., (Belmont, Calif.: Wadsworth Publishing, 1979), p. 167.

16. Leslie Kish, *Survey Sampling,* (New York: John Wiley and Sons, 1965).

17. Hy Mariampoloki, "Community-Based Methods for Multicultural Research," *Quirk's Marketing Research* (Jan. 1994): 6, 7, 26.

CHAPTER 12

1. For excellent discussions of the various issues discussed in this chapter, see Seymour Sudman, *Applied Sampling* (New York: Academic Press, 1976); Morris Slonim, *Sampling in a Nutshell* (New York: Simon and Schuster, 1960); and Gerald Keller, Brian Warrack, and Henry Bartle, *Statistics for Management and Economics* (Belmont, Calif.: Wadsworth Publishing company, 1990), p. 455.

2. Thomas Semon, "Save a Few Bucks on Sample Size, Risk Millions in Opportunity Loss," *Marketing News* (Jan. 3, 1993): 19.

3. Benjamin Sackmary, "Deciding Sample Size Is a Difficult Task," *Marketing News* (September 13, 1985), pp. 30, 458.

4. For discussions of these techniques, see Bill Williams, *A Sampler on Sampling* (New York: John Wiley and Sons, 1978) or Richard Jaeger, *Sampling in Education and the Social Sciences* (New York: Longmans, 1984).

CHAPTER 13

1. Harriet R. Beegle, "How Does the Field Rate?" *Advertising Age* (October 20, 1980), pp. 518–526; "Need Honesty, Better Quality from Research Suppliers, Field Services," *Marketing News* (September 18, 1981), p. 4.

2. Ibid.

3. D. W. Steward, "Filling the Gap: A Review of the Missing Data Problem," *An Assessment of Marketing Thought and Practice* (Chicago: American Marketing Association, 1982), pp. 395–399.

4. E. R. Morrissey, "Sources of Error in the Coding of Questionnaire Data," *Sociological Methods and Research* 1 (1982): 75–77; James McDonald, "Assessing Intercoder Reliability and Resolving Reliability and Resolving Discrepancies," in B. J. Walker et al., *An Assessment of Marketing Thought and Practice* (Chicago: American Marketing Association, 1982), pp. 435–438.

5. J. A. Sonquist and W. C. Dunkelberg, *Survey and Opinion Research: Procedures for Processing and Analysis* (Englewood Cliffs, N.J.: Prentice-Hall, 1977), pp. 100–105.

6. Norman Frendberg, "Scanning Questionnaires Efficiently," *Marketing Research* (Spring 1993): 38–42.

7. Steven Struhl, "Statistics Software Meets Windows," *Quirk's Marketing Research* (May 1993): 8, 9, 28–39.

8. For a discussion of these issues see Alan Roberts, "Understanding Data Requires Recognition of Types of Error," *Quirk's Marketing Research Review* (May 1987): 20–59; Michael Sullivan, "Controlling Non-Response Bias and Item Non-Response Bias Using CATI Techniques," *Quirk's Marketing Research Review* (November 1991): 10–49; Emmet J. Hoffman, "Continuing Analysis of Shopping Habits in San Diego," *Quirk's Marketing Research Review* (April 1987): 10–25.

9. For a discussion of these issues, see Paul Green and Donald Tull, *Research for Marketing Decisions,* 5th ed. (Englewood Cliffs, N.J.: Prentice-Hall, 1988), pp. 386–399.

10. For an excellent discussion on creating graphics presentations, see Gus Venditto, "Twelve Tips for Better Presentations," *PC Magazine* (January 28, 1992), pp. 253–260.

11. Michael Baumgardner and Ron Tatham, "Statistical Significance Testing May Hinder Proper Decision Making," *Quirk's Marketing Research Review* (May 1987): 16–19.

12. W. G. Cochran, "The χ^2 Test of Goodness of Fit," *Annals of Mathematical Statistics* 23 (1952): 315–345; Tony Babinec, "How to Think About Your Tables," *Quirk's Marketing Research Review* (January 1991): 10–12.

13. Gary M. Mullet, "Correctly Estimating the Variances of Proportions," *Marketing Research* (June 1991): 47–51.

CHAPTER 14

1. Joseph Hair, Rolph Anderson, Ron Tatham, and William Black *Multivariate Data Analysis,* 3d ed. (New York: Macmillan, 1992), p. 4.

2. Robert Pindyck and Daniel Rubinfield, *Econometric Models and Economic Forecasts,* 2d ed. (New York: McGraw-Hill, 1981), pp. 273–312.

3. For an excellent and highly understandable presentation of all the multivariate techniques presented in this chapter, see Hain et al., *Multivariate Data Analysis.*

4. For a thorough discussion of regression analysis, see Norman Draper and Harry Smith, *Applied Regression Analysis* (New York: John Wiley and Sons, 1966).

5. Charlotte H. Mason and William D. Perreault, Jr., "Collinear, Power and Interpretation of Multiple Regression Analysis," *Journal of Marketing Research* (August 1991): 268–280.

6. See Hair et al., *Multivariate Data Analysis,* p. 46.

CHAPTER 15

1. Jamal Din, "For GE Medical Systems Each Customer Is . . . A Market of One," *Quirk's Marketing Research Review* (October 1993): 6–7, 30–31.

2. Rohit Deshpande and Gerald Zaltman, "A Comparison of Factors Affecting Researcher and Manager Perceptions of Market Research Use," *Journal of Marketing Research* (February 1984): 37.

3. Richard Kitaeff, "Writing the Marketing Research Report," *Marketing Research* (Winter 1993): 4.

4. This section is partially taken from James H. Nelems, "Report Results, Implications, and Not Just Pounds of Data," *Marketing News* (January 12, 1979): 7.

5. Howard L. Gordon, "Eight Ways to Dress

a Research Report," *Advertising Age* (October 20, 1980): 5, 37. Reprinted with permission from Advertising Age, October 20, 1980, Copyright Crain Communications, Inc. All rights reserved.

6. Thomas T. Semon, "A Bad Picture Is Worth Very Few Words," *Marketing News* (May 24, 1993): 11.

7. Adapted from "Noelle-Neumann Blames Cost Cuts for Regression Research Quality," *Marketing News* (May 4, 1979): 5; also

see Elizabeth H. Stephen and Beth Soldo, "How to Judge the Quality of a Survey," *American Demographics* (April 1990): 42–43.

8. Philip H. Abelson, "Communicating with the Publics," *Science* 194 (November 5, 1976): 565.

9. Peter Eder, "Merchandise All Research Results within Corporation," *Marketing News* (January 4, 1985): 40.

10. Anil Menon, "Are We Squandering Our Intellectual Capital?" *Marketing Research,*

Vol. 5, No. 3 (Summer 1994): 18–22.

11. Steven Perkins and Ram Rao, "The Role of Experience in Information Use and Decision Making by Marketing Managers," *Journal of Marketing Research* (February 1990): 1–10.

12. Ibid.

13. Vincent Barabba and Gerald Zaltman, *Hearing the Voice of the Market* (Boston: Harvard Busines School Press, 1991), pp. 116–122.

INDEX